KEY INDICATORS
FOR ASIA AND THE PACIFIC
2023
54TH EDITION

ASIAN DEVELOPMENT BANK

ADB

6 ADB Avenue, Mandaluyong City, 1550 Metro Manila, Philippines
Tel +63 2 8632 4444; Fax +63 2 8636 2444
www.adb.org

ISBN 978-92-9270-283-0 (print); 978-92-9270-284-7 (electronic); 978-92-9270-285-4 (ebook)
ISSN 0116-3000
Publication Stock No. FLS230311-3
DOI: http://dx.doi.org/10.22617/FLS230311-3

Notes:
In this publication, "$" refers to United States dollars.
ADB recognizes "Korea" as the Republic of Korea and "Hanoi" as Ha Noi.
Photos: All photos by the Asian Development Bank unless otherwise indicated.

Cover design by Mike Cortes.

Contents

Table

Box

Sustainable Development Goals Tables

PART II: Regional Trends and Tables

Figures

Box

People

Economy and Output

Transport and Communication

Energy and Electricity

Environment

Government and Governance

PART III: Dollar Price Wedge between Nominal and Real Global Value Chain Participation

Figures

Tables

PART IV: Stories Behind Data—Using Price Data and Statistics to Track Socioeconomic Development

Figures

Tables

Box

Definitions

Foreword

At the halfway stage of implementing the 2030 Agenda for Sustainable Development, Asia and the Pacific is behind the pace for achieving many of the Sustainable Development Goals (SDGs). In addition, the Russian invasion of Ukraine in 2022 and high inflation have dented hopes for a full recovery from the coronavirus disease (COVID-19) pandemic. As a result, millions of people in developing Asia are at risk of falling back into poverty.

The *Key Indicators for Asia and the Pacific* series provides comprehensive social, economic, financial, environmental, trade, and SDG indicators for the 49 regional members of the Asian Development Bank (ADB). The reports are a vital source of socioeconomic data and information used by policymakers, government officials, development professionals, researchers, and students in the region and the rest of the world.

This 54th edition of *Key Indicators for Asia and the Pacific* offers an in-depth examination of the premium that poor and vulnerable populations pay for goods and services compared to other income groups. It explores the economic consequences of the current price shocks and the importance of quality price data gathering to inform policymakers. The report identifies actions that can be taken to address long-term development challenges that have grown deeper due to the sharp rise in the cost of living. These include strengthening social protection systems, developing the agriculture sector, expanding infrastructure investments, improving access to financial services, and helping low-income groups gain better access to new technologies and innovations. These measures can help to create new socioeconomic opportunities, especially for the most vulnerable groups.

Better and more timely data on international trade and shipping are needed to support government policy in trade-reliant developing economies. This year's *Key Indicators for Asia and the Pacific* highlights the importance of compiling statistics on global value chains in nominal and real terms, especially during periods of significant inflation. A special supplement to the report (to be released in October 2023) examines how information on location and cargo sent by ships every few seconds can provide a near real-time analysis of international shipping.

Key Indicators for Asia and the Pacific is the result of long-standing partnerships with ADB members. I deeply appreciate their sharing of data from official sources. I am also grateful to other international agencies for data that is used throughout this report. I am confident that the data and insights collected here will help governments design and implement actions that enable Asia and the Pacific to get back on track to meet the SDGs and achieve strong, lasting, and inclusive growth.

Masatsugu Asakawa
President
Asian Development Bank

Acknowledgments

This 54th annual edition of *Key Indicators for Asia and the Pacific* was prepared by the Statistics and Data Innovation Unit (EROD-SDI) within the Economic Research and Development Impact Department (ERDI) at the Asian Development Bank (ADB). The publication team was led by Arturo Martinez Jr, under the overall direction of Elaine S. Tan. Joseph Albert Niño Bulan, Rose Anne Dumayas, Karen Firshan, Aileen Oliveros-Guyos, Melissa Pascua, and Eric Suan provided technical and coordination support in preparing the publication.

The statistical tables presenting development indicators for ADB's regional member economies in Parts I and II of the printed publication (also available online via kidb.adb.org), as well as the 49 tables for individual economies available exclusively online, were prepared by EROD-SDI staff and consultants, under the supervision of Daniel Boller, Kaushal Joshi, Mahinthan Joseph Mariasingham, Arturo Martinez Jr, and Stefan Schipper. The research team included Mildred Addawe, Raymond Adofina, Maria Concordia Alfonso, Remedios Baes-Espineda, Nalwino Billones, Joseph Albert Niño Bulan, Criselda De Dios, Dennis Dizon, Madeline Dumaua-Cabauatan, Rose Anne Dumayas, Anna Marie Fernando, Aileen Oliveros-Guyos, Pamela Lapitan, Rica Cynthia Maddawin, Jayzon Mag-Atas, Kristine Faith Maningding, Marymell Martillan, Melissa Pascua, Andrea Felice Quinial, Christian Flora Mae Soco, Eric Suan, and Mar Andriel Umali. Proofreading of statistical tables was done by Ma. Roselia Babalo, Rose Anne Dumayas, and Aileen Gatson. The analyses of Sustainable Development Goal indicators in Part I were prepared by Raymond Adofina, Maria Concordia Alfonso, Nalwino Billones, Joseph Albert Niño Bulan, Aileen Oliveros-Guyos, Rica Cynthia Maddawin, Kristine Faith Maningding, Arturo Martinez Jr., Andrea Felice Quinial, and Mar Andriel Umali. Part II was written by Maria Concordia Alfonso, Madeline Dumaua-Cabauatan, Dennis Dizon, Anna Marie Fernando, Kristine Faith Maningding, and Arturo Martinez Jr. Valuable research assistance was also received from Ephraim Cuya, Ron Lester Durante, and James Matthew Miraflor.

Abdul Abiad, Cynthia Arceo Ambe, Lawrence Dacuycuy, Gaurav Datt, Rajesh Deol, Sudhir Gota, Carla Ferreira, Rana Hasan, Jules Hugot, Oleksiy Ivaschenko, Matteo Lanzafame, Editha Lavina, Hong Soo Lee, Maria Lourdes Lopez, Cholpon Mambetova, Mercedes Martin, Remrick Patagan, Dave Pipon, Iva Sebastian-Samaniego, Kiyoshi Taniguchi, Frank Thomas, Maria Carina Tinio, Natsuko Totsuka, James Villafuerte, Priscille Villanueva, and Mai Lin Villaruel provided insightful feedback.

Mahinthan Joseph Mariasingham led the team that prepared the statistical tables for Part III. The multiregional input-output tables were consolidated by John Arvin Bernabe, Jenny Lou De Las Alas, Lora Kryz Baje, Julieta Magallanes, Grant Rene Mesa, Irene Talam, Janel Asley Raviz, and Ana Francesca Rosales. Valuable contributions were made by Gienneen Antonio, Leila Rahnema-Badr, Ridhima Bahl, Faith Hyacinth Balisacan, John Arvin Bernabe, Danileen Parel-Cadag, Miro Frances Capili, Jenny Lou De Las Alas, Janine De Vera, Madeth Gayosa, Arushi Gupta, Xue Han, Christian Regie Jabagat, Sameeksha Jain, Julieta Magallanes, Sarah Mae Manuel, Faulene Mae Manzanilla, Grant Rene Mesa, Elyssa Mariel Mores, Ed Kieran Reyes, Ana Francesca Rosales, Anna Monina Sanchez, Maegan Saroca, Michelle Sianghio, Irene Talam, Dieco Von Velasco, Dean Joseph Villanueva, and Christian Marvin Zamora.

Part III was written by Mahinthan Joseph Mariasingham, Christian Regie Jabagat, Angelo Jose Lumba, Elyssa Mariel Mores, Jenny Lou De Las Alas, Janel Asley Raviz, and Ana Francesca Rosales. Neil Foster-McGregor, Eric Suan, and Elaine Tan provided insightful comments and suggestions. Kaushal Joshi and

Criselda De Dios summarized the key findings presented in Part IV, with assistance and inputs from Raymond Adofina, Paolo Kris Adriano, Rhea-Ann Bautista, Nalwino Billones, Joseph Albert Niño Bulan, Madeline Dumaua-Cabauatan, Virginia Ganac, Aileen Oliveros-Guyos, Mario Ilagan II, Rica Maddawin, Arturo Martinez Jr, and D.S. Prasada Rao.

We are grateful for the support and guidance of Joseph E. Zveglich Jr and Chia-Hsin Hu; and feedback from ERDI colleagues throughout the process. The ADB Japanese Representative Office, Pacific Liaison and Coordination Office, Philippines Country Office, and Pacific Subregional Office also provided help with the data compilation. We are very grateful for the contributions of ERDI's statistical partners—ADB regional members and international organizations who generously shared their data for the statistical tables on Sustainable Development Goal indicators (Part I), regional tables (Part II), global value chains (Part III), uses of price data (Part IV), and individual economy tables.

ADB resident missions and/or support teams in Afghanistan, Armenia, Azerbaijan, Bangladesh, Bhutan, Cambodia, Georgia, India, Indonesia, Kazakhstan, the Kyrgyz Republic, the Lao People's Democratic Republic, Mongolia, Maldives, Myanmar, Nepal, Pakistan, Papua New Guinea, the People's Republic of China, the Philippines, Sri Lanka, Tajikistan, Thailand, Timor-Leste, Turkmenistan, Uzbekistan, and Viet Nam provided support in compiling the data for their respective economies. We greatly appreciate the continuing cooperation of the governments of ADB member economies and other international agencies.

Paul Dent and Michael Barker edited *Key Indicators for Asia and the Pacific 2023*. The cover design, publication dividers, and infographics were prepared by Mike Cortes, with assistance from Raymond Adofina, Miro Frances Capili, Dennis Dizon, Anna Marie Fernando, Christian Regie J. Jabagat, Arturo Martinez Jr, and Andrea Felice Quinial. Mark Ganaban, Joseph Manglicmot, and Rommel Marilla assisted with typesetting, with guidance from Rhommell Rico. Staff from ADB's Information Technology Department provided database management and technology support in coordination with the Key Indicators Database team, comprising Ephraim Cuya, Karen Firshan, Pamela Lapitan, James Montecillo, Jeffrey Napoles, Le Kim Nguyen, and Lea Rotairo under the leadership of Stefan Schipper. The Logistics Management Unit of the Corporate Services Department facilitated the timely and smooth production of the publication. Terje Langeland and Lean Alfred Santos, with the assistance of ADB's Department of Communications and Knowledge Management staff, including Robert Alcala, Antonio Chua, Ma. Melissa Dela Torre, Ruel Gatchalian, Mira Catherine Gloria, Kristel Marie Gonzales, Luca Lamorte, Duncan Mcleod, Andrew Perrin, and Anna Katharine Sherwood provided general guidance on production issues and organized promotional and awareness activities.

Albert Park
Chief Economist and Director General
Economic Research and Development Impact Department
Asian Development Bank

Statistical Partners

The preparation and publication of *Key Indicators for Asia and the Pacific 2023* would not have been possible without the support, assistance, and cooperation of statistical partners in Asian Development Bank member economies throughout the Asia and Pacific region, along with the invaluable contributions of international, private, and nongovernment organizations. These partners—who share their data, knowledge, expertise, and other information—help provide the Asian Development Bank, policymakers, and other data users with a better understanding of the performance of economies across the region, encouraging the design, formulation, and monitoring of better policies to improve the quality of life for people in this part of the world.

REGIONAL MEMBERS

Armenia	Central Bank of Armenia (https://www.cba.am) Ministry of Finance of the Republic of Armenia (https://www.minfin.am) Statistical Committee of the Republic of Armenia (https://www.armstat.am)
Australia	Australian Bureau of Statistics (https://www.abs.gov.au) Department of Climate Change, Energy, the Environment and Water (https://www.dcceew.gov.au/) Reserve Bank of Australia (https://www.rba.gov.au)
Azerbaijan	Central Bank of the Republic of Azerbaijan (https://www.cbar.az) Ministry of Finance (http://www.maliyye.gov.az) State Statistical Committee of the Republic of Azerbaijan (https://www.stat.gov.az)
Bangladesh	Bangladesh Bank (https://www.bb.org.bd) Bangladesh Bureau of Statistics (http://www.bbs.gov.bd) Ministry of Finance (https://mof.gov.bd)
Bhutan	Ministry of Finance (https://www.mof.gov.bt) Ministry of Industry, Commerce & Employment (https://www.moice.gov.bt/) National Statistics Bureau (https://www.nsb.gov.bt) Royal Monetary Authority of Bhutan (https://www.rma.org.bt)
Brunei Darussalam	Brunei Darussalam Central Bank (https://www.bdcb.gov.bn) Department of Economic Planning and Statistics (https://deps.mofe.gov.bn) Ministry of Finance and Economy (https://www.mofe.gov.bn)
Cambodia	Electricity Authority of Cambodia (https://eac.gov.kh) Ministry of Economy and Finance (https://mef.gov.kh) National Bank of Cambodia (https://www.nbc.org.kh) National Institute of Statistics (https://nis.gov.kh)

China, People's Republic of	National Bureau of Statistics of China (https://www.stats.gov.cn) The People's Bank of China (https://www.pbc.gov.cn) State Administration of Foreign Exchange (https://www.safe.gov.cn)
Cook Islands	Cook Islands Statistics Office under Ministry of Finance and Economic Management (http://www.mfem.gov.ck)
Fiji	Bureau of Statistics (http://www.statsfiji.gov.fj) Reserve Bank of Fiji (http://www.rbf.gov.fj) Ministry of Economy (http://www.economy.gov.fj)
Georgia	Ministry of Finance of Georgia (https://www.mof.ge) National Bank of Georgia (https://www.nbg.gov.ge) National Statistics Office of Georgia (https://www.geostat.ge)
Hong Kong, China	Census and Statistics Department (https://www.censtatd.gov.hk) Financial Services and the Treasury Bureau (https://www.fstb.gov.hk)
India	National Statistical Office under the Ministry of Statistics and Programme Implementation (https://www.mospi.gov.in) Department of Economic Affairs, Ministry of Finance (https://dea.gov.in/) Reserve Bank of India (http://www.rbi.org.in)
Indonesia	Bank Indonesia (https://www.bi.go.id) Badan Pusat Statistik-Statistics Indonesia (https://www.bps.go.id) Ministry of Energy and Mineral Resources (https://www.esdm.go.id) Ministry of Finance (https://www.kemenkeu.go.id) Pertamina (https://www.pertamina.com)
Japan	Bank of Japan (https://www.boj.or.jp) Economic and Social Research Institute (https://www.esri.cao.go.jp) Japan Customs (https://www.customs.go.jp) Japan Statistics Bureau (https://www.e-stat.go.jp) Ministry of Economy, Trade and Industry (https://www.meti.go.jp) Ministry of Finance (https://www.mof.go.jp) The Institute of Energy Economics, Japan (https://oil-info.ieej.or.jp)
Kazakhstan	Bureau of National Statistics, Agency for Strategic Planning and Reforms of the Republic of Kazakhstan (https://stat.gov.kz) Ministry of Finance of the Republic of Kazakhstan (https://www.gov.kz/memleket/entities/minfin?lang=en) National Bank of Kazakhstan (https://nationalbank.kz)

Kiribati	Kiribati National Statistics Office (https://nso.gov.ki/)
Korea, Republic of	Bank of Korea (https://bok.or.kr) Statistics Korea (http://kostat.go.kr)
Kyrgyz Republic	National Bank of the Kyrgyz Republic (https://www.nbkr.kg) National Statistical Committee of the Kyrgyz Republic (http://www.stat.kg)
Lao People's Democratic Republic	Bank of the Lao PDR (https://www.bol.gov.la) Lao Statistics Bureau (https://www.lsb.gov.la) Ministry of Finance (https://www.mof.gov.la)
Malaysia	Bank Negara Malaysia (https://www.bnm.gov.my) Department of Statistics Malaysia (https://www.dosm.gov.my) Ministry of Finance Malaysia (https://www.mof.gov.my)
Maldives	National Bureau of Statistics (https://statisticsmaldives.gov.mv) Maldives Monetary Authority (https://www.mma.gov.mv) Ministry of Finance (https://www.finance.gov.mv)
Marshall Islands	Economic Policy, Planning and Statistics Office (https://www.rmieppso.org)
Micronesia, Federated States of	Division of Statistics (http://www.fsmstatistics.fm)
Mongolia	The Bank of Mongolia (https://www.mongolbank.mn) The Ministry of Finance Mongolia (https://mof.gov.mn) National Statistics Office of Mongolia (https://en.nso.mn/)
Nauru	Ministry of Finance and Economic Planning (http://www.naurugov.nr) Nauru Bureau of Statistics (https://nauru.prism.spc.int)
Nepal	Central Bureau of Statistics (https://cbs.gov.np) Office of the Controller General of Accounts, Ministry of Finance (https://www.fcgo.gov.np) Nepal Rastra Bank (https://www.nrb.org.np) Water and Energy Commission Secretariat (www.wecs.gov.np) Ministry of Energy, Water Resources and Irrigation (www.moewri.gov.np) Ministry of Industry, Commerce and Supplies (https://moics.gov.np) Ministry of Industry, Commerce and Supplies, Department of Mines and Geology (http://www.dmgnepal.gov.np)

New Zealand	Ministry of Business, Innovation and Employment (https://www.mbie.govt.nz) Reserve Bank of New Zealand (https://www.rbnz.govt.nz) Stats NZ Tatauranga Aotearoa (https://www.stats.govt.nz)
Niue	Niue Statistics Office (https://niuestatistics.nu/)
Pakistan	Ministry of Finance and Revenue (http://www.finance.gov.pk) Pakistan Bureau of Statistics (https://www.pbs.gov.pk) State Bank of Pakistan (https://www.sbp.org.pk)
Palau	Bureau of Budget and Planning, Ministry of Finance (https://www.palaugov.pw/mof)
Papua New Guinea	Bank of Papua New Guinea (https://www.bankpng.gov.pg) Department of Treasury (http://www.treasury.gov.pg) National Statistical Office (https://www.nso.gov.pg)
Philippines	Bangko Sentral ng Pilipinas (http://www.bsp.gov.ph) Bureau of Local Government Finance (https://blgf.gov.ph) Bureau of the Treasury (http://www.treasury.gov.ph) Department of Budget and Management (http://www.dbm.gov.ph) Department of Energy (https://www.doe.gov.ph) Philippine Statistics Authority (https://www.psa.gov.ph)
Samoa	Samoa Bureau of Statistics (https://www.sbs.gov.ws) Central Bank of Samoa (https://www.cbs.gov.ws)
Singapore	Department of Statistics Singapore (https://www.tablebuilder.singstat.gov.sg) Enterprise Singapore (https://www.enterprisesg.gov.sg) Ministry of Finance (https://www.mof.gov.sg) Ministry of Manpower (https://www.mom.gov.sg) Ministry of Trade and Industry (https://www.mti.gov.sg) Monetary Authority of Singapore (https://www.mas.gov.sg)
Solomon Islands	Central Bank of Solomon Islands (https://www.cbsi.com.sb) Solomon Islands National Statistics Office (https://www.statistics.gov.sb)
Sri Lanka	Central Bank of Sri Lanka (https://www.cbsl.gov.lk) Department of Census and Statistics (http://www.statistics.gov.lk)
Taipei,China	Central bank of Taipei,China Directorate-General of Budget, Accounting and Statistics Ministry of Finance

Tajikistan	National Bank of Tajikistan (https://www.nbt.tj) Agency on Statistics under President of the Republic of Tajikistan (https://www.stat.tj)
Thailand	Bank of Thailand (https://www.bot.or.th) Ministry of Finance (https://www2.mof.go.th) National Economic and Social Development Council (https://www.nesdc.go.th) National Statistical Office (https://www.nso.go.th) Ministry of Energy, Energy Policy and Planning Office (https://www.eppo.go.th)
Timor-Leste	Central Bank of Timor-Leste (https://www.bancocentral.tl) Ministry of Finance (https://www.mof.gov.tl) National Institute of Statistics of Timor-Leste (https://inetl-ip.gov.tl)
Tonga	Ministry of Finance (http://www.finance.gov.to) National Reserve Bank of Tonga (http://www.reservebank.to) Tonga Statistics Department (https://tongastats.gov.to)
Turkmenistan	Central Bank of Turkmenistan (https://www.cbt.tm) Ministry of Finance and Economy of Turkmenistan (https://www.fineconomic.gov.tm) State Committee on Statistics of Turkmenistan (https://www.stat.gov.tm)
Tuvalu	Central Statistics Division (https://tuvalu.prism.spc.int)
Uzbekistan	Central Bank of the Republic of Uzbekistan (https://www.cbu.uz) Ministry of Finance of the Republic of Uzbekistan (https://imv.uz) State Committee of the Republic of Uzbekistan on Statistics (https:/stat.uz/en)
Vanuatu	Department of Finance and Treasury (https://doft.gov.vu) Reserve Bank of Vanuatu (https://www.rbv.gov.vu) Vanuatu National Statistics Office (http://www.vnso.gov.vu)
Viet Nam	General Statistics Office (https://www.gso.gov.vn) Ministry of Finance (https://www.mof.gov.vn) State Bank of Viet Nam (https://www.sbv.gov.vn)

INTERNATIONAL, PRIVATE, AND NONGOVERNMENT ORGANIZATIONS

Association of Southeast Asian Nations
Food and Agriculture Organization of the United Nations
International Labour Organization
International Monetary Fund
International Telecommunication Union
Interstate Statistical Committee of the Commonwealth of Independent States
Joint United Nations Programme on HIV/AIDS
Organisation for Economic Co-operation and Development
Secretariat of the Pacific Community
Transparency International
United Nations Children's Fund (UNICEF)
United Nations Conference on Trade and Development
United Nations Department of Economic and Social Affairs
United Nations Development Programme
United Nations Economic Commission for Europe
United Nations Economic and Social Commission for Asia and the Pacific
United Nations Educational, Scientific and Cultural Organization (UNESCO) Institute for Statistics
United Nations Environment Programme
United Nations Human Settlements Programme
United Nations Office on Drugs and Crime
United Nations Population Division
United Nations Statistics Division
United Nations World Tourism Organization
United States Agency for International Development
United States Census Bureau
United States Bureau of Economic Analysis
WHO/UNICEF Joint Monitoring Programme for Water Supply, Sanitation and Hygiene
World Bank
World Federation of Exchanges
World Health Organization
World Trade Organization

Guide for Users

Key Indicators for Asia and the Pacific 2023 begins with a Highlights section that presents key messages from various parts of the publication.

Part I comprises data tables and data stories describing trends of selected indicators for the Sustainable Development Goals (SDGs) for which data were available. The indicators are presented according to the United Nations' SDG global indicator framework.

Part II presents specific indicators on social, economic, and environmental developments in member economies of the Asian Development Bank (ADB) located in Asia and the Pacific. The tables containing these indicators are grouped into eight themes: People; Economy and Output; Money, Finance, and Prices; Globalization; Transport and Communications; Energy and Electricity; Environment; and Government and Governance.

The SDGs in Part I and the themes in Part II are preceded by data stories, which are complemented by figures and charts describing the status of economies with respect to key trends of selected targets and indicators. The scales used in some figures and charts are adjusted to show very small numbers. In addition, figures and charts appearing in this publication are also provided with a digital object identifier to facilitate easier access to data.

The SDGs and regional tables presented in Parts I and II cover 49 national economies across Asia and the Pacific, all of which are members of ADB. The terms "country" and "national", used interchangeably with "economy", is not intended to make any judgment as to the legal or other status of any territory or area. The 49 economies have been broadly grouped into developing ADB member economies and developed ADB member economies. The term "developing Asia" refers to the 46 developing member economies of ADB. The developed economies refer to the economies of Australia, Japan, and New Zealand. Based on ADB's geographic operations, the 46 developing ADB member economies are divided into five subregions within the Asia and Pacific region. These subregions are Central and West Asia, East Asia, South Asia, Southeast Asia, and the Pacific. Economies are listed alphabetically within each subregion. The term "regional members", often used interchangeably with "Asia and the Pacific", refers to all 49 ADB members, both developing and developed. Indicators are shown for the most recent year (usually 2022) or period for which data were available and, in most tables, for a starting year or period (usually 2010). Depending on available data, the starting point may be a year nearest to 2010, and the most recent year (usually the year nearest to 2022). There may, however, be some exceptions to these general principles. In the tables, aggregates for regions include economies with available data and are shown if the indicator is available for more than half of the economies and if more than two-thirds of the reference population is represented.

Part III contains selected indicators for depicting participation by economies of Asia and the Pacific in global value chains, and the sector-specific comparative advantage of each economy in terms of exports. Typical indicators of international trade, which mainly refer to the value of exports and imports of goods and services, can be traced back to the traditional trading of final goods across borders. Today's globalization has made many economies more open to trade, providing opportunities for firms to scale up production and allocate their resources more efficiently by moving production chains across borders where there is comparative advantage. Analysis of global value chains provides detailed cross-border trading transactions of inputs used in different stages of production—from raw materials, to intermediate inputs, to the final products purchased by the end consumers.

Part IV provides stories behind the data and focuses on initiatives of the region's national statistics offices to provide data as the basis for actionable insights on development planning and policymaking.

This publication is also available on ADB's website at adb.org/ki-2023, along with individual statistical tables for each of the 49 ADB regional members. The publication's vitally important data and time series are also accessible in digitized format via the Key Indicators Database (kidb.adb.org), which also presents longer data series (usually starting from 2000) for each indicator. Data for the SDG indicators, regional tables, and individual member tables were obtained mainly from two sources: (i) ADB's statistical partners linked to regional member economies, and (ii) international statistics agencies, particularly from the United Nations' SDG Global Database, a master set of data prepared by the Department of Economic and Social Affairs of the United Nations Secretariat. The term "economies' official sources", cited as a source in some tables, refers to data provided by the statistical partners linked to the ADB regional member economies.

The data presented for indicators in Part I were derived from either official economy sources, the SDG Global Database, or databases maintained by international agencies that, based on their areas of expertise, prepared one or more of the series of statistical indicators included in the SDG Global Database. The data presented in Part III were drawn mainly from the ADB Multiregional Input-Output Database and Key Indicators Database. The results of a survey conducted by ADB's Statistics and Data Innovation Unit informed the discussion presented in Part IV.

Data produced and disseminated by international agencies are generally based on data produced and disseminated by an individual economy (including data adjusted by the economy to meet international standards). However, it should be noted that national data may be compiled using national standards and practices and, as such, international agencies often adjust the data for international comparability. In such cases, data disseminated by the international agencies may differ from data available from national sources. In other cases, when data for a specific year, or set of years, are not available; or they are available from multiple national sources (surveys, administrative data sources, and other sources); or when there are data quality issues; the relevant international agency may estimate the data. Some indicators are regularly produced for the purpose of global monitoring by the designated agency, and there are no corresponding data at the national level (e.g., population living on less than $2.15 a day at 2017 purchasing power parity). In other cases, the differences between data from national and international agencies may be because the most recent and/or revised data available at the national level are not yet available with the relevant international agency. Some data gaps are filled by supplementing or deriving data collected through sample surveys financed and carried out by international agencies. For example, many of the health indicators are estimated using data from the Multiple Indicator Cluster Surveys and Demographic and Health Surveys. Data on money and interest rates, featured in several individual economy tables, are presented based on the International Monetary Fund's 2016 *Monetary and Financial Statistics Manual and Compilation Guide*, but there are a few economies that continue to present their data using the format applied in *Key Indicators for Asia and the Pacific 2020* and prior editions. *Key Indicators for Asia and the Pacific* now also features additional transport and communications indicators from ADB's Asian Transportation Outlook Database.

ADB exercises due care and caution in collecting data before publication. Nevertheless, data from international sources presented in this publication may differ from those available within individual member economies. Thus, for a detailed description of how the indicators are compiled by the international agencies, readers may refer to the metadata available from databases of the individual international agencies, or to the SDG Global Database website for metadata of SDG indicators. Modeled estimates as presented in the SDG Global Database are also identified. Comparable and standardized national data gathered through a robust data-reporting mechanism of the international agencies serve as the basis for all data in the global monitoring databases.

Data obtained from ADB member economies are comparable to the extent that the ADB members follow standard statistical concepts, definitions, and estimation methods recommended by the United Nations and other applicable international agencies. Nevertheless, member economies invariably develop and use their own concepts, definitions, and estimation methodologies to suit their individual circumstances, and these may not necessarily comply with recommended international standards. Therefore, even though attempts are made to present the data in a comparable and uniform format, the data are subject to variations in the statistical methods used by individual economies, so full comparability may not be possible. These variations are reflected in the footnotes of the statistical tables or noted in the Data Issues and Comparability sections. Information about changes in compilation methodology is also provided in the footnotes. In addition, some indicators are expressed as functions of two or more indicators (e.g., indicators expressed as a proportion of gross domestic product). Hence, a change in the compilation methodology of one component indicator might affect other indicators based upon it. Hence, readers are encouraged to refer to the footnotes before making comparisons between economies and/or over time.

Moreover, the aggregates shown in some tables for the developing ADB member economies and ADB regional members are treated as approximations of the actual total or average, or growth rates, due to missing data from the primary source. For a description of the regional aggregation method, readers may refer to the footnotes presented in the tables and/or the metadata in the Key Indicators Database (kidb.adb.org). Footnotes also provide information for earlier years (earlier than 2000), which are relevant for the longer data series presented in the Key Indicators Database. Aggregates for the World were sourced from international agencies, and readers may refer to the metadata available from databases of the individual international agencies.

The data published by ADB do not constitute any form of advice or recommendation. For answers to any questions on the data, users of this publication are requested to seek advice from the relevant data source or organization.

Fiscal Year

There are 25 regional members of the Asian Development Bank with fiscal years that do not coincide with the calendar year. Whenever statistical series (for example, national accounts or government finance) are compiled on the basis of a fiscal year, these series are presented in the column for the single-year during which most of the fiscal year occurred. The 25 fiscal year definitions for 2022 are outlined below.

Regional Member	Fiscal Year	Year Caption
Afghanistan* (fiscal year since 2021)	21 March 2022 to 20 March 2023	2022
Brunei Darussalam (fiscal year since 2002) Hong Kong, China India Japan New Zealand Singapore	1 April 2022 to 31 March 2023	2022
Fiji	1 August 2021 to 31 July 2022	2022
Australia Bangladesh Bhutan Cook Islands Kiribati Nauru Niue Pakistan Samoa Tonga	1 July 2021 to 30 June 2022	2022
Nepal	16 July 2021 to 15 July 2022	2022
Lao People's Democratic Republic Marshall Islands Micronesia, Federated States of Myanmar** Palau Thailand	1 October 2021 to 30 September 2022	2022

* ADB placed its regular assistance to Afghanistan on hold effective 15 August 2021, but in 2022 supported the economic and social development of the Afghan people through a special arrangement with the United Nations to address basic human needs. ADB did not make any consultations with Afghanistan for the data in this publication.

** Effective 1 February 2021, ADB placed a temporary hold on sovereign project disbursements and new contracts in Myanmar. The bank continues to closely monitor the situation in the country and remains committed to supporting its people. ADB did not make any consultations with Myanmar for the data in this publication.

Key Symbols

...	data not available
–	magnitude equals zero
(-/+) 0 or 0.0	magnitude is less than half of unit employed
*	provisional/preliminary/estimate/budget figure
|	marks break in series
>	greater than
<	less than
%	percentage

Units of Measurement

GWh	gigawatt-hour
kg	kilogram
km	kilometer
km^2	square kilometer
kWh	kilowatt-hour
kt	kiloton
L	liter
m^3	cubic meter
mj	megajoule
PM	particulate matter
teu	twenty-foot equivalent unit
t	metric ton
$\mu g/m^3$	micrograms per cubic meter

Abbreviations

ADB	Asian Development Bank
ADBI	Asian Development Bank Institute
AIDS	acquired immunodeficiency syndrome
BPM5	Balance of Payments Manual (Fifth Edition)
BPM6	Balance of Payments and International Investment Position Manual (Sixth Edition)
CIF	cost, insurance, and freight
CO_2	carbon dioxide
COICOP	Classification of Individual Consumption by Purpose
COVID-19	coronavirus disease
CPI	consumer price index
CSO	Central Statistical Organization
DHS	Demographic and Health Survey
EROD-SDI	Economic Research and Development Impact Department, Statistics and Data Innovation Unit
FAO	Food and Agriculture Organization of the United Nations
FDI	foreign direct investment
FOB	free on board
FVA	foreign value-added
GDP	gross domestic product
GNI	gross national income
GVA	gross value-added
GVC	global value chain
HIV	human immunodeficiency virus
ICP	International Comparison Program
ICT	information and communication technology
IEA	International Energy Agency
IDA	International Development Association
IHR	International Health Regulations
ILO	International Labour Organization
IMF	International Monetary Fund
ISIC	International Standard Industrial Classification
ITU	International Telecommunication Union
JRC	Joint Research Center
KIDB	Key Indicators Database
LSCI	Liner Shipping Connectivity Index
MICS	Multiple Indicator Cluster Survey
MOF	Ministry of Finance
MRIOT	multiregional input-output table
NPL	nonperforming loan
NSO	national statistics office; national statistical office
ODA	official development assistance
OECD	Organisation for Economic Co-operation and Development
PARIS21	Partnership in Statistics for Development in the 21st Century
PLI	price level index
PPP	purchasing power parity

PRC	People's Republic of China
PSA	Philippine Statistics Authority
SCI	statistical capacity indicator
SDG	Sustainable Development Goal
SNA	System of National Accounts
UN	United Nations
UNAIDS	Joint United Nations Programme on HIV/AIDS
UNESCAP	United Nations Economic and Social Commission for Asia and the Pacific
UNICEF	United Nations Children's Fund
UNSD	United Nations Statistics Division
UNWTO	United Nations World Tourism Organization
US	United States
WHO	World Health Organization

Unless otherwise indicated, "$" refers to United States dollars.

PART I: SUSTAINABLE DEVELOPMENT GOALS

Tackling Cost of Living Challenges to Meet the SDGs

More resources needed to accelerate economic recovery and address post-pandemic development challenges, including increased cost of living

Spending needed to eradicate poverty and achieve other related SDGs in Asia and the Pacific estimated at over $669 billion a year for 2016-2030.

Sources: Figure 1.14 and Page 12.

Poor hurt most by high cost of living

In most economies, the bottom 50% spent more than half their budget on food and 10% more on energy than an average household.

Sources: Figures 1.9 and 1.11.

Increased cost of living crisis and the pandemic pushed millions of Asians into extreme poverty

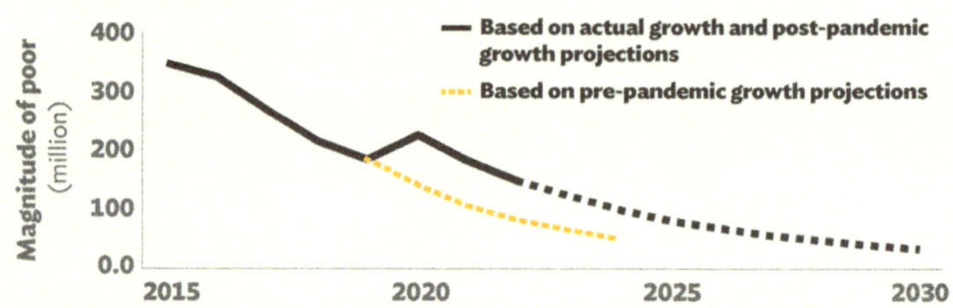

Compared to pre-pandemic estimates for 2022, an extra 67.8 million people were estimated to be extremely poor in developing Asia in 2022.

Source: Table 1.1.

Being poor is expensive

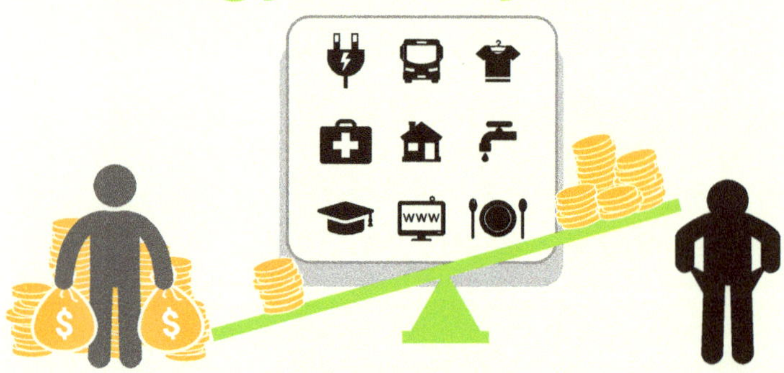

Poor people encounter poverty premium where they pay more for several goods and services.

Source: Page 17.

Poverty premium takes many forms

Transport and location barriers can raise costs for poor people.

Source: Box 1.1.

PART I: SUSTAINABLE DEVELOPMENT GOALS

Tackling Cost of Living Challenges to Meet the SDGs

In 2020, less than half of the population in 26 of 40 economies were covered by at least one social protection measure

Some economies have responded to recent crises with social protection measures but coverage needs to go beyond one-off protection.

Source: Figure 1.13.

Extreme poverty to fall from 3.9% in 2022 to 1% by 2030

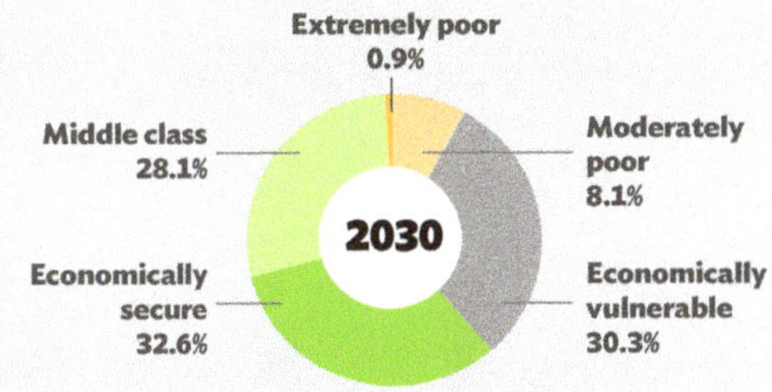

But over a third of the region will experience moderate poverty and economic vulnerability.

Source: Figure 1.7.

Surge of rural-urban migration may worsen urban poverty if not managed properly

The urban population will outstrip the rural population by about 1.5 billion in 2050.

Sources: Page 40 and Figure 1.23.

Internet access has doubled in the past decade

New technologies can narrow poverty premium by broadening access to services and opportunities

Sources: Figure 1.25 and Page 44.

PART II: REGIONAL TABLES

Navigating Inflationary Pressures and Economic Uncertainties

High inflation has exacerbated COVID-19 impacts

In 2022, inflation in developing Asia reached 4.4%, a level unseen in almost a decade.

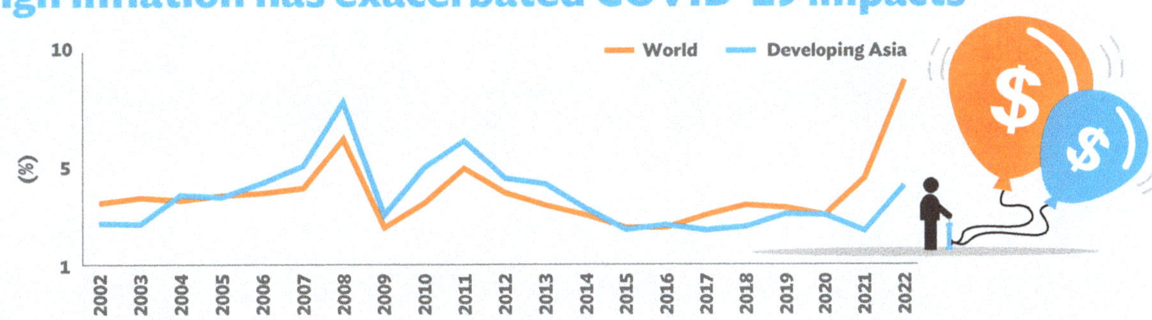

Source: Figure 2.1.

Food and energy prices surged in 2022

Food and nonalcoholic drinks prices rose at least 10% in 15 regional economies, with fuel prices up at least 8% in 15 economies.

Sources: Pages 112–113.

Policy measures to mitigate COVID-19 may have contributed to inflation

One-third of economies still recorded a money supply increase of at least 10% in 2022, following fiscal stimulus packages in previous years.

Sources: Page 113 and Figure 2.4.

PART II: REGIONAL TABLES

Navigating Inflationary Pressures and Economic Uncertainties

Higher interest rates imposed to curb inflation

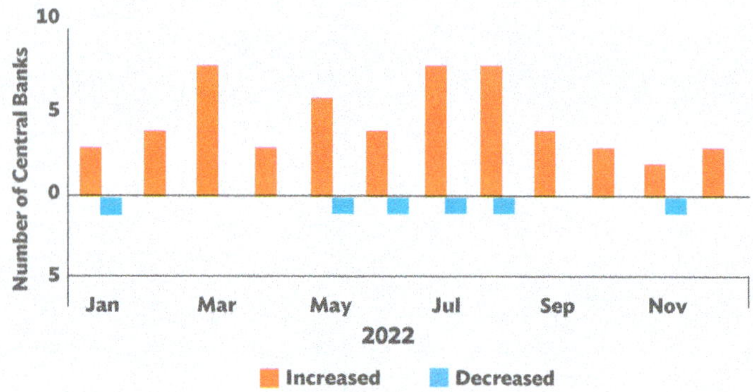

Central banks in 18 of 22 economies hiked interest rates at least once in 2022.

Source: Figure 2.5.

As inflation accelerated, economic recovery in most economies slowed

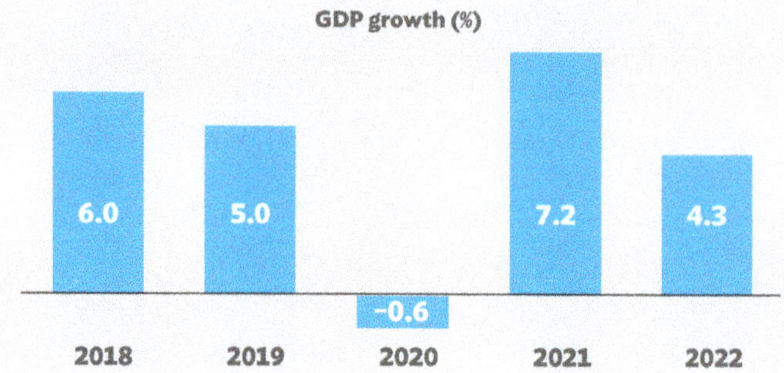

Growth in developing Asia slowed sharply in 2022 to 4.2%.

Source: Figure 2.6.

Nearly a quarter of regional economies had local currency depreciations of at least 10% in 2022

Currency exchange rates respond to changes in interest rates.

Source: Figure 2.7.

9 out of 12 economies recorded stock price index declines in 2022

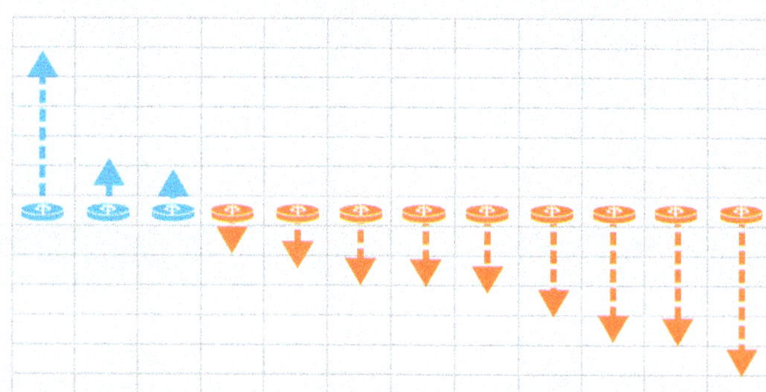

High interest rates increase borrowing costs and can cause declines in investments and stock prices.

Source: Figure 2.7.

Debt levels in some parts of Asia and the Pacific remained above pre-pandemic levels

External debt in 15 regional economies in 2022 exceeded 2019 levels by at least 20%.

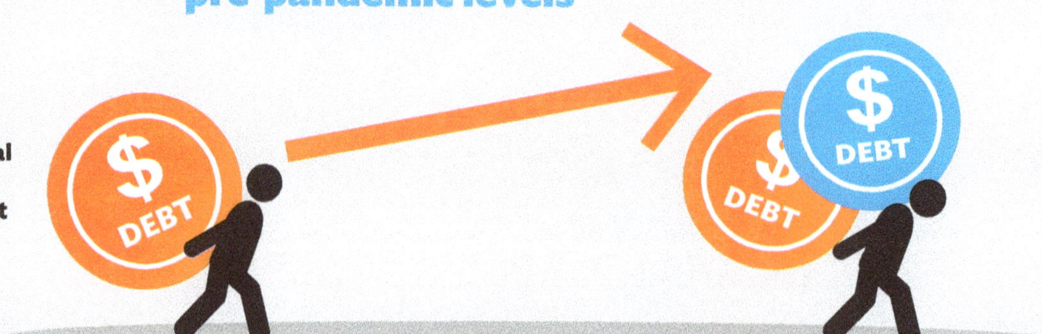

Source: Figure 2.8.

PART III: GLOBAL VALUE CHAINS

Price Change Impacts on GVC Indicators

Effect of inflationary trend on GVC participation started in 2020 and was more pronounced in 2022

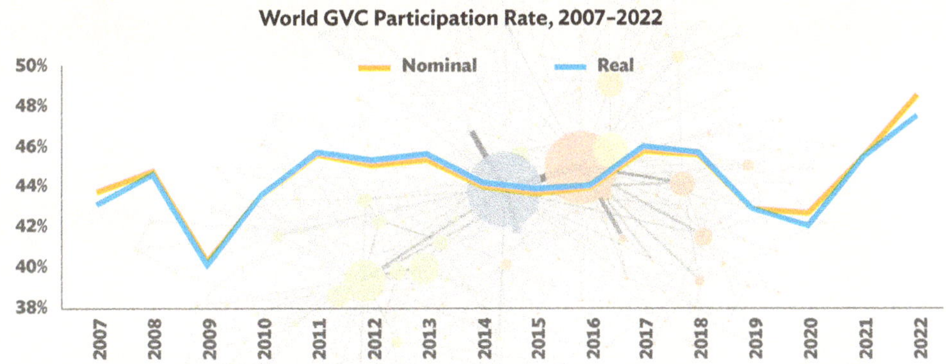

Source: Figure 3.2.

Differences in nominal and real GVC participation rates reflect changing effective prices faced by Developing Asia

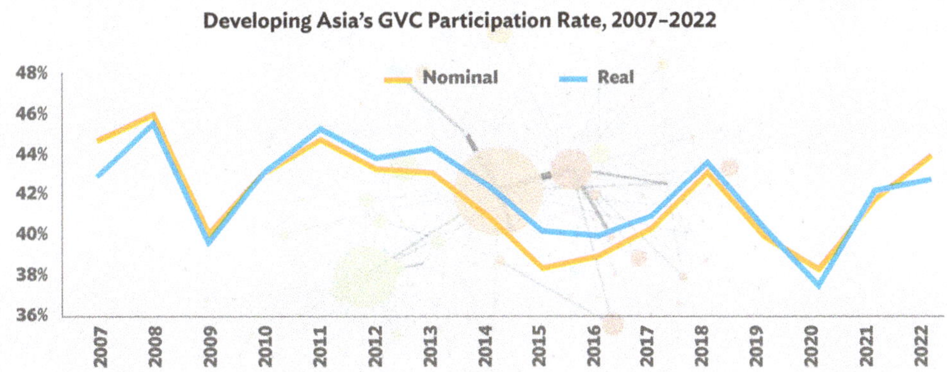

Source: Figure 3.3.

PART IV: STORIES BEHIND DATA

Using Price Data to Track Socioeconomic Development

National statistical systems are vital for price data collection and dissemination

Monthly CPI data provides timely price change information for policy makers.

Sources: Pages 253–255.

The International Comparison Program compiles global PPPs and measures of real outputs

Asia and the Pacific is critical to ICP, accounting for more than half of the world's population and two-fifths of global output in purchasing power parity (PPP) terms.

Sources: Pages 259 and 266.

Introduction

Introduction

Since 2022, the socioeconomic landscape in many parts of the world, including Asia and the Pacific, has been shaped by mixed forces of recovery, the lingering impact of the coronavirus disease (COVID-19) pandemic, and other external factors that have stalled economic growth. Most parts of the world have managed to fully reopen their economies after calibrating strategies to balance containment of COVID-19 infections, while still conducting business activities. This approach helped them cope with the aftermath of impacts from lockdowns and business shutdowns which characterized the first two years of the pandemic.

However, the optimism for a rapid economic recovery slowed as new variants emerged. Strict COVID-19 policies of key actors in global trade, such as the People's Republic of China, affected global supply chains, as it resulted in closed factories and ports. The Russian invasion of Ukraine, which started at the beginning of 2022, further reinforced shocks caused by the pandemic and added to looming uncertainties by causing severe disruptions in food and energy markets. The initial assumption of temporary upward pressure on prices was not well anchored, as inflation surged above the policy targets of many governments for extended periods. These factors, combined with the impact of fiscal stimulus provided at the height of the pandemic, have contributed to inflationary levels unseen since the global financial crisis (ADB 2022c; de Soyres et al. 2022; IMF 2022).

Compared to other regions, initial economic forecasts indicated that inflationary pressures would have benign effects on Asia and the Pacific (EIU 2021; Shevlin and Lam 2021). However, cost of living pressures also rose across the region as prices of food, energy and housing hit all-time highs as 2022 unfolded. This stalled developing Asia's economic performance which only managed to grow by 4.2% by the end of the year, lower than initial forecasts suggested (ADB 2023d). Across the globe, a number of central banks and monetary authorities raised interest rates to combat surging prices.

With inflation of prices of basic commodities and services at record highs, recovery from the pandemic became challenging for low-income groups, and those who just escaped from poverty could be pushed back into it due to reduced purchasing power. Poor people are most likely to be hit hardest due to the higher share of energy and food costs in their budget compared to other income groups. High inflation can also exacerbate economic inequalities as the impact of high prices affects the income and savings of poor people more than wealthier counterparts (Gill and Nagle 2022). An economic slowdown may also constrain national capacities to invest in poverty-reducing activities in areas such as health, education, and infrastructure (UN 2023b).

Even without surging prices, previous studies suggest that living in poverty may be expensive due to the premium, or penalty, paid by the poor (Caplovitz 1963; Corfe and Keohane 2018; Hirsch 2013; Mendoza 2011). The poverty premium manifests in various ways. For example, poor people may end up paying higher unit prices for select food items because they cannot afford to buy in bulk (Hossain 2020), because they have limited facilities to store food at home (Gauri, Jindal, and Ma 2021), or they do not have time and resources to look for cheaper and more nutritious food (French et.al. 2019).

Likewise, poor people may also pay more for commuting to work and other important establishments. For instance, a study suggests that in several cities, a considerable number of poor residing in informal settlements face long and expensive trips to work, often exceeding 3-4 hours per day (Starkey and Hine 2014). This time spent commuting to work deprives them from taking part in more productive activities (Lorenz 2018).

Poor people also face higher costs for accessing financial services. A study from (Cavoli and Shreshta 2020) estimated that in 2017, 18% of adults did not have access to a bank account because financial services were too expensive, while 13% said they were too far away from a physical bank facility. On the other hand, in developing Asia, access to credit for small firms, which provide a major source of employment for people of lower incomes, is constrained due to unfavorable interest rates, complex application procedures, and high collateral requirements (ADB 2015).

As the elevated cost of living pushes millions of Asians into economic hardship, there is a need to galvanize efforts to ensure poor people are able to cope with inflationary pressures and looming economic uncertainties. Furthermore, development practitioners and policymakers must also recognize the need of the poor for additional protection, even beyond the increased cost-of-living crisis. Addressing other development challenges and sources of socioeconomic disadvantage should constitute an important policy agenda as Asia and the Pacific moves closer to Sustainable Development Goal (SDG) reckoning in 2030.

The first half of Part I of *Key Indicators for Asia and the Pacific 2023* presents stylized facts on how previous and ongoing challenges associated with the poverty premium and penalty, and soaring cost of living, affect the most vulnerable populations in developing Asia. To examine these topics, featured data stories cite different examples of poverty premium and penalty. The discussion on poverty premium and penalty illustrates how its different forms may materialize. Data stories also provide a glimpse into how stronger social protection systems may help poor people navigate the increased cost-of-living crisis. The second half of Part I provides an overview of other development challenges confronted by people living in poverty. The section briefly discusses how boosting agricultural development, enhancing financial inclusion, and providing support for innovation and human capital development can potentially level up the playing field for the most vulnerable segments of society.

Part II presents other key indicators compiled by national statistical systems, accompanied by commentaries on the dynamics of inflation, economic growth, stock markets, and monetary policies in the form of interest rates and foreign exchange. These data stories also examine the potential implications of the current socioeconomic landscape on the sustainability of developing Asia's debt levels moving forward.

Part III discusses trends on global value chain participation expressed in nominal and real terms, providing relevant policy insights especially during periods of significant inflation.

Part IV documents how data and statistics on prices serve a wide range of purposes for development practitioners and policymakers, with a specific focus on the International Comparison Program which compiles purchasing power parities. Since the COVID-19 pandemic struck, prices of specific goods and services have fluctuated significantly, highlighting the need for timely intervention. Given the important role of price data as a key input for policymaking, there is a need to reflect on how national statistical systems currently compile data on prices, and how they can further push frontiers of price data collection to provide more timely, granular and spatially comparable information.

As Asia and the Pacific navigates its way through an uncertain economic environment, marked by an elevated cost of living, it is important to generate data driven-insights on other challenges confronting developing and frontier markets. *Key Indicators for Asia and the Pacific 2023* aims to support development practitioners by providing high-quality and timely data that can be used as inputs in designing targeted interventions and policies.

PART I

Sustainable Development Goals Trends and Tables

Pursuing Sustainable Development by Managing the Cost of Living in Poverty

Over the past 6 decades, developing Asia has undergone a significant transition from widespread poverty to general prosperity. From being a collection of agrarian, low-income economies in the 1960s, Asian Development Bank (ADB) data shows the region has evolved into the world's manufacturing powerhouse and now boasts diverse exports, expanding innovation, a growing skilled labor force, and a large consumer base (ADB 2020).

In 1960, the contribution of the region to total global output was just 4.4%. By 2021, estimates suggest that it exceeded 28.6%, in nominal terms.[1] Over these years, gross domestic product (GDP) per capita also grew by 4.7%, far higher than the world average of 1.9% (ADB 2020). The period has also seen a sharp reduction in the incidence of poverty, a rise in life expectancy, a decline in infant mortality, an impressive increase in educational attainment, and substantial improvement in delivery of basic services (Figure 1.1).

Figure 1.1: Improvement in Living Conditions of Asians Over Time

Living conditions in developing Asia improved markedly over the 60 years leading into the COVID-19 pandemic.

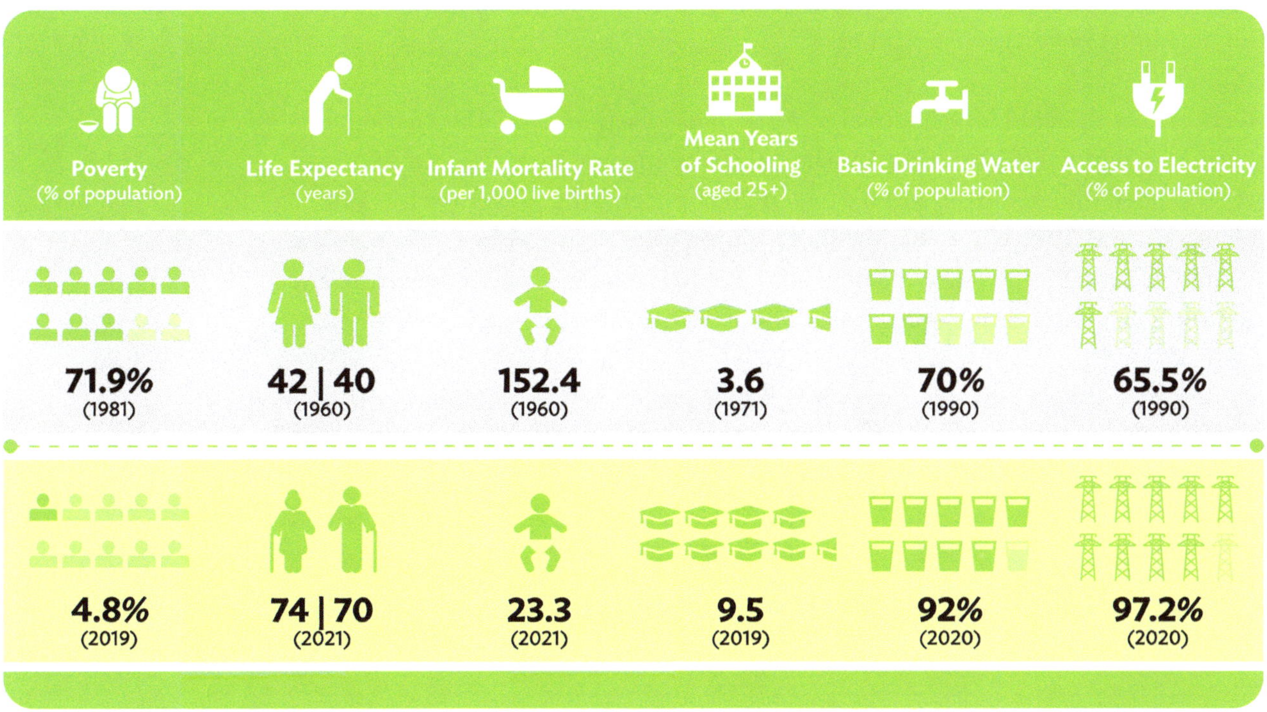

Notes: Poverty refers to the prevalence of extreme poverty using the $2.15/day international poverty line at 2017 purchasing power parity (PPP). Life expectancy refers to life expectancy at birth in years. The infant mortality rate refers to infant deaths per 1,000 live births. Mean years of schooling are for those aged 25 and over. Basic drinking water refers to percentage of population using at least basic drinking water services. Access to electricity is the percentage of population with access to electricity.

Sources: Asian Development Bank estimates and visualization using data from the Asian Development Bank's Key Indicators Database, the World Bank Group's World Development Indicators Database and Poverty and Inequality Platform Database, and the United Nations Educational, Scientific and Cultural Organization Institute for Statistics Database (accessed 1 June 2023).

---

1 The region accounts for about 40% of global GDP, when converted using purchasing power parities (Joshi et al. 2021).

In spite of these achievements, the COVID-19 pandemic and its after-effects pushed developing Asia into its first regional economic recession in 60 years, with millions of Asians driven into severe hardship (ADB 2021c). In 2023, more than 3 years since the pandemic first struck, the region is at a critical juncture. The most vulnerable and poorest populations face multiple dimensions of inequality, grappling with a global cost-of-living crisis, high inflation, and the impacts of longer-term challenges such as climate change (ADB 2023b). With already tight household budgets, poor communities are being confronted by higher costs of food, other basic commodities, and essential services, further absorbing a disproportionate share of their meagre financial resources.

Indeed, studies conducted by the United Nations Development Programme (UNDP) and the World Bank in 2022 estimated that millions of people in the world's poorest economies had been pushed into extreme poverty in the first quarter of 2022 due to increased cost of living pressures (UNDP 2022a; Mahler et al. 2022). To prevent global poverty targets from slipping out of reach, there is an urgent need for action as we cross the halfway point in the 2030 Agenda for Sustainable Development (UN 2023a).

The first half of Part I of *Key Indicators for Asia and the Pacific 2023* takes stock of how developing Asia is faring with respect to selected targets under Sustainable Development Goal (SDG) 1, including reduction of monetary and multidimensional poverty.

The section uses updated international poverty lines based on 2017 International Comparison Program (ICP) results. In particular, the income threshold for extreme poverty has been updated from $1.90 a day in 2011 purchasing power parity (PPP) to $2.15 a day in 2017 PPP, while the threshold for moderate poverty has changed from $3.20 a day in 2011 PPP to $3.65 a day in 2017 PPP. It also discusses nowcasting and forecasting of poverty in developing Asia under varying inflation scenarios.

The second half of Part I also discusses minimizing the poverty premium in the context of selected indicators of SDG 2 (zero hunger), SDG 8 (decent work and economic growth), and SDG 11 (sustainable cities and communities).

Jrgent action needed. At the halfway point of implementation of the SDGs, there is a need to mobilize resources and galvanize ·fforts of development community if we are to eradicate poverty in developing Asia by 2030 (photo by Skanda Gautam/ADB).

Why Is Sustainable Development Goal 1 Important and How Is Developing Asia Faring?[2]

Given the high cost of addressing multiple dimensions of poverty there is a need to focus resources on addressing some of the persistent sources of socioeconomic disadvantage among the poor.

SDG 1 aims to end poverty in all its forms everywhere by 2030. Its targets include eradication of extreme poverty, reduction of multidimensional poverty, and building better social safety nets (UN n.d.) To achieve SDG 1, there is a need to mobilize resources via governments and the wider development community.

Figure 1.2 presents estimates of prevalence of poverty and the poverty gap (or the average income shortfall from the poverty line expressed as a percentage of the poverty line) in developing Asia from 2015 to 2019.

2 Unless stated otherwise, most of the analyses of monetary poverty for developing Asia presented in this section are based on information from 29 Asian Development Bank regional member economies for which data needed for poverty calculations are available: Armenia, Azerbaijan, Bangladesh, Bhutan, Fiji, Georgia, India, Indonesia, Kazakhstan, the Kyrgyz Republic, the Lao People's Democratic Republic, Malaysia, Maldives, Mongolia, Myanmar, Nepal, Pakistan, Papua New Guinea, the People's Republic of China, the Philippines, Samoa, Solomon Islands, Sri Lanka, Tajikistan, Thailand, Tonga, Uzbekistan, Vanuatu, and Viet Nam.

In 2019, the poverty gap was 0.9%. Multiplying this number with the region's population size, number of days per year, and poverty line gives us a monetary equivalent of the cost to eradicate extreme poverty in developing Asia.

A study by the United Nations Economic and Social Commission for Asia and the Pacific (UNESCAP 2019) indicates that total spending to achieve poverty eradication and other goals such as zero hunger (SDG 2) and building human capabilities (SDGs 3 and 4) exceeds $669 billion (or less than 2% of average GDP of developing economies in the region) per year for 2016–2030. With this amount well beyond the reach of many developing economies (UNESCAP 2019), there is a need to focus resources on addressing some of the persistent sources of socioeconomic disadvantage among the poor. For instance, current estimates of total official development assistance grants that focus on poverty reduction as presented in Table 1.1.2, suggest that on average only a small portion of donors gross national income are channeled into poverty reduction. As the latest special edition of UN's SDG Report notes, there is a need for a fundamental shift in commitment, solidarity, financing, and action, as the world maneuvers its way back to a virtuous path of development (UN 2023a).

Although 2017 PPP estimates confirm developing Asia reduced monetary poverty from 1990 to 2019, the prevalence of extreme poverty was higher in 2019 compared to 2011 PPP estimates.

In compiling statistics on monetary poverty, it is important to capture the effects of the cost of living. A typical approach adopted by national statistics offices is to identify a bundle of goods and services deemed essential to meet basic consumption needs then estimate the cost of the bundle (World Bank [WBG] 2022a). In some instances, the composition and pricing of the bundle may vary across different geographic areas within an economy and over time. This approach aims to capture differences in the minimum cost needed for a person to get by. Likewise, the World Bank updates international poverty lines by drawing results from ICP benchmark years (Figure 1.3).

Using the new extreme poverty line of $2.15 a day (2017 PPP), it is estimated that 4.8% of developing Asia's population fell below this threshold in 2019 (up from 4.5% in earlier estimates), meaning 13 million more people are now classified as living in extreme poverty. There are, however, variations across economies as shown in Figure 1.4.

When using the moderate poverty threshold of $3.65 a day (2017 PPP), the average national poverty line of lower-middle income economies, nearly a quarter of developing Asia's population were considered poor in 2019. Under the $6.85 a day (2017 PPP) threshold for economic vulnerability, the average national poverty line of upper-middle income economies, more than half of all Asians were regarded as poor in 2019.

Figure 1.2: Pre-Pandemic Trends of Prevalence of Poverty and the Poverty Gap in Developing Asia

In 2019, about 4.8% of developing Asia's population were living in extreme poverty while the poverty gap was 0.9%.

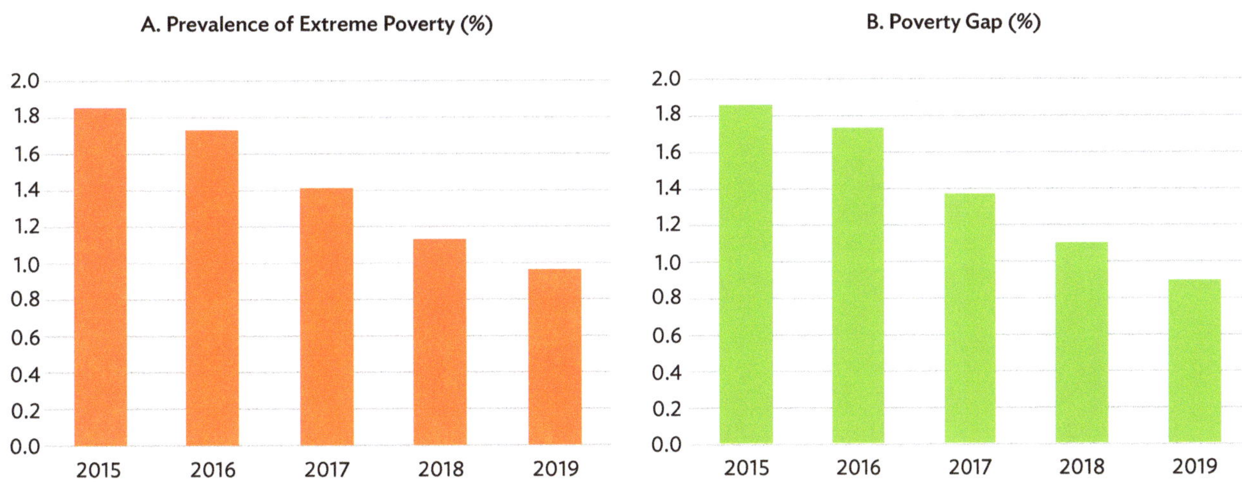

Source: Asian Development Bank estimates using data from the World Bank Poverty and Inequality Platform (accessed 1 June 2023).

Figure 1.3: Evolution of Thresholds for Extreme Poverty Measurement

International poverty lines are updated to capture how differences in price levels evolve across the globe.

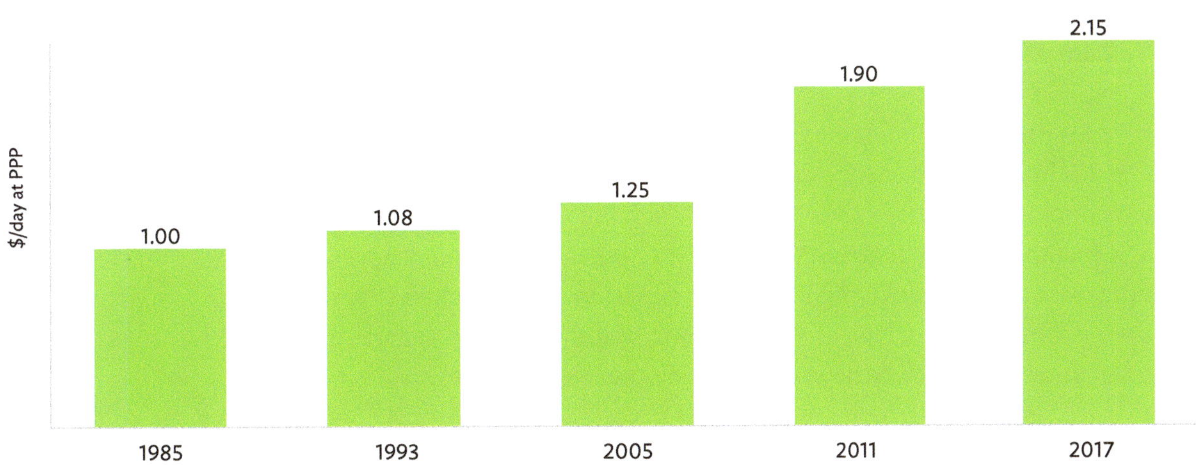

Notes: In general, the determination of the threshold for extreme poverty is based on the national poverty line from some of the poorest economies in the world, expressed in a common currency using purchasing power parity conversion factors. When the international poverty line was first set in 1990, researchers from the World Bank noted that the value of the national poverty line was about $1 per day per person in six of the poorest economies in the 1980s. On the other hand, $1.25 represents the poverty line in the early 1990s, while $1.90 was derived as the average of the national poverty line of 15 poor economies based on the 2011 ICP benchmark year. The $2.15 is the median of the national poverty lines of 28 of the poorest economies across the globe based on the 2017 ICP benchmark year (WBG 2022a).

Source: Asian Development Bank visualization.

Figure 1.4: Prevalence of Extreme Poverty and Comparison of Economy-Level Estimates, 2011 and 2017 PPP

Developing Asia significantly reduced extreme poverty prior to the COVID-19 pandemic, but new international poverty lines reveal that there are more extremely poor people than initially thought.

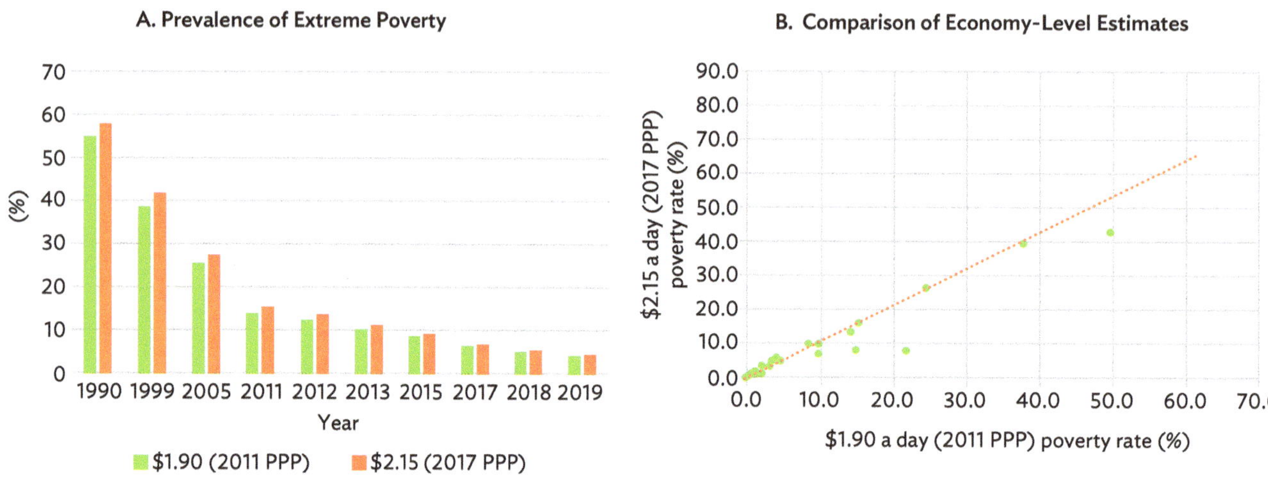

Notes: The estimates are based on 29 developing Asian Development Bank regional member economies with available data required for calculations.

Sources: Asian Development Bank estimates using data presented in Table 1.1.1 of *Key Indicators for Asia and the Pacific 2023* and simulated data derived from the World Bank's Poverty and Inequality Platform (accessed 1 June 2023).

It is important to note that poverty goes beyond lack of income or the absence of financial resources to meet basic needs.

There can be multiple complex issues and situations that converge to push people into poverty. An integrated measure of multidimensional poverty, the Global Multidimensional Poverty Index, has therefore been incorporated into the SDGs to complement income poverty metrics. This measure takes into account non-monetary poverty indicators that people living in poverty experience simultaneously, such as malnutrition, poor sanitation, lack of employment, insufficient health care, limited access to education and other basic services, and other deprivations.

A paper prepared by the UNDP (2022b) notes that about one-third of reporting economies in the Asia and Pacific region had at least 20% of their population considered multidimensionally poor in 2016–2021 (Figure 1.5). The report also assessed the intensity of multidimensional poverty by calculating an average deprivation score based on various poverty dimensions such as the availability of adequate nutrition, cooking fuel, sanitation, and housing. Figure 1.5 also shows that the average intensity of deprivation across selected economies in the region was 41% for 2016–2021.

Figure 1.5: Prevalence and Intensity of Multidimensional Poverty in Asia and the Pacific

The average score for intensity of deprivation exceeded 40% in half of the reporting economies of Asia and the Pacific.

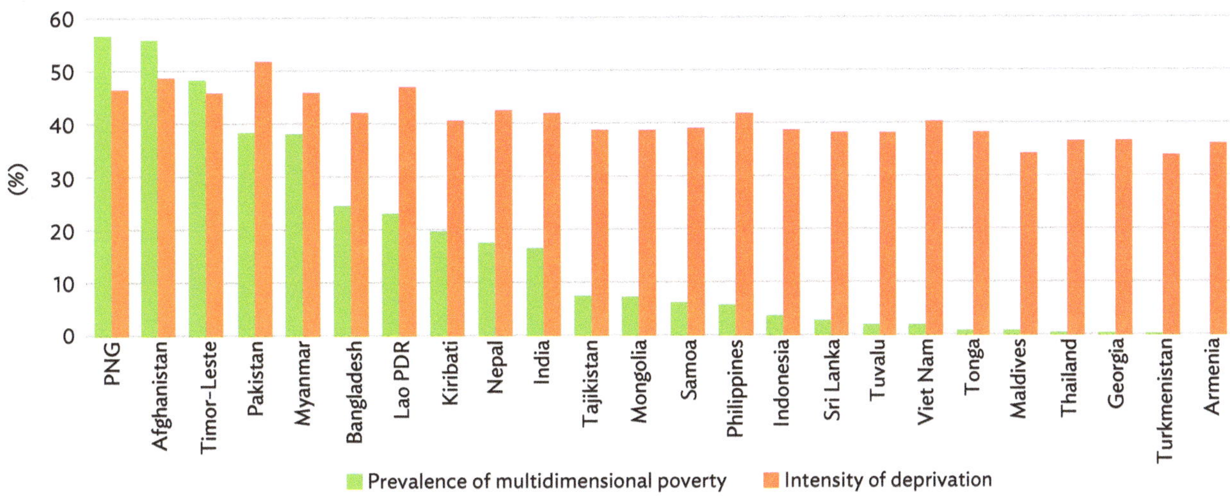

Lao PDR = Lao People's Democratic Republic, PNG = Papua New Guinea.

Notes: The prevalence of multidimensional poverty refers to the percentage of the population with a deprivation score of at least 33.3%. Meanwhile, the intensity of multidimensional poverty denotes the average deprivation score among multidimensionally poor people. In this case, the intensity of more than 40% implies that, on average, multidimensionally poor individuals are experiencing deprivation in approximately 40% of the dimensions or indicators used to measure poverty.

Sources: Estimates from the Multidimensional Poverty Index of the United Nations Development Programme and Oxford Poverty and Human Development Initiative (accessed 14 April 2023).

Figure 1.6: Relative Changes in Household Consumption or Income Per Capita and Proportion of People Living in Poverty Based on National Definitions

Households with low incomes appear to be more impacted by the COVID-19 pandemic, while several economies reported a higher incidence of nationally defined poverty from 2020 onward.

A. Relative Changes in Household Consumption or Income Per Capita

Economy	Year	Overall Mean (in 2017) PPP)	D1	D2	D3	D4	D5	D6	D7	D8	D9	D10
Armenia	2019-2021	0.00	2.03	1.70	1.74	0.88	0.21	-0.01	-0.37	-0.49	-0.19	-4.19
Georgia	2019-2021	-2.72	-2.26	-0.62	-0.82	-0.72	-0.50	-0.99	-1.92	-2.87	-3.04	-5.16
Indonesia	2019-2021	1.99	1.85	2.00	2.11	2.08	1.94	1.54	1.05	1.10	1.36	3.09
Kyrgyz Republic	2019-2020	-9.00	-11.21	-11.24	-9.60	-9.03	-7.36	-6.43	-5.17	-4.56	-4.22	-15.34
Philippines	2018-2021	-2.39	-2.82	-1.78	-1.59	-1.68	-1.92	-2.15	-2.26	-2.39	-2.61	-2.81
Thailand	2019-2021	1.79	0.51	1.20	1.64	1.68	1.63	1.69	1.98	2.05	1.98	1.86
Vanuatu	2010-2019	0.28	1.62	1.40	1.42	1.35	1.37	1.40	1.11	0.62	0.08	-1.53
Viet Nam	2018-2020	5.74	5.98	4.57	4.35	4.06	4.24	4.55	5.08	5.43	5.72	7.72

B. Proportion of People Living in Poverty Based on National Definitions

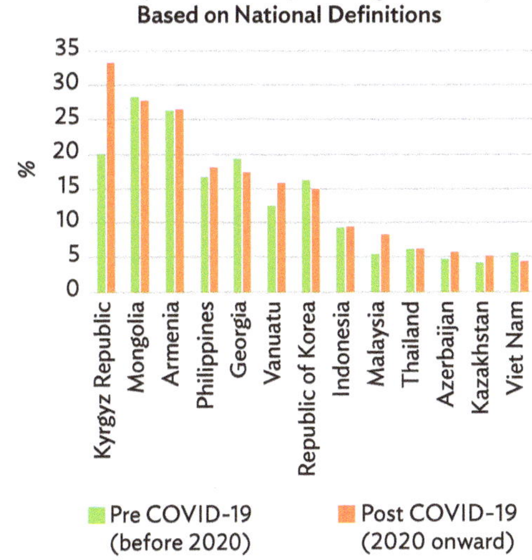

D = decile.

Notes: Cells are highlighted green when the corresponding change is higher than the change in the specific economy's overall mean household consumption per capita and yellow if the change is lower. The reference periods for the bar chart are 2019-2021 (Armenia, Azerbaijan, Georgia, Kazakhstan, Republic of Korea, Kyrgyz Republic, Thailand and Viet Nam); 2019-2022 (Indonesia); 2018-2021 (Philippines); 2019-2020 (Malaysia); 2018-2020 (Mongolia); and 2010-2020 (Vanuatu).

Sources: Asian Development Bank estimates using economy sources, survey reports, and data provided by statistical partners and from the World Bank's Poverty and Inequality Platform (accessed 30 June 2023).

The COVID-19 crisis has made the eradication of poverty even more challenging, with updated data suggesting that the pandemic's impacts on poverty may have been underestimated.

ADB has estimated that an additional 75 to 80 million people in developing Asia were pushed into extreme poverty (based on 2011 PPP) in 2020, compared to the scenario without COVID-19 (ADB 2021c). It has also been estimated that students from the bottom 20% may incur losses in future earnings that are 47% higher than those of their counterparts from the top 20% (ADB 2022b; ADB 2022d).

It should, however, be noted that some previous estimates of the pandemic's socioeconomic impacts, particularly on poverty, relied on simulations and simplified assumptions that all households within an economy experienced the same percentage decline in their per capita consumption expenditure and/or income (ADB 2022d). In some economies, where household survey data have been collected from 2020 onward, the data shows that households with low incomes in fact experienced more severe impacts on consumption than did higher income deciles (Figure 1.6). This is supported by the fact that the prevalence of poverty, based on national definitions, actually increased in several reporting economies (Figure 1.6).

While extreme poverty in developing Asia is forecast to shrink to 1% of the population by 2030, rates of moderate poverty and economic vulnerability will remain disturbingly high.

The rates of extreme and moderate poverty (based on 2017 PPP) in developing Asia for 2022 have been estimated at 3.9% and 18.8%, respectively. The latest forecasts suggest that, by 2030, only 1% of the population (or 37.9 million people) in the region will be living in extreme poverty but 8% (or 336 million people) will still be moderately poor. Additionally, 30.3% of the region's population (or 1.26 billion people) are forecast to be economically vulnerable in 2030 (Figure 1.7).

While developing Asia recovered from the COVID-19 pandemic, other factors such as the Russian invasion of Ukraine, increased trade tensions, and global supply chain disruptions contributed to stalled growth and price pressures in 2022.

For many households, sharp increases in prices of food and other essential commodities and services in 2022 significantly devalued real wages. Compared to wealthier households, even a modest increase in the cost of essential goods and services leaves lower-income households with less money for savings, food, energy, rent, health care expenses, and/or child education. Persistent inflation, moreover, could generate longer-term poverty traps (Nuguer and Parado 2021).

Figure 1.7: Income Groupings in Developing Asia by 2030

Growth projections suggest that developing Asia can reduce the prevalence of extreme and moderate poverty to 9% by 2030, but almost 30% of its population may still be economically vulnerable.

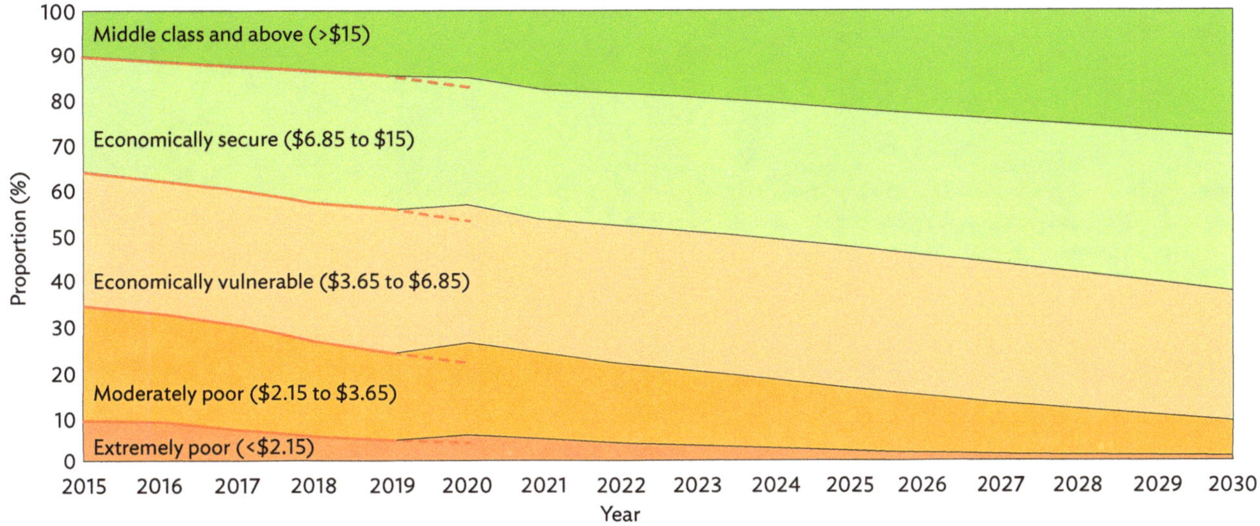

Note: Each income grouping is calculated as the percentage of people in developing Asia. These are based on 29 developing Asian Development Bank member economies with available data required for calculations. Income thresholds are expressed in 2017 purchasing power parities. The dotted lines represent counterfactual estimates under the scenario that the coronavirus disease (COVID-19) pandemic did not happen.

Sources: Asian Development Bank estimates using data presented in Table 1.1.1 of *Key Indicators for Asia and the Pacific 2023* and simulated data derived from the World Bank's Poverty and Inequality Platform (accessed 1 June 2023).

How Expensive Is It to Be Poor?

It is crucial that governments address the socioeconomic disadvantage of the poor paying more to buy certain goods and services.

There is paradoxical evidence suggesting it may cost more to be poor, especially during periods of crisis and uncertainty.

Studies on multidimensional poverty have found that people living with multiple deprivations in poorer regions are more likely to face health shocks and are less likely to be able to afford professional medical services because of their low income and lack of knowledge of the importance of preventive health care (Mohanty et al. 2017). During the COVID-19 pandemic, poorer communities exhibited lower compliance with mobility restrictions (Yechezkel et al. 2021) largely because many low-wage individuals, with little to no savings and a lack of access to credit, had no choice but to leave their homes to earn income. This increased the risk of transmission of the virus and led to unexpected or additional health-related expenses.

Other research indicates that there are instances when the poorest households may pay a premium for selected goods and services during "normal" periods (Corfe and Keohane 2018; Hirsch 2013; Mendoza 2011).

Uncontrolled inflation could generate poverty traps. The poor are most likely to be hit hardest due to the higher share of energy and food costs in their budget compared to other income groups (photo by Al Benavente/ADB).

Figure 1.8 illustrates examples of when prices paid by the poor exceed those of the general population. The orange bar represents the proportion of items whose prices collected from a poverty-specific survey were lower than the prices collected from the ICP's general survey. The green bar represents the proportion of items whose poverty-specific survey prices were higher by up to 20%. The blue bar represents the proportion of items whose poverty-specific survey prices were higher by more than 20%. Although, in most cases, prices from the poverty-specific survey were lower than from the general survey, there were many instances when the poor were paying significantly higher prices for certain items and hence, poverty premium remains an important concern (ADB 2008).

Box 1.1 elaborates on the concept of a poverty premium or penalty, and outlines factors that contribute to its existence, providing some specific examples.[3]

---

[3] The concept of poverty premium was first introduced by Prahalad and Hammond (2002) who postulated that poor people may pay more for the same goods and services than wealthier individuals, which creates an opportunity for companies, particularly large corporations with efficient supply chains, to offer higher quality products at lower prices to this market and increase market share while still maintaining profit margins (Prahalad 2004).

Figure 1.8: Comparison of Prices Paid by the General Population and the Poor

There are instances when the poor may be paying more for several types of goods and services.

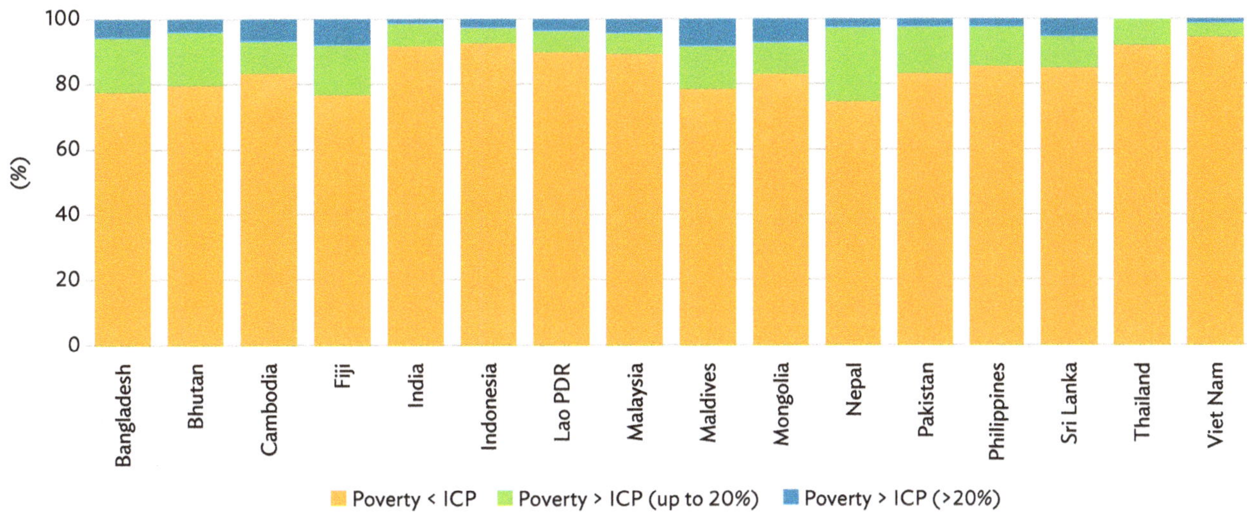

Lao PDR = Lao People's Democratic Republic.
Poverty = Poverty-specific survey, ICP = general ICP price survey collected for 2005 ICP round
Notes: The chart shown here is simply intended to illustrate that there are instances when poor people pay more for select items. The degree of premium paid by the poor may have already changed since the data presented here were collected.
Source: Asian Development Bank estimates using data presented in the Asian Development Bank *Research Study on Poverty-Specific Purchasing Power Parities for Selected Countries in Asia and the Pacific* (ADB 2008).

Box 1.1: Examples of Poverty Premium and Penalty

Studies suggest that the premium or penalty imposed on the poor as consumers may take different forms. For example: (i) products sold at similar prices are of poorer quality, (ii) the same or similar products are priced higher, and/or (iii) products are priced so high they are completely unaffordable for the poor. Where the consumption of a specific good or service is a necessity (e.g., health care) and the poor are unable to afford it, these people could be faced with the difficult choice of forgoing treatment or incurring debt to finance such spending (Mendoza 2011).

There are also indirect forms of poverty premium or penalty. For instance, the poor may be forced to live in less-expensive informal settlements where they are exposed to greater health hazards, or to choose cheaper commuting options that result in longer travel times, which could have been used to undertake more economically productive activities.

Nevertheless, there are studies suggesting that technological advancements and more competitive markets may allow the poor access to better-quality products at the same price or lower prices (Mendoza 2011).

Do poor people pay higher prices for food?

The figure below shows that in a number of developing economies in Asia and the Pacific, at least a quarter of matched food items were being sold to poor populations at prices 20% higher than those offered to the general population. There are several compelling arguments about how the poor may incur a poverty premium on the purchase of food. Studies show that households in low-income categories spend more money on similar products compared to wealthier households because of liquidity constraints (Rao 2000). Limited financial resources may require that smaller quantities of food are purchased each time, forfeiting the cost-efficiencies of buying in larger quantities or in bulk (Hossain 2020).

Another factor in the poverty penalty on food is a lack of access to transportation, which may prevent poor people from shopping around for the best prices and/or more nutritious food. Research by (Boonyabancha et.al. 2019.) shows that low-income households in urban areas of Cambodia and Nepal preferred purchasing in small shops located within their communities and settlements.

(continued on next page)

Box 1.1: Examples of Poverty Premium and Penalty *(continued)*

Poor people may also have limited facilities to safely store or freeze food at home, making them more reliant on prepackaged or convenience foods that are often more expensive and/or less nutritious. As shown in the left figure below, poorer areas have a lower prevalence of refrigerator ownership (Dhanaraj, Mahambare, and Munjal 2017). Limited access to refrigeration may also contribute to time poverty among women as they generally do unpaid domestic work and have to spend longer on food purchasing and preparation, as shown in the right figure below (ADB 2015).

Comparison of Food Prices in Poverty-Specific and General Price Surveys

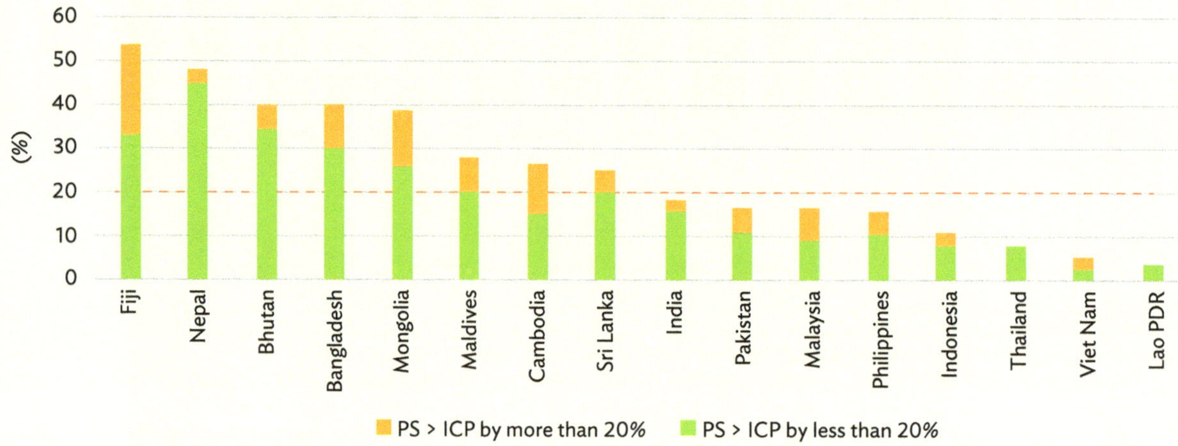

PS = poverty-specific survey, ICP = (general) ICP survey
Lao PDR = Lao People's Democratic Republic.

Notes: This chart is simply intended to illustrate that there are instances when poor people pay more for select food items. The degree of premium paid by the poor on select food items may have already changed since the data presented here were collected.

Source: Asian Development Bank estimates based on data presented in Table 16 of the Asian Development Bank *Research Study on Poverty-Specific Purchasing Power Parities for Selected Countries in Asia and the Pacific* (ADB 2008).

A. Proportion of Poorer Households Owning a Refrigerator

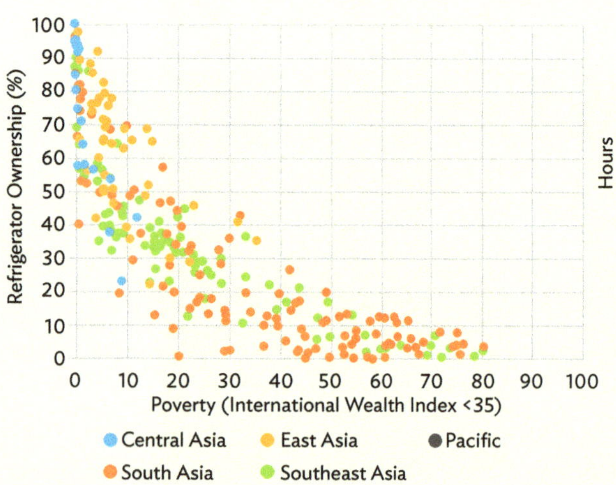

B. Average Number of Hours Worked Per Day by Gender

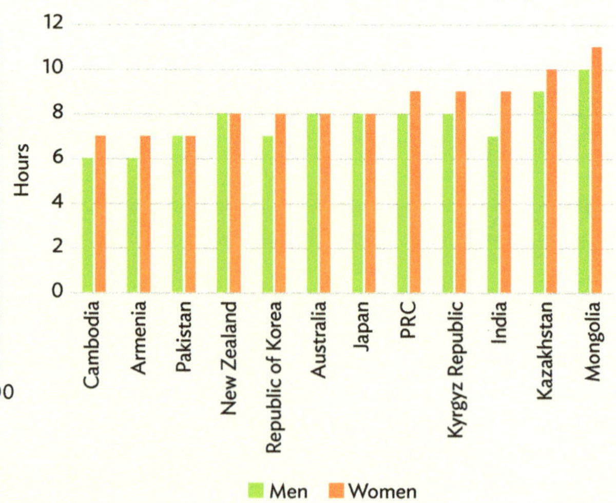

PRC = People's Republic of China.

Notes: In chart A, the y-axis corresponds to the proportion of households in a given area that own a refrigerator, while the x-axis represents the proportion of households in a given area which are poor, as indicated by a value lower than 35 in their International Wealth Index. In chart B, the height of the bar represents total time spent doing paid and unpaid market and non-market work.

Source: Asian Development Bank visualization using data from the Global Data Lab (accessed 1 June 2023) and data from from the Asian Development Bank publication *Balancing the Burden? Desk Review of Women's Time Poverty and Infrastructure in Asia and the Pacific* (ADB 2015).

(continued on next page)

Box 1.1: Examples of Poverty Premium and Penalty *(continued)*

Is transportation less affordable for the poor?

Although people with lower incomes tend to prefer cheaper commuting options, they still may end up paying transportation premiums (Helling 1998).

According to the United Nations Human Settlements Programme (UN-Habitat) and ODI, a significant proportion of poor individuals live in outer suburban areas, often due to involuntary resettlement, or in informal settlements on the remote fringes of cities (Starkey and Hine 2014). These individuals may have to travel long distances and spend significant amounts of time and money commuting to work. There is also evidence that in economies such as the Philippines, the bottom 30% of households faced higher price hikes for transport-related goods and services during the COVID-19 pandemic than did the general population. This is evident from the left figure below.

Inferior quality of roads in poorer areas, as indicated in the right figure below for the Philippines, may also contribute to a transportation penalty or premium through longer travel times and increased vehicle maintenance costs (Thegeya et al. 2022). In some cases, poor communities may have no access at all to affordable and reliable transportation, and walking or cycling long distances are a substantial poverty penalty in terms of commuting times.

Consumer Price Inflation in the Philippine Transport Sector and Road Ratings by Socioeconomic Region in the Philippines

A. Consumer Price Inflation in the Philippines Transport Sector

Transport	2019		2020		2021		2022	
	All HH	Bottom 30%	All HH	Bottom 30%	All HH	Bottom 30%	All HH	Bottom 30%
All	1.1	1.5	1.5	3.9	9.3	11.7	12.9	10.8
Purchase of Vehicles	1.7	1.9	3.4	3.1	3.1	2.0	1.4	1.3
Operation of Personal Transport Equipment	-0.9	0.5	-9.6	-8.1	16.8	17.2	33.7	29.5
Passenger Transport Services	2.2	1.9	7.5	9.6	7.8	11.2	5.5	4.6
Transport Services of Goods	4.6	2.6	0.0	0.2	0.0	0.1	0.2	0.2

B. Road Ratings by Geographic Region in the Philippines

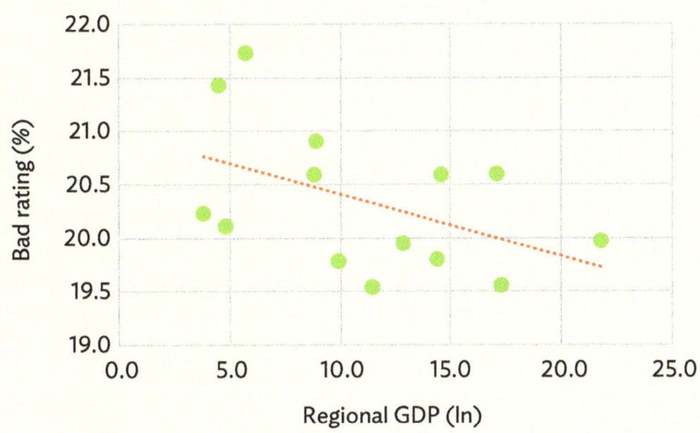

Note: Outliers were excluded from the scatter plot.

Sources: For table A: Asian Development Bank estimates based on data from the Philippine Statistics Authority (accessed 1 June 2023). For chart B: visualization of data from the A. Thegeya et al. 2022 study *Application of Machine Learning Algorithms on Satellite Imagery for Road Quality Monitoring.*

Is there an extra cost for the poor to access reliable energy?

Energy poverty is a term used to describe when individuals or households lack access to, or are unable to afford, adequate heating or other essential energy services within their residences (Pye et al. 2015). One factor that can affect energy poverty is geographic location. Some studies found that the supply of electricity in rural Cambodia was at least six times more expensive than in the economy's urban areas. This discrepancy can be attributed to limitations in infrastructure, high distribution costs, and low consumption levels (Phoumin and Kimura 2019). Similarly, an empirical study by Acharya and Sadath (2019) revealed that energy poverty was higher in rural India than in its urban areas.

(continued on next page)

Box 1.1: Examples of Poverty Premium and Penalty *(continued)*

An alternative source of energy such as kerosene also costs more for the poor as shown in the left figure below, where kerosene was more expensive for poor households in 10 of 15 economies with available data. In some even poorer areas, households are deprived of cooking fuel, meaning they must cook with dung, charcoal, or wood (UNDP 2022b). As shown in the right figure below, 12 of 27 economies in Asia and the Pacific had at least 10% of the population deprived of access to cooking fuel in 2022. These alternative sources of energy can have severe negative impacts on the health of household members, further adding to overall expenses for low-income households (Sadath and Acharya 2017).

Price Ratio of Kerosene in Poverty-Specific and General Price Surveys, and Proportion of Poor People Deprived of Cooking Fuel

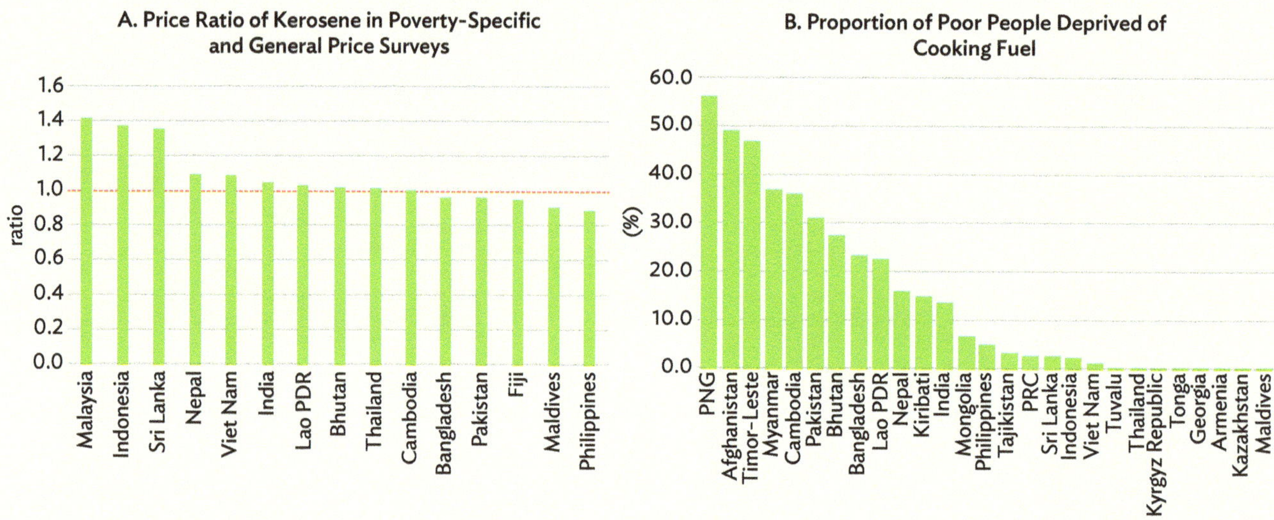

Lao PDR = Lao People's Democratic Republic, PNG = Papua New Guinea, PRC = People's Republic of China.

Note: For chart A, the ratio of the price of kerosene collected from the poverty-specific survey and general ICP survey were compiled from the 2005 ICP round. The degree of difference in prices paid by the poor and the general population may have already changed since the data presented here were collected. For chart B, a person is deprived of cooking fuel if living in a household using solid fuel such as dung, agricultural crop, shrubs, wood, charcoal, or coal for cooking. The global Multidimensional Poverty Index is an international measure of acute multidimensional poverty covering 100 developing economies. It complements traditional monetary poverty measures by capturing acute deprivations in health, education, and living standards that a person faces simultaneously. Cooking fuel is one of the six indicators in the living standard dimension of poverty.

Source: For chart A: Asian Development Bank estimates using data presented in the Asian Development Bank *Research Study on Poverty-Specific Purchasing Power Parities for Selected Countries in Asia and the Pacific* (ADB 2008). For chart B: Global Multidimensional Poverty Index Databank 2022 developed by Ayush Patel using data by Alkire, Kanagaratnam and Suppa (2022a and 2022b).

Is access to financial services more expensive for the poor?

Across developing Asia, poor people and families may not qualify for bank loans or other forms of credit due to a lack of collateral or credit history. They also may not have the necessary documents or identification to open a bank account. The Economic Research Institute for ASEAN and East Asia reported that, in 2017, a significant number of people globally were unable to access a bank account due to factors including the high cost of financial services and lack of proximity to financial institutions (Cavoli and Shrestha 2020).

(continued on next page)

Box 1.1: Examples of Poverty Premium and Penalty *(continued)*

An ADB study also noted that small businesses in developing Asia often face challenges in accessing credit, with 14.75% citing unfavorable interest rates, 10.81% reporting complex application procedures, and 8.21% citing collateral requirements as barriers to obtaining loans (Ayyagari and Beck 2015). Poor people may therefore have to rely on high-cost alternative lenders to meet their financial needs, further contributing to financial instability and poverty. While a number of technological innovations show promise in extending financial access to previously excluded groups, the right figure below suggests that the gap between the rich and poor for these technologies is wider in Asia than in other regions of the world (Jahan et al. 2018).

Reported Challenges When Accessing Credit and Proportion of People with Access to Mobile Money

A. Reported Challenges When Accessing Credit

B. Proportion of People with Access to Mobile Money

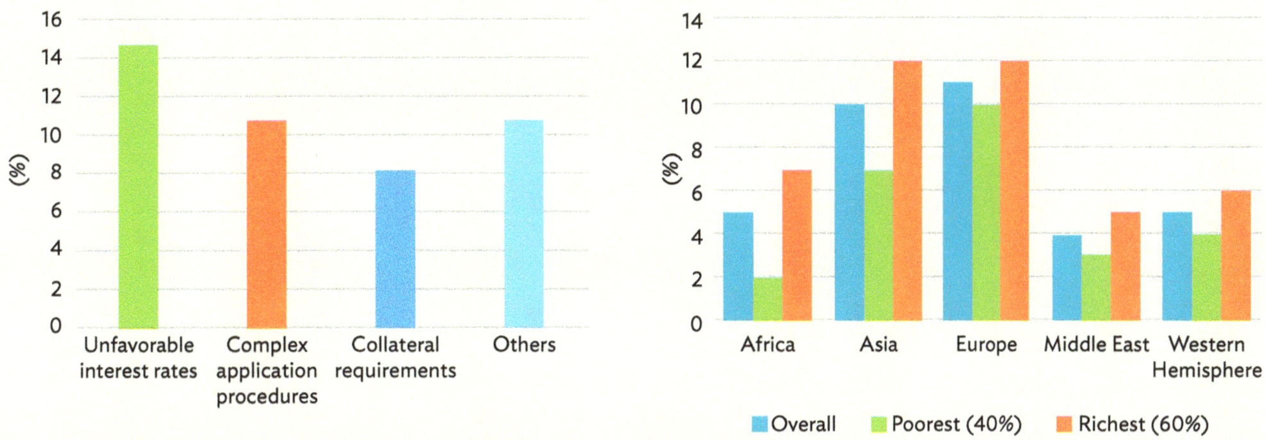

Source: For chart A: Asian Development Bank visualization adopted from Ayyagari and Beck (2015). For chart B: Asian Development Bank visualization adopted from Jahan et al. (2018).

Are there arguments that challenge the existence and/or relevance of the poverty premium?

Some practitioners argue that incidences of poor people paying higher prices for everyday goods occur only in a limited set of circumstances and may depend on the specific context and characteristics of the market. In some cases, traditional products or practices may provide a cheaper (or even free) option to newer goods or services, or greater competition may drive down prices. In other cases, market development, innovation, and/or state intervention have either reduced the costs for the poor or totally erased poverty premiums (Kay and Lewenstein 2013).

Others argue that the focus should be on addressing the issue of "poor mindset", or bad decisions around handling money and making purchases (Mullainathan and Shafir 2013). More generally, Nobel laureates such as Abhijit Banerjee and Esther Duflo, and other proponents of the concept of "poor economics" argue that the poor are actually sensible with money, but that purchasing decisions outside of meeting their basic needs are more likely to be perceived as "counterproductive" (Banerjee and Duflo 2011; Duflo, Kremer and Robinson 2011; Banerjee and Mullainathan 2010). Bruijn and Antonides (2021) also suggest that poverty can have several negative impacts on the poor's economic behavior, some of which may be construed as irrational. Poverty can cause individuals to save little and overborrow to meet basic needs. It can also force individuals to prioritize meeting their basic needs over thinking about long-term outcomes.

(continued on next page)

Box 1.1: Examples of Poverty Premium and Penalty *(continued)*

Some proponents argue these behaviors reflect the poor's preferences and should be seen as rational adaptations to their economic circumstances. Others contend that the poor's norms, values, and attitudes deviate from others and shape their preferences and behaviors, known as the "culture-of-poverty view". These interpretations are subject to debate. The human capital view suggests that behaviors of the poor result from a lack of education, work experience, and financial literacy (Brujin and Antonides 2021). As the poor prioritize making ends meet, they may be limited in their ability to invest in education or other opportunities that can provide long-term benefits, improve their economic situation, and help them escape poverty. This suggests a larger role for government investment in education for the poor.

There is evidence to suggest that behavioral coaching sessions incorporated into wider poverty reduction initiatives may contribute to improved decision-making by the poor (Bryan and Udry 2016; Schelzig and Jilani 2021). Women may benefit significantly from coaching sessions on more efficient consumption patterns, with data showing that women tend to have the final say in making household purchases, particularly on daily purchases, as shown in the figure below.

Proportion of Households in which Women have the Final Say on Making Purchases

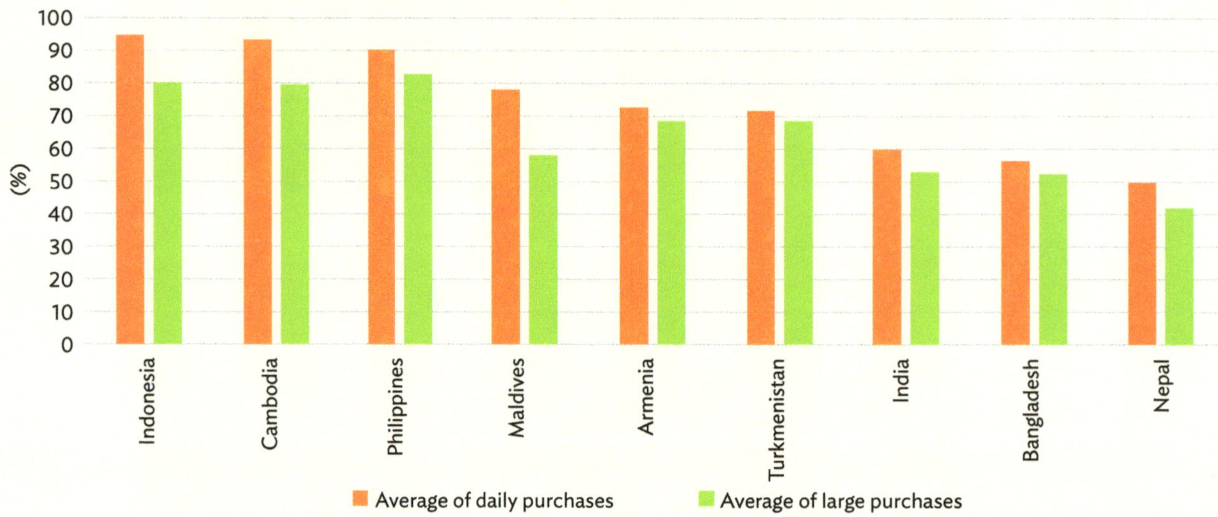

Source: International Classification of Functioning, Disability and Health (ICF). 2015. The DHS Program STATcompiler. Funded by USAID. http://www.statcompiler.com (accessed July 25, 2023).

References

R. Acharya and A. Sadath. 2019. Energy poverty and economic development: Household-level evidence from India. *Energy and Buildings*. 183. 15 January. pp. 785-791.

Asian Development Bank (ADB). 2015. Balancing the Burden? Desk Review of Women's Time Poverty and Infrastructure in Asia and the Pacific. https://www.adb.org/sites/default/files/publication/177465/sdcc-balancing-burden.pdf.

M. Ayyagari and T. Beck. 2015. Financial Inclusion in Asia: An Overview. *ADB Economics Working Paper Series*. 449. https://www.adb.org/sites/default/files/publication/173377/ewp-449.pdf.

A. Banerjee and E. Duflo. 2011. Poor Economics: A Radical Rethinking of the Way to Fight Global Poverty. *Population and Development Review*. 37.4. pp. 796-797.

A. Banerjee and S. Mullainathan. 2010. The Shape of Temptation: Implications of the Economic Lives of the Poor. *National Bureau of Economic Research Working Paper*. No. 15973. https://www.nber.org/papers/w15973.

S. Boonyabancha, T. Kerr, J. Lumanti, J., and C. Tacoli. 2019. How the urban poor define and measure food security in Cambodia and Nepal. *Environment and Urbanization*. Vol 31. July. pp. 517–532. https://www.researchgate.net/publication/334563000_How_the_urban_poor_define_and_measure_food_security_in_Cambodia_and_Nepal.

E. Bruijn and G. Antonides. 2021. Poverty and Economic Decision Making: A Review of Scarcity Theory. *Theory and Decision*. 92. pp. 50-37. https://link.springer.com/article/10.1007/s11238-021-09802-7.

G. Bryan and C. Udry. 2016. The Impact of Cognitive Behavioral Therapy on Low-Income Individuals in Rural Ghana. J-PAL. https://www.povertyactionlab.org/evaluation/impact-cognitive-behavioral-therapy-low-income-individuals-ruralghana.

Box 1.1: Examples of Poverty Premium and Penalty *(continued)*

T. Cavoli and R. Shrestha. 2020. The Nature and Landscape of Financial Inclusion. *ERIA Discussion Paper Series.* No. 340. https://www.eria.org/uploads/media/discussion-papers/1-The-Nature-and-Landscape-of-Financial-Inclusion-in-Asia.pdf.

S. Dhanaraj, V. Mahambare, and P. Munjal. 2017. From Income to Household Welfare: Lessons from Refrigerator Ownership in India. *Journal of Quantitative Economics.* pp. 573–588. https://link.springer.com/article/10.1007/s40953-017-0084-5.

E. Duflo, M. Kremer, J. Robinson. 2011. Nudging Farmers for Use Fertilizer: Theory and Experimental Evidence from Kenya. *American Economic Review.* Vol 101. No.6. pp. 2,350-2,390. https://www.aeaweb.org/articles?id=10.1257/aer.101.6.2350.

A. Helling. 1998. Changing intra-metropolitan accessibility in the US: Evidence from Atlanta. *Progress in Planning.* Vol 49. Issue 2. pp. 57-103. https://doi.org/10.1016/S0305-9006(97)00032-9.

M. Hossain. 2020. Less is More Expensive: Income Differences in Bulk Buying. Philadelphia. https://www.mallickhossain.com/papers/BulkBuyingInequality.pdf.

S. Jahan, E. Loukoianova, C. Sullivan, Y. Yang. 2018. Asia Needs More Access to Financial Services to Grow. IMF Blog. https://www.imf.org/en/Blogs/Articles/2018/09/18/asia-needs-more-access-to-financial-services-to-grow.

E. Kay and W. Lewenstein. 2013. The Problem with the "Poverty Premium". *Harvard Business Review Magazine.* April. https://hbr.org/2013/04/the-problem-withthe-poverty-premium.

R. Mendoza. 2011. Why do the poor pay more? Exploring the poverty penalty concept. Journal of International Development. 23.1. pp. 1–28. https://onlinelibrary.wiley.com/doi/10.1002/jid.1504.

S. Mullainathan and E. Shafir. 2013. Scarcity: Why having too little means so much. Times Books / Henry Holt and Company.

H. Phoumin, and F. Kimura. 2019. The impacts of energy insecurity on household welfare in Cambodia: Empirical evidence and policy implications. *Economic Modelling,* 82(C), pp. 35-41. https://www.sciencedirect.com/science/article/pii/S0264999319307904.

K. Schelzig and A. Jilani. 2021. Assessing the Impact of the Graduation Approach in the Philippines. *ADB Briefs.* No.169. March. https://www.adb.org/sites/default/files/publication/682781/adb-brief-169-impact-graduation-approachphilippines.pdf.

P. Starkey and J. Hine. 2014. Poverty and Sustainable Transport. How Transport Affects Poor People with Policy Implications for Poverty Reduction. *Literature Review UN-Habitat.* October. https://sustainabledevelopment.un.org/content/documents/1767Poverty%20and%20sustainable%20transport.pdf.

UN-Habitat. October (2014). https://sustainabledevelopment.un.org/content/documents/1767Poverty%20and%20sustainable%20transport.pdf.

A. Thegeya, T. Mitterling, A. Martinez, J. Bulan, R. Durante, and J. Mag-atas. 2022. Application of Machine Learning Algorithms on Satellite Imagery for Road and Quality Monitoring. *ADB Economics Working Paper Series.* No. 675. December. https://www.adb.org/sites/default/files/publication/849926/ewp-675-machinelearning-satellite-image-road-quality.pdf.

V. Rao. 2000. Price Heterogeneity and "Real" Inequality: A Case Study of Prices and Poverty in Rural South India. *The Review of Income and Wealth,* 46(2), pp. 201-211.

A. Sadath and R. Acharya. 2017. Assessing the extent and intensity of energy poverty using Multidimensional Poverty Index: Empirical evidence from households in India. *Energy Policy.* 102. March. pp. 540-550.

S. Alkire, U. Kanagaratnam, and N. Suppa. 2023a. The global Multidimensional Poverty Index (MPI) 2023 country results and methodological note. OPHI MPI Methodological Note 55, Oxford Poverty and Human Development Initiative (OPHI), University of Oxford.

S. Alkire, U. Kanagaratnam, and N. Suppa. 2023a. The global Multidimensional Poverty Index (MPI) 2023 disaggregation results and methodological note. OPHI MPI Methodological Note 56, Oxford Poverty and Human Development Initiative (OPHI), University of Oxford.

UNDP. 2022b. Global Multidimensional Poverty Index 2022. Unpacking Deprivation Bundles to Reduce Multidimensional Poverty. https://hdr.undp.org/system/files/documents/hdp-document/2022mpireportenpdf.pdf.

Assessing the Impacts of Inflation on Poverty under Varying Scenarios

Although disruptions caused by the COVID-19 pandemic have moderated, high and persistent inflation has emerged as one of the major challenges confronting policymakers in developing Asia.

For instance, estimates suggest that surging food prices experienced due to the pandemic and other external factors pushed roughly 100 million more people into hunger around the world. This would put the estimated total of undernourished people to over one billion globally (ADB n.d.).

Households with lower incomes spend a higher proportion of their budgets on essential goods and services, making them more vulnerable to price surges on these items.

Figure 1.9 contrasts the poor's average proportion of expenditure on food with the rest of the population in selected economies of developing Asia. The data indicate that this proportion is around 23% higher for the region's poorest quartile, making these households particularly vulnerable when food prices spike. As food prices increase, the cost of a healthy diet also becomes less affordable. In fact, the cost of a healthy diet in developing Asia had already increased from 2017 to 2020, before the current cost-of-living crisis (FAO et al. 2022).

Figure 1.9: Share of Expenditure on Food to Total Consumption and Increase in Cost of a Healthy Diet

The bottom half of the population in most economies spent more than half of their total budget on food, while the cost of a healthy diet increased more in Asia than in other parts of the world at the onset of the COVID-19 pandemic.

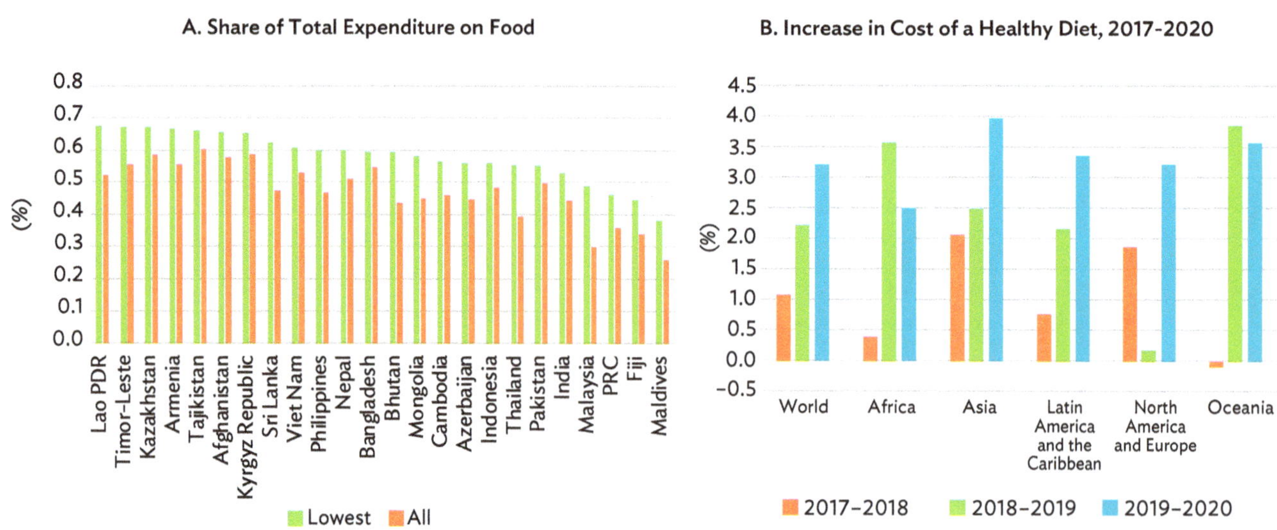

Lao PDR = Lao People's Democratic Republic, PRC = People's Republic of China.

Sources: For chart A: Asian Development Bank estimates using data from the World Bank Global Consumption Database (accessed 1 June 2023). For chart B: visualization adopted from the Food and Agriculture Organization study on *The State of Food Security and Nutrition in the World 2022* (FAO et al. 2022) (accessed 6 March 2023).

An ADB (2011) study emphasized that in addition to potentially increasing the prevalence of poverty, higher food prices lower the living standards of those already living below the poverty line. Simulation from that study suggests an increase in domestic food prices in developing Asia by 10%, 20%, and 30% at that time may have resulted in an increase of 1.4, 2.7, and 4.1 percentage points, respectively, in the (extreme) poverty gap ratio (Figure 1.10). As shown in Table 2.3.2 on food price inflation, a substantial number of the region's economies experienced 5% to 10% food price inflation in 2022, but there were economies that experienced substantially higher rates of food price increases.

Similarly for energy, in 16 of 24 economies across developing Asia, the poorest half spent proportionately more (Figure 1.11). These poorer households are therefore more vulnerable to energy price hikes, with estimates showing that the energy crisis triggered by the Russian invasion of Ukraine may have increased total energy costs of households around the world between 63% to 113% (Guan et al. 2023).

Compared to pre-pandemic numbers, estimates show an additional 67.8 million more people living in extreme poverty in developing Asia in 2022.

In general, high inflation has an adverse effect on economic growth, which in turn hampers an economy's ability to reduce poverty (Ames et al. 2001). To estimate how higher inflation compounded the impact of the pandemic on the prevalence of poverty in 2022, ADB economists and statisticians conducted a simple simulation exercise using grouped distribution data on household or consumption expenditures per capita for 29 developing ADB member economies and different sets of GDP growth numbers.

Figure 1.10: Simulated Increase in Poverty Gap in Developing Asia under Varying Scenarios of Food Price Increases

Higher food prices further erode the living standards of people already living below the poverty line.

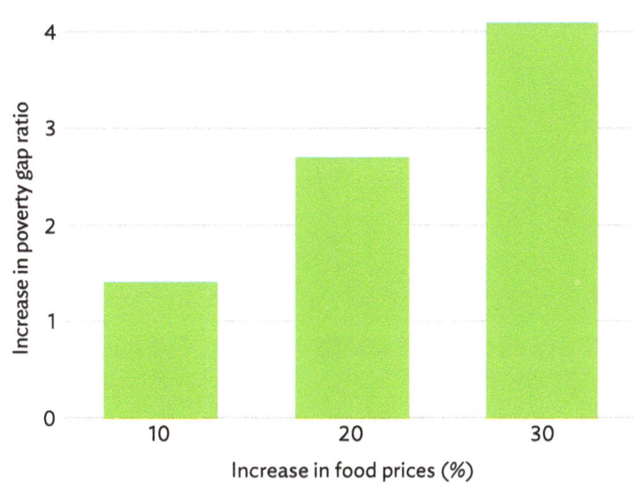

Notes: The estimates presented here are based on $1.25 a day (expressed in 2005 PPP) poverty line.

Source: Asian Development Bank estimates using data from *Global Food Price Inflation and Developing Asia* (ADB 2011).

Figure 1.11: Share of Expenditure on Energy to Total Consumption

As a proportion of their total expenditure, the poorest half spends about 10% more on energy than an average household does.

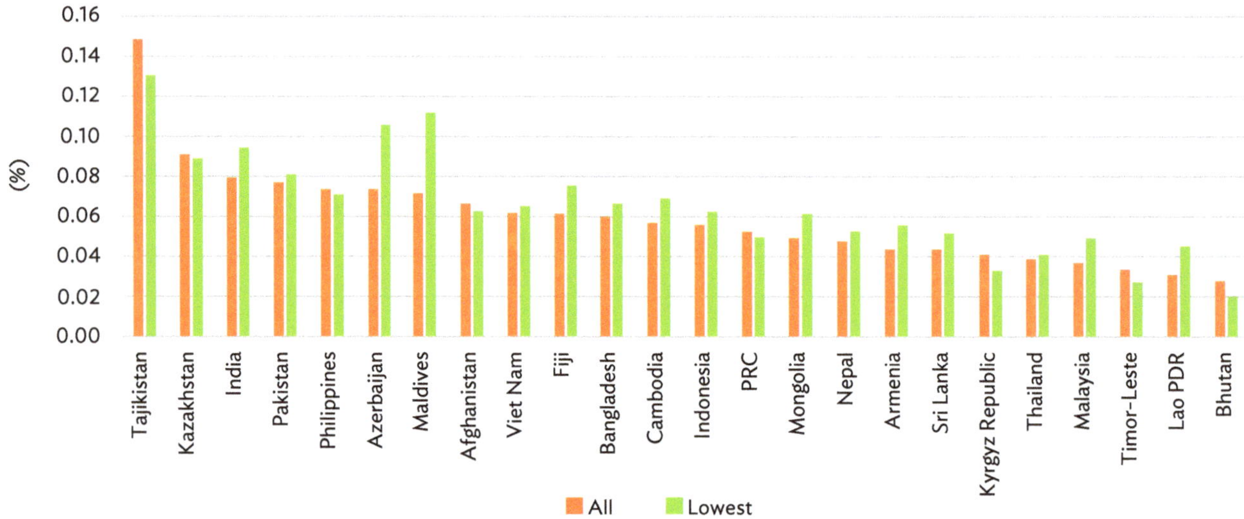

Lao PDR = Lao People's Democratic Republic, PRC = People's Republic of China.
Source: Asian Development Bank visualization using data from the World Bank Global Consumption Database (accessed 1 June 2023).

Table 1.1 presents multiple sets of poverty estimates for developing Asia. The first is based on pre-pandemic growth forecasts for the year 2022, while the next scenarios are based on the actual GDP growth recorded in 2022. The results suggest that the prevalence of extreme poverty in the region in 2022 may have been at least 1.7 percentage points higher compared to the pre-pandemic scenario which assumed a better development picture. However, this estimate assumes that all households within an economy are equally affected by rising prices, and hence, their purchasing power declines at the same rate. Yet, we know that prices paid by poorer people for some goods and services may increase faster.

For instance, Figure 1.12 illustrates that in three economies where a consumer price index is compiled for different income groups, lower-income individuals generally experienced slightly higher consumer price inflation from 2009 to 2022, compared to the overall population. If the same is experienced in a substantial number of economies, the estimated impact of inflation on poverty may be much higher than what the first few rows of Table 1.1 suggest.

One way to capture the impact of higher inflation faced by people with lower incomes is to vary the inflation shocks by the bottom 10% of the income distribution, while keeping an economy's average household consumption per capita growth unchanged. We consider situations wherein due to varying inflation shocks, real consumption of the bottom 10% grows slower than that of the average household (i.e., 0.8, or 0.9 times the growth of the consumption per capita of a typical household). Here, the difference in the estimated prevalence of extreme poverty from the baseline scenario increases by as much as 1.9 percentage points, compared to pre-pandemic numbers. However, it is important

Table 1.1: Simulated Distribution of Income within Economies of Developing Asia in 2022

Compared to the pre-pandemic economic scenario, the prevalence of extreme poverty in developing Asia may have been at least 1.7 percentage points higher, or the equivalent of 67.76 million more people in extreme poverty in the region, compared to a counterfactual scenario based on economic scenarios forecast before the pandemic and increased cost-of-living crisis.

Economic Scenario	<$2.15	[$2.15, $3.65)	[$3.65, $6.85)	[$6.85, $17.1)	[$17.1, $24.36),	>= $24.36
Based on Pre-pandemic Scenario (neutral distribution assumption)	2.2	14.8	32.2	34.1	8.4	8.4
Based on Actual Economic Scenario (neutral distribution assumption)	3.9	18.8	30.2	31.7	7.9	7.6
Based on Actual Economic Scenario (growth of bottom 10% is 0.8 times growth of overall mean)	4.1	19.0	28.9	32.3	8.0	7.7
Based on Actual Economic Scenario (growth of bottom 10% is 0.9 times growth of overall mean)	4.0	19.1	28.9	32.3	8.0	7.7

$ = 2017 PPP dollars.

Note: " < $2.15" represents those living on less than $2.15 a day commonly referred to as extreme poverty; "[$2.15, $3.65)" represents those living on at least $2.15 but less than $3.65 a day, commonly referred to as moderate poverty; "[$3.65, $6.85)" represents those living on at least $3.65 but less than $6.85 a day and "> $6.85" represents those living on more than $6.85 a day.
Baseline Scenario # 1 is based on the economy-level forecast for GDP growth for the year 2022, as published in the *Asian Development Outlook April 2021,* while Baseline Scenario # 2 is based on the economy-level forecast for GDP growth for the year 2022, as published in the *Asian Development Outlook Update September 2021*. The Actual Economic Scenario is based on the actual economy-level GDP growth rate in 2022. These three scenarios assume that all households within an economy experience the same percentage decline in their per capita consumption expenditure and/or income as predicted based on GDP per capita growth numbers.

Sources: Asian Development Bank estimates using simulated data derived from the World Bank's Poverty and Inequality Platform (accessed 12 June 2023), and GDP growth forecasts from the *Asian Development Outlook 2021* and *Asian Development Outlook Update 2021*.

Figure 1.12: Inflation Experienced by Low-Income People versus the General Population

In economies with available data, households with lower incomes experienced slightly faster inflation.

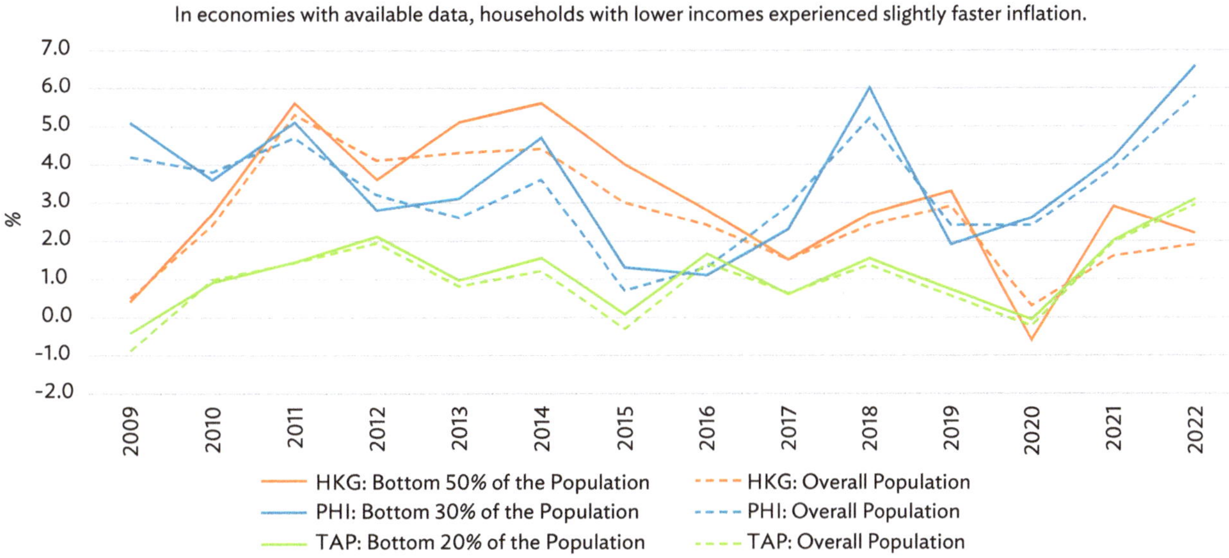

CPI = consumer price index; HKG = Hong Kong, China; PHI = Philippines; TAP = Taipei,China.

Sources: For CPI overall population: Asian Development Bank data presented in Table 2.3.1 of *Key Indicators of Asia and the Pacific 2023.*
For CPI bottom population, For TAP: Government of Taipei,China. Directorate-General of Budget, Accounting and Statistics;
For HKG: The Government of the Hong Kong Special Administrative Region of the People's Republic of China. Census and Statistics Department. https://www.censtatd.gov.hk/en/web_table.html?id=510-60003# (accessed 24 July 2023); For PHI: Philippine Statistics Authority.https://openstat.psa.gov.ph/Database/Prices/Price-Indices (accessed 24 July 2023).

to note that, even if the non-neutral distribution assumption is made, these estimates may not fully capture the full impact of the pandemic and increased cost of living on poverty, and may be sensitive to assumptions used in calculation.

On the other hand, it is also possible that some poor people (particularly rural households) may benefit from higher food prices if they are net sellers of food. Furthermore, households may also adjust their consumption patterns when confronted with higher prices. These factors may diminish the impact of higher prices on poor people's living conditions (Mahler et al. 2022).

Social protection policies can mitigate some of the impact of higher prices on the poor.

ADB studies (ADB 2019; ADB 2022d) note that there is diversity in social protection systems across developing Asia. Some are mainly dependent on contributory social insurance and provident funds, while others provide additional assistance for vulnerable demographic groups in the form of food vouchers, child benefits, caregiver allowances, and disability grants.

Amid this diversity, data show that a substantial number of economies expanded social protection coverage in 2020, during the COVID-19 pandemic (Figure 1.13). This came in the form of new or modified cash transfers, new unemployment programs, unemployment insurance, food subsidies, and sickness benefits (ADB 2022d). However, a number of economies in the region still have less than half of their population covered by at least one social protection measure and in general, economies that were more severely affected by the pandemic were those without strong social protection systems (McConnell 2022).

Figure 1.13: Proportion of Population Covered by at Least One Social Protection Benefit, 2020

In 2020, less than half of the population in 26 of 40 economies were covered by at least one social protection measure.

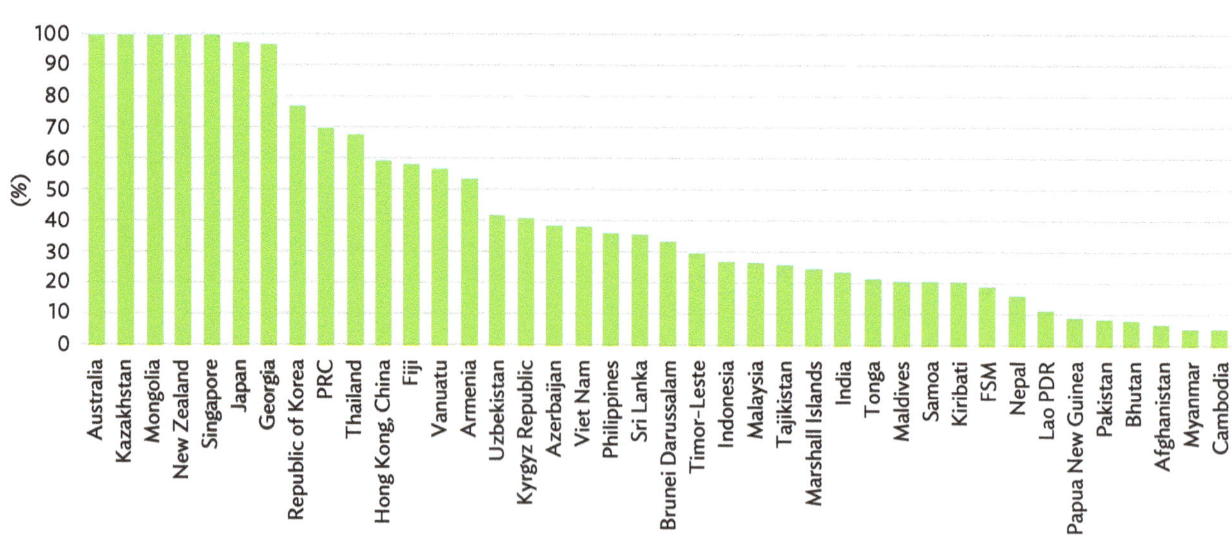

FSM = Federated States of Micronesia, Lao PDR = Lao People's Democratic Republic, PRC = People's Republic of China.

Source: Asian Development Bank data from Table 1.1.2 of *Key Indicators for Asia and the Pacific 2023* and Key Indicators Database (accessed 7 July 2023).

In the face of the increased cost-of-living crisis that emerged in 2022, a number of economies announced social protection and other related measures to counter inflation (UN 2023a). A World Bank study notes that, globally, the provision of subsidies (on fuel, food, fertilizers, and others) was the most common countermeasure against inflation, representing about 34% of measures recorded (Gentilini et al. 2023).[4] Social assistance in the forms of unconditional and conditional cash transfers accounted for about 29% of such measures (Gentilini et al. 2023).

Because hikes in prices of food staples, fuel, and other essential commodities have greater impact on the most vulnerable segments of society, strengthening social protection systems (including fair wage policies) can help lessen the adverse impacts of the cost-of-living crisis.

Navigating Other Development Challenges Faced by the Poor

In addition to the increased cost-of-living crisis, a number of other development challenges are threatening SDG progress.

Asia and the Pacific, along with the rest of the world, is grappling with a polycrisis which includes high cost of living, climate change, lingering impacts from the COVID-19 pandemic, and the Russian invasion of Ukraine (Figure 1.14). These factors are resulting in fragile and slow progress in achieving the Sustainable Development Goals (SDGs). At the global level, UN (2023a) notes that half of the approximately 140 SDG targets whose progress can be assessed point to moderate or severe deviations from the desired trajectory. Almost a third of these targets show no progress or even regression below baseline numbers when SDG implementation started in 2015 (UN 2023a). Likewise, a report released by UNESCAP, ADB, and UNDP also notes that the convergence of these multiple global crises constrains Asia and the Pacific's ability to achieve the SDGs (ADB 2023b).

To help the poorest and most vulnerable segments of societies navigate this polycrisis requires tackling multiple sources of socioeconomic disadvantage. This section of the report explores the development challenges and potential policy measures that could be taken in response. This includes scaling up investment in the agriculture sector, which analysis by the International Fund for Agricultural Development, World Bank and the International Food Policy Research Institute has shown is 2.5 to 3.0 times more effective in increasing the income of the poor than nonagricultural investments (Cleaver 2012). The broader rollout of new technologies and innovations in rural areas

4 This includes a total of 1,016 social protection and related measures that were either announced or implemented across 170 economies around the world as of November 2022 (Gentilini et al. 2023).

to reduce costs and increase access to services for remote communities can also aid faster socioeconomic development and help reduce the poverty premium.

Among innovations that have shown promise for farmers are the use of satellite data to monitor crop growth and water resources and big data analytics to optimize use of agricultural resources, enabling savings in areas such as seeds and fertilizer. E-learning and the adoption of online health services and other technologies are also key to improving access to public services and helping cut costs for the poor (OECD 2020). To benefit from these measures will require improved information and communications technology connectivity in remote areas.

Figure 1.14: Interconnected Impacts of Development Challenges

Source: Adopted from *Delivering on the Sustainable Development Goals through Solutions at the Energy, Food and Finance Nexus: 2023.* Asia–Pacific SDG Partnership Report, copublished by ADB, UNESCAP and UNDP (ADB 2023b).

Scaling Up Solutions to Boost Agricultural Development

Agricultural productivity plays a central role in helping developing Asia achieve the Sustainable Development Goals of reduced poverty and zero hunger by 2030.

Although the proportion of developing Asia's population living in rural areas has declined considerably over time, the total number of Asians living in rural areas has actually grown from over 1.5 billion in 1970 to over 2 billion in 2020 (equivalent to 25% of the world's total population) as shown in Figure 1.15.

Furthermore, statistics suggest that one in three workers in developing Asia depend on agriculture for their livelihoods (ADB 2021d) and the sector accounts for as much as 19.5% of total employment in 41 of 46 economies with available data (Table 2.1.5).

Strengthening agriculture in developing Asia. To minimize the rural poverty premium, it is important to strengthen links between producers of agricultural products and their markets (photo by Gerhard Joren/ADB).

Figure 1.15: Rural Population in Developing Asia and the World, 1970–2020

Despite rapid urbanization, approximately 500 million more Asians resided in rural areas in 2020 compared to 50 years prior.

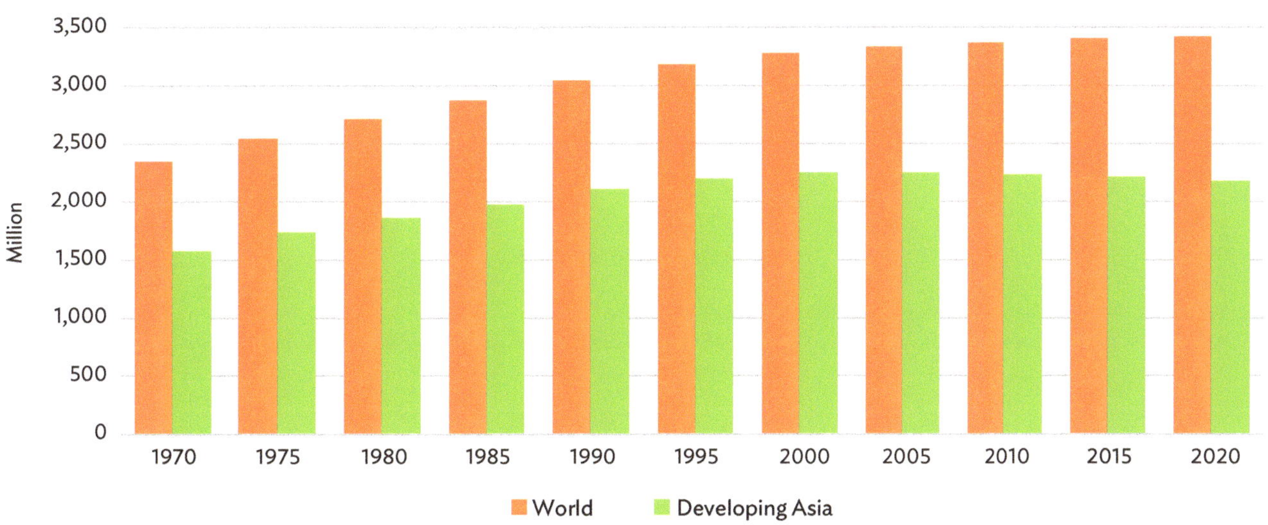

Source: Asian Development Bank estimates using data from the United Nations. World Urbanization Prospects 2018. https://population.un.org/wup/Download/ (accessed 7 July 2023).

However, the sector confronts a number of issues such as low productivity and meager incomes (ADB 2021d).

In general, those living in rural areas and/or relying on the agriculture sector tend to be more exposed to various forms of socioeconomic disadvantage. In fact, approximately three out of every five persons living in extreme poverty in developing Asia are found in rural areas (WBG 2022a), with some studies suggesting that the most chronic or persistent forms of socioeconomic disadvantage is associated with being born in a rural or remote area in a low-income economy (Kharas et al. 2019). Indicators of such poverty can include limited access to basic services such as safe drinking water and proper sanitation as seen in Figure 1.16.

Figure 1.16: Proportion of Rural Population with Access to Safely Managed Drinking Water and Sanitation Services

In several economies of developing Asia, more than half the rural population did not have access to either safely managed drinking water or sanitation services.

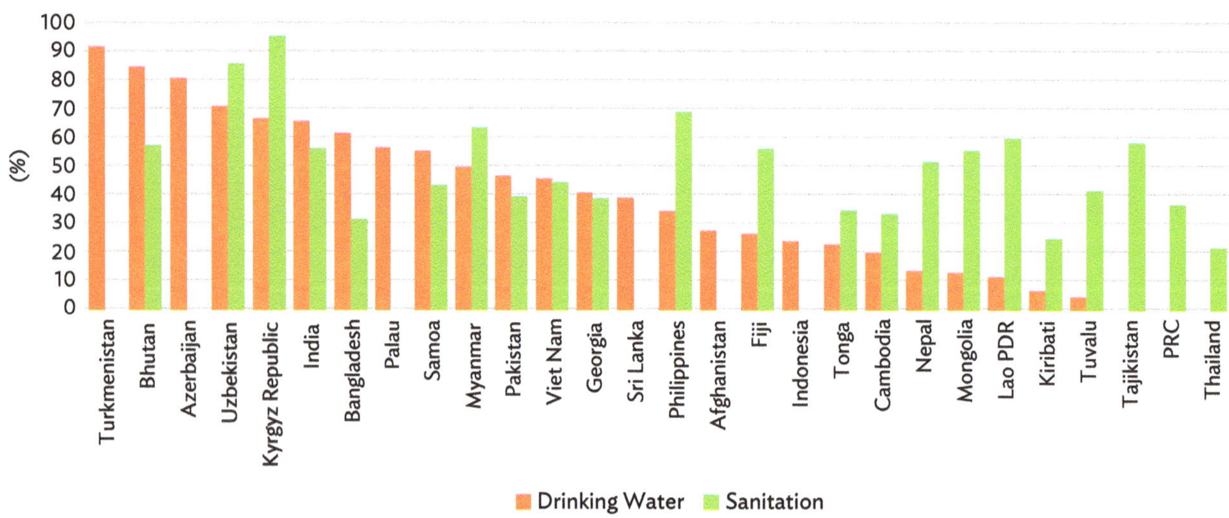

Lao PDR = Lao People's Democratic Republic, PRC = People's Republic of China.
Source: Asian Development Bank estimates using data presented in Table 1.6.1 of *Key Indicators for Asia and the Pacific 2023*.

The polycrisis compounds these persistent forms of socioeconomic disadvantage. For instance, agricultural households must contend with shocks in prices of agricultural inputs. Additionally, in rural areas that are not well connected to economic hubs, the poverty premium may be higher due to increased costs of transporting goods and services to markets. Disruptions caused by extreme weather events and climate change can severely affect agricultural yields, hurting small scale farmers and agricultural workers the most.

Policy measures such as boosting development of the agriculture sector and strengthening the resilience of agricultural households to price shocks and other types of disruptions can be a powerful tool for facilitating faster poverty reduction.

Furthermore, as developing Asia continues to urbanize rapidly, supplying growing cities with adequate and affordable food will require greater use of innovative technologies on farms and stepped up investments in the agriculture sector (ADB 2021d).

Trends in the Agriculture Orientation Index show a mixed picture of progress across developing Asia.

SDG indicator 2.a.1, as reflected in the Agriculture Orientation Index, measures the ratio of government expenditure on agriculture to the share of agriculture value-added in GDP. Values exceeding 1 suggest a higher orientation towards the agriculture sector as the sector receives a higher share of government spending relative to its economic value-added.

Figure 1.17 reflects a lower orientation towards agriculture for most of developing Asia's economies from 2001 to 2021. It is important to assess the need to further improve orientation towards the agriculture sector to accelerate poverty reduction, as a significant fraction of the poor rely on the agriculture sector for livelihoods and income.

Data highlighting the benefits of agriculture sector investment are clear. Analyses by the International Fund for Agricultural Development, World Bank, and International Food Policy Research Institute show a correlation between the developing economies with the largest reductions in poverty rates and those with the most rapid agricultural

Figure 1.17: Agriculture Orientation Index in Selected Economies of Developing Asia

Developing Asia generally recorded Agriculture Orientation Index values below 1, albeit with significant variation across economies.

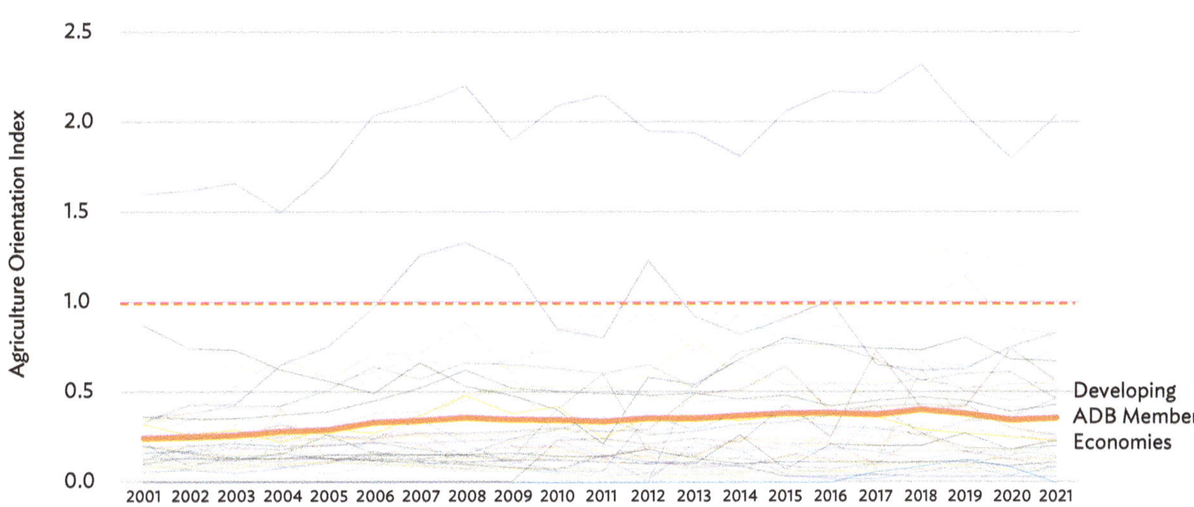

Note: An Agriculture Orientation Index (AOI) greater than 1 reflects a higher orientation towards the agriculture sector, which receives a higher share of government spending relative to its contribution to economic value-added. An AOI less than 1 reflects a lower orientation to agriculture, while an AOI equal to 1 reflects neutrality in a government's orientation to the agriculture sector.

Source: Asian Development Bank estimates using data presented in Table 1.2.2 of *Key Indicators for Asia and the Pacific 2023* and data from United Nations. SDG Global Database. https://unstats.un.org/sdgs/dataportal (accessed 11 July 2023).

growth. For example, a 1 percentage point per annum increase in agricultural growth, on average associates with a 2.7 percent increase in the income of people in the lowest three income deciles in developing Asia. Data also shows that investment in agriculture is 2.5 to 3.0 times more effective in increasing the income of the poor than is nonagricultural investment (Cleaver 2012).

Policymakers can consider minimizing the rural poverty premium by reducing environmental stresses and enhancing the efficiency of agricultural value chains.

Farmers and agricultural workers may pay a productivity poverty premium in terms of being able to produce limited output. This may be due to factors such as degraded land, additional costs for farming inputs, limited access to modern technology and machinery (WBG 2008), inadequate infrastructure (FAO 2011), lack of education on modern farming practices (Anderson and Feder 2007), limited bargaining power (Barrett 2008), and climate change (Wheeler and von Braun 2013).

Other emerging concerns around agricultural productivity include the aging of rural populations, environmental stresses caused by climate change, and natural resources depletion. These warrant urgent attention to avoid disrupting agricultural value chains (ADB 2019). For instance, deforestation is largely associated with increasing food demand but is among the major causes of soil depletion. Globally, it is estimated that one-third of the world's soil is degraded (UN 2014). Likewise, there have been significant reductions in forest cover in subregions of developing Asia, especially in Southeast Asia, since 2000 (Figure 1.18).

An ADB study (ADB 2023c) also surmises that agricultural losses are the primary pathway by which climate change is expected to harm the lowest-income regions of developing Asia. Equipping agriculture to address simultaneous pressures posed by climate change mitigation policy and unmitigated climate change will be critical for protecting the livelihoods of many of the region's poor (ADB 2023c).

To minimize the rural poverty premium, it is important to strengthen links between producers of agricultural products and their markets. This largely means constructing better-quality roads, with Figure 1.19 indicating that economies in developing Asia had an average score of only 4 on a 7-point scale for road quality (with many economies registering scores of around 3). Other measures needed to strengthen links include providing more reliable and environmentally sustainable power and developing market infrastructure (WBG 2008). There is also a need to integrate innovative technologies that can better connect agricultural producers with markets, reduce post-harvest losses, and improve overall value chain efficiency (ADB 2021d).

Figure 1.18: Forest Cover by Subregion of Developing Asia

Forest cover declined in Southeast Asia and the Pacific from 2000 to 2020.

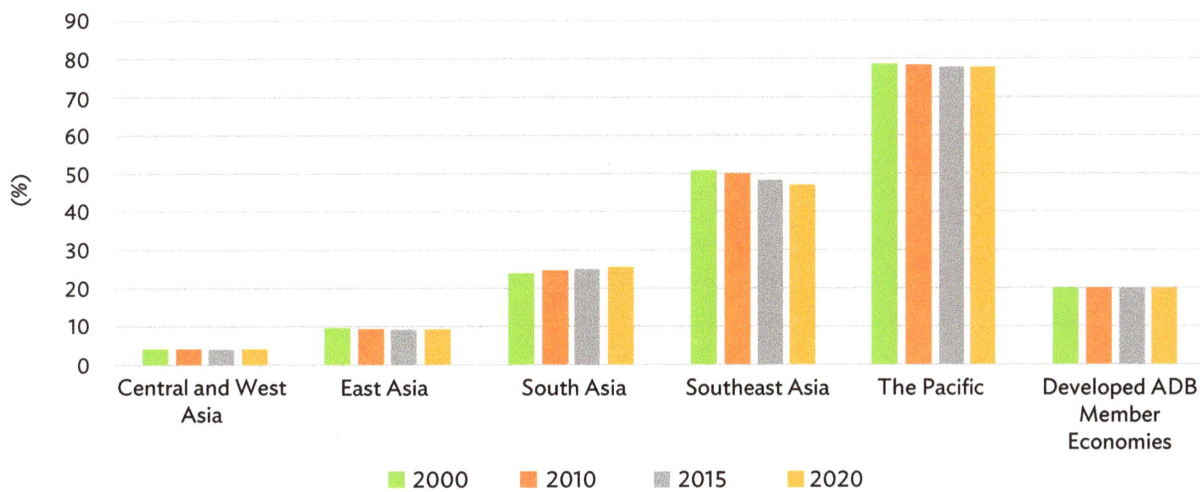

Source: Asian Development Bank estimates using data presented in Table 1.15.1 of *Key Indicators for Asia and the Pacific 2023* and data from United Nations. SDG Global Database. https://unstats.un.org/sdgs/dataportal (accessed 11 July 2023).

Figure 1.19: Quality of Roads in Selected Economies of Developing Asia

Road quality in many developing Asian economies has fallen below that of more developed economies.

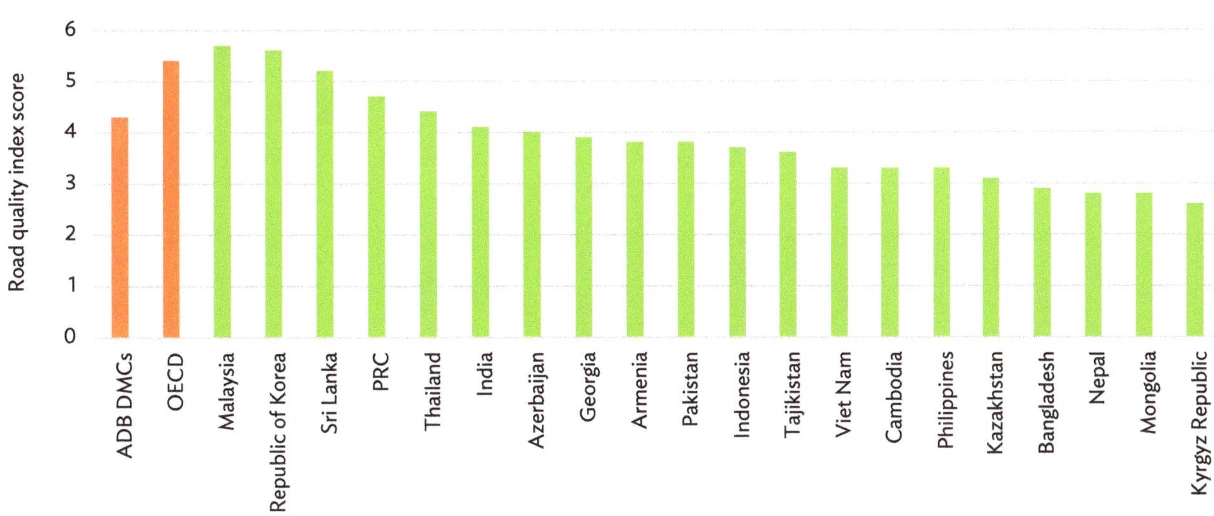

PRC = People's Republic of China.

Source: Asian Development Bank estimates using data from the World Economic Forum. Global Competitiveness Report 2015-2016.

Implementing Urban Development Strategies to Reduce Poverty

Badly managed urbanization may contribute to developing Asia's urban poverty by exposing poor communities to traffic congestion, inadequate waste management, and dangerous air pollution.

More than half the population across Asia and the Pacific (over two billion people) now live in urban areas and forecasts suggest this figure will exceed 60% by 2050 (Figure 1.20). At present, Asia and the Pacific is home to some of the world's most populated cities, including Delhi, Metro Manila, Seoul, Singapore, Shanghai, and Tokyo.

Figure 1.20: Urban Population in Asia and the Pacific, 1970–2050

The urban population in the region is expected to grow to 3.1 billion by 2050, or more than 60% of the world's total urban population.

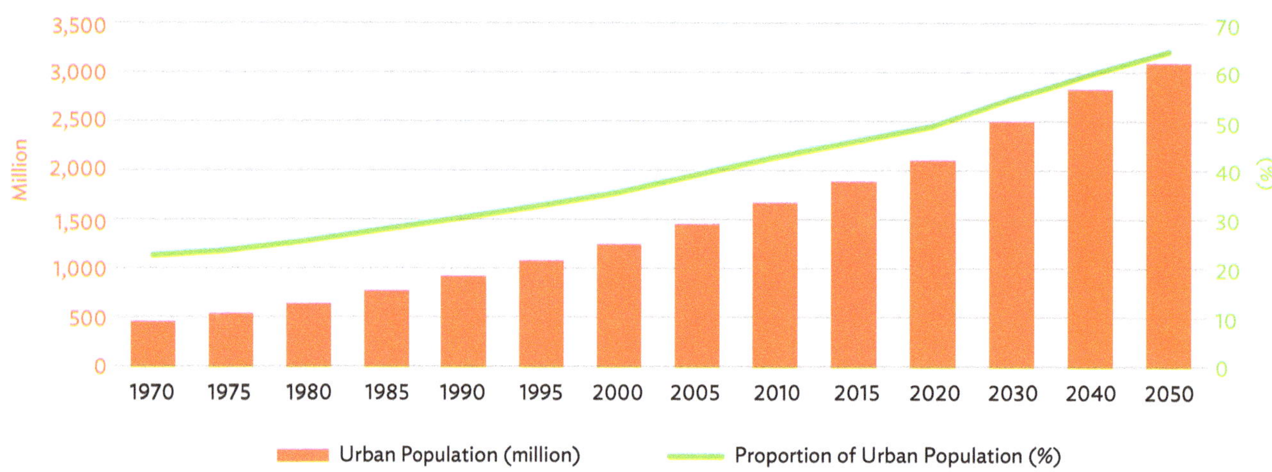

Sources: Asian Development Bank estimates using data from the United Nations World Urbanization Prospects 2018. https://population.un.org/wup/Download/ (accessed 1 March 2023).

This rapid urbanization has contributed to faster economic growth across developing Asia. Large cities have become hubs of economic and social activity and have created economies of scale that boost infrastructure and technology and increase productivity and employment. Some studies have estimated that cities will generate around 80% of Asia's economic growth by 2050 (Leather 2022).

At the same time, rapid and haphazard urbanization has seen some cities expand with poorly coordinated urban planning, including a lack of participation from poor and vulnerable communities, an absence of measures to address climate change, and inadequate provision of affordable housing. The fast growth of cities has also resulted in worsening air and water pollution and inadequate infrastructure (ADB 2021a).

Asian cities are experiencing significant strains on transportation and mobility. While public transport (along with walking and cycling) accounts for 70% of urban passenger trips, the number of motor vehicles on urban roads is doubling every 5 to 7 years (Leather 2022). In Asian economies, road congestion is already responsible for economic losses of 2% to 5% of GDP each year, while up to 80% of the region's urban air pollution is caused by transportation (Leather 2022).

Developing Asia's rapid urbanization has also seen difficulties in managing solid waste in many crowded cities because of inadequate infrastructure (Hondo et al. 2020). This contrasts with effective municipal solid waste collection achieved by many cities in developed economies (Figure 1.21). Poor solid waste management creates poverty premiums in the form of higher health spending because of waste-related diseases. In some cases, it may even promote urban violence (Medina 2010; WBG 2022b).

Figure 1.21: Municipal Solid Waste Collection in Select Areas of Asia and the Pacific, 2015

Cities in developed economies saw almost 100% of municipal solid waste being collected, much higher than in select cities of developing Asia where such data are available.

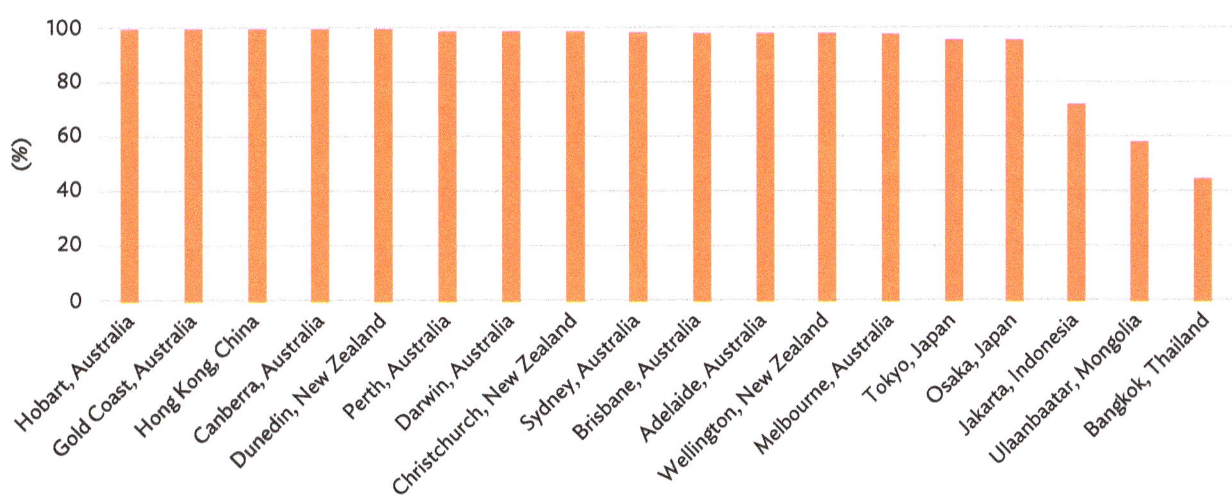

Source: Asian Development Bank estimates using data from UNStats (accessed 19 May 2023).

The same principle applies to urban pollution. Concentrations of fine particulate matter (PM2.5)—the air pollutant that affects more people than any other pollutant and causes cardiovascular and respiratory disease and cancers—are very high in the urban areas of developing Asia, with ranges of up to 76 micrograms per cubic meter (Figure 1.22). This poses health risks that could lead to higher expenditure on pollution-induced diseases. According to the World Health Organization, outdoor air pollution is estimated to have caused 4.2 million premature deaths worldwide in 2016 (UNEP 2022).

Figure 1.22: Concentrations of Fine Particulate Matter in Urban Areas of Developing Asia, 2019
(population-weighted)

A majority of the economies in developing Asia recorded an annual average of more than 10 micrograms per cubic meter of fine particulate matter (PM2.5) in urban areas.

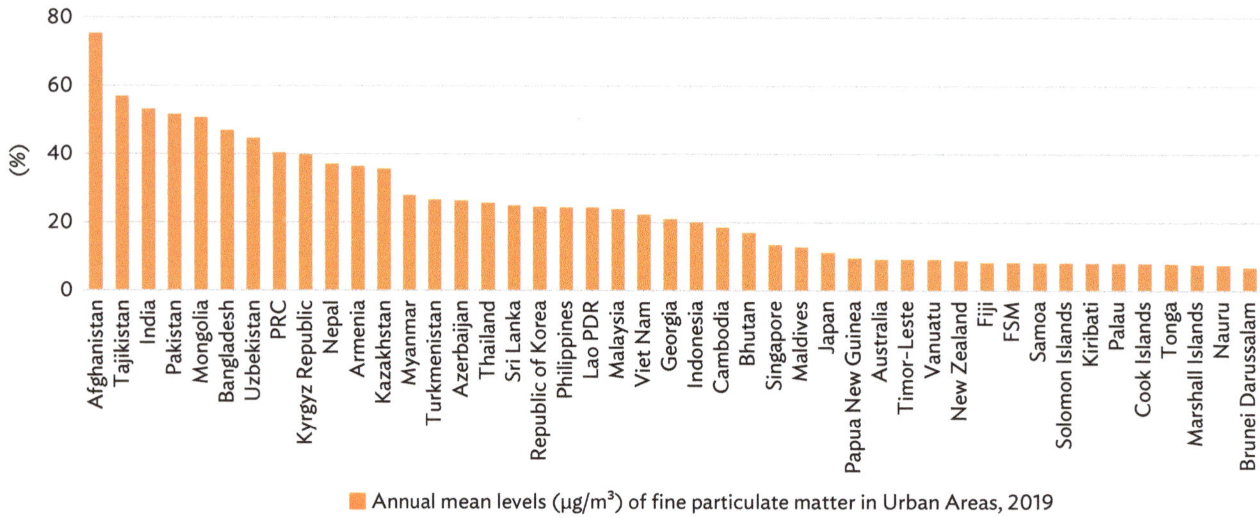

m³ = cubic meter, µg = microgram, FSM = Federated States of Micronesia, Lao PDR = Lao People's Democratic Republic, PRC = People's Republic of China.

Source: Asian Development Bank estimates using data from Table 1.11.1 of *Key Indicators for Asia and the Pacific 2023*.

A higher cost of living in cities puts migrants from rural areas at risk of being trapped in precarious living conditions.

Since about 2000, urban populations in Asia and the Pacific have been growing more quickly than have rural populations, as shown in Figure 1.23. According to the United Nations study, World Urbanization Prospects 2018, the region's total urban population will exceed its rural population by about 1.5 billion people in 2050.

In some economies of developing Asia, more than half of the overall urban growth in 2018, including for areas reclassified as "urban", was attributed to rural-urban migration. The level was as high as 80% in the People's Republic of China and Thailand, and 68% in Indonesia (UNESCAP and UN-Habitat 2019). This surge of rural-urban migration may amplify the risks of urban poverty, with people moving to cities for better job opportunities also needing to pay more for housing, transportation, food, and other essentials. As megacities expand, intra-urban trip distances and traffic congestion also increase. This places pressure on public transportation systems, impacting fare prices, transportation options, travel times and convenience, and pedestrian and travel safety (Starkey and Hine 2014).

The pricing structure of public transportation may disproportionately affect low-income urban dwellers, who cannot afford to purchase more economical long-term passes. The urban poor may also face additional costs related to transportation, such

Figure 1.23: Comparison of Urban and Rural Populations of Asia and the Pacific, 1970–2050

Populations in urban areas have already exceeded those of rural areas.

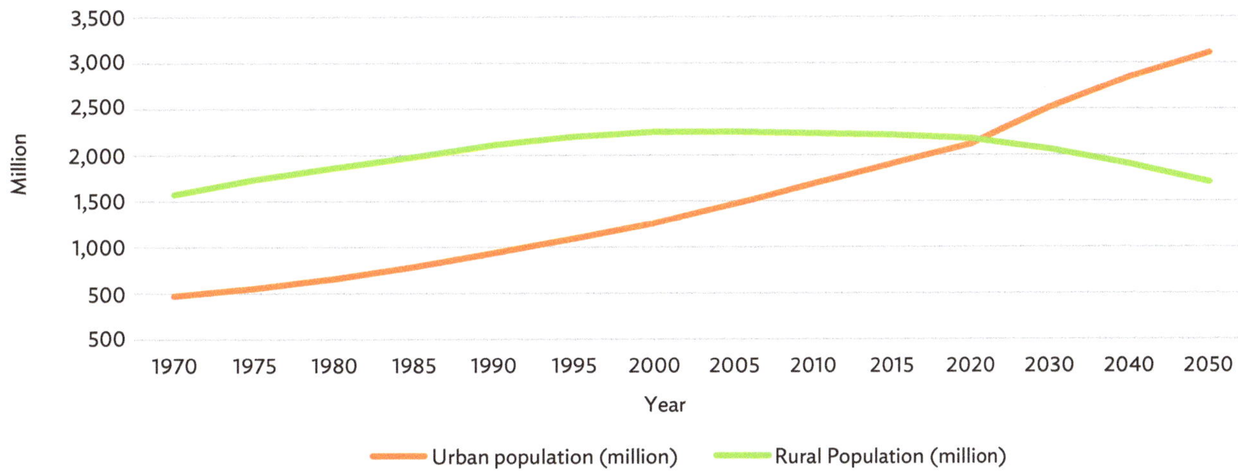

Source: Asian Development Bank estimates using data from the United Nations. World Urbanization Prospects. https://population.un.org/wup/Download/ (accessed 1 March 2023).

as having to travel further to access job opportunities (WBG 2017). These costs can further contribute to the poverty premium in urban public transportation (Lucas 2012).

In developing Asia, many residents with low incomes live in areas that are not served by public transit. Informal transport, such as motorcycles or taxis, may provide an option in these instances, but these services are often unregulated and unsafe. Overall, improving access to safe, reliable, and affordable public transportation for the urban poor should be a policy priority for governments in developing Asia (ADB 2022e).

In terms of the poverty premium in urban housing, a large portion of low-income city-dwellers in developing Asia are tenants paying a significant proportion of their weekly or monthly expenses in rent (UN-Habitat 2003). The urban poor are largely unable to access affordable housing due to their restricted financial resources and inadequate national and local housing policies (Golubchikov and Badyina 2012), with the latter also placing upward inflationary pressure on rents.

Developing Asia still lags the rest of the world in moving urban residents out of slums.

Urbanization in many parts of developing Asia is associated with expanding slums and shelter deprivation, informality of employment, and generally precarious living conditions (UN DESA 2018). Those living in slums and shanty towns in urban areas face limited access to secure housing, services, and livelihoods (Ogra 2016). They often reside in unhealthy and violent environments, without access to social protections, education, or health care.

A study commissioned by UN-Habitat estimates that developing Asia is home to 60% of the world's total slum population, and many more people live in areas with slum-like conditions (ADB 2014; Lee and Singh 2022). As shown in Figure 1.24, which presents trends with respect to SDG 11.1.1, the urban population living in slum households grew by 31.9 million worldwide in 2020, reaching a total of over 1.06 billion. This is despite a downward trend in the proportion of those living in slums to the total urban population, globally (e.g., 27.3% in 2010 versus 24.2% in 2020). In developing Asia, 10 of the 22 economies with available data for 2020 had more than 30% of the total urban population living in slums.

Figure 1.24: Urban Population Living in Slums, Informal Settlements, or Inadequate Housing; World and Developing Asia

Globally, the proportion of the urban population living in slums has gradually declined but estimates suggest there were still at least 150 million more people living in slums in 2020 than in 2000.

In developing Asia, only 8 of 22 reporting economies had less than 10% of the urban population living in slums in 2020.

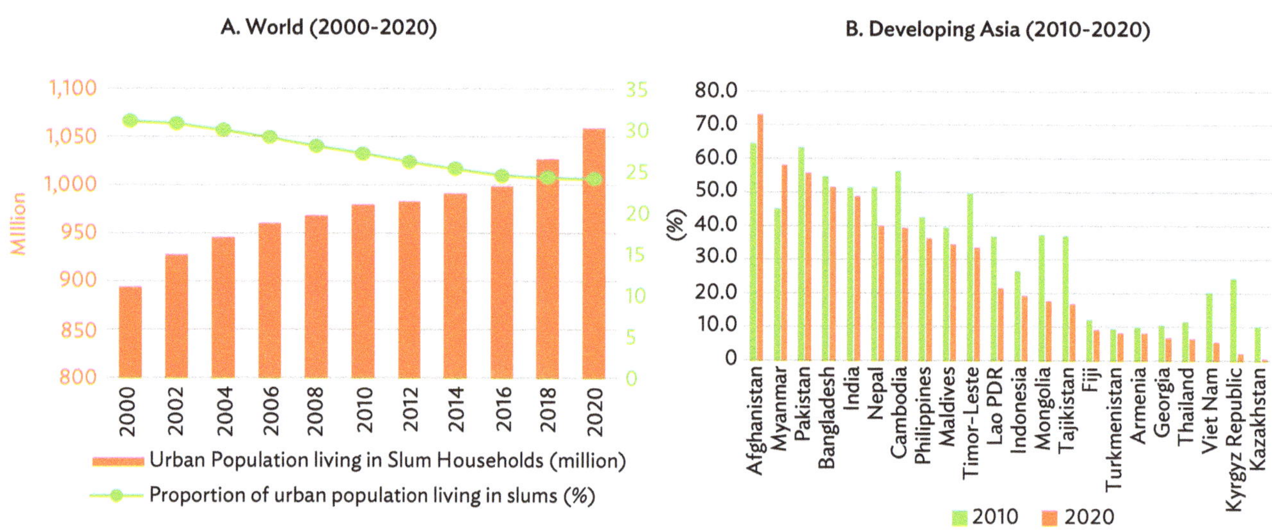

Lao PDR = Lao People's Democratic Republic.

Notes: (a) A "slum household" is a household in which the inhabitants suffer one or more of the following "household deprivations": 1) Lack of access to improved water services; 2) Lack of access to improved sanitation facilities; 3) Lack of sufficient living area; 4) Lack of housing durability and 5) Lack of security of tenure. For these calculations, only the first four deprivations were used.
(b) Slum population (million) based on UN calculations derived from World Urbanization Prospects: The 2018 Revision.

Source: For chart A: Asian Development Bank estimates using data from the United Nations Human Settlement Programme (UN-Habitat), Global Urban Indicators Database 2020 (accessed 3 March 2023). For chart B: Asian Development Bank estimates using data from Table 11.1.1 of *Key Indicators for Asia and the Pacific 2023*.

The global cost-of-living crisis amplifies the plight of the urban poor, particularly those living in slums.

People in urban areas spend more than their rural counterparts on fuel, residential power, and housing, all of which have been greatly affected by higher energy prices and the rental accommodation crisis in some economies. In general, urban dwellers are also more likely to purchase more goods and services to cover their daily basic needs, compared to rural dwellers who may grow their own food and have less need to travel to earn a living. During periods of high inflation, these scenarios have a disproportionate negative impact on low-income earners and the urban poor, who have less disposable income to cover price increases.

The existence of slums involves a trade-off for policy makers. While slums give dwellers access to labor market opportunities in urban areas without the costs associated with infrastructure and formal housing development, they also often occupy valuable land that could be used for other purposes. This may be enhanced by stringent regulations for the supply of formal housing which may raise prices in the sector and increases the demand and value for residential space in slums. Relaxing these distortionary regulations and investing in infrastructure to reduce commuting costs in urban areas are several ways policy makers could help reduce the share of the urban population living in slums (Rivera-Padilla 2021).

Minimizing the urban poverty premium requires large-scale investment to finance urban infrastructure.

In the context of reducing the poverty premium, policymakers should consider strategies aimed at improving urban living conditions. These should include enhancing the coverage, quality, efficiency, and reliability of urban services, with the objective of creating inclusive, sustainable, and energy-efficient infrastructure. Initiatives should embrace low-carbon development, climate-resilience, and disaster management through nature-based solutions, ecosystem enhancement, and capacity building in cities and communities.

Financial sustainability can be improved through integrated urban and regional planning along with innovative financing options, including public-private partnerships, municipal bonds, and capital market instruments. Lastly, strengthening institutional frameworks is essential in supporting improvements in developing Asia's cities.

Advancing Innovation to Create New Opportunities for the Poor

By examining trends with respect to selected indicators under SDG 8 (decent work and economic growth), particularly access to financial services, policymakers can determine how to leverage technology and harness innovation to minimize the poverty premium.

Technology and innovation can play an important role in reducing poverty.

Innovations and developments in technology have enormous potential to impact poor people positively. In rural areas, which are home to a significant proportion of the poor, the adoption of innovative approaches to farming and use of new technologies can support enhanced agricultural productivity, sustainability, and resilience, higher incomes and reduced financial risks. It can also open up new market opportunities and help reduce natural resource depletion and degradation (FAO 2018).

New technologies such as satellite data, big data analytics, drones and artificial intelligence can support 'smart farming', delivering multiple benefits, including improved monitoring of crops and water resources, automated production, and increased efficiency and sustainability of farm practices, saving time and money. This in turn can help increase farmer incomes and make them more resilient to price shocks, especially those related to extreme weather events (OECD 2018).

A number of these policy actions could contribute to reducing the poverty premium in rural areas. For instance, reductions in forest cover and related soil degradation can be addressed through innovative financing to incentivize reforestation initiatives (FAO 2015). Similarly, enhanced farming profitability may be achieved through investment programs supporting mechanization and advanced cropping technologies. Enhancing resilience to food price fluctuations may also be met by decentralizing access to resources, finance, and technology (FAO 2018).

Innovations in energy efficiency and communications technology can lower the costs of essential services.

Innovation in the energy sector, such as use of solar panels and other renewable sources, can reduce the poverty premium and contribute to poverty alleviation by improving the standard of living in poor communities (Bishoge et al. 2020, Olsson 2018). Estimates suggest that the cost of renewable energy has declined dramatically. For example, between 2009 and 2017, the cost of solar panels dropped by 76% (Bogmans 2019). The poor may use the associated long-term savings to invest in education and personal development, cover medical-related expenses, establish bank accounts, reduce the balance of loans, and explore other means of breaking the poverty cycle.

Communication technologies can also narrow the poverty premium by affording poor people greater ease in accessing educational resources, market information, job opportunities, government services, and other resources. From 2000 to 2021, the proportion of Asians using the internet increased substantially, doubling in the past decade (Figure 1.25).

Remote rural communities can benefit from technologies that expand e-Learning opportunities for students unable to commute to educational institutions, while the scaling up of telemedicine and online health services (OECD 2018 and 2020) can improve access to health care in poor communities and reduce the cost of seeking medical treatment.

Figure 1.25: Proportion of Individuals using the Internet in Developing Asia

While there are variations across the region, internet access increased significantly in Asia and the Pacific from 2000 to 2021.

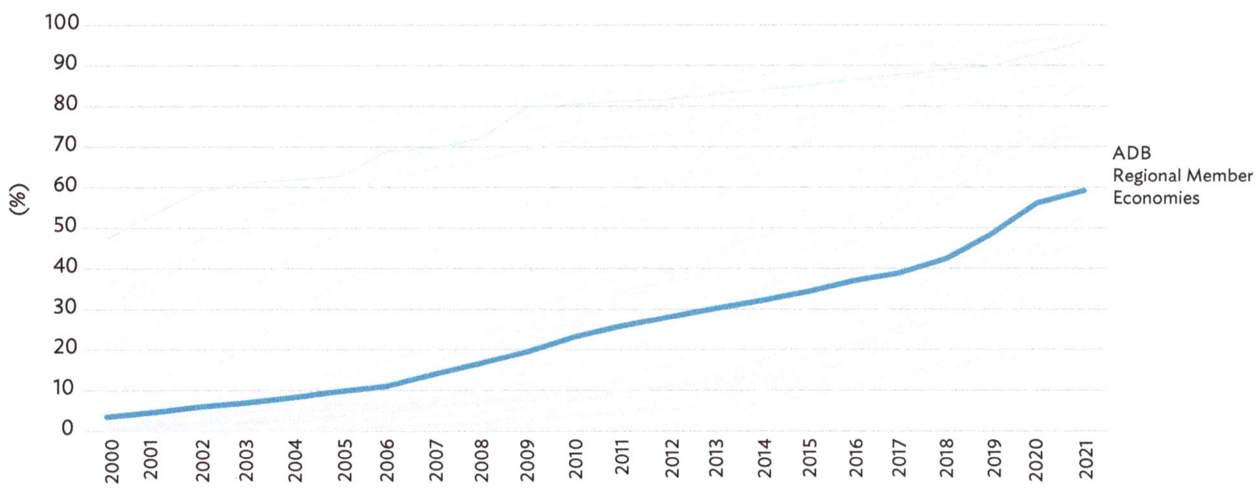

Source: Asian Development Bank estimates using data from the International Telecommunications Union. https://www.itu.int/ (accessed 24 May 2023).

Overall, it is imperative that policies be designed to ensure that energy and communications technologies are continuously accessible and affordable for poor people.

Technology can have a substantial impact on financial inclusion for people living in poverty.

Financial inclusion, or the ability to access financial services, has the potential to drive down poverty rates (Demirguc-Kunt et al. 2015). There are four aspects of effective financial inclusion: access, usage, financial development, and financial technology (fintech) infrastructure. As seen in Figure 1.26, access to financial services tends to reduce poverty and protect households from financial shocks (Demirguc-Kunt et al. 2015).

Fintech infrastructure increases access to financial services, particularly among underserved and marginalized populations, and lowers the costs of financial transactions and services, which is especially beneficial to the poor (Demigurc-Kunt et al. 2018). Financial access, usage, and fintech infrastructure also increases entrepreneurship, enabling the poor to explore business ideas to lift themselves out of poverty (ADB 2021b).

Financial inclusion can also help achieve gender-related targets of the SDGs. Figure 1.26 demonstrates that increasing financial inclusion for women in 2021 improved their indexed level of autonomy and decision-making power. This can help reduce poverty levels for women and gender inequality, while opening up more employment opportunities. For example, some studies show that education spending increased significantly when households headed by women were given access to digital savings accounts (Yamada et al. 2019).

Figure 1.26: Effect of Financial Access on the Incidence of Moderate Poverty and Women's Empowerment

Moderate poverty was significantly lowered, while women's empowerment was substantially strengthened, as financial access improved in 2021.

Note: Women's empowerment is calculated as 1 - gender inequality index. Financial Access - Account is defined as the percentage of respondents who report having an account (by themselves or together with someone else) at a bank or another type of financial institution (see the definition for "financial institution account") or report personally using a mobile money service in the past year (see the definition for "mobile money account").

Sources: Asian Development Bank estimates using data from the World Bank. World Development Indicators. https://databank.worldbank.org/source/world-development-indicators (accessed 14 May 2023) and the United Nations Development Programme. Human Development Report. https://hdr.undp.org/data-center/thematic-composite-indices/gender-inequality-index#/indicies/GII (accessed 14 May 2023).

The integration of innovation into the banking industry, especially in fintech services such as mobile money, presents an enormous opportunity to accelerate the process of financial inclusion.

Trends in SDG indicator 8.10.2 show that, in developing Asian economies, the proportion of adults with an account at a bank or other financial institution, or with a mobile-money service provider, increased significantly from 2011 to 2021 (Figure 127). By 2021, East Asia had the highest proportion with 98.9%, while Southeast Asia and

South Asia rose from around 40% in 2011 to almost 70% in 2021. Central and West Asia needs to lift its rate of financial inclusion, but its proportion has risen impressively from 17.3% in 2011 to 45.8% in 2021. There is also a need to close the financial inclusion gap between men and women, in select areas, particularly Central and West, and South Asia.

Figure 1.27: Proportion of Adults (15 Years and Older) with an Account at a Bank or Other Financial Institution or with a Mobile-Money Service Provider by Subregion of Developing Asia

Developing Asia's rate of financial inclusion rose to above 40% of the total adult population in 2021 but there is still a need to close the gap between men and women in select areas.

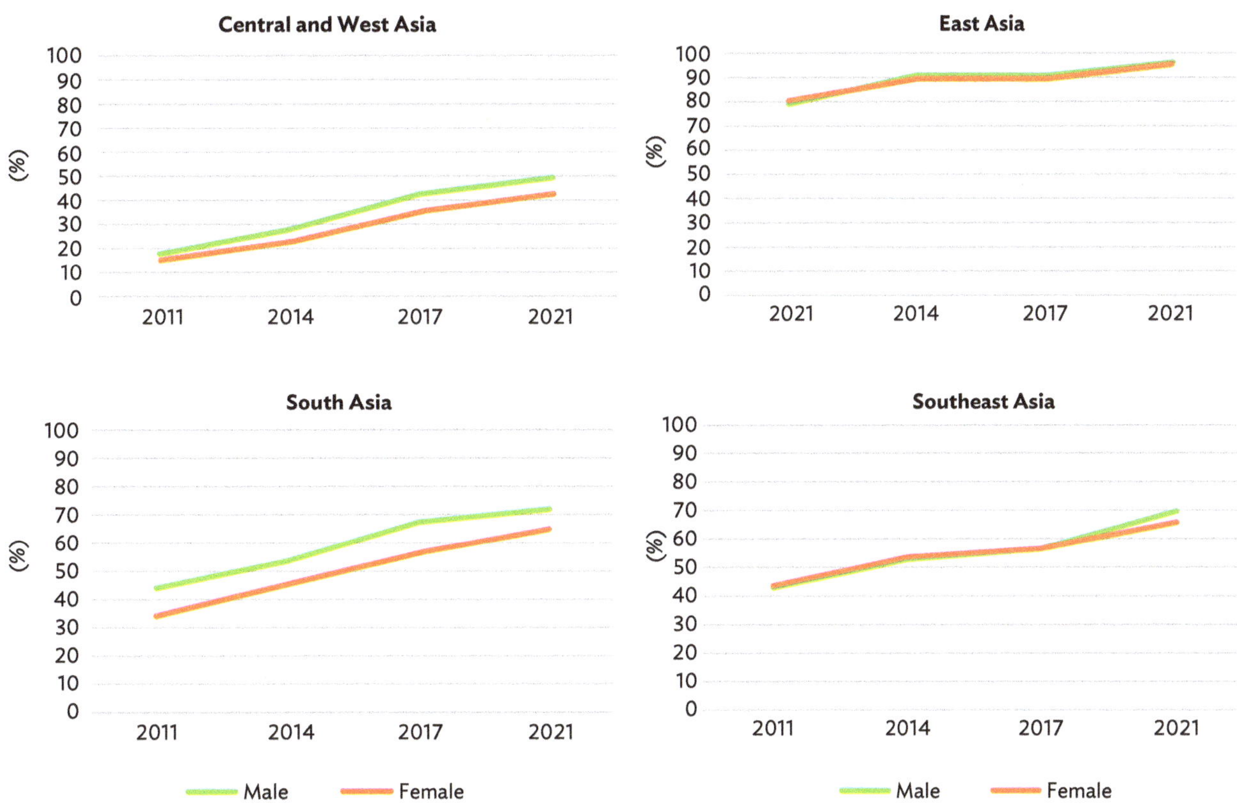

Source: Asian Development Bank estimates using data from the World Bank. World Development Indicators. https://databank.worldbank.org/source/world-development-indicators (accessed 25 May 2023).

References

R. Acharya and A. Sadath. 2019. Energy poverty and economic development: Household-level evidence from India. *Energy and Buildings*. 183. 15 January. pp. 785-791.

J. Anderson and G. Feder. 2007. Agricultural Extension. *Handbook of Agricultural Economics*. Vol.3. Chapter 44. pp. 2343-2378. https://econpapers.repec.org/bookchap/eeehagchp/5-44.htm.

Asian Development Bank (ADB). (no date). *ADB's Work in Agriculture and Food Security. What We Do.* Manila. https://www.adb.org/what-we-do/topics/agriculture/overview.

ADB. 2008. *Research Study on Poverty-Specific Purchasing Power Parities for Selected Countries in Asia and the Pacific.* Manila. https://www.adb.org/sites/default/files/publication/29130/poverty-specific-ppp.pdf.

ADB. 2011. *Global Food Price Inflation and Developing Asia.* Manila. https://www.adb.org/sites/default/files/publication/28626/food-price-inflation.pdf.

ADB. 2014. *Urban Poverty in Asia.* Manila. https://www.adb.org/sites/default/files/publication/59778/urban-poverty-asia_0.pdf.

ADB. 2015. *Balancing the Burden? Desk Review of Women's Time Poverty and Infrastructure in Asia and the Pacific.* Manila. https://www.adb.org/sites/default/files/publication/177465/sdcc-balancing-burden.pdf Star.

ADB. 2019. *Modernizing Agriculture and Rural Development. Asia's Journey to Prosperity: Policy, Market and Technology over 50 Years.* Chapter 4. pp. 1-34. Manila. https://www.adb.org/sites/default/files/publication/549191/asias-journey-chapter-4.pdf.

ADB. 2020. *Asia's Journey to Prosperity: Policy Market, And Technology Over 50 Years.* Manila. https://www.adb.org/sites/default/files/publication/549191/asias-journey-prosperity.pdf.

ADB. 2021a. *Creating Livable Asian Cities.* B. Susantono and R.Guild (eds). Manila. https://www.adb.org/sites/default/files/publication/697006/creating-livable-asian-cities.pdf.

ADB. 2021b. Emerging Priorities in the Covid-19 Era. *Asia-Pacific Financial Inclusion Forum.* Manila. https://www.adb.org/sites/default/files/publication/761211/asia-pacific-financial-inclusion-forum-2021.pdf.

ADB. 2021c. *Asian Development Outlook 2021: Financing a Green and Inclusive Recovery.* Manila. https://www.adb.org/sites/default/files/publication/692111/ado2021.pdf.

ADB. 2021d. *Asian Development Outlook 2021 Update. Theme Chapter: Transforming Agriculture in Asia.* Manila. https://www.adb.org/sites/default/files/publication/726556/ado2021-update-theme-chapter.pdf.

ADB. 2022a. *Asian Development Outlook (ADO) Update 2022: Entrepreneurship in the Digital Age.* Manila. https://www.adb.org/sites/default/files/publication/825166/ado2022-update.pdf.

ADB. 2022b. *Asian Development Outlook (ADO) 2022: Mobilizing Taxes for Development.* Manila. https://www.adb.org/sites/default/files/publication/784041/ado2022.pdf.

ADB. 2022c. *Asian Development Outlook 2022 Supplement: Global Gloom Dims Asian Prospects.* Manila. https://www.adb.org/sites/default/files/publication/844296/ado-supplement-december-2022.pdf.

ADB. 2022d. *Key Indicators for Asia and the Pacific 2022. 53rd Edition.* Manila. https://www.adb.org/sites/default/files/publication/812946/ki2022.pdf.

ADB. 2022e. *Reimagining the Future of Transport Across Asia and the Pacific.* Manila. https://www.adb.org/sites/default/files/publication/744376/future-transport-asia-pacific-trend-cards.pdf.

ADB. 2023a. *Asian Development Outlook 2023.* Manila. https://www.adb.org/sites/default/files/publication/863591/asian-development-outlook-april-2023.pdf.

ADB. 2023b. *Delivering on the Sustainable Development Goals through Solutions at the Energy, Food and Finance Nexus.* Asia-Pacific SDG Partnership Report copublished by ADB, United Nations Economic and Social Commission for Asia and the Pacific and the United Nations Development Programme. Thailand. https://www.adb.org/sites/default/files/institutional-document/870986/2023-asia-pacific-sdg-partnership-report.pdf.

ADB. 2023c. *Asia in the Global Transition to Net Zero: Asian Development Outlook 2023 Thematic Report*. Manila. https://www.adb.org/sites/default/files/publication/876891/ado-2023-thematic-report.pdf.

ADB. 2023d. *Asian Development Outlook July 2023.* Asian Development Bank.

B. Ames, W. Brown, S. Devarajan and A. Izquierdo. 2001. Macroeconomic Policy and Poverty Reduction. *International Monetary Fund.* https://www.imf.org/external/pubs/ft/exrp/macropol/eng/.

M. Ayyagari and T. Beck. 2015. Financial Inclusion in Asia: An Overview. *ADB Economics Working Paper Series.* 449. https://www.adb.org/sites/default/files/publication/173377/ewp-449.pdf.

A. Banerjee and E. Duflo. 2011. Poor Economics: A Radical Rethinking of the Way to Fight Global Poverty. *Population and Development Review.* 37.4. pp. 796-797.

A. Banerjee and S. Mullainathan. 2010. The Shape of Temptation: Implications of the Economic Lives of the Poor. *National Bureau of Economic Research Working Paper* No. 15973. https://www.nber.org/papers/w15973.

C. Barrett. 2008. Smallholder Market Participation: Concepts and Evidence from Eastern and Southern Africa. Food Policy. *ScienceDirect.* 33.4. pp. 299-317. https://www.sciencedirect.com/science/article/abs/pii/S0306919207000607.

V. Bérenger and A. Verdier-Chouchane. 2017. Multidimensional Measures of Well-Being: Standard of Living and Quality of Life Across Countries. *World Development.* 35. 7. pp. 1,259-1,276. https://www.sciencedirect.com/science/article/abs/pii/S0305750X07000563?via%3Dihub.

O. Bishoge, G. Kombe and B. Mvile. 2020. Community Participation in the Renewable Energy Sector in Tanzania. International Journal of Sustainable Energy Planning and Management. June. https://www.semanticscholar.org/paper/Community-participation-in-the-renewable-energy-in-Bishoge-Kombe/c36b897c54ffc38e68407166c670b67172ab5112.

D.J. Bertulfo. 2020. COVID-19 labor market impact in the Philippines: Assessment and national policy responses. *International Labour Organization*. https://www.ilo.org/wcmsp5/groups/public/---asia/---ro-bangkok/---ilo-manila/documents/publication/wcms_762209.pdf.

C. Bogmans. 2019. Falling Costs Make Wind, Solar More Affordable. *IMF Blog*. 26 April. https://www.imf.org/en/Blogs/Articles/2019/04/26/falling-costs-make-wind-solar-more-affordable.

S. Boonyabancha, T. Kerr, J. Lumanti, J., and C. Tacoli. 2019. How the urban poor define and measure food security in Cambodia and Nepal. *Environment and Urbanization*. Vol 31. July. pp. 517–532. https://www.researchgate.net/publication/334563000_How_the_urban_poor_define_and_measure_food_security_in_Cambodia_and_Nepal.

E. Bruijn and G. Antonides. 2021. Poverty and Economic Decision Making: A Review of Scarcity Theory. *Theory and Decision*. 92. pp. 50-37 https://link.springer.com/article/10.1007/s11238-021-09802-7.

G. Bryan and C. Udry. 2016. The Impact of Cognitive Behavioral Therapy on Low-Income Individuals in Rural Ghana. *J-PAL*. https://www.povertyactionlab.org/evaluation/impact-cognitive-behavioral-therapy-low-income-individuals-rural-ghana.

D. Caplovitz.1963. The Poor Pay More. Consumer Practices of Low-Income Families. *The Free Press of Glencoe, Collier-Macmillan Limited*. https://babel.hathitrust.org/cgi/pt?id=mdp.39015061002310&view=1up&seq=7&q1=premium.

T. Cavoli and R. Shrestha. 2020. The Nature and Landscape of Financial Inclusion. *ERIA Discussion Paper Series*. No. 340. https://www.eria.org/uploads/media/discussion-papers/1-The-Nature-and-Landscape-of-Financial-Inclusion-in-Asia.pdf.

K. Cleaver. 2012. Investing in Agriculture to Reduce Poverty and Hunger. Scaling Up in Agriculture, Rural Development, and Nutrition. Focus 19. Brief 2. https://ebrary.ifpri.org/utils/getfile/collection/p15738coll2/id/126979/filename/127190.pdf

S. Corfe and N. Keohane. 2018. Measuring the Poverty Premium. The Social Market Foundation. https://www.smf.co.uk/wp-content/uploads/2018/03/Measuring-the-Poverty-Premium.pdf

D. R.Cox, C. Kartsonaki, and R.H. Keogh. 2018. Big data: Some statistical issues. Statistics & probability letters, 136, 111–115. https://doi.org/10.1016/j.spl.2018.02.015

A. Demigurc-Kunt, L. Klapper, D. Singer and P. Van Oudheusden. 2015. Global Findex Database 2014. Measuring Financial Inclusion around the World. *World Bank*. Washington, D.C. https://thedocs.worldbank.org/en/doc/681361466184854434-0050022016/original/2014GlobalFindexReportDKSV.pdf.

A. Demirguc-Kunt, L. Klapper, D. Singer, S. Ansar, and J. Hess. 2018. The Global Findex Database 2017. Measuring Financial Inclusion and the Fintech Revolution. *World Bank*. Washington, D.C. https://openknowledge.worldbank.org/entities/publication/ed800062-e062-5a05-acdd-90429d8a5a07.

F. de Soyres, A. M. Santacreu, and H. Young. 2022. Fiscal Policy and Excess Inflation During Covid-19: A Cross-country View. *US Federal Reserve.* https://www.federalreserve.gov/econres/notes/feds-notes/fiscal-policy-and-excess-inflation-during-covid-19-a-cross-country-view-20220715.html.

S. Dhanaraj, V. Mahambare, and P. Munjal. 2017. From Income to Household Welfare: Lessons from Refrigerator Ownership in India. *Journal of Quantitative Economics.* pp. 573–588. https://link.springer.com/article/10.1007/s40953-017-0084-5.

E. Duflo, M. Kremer, J. Robinson. 2011. Nudging Farmers for Use Fertilizer: Theory and Experimental Evidence from Kenya. *American Economic Review.* Vol 101. No.6. pp. 2,350-2,390. https://www.aeaweb.org/articles?id=10.1257/aer.101.6.2350.

Food and Agriculture Organization of the United Nations (FAO). 2011. *Innovative Policies and Institutions to Support Agro-Industries Development.* https://www.fao.org/sustainable-food-value-chains/library/details/ar/c/267095/.

FAO. 2015. *Global Guidelines for the Restoration of Degraded Forests and Landscapes in Drylands: Building Resilience and Benefiting Livelihoods.* FAO Forestry Paper. No. 175. Rome. https://www.fao.org/3/i5036e/i5036e.pdf.

FAO. 2018. *Transforming Food and Agriculture to Achieve the SDGs: 20 Interconnected Actions to Guide Decision Makers.* Rome. https://www.fao.org/3/I9900EN/i9900en.pdf.

FAO, International Fund for Agricultural Development, United Nations Children's Fund, World Food Programme, and World Health Organization. 2022. *The State of Food Security and Nutrition in the World 2022. Repurposing food and agricultural policies to make healthy diets more affordable.* Rome. https://www.fao.org/documents/card/en/c/cc0639en.

S. French, C. Tangney, M. Crane, Y. Wang and B. Applehans. 2019. Nutrition Quality of Food Purchases Varies by Household Income: the SHoPPER Study. *BMC Public Health.* https://bmcpublichealth.biomedcentral.com/articles/10.1186/s12889-019-6546-2.

D. Gauri, R. Jindal, M. Yu. 2021. Higher Prices and Fewer Deals: Low-Income Customers Face Post-Pandemic Disparities. *Progressive GROCER.* https://progressivegrocer.com/higher-prices-and-fewer-deals-low-income-customers-face-post-pandemic-disparities.

U. Gentilini, M. Almenfi, H. Iyengar, Y. Okamura, Y. Urteaga, E. Raul, G. Valleriani, S. Aziz, M. Al Azim Bin Noruzi, M. Chu. 2023. Tracking Global Social Protection Responses to Inflation. Living Paper. v.5. *World Bank Group Social Protection & Jobs Discussion Paper.* No. 2305. June. https://openknowledge.worldbank.org/server/api/core/bitstreams/54eb895b-3cb3-4322-b342-af377b52e3bd/content.

U. Gentilini, M.Almenfi, H. Iyengar, Y. Okamura, G.Valleriani, E. Urteaga, Sheraz Aziz. 2022. Tracking Global Social Protection Responses to Inflation. Living Paper. v.4. *World Bank Group Social Protection & Jobs Discussion Paper.* No. 2215. December. https://documents1.worldbank.org/curated/en/099400012222223378/pdf/P176585074ebcd0260a3ca04efbbb3c25c0.pdf.

I. Gill and P. Nagle. 2022. Inflation Could Wreak Vengeance on the World's Poor. *Brookings Institution.* 18 March. https://www.brookings.edu/articles/inflation-could-wreak-vengeance-on-the-worlds-poor/.

O. Golubchikov, A. Badyina. 2012. Sustainable Housing for Sustainable Cities: A Policy Framework for Developing Countries. *UN-Habitat.* Nairobi. https://papers.ssrn.com/sol3/papers.cfm?abstract_id=2194204.

Y. Guan, J. Yan, Y. Shan, Y. Zhou, Y. Hang, R. Li, Y. Li, B. Liu, Q. Nie, B. Bruckner, K. Feng, K. Hubacek. 2023. Burden of the Global Energy Price Crisis on Households. *Nature Energy.* Article. https://www.nature.com/articles/s41560-023-01209-8.

A. Helling. 1998. Changing intra-metropolitan accessibility in the US: Evidence from Atlanta. *Progress in Planning.* Vol 49. Issue 2. pp. 57-103. https://doi.org/10.1016/S0305-9006(97)00032-9.

D. Hirsch. 2013. Addressing the poverty premium. Approaches to regulation. *Consumer Futures.* London. https://repository.lboro.ac.uk/articles/report/Addressing_the_poverty_premium_approaches_to_regulation/9598631

D. Hondo, L. Arthur, and P. Gamaralalage. 2020. Solid Waste Management in Developing Asia: Prioritizing Waste Separation. *ADBI Policy Brief.* No. 2020. 7 November. https://www.adb.org/sites/default/files/publication/652121/adbi-pb2020-7.pdf.

M. Hossain. 2020. Less is More Expensive: Income Differences in Bulk Buying. Philadelphia. https://www.mallickhossain.com/papers/BulkBuyingInequality.pdf.

International Labour Organization (ILO 2022). Social Protection at the Crossroads – in Pursuit of a Better Future. *World Social Protection Report 2020-22.* https://www.ilo.org/wcmsp5/groups/public/@ed_protect/@soc_sec/documents/publication/wcms_817572.pdf.

International Monetary Fund. 2022. (IMF 2022). Regional Economic Outlook: Asia and the Pacific, October 2022: *Sailing into Headwinds.* https://www.imf.org/en/Publications/REO/APAC/Issues/2022/10/13/regional-economic-outlook-for-asia-and-pacific-october-2022.

International Monetary Fund (IMF), International Labour Organization, Statistical Office of the European Union, United Nations Economic Commission for Europe, Organisation for Economic Co-operation and Development, and the World Bank. 2020. Consumer price index manual: concepts and methods. Washington, DC: IMF. https://unece.org/statistics/documents/2020/12/standards/consumer-price-index-manual-concepts-and-methods-2020.

S. Jahan, E. Loukoianova, C. Sullivan, Y. Yang. 2018. Asia Needs More Access to Financial Services to Grow. *IMF Blog.* https://www.imf.org/en/Blogs/Articles/2018/09/18/asia-needs-more-access-to-financial-services-to-grow.

K. Joshi, M. Accad, and I. Song. 2021. Prices Matter When Tracking Economic Development and Recovery After the Pandemic. Asian Development Bank Blog. 19 April. https://blogs.adb.org/blog/prices-matter-when-tracking-economicdevelopment-and-recovery-after-pandemic.

E. Kay and W. Lewenstein. 2013. The Problem with the “Poverty Premium”. *Harvard Business Review Magazine.* April. https://hbr.org/2013/04/the-problem-with-the-poverty-premium.

H. Kharas, I. Ohno, J. McArthur (eds). 2019. Leave No one Behind. Time for Specifics on the Sustainable Development Goals. *Brookings Institution Press.* https://www.google.com.hk/books/edition/Leave_No_One_Behind/h9SiDwAAQBAJ?hl=en&gbpv=0.

R. Latimaha, N. Ismail, and Z. Bahari. 2020. Cost of Living and Standard of Living Nexus: The Determinants of Cost of Living. *Jurnal Ekonomi Malaysia.* 54. 3. pp. 1–14. https://www.ukm.my/jem/article/cost-of-living-and-standard-of-living-nexus-the-determinants-of-cost-of-living/.

J. Leather. 2022. Asia's Cities Need Quality Public Transport. *ADB Blogs.* March 25. https://blogs.adb.org/blog/asia-s-cities-need-quality-public-transport.

H.S. Lee and A. Singh. 2022. Adequate and Affordable Housing. Enhancing ADB's Support to Developing Member Countries. *ADB Sustainable Development Working Paper Series.* No. 82. September. Manila. https://www.adb.org/sites/default/files/publication/822346/sdwp-082-adequate-affordable-housing-adb-support.pdf.

O. Lorenz. 2018. Does commuting matter to subjective well-being? *Journal of Transport Geography.* Vol 66. January. pp. 180-199.

K. Lucas. 2012. Transport and Social Exclusion: Where are We Now? Transport Policy. *ScienceDirect.* Vol 20. March. pp.105-113. https://www.sciencedirect.com/science/article/pii/S0967070X12000145.

D. Mahler, N. Yonzan, R. Hill, C.Lakner, H. Wu and N. Yoshida. 2022. Pandemic Prices and Poverty. *World Bank Blogs.* April. https://blogs.worldbank.org/opendata/pandemic-prices-and-poverty.

M. McConnell. 2022. What Covid Teaches Us About the Cost-of-Living Crisis? https://www.hrw.org/news/2022/12/20/what-covid-teaches-us-about-cost-living-crisis

M. Medina. 2010. Solid Wastes, Poverty and the Environment in Developing Country Cities: Challenges and Opportunities. *United Nations University, World Institute for Development Economics Research Working Paper.* No. 2010/23. https://www.wider.unu.edu/sites/default/files/wp2010-23.pdf.

R. Mendoza. 2011. Why do the poor pay more? Exploring the poverty penalty concept. *Journal of International Development.* 23.1. pp. 1–28. https://onlinelibrary.wiley.com/doi/10.1002/jid.1504.

S. Mohanty, N. Agrawal, B. Mahapatra, D. Choudhury, S. Tuladhar and E. Valdemar Holmgren. 2017. Multidimensional Poverty and Catastrophic Health Spending in the Mountainous Regions of Myanmar, Nepal and India. *International Journal for Equity in Health.* Article No. 21. https://equityhealthj.biomedcentral.com/articles/10.1186/s12939-016-0514-6#citeas.

S. Mullainathan and E. Shafir. 2013. Scarcity: Why having too little means so much. Times Books / Henry Holt and Company.

V. Nuguer and E. Parado. 2021. Inflation and its Impact on the Poor in the Era of COVID-19. *IDB Blog.* October. https://blogs.iadb.org/ideas-matter/en/inflation-and-its-impact-on-the-poor-in-the-era-of-covid-19/.

S. Nakamura, R. Harati,. S. Lall, Y. Dikhanov, N. Hamadeh, W. Oliver, M. Rissanen, and M. Yamanaka. 2020. Comparing Costs of Living across World Cities. *The World Bank Economic Review.* Vol 34. Issue Supplement 1, pp. S79-S88. https://academic.oup.com/wber/article/34/Supplement_1/S79/5671691.

Organisation for Economic Co-operation and Development (OECD). 2018. Rural Regions of the Future: Seizing Technological Change. *OECD iLibrary.* https://www.oecd-ilibrary.org/sites/ae6bf9cd-en/index.html?itemId=/content/component/ae6bf9cd-en#chapter-d1e19840.

OECD. 2020. Rural Well-being: Geography of Opportunities. https://www.oecd.org/cfe/rural-well-being-d25cef80-en.htm

A. Ogra. 2016. Sustainable Transport for Urban Poor: A Case of Johannesburg. 7th Planning Africa Conference. Johannesburg. https://www.researchgate.net/publication/310832246_Sustainable_Transport_for_Urban_Poor_A_Case_of_Johannesburg.

G. Olsson. 2018. Clean Water Using Solar and Wind. Outside the Power Grid. *IWA Publishing.* United Kingdom. https://pdfs.semanticscholar.org/0024/e3b2d8723ed723073900a2241ceb230759e2.pdf?_gl=1*1ra9ipw*_ga*MzM3MjUyODg5LjE2NzgwNjg5MDA.*_ga_H7P4ZT52H5*MTY3OTI4MTEwOC42LjAuMTY3OTI4MTkxMy4wLjAuMA.

H. Phoumin, and F. Kimura. 2019. The impacts of energy insecurity on household welfare in Cambodia: Empirical evidence and policy implications. *Economic Modelling,* 82(C), pp. 35-41. https://www.sciencedirect.com/science/article/pii/S0264999319307904.

C. Prahalad. 2004. *The Fortune at the Bottom of the Pyramid: Eradicating Poverty Through Profits.* Wharton School Publishing.

C. Prahalad, and A. Hammond. 2002. Serving the world's poor, profitably. *Haravard Business Review,* 80(9). pp. 48-57, 124.

S. Pye, A. Dobbins, C. Baffert, J. Brajkovic, P. Deane, R. de Miglio. 2015. Addressing Energy Poverty and Vulnerable Consumers in the Energy Sector Across the EU. *L'Europe En Formation.* 4. 378. pp. 64-89.

V. Rao. 2000. Price Heterogeneity and "Real" Inequality: A Case Study of Prices and Poverty in Rural South India. *The Review of Income and Wealth,* 46(2), pp. 201-211.

A. Sadath and R. Acharya. 2017. Assessing the extent and intensity of energy poverty using Multidimensional Poverty Index: Empirical evidence from households in India. *Energy Policy.* Vol. 102. March. pp. 540-550.

K. Schelzig and A. Jilani. 2021. Assessing the Impact of the Graduation Approach in the Philippines. *ADB Briefs.* No.169. March. https://www.adb.org/sites/default/files/publication/682781/adb-brief-169-impact-graduation-approach-philippines.pdf.

A. Shevlin and C. Lam. 2021. Inflation in Asia Pacific - A Different Phenomenon. *J.P. Morgan Asset Management.* https://am.jpmorgan.com/sg/en/asset-management/liq/insights/liquidity-insights/updates/inflation-in-asia-pacific-a-different-phenomenon/

P. Starkey and J. Hine. 2014. Poverty and Sustainable Transport. How Transport Affects Poor People with Policy Implications for Poverty Reduction. *Literature Review UN-Habitat.* October. https://sustainabledevelopment.un.org/content/documents/1767Poverty%20and%20sustainable%20transport.pdf.

A. Rivera-Padilla. 2021. Slums, Allocation of Talent and Barriers to Urbanization. *European Economic Review.* Vol 140. https://www.sciencedirect.com/science/article/abs/pii/S0014292121002166.

K. Tan, H. Chuah, and N. Luu. 2018. A case study on Malaysia and Singapore: Nexus amongst competitiveness, cost of living, wages, purchasing power and livability. *Competitiveness Review: An International Business Journal.* 28.2. pp. 172–193. https://www.semanticscholar.org/paper/A-case-study-on-Malaysia-and-Singapore%3A-Nexus-cost-Tan-Chuah/843ebe9d704c19bf6c9529ad2db3feab939c8e1d.

The Economist Intelligence Unit (EIU). 2021. *Will Inflation Stay Under Control in Asia?.* March. https://www.eiu.com/n/will-inflation-stay-under-control-in-asia/.

The Lancet Public Health. 2022. The cost of living: an avoidable public health crisis. *The Lancet Public Health.* 7. 6. https://www.thelancet.com/journals/lanpub/article/PIIS2468-2667(22)00120-7/fulltext.

A. Thegeya, T. Mitterling, A. Martinez, J. Bulan, R. Durante, and J. Mag-atas. 2022. Application of Machine Learning Algorithms on Satellite Imagery for Road and Quality Monitoring. *ADB Economics Working Paper Series.* No. 675. December. https://www.adb.org/sites/default/files/publication/849926/ewp-675-machine-learning-satellite-image-road-quality.pdf.

United Nations (UN). (no date). *End Poverty in all its forms everywhere.* https://sdgs.un.org/goals/goal1.

UN. 2014. UN Agency Calls for Urgent Action to Protect Global Soil from Depletion, Degradation. *UN News.* 24 July. https://news.un.org/en/story/2014/07/473762.

UN. 2023a. *The Sustainable Development Goals Report: Special Edition.* https://unstats.un.org/sdgs/report/2023/The-Sustainable-Development-Goals-Report-2023.pdf.

UN. 2023b. *World Economic Situation and Prospects.* United Nations Department of Economic and Social Affairs (UN DESA). https://unctad.org/system/files/official-document/wesp2023_en.pdf.

UN DESA. 2018 Review of SDGs Implementation: SDG 11 – Make Cities and Human Settlements Inclusive, Safe, Resilient and Sustainable. *High-Level Political Forum on Sustainable Development.* https://sdgs.un.org/sites/default/files/documents/197282018_background_notes_SDG_11_v3.pdf.

United Nations Development Programme (UNDP). 2022a. *Addressing the cost-of-living crisis in developing countries: Poverty and Vulnerability Projections and Policy Responses.* https://www.undp.org/publications/addressing-cost-living-crisis-developing-countries-poverty-and-vulnerability-projections-and-policy-responses.

UNDP. 2022b. *Global Multidimensional Poverty Index 2022. Unpacking Deprivation Bundles to Reduce Multidimensional Poverty.* https://hdr.undp.org/system/files/documents/hdp-document/2022mpireportenpdf.pdf.

United Nations Economic and Social Commission for Asia and the Pacific (UNESCAP). 2019. *Economic and Social Survey of Asia and the Pacific 2019: Ambitions Beyond Growth.* 4 April. https://www.unescap.org/sites/default/files/publications/Economic_Social_Survey%202019.pdf.

United Nations Economic and Social Commission for Asia and the Pacific (UNESCAP) and United Nations Human Settlements Programme (UN-Habitat). 2019. *The Future of Asian & Pacific Cities: Transformative Pathways towards Sustainable Urban Development.* https://unhabitat.org/sites/default/files/2019/10/future_of_ap_cities_report_2019_compressed.pdf.

United Nations Environment Programme. (UNEP). 2022. Collective Action Needed to Improve Quality of the Air We Share. *UNEP Article.* August. https://www.unep.org/news-and-stories/story/collective-action-needed-improve-quality-air-we-share.

United Nations Human Settlements Programme (UN-Habitat). 2003. *Rental Housing: An Essential Option for the Urban Poor in Developing Countries.* Nairobi. https://www.humanitarianlibrary.org/sites/default/files/2015/06/Rental%20housing%20an%20essential%20option%20for%20urban%20poor%20in%20developing%20countries%20%28compressed%29.pdf.

T. Wheeler and J. von Braun. 2013. Climate Change Impacts on Global Food Security. *Science AAAS.* 508. https://denning.atmos.colostate.edu/readings/Impacts/FoodSecurity.Science-2013-Wheeler-508-13.pdf.

World Bank. (WBG). (no date). *Agriculture and Food: Overview.* https://www.worldbank.org/en/topic/agriculture/overview.

WBG. (no date). *Poverty and Inequality Platform Methodology Handbook.* https://datanalytics.worldbank.org/PIP-Methodology/.

WBG. 2008. *World Development Report. Agriculture for Development.* https://documents1.worldbank.org/curated/en/587251468175472382/pdf/41455optmzd0PA18082136807701PUBLIC1.pdf.

WBG. 2017. East Asia and Pacific Cities: Expanding Opportunities for the Urban Poor. *World Bank Urban Development Series.* https://openknowledge.worldbank.org/server/api/core/bitstreams/5ec7c925-2200-57d9-9b1b-6f5cb06f3e60/content.

WBG 2022a. *Poverty and Shared Prosperity 2022. Correcting Course.* https://www.worldbank.org/en/publication/poverty-and-shared-prosperity.

WBG. 2022b. Solid Waste Management. *World Bank Brief.* February. https://www.worldbank.org/en/topic/urbandevelopment/brief/solid-waste-management#:~:text=These%20practices%20create%20serious%20health,can%20even%20promote%20urban%20violence.

World Population Review. (no date). World City Populations 2023. https://worldpopulationreview.com/world-cities.

E. Yamada, E. Sioson, E. Murakami, A. Murata. 2019. "No Woman Left Excluded from Financial Services" in Leave No One Behind: Time for Specifics on the Sustainable Development Goals. *Brookings Institution Press.* pp. 149-168. https://www.brookings.edu/wp-content/uploads/2019/09/LNOB_Chapter8.pdf.

M. Yechezkel, A. Weiss, I. Rejwan, E. Shahmoon, S. Ben-Gal and Dan Yamin. 2021. Human Mobility and Poverty as Key Drivers of COVID-19 Transmission and Control. *BMC Public Health.* Article No. 596. https://bmcpublichealth.biomedcentral.com/articles/10.1186/s12889-021-10561-x#citeas.

Goal 1. End poverty in all its forms everywhere

Table 1.1.1: Selected Indicators for Sustainable Development Goal 1—No Poverty

ADB Regional Member	Target 1.1: By 2030, eradicate extreme poverty for all people everywhere, measured as people living below the international poverty line of $2.15 a day (2017 PPP)						
	1.1.1.a: Proportion of Population Living below the $2.15 a Day (2017 PPP) Poverty Line[a,b] (%)		1.1.1.b: Proportion of Employed Population Living below the International Poverty Line, by Age Group and Sex[c,d] (%) 2019 Age Group				
			15+			15–24	25+
	2010	2020	Total (2022)	Female	Male		
Developing ADB Member Economies							
Central and West Asia							
Afghanistan	...	...	...	...	...	...	...
Armenia	1.0	0.5 (2021)	0.4	0.4	0.2	0.2	0.3
Azerbaijan[e]	0.0 (2005)	...	0.1	0.1	0.1	0.1	0.1
Georgia	14.4	5.5 (2021)	2.4	2.8	3.3	3.6	3.0
Kazakhstan	0.2	0.0 (2018)	0.1	0.0	0.0	0.0	0.0
Kyrgyz Republic	3.5	1.3	0.3	0.1	0.2	0.2	0.2
Pakistan	9.4	4.9 (2018)	2.4	3.7	3.0	3.0	3.2
Tajikistan	6.8 (2009)	6.1 (2015)	1.6	2.5	2.0	2.0	2.2
Turkmenistan	...	...	0.6	0.6	0.4	0.8	0.5
Uzbekistan[e]	81.5 (2003)	...	6.6	6.7	9.0	8.3	8.1
East Asia							
China, People's Republic of	13.9	0.1 (2019)	0.1	0.1	0.1	0.2	0.1
Hong Kong, China[g]	...	...	...	...	...	...	...
Korea, Republic of[g]	0.5	0.2 (2016)	0.0	0.0	0.0	0.0	0.0
Mongolia	1.1	0.7 (2018)	0.1	0.0	0.1	0.1	0.1
Taipei,China	0.2	0.0 (2016)	...	...	...	...	...
South Asia							
Bangladesh	18.2	13.5 (2016)	2.7	5.4	6.9	6.3	6.5
Bhutan	1.7 (2012)	0.9 (2017)	1.1	0.8	0.7	1.1	0.7
India	22.5 (2011)	10.0 (2019)	5.7	9.8	8.7	11.2	8.7
Maldives	3.8 (2009)	0.0 (2019)	0.1	0.1	0.1	0.1	0.1
Nepal	8.2	...	5.1	5.1	4.8	4.9	4.9
Sri Lanka	3.5 (2009)	1.0 (2019)	0.4	0.3	0.4	0.4	0.4
Southeast Asia							
Brunei Darussalam	...	...	...	...	...	...	...
Cambodia[j]	...	...	14.2	13.1	16.9	17.7	14.5
Indonesia	18.3	2.5 (2022)	2.3	3.3	3.1	3.4	3.2
Lao People's Democratic Republic	10.9 (2012)	7.1 (2018)	10.0	10.8	8.7	15.0	8.1
Malaysia	0.1 (2011)	0.0 (2018)	0.1	0.0	0.0	0.0	0.0
Myanmar	...	2.0 (2017)	...	0.9	1.0	1.4	0.8
Philippines	11.3 (2009)	3.0 (2021)	2.2	2.0	2.8	3.0	2.4
Singapore	...	...	...	...	...	...	...
Thailand	0.3	0.0 (2021)	0.1	0.0	0.1	0.2	0.0
Timor-Leste	40.9 (2007)	24.4 (2014)	14.2	15.5	19.2	20.8	16.8
Viet Nam	2.9	0.7	1.2	1.7	1.5	2.9	1.4
The Pacific							
Cook Islands	...	...	...	...	...	...	...
Fiji	1.0 (2008)	1.3 (2019)	2.3	0.4	0.5	0.6	0.4
Kiribati	14.0 (2006)	1.7 (2019)	...	...	...	...	...
Marshall Islands	...	0.9 (2019)	...	...	...	...	...
Micronesia, Federated States of	16.0 (2013)	...	...	...	...	...	...
Nauru	1.7 (2012)	...	...	...	...	...	...
Niue	...	...	...	...	...	...	...
Palau	...	...	...	...	...	...	...
Papua New Guinea	39.7 (2009)	...	24.4	30.0	18.2	33.7	21.2
Samoa[e]	1.1 (2008)	...	...	...	...	...	...
Solomon Islands	26.6 (2012)	...	23.1	17.8	22.7	26.5	18.1
Tonga	1.3 (2009)	1.8 (2015)	...	...	...	...	...
Tuvalu	3.6	...	...	...	...	...	...
Vanuatu	14.7	10.0 (2019)	...	...	...	...	...
Developed ADB Member Economies							
Australia	...	...	...	...	...	...	...
Japan	...	...	...	...	...	...	...
New Zealand	...	...	...	...	...	...	...

Table 1.1.1: Selected Indicators for Sustainable Development Goal 1—No Poverty *(continued)*

ADB Regional Member	Target 1.2: By 2030, reduce at least by half the proportion of men, women, and children of all ages living in poverty in all its dimensions according to national definitions — 1.2.1: Proportion of Population Living below the National Poverty Line, by Urban–Rural Location[a] (%)					
	2010			2020		
	Total	Urban	Rural	Total	Urban	Rural
Developing ADB Member Economies						
Central and West Asia						
Afghanistan	38.3 (2011)	...	...	49.4	41.6 (2016)	58.6 (2016)
Armenia	35.8	35.7	36.0	26.5 (2021)	21.8 (2021)	33.0 (2021)
Azerbaijan[e]	9.1	...	...	5.9 (2021)	...	...
Georgia	37.3[f]	32.7[f]	43.3[f]	15.6 (2022)	12.3 (2022)	20.6 (2022)
Kazakhstan	6.5	3.7	10.1	5.2 (2022)	4.0 (2022)	7.3 (2022)
Kyrgyz Republic	33.7	23.6	39.5	33.3 (2021)	29.3 (2015)	33.6 (2015)
Pakistan	36.8	18.2 (2013)	35.6 (2013)	21.9 (2018)	12.5 (2015)	30.7 (2015)
Tajikistan	34.3 (2013)	...	...	26.3 (2019)	...	...
Turkmenistan	...	...	...	...	...	...
Uzbekistan[e]	17.7	...	...	14.1 (2022)	...	...
East Asia						
China, People's Republic of	...	...	17.2	...	...	–
Hong Kong, China[g]	15.7	...	...	17.3	...	...
Korea, Republic of[g]	18.6 (2011)	...	...	15.1 (2021)	...	...
Mongolia	38.8	33.2	49.0	27.8	27.2 (2018)	30.8 (2018)
Taipei,China	1.2[h]	...	...	1.3 (2021)	...	...
South Asia						
Bangladesh	31.5	21.3	35.2	20.5 (2019)	...	...
Bhutan	12.0 (2012)	1.8 (2012)	16.7 (2012)	12.4 (2022)	4.2 (2022)	17.5 (2022)
India	21.9[i] (2011)	13.7[i] (2011)	25.7[i] (2011)	...	...	...
Maldives	...	...	...	5.4 (2019)	...	...
Nepal	25.2	15.5	27.4	...	...	...
Sri Lanka	6.7 (2012)	2.1 (2012)	7.6 (2012)	14.3 (2019)	1.9 (2016)	4.3 (2016)
Southeast Asia						
Brunei Darussalam	...	...	...	...	...	...
Cambodia[j]	21.1	17.0	22.7	17.8 (2019)	12.6 (2019)	22.8 (2019)
Indonesia	13.3	9.9	16.6	9.5[k] (2022)	7.5[k] (2022)	12.3[k] (2022)
Lao People's Democratic Republic	24.6 (2013)	7.9 (2013)	31.4 (2013)	18.3 (2019)	7.0 (2019)	23.8 (2019)
Malaysia	1.7 (2011)	1.0 (2012)	...	8.4	0.2 (2016)	1.0 (2016)
Myanmar	42.4	...	...	24.8 (2017)	11.3 (2017)	30.2 (2017)
Philippines	25.2 (2012)	13.0 (2012)	...	18.1[k] (2021)	11.6 (2021)	25.7 (2021)
Singapore	...	...	...	...	...	...
Thailand	16.4	...	...	6.3 (2021)	...	...
Timor-Leste	41.8 (2014)	28.3 (2014)	47.1 (2014)	...	...	...
Viet Nam	14.2	6.9	17.4	4.2 (2022)	1.5 (2022)	5.9 (2022)
The Pacific						
Cook Islands	...	...	...	...	...	...
Fiji	28.1[l] (2013)	19.8[l] (2013)	36.7[l] (2013)	24.1 (2019)	14.0 (2019)	36.5 (2019)
Kiribati	...	...	...	21.9 (2019)	...	...
Marshall Islands	...	...	...	7.2 (2019)	2.5 (2019)	21.2 (2019)
Micronesia, Federated States of	41.2[l] (2013)	...	...	...	...	...
Nauru	24.0[l] (2013)	...	...	...	...	...
Niue	...	...	...	...	...	...
Palau	...	...	...	...	...	...
Papua New Guinea	...	...	...	37.5 (2017)	...	...
Samoa[e]	18.8[l] (2013)	...	...	22.7 (2018)	...	...
Solomon Islands	12.7[m] (2013)	9.1[m] (2013)	13.6[m] (2013)	...	...	...
Tonga	...	...	...	27.0 (2015)	...	...
Tuvalu	19.7[l]	19.8[l]	19.7[l]	...	...	...
Vanuatu	12.7[l]	...	10.0[l]	...	...	...
Developed ADB Member Economies						
Australia	...	...	...	...	...	...
Japan	...	...	...	...	...	...
New Zealand	...	...	...	...	...	...

... = data not available, – = magnitude equals zero, 0.0 = magnitude is less than half of unit employed, $ = United States dollars, ADB = Asian Development Bank, PPP = purchasing power parity.

a For Indicator 1.1.1.a and Indicator 1.2.1, the year indicated in the table refers to the year when the household survey data were collected. For economies in which the household survey data collection period bridged 2 calendar years, the table reports the first year.
b For Indicator 1.1.1.a, data are consumption-based, except for Malaysia; the Philippines, the Republic of Korea; and Taipei,China, whose estimates are income-based. The World Bank has updated the international poverty lines using 2017 purchasing power parity (PPP), however, 2011-based PPP poverty estimates are still released for SDG monitoring.
c For Indicator 1.1.1.b, the estimates are based on the international poverty line of $1.90 a day (2011 PPP).
d Data are taken from estimates and projections modeled by the International Labour Organization (ILO). These modeled estimates present an internationally comparable series, which consists of economy-sourced estimates and imputations for missing data. Global and regional estimates are updated by the ILO annually.
e For Indicator 1.1.1.a, the latest available estimate for Azerbaijan is for 2005: 0.0%; for Samoa, the latest available estimate is for 2013: 1.2%; for Uzbekistan, the latest available estimate is for 2003: 81.5%.
f Refers to absolute poverty or the share of the population under the absolute poverty line.
g For Indicator 1.2.1 for Hong Kong, China, data refer to the poverty rate after policy intervention (recurrent cash); for the Republic of Korea, data refer to the relative poverty rate.
h Refers to the percentage of the low-income population to the total population.
i Based on the Tendulkar methodology, using mixed reference period.
j The urban and rural poverty estimates refer to other areas excluding Phnom Penh.
k Reference period is first semester poverty estimates.
l Data refer to the percentage of the population living below the basic-needs poverty line.
m Refers to the poverty headcount ratio using the upper poverty line, which serves as spatial deflator with respect to Honiara (the Solomon Islands capital).

Sources: For Indicator 1.1.1.a: World Bank. Poverty and Inequality Platform. https://pip.worldbank.org/ (accessed 17 April 2023). For Indicator 1.1.1.b: International Labour Organisation. ILOSTAT. http://www.ilo.org/ilostat (accessed 27 July 2023). For Indicator 1.2.1: Economies' official sources; United Nations Statistics Division. Sustainable Development Goals (SDGs), SDG Indicators, Global Database. http://unstats.un.org/sdgs/indicators/database/ (accessed 11 July 2023); and Secretariat of the Pacific Community. National Minimum Development Indicators. https://www.spc.int/nmdi/ (accessed 11 July 2023).

Goal 1. End poverty in all its forms everywhere

Table 1.1.2: Selected Indicators for Sustainable Development Goal 1— Social Protection and Official Development Assistance

ADB Regional Member	Target 1.3: Implement nationally appropriate social protection systems and measures for all, including floors, and by 2030 achieve substantial coverage of the poor and the vulnerable						
	1.3.1.a: Proportion of Population Covered by at least One Social Protection Benefit (%)		1.3.1.b: Proportion of Population above Statutory Pensionable Age Receiving a Pension (%)			1.3.1.c: Proportion of Poor Population Receiving Social Assistance Cash Benefit (%)	
	2016	2020	2000	2016	2020	2016	2021
Developing ADB Member Economies							
Central and West Asia							
Afghanistan	...	7.5	5.0	...	24.7	...	...
Armenia	47.3	54.4	87.0	68.5	65.2	38.2	100.0 (2018)
Azerbaijan	40.3	39.0	97.0	81.1	72.8	100.0	100.0 (2018)
Georgia	28.6	97.1	80.0	91.9	90.9	100.0	100.0 (2018)
Kazakhstan	100.0	100.0	100.0	82.6	99.6	28.9	...
Kyrgyz Republic	...	41.7	86.0	100.0	100.0	...	89.4 (2018)
Pakistan	...	20.1 (2022)	2.0 (2005)	...	17.4 (2022)	...	69.2 (2018)
Tajikistan	...	26.6	88.0 (2005)	92.8	93.7	...	28.1 (2018)
Turkmenistan	...	44.2 (2021)	...	...	77.2 (2021)	...	...
Uzbekistan	...	42.7	100.0	100.0 (2017)	100.0	68.0 (2017)	82.5 (2018)
East Asia							
China, People's Republic of	63.0	70.8	24.0	100.0	100.0	51.6	100.0
Hong Kong, China	...	59.7	76.0	72.9	73.2	...	...
Korea, Republic of	65.7	77.3	...	100.0 (2018)	100.0	21.4	...
Mongolia	72.4	100.0	80.0	100.0	100.0	94.9	100.0 (2018)
Taipei,China	...	...	...	...	...	...	...
South Asia							
Bangladesh	28.4	22.5 (2021)	6.0 (2002)	33.4	56.9 (2021)	11.0	60.8 (2021)
Bhutan	...	8.8	...	...	18.8 (2019)	...	60.2 (2018)
India	22.0	24.4	7.0	25.2	42.5	...	...
Maldives	...	21.2	...	...	100.0	...	100.0 (2018)
Nepal	...	16.9	33.0	...	80.2	...	70.1 (2018)
Sri Lanka	30.4	36.4	19.0	25.2	35.7	51.5	100.0 (2018)
Southeast Asia							
Brunei Darussalam	...	34.1	...	...	100.0	...	...
Cambodia	...	6.2	1.0	3.2	6.6 (2018)	...	48.4 (2018)
Indonesia	...	27.8	6.0 (2002)	14.0	14.8	...	100.0 (2018)
Lao People's Democratic Republic	...	12.1	3.0	...	6.3	...	0.1 (2018)
Malaysia	...	27.3	15.0	19.8 (2018)	18.6	...	100.0 (2018)
Myanmar	...	6.3	...	0.9	14.9	...	0.8 (2018)
Philippines	47.1	36.7	20.0	39.8	20.5	...	100.0 (2018)
Singapore	...	100.0	...	48.9 (2018)	33.1	...	...
Thailand	...	68.0	5.0	83.0	89.1	...	100.0 (2019)
Timor-Leste	...	30.6	...	89.7	100.0	...	94.9 (2018)
Viet Nam	37.9	38.8	16.0	39.9	40.9	...	100.0 (2018)
The Pacific							
Cook Islands	...	86.3 (2019)	...	100.0 (2018)	100.0	...	...
Fiji	...	58.9	9.0	10.6 (2015)	92.1	...	68.0 (2018)
Kiribati	...	21.0	...	...	93.8	...	15.9 (2018)
Marshall Islands	...	25.2	62.0	...	62.7	...	...
Micronesia, Federated States of	...	19.4	...	...	100.0	...	...
Nauru	...	45.4 (2019)	64.0	...	95.7	...	...
Niue	...	...	...	...	...	...	...
Palau	...	35.8 (2019)	48.0 (2010)	...	100.0	...	56.0 (2018)
Papua New Guinea	...	9.6	1.0	...	22.3	...	...
Samoa	...	21.1	...	...	91.4	...	69.2 (2018)
Solomon Islands	...	1.1 (2019)	10.0	...	20.5 (2019)	...	2.9 (2018)
Tonga	...	22.2	...	73.3 (2018)	90.0	...	16.7 (2018)
Tuvalu	...	...	15.0	...	...	...	...
Vanuatu	...	57.4	2.0	...	8.5 (2019)	...	100.0 (2018)
Developed ADB Member Economies							
Australia	82.0	100.0	80.0	74.3	100.0	100.0	...
Japan	75.4	98.0	74.0	100.0 (2018)	100.0	...	...
New Zealand	66.6	100.0	100.0	100.0	100.0	37.4	...

Table 1.1.2: Selected Indicators for Sustainable Development Goal 1— Social Protection and Official Development Assistance *(continued)*

ADB Regional Member	Target 1.3: Implement nationally appropriate social protection systems and measures for all, including floors, and by 2030 achieve substantial coverage of the poor and the vulnerable				Target 1.a: Ensure significant mobilization of resources from a variety of sources, including through enhanced development cooperation, in order to provide adequate and predictable means for developing countries, in particular least developed countries, to implement programmes and policies to end poverty in all its dimensions	
	1.3.1.d: Proportion of Vulnerable Population Receiving Social Assistance Cash Benefit (%)		1.3.1.e: Proportion of Children/ Households Receiving Child/ Family Cash Benefit (%)		1.a.1: Official Development Assistance Grants for Poverty Reduction, by Recipient Countries (percentage of GNI)	
	2016	2020	2016	2020	2015	2021
Developing ADB Member Economies						
Central and West Asia						
Afghanistan	...	5.9	...	0.4	1.6	2.1 (2020)
Armenia	16.2	19.6	21.4	30.2	0.1	0.1
Azerbaijan	12.6	13.4	...	16.9	0.0	0.0
Georgia	12.0	92.9	...	48.1	0.1	0.2
Kazakhstan	100.0	74.2	100.0	57.4	0.0	0.0
Kyrgyz Republic	...	14.1	17.8	16.9	0.6	0.8
Pakistan	...	17.6 (2022)	...	5.7 (2021)	0.1	0.2
Tajikistan	...	7.5	6.4	14.0	0.6	1.3
Turkmenistan	...	10.9 (2021)	...	15.3 (2021)	0.0	0.0 (2019)
Uzbekistan	16.0 (2017)	15.6	22.0 (2017)	29.2	0.0	0.1
East Asia						
China, People's Republic of	31.0 (2017)	33.2	2.2	3.0	0.0	0.0
Hong Kong, China	...	28.3	...	...	...	...
Korea, Republic of	26.3 (2018)	48.9	...	40.0	...	...
Mongolia	35.1	88.5	100.0	85.0	0.2	0.5
Taipei,China	...	...	...	...	...	...
South Asia						
Bangladesh	4.3	20.9 (2021)	29.4	45.9 (2021)	0.2	0.1
Bhutan	...	5.0	...	13.5	0.3	0.5 (2020)
India	10.4	16.4	...	24.1	0.0	0.0
Maldives	...	8.1	...	8.2	0.1	0.6
Nepal	...	17.1	...	22.9	0.7	0.7
Sri Lanka	4.4	16.0	...	32.0	0.0	0.1
Southeast Asia						
Brunei Darussalam	...	14.7	...	...	...	...
Cambodia	...	4.3	...	4.5	0.6	0.6
Indonesia	...	16.5	...	25.6	0.0	0.0
Lao People's Democratic Republic	– (2018)	7.7	...	...	0.6	0.8
Malaysia	...	2.1	...	2.8	0.0	0.0
Myanmar	...	1.1	...	2.1	0.3	0.3
Philippines	7.8	22.4	13.6	31.1	0.1	0.1
Singapore	...	100.0	...	...	...	...
Thailand	...	54.3	18.9	21.0	0.0	0.0
Timor-Leste	...	26.5	30.7	38.2	1.0	3.0
Viet Nam	10.0	24.6	...	1.0 (2019)	0.0	0.1
The Pacific						
Cook Islands	...	85.8	100.0 (2018)	100.0	...	...
Fiji	...	28.2	...	2.6	0.4	0.9
Kiribati	...	5.1	1.3 (2018)	1.3	4.1	4.7 (2020)
Marshall Islands	...	1.7	...	...	0.6	0.6
Micronesia, Federated States of	...	2.2	...	6.8	0.7	0.6
Nauru	...	45.4	...	...	8.0	0.6
Niue	...	...	...	...	...	...
Palau	...	17.8	...	60.0 (2019)	0.4	2.7 (2020)
Papua New Guinea	...	...	...	...	0.3	0.9
Samoa	...	5.3	...	– (2018)	2.9	1.4
Solomon Islands	...	0.4 (2019)	...	...	2.6	1.9
Tonga	...	6.2	...	3.3	1.4	1.7 (2020)
Tuvalu	...	...	...	...	5.5	8.1
Vanuatu	...	53.3	...	12.9 (2019)	2.4	2.2
Developed ADB Member Economies						
Australia	53.0	100.0	100.0	100.0	...	...
Japan	...	100.0	...	85.4	...	...
New Zealand	9.7	100.0	...	67.1	...	...

... = data not available, – = magnitude equals zero, 0.0 = magnitude is less than half of unit employed, ADB = Asian Development Bank, GNI = gross national income.

Note: The population covered by at least one social protection benefit (effective coverage) refers to the proportion of the total population receiving at least one contributory or noncontributory cash benefit, or actively contributing to at least one social security scheme. For children, older persons, and the poor and vulnerable, effective coverage is expressed as a share of the respective population..

Source: United Nations. SDG Global Database. https://unstats.un.org/sdgs/dataportal (accessed 11 July 2023).

Goal 2. End hunger, achieve food security and improved nutrition, and promote sustainable agriculture

Table 1.2.1: Selected Indicators for Sustainable Development Goal 2—Zero Hunger

ADB Regional Member	Target 2.1: By 2030, end hunger and ensure access by all people, in particular the poor and people in vulnerable situations, including infants, to safe, nutritious, and sufficient food all year round		Target 2.2: By 2030, end all forms of malnutrition, including achieving, by 2025, the internationally agreed targets on stunting and wasting in children under 5 years of age, and address the nutritional needs of adolescent girls, pregnant and lactating women, and older persons					
	2.1.1: Prevalence of Undernourishment (%)		2.2.1: Prevalence of Stunting among Children under 5 Years of Age[a] (%)		2.2.2.c: Prevalence of Malnutrition (Overweight) among Children under 5 Years of Age[a] (%)		2.2.2.d: Prevalence of Malnutrition (Wasting) among Children under 5 Years of Age (%)	
	2010[b]	2021[c]	2010	2021[d]	2010	2021[d]	2010	2020
Developing ADB Member Economies								
Central and West Asia[e]	**...**	**...**	**39.8**	**29.1**	**5.9**	**3.6**	**...**	**...**
Afghanistan	20.5	30.1	47.4	34.0	5.2	3.8	9.1 (2004)	5.1 (2018)
Armenia	2.8	<2.5	16.4	7.5	15.6	11.3	4.1	4.4 (2016)
Azerbaijan	<2.5	<2.5	19.3	13.5	12.1	10.1	6.6 (2011)	3.2 (2013)
Georgia	4.2	2.9	10.4	5.0	16.6	5.3	1.3 (2009)	0.6 (2018)
Kazakhstan	3.1	<2.5	12.7	5.4	12.7	7.9	4.1	3.1 (2015)
Kyrgyz Republic	7.4	4.8	17.8	10.7	8.5	6.2	1.4 (2009)	2.0 (2018)
Pakistan	15.1	18.5	45.1	34.9	4.9	2.9	14.9 (2011)	7.1 (2018)
Tajikistan	26.8	9.3	29.0	13.8	6.4	3.0	4.2 (2009)	5.6 (2017)
Turkmenistan	5.9	5.7	14.4	7.0	6.1	3.5	7.2 (2006)	4.1 (2019)
Uzbekistan	5.8	<2.5	15.4	7.3	9.1	4.2	4.4 (2006)	2.4 (2021)
East Asia[e]	**...**	**...**	**8.7**	**4.8**	**6.7**	**8.5**	**...**	**...**
China, People's Republic of	<2.5	<2.5	8.9	4.9	6.7	8.6	2.3	1.9 (2017)
Hong Kong, China	<2.5	<2.5	...	...	...	...	...	...
Korea, Republic of	<2.5	<2.5	2.0	1.7	7.0	5.5	0.5 (2011)	0.2
Mongolia	16.0	8.0	15.3	6.5	9.4	10.5	1.6	0.9 (2018)
Taipei,China	4.7	3.0	...	...	...	...	...	...
South Asia[e]	**...**	**...**	**43.5**	**31.7**	**2.1**	**2.6**	**...**	**...**
Bangladesh	15.2	11.2	42.2	27.5	1.6	2.2	15.7 (2011)	9.8 (2019)
Bhutan	...	...	32.8	23.2	6.5	6.7	5.9	...
India	15.7	16.6	44.0	32.5	2.2	2.7	20.0 (2006)	18.7
Maldives	...	...	18.1	14.1	6.3	3.5	10.6 (2009)	9.1 (2017)
Nepal	10.1	5.4	43.4	27.8	1.1	1.7	11.2 (2011)	7.7 (2022)
Sri Lanka	13.0	5.3	17.2	16.1	1.2	1.3	11.8 (2009)	15.1 (2016)
Southeast Asia[e]	**...**	**...**	**31.6**	**26.7**	**5.6**	**7.7**	**...**	**...**
Brunei Darussalam	...	...	18.4	11.3	8.4	9.1	2.9 (2009)	...
Cambodia	11.1	4.8	37.4	23.0	2.1	3.4	11.0	9.6 (2021)
Indonesia	13.2	5.9	35.9	31.4	7.9	11.2	12.3	10.2 (2018)
Lao People's Democratic Republic	14.5	4.7	43.4	28.7	2.1	3.7	5.9 (2011)	9.0 (2017)
Malaysia	4.7	2.7	17.4	21.7	6.2	5.7	13.2 (2006)	9.7 (2019)
Myanmar	10.2	3.8	33.0	24.8	2.2	0.8	7.9 (2009)	7.4 (2018)
Philippines	12.3	5.2	32.6	29.0	3.2	4.6	7.0 (2011)	5.8 (2019)
Singapore	...	...	3.6	3.0	2.9	3.7	3.6 (2000)	...
Thailand	9.6	5.2	15.2	11.9	8.7	8.7	6.7 (2012)	7.7 (2019)
Timor-Leste	32.9	22.3	54.8	45.6	2.8	1.3	18.9 (2009)	8.3
Viet Nam	9.9	5.0	27.4	19.8	3.8	7.7	4.1	4.7
The Pacific[e]	**...**	**...**	**41.3**	**44.7**	**8.4**	**13.9**	**...**	**...**
Cook Islands	...	...	...	...	...	...	...	...
Fiji	6.9	6.6	9.0	7.1	5.8	7.5	6.4 (2004)	4.6 (2021)
Kiribati	12.6	12.1	17.1	14.5	2.1	1.9	...	3.5 (2018)
Marshall Islands	...	...	38.7	31.2	4.0	4.3	...	3.5 (2017)
Micronesia, Federated States of	...	...	...	...	...	...	...	...
Nauru	...	...	22.7	15.3	3.9	4.5	1.0 (2007)	...
Niue	...	...	...	...	...	...	...	...
Palau	...	...	...	...	...	...	...	...
Papua New Guinea	26.1	23.4	47.3	51.0	9.2	15.8	14.1	...
Samoa	5.4	4.6	4.8	7.2	5.7	7.7	...	3.1 (2019)
Solomon Islands	15.6	19.0	32.5	29.9	3.2	5.3	4.3 (2007)	8.5 (2015)
Tonga	...	...	8.9	2.0	15.9	11.3	5.2 (2012)	1.1 (2019)
Tuvalu	...	...	8.7	5.4	5.4	4.3	3.3 (2007)	2.8 (2019)
Vanuatu	9.3	9.5	26.5	31.2	4.8	5.1	5.9 (2008)	4.7 (2013)
Developed ADB Member Economies[e]	**...**	**...**	**6.2**	**4.6**	**3.9**	**7.0**	**...**	**...**
Australia	<2.5	<2.5	3.1	3.3	12.1	21.1	0.2 (2007)	...
Japan	2.8	3.2	7.0	5.1	1.7	2.0	2.3	...
New Zealand	<2.5	<2.5	...	...	...	...	...	...
DEVELOPING ADB MEMBER ECONOMIES[e]	**...**	**...**	**31.9**	**23.8**	**4.4**	**5.2**	**...**	**...**
ALL ADB REGIONAL MEMBERS[e]	**...**	**...**	**31.4**	**23.4**	**4.4**	**5.2**	**...**	**...**
WORLD	**8.6**	**9.2 (2022)**	**27.9**	**22.5**	**5.5**	**5.6**	**...**	**6.8 (2022)**

... = data not available, < = less than, ADB = Asian Development Bank.

a Refers to modeled estimates from the Joint Child Malnutrition Estimates Database.
b Economy level data refer to the 3-year average for 2009–2011. World estimate refers to annual value.
c Economy level data refer to the 3-year average for 2020–2022. World estimate refers to annual value.
d The 2021 data was presented due to the unavailability of the 2022 weights used for calculating regional aggregates. Users can access and retrieve the 2022 economy-level data from the Key Indicators Database.
e For indicators 2.2.1 and 2.2.2.c, estimated as weighted averages using total population of children aged 0–5 years from the United Nations' World Population Prospects 2022 as weightings.

Source: For Indicator 2.1.1: Food and Agriculture Organization of the United Nations. FAOSTAT Database. http://www.fao.org/faostat/en/#data/FS (accessed 25 July 2023). For Indicator 2.2.1, Indicator 2.2.2.c, and Indicator 2.2.2.d: United Nations. SDG Global Database. https://unstats.un.org/sdgs/dataportal (accessed 18 July 2023); and United Nations Children's Fund (UNICEF). Malnutrition Data. https://data.unicef.org/resources/dataset/malnutrition-data/ (accessed 18 July 2023). For total population of children 0–5 years old used as weightings: United Nations. World Population Prospects 2022. https://population.un.org/wpp/Download/Standard/Interpolated/ (accessed 18 July 2023).

Table 1.2.2: Selected Indicators for Sustainable Development Goal 2—Improved Agricultural Investment

ADB Regional Member	Target 2.a: Increase investment, including through enhanced international cooperation, in rural infrastructure, agricultural research and extension services, technology development, and plant and livestock gene banks in order to enhance agricultural productive capacity in developing countries (or economies), in particular least developed countries (or economies)					
	2.a.1: The Agriculture Orientation Index for Government Expenditures			2.a.2: Total Official Flows to the Agriculture Sector[a] (constant 2021 $ million)		
	2010	2015	2021	2010	2015	2021
Developing ADB Member Economies						
Central and West Asia	...	...	...	**1,250.6**	**1,067.8**	**827.4**
Afghanistan	0.2	0.2	0.2	768.9	372.5	120.6
Armenia	0.3	0.1	0.2	93.4	41.7	32.4
Azerbaijan	0.5	0.5	0.5	18.3	58.4	25.0
Georgia	0.1	0.4	0.5	18.2	47.1	61.4
Kazakhstan	0.9	0.9	0.8	60.2	73.9	15.6
Kyrgyz Republic	0.1	0.1	0.1	24.8	27.4	17.8
Pakistan	0.1	0.1	0.1	175.6	331.4	235.0
Tajikistan	0.1	0.0	0.0	55.5	37.2	51.0
Turkmenistan	...	...	...	1.2	0.1	2.5
Uzbekistan	0.2	0.2	0.1	34.4	78.1	266.1
East Asia	...	...	...	**386.8**	**454.3**	**539.8**
China, People's Republic of	0.9	1.1	1.2	341.8	434.8	512.6
Hong Kong, China	2.7	1.8	1.6	...	...	...
Korea, Republic of	2.1	2.1	2.0	...	...	...
Mongolia	0.4	0.1	0.1	45.0	19.4	27.2
Taipei,China	...	...	...	...	...	...
South Asia	...	...	...	**1,147.9**	**1,624.1**	**1,449.0**
Bangladesh	0.5	0.6	0.6	204.0	276.9	350.5
Bhutan	0.7	0.8	0.8	6.7	7.4	9.9
India	0.5	0.5	0.4	788.8	1,186.2	891.2
Maldives	0.2	0.0	0.1	0.0	0.7	15.1
Nepal	0.3	0.3	0.2	110.7	114.7	84.3
Sri Lanka	0.6	0.8	0.5	37.7	38.3	98.0
Southeast Asia	...	...	...	**1,701.1**	**1,035.1**	**1,219.1**
Brunei Darussalam	...	...	...	...	...	...
Cambodia	0.0	0.1	0.1	82.7	126.8	149.5
Indonesia	0.1	0.2	0.3	1,045.3	244.3	492.1
Lao People's Democratic Republic	...	0.1 (2017)	0.1 (2020)	57.5	75.9	89.6
Malaysia	0.3	0.4	0.2	2.5	5.3	1.7
Myanmar	0.2	0.2	0.2	41.6	154.7	87.1
Philippines	0.4	0.4	0.2	139.3	124.1	131.9
Singapore	6.8	7.7	6.9	...	...	...
Thailand	0.4	0.8	0.7	12.3	8.2	15.1
Timor-Leste	0.1	0.1	0.1	28.1	27.5	18.3
Viet Nam	0.3	0.3	0.3	292.1	268.3	233.8
The Pacific[b]	...	...	...	**60.8**	**91.8**	**139.7**
Cook Islands	0.9	0.9	0.8	1.3	0.3	0.8 (2019)
Fiji	0.3	0.6	0.3	3.4	22.9	36.7
Kiribati	0.1	0.1	0.1	3.2	2.8	6.1
Marshall Islands	0.2	0.2	0.1	3.8	1.6	3.3
Micronesia, Federated States of	0.1	0.1	0.2	1.1	2.1	2.8
Nauru	...	0.5	0.6	0.6	0.5	1.0
Niue	...	...	...	0.2	0.2	0.4
Palau	0.1	0.1	0.1	0.6	0.8	3.8
Papua New Guinea	0.1	0.1	0.1	23.2	33.5	47.5
Samoa	0.2	0.4	0.6	1.6	4.3	3.7
Solomon Islands	0.1	0.1	0.1	12.1	14.1	14.0
Tonga	0.4	0.2	0.3	2.4	2.0	4.1
Tuvalu	...	...	...	0.9	2.4	3.8
Vanuatu	0.1	0.2	0.1	6.4	4.3	12.5
Developed ADB Member Economies	...	...	...	...	...	...
Australia	0.5	0.3	0.2	...	...	...
Japan	2.1	2.2	2.1	...	...	...
New Zealand	0.2	0.1	0.2	...	...	...
DEVELOPING ADB MEMBER ECONOMIES	...	...	...	**4,547.2**	**4,273.1**	**4,175.0**

... = data not available, 0.0 = magnitude is less than half of unit employed, $ = United States dollars, ADB = Asian Development Bank.

a Total official flows refer to official development assistance plus other official flows. Data refer to gross disbursements.

b Includes only reporting economies with data corresponding to the year heading.

Source: United Nations. SDG Global Database. https://unstats.un.org/sdgs/dataportal (accessed 13 July 2023).

Goal 3. Ensure healthy lives and promote well-being for all at all ages

Table 1.3.1: Selected Indicators for Sustainable Development Goal 3—Maternal and Child Health

ADB Regional Member	Target 3.1: By 2030, reduce the global maternal mortality ratio to less than 70 per 100,000 live births				Target 3.2: By 2030, end preventable deaths of newborns and children under 5 years of age, with all countries (or economies) aiming to reduce neonatal mortality to at least as low as 12 per 1,000 live births and under-5 mortality to at least as low as 25 per 1,000 live births			
	3.1.1: Maternal Mortality Ratio[a,b] (per 100,000 live births)		3.1.2: Proportion of Births Attended by Skilled Health Personnel[c] (%)		3.2.1: Under-5 Mortality Rate[a,b] (per 1,000 live births)		3.2.2: Neonatal Mortality Rate[a,b] (per 1,000 live births)	
	2010	2020	2010	2021	2010	2021	2010	2021
Developing ADB Member Economies								
Central and West Asia	**275**	**194**	**...**	**...**	**76**	**53**	**43**	**33**
Afghanistan	899	620	34.3	61.8 (2020)	88	56	47	34
Armenia	33	27	99.5	99.8 (2016)	19	11	10	6
Azerbaijan	33	41	99.4	99.9	37	19	20	10
Georgia	41	28	99.6	99.8	14	10	10	5
Kazakhstan	20	13	99.4	99.9 (2018)	20	10	12	5
Kyrgyz Republic	72	50	98.3	100.0 (2020)	30	17	17	12
Pakistan	230	154	43.0 (2011)	68.0 (2020)	87	63	50	39
Tajikistan	32	17	87.7	94.8 (2017)	43	31	20	14
Turkmenistan	9	5	99.5 (2006)	100.0 (2019)	43	41	23	24
Uzbekistan	38	30	100.0	99.0 (2022)	28	14	15	8
East Asia	**32**	**23**	**...**	**...**	**16**	**7**	**8**	**3**
China, People's Republic of	33	23	99.6	99.9 (2016)	16	7	8	3
Hong Kong, China	1	8* (2021)	...	...	...	...	1	1*
Korea, Republic of	8	8	99.9 (2009)	...	4	3	2	1
Mongolia	65	39	98.8	99.3 (2018)	26	15	12	8
Taipei,China	4	14 (2021)	...	...	...	...	3	2 (2020)
South Asia	**193**	**106**	**...**	**...**	**56**	**30**	**31**	**19**
Bangladesh	301	123	26.5	59.0 (2019)	49	27	29	16
Bhutan	117	60	64.5	98.9	42	27	23	15
India	179	103	52.3 (2008)	89.4	58	31	32	19
Maldives	60	57	98.2	99.5 (2017)	14	6	8	4
Nepal	349	174	36.0 (2011)	77.2 (2019)	46	27	26	16
Sri Lanka	37	29	98.6 (2007)	99.5 (2016)	11	7	6	4
Southeast Asia	**169**	**131**	**...**	**...**	**33**	**23**	**16**	**12**
Brunei Darussalam	42	44	99.8	99.6	10	12	5	6
Cambodia	276	218	71.0 (2011)	98.7 (2022)	44	25	21	13
Indonesia	219	173	83.1 (2012)	94.7 (2019)	34	22	17	11
Lao People's Democratic Republic	284	126	40.1 (2012)	64.4 (2017)	68	43	29	21
Malaysia	25	21	98.6	99.6 (2019)	8	8	4	4
Myanmar	293	179	70.6	60.2 (2016)	63	42	28	22
Philippines	105	78	72.2 (2011)	84.4 (2017)	32	26	15	12
Singapore	8	7	99.7	99.6	3	2	1	1
Thailand	35	29	99.4 (2009)	99.1 (2019)	14	8	8	5
Timor-Leste	376	204	29.3	56.7 (2016)	71	51	28	22
Viet Nam	88	124	91.9 (2011)	96.1	23	21	12	11
The Pacific	**246**	**170**	**...**	**...**	**51**	**39**	**23**	**19**
Cook Islands	...	...	100.0 (2009)	...	11	7	6	4
Fiji	42	38	99.7	99.8	24	28	9	14
Kiribati	131	76	98.3	91.9 (2019)	65	48	25	21
Marshall Islands	...	...	90.0	92.4 (2017)	39	30	18	14
Micronesia, Federated States of	46	74	100.0 (2009)	...	35	25	18	13
Nauru	...	...	97.4 (2007)	...	38	28	24	18
Niue	...	...	100.0	...	34	24	18	13
Palau	...	...	99.6	97.2 (2020)	23	16	12	9
Papua New Guinea	289	192	53.0 (2006)	56.4 (2018)	58	43	26	21
Samoa	62	59	80.8 (2009)	88.9 (2020)	19	17	8	7
Solomon Islands	147	122	85.5 (2007)	...	26	19	11	8
Tonga	93	126	99.0	98.3 (2019)	13	11	6	5
Tuvalu	...	...	93.1 (2007)	99.5 (2020)	31	21	16	10
Vanuatu	93	94	89.4 (2013)	...	29	23	12	10
Developed ADB Member Economies	**6**	**4**	**...**	**...**	**4**	**3**	**2**	**1**
Australia	5	3	99.1	96.0 (2020)	5	4	3	2
Japan	6	4	99.8	99.8	3	2	1	1
New Zealand	10	7	96.8	96.5 (2019)	6	5	3	3
DEVELOPING ADB MEMBER ECONOMIES	**158**	**107**	**...**	**...**	**44**	**27**	**24**	**17**
ALL ADB REGIONAL MEMBERS	**154**	**105**	**...**	**...**	**43**	**27**	**24**	**16**
WORLD	**254**	**223**	**74.9 (2011)**	**86.2 (2022)**	**51**	**38**	**22**	**18**

... = data not available; * = provisional, preliminary; ADB = Asian Development Bank.

a Regional aggregates are weighted averages estimated using population of annual live births for the respective year headings. The data for maternal, under-5, and neonatal deaths are from United Nations databases. For Taipei,China, maternal and neonatal deaths data are from the Government of Taipei,China's Ministry of Health and Welfare. Aggregates are derived for reporting economies only. Aggregates for East Asia exclude Hong Kong, China. For under-5 mortality rate, aggregates also exclude Taipei,China.

b Data are estimates as published on the United Nations' SDG Global Database.

c Based on data from national-level household surveys and routine service statistics.

Sources: For Indicators 3.1.1, 3.1.2, 3.2.1, and 3.2.2: United Nations. SDG Global Database. https://unstats.un.org/sdgs/dataportal (accessed 21 July 2023). For Indicator 3.1.1 for Hong Kong, China: Government of the Hong Kong Special Administrative Region of the People's Republic of China. Centre for Health Protection Statistics. https://www.chp.gov.hk/en/statistics/data/10/27/110.html (accessed 21 July 2023). For Indicator 3.1.1 for Taipei,China: Government of Taipei,China, Directorate-General of Budget, Accounting and Statistics. For Indicator 3.2.2 for Hong Kong, China: Government of the Hong Kong Special Administrative Region of the People's Republic of China, Department of Health. Health Facts of Hong Kong 2022 Edition; past editions. https://www.dh.gov.hk/english/statistics/statistics_hs/files/2021.pdf (accessed 21 July 2023). For Indicator 3.2.2 for Taipei,China: Government of Taipei,China, Ministry of Health and Welfare. 2020 Cause of Death Statistics.

Table 1.3.2: Selected Indicators for Sustainable Development Goal 3—Incidence of Communicable Diseases

ADB Regional Member	Target 3.3: By 2030, end the epidemics of AIDS, tuberculosis, malaria, and neglected tropical diseases; and combat hepatitis, water-borne diseases, and other communicable diseases					
	3.3.1: Number of New HIV Infections[a] (per 1,000 uninfected population)		3.3.2: Tuberculosis Incidence[b] (per 100,000 population)		3.3.3: Malaria Incidence[c] (per 1,000 population)	
	2010	2022	2010	2021	2010	2021
Developing ADB Member Economies						
Central and West Asia						
Afghanistan	0.03	0.03	189.0	189.0	13.4	6.3
Armenia	0.13	0.19	61.0	27.0	–	–
Azerbaijan	0.08	0.05	104.0	63.0	0.2	–
Georgia	0.14	0.14	127.0	64.0	–	–
Kazakhstan	...	...	144.0	74.0	–	–
Kyrgyz Republic	0.13	0.11	120.0	130.0	0.0	–
Pakistan	...	...	276.0	264.0	7.6	2.2
Tajikistan	0.09	0.10	128.0	88.0	0.0	–
Turkmenistan	...	...	79.0	47.0	–	–
Uzbekistan	...	...	97.0	62.0	0.1	–
East Asia						
China, People's Republic of	...	...	76.0	55.0	0.0	–
Hong Kong, China	...	...	80.0	57.0	...	...
Korea, Republic of	...	...	97.0	44.0	0.4	0.1
Mongolia	0.02	0.01	428.0	428.0	...	...
Taipei,China	...	...	...	...	...	...
South Asia						
Bangladesh	<0.01	<0.01	221.0	221.0	4.3	0.5
Bhutan	0.12	0.08	232.0	164.0	0.8	0.0
India	...	0.05	292.0	210.0	17.5	3.2
Maldives	<0.01	<0.01	32.0	38.0	...	...
Nepal	0.08	0.02	311.0	229.0	3.8	0.0
Sri Lanka	0.02	<0.01	66.0	63.0	0.1	–
Southeast Asia						
Brunei Darussalam	...	...	69.0	61.0	...	...
Cambodia	0.15	0.08	438.0	288.0	34.8	1.6
Indonesia	0.21	0.09	342.0	354.0	8.2	3.0
Lao People's Democratic Republic	0.17	0.14	221.0	143.0	13.3	1.7
Malaysia	0.20	0.09	75.0	97.0	4.5	–
Myanmar	0.35	0.21	500.0	360.0	51.3	9.1
Philippines	0.05	0.21	531.0	650.0	1.0	0.2
Singapore	...	...	35.0	48.0	...	...
Thailand	0.25	0.13	181.0	143.0	2.5	0.2
Timor-Leste	0.09	0.07	498.0	486.0	93.2	–
Viet Nam	0.16	0.06	231.0	173.0	0.4	0.0
The Pacific						
Cook Islands	...	...	–	13.0	...	...
Fiji	0.09	0.33	27.0	66.0	...	...
Kiribati	...	...	347.0	424.0	...	...
Marshall Islands	...	...	428.0	483.0	...	...
Micronesia, Federated States of	...	...	191.0	80.0	...	...
Nauru	...	...	34.0	193.0	...	...
Niue	...	...	–	48.0	...	...
Palau	...	...	118.0	51.0	...	...
Papua New Guinea	0.37	0.65	432.0	424.0	142.3	124.3
Samoa	...	...	8.3	6.8	...	...
Solomon Islands	...	...	78.0	65.0	170.9	216.1
Tonga	...	...	12.0	7.6	...	...
Tuvalu	...	...	153.0	296.0	...	...
Vanuatu	...	...	69.0	34.0	85.4	1.8
Developed ADB Member Economies						
Australia	0.05	0.01 (2021)	6.6	6.5	...	...
Japan	...	...	20.0	11.0	...	...
New Zealand	0.03	<0.01	8.0	6.8	...	...

.. = data not available, < = less than, – = magnitude equals zero, 0.0 = magnitude is less than half of unit employed, ADB = Asian Development Bank.

a Figures are based on modeled HIV estimates. For more information on the HIV estimates methodology, please see https://www.unaids.org.

b Estimates of tuberculosis incidence are produced through a consultative and analytical process led by the World Health Organization and are published annually. These estimates are based on annual case notifications, assessments of the quality and coverage of tuberculosis notification data, national surveys of the prevalence of tuberculosis disease, and information from death (vital) registration systems. For the period 2000–2019, estimates of incidence for each economy are derived, using one or more of the following approaches, depending on available data: (i) incidence = case notifications and/or estimated proportion of cases detected; (ii) capture-recapture modelling, (iii) incidence = prevalence and/or duration of condition. For 2020 and 2021 specifically, these methods were retained for most economies. However, for economies with large absolute reductions in the reported number of people newly diagnosed with tuberculosis in 2020 or 2021 relative to pre-2020 trends (which suggested major disruptions to access to tuberculosis diagnosis and treatment during the COVID-19 pandemic), dynamic models were used in replacement of the methods used for 2000–2019.

c Malaria incidence is expressed as the number of new cases per 100,000 population per year, with the population of each economy derived from projections made by the United Nations Population Division and the total proportion at risk estimated by an economy's national malaria control program. More specifically, the economy estimates the total proportion of the population at risk of malaria and then, for each year, the total population at risk is estimated as the United Nations population figure for that year times the proportion of the population at risk.

Sources: For Indicator 3.3.1: Joint United Nations Programme on HIV/AIDS (UNAIDS). AIDSinfo. https://aidsinfo.unaids.org/ (accessed 18 July 2023).
For Indicators 3.3.2 and 3.3.3: United Nations. SDG Global Database. https://unstats.un.org/sdgs/dataportal (accessed 18 July 2023).

Goal 3. Ensure healthy lives and promote well-being for all at all ages

Table 1.3.3: Selected Indicators for Sustainable Development Goal 3—Mortality Rates, Reproductive Health

ADB Regional Member	Target 3.4: By 2030, reduce by one-third premature mortality from noncommunicable diseases through prevention and treatment, and promote mental health and well-being					Target 3.6: By 2020, halve the number of global deaths and injuries from road traffic accidents	
	3.4.1: Mortality Rate Attributed to Cardiovascular Disease, Cancer, Diabetes, or Chronic Respiratory Disease[a] (%)		3.4.2: Suicide Mortality Rate[a] (per 100,000 population)			3.6.1: Death Rate Due to Road Traffic Injuries[a] (per 100,000 population)	
	2010	2019	2019			2010	2019
			Total	Female	Male		
Developing ADB Member Economies							
Central and West Asia							
Afghanistan	37.8	35.3	4.1	3.6	4.6	14.4	15.9
Armenia	25.0	19.9	3.3	1.3	5.6	18.0	20.0
Azerbaijan	29.8	27.2	4.1	1.6	6.6	11.4	6.7
Georgia	27.1	24.9	9.2	3.0	16.0	17.2	12.4
Kazakhstan	31.4	22.4	17.6	6.8	29.0	25.9	12.7
Kyrgyz Republic	27.9	20.3	7.4	3.2	11.7	18.0	12.7
Pakistan	31.8	29.4	8.9	4.3	13.3	14.7	13.0
Tajikistan	30.5	28.3	4.3	2.8	5.7	18.7	15.7
Turkmenistan	33.1	27.7	5.7	2.6	8.8	16.9	13.5
Uzbekistan	28.9	25.3	8.0	4.8	11.3	11.3	11.7
East Asia							
China, People's Republic of	19.0	15.9	8.1	6.2	9.8	20.3	17.4
Hong Kong, China	...	...	...	...	...	1.7[e]	1.2[e] (2022)
Korea, Republic of	10.6	7.3	28.6	16.9	40.2	13.7	8.6
Mongolia	41.6	35.0	17.9	5.4	30.7	18.6	21.0
Taipei,China	...	...	15.5 (2020)	...	...	...	...
South Asia							
Bangladesh	21.5	18.9	3.7	1.7	5.7	16.9	15.3
Bhutan	19.4	18.5	4.6	2.7	6.3	13.6	16.2
India	23.7	21.9	12.7	11.1	14.1	17.2	15.6
Maldives	16.5	11.6	2.7	0.8	3.9	3.0	1.6
Nepal	20.2	21.5	9.0	2.7	16.4	15.8	16.3
Sri Lanka	17.0	13.2	14.0	6.2	22.3	14.2	19.7
Southeast Asia							
Brunei Darussalam	19.9	18.5	2.7	0.8	4.4	7.7	7.5
Cambodia	23.7	22.5	4.9	2.8	7.0	18.1	19.6
Indonesia	26.1	24.8	2.4	1.1	3.7	13.7	11.3
Lao People's Democratic Republic	28.3	26.8	5.4	3.2	7.6	14.3	17.9
Malaysia	18.9	18.4	5.7	2.3	8.9	25.1	22.5
Myanmar	28.3	24.9	2.9	1.1	4.9	19.1	20.4
Philippines	24.4	24.5	2.2	1.2	3.1	11.5	12.0
Singapore	11.0	9.5	11.2	7.1	15.0	5.1	2.1
Thailand	14.9	13.7	8.8	2.9	15.0	38.3	32.2
Timor-Leste	19.9	19.9	3.7	2.0	5.3	15.3	11.9
Viet Nam	22.4	21.2	7.5	4.7	10.4	25.6	30.6
The Pacific							
Cook Islands	...	...	...	...	...	...	...
Fiji	39.6	37.7	9.0	5.7	12.2	9.8	13.5
Kiribati	53.0	50.8	28.3	8.6	48.6	5.8	1.9
Marshall Islands	...	...	...	...	...	...	...
Micronesia, Federated States of	44.6	46.3	28.2	12.7	43.2	2.9	0.2
Nauru	...	30.0 (2017)	...	...	...	...	...
Niue	...	18.5 (2016)	...	...	...	...	...
Palau	...	...	...	...	...	...	...
Papua New Guinea	35.4	36.0	2.9	1.6	4.2	17.1	12.6
Samoa	32.4	31.2	12.6	6.7	18.0	12.9	13.0
Solomon Islands	40.4	39.2	14.7	1.9	27.0	17.8	16.5
Tonga	26.3	24.8	3.8	2.6	5.0	5.8	33.0
Tuvalu	...	...	...	...	...	...	...
Vanuatu	40.4	39.7	18.0	7.6	28.1	13.5	14.9
Developed ADB Member Economies							
Australia	9.9	8.6	12.5	6.4	18.6	6.5	4.9
Japan	9.5	8.3	15.3	9.2	21.8	5.3	3.6
New Zealand	11.8	10.3	11.0	5.8	16.5	9.3	9.6

Table 1.3.3: Selected Indicators for Sustainable Development Goal 3—Mortality Rates, Reproductive Health *(continued)*

ADB Regional Member	Target 3.7: By 2030, ensure universal access to sexual and reproductive health-care services, including for family planning, information, and education, and the integration of reproductive health into natural strategies and programs				Target 3.8: Achieve universal health coverage, including financial risk protection; access to quality essential health-care services; and access to safe, effective, quality, and affordable essential medicines and vaccines for all	Target 3.9: By 2030, substantially reduce the number of deaths and illnesses from hazardous chemicals and air, water, and soil pollution and contamination	
	3.7.1: Proportion of Women of Reproductive Age (Aged 15–49 Years) Who Have Their Need for Family Planning Satisfied with Modern Methods		3.7.2: Adolescent Birth Rate (Aged 15–19 Years) per 1,000 Women in That Age Group		3.8.1: Coverage of Essential Health Services[b] (index in a unitless scale of 0 to 100)	3.9.1: Mortality Rate Attributed to Household and Ambient Air Pollution (per 100,000 population)	3.9.2: Mortality Rate Attributed to Unsafe Water, Unsafe Sanitation, and Lack of Hygiene (per 100,000 population)
	2010	2019	2010	2019	2021	2019	2019
Developing ADB Member Economies							
Central and West Asia							
Afghanistan	42.1[c] (2015)	...	81.1 (2009)	62.1 (2017)	41.0	266.0	16.6
Armenia	39.4	...	27.1	13.9 (2020)	68.0	75.0	5.8
Azerbaijan	21.5[c] (2006)	...	48.6	41.6 (2020)	66.0	125.0	3.6
Georgia	52.8[c,d]	51.3[c] (2018)	48.4	27.2 (2020)	68.0	93.0	3.3
Kazakhstan	79.6[c,d]	73.2[c,d] (2018)	28.5	22.9 (2021)	80.0	83.0	3.2
Kyrgyz Republic	62.1 (2012)	64.6 (2018)	32.7	32.6 (2020)	69.0	125.0	2.3
Pakistan	47.0[c] (2012)	48.5[c,d] (2017)	49.0 (2009)	54.0 (2018)	45.0	192.0	38.8
Tajikistan	50.8[c] (2012)	52.1[c] (2017)	47.5	41.7	67.0	204.0	9.0
Turkmenistan	75.6[c] (2015)	79.6[c]	26.2 (2011)	27.5 (2017)	75.0	88.0	5.7
Uzbekistan	...	...	24.1 (2013)	34.3 (2021)	75.0	152.0	2.9
East Asia							
China, People's Republic of	96.6[c,d] (2001)	...	6.2 (2011)	6.1 (2020)	81.0	95.0	2.2
Hong Kong, China	...	...	3.5 (2009)	1.3 (2021)	...	...	...
Korea, Republic of	...	...	1.8	0.7 (2020)	89.0	19.0	5.2
Mongolia	65.3[c,d]	63.6 (2018)	20.3 (2009)	26.9 (2020)	65.0	215.0	3.2
Taipei,China	...	...	...	...	...	...	...
South Asia							
Bangladesh	69.7[c] (2011)	77.4[c]	137.5	74.0 (2020)	52.0	144.0	18.2
Bhutan	84.6[c,d]	...	19.6 (2011)	8.1 (2020)	60.0	94.0	15.7
India	63.9[c] (2007)	...	62.8 (2011)	10.6	63.0	139.0	36.4
Maldives	42.7[c] (2009)	29.2 (2016)	15.7	5.1	61.0	32.0	2.3
Nepal	56.2 (2011)	61.9[c]	86.6 (2012)	63.1 (2018)	54.0	178.0	17.8
Sri Lanka	69.4[c,d] (2006)	74.3[c] (2016)	22.8 (2009)	...	67.0	92.0	4.8
Southeast Asia							
Brunei Darussalam	...	...	14.2 (2011)	7.9 (2020)	78.0	20.0	1.7
Cambodia	51.6[c]	...	53.8	...	58.0	163.0	17.1
Indonesia	79.0 (2012)	77.0 (2017)	48.0	36.1 (2016)	55.0	96.0	15.8
Lao People's Democratic Republic	60.5 (2011)	72.3 (2017)	94.5	83.4 (2016)	52.0	195.0	20.5
Malaysia	...	...	14.0	7.8 (2020)	76.0	76.0	14.4
Myanmar	74.9 (2015)	...	39.8 (2008)	24.5	52.0	184.0	12.9
Philippines	54.0[c] (2011)	56.0 (2017)	41.5 (2009)	34.8	58.0	203.0	16.9
Singapore	...	...	4.5	2.4 (2020)	89.0	23.0	8.5
Thailand	89.2[c] (2012)	88.2	49.0	27.4 (2020)	82.0	46.0	11.8
Timor-Leste	38.4 (2009)	45.9 (2016)	41.0	...	52.0	186.0	20.4
Viet Nam	73.1[c,d]	72.1[c] (2020)	41.7 (2011)	29.0 (2020)	68.0	103.0	6.9
The Pacific							
Cook Islands	...	...	51.1	32.5 (2017)	46.0	...	...
Fiji	...	...	32.5 (2011)	31.1	58.0	119.0	10.8
Kiribati	35.8[c] (2009)	53.1 (2018)	37.8	50.6 (2017)	48.0	247.0	37.4
Marshall Islands	80.5[c] (2007)	...	82.2	...	59.0	...	...
Micronesia, Federated States of	...	...	33.0 (2009)	...	48.0	254.0	14.0
Nauru	42.5[c] (2007)	...	60.5	...	60.0	...	...
Niue	...	...	...	...	44.0	...	...
Palau	...	...	30.6 (2012)	34.5	65.0	...	...
Papua New Guinea	40.6[c] (2006)	49.2 (2016)	91.3	67.8 (2016)	30.0	190.0	24.9
Samoa	34.9[c] (2009)	27.0	40.1 (2011)	54.9 (2018)	55.0	145.0	8.2
Solomon Islands	60.0[c] (2006)	...	41.7 (2009)	...	47.0	281.0	32.7
Tonga	47.9[c] (2012)	49.9	24.0	...	57.0	52.0	7.1
Tuvalu	41.0[c] (2007)	44.9 (2020)	29.9 (2012)	40.3 (2017)	52.0	...	...
Vanuatu	50.7[c] (2013)	...	78.0 (2011)	...	47.0	259.0	25.0
Developed ADB Member Economies							
Australia	...	...	15.8	7.8 (2020)	87.0	10.0	1.9
Japan	...	...	4.6	2.5 (2020)	83.0	12.0	8.4
New Zealand	...	...	25.8 (2011)	10.1 (2021)	85.0	12.0	2.1

... = data not available, ADB = Asian Development Bank.

a For detailed information regarding the nature of the data, please refer to the United Nations' SDG Global Database at https://unstats.un.org/sdgs/dataportal.

b The universal health coverage service coverage index is calculated as the geometric mean of 14 tracer indicators of health service coverage. The index is reported on a unitless scale of 0 to 100, with 100 being the optimal value. The reported values do not directly translate to the percentage of the population covered by universal health coverage services, but they can be viewed as performance scores.

c The global indicator represents all women of reproductive age: this survey estimate represents women who are married or in a union.

d For additional information regarding the data, please refer to the United Nations' SDG Global Database at https://unstats.un.org/sdgs/dataportal.

e Estimated by ADB using Road Traffic Accident Statistics data of the Transport Department and Population Estimates data of the Census and Statistics Department of the Government of the Hong Kong Special Administrative Region of the People's Republic of China.

Sources: For Indicators 3.4.1, 3.4.2, 3.6.1, 3.7.1, 3.7.2, 3.8.1, 3.9.1, and 3.9.2: United Nations. SDG Global Database. https://unstats.un.org/sdgs/dataportal (accessed 20 July 2023). For Indicator 3.4.1 for Nauru and Niue: Pacific Community. Pacific Data Hub. Explorer. https://stats.pacificdata.org/ (accessed 20 July 2023). For Indicator 3.4.2 for Taipei,China: Government of Taipei,China, Ministry of Health and Welfare. 2020 Cause of Death Statistics. For Indicator 3.6.1 for Hong Kong, China: Government of the Hong Kong Special Administrative Region of the People's Republic of China. Road Traffic Accident Statistics. https://www.td.gov.hk/en/road_safety/road_traffic_accident_statistics/accident_trend_since_1953/index.html (accessed 20 July 2023).

Goal 3. Ensure healthy lives and promote well-being for all at all ages

Table 1.3.4: Selected Indicators for Sustainable Development Goal 3—Health Workforce and National and Global Health Risks

ADB Regional Member	Target 3.c: Substantially increase health financing and the recruitment, development, training, and retention of the health workforce in developing countries, especially in least developed countries and small island developing states						Target 3.d: Strengthen the capacity of all countries, in particular developing countries, for early warning, risk reduction, and management of national and global health risks
	3.c.1: Health Worker Density, by Type of Occupation[a,b] (per 10,000 population)						3.d.1: International Health Regulations Capacity and Health Emergency Preparedness[b,c,d] (%)
	Density of Medical Doctors			Density of Nursing and Midwifery Personnel			Average of 15 International Health Regulations Core Capacity Scores
	2010	2015	2020	2010	2015	2020	2022
Developing ADB Member Economies							
Central and West Asia	**12.7**	**13.3**	**...**	**24.8**	**23.1**	**...**	**67**
Afghanistan	2.5	2.9	2.5	6.3 (2009)	1.3	4.5 (2018)	40[e]
Armenia	27.8	29.6	...	51.2	50.3	...	84
Azerbaijan	35.8	32.9	31.1 (2019)	71.9	62.8 (2014)	...	81
Georgia	47.5	53.4	54.1 (2021)	42.2	42.9	58.8 (2021)	71
Kazakhstan	38.4	39.1	40.3	75.5	71.9	...	80
Kyrgyz Republic	23.1	22.3 (2014)	21.7 (2019)	55.8	59.8 (2014)	56.8 (2019)	48
Pakistan	7.5	8.8	10.8 (2019)	5.2	4.5	4.7 (2019)	50
Tajikistan	16.8	17.1 (2014)	...	39.0	47.1 (2014)	...	63
Turkmenistan	22.0	21.5 (2014)	...	43.6	42.7 (2014)	...	81
Uzbekistan	25.4	23.7 (2014)	...	113.4	112.7 (2014)	...	70
East Asia	**14.8**	**18.2**	**23.9**	**16.3**	**24.6**	**34.9**	**88**
China, People's Republic of	14.6	18.0	23.9	15.2	23.3	33.1	93
Hong Kong, China	...	...	...	...	...	...	...
Korea, Republic of	20.1	22.4	25.1	47.1	59.6	85.3	99
Mongolia	27.7	32.6	38.6 (2018)	36.5	41.4	42.2 (2018)	72
Taipei,China	...	...	...	...	...	...	...
South Asia	**...**	**...**	**7.3**	**...**	**19.0**	**16.5**	**64**
Bangladesh	3.6	4.8	6.7 (2021)	1.8	2.7	6.1 (2021)	68
Bhutan	2.7 (2012)	3.4	5.6 (2021)	10.2 (2012)	14.4	22.1 (2021)	63
India	...	...	7.3	...	20.8 (2017)	17.3	85
Maldives	14.5	12.9 (2016)	21.6 (2019)	51.7	68.6	49.0	56
Nepal	5.1 (2012)	8.9 (2017)	8.7 (2021)	15.8 (2012)	20.9 (2014)	34.9 (2021)	47
Sri Lanka	7.1	8.5	11.9 (2021)	17.1	19.2	24.4 (2021)	66
Southeast Asia	**5.3**	**5.4**	**8.4**	**27.0**	**21.4**	**...**	**70**
Brunei Darussalam	14.2	17.5	19.1 (2021)	73.4	65.4	67.1 (2021)	...
Cambodia	2.3	1.9 (2014)	2.1 (2019)	8.5	5.9	10.3 (2019)	60
Indonesia	1.4	2.7	7.0 (2021)	...	13.0	11.2 (2021)	72
Lao People's Democratic Republic	3.3	4.0	3.3 (2021)	8.5	12.1	11.8	53
Malaysia	11.5	15.0	22.3	31.4	40.8	33.9 (2019)	89
Myanmar	5.4	6.3 (2016)	7.5 (2019)	9.2	10.6 (2016)	11.0 (2019)	61
Philippines	12.6	6.7 (2017)	7.9 (2021)	56.2 (2009)	47.3 (2017)	47.6 (2021)	67
Singapore	17.5	22.1	24.3 (2019)	56.8	59.5	...	94
Thailand	3.8	4.6	9.3	20.3	23.2	30.8 (2019)	87
Timor-Leste	...	6.9	7.7	11.5	14.7	17.7	68
Viet Nam	7.2	8.0	...	12.4	14.3	...	52
The Pacific	**1.3**	**...**	**...**	**8.8**	**...**	**...**	**60**
Cook Islands	14.5 (2009)	14.1 (2014)	13.5 (2019)	69.9 (2009)	67.8	81.9 (2019)	71
Fiji	4.1 (2009)	8.1	...	21.7 (2009)	28.6	38.4 (2019)	48
Kiribati	3.8	1.9 (2013)	...	37.4	54.7 (2013)	36.2 (2018)	64 (2021)
Marshall Islands	6.0	...	...	23.8	...	42.4 (2018)	...
Micronesia, Federated States of	6.7 (2012)	...	9.6	...	...	22.0 (2019)	53
Nauru	10.8	12.5	...	68.0 (2011)	62.5	70.6 (2018)	...
Niue	16.7 (2008)	...	...	88.9 (2008)	...	105.3 (2018)	69
Palau	15.7	14.1 (2014)	17.8	64.3	62.4 (2014)	65.0	47 (2021)
Papua New Guinea	0.5	...	0.6 (2021)	4.8	...	5.1 (2021)	...
Samoa	3.3	3.3 (2016)	5.5	14.7	17.7 (2014)	30.2	55
Solomon Islands	2.0 (2011)	1.9 (2016)	...	17.5 (2011)	19.6 (2013)	21.4 (2018)	51 (2021)
Tonga	5.4	5.1 (2013)	10.1 (2021)	37.2	38.1 (2013)	41.8 (2021)	70
Tuvalu	11.5 (2009)	9.2 (2014)	12.6	62.1 (2008)	37.6 (2014)	36.9	61 (2021)
Vanuatu	1.8 (2012)	1.6 (2016)	1.6 (2019)	17.8 (2012)	...	14.0 (2019)	54
Developed ADB Member Economies	**23.9**	**26.1**	**28.9**	**103.4**	**116.7**	**128.2**	**91**
Australia	33.6	35.1	41.0	104.7	122.6	148.2 (2021)	89
Japan	22.1	24.3 (2016)	26.1	103.1	115.9 (2016)	124.5	99
New Zealand	26.3	30.5	35.2 (2021)	106.3	108.3	114.4 (2021)	85
DEVELOPING ADB MEMBER ECONOMIES	**...**	**...**	**...**	**...**	**21.5**	**...**	**68**
ALL ADB REGIONAL MEMBERS	**...**	**...**	**...**	**...**	**25.1**	**...**	**70**
WORLD	**...**	**...**	**16.3**	**...**	**...**	**39.4**	**67**

... = data not available, ADB = Asian Development Bank.

a Regional aggregates are population weighted averages of the densities of the economies calculated by ADB. The data for number of doctors and nurses and midwifery personnel are from the World Health Organization's Global Health Workforce Database.

b Aggregates are derived for reporting economies only.

c The scores are based on self-assessment and self-reporting by the economy and the World Health Organization (WHO) may need to provide more technical support guidance to ensure data quality. In 2018, WHO introduced a new State Parties Self-Assessment Annual Reporting Tool (SPAR), which has been in use since. For 2021 onward, the tool uses the second edition of the SPAR questionnaire. Caution should be exercised in comparing SPAR data for 2018–2022 submission that used the SPAR first edition, and the 2010–2017 SPAR submission that used the International Health Regulations questionnaire.

d Regional aggregates are averages of the scores of the economies calculated by ADB.

e Data provided by the WHO Country Office in Afghanistan.

Sources: For Indicator 3.c.1: United Nations. SDG Global Database. https://unstats.un.org/sdgs/dataportal (accessed 18 July 2023). For Indicator 3.d.1: World Health Organization. The Global Health Observatory. https://www.who.int/data/gho (accessed 20 July 2023). For Indicator 3.d.1 for World: World Health Organization. Electronic State Parties Self-Assessment Annual Reporting Tool (e-SPAR). https://extranet.who.int/e-spar/ (accessed 20 July 2023).

Table 1.4.1: Selected Indicators for Sustainable Development Goal 4—Proficiency in Reading and Mathematics

ADB Regional Member	Target 4.1: By 2030, ensure that all girls and boys complete free, equitable, and quality primary and secondary education leading to relevant and effective learning outcomes			
	4.1.1.b: Proportion of Children and Young People at the End of Primary School Achieving at Least a Minimum Proficiency Level (%)		4.1.1.c: Proportion of Children and Young People at the End of Lower Secondary School Achieving at Least a Minimum Proficiency Level (%)	
	Reading	Mathematics	Reading	Mathematics
	2019	2019	2019	2019
Developing ADB Member Economies				
Central and West Asia				
Afghanistan	...	...	...	...
Armenia	...	64.3	...	50.4 (2015)
Azerbaijan[a]	80.8 (2016)	71.7	...	...
Georgia	86.5 (2016)	55.8	35.6 (2018)	38.9 (2018)
Kazakhstan	98.1 (2016)	70.8	35.8 (2018)	50.9 (2018)
Kyrgyz Republic	...	...	...	...
Pakistan	...	7.5	...	...
Tajikistan	...	...	...	...
Turkmenistan	...	...	...	...
Uzbekistan	...	...	...	...
East Asia				
China, People's Republic of	...	...	...	...
Hong Kong, China	98.6 (2016)	95.6	87.4 (2018)	90.8 (2018)
Korea, Republic of	...	95.2	84.9 (2018)	85.0 (2018)
Mongolia[b]	...	...	...	...
Taipei,China	...	...	...	...
South Asia				
Bangladesh	...	...	...	...
Bhutan	...	...	...	...
India	...	...	...	...
Maldives	...	...	...	...
Nepal	...	...	...	...
Sri Lanka	...	...	...	...
Southeast Asia				
Brunei Darussalam	...	...	48.2 (2018)	52.1 (2018)
Cambodia	11.0	18.0	7.5 (2017)	9.9 (2017)
Indonesia	66.2 (2011)	17.5 (2015)	30.1 (2018)	28.1 (2018)
Lao People's Democratic Republic	2.0	7.9	...	...
Malaysia	58.0	64.0	54.2 (2018)	58.5 (2018)
Myanmar	11.0	12.0	...	...
Philippines	10.0	17.0	19.4 (2018)	19.3 (2018)
Singapore	97.3 (2016)	95.5	88.8 (2018)	91.8
Thailand	...	43.4 (2011)	40.5 (2018)	47.3 (2018)
Timor-Leste	...	...	...	...
Viet Nam	82.0	91.0	90.5 (2018)	84.3 (2018)
The Pacific				
Cook Islands	...	...	...	...
Fiji	...	...	...	...
Kiribati	...	...	...	...
Marshall Islands	...	...	...	...
Micronesia, Federated States of	...	...	...	...
Nauru	...	...	...	...
Niue	...	...	...	...
Palau	...	...	...	...
Papua New Guinea	...	...	...	...
Samoa	...	...	...	...
Solomon Islands	...	...	...	...
Tonga	...	...	...	...
Tuvalu	...	...	...	...
Vanuatu	...	...	...	...
Developed ADB Member Economies				
Australia	...	68.0	80.4 (2018)	77.6 (2018)
Japan	...	...	...	...
New Zealand	90.0 (2016)	55.9	81.0 (2018)	78.2 (2018)

... = data not available, ADB = Asian Development Bank.

a For Indicator 4.1.1.c (Reading), the latest available estimate is for 2009: 27.2%. For Indicator 4.1.1.c (Mathematics), the latest available estimate is for 2009: 54.7%.

b For Indicator 4.1.1.b (Mathematics), the latest available estimate is for 2007: 33.9%. For Indicator 4.1.1.c (Mathematics), the latest available estimate is for 2007: 31.2%.

Source: United Nations. SDG Global Database. https://unstats.un.org/sdgs/dataportal (accessed 27 July 2023).

Goal 4. Ensure inclusive and equitable quality education and promote lifelong learning opportunities for all

Table 1.4.2: Selected Indicators for Sustainable Development Goal 4—Education Completion

ADB Regional Member	Target 4.1: By 2030, ensure that all girls and boys complete free, equitable, and quality primary and secondary education leading to relevant and effective learning outcomes											
	4.1.2: Completion Rate (Primary Education, Lower Secondary Education, Upper Secondary Education)[a] (%)											
	Primary											
	2010						2020					
	Total		Q1		Q2		Total		Q1		Q2	
Developing ADB Member Economies												
Central and West Asia												
Afghanistan	41.00		21.00	(2011)	26.00	(2011)	65.00		45.00	(2015)	46.00	(2015)
Armenia	100.00		99.00		100.00		100.00		99.00	(2018)	99.00	(2018)
Azerbaijan	98.00		95.00	(2006)	99.00	(2006)	98.70		...		...	
Georgia	99.00		100.00	(2013)	98.00	(2013)	100.00		100.00	(2018)	100.00	(2018)
Kazakhstan	100.00		99.00		100.00		100.00		100.00	(2015)	100.00	(2015)
Kyrgyz Republic	99.00		100.00	(2012)	99.00	(2012)	99.00		100.00	(2018)	100.00	(2018)
Pakistan	48.00		24.00	(2012)	50.00	(2012)	54.00		28.00	(2018)	48.00	(2018)
Tajikistan	98.00		97.00	(2012)	97.00	(2012)	99.00		98.00	(2017)	99.00	(2017)
Turkmenistan	100.00		100.00	(2006)	100.00	(2006)	100.00		99.00	(2019)	100.00	(2019)
Uzbekistan	100.00		100.00	(2006)	100.00	(2006)	100.00	(2021)	100.00	(2021)	100.00	(2021)
East Asia												
China, People's Republic of	97.00		93.00		95.00		98.00		93.00	(2016)	98.00	(2016)
Hong Kong, China	...		...		...		...		...		...	
Korea, Republic of	100.00		100.00	(2012)	100.00	(2012)	100.00		...		...	
Mongolia	97.00		90.00		95.00		99.00		97.00	(2018)	99.00	(2018)
Taipei,China	...		...		...		...		...		...	
South Asia												
Bangladesh	72.00		47.00	(2011)	69.00	(2011)	85.00		70.00	(2019)	80.00	(2019)
Bhutan	68.00		42.00		55.00		88.20		...		...	
India	87.00		84.00	(2011)	85.00	(2011)	94.00	(2021)	87.00	(2021)	94.00	(2021)
Maldives	97.00		94.00	(2009)	96.00	(2009)	99.00		97.00	(2017)	96.00	(2017)
Nepal	65.00		58.00	(2011)	67.00	(2011)	82.00		74.00	(2019)	75.00	(2019)
Sri Lanka	98.00	(2006)	96.00	(2006)	99.00	(2006)	...		...		...	
Southeast Asia												
Brunei Darussalam	...		...		...		...		...		...	
Cambodia	71.00		43.00		61.00		79.00		...		...	
Indonesia	94.00		87.00	(2012)	95.00	(2012)	97.00		91.00	(2017)	97.00	(2017)
Lao People's Democratic Republic	58.00		28.00	(2011)	54.00	(2011)	86.10		58.00	(2017)	80.00	(2017)
Malaysia	98.30		...		...		99.60		...		...	
Myanmar	63.00		...		...		84.00		65.00	(2016)	83.00	(2016)
Philippines	87.00		60.00	(2008)	83.00	(2008)	91.00		79.00	(2018)	92.00	(2018)
Singapore	...		...		...		...		...		...	
Thailand	97.00		98.00	(2012)	98.00	(2012)	99.00		97.00	(2019)	97.00	(2019)
Timor-Leste	64.00		39.00	(2009)	48.00	(2009)	77.00		60.00	(2016)	71.00	(2016)
Viet Nam	96.00		89.00		95.00		98.00	(2021)	95.00	(2021)	99.00	(2021)
The Pacific												
Cook Islands	...		...		...		...		...		...	
Fiji	98.00		...		...		98.00	(2021)	98.00	(2021)	96.00	(2021)
Kiribati	92.00		...		...		93.00		88.00	(2019)	93.00	(2019)
Marshall Islands	...		...		...		...		...		...	
Micronesia, Federated States of	...		...		...		...		...		...	
Nauru	...		...		...		...		...		...	
Niue	...		...		...		...		...		...	
Palau	...		...		...		...		...		...	
Papua New Guinea	54.00		...		...		59.00		39.00	(2018)	49.00	(2018)
Samoa	98.00		...		...		98.00		97.00	(2019)	97.00	(2019)
Solomon Islands	...		...		...		...		...		...	
Tonga	98.00		...		...		99.00		97.00	(2019)	98.00	(2019)
Tuvalu	98.00		...		...		99.00		100.00		100.00	
Vanuatu	78.00		64.00	(2007)	81.00	(2007)	82.60		...		...	
Developed ADB Member Economies												
Australia	100.00		98.00		100.00		100.00		87.00	(2018)	85.00	(2018)
Japan	100.00		...		...		100.00	(2018)	...		...	
New Zealand	...		...		...		...		...		...	

Table 1.4.2: Selected Indicators for Sustainable Development Goal 4—Education Completion *(continued)*

ADB Regional Member	Target 4.1: By 2030, ensure that all girls and boys complete free, equitable, and quality primary and secondary education leading to relevant and effective learning outcomes — 4.1.2: Completion Rate (Primary Education, Lower Secondary Education, Upper Secondary Education) (%) — Lower Secondary											
	2010						2020					
	Total		Q1		Q2		Total		Q1		Q2	
Developing ADB Member Economies												
Central and West Asia												
Afghanistan	29.00		8.00	(2011)	12.00	(2011)	49.00		25.00	(2015)	29.00	(2015)
Armenia	94.00		94.00		88.00		98.00		96.00	(2018)	96.00	(2018)
Azerbaijan	92.00		84.00	(2006)	86.00	(2006)	95.60		...		...	
Georgia	98.00		98.00	(2013)	97.00	(2013)	99.00		93.00	(2018)	97.00	(2018)
Kazakhstan	99.00		98.00		98.00		100.00		99.00	(2015)	100.00	(2015)
Kyrgyz Republic	98.00		98.00	(2012)	97.00	(2012)	98.00		96.00	(2018)	100.00	(2018)
Pakistan	40.00		11.00	(2012)	31.00	(2012)	48.00		13.00	(2018)	34.00	(2018)
Tajikistan	88.00		83.00	(2012)	86.00	(2012)	98.00		95.00	(2017)	92.00	(2017)
Turkmenistan	99.00		97.00	(2006)	98.00	(2006)	100.00		97.00	(2019)	99.00	(2019)
Uzbekistan	98.00		95.00	(2006)	96.00	(2006)	99.00	(2021)	99.00	(2021)	99.00	(2021)
East Asia												
China, People's Republic of	85.00		66.00		85.00		91.00		84.00	(2016)	91.00	(2016)
Hong Kong, China	...		...		...		...		...		...	
Korea, Republic of	100.00		100.00	(2012)	100.00	(2012)	100.00		...		...	
Mongolia	85.00		49.00		80.00		99.00		83.00	(2018)	93.00	(2018)
Taipei,China	...		...		...		...		...		...	
South Asia												
Bangladesh	50.00		16.00	(2011)	36.00	(2011)	68.00		43.00	(2019)	58.00	(2019)
Bhutan	39.00		16.00		19.00		61.90		...		...	
India	73.00		70.00	(2011)	71.00	(2011)	86.00	(2021)	70.00	(2021)	83.00	(2021)
Maldives	79.00		64.00	(2009)	70.00	(2009)	94.00		82.00	(2017)	90.00	(2017)
Nepal	52.00		36.00	(2011)	49.00	(2011)	71.00		60.00	(2019)	68.00	(2019)
Sri Lanka	88.00	(2006)	77.00	(2006)	86.00	(2006)	...		...		...	
Southeast Asia												
Brunei Darussalam	...		...		...		...		...		...	
Cambodia	37.00		12.00		18.00		46.00		...		...	
Indonesia	75.00		51.00	(2012)	67.00	(2012)	89.00		66.00	(2017)	82.00	(2017)
Lao People's Democratic Republic	42.00		4.00	(2011)	16.00	(2011)	64.80		16.00	(2017)	39.00	(2017)
Malaysia	91.80		...		...		97.20		...		...	
Myanmar	41.00		...		...		53.00		13.00	(2016)	24.00	(2016)
Philippines	71.00		27.00	(2008)	57.00	(2008)	72.00		52.00	(2018)	76.00	(2018)
Singapore	...		...		...		...		...		...	
Thailand	84.00		77.00	(2012)	80.00	(2012)	89.00		68.00	(2019)	86.00	(2019)
Timor-Leste	49.00		24.00	(2009)	29.00	(2009)	62.00		34.00	(2016)	46.00	(2016)
Viet Nam	81.00		67.00		73.00		87.00	(2021)	67.00	(2021)	82.00	(2021)
The Pacific												
Cook Islands	...		...		...		...		...		...	
Fiji	88.00		...		...		89.00	(2021)	78.00	(2021)	87.00	(2021)
Kiribati	76.00		...		...		79.00		62.00	(2019)	72.00	(2019)
Marshall Islands	...		...		...		...		...		...	
Micronesia, Federated States of	...		...		...		...		...		...	
Nauru	...		...		...		...		...		...	
Niue	...		...		...		...		...		...	
Palau	...		...		...		...		...		...	
Papua New Guinea	22.00		...		...		30.00		26.00	(2018)	37.00	(2018)
Samoa	96.00		...		...		97.00		95.00	(2019)	97.00	(2019)
Solomon Islands	...		...		...		...		...		...	
Tonga	81.00		...		...		86.00		87.00	(2019)	88.00	(2019)
Tuvalu	74.00		...		...		85.00		76.00		83.00	
Vanuatu	36.00		11.00	(2007)	18.00	(2007)	45.70		...		...	
Developed ADB Member Economies												
Australia	99.00		97.00		99.00		99.00		98.00	(2018)	100.00	(2018)
Japan	93.00		–	(2009)	–	(2011)	94.00	(2018)	...		...	
New Zealand	...		...		...		...		...		...	

Table 1.4.2: Selected Indicators for Sustainable Development Goal 4—Education Completion *(continued)*

ADB Regional Member	Target 4.1: By 2030, ensure that all girls and boys complete free, equitable, and quality primary and secondary education leading to relevant and effective learning outcomes — 4.1.2: Completion Rate (Primary Education, Lower Secondary Education, Upper Secondary Education) (%) — Upper Secondary											
	2010						2020					
	Total		Q1		Q2		Total		Q1		Q2	
Developing ADB Member Economies												
Central and West Asia												
Afghanistan	21.00		3.00	(2011)	4.00	(2011)	34.00		13.00	(2015)	15.00	(2015)
Armenia	60.00		31.00		43.00		97.00		75.00	(2018)	74.00	(2018)
Azerbaijan	84.00		54.00	(2006)	71.00	(2006)	90.20		...		...	
Georgia	90.00		89.00	(2013)	93.00	(2013)	92.00		54.00	(2018)	69.00	(2018)
Kazakhstan	91.00		85.00		88.00		98.00		88.00	(2015)	92.00	(2015)
Kyrgyz Republic	93.00		89.00	(2012)	85.00	(2012)	96.00		78.00	(2018)	84.00	(2018)
Pakistan	19.00		3.00	(2012)	9.00	(2012)	24.00		2.00	(2018)	8.00	(2018)
Tajikistan	61.00		51.00	(2012)	52.00	(2012)	76.00		66.00	(2017)	68.00	(2017)
Turkmenistan	93.00		10.29	(2006)	10.09	(2006)	94.00		91.00	(2016)	98.00	(2016)
Uzbekistan	85.00		65.00	(2006)	68.00	(2006)	95.00	(2021)	90.00	(2021)	95.00	(2021)
East Asia												
China, People's Republic of	44.00		27.00		35.00		75.00		51.00	(2016)	61.00	(2016)
Hong Kong, China	...		...		...		...		...		...	
Korea, Republic of	98.00		95.00		98.00		99.00		92.00	(2016)	97.00	(2016)
Mongolia	63.00		26.00		50.00		88.00		51.00	(2018)	62.00	(2018)
Taipei,China	...		...		...		...		...		...	
South Asia												
Bangladesh	15.00		–	(2011)	3.00	(2011)	33.00		12.00	(2019)	20.00	(2019)
Bhutan	21.00		6.00		8.00		35.70		...		...	
India	41.00		24.00	(2011)	24.00	(2011)	51.00	(2021)	20.00	(2021)	35.00	(2021)
Maldives	21.00		5.00	(2009)	4.00	(2009)	34.00		19.00	(2017)	28.00	(2017)
Nepal	28.00		1.00	(2007)	2.00	(2007)	36.00		10.00	(2019)	14.00	(2019)
Sri Lanka	25.00	(2006)	8.00	(2006)	13.00	(2006)	...		...		...	
Southeast Asia												
Brunei Darussalam	...		...		...		...		...		...	
Cambodia	17.00		1.00		4.00		22.00		...		...	
Indonesia	49.00		22.00	(2012)	35.00	(2012)	67.00		31.00	(2017)	46.00	(2017)
Lao People's Democratic Republic	24.00		1.00	(2011)	6.00	(2011)	40.70		4.00	(2017)	16.00	(2017)
Malaysia	48.10		...		...		63.10		...		...	
Myanmar	16.00		...		...		22.00		2.00	(2016)	6.00	(2016)
Philippines	66.00		21.00	(2008)	49.00	(2008)	71.00		48.00	(2018)	71.00	(2018)
Singapore	...		...		...		...		...		...	
Thailand	55.00		31.00	(2012)	43.00	(2012)	65.00		40.00	(2019)	61.00	(2019)
Timor-Leste	49.00		27.00	(2009)	33.00	(2009)	52.00		19.00	(2016)	28.00	(2016)
Viet Nam	48.00		20.00		33.00		58.00	(2021)	30.00	(2021)	41.00	(2021)
The Pacific												
Cook Islands	...		...		...		...		...		...	
Fiji	79.00		...		...		55.00	(2021)	30.00	(2021)	41.00	(2021)
Kiribati	12.00		...		...		19.00		–	(2019)	–	(2019)
Marshall Islands	...		...		...		...		...		...	
Micronesia, Federated States of	...		...		...		...		...		...	
Nauru	...		...		...		...		...		...	
Niue	...		...		...		...		...		...	
Palau	...		...		...		...		...		...	
Papua New Guinea	11.00		...		...		13.00		–	(2018)	–	(2018)
Samoa	50.00		...		...		57.00		39.00	(2019)	44.00	(2019)
Solomon Islands	...		...		...		...		...		...	
Tonga	80.00		...		...		86.00		14.00	(2019)	16.00	(2019)
Tuvalu	42.00		...		...		55.00		30.00		47.00	
Vanuatu	9.00		–	(2007)	1.00	(2007)	11.90		...		...	
Developed ADB Member Economies												
Australia	85.00		73.00		77.00		88.00		85.00	(2018)	84.00	(2018)
Japan	94.00		56.00	(2009)	55.00	(2009)	96.00	(2018)	...		...	
New Zealand	...		...		...		...		...		...	

... = data not available, – = magnitude equals zero, ADB = Asian Development Bank, Q = wealth quintile.

a Refers to the "percentage of a cohort of children or young people aged 3–5 years above the intended age for the last grade of each level of education who have completed that grade" as defined by the United Nations Educational, Scientific and Cultural Organization (UNESCO) Institute for Statistics.

Source: United Nations. SDG Global Database. https://unstats.un.org/sdgs/dataportal (accessed 20 July 2023).

Table 1.4.3: Selected Indicators for Sustainable Development Goal 4—Early Childhood Education

ADB Regional Member	Target 4.2: By 2030, ensure that all girls and boys have access to quality early childhood development, care, and preprimary education, so that they are ready for primary education					
	4.2.2: Participation Rate in Organized Learning (1 Year before the Official Primary Entry Age)[a,b] (%)					
	2010			2021		
	Total	Female	Male	Total	Female	Male
Developing ADB Member Economies						
Central and West Asia						
Afghanistan	...	...	...	...	...	...
Armenia	...	...	...	38.1	39.4	37.0
Azerbaijan	30.4	29.7	30.9	83.8	83.6	84.0
Georgia	47.8 (2007)	50.5 (2007)	45.5 (2007)	...	...	...
Kazakhstan	99.2 (2011)	100.0 (2011)	98.4 (2011)	77.7 (2020)	77.5 (2020)	78.0 (2020)
Kyrgyz Republic	54.0	55.5	52.5	84.4	84.6	84.2
Pakistan	...	...	...	94.3 (2019)	88.1 (2019)	100.0 (2019)
Tajikistan	8.0	7.4	8.6	12.5 (2017)	11.6 (2017)	13.4 (2017)
Turkmenistan	...	...	...	...	...	...
Uzbekistan	33.8	34.3	33.3	68.9	68.1	69.6
East Asia						
China, People's Republic of	...	...	...	...	...	...
Hong Kong, China	98.2 (2012)	100.0 (2012)	96.5 (2012)	99.9 (2020)	100.0 (2020)	96.4 (2020)
Korea, Republic of	...	...	...	89.8 (2020)	89.8 (2020)	89.8 (2020)
Mongolia	98.0	99.1	96.8	95.5	95.0	96.1
Taipei,China	...	...	...	...	...	...
South Asia						
Bangladesh	37.0	37.4	36.6	90.8	93.7	88.0
Bhutan	4.3 (2000)	4.2 (2000)	4.4 (2000)	85.1	85.5	84.8
India	...	...	...	94.5 (2022)	96.3 (2022)	92.8 (2022)
Maldives	86.1	88.6	83.9	91.9 (2020)	94.5 (2020)	89.5 (2020)
Nepal	82.2 (2011)	86.9 (2011)	77.8 (2011)	70.8 (2022)	67.1 (2022)	74.4 (2022)
Sri Lanka	...	...	...	...	...	...
Southeast Asia						
Brunei Darussalam	99.4	98.8	100.0	94.8 (2020)	94.5 (2020)	95.0 (2020)
Cambodia	36.8	37.0	36.5	70.5 (2020)	70.6 (2020)	70.4 (2020)
Indonesia	86.5	88.6	84.6	95.8 (2018)	100.0 (2018)	91.8 (2018)
Lao People's Democratic Republic	35.6	35.9	35.3	70.6	71.4	69.9
Malaysia	85.9	88.4	83.6	86.1	0.0	85.5
Myanmar	8.8	9.0	8.5	11.8 (2018)	11.8 (2018)	11.7 (2018)
Philippines	41.5 (2009)	42.1 (2009)	40.9 (2009)	66.4	67.7	65.2
Singapore	...	...	...	96.9 (2020)	...	...
Thailand	98.5	100.0	97.1	96.5 (2022)	96.2 (2022)	96.9 (2022)
Timor-Leste	...	...	...	60.1 (2020)	62.8 (2020)	57.5 (2020)
Viet Nam[c]	90.4	...	...	99.9 (2018)	99.8 (2018)	100.0 (2018)
The Pacific						
Cook Islands	...	...	...	87.9	85.5	90.2
Fiji	49.6 (2006)	50.6 (2006)	48.7 (2006)	89.3	88.5	90.0
Kiribati	...	...	...	97.7 (2020)	100.0 (2020)	95.6 (2020)
Marshall Islands	69.5 (2002)	69.7 (2002)	69.3 (2002)	58.8	60.2	57.5
Micronesia, Federated States of	...	...	...	12.6	13.0	12.3
Nauru	88.1 (2012)	76.0 (2012)	100.0 (2012)	96.0 (2020)	100.0 (2020)	92.0 (2020)
Niue	...	...	...	90.9	81.8	100.0
Palau	...	...	...	89.3 (2020)	100.0 (2020)	80.0 (2020)
Papua New Guinea	...	...	...	71.4 (2018)	71.2 (2018)	71.6 (2018)
Samoa	25.6	28.5	22.8	34.9	36.5	33.3
Solomon Islands[d]	66.7	...	...	65.6 (2019)	67.0 (2019)	64.3 (2019)
Tonga	...	...	...	94.6 (2020)	88.9 (2020)	100.0 (2020)
Tuvalu	...	...	...	89.0	77.5	100.0
Vanuatu[e]	66.7 (2011)	...	...	98.0 (2020)	100.0 (2020)	96.2 (2020)
Developed ADB Member Economies						
Australia	52.6	52.1	53.0	82.0 (2020)	81.8 (2020)	82.2 (2020)
Japan	...	...	...	91.8 (2015)	...	...
New Zealand	...	...	...	89.6 (2020)	88.7 (2020)	90.5 (2020)

... = data not available, 0.0 = magnitude is less than half of unit employed, ADB = Asian Development Bank.

a According to the United Nations Educational, Scientific and Cultural Organization (UNESCO), this is the percentage of children who participate in one or more organized learning programs, including programs that offer a combination of education and care, 1 year before the official age for entry to primary education (varies by economy). An organized learning program is one that consists of a coherent set or sequence of educational activities designed with the intention of achieving predetermined learning outcomes or the accomplishment of a specific set of educational tasks.

b The figures for the following economies and years are estimates by the UNESCO Institute for Statistics (UIS) as published on the Global SDG Indicators Database: Azerbaijan; Bangladesh (2009); Cambodia (2006 and 2015); Hong Kong, China (2012–2019); Indonesia (2009, 2014, 2018); Nepal (2013); Pakistan (2014–2019); Samoa (2000–2001); Singapore (2018–2020); Tuvalu (2018); Viet Nam (2013–2014). For the purposes of estimating participation rates by age, the UIS may make one or more of the following: (i) an adjustment to account for over- or under-reporting in enrolments; (ii) an estimate of the number of enrolments in a given age group; (iii) a redistribution of enrolments of unknown age (across known ages); or (iv) for small economies, an estimate of the population in the official age group. In all cases, estimates are based on evidence from the economy itself.

c Earliest year available with female-male breakdown is 2014.

d Earliest year available with female-male breakdown is 2013.

e Earliest year available with female-male breakdown is 2019.

Source: United Nations. SDG Global Database. https://unstats.un.org/sdgs/dataportal (accessed 17 July 2023).

Goal 4. Ensure inclusive and equitable quality education and promote lifelong learning opportunities for all

Table 1.4.4: Selected Indicators for Sustainable Development Goal 4—Teacher Training and Supply

ADB Regional Member	Target 4.c: By 2030, substantially increase the supply of qualified teachers, including through international cooperation for teacher training in developing countries (or economies), especially least developed countries (or economies) and small island developing states															
	Proportion of Teachers Who Have Received at Least the Minimum Organized Teacher Training, by Education Level (% of total teachers)															
	4.c.1.a: Preprimary				4.c.1.b: Primary				4.c.1.c: Lower Secondary				4.c.1.d: Upper Secondary			
	2010		2021		2010		2021		2010		2021		2010		2021	
Developing ADB Member Economies																
Central and West Asia																
Afghanistan	...		...		...		...		...		...		...		...	
Armenia[a]	87.8		74.7		77.5	(2005)	73.9		...		73.8		...		76.0	
Azerbaijan[a,b]	90.9		91.3		100.0		99.7		...		99.6		...		96.7	
Georgia	96.6	(2003)	...		94.6	(2009)	...		94.6	(2009)	...		94.8	(2009)	...	
Kazakhstan[c,d]	...		...		...		100.0	(2020)	...		...		...		...	
Kyrgyz Republic	42.7		...		68.4		95.4	(2017)	...		...		...		...	
Pakistan[b]	...		...		84.2		77.3	(2019)	...		58.6	(2019)	88.1	(2011)	84.7	(2017)
Tajikistan	85.2		100.0	(2016)	92.9		100.0	(2017)	94.0	(2003)	...		94.3	(2003)	...	
Turkmenistan	...		...		...		99.6		...		...		...		...	
Uzbekistan	100.0		100.0		100.0		100.0		...		99.0	(2017)	...		93.4	(2017)
East Asia																
China, People's Republic of	...		...		...		...		...		...		...		...	
Hong Kong, China	95.1		97.4		95.6		96.1		...		...		...		...	
Korea, Republic of	100.0	(2011)	100.0	(2020)	100.0		100.0	(2020)	...		...		100.0		100.0	(2020)
Mongolia	89.9		95.7	(2019)	97.6		88.9	(2019)	100.0	(2007)	...		100.0	(2006)	...	
Taipei,China	...		...		...		...		...		...		...		...	
South Asia																
Bangladesh	...		...		57.7	(2011)	50.4	(2017)	58.5		62.7		40.7		61.9	
Bhutan	93.8	(2000)	100.0	(2020)	91.5	(2008)	100.0		90.2	(2008)	100.0	(2020)	72.2	(2008)	100.0	(2018)
India[a,b,c,d]	...		94.8	(2022)	...		88.7	(2022)	...		88.6	(2022)	...		92.1	(2022)
Maldives	39.0		66.2	(2019)	77.0		88.8	(2019)	97.6		94.1	(2019)	94.5		91.3	(2019)
Nepal	81.5		82.4		73.7		97.2		57.2		86.0		72.3		43.1	
Sri Lanka[a,b]	83.1		81.5	(2020)	82.1		82.6	(2020)	...		83.7	(2020)	...		78.9	(2020)
Southeast Asia																
Brunei Darussalam[a,b]	73.0		58.1	(2020)	87.1		85.2	(2020)	...		89.5	(2019)	...		90.5	(2020)
Cambodia	98.3		100.0		99.1		100.0		99.8		100.0		99.8	(2007)	100.0	
Indonesia	...		...		...		...		...		...		...		...	
Lao People's Democratic Republic	97.5		94.5		95.4		99.1		99.3		99.7		99.4		99.7	
Malaysia[d]	...		37.1		95.4		97.1		...		...		...		...	
Myanmar	58.5		81.4	(2018)	99.9		95.3	(2018)	98.3		89.5	(2018)	100.0		87.7	(2018)
Philippines[a,b,c,d]	...		100.0	(2020)	...		100.0	(2020)	...		100.0	(2020)	...		100.0	(2020)
Singapore	...		...		98.6	(2009)	98.2	(2020)	...		...		...		...	
Thailand[a,b,c,d]	...		100.0	(2022)	...		100.0	(2022)	...		100.0	(2022)	...		100.0	(2022)
Timor-Leste	...		...		...		...		...		...		...		...	
Viet Nam	98.5	(2011)	81.7		98.3		69.6		99.1		83.3		...		...	
The Pacific																
Cook Islands	69.7	(2011)	90.0		96.6	(2011)	97.4		...		...		...		...	
Fiji[d]	...		94.9		100.0	(2011)	50.1		...		...		94.8	(2008)	...	
Kiribati	...		93.6	(2020)	94.1		90.5	(2020)	79.2	(2008)	85.9	(2020)	33.6	(2008)	47.0	(2016)
Marshall Islands[a]	100.0	(2002)	...		...		51.4		...		46.9	(2020)	...		85.5	
Micronesia, Federated States of[a,d]	...		26.4		...		38.0		...		31.7		...		30.3	
Nauru	82.1	(2007)	100.0	(2016)	74.2	(2007)	100.0	(2016)	...		100.0	(2016)	...		100.0	(2016)
Niue[a,b,c,d]	...		100.0		...		100.0		...		100.0		...		...	
Palau	...		...		...		100.0		...		...		...		100.0	
Papua New Guinea	...		...		...		...		...		...		...		...	
Samoa[d]	...		100.0	(2018)	...		...		...		...		71.9	(2009)	54.7	(2020)
Solomon Islands	61.3	(2011)	...		58.0		82.4	(2019)	70.8		93.9	(2019)	70.9		...	
Tonga[c,d]	...		52.7	(2020)	...		94.1	(2020)	...		...		...		...	
Tuvalu[a,b,c,d]	...		100.0		...		62.0		...		67.1	(2018)	...		62.0	(2018)
Vanuatu	44.6		100.0		55.1		100.0		...		...		...		...	
Developed ADB Member Economies																
Australia	...		...		...		...		...		...		...		...	
Japan	...		...		...		...		...		...		...		...	
New Zealand	...		...		...		...		...		...		...		...	

... = data not available, ADB = Asian Development Bank.

a For Indicator 4.c.1.d, the earliest available estimate for Armenia is for 2019: 75.4%. For Azerbaijan, the earliest available estimate is for 2018: 94.9%. For India, the earliest available estimate is for 2017: 76.4%. For Sri Lanka, the earliest available estimate is for 2016: 77.3%. For Brunei Darussalam, the earliest available estimate is for 2014: 90.4%. For the Philippines, the earliest available estimate is for 2016: 100%. For Thailand, the earliest available estimate is for 2015: 100%. For Niue, the earliest available estimate is for 2015: 100%. For the Marshall Islands, the earliest available estimate is for 2020: 66.9%. For the Federated States of Micronesia, the earliest available estimate is for 2013: 1.7%. For Tuvalu, the earliest available estimate is for 2016: 34.6%.

b For Indicator 4.c.1.c, the earliest available estimate for Azerbaijan is for 2016: 91.6%. For Pakistan, the earliest available estimate is for 2015: 61.2%. For India, the earliest available estimate is for 2016: 77.0%. For Sri Lanka, the earliest available estimate is for 2013: 72.1%. For Brunei Darussalam, the earliest available estimate is for 2014: 94.0%. For the Philippines, the earliest available estimate is for 2016: 100%. For Thailand, the earliest available estimate is for 2015: 100%. For Niue, the earliest available estimate is for 2015: 100%. For Tuvalu, the earliest available estimate is for 2016: 52.4%.

c For Indicator 4.c.1.b, the earliest available estimate for Kazakhstan is for 2014: 100%. For India, the earliest available estimate is for 2017: 69.8%. For the Philippines, the earliest available estimate is for 2014: 100%. For Thailand, the earliest available estimate is for 2014: 100%. For Niue, the earliest available estimate is for 2015: 100%. For Tonga, the earliest available estimate is for 2013: 99.6%. For Tuvalu, the earliest available estimate is for 2016: 76.6%.

d For Indicator 4.c.1.a, the earliest available estimate for the Kazakhstan is for 2014: 100%. For India, the earliest available estimate is for 2020: 83.8%. For Malaysia, the earliest available estimate is for 2017: 36.8%. For the Philippines, the earliest available estimate is for 2015: 100%. For Thailand, the earliest available estimate is for 2021: 100%. For Fiji, the earliest available estimate is for 2020: 93.5%. For the Federated States of Micronesia, the earliest available estimate is for 2018: 26.7%. For Niue, the earliest available estimate is for 2015: 100%. For Samoa, the earliest available estimate is for 2014: 100%. For Tonga, the earliest available estimate is for 2012: 100%. For Tuvalu, the earliest available estimate is for 2012: 100%.

Source: United Nations. Sustainable Development Goals Global Database. https://unstats.un.org/sdgs/dataportal (accessed 15 June 2023).

Table 1.5.1: Selected Indicators for Sustainable Development Goal 5—Early Marriage and Women in Leadership

ADB Regional Member	Target 5.3: Eliminate all harmful practices such as child, early, and forced marriage, and female genital mutilation				Target 5.5: Ensure women's full and effective participation in, and equal opportunities for leadership at, all levels of decision-making in political, economic, and public life		
	5.3.1: Proportion of Women Aged 20–24 Years Who Were Married or in a Union (%)				5.5.1.a: Proportion of Seats Held by Women in National Parliaments (%)		5.5.2: Proportion of Women in Managerial Positions (%)
	Before Age 15		Before Age 18				
	2010	2018	2010	2018	2010	2022	2021
Developing ADB Member Economies							
Central and West Asia[a]					**18.7**	**24.2**	...
Afghanistan	...	4.2 (2017)	...	28.3 (2017)	27.3	27.0	4.9 (2020)
Armenia	...	0.0 (2016)	...	5.3 (2016)	9.2	34.6	29.7
Azerbaijan	1.9 (2011)	...	11.0 (2011)	...	11.4	18.3	36.2
Georgia	1.1	0.3	14.0	13.9	5.1	19.1	36.1 (2020)
Kazakhstan	...	0.2 (2015)	...	7.0 (2015)	17.8	27.4	41.1 (2020)
Kyrgyz Republic	0.9 (2014)	0.3	11.6 (2014)	12.9	25.6	20.5	42.8
Pakistan	2.8 (2013)	3.6	21.0 (2013)	18.3	22.2	20.5	5.7
Tajikistan	...	0.1 (2017)	...	8.7 (2017)	17.5	27.0	...
Turkmenistan	...	0.2 (2019)	...	6.1 (2019)	16.8	25.9	...
Uzbekistan	0.3 (2006)	...	7.2 (2006)	...	22.0	33.3	...
East Asia[a]					**20.3**	**24.2**	...
China, People's Republic of	...	0.1 (2020)	...	2.8 (2020)	21.3	24.9	...
Hong Kong, China	...	...	...	...	...	...	38.3 (2022)
Korea, Republic of	...	...	...	...	14.7	18.6	14.6 (2022)
Mongolia	0.1 (2013)	0.9	5.2 (2013)	12.0	4.0	17.1	41.9 (2022)
Taipei,China	...	...	...	...	...	...	30.5 (2020)
South Asia[a]					**18.7**	**17.6**	...
Bangladesh	22.4 (2014)	15.5 (2019)	58.6 (2014)	51.4 (2019)	18.6	20.9	10.7 (2017)
Bhutan	6.2	...	25.8	...	8.5	17.4	39.7
India	...	6.8 (2016)	...	27.3 (2016)	10.8	14.9	16.6
Maldives	0.3 (2009)	0.0 (2017)	3.9 (2009)	2.2 (2017)	6.5	4.6	18.7 (2019)
Nepal	...	7.9 (2019)	...	32.8 (2019)	33.2	33.6	13.2 (2017)
Sri Lanka	...	0.9 (2016)	...	9.8 (2016)	5.8	5.3	27.0 (2020)
Southeast Asia[a]					**19.3**	**25.5**	...
Brunei Darussalam	...	...	...	...	...	9.1	42.6
Cambodia	1.9 (2014)	...	18.5 (2014)	...	21.1	20.8	29.2
Indonesia	...	0.6	...	11.2	18.0	21.9	31.7 (2022)
Lao People's Democratic Republic	...	7.1 (2017)	...	32.7 (2017)	25.2	22.0	59.0 (2017)
Malaysia	...	...	...	...	9.9	15.0	24.9 (2020)
Myanmar	...	1.9 (2016)	...	16.0 (2016)	4.3 (2011)	15.3	27.8 (2020)
Philippines	...	2.2 (2017)	...	16.5 (2017)	21.0	27.7	53.4
Singapore	...	– (2020)	...	0.1 (2020)	23.4	29.1	38.1
Thailand	...	3.0 (2019)	...	20.2 (2019)	13.3	15.8	36.9 (2022)
Timor-Leste	...	2.6 (2016)	...	14.9 (2016)	29.2	40.0	13.3
Viet Nam	0.9 (2014)	...	10.6 (2014)	...	25.8	30.3	25.6 (2022)
The Pacific[a]					**2.5**	**5.9**	...
Cook Islands	...	...	...	...	...	...	59.8 (2019)
Fiji	...	...	...	...	8.5 (2006)	19.6	38.9 (2016)
Kiribati	2.8 (2009)	2.4 (2019)	20.3 (2009)	18.4 (2019)	4.4	6.7	43.3 (2020)
Marshall Islands	5.5 (2007)	...	26.3 (2007)	...	3.0	6.1	33.3
Micronesia, Federated States of	...	...	...	...	–	7.1	20.3 (2014)
Nauru	1.9 (2007)	...	26.8 (2007)	...	–	10.5	57.6
Niue	...	...	...	...	...	...	39.8 (2017)
Palau	...	...	...	...	–	6.3	46.8 (2020)
Papua New Guinea	2.1 (2006)	8.0	21.3 (2006)	27.3	0.9	–	18.1 (2010)
Samoa	0.7 (2014)	0.9 (2020)	10.8 (2014)	7.4 (2020)	8.2	7.8	43.1 (2017)
Solomon Islands	...	5.6 (2015)	...	21.3 (2015)	–	8.0	25.7 (2013)
Tonga	0.3 (2012)	0.4 (2019)	5.6 (2012)	10.1 (2019)	3.1	3.7	44.3
Tuvalu	– (2007)	– (2020)	9.9 (2007)	1.8 (2020)	–	6.3	37.0 (2017)
Vanuatu	2.5 (2013)	...	21.4 (2013)	...	3.9	–	36.4 (2020)
Developed ADB Member Economies[a]					**18.1**	**20.6**	...
Australia	...	...	...	...	27.3	31.1	39.7
Japan	...	...	...	...	11.3	9.7	12.9 (2022)
New Zealand	...	...	...	...	33.6	49.2	...
DEVELOPING ADB MEMBER ECONOMIES[a]					**18.7**	**22.5**	...
ALL ADB REGIONAL MEMBERS[a]					**18.6**	**22.3**	...

... = data not available, 0.0 = magnitude is less than half of unit employed, – = magnitude equals zero, ADB = Asian Development Bank.

a For proportion of seats held by women in national parliaments, regional aggregates are estimated as weighted averages based on the number of parliament seats in reporting economies.

Sources: United Nations. SDG Global Database. https://unstats.un.org/sdgs/dataportal (accessed 22 July 2023). For Indicator 5.5.1.a for Afghanistan, Bangladesh, and Nepal: Inter-Parliamentary Union. Women in National Parliaments. http://archive.ipu.org/wmn-e/classif-arc.htm (accessed 22 July 2023). For Indicator 5.5.2: International Labour Organization. ILOSTAT Database. https://ilostat.ilo.org/data (accessed 22 July 2023).

Goal 6. Ensure availability and sustainable management of water and sanitation for all

Table 1.6.1: Selected Indicators for Sustainable Development Goal 6—Clean Water and Sanitation

ADB Regional Member	Target 6.1: By 2030, achieve universal and equitable access to safe and affordable drinking water for all 6.1.1: Proportion of Population Using Safely Managed Drinking Water Services (%)					
	2010			2022		
	Total	Urban	Rural	Total	Urban	Rural
Developing ADB Member Economies						
Central and West Asia						
Afghanistan	19.0	28.0	17.0	30.0	36.0	28.0
Armenia	83.0	...	...	82.0	...	...
Azerbaijan	65.0	91.0	58.0	72.0	92.0	81.0
Georgia	66.0	88.0	39.0	69.0	88.0	41.0
Kazakhstan	78.0	...	...	89.0 (2021)	...	...
Kyrgyz Republic	58.0	88.0	41.0	76.0	92.0	67.0
Pakistan	38.0	50.0	32.0	51.0	57.0	47.0
Tajikistan	47.0	...	...	55.0	...	...
Turkmenistan	82.0	92.0	73.0	95.0	97.0	92.0
Uzbekistan	67.0	87.0	47.0	80.0	89.0	71.0
East Asia						
China, People's Republic of	...	90.0	...	...	98.0	...
Hong Kong, China	99.0	99.0	...	100.0	100.0	...
Korea, Republic of	98.0	...	...	99.0	...	...
Mongolia	29.0	40.0	5.0	39.0	51.0	13.0
Taipei,China	...	...	...	...	...	...
South Asia						
Bangladesh	55.0	42.0	61.0	59.0	54.0	62.0
Bhutan	26.0	41.0	19.0	73.0	59.0	85.0
India	...	...	44.0	...	...	66.0
Maldives	...	...	...	...	...	...
Nepal	29.0	38.0	28.0	16.0	23.0	14.0
Sri Lanka	46.0	88.0	37.0	47.0	83.0	39.0
Southeast Asia						
Brunei Darussalam	...	...	...	...	...	...
Cambodia	22.0	51.0	15.0	29.0	58.0	20.0
Indonesia	27.0	33.0	21.0	30.0	35.0	24.0
Lao People's Democratic Republic	14.0	24.0	9.0	18.0	27.0	12.0
Malaysia	93.0	...	...	94.0	...	...
Myanmar	43.0	68.0	33.0	57.0	72.0	50.0
Philippines	45.0	61.0	32.0	48.0	62.0	35.0
Singapore	100.0	100.0	...	100.0	100.0	...
Thailand	...	...	...	...	...	...
Timor-Leste	...	...	...	...	...	...
Viet Nam	51.0	75.0	41.0	58.0	76.0	46.0
The Pacific						
Cook Islands	...	...	...	...	...	...
Fiji	40.0	52.0	27.0	42.0	53.0	27.0
Kiribati	12.0	18.0	6.0	14.0	20.0	7.0
Marshall Islands	...	...	...	...	...	...
Micronesia, Federated States of	...	...	...	...	...	...
Nauru	...	...	...	...	...	...
Niue	97.0	...	...	94.0	...	...
Palau	76.0	83.0	56.0	90.0	98.0	57.0
Papua New Guinea	...	...	...	...	...	...
Samoa	61.0	85.0	55.0	62.0	90.0	56.0
Solomon Islands	...	...	...	...	...	...
Tonga	29.0	50.0	23.0	30.0	51.0	23.0
Tuvalu	8.0	10.0	5.0	9.0	10.0	5.0
Vanuatu	...	55.0	...	...	56.0	...
Developed ADB Member Economies						
Australia	...	99.0	...	...	100.0	...
Japan	98.0	...	...	99.0	...	...
New Zealand	89.0	...	...	100.0	...	...

Table 1.6.1: Selected Indicators for Sustainable Development Goal 6—Clean Water and Sanitation *(continued)*

ADB Regional Member	Target 6.2: By 2030, achieve access to adequate and equitable sanitation and hygiene for all and end open defecation, paying special attention to the needs of women and girls and those in vulnerable situations 6.2.1a: Proportion of Population Using Safely Managed Sanitation Services (%)					
	2010			2022		
	Total	Urban	Rural	Total	Urban	Rural
Developing ADB Member Economies						
Central and West Asia						
Afghanistan	...	...	...	...	...	...
Armenia	13.0	3.0	...	11.0	–	...
Azerbaijan	60.0	49.0	...	69.0 (2019)	63.0	...
Georgia	34.0	23.0	48.0	24.0	14.0	39.0
Kazakhstan	...	87.0	...	...	84.0	...
Kyrgyz Republic	89.0	81.0	93.0	93.0	86.0	96.0
Pakistan	...	...	20.0	...	...	40.0
Tajikistan	...	...	57.0	...	...	59.0
Turkmenistan	...	...	...	...	...	...
Uzbekistan	74.0	65.0	83.0	75.0	63.0	86.0
East Asia						
China, People's Republic of	34.0	53.0	15.0	67.0	85.0	37.0
Hong Kong, China	75.0	75.0	...	97.0	97.0	...
Korea, Republic of	94.0	...	...	99.0	...	...
Mongolia	53.0	62.0	36.0	66.0	70.0	56.0
Taipei,China	...	...	...	...	...	...
South Asia						
Bangladesh	18.0	26.0	15.0	31.0	29.0	32.0
Bhutan	46.0	47.0	46.0	51.0	41.0	58.0
India	26.0	30.0	24.0	52.0	43.0	57.0
Maldives	...	...	...	...	...	...
Nepal	27.0	28.0	27.0	51.0	45.0	52.0
Sri Lanka	...	...	...	...	...	...
Southeast Asia						
Brunei Darussalam	...	...	...	...	...	...
Cambodia	19.0	36.0	15.0	37.0	45.0	34.0
Indonesia	...	...	...	...	...	...
Lao People's Democratic Republic	44.0	55.0	39.0	61.0	63.0	60.0
Malaysia	79.0	...	...	86.0	...	...
Myanmar	61.0	61.0	61.0	61.0	53.0	64.0
Philippines	51.0	49.0	52.0	63.0	56.0	69.0
Singapore	100.0	100.0	...	100.0	100.0	
Thailand	23.0	26.0	20.0	26.0	30.0	22.0
Timor-Leste	...	...	...	...	...	...
Viet Nam	38.0	40.0	37.0	44.0	41.0	45.0
The Pacific						
Cook Islands	...	...	...	...	...	...
Fiji	46.0	43.0	51.0	49.0	43.0	57.0
Kiribati	22.0	25.0	20.0	25.0	25.0	25.0
Marshall Islands	...	...	...	...	...	...
Micronesia, Federated States of	...	...	...	...	...	...
Nauru	...	...	...	...	...	...
Niue	...	...	...	...	...	...
Palau	...	...	...	...	...	...
Papua New Guinea	...	30.0	...	...	28.0	...
Samoa	49.0	43.0	51.0	43.0	37.0	44.0
Solomon Islands	...	...	...	...	...	...
Tonga	37.0	29.0	39.0	32.0	22.0	35.0
Tuvalu	44.0	37.0	51.0	37.0	35.0	42.0
Vanuatu	...	38.0	...	...	30.0	...
Developed ADB Member Economies						
Australia	95.0	...	...	96.0	...	...
Japan	98.0	...	...	99.0	...	...
New Zealand	86.0	...	...	89.0	...	...

Goal 6: Ensure availability and sustainable management of water and sanitation for all

Table 1.6.1: Selected Indicators for Sustainable Development Goal 6—Clean Water and Sanitation *(continued)*

ADB Regional Member	Target 6.4: By 2030, substantially increase water-use efficiency across all sectors and ensure sustainable withdrawals and supply of freshwater to address water scarcity and substantially reduce the number of people suffering from water scarcity 6.4.2: Level of Water Stress, Freshwater Withdrawal as a Proportion of Available Freshwater Resources (%)			Target 6.a: By 2030, expand international cooperation and capacity-building support to developing countries in water- and sanitation-related activities and programmes, including water harvesting, desalination, water efficiency, wastewater treatment, and recycling and reuse technologies 6.a.1: Amount of Water- and Sanitation-Related Official Development Assistance as Part of a Government-Coordinated Spending Plan ($ million)		
	2010	2015	2020	2010	2015	2021
Developing ADB Member Economies						
Central and West Asia						
Afghanistan	54.8	54.8	54.8	114.6	82.8	79.5
Armenia	42.9	66.0	57.1	87.9	42.7	22.5
Azerbaijan	48.4	51.6	55.6	18.8	73.2	6.3
Georgia	5.8	5.3	5.4	56.3	49.2	37.1
Kazakhstan	33.0	30.0	34.1	20.9	0.2	0.4
Kyrgyz Republic	50.0	50.0	50.0	12.0	24.4	70.5
Pakistan	113.7	120.8	116.3	85.8	310.2	196.0
Tajikistan	71.6	68.7	69.9	23.7	45.2	102.5
Turkmenistan	144.1	144.7	135.2	0.0	...	0.0
Uzbekistan	143.1	158.1	168.9	33.7	117.3	126.8
East Asia						
China, People's Republic of	42.9	43.2	41.5	294.6	216.3	63.2
Hong Kong, China	...	...	...	...	...	...
Korea, Republic of	85.2	85.2	85.2	...	...	...
Mongolia	3.9	3.2	3.4	25.8	8.4	29.9
Taipei,China	...	...	...	...	...	...
South Asia						
Bangladesh	5.7	5.7	5.7	189.6	217.9	283.9
Bhutan	1.4	1.4	1.4	3.0	7.4	11.4
India	66.5	66.5	66.5	465.1	483.6	420.2
Maldives	3.4	15.7	15.7	2.2	8.2	25.8
Nepal	8.3	8.3	8.3	81.3	116.7	185.2
Sri Lanka	90.8	90.8	90.8	168.6	163.1	133.0
Southeast Asia						
Brunei Darussalam	3.5	3.5	3.5	...	...	...
Cambodia	1.0	1.0	1.0	42.8	85.7	309.4
Indonesia	24.2	28.8	29.7	285.7	134.3	204.2
Lao People's Democratic Republic	3.8	5.1	4.8	28.8	114.8	75.4
Malaysia	3.1	3.2	3.4	58.4	70.9	0.6
Myanmar	5.8	5.8	5.8	22.0	82.9	42.4
Philippines	25.5	26.4	26.3	48.3	29.0	45.9
Singapore	219.9	84.6	83.1	...	...	...
Thailand	23.0	23.0	23.0	7.3	8.3	1.9
Timor-Leste	28.3	28.3	28.3	19.0	17.9	3.3
Viet Nam	18.1	18.1	18.1	402.5	602.8	413.3
The Pacific						
Cook Islands	...	...	...	0.6	4.7	2.0 (2019)
Fiji	0.3	0.3	0.3	1.9	3.6	12.8
Kiribati	...	...	...	0.1	7.2	10.9
Marshall Islands	...	...	...	0.2	1.1	1.1
Micronesia, Federated States of	...	...	...	0.1	2.0	1.5
Nauru	...	...	...	0.2	5.7	0.0
Niue	...	...	...	0.4	0.0 (2016)	0.0
Palau	...	...	...	0.2	1.4	1.4
Papua New Guinea	0.1	0.1	0.1	14.6	6.8	21.4
Samoa	...	...	...	16.2	21.1	0.7
Solomon Islands	...	...	...	6.4	8.5	10.9
Tonga	...	...	...	1.1	1.8	1.2
Tuvalu	...	...	...	0.0	3.0	3.3
Vanuatu	...	...	...	0.9	3.4	9.8
Developed ADB Member Economies						
Australia	5.3	3.7	3.5	...	...	...
Japan	37.2	36.7	36.1	...	...	...
New Zealand	4.2	8.1	8.1	...	...	...

... = data not available, 0.0 = magnitude is less than half of unit employed, $ = United States dollars, ADB = Asian Development Bank.

Source: United Nations. SDG Global Database. https://unstats.un.org/sdgs/dataportal (accessed 12 July 2023).

Table 1.7.1: Selected Indicators for Sustainable Development Goal 7—Affordable and Clean Energy

ADB Regional Member	Target 7.1: By 2030, ensure universal access to affordable, reliable, and modern energy services								Target 7.2: By 2030, increase substantially the share of renewable energy in the global energy mix		Target 7.3: By 2030, double the global rate of improvement in energy efficiency	
	7.1.1: Proportion of Population with Access to Electricity (%)						7.1.2: Proportion of Population with Primary Reliance on Clean Fuels and Technology (%)		7.2.1: Renewable Energy Share in Total Final Energy Consumption (%)		7.3.1: Energy Intensity Measured in Terms of Primary Energy and GDP (MJ/$ 2011 PPP GDP)	
	Total		Urban		Rural							
	2010	2021	2010	2021	2010	2021	2010	2021	2010	2020	2010	2020
Developing ADB Member Economies												
Central and West Asia												
Afghanistan	42.7	97.7	82.8	99.5	30.2	97.1	20.0	35.0	15.2	17.6	2.5	2.6
Armenia	99.8	100.0	99.7	99.9	100.0	100.0	>95	>95	9.4	8.4	3.9	4.0
Azerbaijan	99.9	100.0	100.0	100.0	99.9	100.0	93.0	>95	4.5	1.2	3.9	4.7
Georgia	100.0	100.0	100.0	99.9	100.0	100.0	66.0	91.0	39.2	23.5	3.6	4.0
Kazakhstan	100.0	100.0	100.0	100.0	100.0	100.0	92.0	94.0	1.4	1.8	8.6	5.8
Kyrgyz Republic	99.0	99.7	99.1	99.8	98.9	99.6	71.0	78.0	25.6	30.0	5.1	5.1
Pakistan	87.1	94.9	96.5	99.9	82.1	91.9	35.0	51.0	47.4	46.6	4.5	4.0
Tajikistan	98.8	99.6	99.4	98.9	98.6	99.8	69.0	86.0	61.8	38.8	5.1	4.4
Turkmenistan	100.0	100.0	100.0	100.0	100.0	100.0	>95	>95	0.1	0.1	21.7	11.1
Uzbekistan	99.6	99.9	100.0	100.0	99.2	99.8	86.0	83.0	1.4	1.0	13.4	7.5
East Asia												
China, People's Republic of	99.7	100.0	100.0	100.0	99.4	100.0	58.0	83.0	12.3	14.8	8.9	6.4
Hong Kong, China	100.0	100.0	100.0	100.0	100.0	100.0	..	..	0.2	0.3	1.6	1.3
Korea, Republic of	100.0	100.0	100.0	100.0	100.0	100.0	>95	>95	1.3	3.6	6.1	5.3
Mongolia	78.5	100.0	96.1	100.0	41.9	100.0	35.0	53.0	4.5	4.0	8.1	6.6
Taipei,China	..	..	..	..	..	..	..	..	1.6	..	..	..
South Asia												
Bangladesh	55.3	99.0	90.1	99.7	40.0	98.5	13.0	26.0	40.3	28.0	2.5	2.0
Bhutan	73.3	100.0	99.3	100.0	59.4	100.0	64.0	87.0	90.8	88.4	10.1	8.3
India	76.3	99.6	94.0	100.0	68.4	99.3	36.0	71.0	36.2	35.8	5.3	4.3
Maldives	99.0	100.0	99.6	100.0	98.7	100.0	93.0	>95	1.4	1.3	2.3	3.4
Nepal	68.6	89.9	95.5	94.2	63.2	93.5 (2018)	21.0	35.0	87.3	74.5	5.9	5.7
Sri Lanka	85.3	100.0	95.6	100.0	83.0	100.0	22.0	33.0	61.9	49.3	2.2	1.7
Southeast Asia												
Brunei Darussalam	100.0	100.0	100.0	100.0	100.0	100.0	>95	>95	–	0.0	5.2	6.1
Cambodia	31.1	82.5	91.3	98.9	15.8	77.1	12.0	44.0	64.8	51.4	5.1	5.1
Indonesia	94.2	99.2	99.0	99.9	89.4	98.2	41.0	87.0	36.0	22.0	4.3	3.1
Lao People's Democratic Republic	70.2	100.0	97.3	100.0	58.6	100.0	<5	9.0	64.9	49.9	3.3	4.3
Malaysia	99.5	100.0	99.6	100.0	99.0	100.0	>95	94.0	2.0	5.8	5.2	4.5
Myanmar	48.8	72.5	89.0	93.6	32.5	62.8	10.0	44.0	84.9	59.8	4.2	3.6
Philippines	85.5	97.5	93.9	98.6	78.5	96.5	41.0	48.0	32.6	29.1	3.1	2.8
Singapore	100.0	100.0	100.0	100.0	100.0	100.0	>95	>95	0.5	0.9	2.5	2.5
Thailand	99.7	100.0	100.0	99.8	99.5	100.0	73.0	85.0	22.8	20.8	5.1	4.6
Timor-Leste	38.0	100.0	83.4	100.0	20.6	100.0	<5	15.0	34.8	11.4	1.4	1.8
Viet Nam	97.4	100.0	99.9	100.0	96.4	100.0	51.0	>95	34.6	19.1	4.4	4.1
The Pacific												
Cook Islands	99.1	100.0	99.0	100.0	..	..	82.0	79.0	7.3	13.1	..	..
Fiji	92.4	92.1	96.9	96.0	87.4	86.8	33.0	51.0	28.0	31.8	2.2	2.0
Kiribati	63.2	92.8	89.5	88.3	39.4	94.3 (2020)	<5	12.0	50.2	42.8	7.0	6.5
Marshall Islands	89.4	99.8	92.4	96.0	81.1	100.0	54.0	67.0	13.7	12.0	10.5	9.7
Micronesia, Federated States of	64.5	83.6	84.6	97.6	58.8	79.4	12.0	13.0	2.0	2.0	4.1	5.6
Nauru	99.2	100.0	98.4	100.0	100.0 (2015)	100.0 (2020)	>95	>95	0.0	1.4	8.7	5.1
Niue	99.4	99.5	99.7	100.0	..	..	94.0	>95	26.7	22.7	..	..
Palau	98.8	100.0	99.4	100.0	96.9	100.0	51.0	43.0	–	0.9	10.6	10.5
Papua New Guinea	19.5	20.9	71.2	65.2	11.8	14.0	8.0	10.0	55.3	54.3	5.7	5.5
Samoa	96.4	98.3	98.9	100.0	95.8	97.9	27.0	37.0	41.3	37.5	3.8	4.1
Solomon Islands	35.4	76.3	65.4	79.2	27.9	75.4	8.0	9.0	45.1	49.0	6.2	4.4
Tonga	92.8	100.0	97.9	100.0	91.2	100.0	60.0	87.0	1.0	1.9	3.1	4.0
Tuvalu	96.7	99.7	98.1	100.0	95.1	99.1	47.0	75.0	0.5	6.7	3.9	2.6
Vanuatu	44.1	70.0	82.3	97.0	31.7	60.7	12.0	7.0	38.1	26.0	3.7	4.3
Developed ADB Member Economies												
Australia	100.0	100.0	100.0	100.0	100.0	100.0	>95	>95	8.2	10.9	5.3	4.4
Japan	100.0	100.0	100.0	100.0	100.0	100.0	>95	>95	4.7	8.5	4.3	3.2
New Zealand	100.0	100.0	100.0	100.0	100.0	100.0	>95	>95	29.4	28.6	4.6	3.9
	83.6	91.4	95.9	97.7	72.9	84.5	57.0	71.0	16.0	19.1	5.5	4.6
WORLD	**83.6**	**91.4**	**95.9**	**97.7**	**72.9**	**84.6**	**57.0**	**71.0**	**16.0**	**19.1**	**5.5**	**4.6**

... = data not available, – = magnitude equals zero, 0.0 = magnitude is less than half of unit employed, < = less than, > = greater than, $ = United States dollars, ADB = Asian Development Bank, GDP = gross domestic product, MJ = megajoule, PPP = purchasing power parity.

Sources: United Nations. SDG Global Database. https://unstats.un.org/sdgs/dataportal (accessed 16 July 2023). For Indicator 7.2.1 for Taipei,China: World Bank. DataBank: Sustainable Energy for All. https://databank.worldbank.org/source/sustainable-energy-for-all# (accessed 16 July 2023).

Goal 8. Promote sustained, inclusive, and sustainable economic growth; full and productive employment; and decent work for all

Table 1.8.1: Selected Indicators for Sustainable Development Goal 8—Decent Work and Economic Growth

ADB Regional Member	Target 8.1: Sustain per capita economic growth in accordance with national circumstances and, in particular, at least 7% gross domestic product per annum in the least developed countries (or economies)			Target 8.2: Achieve higher levels of economic productivity through diversification, technological upgrading, and innovation, including through a focus on high-value-added and labor-intensive sectors		
	8.1.1: Annual Growth Rate of Real GDP per Capita at Constant 2015 $ (%)			8.2.1: Annual Growth Rate of Real GDP per Employed Person at Constant 2015 $[a] (%)		
	2010	2015	2021	2010	2015	2022
Developing ADB Member Economies						
Central and West Asia						
Afghanistan	2.3	-4.5	-23.0	10.4	-1.5	1.9
Armenia	2.8	3.6	6.3	2.9	4.1	6.8
Azerbaijan	3.7	-0.1	5.3	3.5	-1.0	2.7
Georgia	6.8	3.1	10.6	4.6	0.8	8.6
Kazakhstan	5.8	-0.2	2.9	5.5	0.6	0.9
Kyrgyz Republic	-1.7	2.1	4.5	-2.2	2.9	1.5
Pakistan	0.5	4.6	4.6	-2.0	3.0	3.4
Tajikistan	4.4	3.5	6.9	3.3	2.9	3.1
Turkmenistan	14.3	1.1	3.1	7.8	5.2	-0.1
Uzbekistan	8.2	5.5	5.7	6.0	6.1	3.5
East Asia						
China, People's Republic of	9.9	6.4	8.0	10.4	6.9	3.4
Hong Kong, China	6.2	1.7	6.4	6.7	1.5	-0.5
Korea, Republic of	6.3	1.9	4.2	5.4	1.5	-0.1
Mongolia	5.0	-0.9	-0.2	4.2	1.4	0.3
Taipei,China	...	...	...	1.7 (2011)	0.3	3.5
South Asia						
Bangladesh	6.3	7.2	5.7	2.2	4.6	4.1
Bhutan	10.7	5.7	-4.0	11.4	3.8	0.9
India	7.0	6.7	7.8	6.2	7.9	3.1
Maldives	3.6	-1.6	39.8	-0.5	-4.6	6.2
Nepal	5.7	3.4	1.9	3.6	2.7	-0.5
Sri Lanka	7.0	4.5	3.4	6.2	3.6	-6.2
Southeast Asia						
Brunei Darussalam	1.1	-1.5	-2.4	0.8	-0.1	-0.5
Cambodia	4.4	5.6	1.8	5.2	3.1	3.6
Indonesia	4.9	3.7	3.0	3.2	4.0	2.8
Lao People's Democratic Republic	6.5	5.8	2.0	6.2	5.7	-0.6
Malaysia	5.6	3.5	2.0	4.2	2.8	2.7
Myanmar	7.0	5.6	-18.5	9.4	2.5	1.2
Philippines	5.4	4.6	4.1	4.5	4.7	1.2
Singapore	11.3	1.5	7.1	7.4	-0.2	2.8
Thailand	6.8	2.6	1.4	7.0	3.2	3.0
Timor-Leste	7.3	1.0	-0.1	6.9	0.3	-0.2
Viet Nam	10.4	5.9	1.7	3.6	6.2	4.8
The Pacific						
Cook Islands	-8.1	6.5	-10.3	...	...	...
Fiji	2.6	4.5	-5.5	0.5	5.3	10.1
Kiribati	-3.0	8.2	5.9	...	...	...
Marshall Islands	6.8	3.8	5.4	...	...	...
Micronesia, Federated States of	2.5	4.2	-4.1	...	...	...
Nauru	13.5	33.5	-0.9	...	...	...
Niue	...	...	...	...	...	...
Palau	1.9	8.9	-13.6	...	...	...
Papua New Guinea	6.9	3.9	-0.9	12.0	3.9	1.3
Samoa	0.8	5.2	-4.0	1.2	3.6	-6.5
Solomon Islands	7.2	-0.9	-2.6	5.6	-1.4	-6.2
Tonga	0.6	1.7	-3.4	0.7	1.9	-2.9
Tuvalu	-4.6	10.6	0.5	...	...	...
Vanuatu	-0.8	-2.2	-2.2	-1.4	-1.8	-1.4
Developed ADB Member Economies						
Australia	0.7	1.2	2.6	0.1	0.2	0.1
Japan	4.1	1.7	2.2	4.5	1.3	1.6
New Zealand	-0.1	2.5	2.3	1.3	1.6	0.3

... = data not available, $ = United States dollars, ADB = Asian Development Bank, GDP = gross domestic product.

a Modeled data based on GDP per person engaged, constant 2015 United States dollars.

Sources: United Nations. SDG Global Database. https://unstats.un.org/sdgs/dataportal (accessed 24 July 2023). For Taipei,China: International Labour Organization. ILOSTAT Database. https://ilostat.ilo.org/data/ (accessed 24 July 2023).

Goal 8. Promote sustained, inclusive, and sustainable economic growth; full and productive employment; and decent work for all

Table 1.8.2: Selected Indicators for Sustainable Development Goal 8—Unemployment

ADB Regional Member	Target 8.5: By 2030, achieve full and productive employment and decent work for all women and men, including for young people and persons with disabilities, and equal pay for work of equal value 8.5.2.a: Unemployment Rate for Age Group 15+ Years, by Sex (%)					
	2010			2021		
	Total	Female	Male	Total	Female	Male
Developing ADB Member Economies						
Central and West Asia						
Afghanistan	1.7 (2012)	3.3 (2012)	1.4 (2012)	5.6	5.5	5.6
Armenia	19.0	21.2	17.0	10.0	7.3	13.0
Azerbaijan	5.6	6.9	4.4	6.0	7.0	4.9
Georgia	20.2	17.6	22.5	11.7 (2020)	10.2 (2020)	13.1 (2020)
Kazakhstan	5.8	6.6	4.9	4.9 (2020)	5.4 (2020)	4.4 (2020)
Kyrgyz Republic[a]	6.0	6.3	5.7	4.1	4.3	4.0
Pakistan	0.7	0.6	0.7	6.3	9.2	5.5
Tajikistan	11.5 (2009)	10.5 (2009)	12.3 (2009)	6.9 (2016)	5.5 (2016)	7.9 (2016)
Turkmenistan	4.0	2.3	5.3	...	...	...
Uzbekistan[b]	5.4	6.3	4.6	5.3 (2020)	7.7 (2020)	3.9 (2020)
East Asia						
China, People's Republic of	4.1	...	...	5.1	...	...
Hong Kong, China	4.3	3.5	5.1	4.3 (2022)	3.5 (2022)	5.1 (2022)
Korea, Republic of	3.3	2.8	3.7	2.9 (2022)	3.0 (2022)	2.7 (2022)
Mongolia	6.6	5.9	7.1	6.2 (2022)	5.4 (2022)	7.0 (2022)
Taipei,China	5.2	4.5	5.8	3.8 (2020)	3.8 (2020)	3.9 (2020)
South Asia						
Bangladesh	3.4	4.4	3.0	4.4 (2017)	6.7 (2017)	3.3 (2017)
Bhutan	3.3	4.0	2.7	6.0 (2022)	7.9 (2022)	4.4 (2022)
India	3.1	3.8	2.9	6.4	5.4	6.7
Maldives[c]	11.7 (2009)	13.8 (2009)	10.4 (2009)	4.6 (2019)	3.9 (2019)	5.0 (2019)
Nepal	1.3 (2008)	1.1 (2008)	1.6 (2008)	10.7 (2017)	12.0 (2017)	9.8 (2017)
Sri Lanka[b]	4.8	7.4	3.4	5.4 (2020)	8.2 (2020)	3.9 (2020)
Southeast Asia						
Brunei Darussalam	6.9 (2014)	7.8 (2014)	6.1 (2014)	4.9	6.4	3.9
Cambodia	0.8	0.8	0.8	0.4	0.4	0.4
Indonesia	5.6	6.4	5.1	3.5 (2022)	3.2 (2022)	3.7 (2022)
Lao People's Democratic Republic	0.7	0.7	0.8	3.3 (2017)	2.8 (2017)	3.7 (2017)
Malaysia	3.4	3.3 (2011)	2.9 (2011)	4.5 (2020)	4.7 (2020)	4.5 (2020)
Myanmar	...	...	...	1.5 (2020)	2.1 (2020)	1.0 (2020)
Philippines	3.6	3.8	3.5	3.4	3.8	3.1
Singapore[a]	4.1	4.4	3.9	4.6	5.0	4.3
Thailand	0.6	0.6	0.6	0.9 (2022)	1.1 (2022)	0.8 (2022)
Timor-Leste	3.3	4.3	2.9	2.3	3.0	1.9
Viet Nam	1.1	1.1	1.2	1.5 (2022)	1.4 (2022)	1.6 (2022)
The Pacific						
Cook Islands	8.2 (2011)	8.1 (2011)	8.2 (2011)	1.3 (2019)	0.9 (2019)	1.6 (2019)
Fiji	8.9	4.6 (2011)	4.3 (2011)	4.3 (2016)	5.5 (2016)	3.7 (2016)
Kiribati	30.6	34.1	27.6	11.0 (2020)	12.3 (2020)	9.9 (2020)
Marshall Islands	4.7 (2011)	4.5 (2011)	4.9 (2011)	9.8	11.5	8.9
Micronesia, Federated States of	8.9 (2014)	13.9 (2014)	5.4 (2014)	...	...	...
Nauru	23.0 (2011)	25.5 (2011)	21.4 (2011)	5.1	5.2	4.9
Niue	2.2 (2001)	2.1 (2001)	2.3 (2001)	0.8 (2017)	- (2017)	- (2017)
Palau	1.4 (2014)	1.8 (2014)	1.1 (2014)	0.8 (2020)	1.0 (2020)	0.6 (2020)
Papua New Guinea	2.0	1.3	2.7	...	...	...
Samoa	5.7 (2011)	6.8 (2011)	5.2 (2011)	9.4 (2017)	14.5 (2017)	6.3 (2017)
Solomon Islands	2.0 (2009)	1.8 (2009)	2.3 (2009)	...	...	...
Tonga	1.1 (2006)	7.4 (2003)	3.8 (2003)	2.1	2.5	1.8
Tuvalu	6.5 (2002)	8.6 (2002)	5.0 (2002)	26.6 (2017)	28.2 (2017)	25.5 (2017)
Vanuatu	1.9	1.6	2.1	4.1 (2020)	4.1 (2020)	4.0 (2020)
Developed ADB Member Economies						
Australia	5.2	5.4	5.1	3.7 (2022)	3.6 (2022)	3.8 (2022)
Japan	5.1	4.6	5.5	2.6 (2022)	2.4 (2022)	2.8 (2022)
New Zealand	6.6	6.9	6.2	3.3 (2022)	3.5 (2022)	3.1 (2022)

Goal 8. Promote sustained, inclusive and sustainable economic growth; full and productive employment; and decent work for all

Table 1.8.2: Selected Indicators for Sustainable Development Goal 8—Unemployment *(continued)*

ADB Regional Member	Target 8.5: By 2030, achieve full and productive employment and decent work for all women and men, including for young people and persons with disabilities, and equal pay for work of equal value — 8.5.2.b: Unemployment Rate for Age Group 15–24 Years, by Sex (%)					
	2010			2021		
	Total	Female	Male	Total	Female	Male
Developing ADB Member Economies						
Central and West Asia						
Afghanistan	2.9 (2012)	4.5 (2012)	2.6 (2012)	8.7	9.4	8.5
Armenia	38.9	48.0	31.9	22.5	19.7	25.2
Azerbaijan	14.9	16.0	13.9	14.2	16.5	12.3
Georgia	41.5	45.7	39.1	31.3 (2020)	32.7 (2020)	30.5 (2020)
Kazakhstan	5.2	5.7	4.8	3.8 (2020)	4.2 (2020)	3.4 (2020)
Kyrgyz Republic[a]	12.0	13.9	10.7	8.3	9.0	7.9
Pakistan	1.3	1.1	1.3	11.1	14.4	10.0
Tajikistan	5.9 (2007)	2.9 (2007)	8.4 (2007)	...	...	...
Turkmenistan	...	...	...	...	...	...
Uzbekistan[b]	...	...	...	13.2 (2020)	21.5 (2020)	8.3 (2020)
East Asia						
China, People's Republic of	...	...	...	14.3	...	...
Hong Kong, China	12.2	10.3	14.1	11.0 (2022)	10.1 (2022)	12.0 (2022)
Korea, Republic of	8.7	7.8	10.2	6.7 (2022)	6.2 (2022)	7.4 (2022)
Mongolia	14.8	14.2	15.2	11.7 (2022)	13.5 (2022)	10.4 (2022)
Taipei,China	13.1	12.7	13.6	11.6 (2020)	12.1 (2020)	11.3 (2020)
South Asia						
Bangladesh	6.4	7.0	6.0	12.8 (2017)	16.8 (2017)	10.8 (2017)
Bhutan	9.2	11.0	7.1	28.6 (2022)	32.8 (2022)	24.4 (2022)
India	9.6	10.4	9.4	20.7	20.1	20.8
Maldives[c]	25.4 (2009)	21.4 (2009)	29.1 (2009)	13.9 (2019)	9.7 (2019)	17.2 (2019)
Nepal	2.2 (2008)	1.6 (2008)	2.9 (2008)	20.5 (2017)	22.5 (2017)	19.2 (2017)
Sri Lanka[b]	19.0	23.8	16.1	25.9 (2020)	34.4 (2020)	21.5 (2020)
Southeast Asia						
Brunei Darussalam	25.3 (2014)	27.9 (2014)	23.4 (2014)	16.3	23.0	12.0
Cambodia	1.0	0.9	1.0	0.8	1.0	0.7
Indonesia	17.6	18.8	16.7	14.1 (2022)	13.7 (2022)	14.5 (2022)
Lao People's Democratic Republic	1.8	1.7	1.9	5.9 (2017)	5.4 (2017)	6.5 (2017)
Malaysia	9.7 (2011)	10.7 (2011)	9.1 (2011)	12.0 (2020)	13.0 (2020)	11.4 (2020)
Myanmar	...	...	...	4.9 (2020)	5.8 (2020)	4.1 (2020)
Philippines	9.9	12.0	8.7	8.5	10.3	7.4
Singapore[a]	9.9	12.5	7.6	10.1	13.2	7.0
Thailand	2.5	3.1	2.2	5.1 (2022)	7.0 (2022)	3.7 (2022)
Timor-Leste	12.4	19.1	8.7	5.5	8.3	3.3
Viet Nam	3.6	3.5	3.6	6.0 (2022)	6.1 (2022)	6.0 (2022)
The Pacific						
Cook Islands	15.5 (2011)	15.3 (2011)	15.6 (2011)	3.5 (2019)	- (2019)	4.6 (2019)
Fiji	14.2 (2011)	18.4 (2011)	12.1 (2011)	15.4 (2016)	22.4 (2016)	11.9 (2016)
Kiribati	54.0	61.8	47.6	27.0 (2020)	32.5 (2020)	23.5 (2020)
Marshall Islands	...	...	...	24.9	25.1	24.8
Micronesia, Federated States of	18.9 (2014)	29.9 (2014)	10.4 (2014)	...	...	...
Nauru	26.6 (2013)	37.5 (2013)	20.9 (2013)	12.0	14.5	10.6
Niue	9.0 (2001)	7.6 (2001)	10.3 (2001)	- (2017)	- (2017)	- (2017)
Palau	5.6 (2014)	- (2014)	- (2014)	3.3 (2020)	3.5 (2020)	3.1 (2020)
Papua New Guinea	3.6	3.0	4.3	...	...	...
Samoa	16.1 (2011)	22.2 (2011)	13.8 (2011)	19.7 (2017)	30.0 (2017)	13.3 (2017)
Solomon Islands	1.3 (2013)	1.6 (2013)	1.1 (2013)	...	...	...
Tonga	...	...	...	6.4	10.1	4.1
Tuvalu	...	...	...	54.9 (2017)	57.6 (2017)	52.8 (2017)
Vanuatu	4.8	4.8	4.8	9.7 (2020)	9.6 (2020)	9.8 (2020)
Developed ADB Member Economies						
Australia	11.6	11.1	12.0	8.2 (2022)	7.2 (2022)	9.1 (2022)
Japan	9.4	8.1	10.8	4.4 (2022)	3.5 (2022)	4.9 (2022)
New Zealand	17.4	17.8	17.1	9.4 (2022)	9.1 (2022)	9.6 (2022)

Goal 8. Promote sustained, inclusive, and sustainable economic growth; full and productive employment; and decent work for all

Table 1.8.2: Selected Indicators for Sustainable Development Goal 8—Unemployment *(continued)*

ADB Regional Member	Target 8.5: By 2030, achieve full and productive employment and decent work for all women and men, including for young people and persons with disabilities, and equal pay for work of equal value 8.5.2.c: Unemployment Rate for Age Group 25+ Years, by Sex (%)					
	2010			2021		
	Total	Female	Male	Total	Female	Male
Developing ADB Member Economies						
Central and West Asia						
Afghanistan	1.2 (2012)	2.7 (2012)	0.9 (2012)	4.4	3.8	4.6
Armenia	15.9	17.5	14.5	9.0	6.4	11.9
Azerbaijan	4.2	5.6	3.0	4.9	5.8	3.9
Georgia	17.6	14.9	20.1	10.1 (2020)	8.7 (2020)	11.2 (2020)
Kazakhstan	5.9	6.8	5.0	5.0 (2020)	5.5 (2020)	4.6 (2020)
Kyrgyz Republic[a]	4.1	4.3	4.0	3.3	3.6	3.1
Pakistan	0.4	0.5	0.4	4.7	7.2	3.9
Tajikistan	1.9 (2007)	0.9 (2007)	2.5 (2007)	...	...	...
Turkmenistan	...	...	...	...	...	...
Uzbekistan[b]	...	...	...	4.2 (2020)	5.6 (2020)	3.3 (2020)
East Asia						
China, People's Republic of	...	...	...	...	...	...
Hong Kong, China	3.6	2.8	4.3	4.0 (2022)	3.2 (2022)	4.8 (2022)
Korea, Republic of	3.0	2.4	3.4	2.7 (2022)	2.8 (2022)	2.6 (2022)
Mongolia	5.1	4.6	5.6	5.7 (2022)	4.7 (2022)	6.6 (2022)
Taipei,China	4.5	3.5	5.3	3.2 (2020)	3.0 (2020)	3.3 (2020)
South Asia						
Bangladesh	2.5	3.3	2.2	2.6 (2017)	4.4 (2017)	1.8 (2017)
Bhutan	2.1	2.4	1.9	3.5 (2022)	4.8 (2022)	2.5 (2022)
India	1.7	2.4	1.4	4.1	3.6	4.3
Maldives[c]	6.6 (2009)	9.9 (2009)	4.7 (2009)	2.8 (2019)	2.8 (2019)	2.8 (2019)
Nepal	1.0 (2008)	0.9 (2008)	1.1 (2008)	8.2 (2017)	9.3 (2017)	7.5 (2017)
Sri Lanka[b]	2.6	4.6	1.5	2.9 (2020)	4.9 (2020)	1.8 (2020)
Southeast Asia						
Brunei Darussalam	4.1 (2014)	4.9 (2014)	3.4 (2014)	3.3	4.2	2.7
Cambodia	0.7	0.7	0.6	0.3	0.3	0.3
Indonesia	3.1	3.7	2.7	1.7 (2022)	1.3 (2022)	1.9 (2022)
Lao People's Democratic Republic	0.4	0.3	0.4	2.5 (2017)	1.9 (2017)	3.0 (2017)
Malaysia	1.5 (2011)	1.4 (2011)	1.5 (2011)	3.0 (2020)	3.0 (2020)	3.1 (2020)
Myanmar	...	...	...	0.8 (2020)	1.2 (2020)	0.4 (2020)
Philippines	2.0	1.8	2.1	2.5	2.8	2.4
Singapore[a]	3.5	3.5	3.5	4.2	4.3	4.1
Thailand	0.3	0.3	0.4	0.5 (2022)	0.5 (2022)	0.5 (2022)
Timor-Leste	2.3	2.4	2.2	2.0	2.3	1.7
Viet Nam	0.6	0.6	0.6	1.0 (2022)	0.9 (2022)	1.1 (2022)
The Pacific						
Cook Islands	6.5 (2011)	6.5 (2011)	6.4 (2011)	0.8 (2019)	- (2019)	- (2019)
Fiji	2.7 (2011)	2.4 (2011)	2.8 (2011)	2.2 (2016)	2.4 (2016)	2.2 (2016)
Kiribati	20.9	22.8	19.2	7.5 (2020)	8.5 (2020)	6.6 (2020)
Marshall Islands	...	...	...	7.3	9.2	6.1
Micronesia, Federated States of	6.1 (2014)	9.0 (2014)	4.0 (2014)	...	...	...
Nauru	9.1 (2013)	13.1 (2013)	6.1 (2013)	3.4	3.4	3.3
Niue	1.0 (2001)	1.2 (2001)	0.8 (2001)	0.7 (2017)	- (2017)	- (2017)
Palau	1.0 (2014)	1.4 (2014)	0.7 (2014)	0.6 (2020)	0.9 (2020)	0.4 (2020)
Papua New Guinea	1.5	0.7	2.2	...	...	...
Samoa	3.0 (2011)	2.8 (2011)	3.0 (2011)	6.5 (2017)	10.1 (2017)	4.4 (2020)
Solomon Islands	0.5 (2013)	0.4 (2013)	0.6 (2013)	...	...	...
Tonga	...	...	...	1.3	1.4	1.3
Tuvalu	...	...	...	17.8 (2017)	18.1 (2017)	17.6 (2017)
Vanuatu	1.1	0.7	1.5	2.8 (2020)	2.9 (2020)	2.7 (2020)
Developed ADB Member Economies						
Australia	3.8	4.0	3.7	2.9 (2022)	2.9 (2022)	2.8 (2022)
Japan	4.7	4.2	5.1	2.4 (2022)	2.2 (2022)	2.6 (2022)
New Zealand	4.5	4.8	4.2	2.3 (2022)	2.6 (2022)	2.0 (2022)

... = data not available, – = magnitude equals zero, ADB = Asian Development Bank.

a For 2021, data were derived using International Labour Organization's ILOSTAT microdata processing.

b For 2020, data were derived using International Labour Organization's ILOSTAT microdata processing.

c For 2009 and 2019, data were derived using International Labour Organization's ILOSTAT microdata processing

Source: International Labour Organization. ILOSTAT Database. https://ilostat.ilo.org/data (accessed 20 July 2023).

Goal 8. Promote sustained, inclusive and sustainable economic growth; full and productive employment; and decent work for all

Table 1.8.3: Selected Indicators for Sustainable Development Goal 8—Youth Participation in Education and Work, Child Labor

ADB Regional Member	Target 8.6: By 2020, substantially reduce the proportion of youth not in employment, education, or training — 8.6.1: Proportion of Youth (Aged 15–24 Years) not in Education, Employment, or Training (%)		Target 8.7: Take immediate and effective measures to eradicate forced labor, end modern slavery and human trafficking, and secure the prohibition and elimination of the worst forms of child labor, including recruitment and use of child soldiers; and, by 2025, end child labor in all its forms — 8.7.1: Proportion of Children (Aged 5–17 Years) Engaged in Child Labor (%)		
	2010	2021	Total 2020	Female 2020	Male 2020
Developing ADB Member Economies					
Central and West Asia					
Afghanistan	35.1 (2014)	62.8	9.0	5.1	12.6
Armenia	44.6 (2011)	26.1 (2020)	3.9 (2015)	2.7 (2015)	4.9 (2015)
Azerbaijan	...	...	...	...	...
Georgia	32.6 (2012)	24.9 (2020)	1.5 (2015)	0.9 (2015)	2.1 (2015)
Kazakhstan	8.2	9.5 (2016)	...	...	...
Kyrgyz Republic	14.9	15.9	20.1 (2018)	15.6 (2018)	24.2 (2018)
Pakistan	31.1	34.6	9.0 (2018)	5.1 (2018)	12.4 (2018)
Tajikistan	42.2 (2009)	...	...	...	...
Turkmenistan	...	...	...	...	...
Uzbekistan	...	...	...	...	...
East Asia					
China, People's Republic of	...	...	...	...	...
Hong Kong, China	7.4 (2009)	...	...	...	...
Korea, Republic of	10.9	20.8 (2019)	...	...	...
Mongolia	17.6	17.2	7.9 (2018)	6.5 (2018)	9.1 (2018)
Taipei,China	...	...	...	...	...
South Asia					
Bangladesh	30.1	27.4 (2017)	5.9 (2019)	3.0 (2019)	8.7 (2019)
Bhutan	...	9.6	1.7 (2010)	1.7 (2010)	1.6 (2010)
India	28.9	30.7 (2020)	4.3 (2012)	3.1 (2012)	5.3 (2012)
Maldives	32.5 (2009)	26.3 (2019)	...	...	...
Nepal	23.1 (2008)	34.8 (2017)	19.0 (2014)	19.3 (2014)	19.2 (2014)
Sri Lanka	26.7	21.5 (2020)	0.8 (2016)	0.6 (2016)	0.9 (2016)
Southeast Asia					
Brunei Darussalam	17.1 (2014)	18.7	...	...	...
Cambodia	5.3	11.4 (2019)	11.5 (2012)	12.2 (2012)	10.8 (2012)
Indonesia	26.7	22.3 (2022)	1.7 (2021)	...	...
Lao People's Democratic Republic	5.1	25.8 (2017)	26.3 (2017)	26.2 (2017)	26.3 (2017)
Malaysia	14.4 (2011)	13.6 (2020)	...	...	...
Myanmar	18.6 (2015)	15.0 (2020)	8.1 (2015)	7.6 (2015)	8.7 (2015)
Philippines	25.3	17.5	1.0	0.7	1.3
Singapore	3.7 (2013)	6.2	...	...	...
Thailand	12.5	14.8	...	...	...
Timor-Leste	19.0	31.2	7.2 (2016)	6.9 (2016)	7.6 (2016)
Viet Nam	8.2	14.9	5.7 (2021)	6.2 (2021)	5.2 (2021)
The Pacific					
Cook Islands	...	12.5 (2019)	...	...	...
Fiji	18.4 (2011)	20.1 (2016)	15.6 (2021)	12.3 (2021)	18.8 (2021)
Kiribati	46.9 (2015)	47.6 (2020)	7.1 (2019)	5.5 (2019)	8.6 (2019)
Marshall Islands	...	42.9 (2019)	...	...	...
Micronesia, Federated States of	28.7 (2014)	...	...	...	...
Nauru	36.4 (2013)	...	...	...	...
Niue	...	...	...	...	...
Palau	13.3 (2014)	18.0 (2020)	...	...	...
Papua New Guinea	35.5	...	...	...	...
Samoa	39.1 (2012)	28.7 (2017)	13.0	10.8	14.9
Solomon Islands	7.0 (2013)	...	13.8 (2015)	13.8 (2015)	13.8 (2015)
Tonga	...	18.7	25.9 (2019)	18.5 (2019)	32.9 (2019)
Tuvalu	...	34.3 (2016)	3.7	4.0	3.4
Vanuatu	31.9	34.5 (2019)	15.0 (2013)	15.8 (2013)	14.2 (2013)
Developed ADB Member Economies					
Australia	11.3	8.9 (2017)	...	...	...
Japan	4.3	3.1 (2019)	...	...	...
New Zealand	13.6	11.9	...	...	...

... = data not available, ADB = Asian Development Bank.

Source: United Nations. SDG Global Database. https://unstats.un.org/sdgs/dataportal (accessed 15 July 2023).

Goal 8. Promote sustained, inclusive, and sustainable economic growth; full and productive employment; and decent work for all

Table 1.8.4: Access to Banking, Insurance and Financial Services, and Trade

ADB Regional Member	Target 8.10: Strengthen the capacity of domestic financial institutions to encourage and expand access to banking, insurance, and financial services for all					
	8.10.1: Number of Commercial Bank Branches and ATMs per 100,000 Adults				8.10.2: Proportion of Adults (15 Years and Older) with an Account at a Bank or Other Financial Institution or with a Mobile-Money Service Provider (%)	
	Commercial Bank Branches		ATMs			
	2010	2021	2010	2021	2011	2021
Developing ADB Member Economies						
Central and West Asia						
Afghanistan	2.4	1.9 (2019)	0.5	1.6 (2019)	9.0	9.7
Armenia	18.6	24.2	34.0	67.1	17.5	55.4
Azerbaijan	9.9	6.5	27.1	37.4	14.9	28.6 (2017)
Georgia	21.2	31.2	48.3	95.4	33.0	70.5
Kazakhstan	3.3	13.1	61.4	92.5	42.1	81.1
Kyrgyz Republic	6.1	7.4	7.3	42.3	3.8	45.1
Pakistan	8.4	10.4	4.3	11.1	10.3	21.0
Tajikistan	5.5	3.4	4.5	23.1	2.5	39.5
Turkmenistan	...	...	...	...	0.4	40.6 (2017)
Uzbekistan	39.2	48.0	8.5 (2014)	52.0	22.5	44.1
East Asia						
China, People's Republic of	7.7 (2012)	8.8	24.9	81.4	63.8	88.7
Hong Kong, China	23.8	19.8	46.9	51.2	88.7	97.8
Korea, Republic of	18.2	13.7	265.4	259.5 (2020)	93.1	98.7
Mongolia	54.6	61.3	18.5	45.8	77.7	98.5
Taipei,China	17.2 (2011)	16.2 (2022)	134.9 (2015)	157.4 (2022)	87.3	94.7
South Asia						
Bangladesh	7.7	9.0	2.1	11.4	31.7	52.8
Bhutan	15.3	20.9	8.9	45.2	33.7 (2014)	...
India	10.0	14.6	7.2	21.4	35.2	77.5
Maldives	11.7	13.8	16.5	39.9	...	79.6 (2017)
Nepal	5.1	22.3	7.4 (2011)	20.3	25.3	54.0
Sri Lanka	14.3	17.3	...	...	68.5	89.3
Southeast Asia						
Brunei Darussalam	23.3	16.2	82.0	73.1	...	...
Cambodia	4.1	12.4	5.3	31.6	3.7	33.4
Indonesia	8.1	15.8	13.0	48.1	19.6	51.8
Lao People's Democratic Republic	2.5	3.1	8.7	28.1	26.8	37.3
Malaysia	10.9	8.7	51.3	54.3	66.2	88.4
Myanmar	1.5	5.6 (2019)	0.1 (2012)	6.9 (2019)	22.8 (2014)	47.8
Philippines	7.5	9.0	15.1	29.4	26.6	51.4
Singapore	9.8	7.0	59.1	54.3	98.2	97.6
Thailand	11.0	9.7	81.9	108.1	72.7	95.6
Timor-Leste	1.8	5.5	2.4	13.4	...	...
Viet Nam	3.2	2.9	17.0	27.1	21.4	30.8 (2017)
The Pacific						
Cook Islands	...	...	...	...	...	...
Fiji	11.1	10.6	33.1	50.5	...	...
Kiribati	6.0 (2011)	...	10.5 (2011)	...	...	...
Marshall Islands	10.6	11.7	1.8	5.0	...	...
Micronesia, Federated States of	15.1	12.5	9.1	11.2	...	...
Nauru	...	...	...	...	...	...
Niue	...	...	...	...	...	...
Palau	...	...	33.4	44.9 (2017)	...	...
Papua New Guinea	1.6	1.5	5.3	7.9	...	...
Samoa	25.3	25.4	25.3	62.0	...	...
Solomon Islands	4.5	3.9 (2020)	11.2	15.1 (2020)	...	...
Tonga	21.5	33.0 (2018)	27.7	40.5 (2018)	...	...
Tuvalu	...	...	...	...	...	...
Vanuatu	20.6	21.1	28.1	56.6	...	...
Developed ADB Member Economies						
Australia	30.8	24.1	168.7	123.6	99.1	99.3
Japan	33.8	33.9	130.9	116.9	96.4	98.5
New Zealand	34.5	17.7	72.2	53.9	99.4	98.8

Goal 8. Promote sustained, inclusive, and sustainable economic growth; full and productive employment; and decent work for all

Table 1.8.4: Access to Banking, Insurance and Financial Services, and Trade *(continued)*

ADB Regional Member	Target 8.10: Strengthen the capacity of domestic financial institutions to encourage and expand access to banking, insurance, and financial services for all — 8.a.1: Aid for Trade (millions of constant 2021 United States dollars)			
	Commitments		Disbursement	
	2010	2021	2010	2021
Developing ADB Member Economies				
Central and West Asia				
Afghanistan	1,938.4	182.2	2,139.3	437.6
Armenia	164.4	211.2	171.6	186.7
Azerbaijan	99.6	9.1	62.5	50.5
Georgia	343.8	90.7	270.5	204.5
Kazakhstan	194.9	8.3	62.3	12.3
Kyrgyz Republic	168.6	185.4	83.3	199.9
Pakistan	828.5	723.2	359.4	1,006.7
Tajikistan	254.8	246.0	177.3	296.0
Turkmenistan	19.5	119.5	3.2	3.6
Uzbekistan	452.3	934.0	90.7	549.2
East Asia				
China, People's Republic of	637.0	240.6	501.0	249.3
Hong Kong, China	...	...	...	...
Korea, Republic of	...	...	...	...
Mongolia	313.8	103.0	139.8	84.7
Taipei,China	...	...	...	...
South Asia				
Bangladesh	1,159.7	3,051.8	482.3	2,436.7
Bhutan	56.5	51.3	84.9	57.5
India	2,880.7	3,670.5	2,126.2	3,683.1
Maldives	14.4	67.9	31.4	37.2
Nepal	489.8	258.5	254.9	528.0
Sri Lanka	318.1	44.5	328.8	284.2
Southeast Asia				
Brunei Darussalam	...	...	...	...
Cambodia	452.2	464.2	215.3	431.0
Indonesia	718.3	282.5	983.7	847.4
Lao People's Democratic Republic	274.4	299.3	147.4	178.2
Malaysia	15.2	6.3	32.5	5.5
Myanmar	34.6	115.8	44.0	477.8
Philippines	125.7	185.0	350.8	806.6
Singapore	...	...	...	...
Thailand	313.5	34.9	168.3	203.2
Timor-Leste	91.4	152.9	45.1	50.1
Viet Nam	1,740.7	591.3	1,630.8	1,040.0
The Pacific				
Cook Islands	5.4	1.0 (2019)	3.1	6.0 (2019)
Fiji	19.9	127.4	10.0	117.1
Kiribati	4.5	24.3	3.9	14.3
Marshall Islands	0.9	49.5	9.5	14.4
Micronesia, Federated States of	1.4	59.3	12.5	10.6
Nauru	0.3	4.2	0.9	12.8
Niue	4.4	5.1	5.2	7.9
Palau	1.5	7.0	6.8	14.4
Papua New Guinea	247.6	181.6	126.4	250.2
Samoa	25.3	15.2	32.1	22.9
Solomon Islands	42.7	140.4	26.1	66.8
Tonga	30.3	95.0	31.3	28.9
Tuvalu	1.3	33.5	1.6	13.7
Vanuatu	20.1	65.3	38.6	42.9
Developed ADB Member Economies				
Australia	...	...	...	...
Japan	...	...	...	...
New Zealand	...	...	...	...

... = data not available, ADB = Asian Development Bank.

Sources: For indicator 8.10.1: United Nations. SDG Global Database. https://unstats.un.org/sdgs/dataportal (accessed 20 July 2023). For indicator 8.10.1: Commercial bank branches for Taipei,China: Central bank of Taipei,China; and ATMs for Taipei,China: Financial Supervisory Commission, Banking Bureau. For Indicator 8.10.2: World Bank. World Development Indicators. https://data.worldbank.org/indicator (accessed 20 July 2023). For indicator 8.a.1: United Nations. SDG Global Database. https://unstats.un.org/sdgs/dataportal (accessed 20 July 2023).

Goal 9. Build resilient infrastructure, promote inclusive and sustainable industrialization, and foster innovation

Table 1.9.1: Selected Indicators for Sustainable Development Goal 9—Air Transport, Passenger and Freight Volume

ADB Regional Member	Target 9.1: Develop quality, reliable, sustainable, and resilient infrastructure, including regional and transborder infrastructure, to support economic development and human well-being, with a focus on affordable and equitable access for all			
	9.1.2: Passenger Volume, by Air Transport[a] (p-km million)		9.1.2: Freight Volume, by Air Transport[b] (t-km million)	
	2017	2021	2017	2021
Developing ADB Member Economies				
Central and West Asia	**51,455.5**	**28,010.1**	**496.8**	**3,333.9**
Afghanistan	1,843.7	300.0	21.5	12.0
Armenia	...	197.7	...	1.3
Azerbaijan	4,204.1	1,401.9	61.6	3,173.7
Georgia	600.0	192.9	0.5	0.1
Kazakhstan	12,597.2	12,413.4	49.5	31.4
Kyrgyz Republic	2,175.8	208.2	0.0	0.0
Pakistan	18,514.6	7,903.3	214.5	75.6
Tajikistan	1,467.7	343.3	2.9	1.0
Turkmenistan	2,939.6	318.2	19.5	0.7
Uzbekistan	7,112.7	4,731.1	126.8	38.0
East Asia[c]	**1,266,268.0**	**682,572.5**	**47,259.0**	**57,767.2**
China, People's Republic of	950,425.2	655,591.6	23,323.6	33,369.2
Hong Kong, China	150,193.8	4,240.2	12,415.2	9,027.9
Korea, Republic of	164,423.6	22,638.1	11,511.8	15,370.0
Mongolia	1,225.4	102.7	8.4	0.2
Taipei,China	...	...	...	...
South Asia[c]	**216,727.2**	**98,700.6**	**2,880.2**	**1,423.6**
Bangladesh	9,087.3	5,180.3	61.7	83.7
Bhutan	389.1	20.1	0.5	0.4
India	190,343.5	88,509.9	2,407.1	907.9
Maldives	768.7	96.7	7.7	1.7
Nepal	1,970.1	2,049.6	4.6	17.3
Sri Lanka	14,168.5	2,844.0	398.5	412.5
Southeast Asia[c]	**605,563.2**	**84,870.9**	**11,429.0**	**7,411.4**
Brunei Darussalam	3,768.1	84.9	132.6	23.1
Cambodia	1,849.6	118.6	0.9	–
Indonesia	111,371.1	35,377.0	1,052.4	772.9
Lao People's Democratic Republic	860.7	76.3	1.5	–
Malaysia	111,058.6	4,442.4	1,455.2	1,119.4
Myanmar	1,711.2	697.8	4.8	18.4
Philippines	63,909.7	10,237.6	753.4	530.3
Singapore	135,587.3	11,596.9	5,063.0	3,666.9
Thailand	119,168.9	9,176.6	2,511.9	604.0
Timor-Leste	...	...	...	...
Viet Nam	56,278.1	13,062.9	453.3	676.5
The Pacific[c]	**8,117.3**	**1,162.9**	**145.5**	**48.4**
Cook Islands	29.8	11.7	0.1	–
Fiji	5,451.8	347.6	102.6	6.4
Kiribati	10.7	8.2	–	–
Marshall Islands	14.2	6.6	0.2	0.1
Micronesia, Federated States of	...	...	...	...
Nauru	151.2	9.6	7.9	3.3
Niue	...	...	...	...
Palau	...	...	...	...
Papua New Guinea	1,747.6	662.9	29.2	38.2
Samoa	21.7	1.0	–	0.0
Solomon Islands	324.6	75.4	3.8	–
Tonga	...	...	...	...
Tuvalu	...	...	...	...
Vanuatu	365.8	39.9	1.6	0.4
Developed ADB Member Economies	**381,168.3**	**86,192.6**	**14,003.1**	**12,509.4**
Australia	155,093.0	29,027.2	1,982.6	1,244.8
Japan	191,538.0	51,369.2	10,684.6	10,947.0
New Zealand	34,537.3	5,796.3	1,336.0	317.6
DEVELOPING ADB MEMBER ECONOMIES[c]	**2,148,131.3**	**895,317.0**	**62,210.4**	**69,984.5**
ALL ADB REGIONAL MEMBERS[c]	**2,529,299.6**	**981,509.7**	**76,213.6**	**82,493.9**

... = data not available, – = magnitude equals zero, 0.0 = magnitude is less than half of unit employed, ADB = Asian Development Bank, p-km = passenger-kilometer, t-km = ton-kilometer.

Note: The numbers shown in the table are modeled estimates as published on the United Nations' SDG Global Database.

a A passenger-kilometer, abbreviated as p-km, is a unit of measurement representing the transport of 1 passenger by a defined mode of transport over 1 kilometer.
b A ton-kilometer, abbreviated as t-km, is a unit of measurement of freight transport representing the transport of 1 metric ton of goods (including packaging and tare weights of intermodal transport units) by a defined mode of transport over 1 kilometer.
c For reporting economies only.

Source: United Nations. SDG Global Database. https://unstats.un.org/sdgs/dataportal (accessed 20 July 2023).

Goal 9. Build resilient infrastructure, promote inclusive and sustainable industrialization, and foster innovation

Table 1.9.2: Selected Indicators for Sustainable Development Goal 9—Growth in Manufacturing

ADB Regional Member	Target 9.2: Promote inclusive and sustainable industrialization; and, by 2030, significantly raise industry's share of employment and GDP, in line with national circumstances, and double its share in least developed countries (or economies)					
	9.2.1: Manufacturing Value-Added[a]				9.2.2: Manufacturing Employment as a Proportion of Total Employment (%)	
	As a Proportion of GDP (%)		Per Capita (at constant 2015 $)			
	2010	2022	2010	2022	2010	2021
Developing ADB Member Economies						
Central and West Asia						
Afghanistan	7.0	7.2	36.6	25.0	6.8 (2012)	6.4
Armenia	9.0	11.4	261.1	585.3	5.7	6.2 (2020)
Azerbaijan	4.6	7.2	235.5	392.7	4.8	5.4
Georgia	8.8	8.4	270.2	453.1	5.3	5.9 (2020)
Kazakhstan	11.3	11.3	985.6	1,326.5	7.0	6.7 (2020)
Kyrgyz Republic	17.4	15.6	166.6	194.3	6.9	10.7
Pakistan	12.6	11.8	148.5	201.3	13.5	14.9
Tajikistan	19.2	19.1	155.6	258.0	5.5 (2009)	5.4 (2018)
Turkmenistan	46.4	32.6	2,487.4	1,907.5	...	...
Uzbekistan	12.3	14.0	261.2	496.4	11.5	11.4 (2020)
East Asia						
China, People's Republic of	27.5	28.3	1,540.2	3,228.3	...	28.7 (2020)
Hong Kong, China	1.3	1.0	492.6	429.4	3.8	2.6
Korea, Republic of	26.8	27.0	6,922.8	9,054.3	16.8	16.0 (2022)
Mongolia	9.0	8.2	240.1	345.1	6.3	7.3
Taipei,China	27.8	35.5	5,583.0	10,025.6	27.3	26.4 (2020)
South Asia						
Bangladesh	15.3	23.9	158.6	509.4	12.4	14.4 (2017)
Bhutan	8.7	6.6	188.3	188.6	3.9	6.8
India	15.3	15.7	193.7	328.6	10.8	10.9 (2020)
Maldives	2.0	1.9	169.3	206.8	9.1 (2009)	9.7 (2019)
Nepal	5.3	4.9	37.0	51.4	0.2 (2008)	14.5 (2017)
Sri Lanka	18.7	16.9	539.6	649.5	17.1	17.5 (2020)
Southeast Asia						
Brunei Darussalam	14.7	18.7	4,832.5	5,408.0	3.7 (2014)	9.1
Cambodia	14.3	15.7	126.7	232.2	10.7	15.1 (2019)
Indonesia	21.5	20.1	578.9	816.9	12.5	14.0 (2022)
Lao People's Democratic Republic	8.0	8.8	125.0	234.2	5.1	5.1 (2017)
Malaysia	22.8	25.0	1,847.8	2,835.5	16.8	16.7 (2020)
Myanmar	19.3	22.5	175.4	258.2	10.9 (2015)	12.2 (2020)
Philippines	20.6	19.8	497.2	699.2	8.3 (2012)	7.9
Singapore	21.0	22.5	10,072.8	14,112.1	14.6 (2011)	2.3
Thailand	30.1	26.8	1,529.0	1,684.1	14.1	15.7
Timor-Leste	0.9	1.7	10.9	27.7	3.2	5.6
Viet Nam	18.7	26.6	379.6	971.1	14.3	21.0
The Pacific						
Cook Islands	2.5	2.5	383.9	373.4	3.9 (2011)	3.8 (2019)
Fiji	11.1	11.1	476.5	561.8	9.3 (2011)	5.6 (2016)
Kiribati	5.1	4.1	66.5	58.2	13.2	4.0 (2020)
Marshall Islands	7.5	2.1	251.9	108.7	0.7	3.1 (2019)
Micronesia, Federated States of	0.4	0.6	13.1	17.3	2.4 (2014)	...
Nauru	25.6	22.2	1,051.2	2,024.8	0.5 (2013)	...
Niue	...	...	...	...	...	...
Palau	0.7	1.1	92.5	130.0	3.2 (2008)	1.5 (2020)
Papua New Guinea	2.6	1.6	55.7	39.9	1.8	...
Samoa	9.3	4.3	361.3	146.0	5.5 (2011)	5.1 (2017)
Solomon Islands	11.7	9.4	238.5	177.9	5.5 (2013)	...
Tonga	6.1	5.2	204.7	210.2	...	17.9
Tuvalu	1.1	0.2	29.4	8.9	...	3.7 (2016)
Vanuatu	5.0	2.7	142.9	70.4	2.3	4.0 (2019)
Developed ADB Member Economies						
Australia	7.5	5.4	3,685.6	3,049.5	8.9	6.9
Japan	20.8	20.1	6,852.2	7,283.3	16.8	15.5 (2022)
New Zealand	12.3	10.4	4,348.9	4,350.9	11.6	8.7

... = data not available, $ = United States dollars, ADB = Asian Development Bank, GDP = gross domestic product.

a United Nations Statistics Division figures calculated from GDP, manufacturing value-added, and population data.

Sources: United Nations. SDG Global Database. https://unstats.un.org/sdgs/dataportal (accessed 23 July 2023). For Taipei,China: United Nations Industrial Development Organization. Statistics Data Portal. https://stat.unido.org/sdg (accessed 23 July 2023).

Goal 9. Build resilient infrastructure, promote inclusive and sustainable industrialization, and foster innovation

Table 1.9.3: Selected Indicators for Sustainable Development Goal 9—Carbon Dioxide Emissions

ADB Regional Member	Target 9.4: By 2030, upgrade infrastructure and retrofit industries to make them sustainable, with increased resource-use efficiency and greater adoption of clean and environmentally sound technologies and industrial processes, with all countries (or economies) taking action in accordance with their respective capabilities — 9.4.1: Carbon Dioxide Emissions[a]			
	Per Unit of GDP (PPP) (kg of CO_2 equivalent per constant 2017 $)		Per Unit of Manufacturing Value-Added (kg of CO_2 equivalent per constant 2015 $)	
	2010	2020	2010	2020
Developing ADB Member Economies				
Central and West Asia				
Afghanistan	...	...	...	...
Armenia	0.15	0.17	0.7	0.3
Azerbaijan	0.18	0.24	0.6	0.9
Georgia	0.14	0.18	0.5	1.0
Kazakhstan	0.65	0.43	3.2	1.0
Kyrgyz Republic	0.27	0.26	0.7	0.4
Pakistan	0.16	0.15	1.3	1.1
Tajikistan	0.13	0.21	0.1 (2012)	0.6
Turkmenistan	1.30	0.63	0.1	0.1
Uzbekistan	0.85	0.44	2.3	0.7
East Asia				
China, People's Republic of	0.66	0.44	1.3	0.7
Hong Kong, China	0.12	0.08	0.5	0.7
Korea, Republic of	0.32	0.25	0.2	0.1
Mongolia	0.70	0.54	1.9	1.2
Taipei,China	...	...	0.3	0.1
South Asia				
Bangladesh	0.10	0.09	0.4	0.2
Bhutan	...	...	...	...
India	0.30	0.24	1.6	1.2
Maldives	...	...	...	...
Nepal	0.06	0.11	1.2	3.0
Sri Lanka	0.07	0.08	0.1	0.1
Southeast Asia				
Brunei Darussalam	0.26	0.34	0.2	0.1
Cambodia	0.12	0.19	0.4	0.3
Indonesia	0.20	0.17	0.9	0.6
Lao People's Democratic Republic	0.08	0.30	1.1	0.4
Malaysia	0.33	0.27	0.6	0.4
Myanmar	0.06	0.12	0.3	0.2
Philippines	0.14	0.14	0.3	0.1
Singapore	0.11	0.08	0.2	0.2
Thailand	0.23	0.20	0.5	0.5
Timor-Leste	...	...	...	...
Viet Nam	0.23	0.29	1.3	1.1
The Pacific				
Cook Islands	...	...	...	...
Fiji	...	...	...	...
Kiribati	...	...	...	...
Marshall Islands	...	...	...	...
Micronesia, Federated States of	...	...	...	...
Nauru	...	...	...	...
Niue	...	...	...	...
Palau	...	...	...	...
Papua New Guinea	...	...	...	...
Samoa	...	...	...	...
Solomon Islands	...	...	...	...
Tonga	...	...	...	...
Tuvalu	...	...	...	...
Vanuatu	...	...	...	...
Developed ADB Member Economies				
Australia	0.40	0.30	0.4	0.4
Japan	0.23	0.20	0.2	0.2
New Zealand	0.19	0.15	0.3	0.3

... = data not available, $ = United States dollars, ADB = Asian Development Bank, CO_2 = carbon dioxide, GDP = gross domestic product, kg = kilogram, PPP = purchasing power parity.

a Refers to carbon dioxide emissions from fuel combustion.

Sources: United Nations. SDG Global Database. https://unstats.un.org/sdgs/dataportal (accessed 20 July 2023). For CO_2 per unit of manufacturing value-added for Taipei,China: United Nations Industrial Development Organization. UNIDO Statistics Data Portal. https://stat.unido.org/SDG (accessed 21 July 2023).

Goal 9. Build resilient infrastructure, promote inclusive and sustainable industrialization, and foster innovation

Table 1.9.4: Selected Indicators for Sustainable Development Goal 9—Research and Development

ADB Regional Member	Target 9.5: Enhance scientific research, upgrade the technological capabilities of industrial sectors in all countries (or economies), in particular developing countries (or economies), including, by 2030, encouraging innovation and substantially increasing the number of research and development workers per 1 million people and public and private research and development spending			
	9.5.1: Research and Development Expenditure as a Proportion of GDP (%)		9.5.2: Researchers (Full-Time Equivalent) (per million inhabitants)	
	2010	2021	2010	2021
Developing ADB Member Economies				
Central and West Asia				
Afghanistan	...	...	...	...
Armenia	0.24	0.21	...	...
Azerbaijan	0.22	0.21	...	1,741
Georgia	0.08 (2013)	0.25	566 (2013)	1,624
Kazakhstan	0.15	0.13	371	630
Kyrgyz Republic	0.16	0.09 (2020)	...	...
Pakistan	0.33 (2011)	0.16	143 (2011)	423
Tajikistan	0.09	0.09 (2020)	...	...
Turkmenistan	...	...	...	...
Uzbekistan	0.15	0.13	545	523
East Asia				
China, People's Republic of	1.71	2.41 (2020)	885	1,585 (2020)
Hong Kong, China	0.75	0.97	3,115	4,553
Korea, Republic of	3.32	4.80 (2020)	5,331	8,714 (2020)
Mongolia	0.24	0.13 (2020)	...	331 (2020)
Taipei,China	...	...	...	...
South Asia				
Bangladesh	...	...	...	...
Bhutan	...	...	...	...
India	0.79	0.66 (2018)	156	253 (2018)
Maldives	...	...	...	...
Nepal	0.30	...	61 (2002)	...
Sri Lanka	0.13	0.12 (2018)	106	106 (2018)
Southeast Asia				
Brunei Darussalam	0.04 (2004)	0.28 (2018)	284 (2004)	...
Cambodia	0.05 (2002)	0.12 (2015)	18 (2002)	30 (2015)
Indonesia	0.08 (2009)	0.28 (2020)	89 (2009)	396 (2020)
Lao People's Democratic Republic	0.04 (2002)	...	16 (2002)	...
Malaysia	1.04	0.95 (2020)	1,462	741 (2020)
Myanmar	0.20 (2002)	0.15	18 (2002)	19
Philippines	0.11 (2011)	0.32 (2018)	84 (2011)	174 (2018)
Singapore	1.93	1.89 (2019)	6,242	7,287 (2019)
Thailand	0.36 (2011)	1.33 (2020)	539 (2011)	2,070 (2020)
Timor-Leste	...	...	...	...
Viet Nam	0.15 (2011)	0.42 (2019)	679 (2013)	757 (2019)
The Pacific				
Cook Islands	...	...	...	...
Fiji	...	...	...	...
Kiribati	...	...	...	...
Marshall Islands	...	...	...	...
Micronesia, Federated States of	...	...	...	...
Nauru	...	...	...	...
Niue	...	...	...	...
Palau	...	...	...	...
Papua New Guinea	...	0.03 (2016)	...	35 (2016)
Samoa	...	...	...	...
Solomon Islands	...	...	...	...
Tonga	...	...	...	...
Tuvalu	...	...	...	...
Vanuatu	...	...	...	...
Developed ADB Member Economies				
Australia	2.37	1.83 (2019)	4,532	...
Japan	3.10	3.27 (2020)	5,104	5,455 (2020)
New Zealand	1.23 (2011)	1.40 (2019)	3,689 (2011)	5,854 (2019)

... = data not available, ADB = Asian Development Bank, GDP = gross domestic product.

Source: United Nations Educational, Scientific and Cultural Organization (UNESCO) Institute for Statistics. UIS.Stat Database. https://data.uis.unesco.org/# (accessed 16 July 2023).

Goal 9. Build resilient infrastructure, promote inclusive and sustainable industrialization, and foster innovation

Table 1.9.5: Selected Indicators for Sustainable Development Goal 9—Official International Support and Industry Value-Added

ADB Regional Member	Target 9.a: Facilitate sustainable and resilient infrastructure development in developing countries through enhanced financial, technological, and technical support to African countries, least developed countries, landlocked developing countries and small island developing States — 9.a.1: Total Official International Support to Infrastructure[a] (constant 2021 $ million)		Target 9.b: Support domestic technology development, research, and innovation in developing countries (or economies), including by ensuring a conducive policy environment for, *inter alia*, industrial diversification and value addition to commodities — 9.b.1: Proportion of Medium and High-Tech Industry Value-Added in Total Value-Added (%)	
	2010	2021	2010	2020
Developing ADB Member Economies				
Central and West Asia	**4,290.6**	**5,738.0**		
Afghanistan	1,380.5	292.9	9.5	8.5
Armenia	243.3	371.4	4.5	8.2
Azerbaijan	230.4	273.0	8.0	15.2
Georgia	370.3	1,234.8	17.0	12.5
Kazakhstan	1,246.9	431.0	12.8	16.9
Kyrgyz Republic	70.9	186.1	3.5	2.2
Pakistan	520.2	1,691.0	24.0	22.9
Tajikistan	133.3	333.1	3.7	2.8
Turkmenistan	1.6	123.3	...	...
Uzbekistan	93.2	801.5	19.7	20.6
East Asia[b]	**2,699.3**	**1,866.5**		
China, People's Republic of	2,601.0	1,731.4	41.4	41.5
Hong Kong, China	...	...	38.1	37.3
Korea, Republic of	...	...	61.2	63.8
Mongolia	98.3	135.1	2.1	3.9
Taipei,China	...	...	64.3	71.0
South Asia	**7,221.4**	**11,838.2**		
Bangladesh	471.6	2,882.0	9.1	7.8
Bhutan	97.6	49.5	...	...
India	5,961.0	7,513.5	38.1	44.6
Maldives	31.2	40.2	2.6	2.6
Nepal	195.6	492.5	8.2	8.6
Sri Lanka	464.3	860.5	9.8	8.3
Southeast Asia[b]	**3,782.6**	**6,505.6**		
Brunei Darussalam	...	...	3.3	3.3
Cambodia	136.0	346.2	0.3	0.3
Indonesia	1,189.1	2,018.4	39.7	35.0
Lao People's Democratic Republic	110.3	90.9	3.8	3.8
Malaysia	25.6	113.1	40.7	43.3
Myanmar	5.4	399.1	27.6	23.7
Philippines	278.8	1,653.7	37.1	47.3
Singapore	...	...	76.0	82.1
Thailand	150.1	523.5	43.8	41.4
Timor-Leste	25.4	35.3	...	...
Viet Nam	1,861.9	1,325.3	23.4	38.3
The Pacific[c]	**255.4**	**912.6**		
Cook Islands	1.7	10.3 (2019)	...	...
Fiji	13.0	151.5	7.9	7.8
Kiribati	1.4	5.8	...	...
Marshall Islands	5.6	73.1	...	...
Micronesia, Federated States of	11.0	7.8	...	...
Nauru	0.2	11.8	...	...
Niue	3.6	4.8	...	...
Palau	6.1	10.7	...	...
Papua New Guinea	107.2	519.6	12.6	12.6
Samoa	25.2	17.7	...	...
Solomon Islands	15.4	51.1	...	...
Tonga	28.2	24.6	1.6	1.6
Tuvalu	0.9	9.2	...	...
Vanuatu	36.0	24.9	...	...
Developed ADB Member Economies	**...**	**...**		
Australia	...	...	27.8	29.8
Japan	...	...	53.7	56.9
New Zealand	...	...	17.6	21.7
DEVELOPING ADB MEMBER ECONOMIES[c]	**18,249.3**	**26,860.9**		

... = data not available, $ = United States dollars, ADB = Asian Development Bank.

a Gross disbursements of total official development assistance and other official flows from all donors in support of infrastructure.

b Includes only reporting economies with data corresponding to the year heading.

c For estimating aggregates, imputation was done for economies with missing data by substituting available data from the nearest years.

Sources: United Nations. SDG Global Database. https://unstats.un.org/sdgs/dataportal (accessed 22 July 2023). For Taipei,China: United Nations Industrial Development Organization. Statistics Data Portal. https://stat.unido.org/sdg (accessed 23 July 2023).

Goal 9. Build resilient infrastructure, promote inclusive and sustainable industrialization, and foster innovation

Table 1.9.6: Selected Indicators for Sustainable Development Goal 9—Coverage by Mobile Networks

ADB Regional Member	Target 9.c: Significantly increase access to information and communications technology and strive to provide universal and affordable access to the internet in least developed countries (or economies) by 2020					
	9.c.1.a: Proportion of Population Covered by 2G Mobile Networks (%)		9.c.1.b: Proportion of Population Covered by 3G Mobile Networks (%)		9.c.1.c: Proportion of Population Covered by LTE Mobile Networks (%)	
	2010	2021	2010	2021	2012	2021
Developing ADB Member Economies						
Central and West Asia						
Afghanistan	80.0	90.0	28.0 (2013)	57.0	– (2014)	26.0
Armenia	98.9	100.0	93.0	100.0	17.5	100.0
Azerbaijan	100.0	100.0	69.2	99.5	6.7	94.0
Georgia	99.0	100.0	74.4 (2012)	100.0	8.9 (2013)	99.7
Kazakhstan	95.0	98.2	45.7 (2012)	96.0	2.7	83.5
Kyrgyz Republic	96.0	99.3	32.0 (2011)	91.0	0.5 (2014)	85.0
Pakistan	75.0 (2012)	89.1	– (2012)	78.1	–	75.4
Tajikistan	60.0 (2015)	90.0	60.0 (2014)	90.0	8.4	80.0
Turkmenistan	60.0 (2015)	97.9	28.5 (2012)	75.8	6.0 (2013)	67.0
Uzbekistan	92.0 (2012)	99.4	40.0 (2012)	95.0	1.0 (2014)	75.0
East Asia						
China, People's Republic of	99.5	99.9	43.6 (2014)	99.9	10.0 (2013)	99.9
Hong Kong, China	100.0	100.0	99.0	99.0	91.7	99.0
Korea, Republic of	99.9	99.9	99.0	99.9	99.0 (2014)	99.9
Mongolia	85.0	100.0	49.8	100.0	6.9 (2016)	99.0
Taipei,China	...	...	...	...	...	...
South Asia						
Bangladesh	96.0	99.6	1.0 (2012)	98.2	59.0 (2014)	98.2
Bhutan	98.0	98.0	15.0	95.0	5.0 (2013)	80.0
India	93.5 (2013)	99.2	36.5 (2012)	98.8	2.0 (2014)	98.7
Maldives	100.0	100.0	57.1	100.0	11.4 (2013)	100.0
Nepal	35.1	93.0	30.0 (2014)	54.1	– (2014)	45.0
Sri Lanka	98.0	99.0	72.0 (2012)	96.0	5.0	96.0
Southeast Asia						
Brunei Darussalam	97.0 (2015)	99.0	80.8 (2012)	96.0	5.0 (2013)	95.3
Cambodia	99.0	99.6	60.0 (2014)	95.7	9.0 (2014)	95.7
Indonesia	100.0 (2011)	97.8	60.0 (2014)	93.9	5.0 (2013)	96.2
Lao People's Democratic Republic	59.0	95.0	17.0	85.0	2.0 (2014)	52.0
Malaysia	95.0	98.5	81.1	95.4	15.0 (2013)	95.4
Myanmar	73.0 (2014)	96.3	9.7 (2012)	94.3	– (2014)	94.3
Philippines	99.0	99.0	69.0	96.0	6.0	80.0 (2020)
Singapore	100.0	100.0	100.0	100.0	99.0 (2014)	100.0
Thailand	100.0 (2011)	98.8	80.0 (2013)	98.8	– (2014)	98.1
Timor-Leste	86.0	96.5	96.0 (2014)	96.5	– (2015)	45.0
Viet Nam	94.0 (2015)	99.8	31.0 (2012)	99.8	– (2014)	99.7
The Pacific						
Cook Islands	...	100.0	20.2 (2014)	55.0	55.0 (2017)	55.0
Fiji	88.0 (2015)	98.0	30.0 (2013)	96.0	15.0 (2014)	80.0 (2020)
Kiribati	70.0 (2015)	75.0	15.0 (2013)	75.0	10.0 (2013)	54.0
Marshall Islands	65.0 (2015)	65.0	...	...	...	...
Micronesia, Federated States of	80.0 (2015)	80.0 (2020)	– (2014)	15.0 (2020)	– (2015)	– (2017)
Nauru	98.0	98.0	98.0	98.0	– (2014)	30.0
Niue	...	...	– (2014)	...	...	...
Palau	95.0	98.0	88.0 (2015)	88.0	...	...
Papua New Guinea	89.0 (2015)	89.0	60.0 (2014)	64.4	7.0 (2014)	50.0
Samoa	97.0 (2015)	97.0	31.4 (2012)	91.0	– (2015)	49.0
Solomon Islands	91.0 (2015)	95.0	27.1 (2012)	45.0	11.5 (2015)	25.0
Tonga	92.0 (2015)	99.0	15.0 (2013)	99.0	– (2014)	96.0
Tuvalu	19.0 (2015)	50.0	19.0 (2015)	48.0	– (2015)	–
Vanuatu	87.0	90.0	23.0 (2011)	70.0	18.0 (2015)	70.0
Developed ADB Member Economies						
Australia	99.0	99.5	99.0	99.5	52.2	99.5
Japan	99.9	99.9	99.9 (2012)	99.9	84.0	99.9
New Zealand	97.0	98.3	97.0	98.3	50.0 (2014)	97.5

... = data not available, – = magnitude equals zero, 2G = second generation, 3G = third generation, ADB = Asian Development Bank, LTE = Long-Term Evolution.

Source: United Nations. SDG Global Database. https://unstats.un.org/sdgs/dataportal (accessed 13 July 2023).

Table 1.10.1: Selected Indicators for Sustainable Development Goal 10—Household Expenditure or Income Growth

ADB Regional Member	Target 10.1: By 2030, progressively achieve and sustain income growth of the bottom 40% of the population at a rate higher than the national average			
	10.1.1.a: Growth Rates of Household Expenditure or Income per Capita among the Bottom 40% of the Population[a,b] (%)		10.1.1.b: Growth Rates of Household Expenditure or Income per Capita[a,b] (%)	
Developing ADB Member Economies				
Central and West Asia				
Afghanistan			…	
Armenia[c]	1.3	(2013–2018)	2.4	(2013–2018)
Azerbaijan	…		…	
Georgia[c]	0.2	(2016–2021)	–0.9	(2016–2021)
Kazakhstan[c]	–0.3	(2013–2018)	–0.2	(2013–2018)
Kyrgyz Republic[c]	0.8	(2015–2020)	1.1	(2015–2020)
Pakistan[c]	1.3	(2013–2018)	1.3	(2013–2018)
Tajikistan[c]	1.3	(2009–2015)	2.7	(2009–2015)
Turkmenistan	…		…	
Uzbekistan	…		…	
East Asia				
China, People's Republic of[c]	7.2	(2014–2019)	6.3	(2014–2019)
Hong Kong, China	…		…	
Korea, Republic of[d]	2.5	(2012–2016)	2.3	(2012–2016)
Mongolia[c]	2.5	(2016–2018)	3.1	(2016–2018)
Taipei,China	…		…	
South Asia				
Bangladesh[c]	1.4	(2010–2016)	1.5	(2010–2016)
Bhutan[c]	1.6	(2012–2017)	1.7	(2012–2017)
India[c]	4.5	(2015–2019)	4.9	(2015–2019)
Maldives	…		…	
Nepal[c]	8.3	(2003–2010)	4.7	(2003–2010)
Sri Lanka[c]	1.7	(2016–2019)	0.7	(2016–2019)
Southeast Asia				
Brunei Darussalam	…		…	
Cambodia	…		…	
Indonesia[c]	3.4	(2017–2022)	2.4	(2017–2022)
Lao People's Democratic Republic[c]	1.9	(2012–2018)	3.1	(2012–2018)
Malaysia[d]	4.1	(2015–2018)	4.4	(2015–2018)
Myanmar[c]	9.5	(2015–2017)	1.3	(2015–2017)
Philippines[d]	3.0	(2015–2021)	0.8	(2015–2021)
Singapore	…		…	
Thailand[c]	0.7	(2015–2019)	0.1	(2015–2019)
Timor-Leste	…		…	
Viet Nam[c]	4.7	(2016–2020)	5.6	(2016–2020)
The Pacific				
Cook Islands	…		…	
Fiji[c]	1.2	(2008–2013)	–0.5	(2008–2013)
Kiribati	…		…	
Marshall Islands	…		…	
Micronesia, Federated States of	…		…	
Nauru	…		…	
Niue	…		…	
Palau	…		…	
Papua New Guinea	…		…	
Samoa	…		…	
Solomon Islands	…		…	
Tonga[c]	–1.8	(2009–2015)	–3.7	(2009–2015)
Tuvalu	…		…	
Vanuatu	…		…	
Developed ADB Member Economies				
Australia[d]	–0.5	(2014–2018)	–0.3	(2014–2018)
Japan	…		…	
New Zealand	…		…	

… = data not available, ADB=Asian Development Bank.

a Based on real mean per capita consumption or income measured at 2011 purchasing power parity using the World Bank's Poverty and Inequality Platform (https://www.pip.worldbank.org). Data reported are based on consumption, except for Australia, Malaysia, the Philippines, and the Republic of Korea, which are based on income.

b For the data collection periods in brackets, the initial year refers to the most recently conducted survey prior to the latest survey (only surveys conducted between 3 and 7 years before the latest survey are considered). The final year refers to the latest survey (those available between 2010 and 2022).

c Estimated from individual consumption data.

d Estimated from individual income data.

Source: United Nations. SDG Global Database. https://unstats.un.org/sdgs/dataportal (accessed 16 July 2023).

Goal 11. Make cities and human settlements inclusive, safe, resilient, and sustainable

Table 1.11.1: Selected Indicators for Sustainable Development Goal 11—Sustainable Cities and Environment

ADB Regional Member	Target 11.1: By 2030, ensure access for all to adequate, safe, and affordable housing and basic services, and upgrade slums — 11.1.1: Proportion of Urban Population Living in Slums, Informal Settlements, or Inadequate Housing (%)		Target 11.5: By 2030, significantly reduce the number of deaths and the number of people affected, and substantially decrease the direct economic losses relative to global gross domestic product caused by disasters, including water-related disasters, with a focus on protecting the poor and people in vulnerable situations — 11.5.2: Direct Economic Loss Attributed to Disasters[a] ($ million)		Target 11.6: By 2030, reduce the adverse per capita environmental impact of cities, including by paying special attention to air quality and municipal and other waste management — 11.6.2: Annual Mean Levels (μg/m^3) of Fine Particulate Matter (e.g., PM2.5 and PM10) in Cities[b] (population weighted)	
					Total	Urban
	2010	2020	2010	2021	2019	2019
Developing ADB Member Economies						
Central and West Asia						
Afghanistan	64.8	73.3	...	567.7 (2019)	62.5	75.2
Armenia	10.4	8.4	7.0	13.9	34.1	36.2
Azerbaijan	26.9	...	...	...	24.6	26.2
Georgia	10.9	7.1	...	11.8	19.1	20.9
Kazakhstan	10.5	0.8	–	52.5 (2020)	26.5	35.4
Kyrgyz Republic	24.8	2.4	81.2	6.7 (2020)	37.6	39.6
Pakistan	63.6	56.0	1,173.8 (2009)	18.2 (2018)	50.1	51.6
Tajikistan	37.5	17.1	...	4.9 (2020)	53.6	56.8
Turkmenistan	9.8	8.5	...	– (2019)	26.4	26.4
Uzbekistan	...	...	...	0.3	41.0	44.5
East Asia						
China, People's Republic of	...	...	...	...	38.2	40.2
Hong Kong, China	...	...	...	...	...	...
Korea, Republic of	...	...	368.3	68.2 (2020)	24.0	24.4
Mongolia	37.7	17.9	41.0	40.8	41.3	50.6
Taipei,China	...	...	...	...	...	...
South Asia						
Bangladesh	55.1	51.9	11,295.3 (2007)	...	46.0	46.8
Bhutan	...	...	0.5	243.0 (2018)	26.1	16.9
India	51.8	49.0	...	...	50.2	53.0
Maldives	39.9	34.8	0.2 (2008)	...	13.0	12.7
Nepal	51.9	40.3	292.8	58.7	36.4	36.9
Sri Lanka	...	...	– (2009)	115.4 (2020)	23.9	24.8
Southeast Asia						
Brunei Darussalam	...	...	...	...	6.9	6.8
Cambodia	56.6	39.7	0.0	–	17.8	18.3
Indonesia	26.9	19.4	859.9	7,742.3 (2020)	19.3	19.9
Lao People's Democratic Republic	37.3	21.8	120.7	...	21.2	24.2
Malaysia	...	...	33.0	780.9	21.5	23.7
Myanmar	45.4	58.3	14.6	794.4	27.2	27.8
Philippines	42.9	36.6	...	55,860.7	22.5	24.2
Singapore	...	...	...	...	13.3	13.3
Thailand	12.0	6.8	...	...	24.6	25.5
Timor-Leste	50.0	33.9	29.6	...	20.5	21.8
Viet Nam	20.6	5.8	988.0	2.3 (2019)	20.9	22.1
The Pacific						
Cook Islands	...	...	...	...	7.8	7.9
Fiji	12.5	9.4	24.6	92.9	7.4	8.1
Kiribati	...	...	...	22.5	7.6	8.0
Marshall Islands	...	...	...	–	7.2	7.5
Micronesia, Federated States of	...	...	...	0.0	7.8	8.1
Nauru	...	...	...	0.0	7.4	7.4
Niue	...	...	...	...	6.7	...
Palau	...	...	– (2011)	17.3	7.8	7.9
Papua New Guinea	...	...	–	1.6 (2020)	8.9	9.5
Samoa	...	...	27.2 (2009)	...	7.8	8.1
Solomon Islands	...	...	12.4 (2013)	1.8 (2020)	7.8	8.7
Tonga	...	...	1.1 (2011)	0.6 (2020)	7.5	7.7
Tuvalu	...	...	– (2011)	8.9 (2020)	6.8	...
Vanuatu	...	...	3.1	–	8.4	9.1
Developed ADB Member Economies						
Australia	...	...	106.3	149.9	8.9	9.1
Japan	...	...	...	2,619.3	10.8	11.1
New Zealand	...	...	...	12.3	8.6	8.7

... = data not available, – = magnitude equals zero, 0.0 = magnitude is less than half of unit employed, $ = United States dollars, ADB = Asian Development Bank, m^3 = cubic meter, PM = particulate matter, μg = microgram.

a The data are submitted to the United Nation's SDG Global Database by the United Nations Office for Disaster Risk Reduction (UNISDR) and have been extracted from two sources: (a) the Sendai Framework Monitoring System as provided by designated national focal points; and (b) Desinventar disaster loss databases. Some of the data have not undergone an official validation process and may be subject to revision at a later date.

b Data are estimates as published on the United Nation's SDG Global Database.

Source: United Nations. SDG Global Database. https://unstats.un.org/sdgs/dataportal (accessed 23 July 2023).

Table 1.12.1: Selected Indicators for Sustainable Development Goal 12—Responsible Consumption and Production

ADB Regional Member	Target 12.2: By 2030, achieve the sustainable management and efficient use of natural resources							
	12.2.1: Material Footprint				12.2.2: Domestic Material Consumption			
	All (t million)		Per Capita (t)		All (t million)		Per Capita (t)	
	2010	2019	2010	2019	2010	2019	2010	2019
Developing ADB Member Economies								
Central and West Asia	**1,412.8**	**1,987.6**	...	...	**1,498.9**	**2,180.8**	...	...
Afghanistan	51.7	52.6	1.8	1.4	46.8	46.6	1.6	1.2
Armenia	18.6	17.6	6.5	6.0	30.0	49.3	10.4	16.7
Azerbaijan	86.5	106.1	9.6	10.6	77.5	96.0	8.4	9.4
Georgia	37.8	41.4	9.2	10.3	24.9	45.1	6.1	11.3
Kazakhstan	478.2	638.3	29.4	34.4	432.3	561.8	26.6	30.3
Kyrgyz Republic	36.6	50.2	6.8	7.8	33.6	55.6	6.2	8.7
Pakistan	500.7	747.8	2.8	3.5	556.9	854.0	3.1	3.9
Tajikistan	22.1	53.6	2.9	5.7	17.9	59.6	2.4	6.4
Turkmenistan	29.0	78.0	5.7	13.1	48.7	80.3	9.6	13.5
Uzbekistan	151.6	202.0	5.3	6.1	230.6	332.5	8.1	10.1
East Asia[a]	**25,157.0**	**33,479.1**	...	...	**27,620.6**	**34,235.8**	...	...
China, People's Republic of	23,584.8	31,480.2	17.2	22.0	26,357.9	32,667.4	19.3	22.8
Hong Kong, China	488.2	837.2	70.1	112.6	69.7	132.1	10.0	17.8
Korea, Republic of	1,056.7	1,127.5	21.3	22.0	779.3	920.4	15.7	18.0
Mongolia	27.3	34.2	10.0	10.6	106.2	239.2	30.2	50.1
Taipei,China	...	...	...	...	307.5	276.7	13.3	11.6
South Asia	**6,112.1**	**7,893.9**	...	...	**6,151.9**	**8,140.6**	...	...
Bangladesh	357.1	470.2	2.4	2.9	372.5	415.8	2.5	2.6
Bhutan	17.6	24.7	25.7	32.4	13.0	21.2	19.0	27.8
India	5,577.6	7,140.1	4.5	5.2	5,595.8	7,457.0	4.5	5.5
Maldives	5.2	6.3 (2017)	14.2	12.8 (2017)	2.2	5.8	6.0	10.9
Nepal	67.0	159.7	2.5	5.6	89.5	160.8	3.3	5.6
Sri Lanka	87.6	92.9	4.3	4.4	79.0	80.1	3.9	3.8
Southeast Asia	**4,118.1**	**5,650.1**	...	...	**4,337.0**	**5,667.3**	...	...
Brunei Darussalam	25.1	37.1	64.7	85.7	7.6	4.4	19.4	10.1
Cambodia	92.2	94.0	6.4	5.7	122.9	124.1	8.6	7.5
Indonesia	1,259.6	1,831.4	5.2	6.8	1,213.1	1,805.6	5.0	6.7
Lao People's Democratic Republic	41.5	69.1	6.6	9.6	51.6	105.2	8.3	14.7
Malaysia	443.1	625.8	15.7	19.6	488.1	675.1	17.3	21.1
Myanmar	105.8	111.5	2.1	2.1	227.8	229.0	4.5	4.2
Philippines	451.2	948.3	4.8	8.8	433.4	887.8	4.6	8.2
Singapore	261.8	292.7	51.0	50.4	114.4	119.8	22.3	20.6
Thailand	676.3	817.9	10.1	11.7	718.6	830.9	10.7	11.9
Timor-Leste	...	...	...	...	2.6	6.1	2.4	4.7
Viet Nam	761.5	822.3	8.7	8.5	957.1	879.3	10.9	9.1
The Pacific[a]	...	...	...	...	**110.5**	**92.8**	...	...
Cook Islands	...	...	...	...	0.1	0.1	4.9	4.1
Fiji	5.1	6.5 (2017)	6.0	7.5 (2017)	8.4	4.8	9.8	5.4
Kiribati	...	...	...	...	0.5	0.6	5.3	5.5
Marshall Islands	...	...	...	...	0.1	0.1	1.9	1.9
Micronesia, Federated States of	...	...	...	...	0.4	0.4	3.7	3.5
Nauru	...	...	...	...	0.4	0.1	43.6	9.5
Niue	...	...	...	...	...	...	...	...
Palau	...	...	...	...	0.1	0.2	6.1	8.8
Papua New Guinea	34.2	45.9	4.7	5.2	92.8	72.0	12.7	8.2
Samoa	1.3	1.6 (2017)	7.2	7.9 (2017)	1.3	1.7	6.7	8.4
Solomon Islands	...	...	...	...	2.4	6.5	4.5	9.7
Tonga	...	...	...	...	1.4	3.8	13.8	36.8
Tuvalu	...	...	...	...	0.0	0.0	0.6	1.0
Vanuatu	1.9	2.1 (2017)	7.9	7.3 (2017)	2.5	2.5	10.7	8.2
Developed ADB Member Economies	**3,668.5**	**3,633.2**	...	...	**2,193.2**	**2,370.4**	...	...
Australia	1,005.9	1,180.1	45.4	46.8	835.9	1,064.6	37.7	42.2
Japan	2,530.3	2,306.3	19.7	18.2	1,208.7	1,142.0	9.4	9.1
New Zealand	132.3	146.8	30.3	30.7	148.6	163.8	34.2	33.0

... = data not available, 0.0 = magnitude is less than half of unit employed, ADB = Asian Development Bank, t = metric ton.

a Regional aggregates include reporting economies only.

Source: For Indicator 12.2.1: Organisation for Economic Co-operation and Development. OECD Statistics-Material Resources. https://stats.oecd.org/viewhtml.aspx?datasetcode=MATERIAL_RESOURCES&lang=en (accessed 27 July 2023). For Indicator 12.2.2: United Nations. SDG Global Database. https://unstats.un.org/sdgs/dataportal (accessed 27 July 2023); and for Taipei,China: Organisation for Economic Co-operation and Development. OECD Statistics-Material Resources. https://stats.oecd.org/viewhtml.aspx?datasetcode=MATERIAL_RESOURCES&lang=en (accessed 27 July 2023).

Goal 13. Take urgent action to combat climate change and its impacts

Table 1.13.1: Selected Indicators for Sustainable Development Goal 13—Impact of Disasters and Risk Reduction Strategies

ADB Regional Member	Target 13.1: Strengthen resilience and adaptive capacity to climate-related hazards and natural disasters in all countries									
	13.1.1.a: Number of Persons Affected by Disaster[a]				13.1.1.b: Number of Deaths Due to Disaster[a]				13.1.2: Countries that Adopt and Implement National Disaster Risk Reduction Strategies in Line with the Sendai Framework for Disaster Risk Reduction 2015–2030[b,c]	
	2010		2021		2010		2021		2021	
Developing ADB Member Economies										
Central and West Asia										
Afghanistan	...		418	(2019)	...		368	(2019)	0.73	(2019)
Armenia	7,641		192,401		155		5,577		0.93	
Azerbaijan	...		...		...		...		...	
Georgia	79		712,286		54		11,395		0.98	
Kazakhstan	–		939		9		15,757		0.78	
Kyrgyz Republic	76,959		81,790	(2020)	158		109		0.90	(2019)
Pakistan	2,963		404	(2020)	2,199		10,599	(2020)	0.80	(2020)
Tajikistan	...		2,085	(2020)	...		8	(2020)	1.00	(2020)
Turkmenistan	...		–	(2019)	...		–	(2019)	0.75	(2019)
Uzbekistan	...		1,953		...		11		1.00	
East Asia										
China, People's Republic of	...		7,300,250	(2020)	...		765		1.00	(2020)
Hong Kong, China	...		...		...		...		...	
Korea, Republic of	93,032		131,737	(2020)	28		1,070	(2020)	1.00	(2020)
Mongolia	9,086		702,706		226		2,230		1.00	(2020)
Taipei,China	...		...		...		...		...	
South Asia										
Bangladesh	...		206		96		20,876		–	
Bhutan	1,711		244	(2018)	2,763		21	(2019)	0.50	(2018)
India	...		14,117,772		7,489		2,206		1.00	(2020)
Maldives	84	(2008)	...		4	(2008)	1	(2019)	...	
Nepal	134,309		45,924		1,002		508		0.75	(2019)
Sri Lanka	1,193,504		63,655	(2020)	50		67		0.93	(2020)
Southeast Asia										
Brunei Darussalam	...		15,317		...		54		0.05	(2018)
Cambodia	5,916		41,475		91		142		0.65	(2019)
Indonesia	333,235		4,225,467		1,630		144,475		0.88	(2020)
Lao People's Democratic Republic	32,952		...		50		...		0.03	
Malaysia	9,882		3,141,148		4		31,954		0.70	
Myanmar	545,156		98,313	(2020)	55		275	(2020)	...	
Philippines	1,489,711		11,305,535		192		58,064		1.00	
Singapore	...		228,667		...		944		...	
Thailand	...		142,780	(2018)	...		81	(2018)	0.68	(2020)
Timor-Leste	19,331		...		10		...		...	
Viet Nam	651,751		359	(2019)	60		5	(2019)	...	
The Pacific										
Cook Islands	...		...		...		...		...	
Fiji	6,644		78,029		3		709		0.98	
Kiribati	85	(2008)	333		...		–		0.93	
Marshall Islands	...		–		...		–		–	(2020)
Micronesia, Federated States of	...		15,010		2	(2011)	–		0.43	
Nauru	...		–		...		–		0.60	
Niue	...		...		...		...		...	
Palau	–	(2011)	20,000		–	(2011)	–		0.73	
Papua New Guinea	–		3,297	(2020)	16		651		0.78	(2020)
Samoa	6,332	(2009)	15		369	(2009)	–		0.73	
Solomon Islands	...		1		...		–		0.73	
Tonga	–		68	(2020)	–	(2011)	–	(2020)	0.50	
Tuvalu	–	(2011)	6		–	(2011)	–		0.45	
Vanuatu	500		1,400		–		–		0.60	
Developed ADB Member Economies										
Australia	251		14,870		38	(2011)	787		0.70	
Japan	...		277,575	(2019)	89		155	(2019)	1.00	
New Zealand	...		2,053		–		19		0.90	

... = data not available, – = magnitude equals zero, ADB = Asian Development Bank.

a The data are submitted to the SDG Global Database by the United Nations Office for Disaster Risk Reduction and have been extracted from two sources: (i) the Sendai Framework Monitoring System as provided by designated national focal points; and (ii) Desinventar disaster loss databases. Some of the data have not undergone an official validation process and may be subject to revision at a later date.

b Economies displaying data in this column have adopted and implemented national disaster risk reduction strategies. Data refer to the score for adoption and implementation of national disaster risk reduction strategies in line with the Sendai Framework. The scores indicate the compliance of alignment of national strategies with the Sendai Framework, based on self-assessments of the economy using 10 criteria for monitoring the progress of national disaster risk reduction strategies. The score ranges are as follows: 1 = comprehensive alignment, 0.75 = substantial alignment, 0.50 = moderate alignment, 0.25 = limited alignment, 0 = no alignment.

c Some of the data have not undergone an official validation process and may be subject to revision at a later date.

Source: United Nations. SDG Global Database. https://unstats.un.org/sdgs/dataportal (accessed 23 July 2023).

Goal 14. Conserve and sustainably use the oceans, seas, and marine resources for sustainable development

Table 1.14.1: Selected Indicators for Sustainable Development Goal 14—Life Below Water

ADB Regional Member	Target 14.5: By 2020, conserve at least 10% of coastal and marine areas, consistent with national and international law and based on the best available scientific information				
	14.5.1: Average Proportion of Marine Key Biodiversity Areas Covered by Protected Areas (%)				
	2010	2015	2020	2021	2022
Developing ADB Member Economies					
Central and West Asia					
Afghanistan	...	...	...	...	...
Armenia	...	...	...	...	...
Azerbaijan	...	...	...	...	...
Georgia	35.6	35.6	35.6	35.6	35.6
Kazakhstan	...	...	...	...	...
Kyrgyz Republic	...	...	...	...	...
Pakistan	14.6	14.6	14.6	14.6	14.6
Tajikistan	...	...	...	...	...
Turkmenistan	...	...	...	...	...
Uzbekistan	...	...	...	...	...
East Asia					
China, People's Republic of	6.8	7.1	7.1	7.1	7.1
Hong Kong, China	32.5	32.5	32.5	32.5	32.5
Korea, Republic of	32.7	36.8	38.7	38.7	38.7
Mongolia	...	...	...	...	...
Taipei,China	...	...	...	...	...
South Asia					
Bangladesh	34.4	34.5	34.5	34.5	34.5
Bhutan	...	...	...	...	...
India	4.2	4.2	4.2	4.2	4.2
Maldives	–	–	–	–	...
Nepal	...	...	...	...	...
Sri Lanka	46.3	50.0	50.0	50.0	50.0
Southeast Asia					
Brunei Darussalam	5.4	5.4	5.4	5.4	5.4
Cambodia	41.2	41.2	51.0	51.0	51.0
Indonesia	16.1	22.8	25.7	25.7	25.7
Lao People's Democratic Republic	...	...	...	...	...
Malaysia	16.1	19.7	19.7	19.7	19.7
Myanmar	9.3	9.3	19.2	19.2	19.2
Philippines	32.5	33.7	46.6	46.6	46.6
Singapore	3.3	3.3	3.3	3.3	3.3
Thailand	36.3	41.6	44.0	44.0	44.0
Timor-Leste	18.7	18.7	19.6	19.6	19.6
Viet Nam	18.7	24.6	24.6	24.6	24.6
The Pacific					
Cook Islands	17.8	17.8	50.1	50.1	50.1
Fiji	16.5	16.5	16.5	16.5	16.5
Kiribati	32.9	32.9	32.9	32.9	32.9
Marshall Islands	6.7	7.8	7.8	7.8	7.8
Micronesia, Federated States of	1.6	1.6	1.6	1.6	1.6
Nauru	–	–	–	–	...
Niue	...	...	...	...	...
Palau	56.7	72.3	72.3	72.3	72.3
Papua New Guinea	1.9	1.9	1.9	1.9	1.9
Samoa	54.2	54.2	54.2	54.2	54.2
Solomon Islands	3.1	3.2	3.2	3.2	3.2
Tonga	19.2	19.2	19.2	19.2	19.2
Tuvalu	...	...	...	...	...
Vanuatu	3.3	3.3	3.3	3.3	3.3
Developed ADB Member Economies					
Australia	54.2	62.1	66.0	66.0	66.0
Japan	45.0	64.6	65.5	66.5	66.5
New Zealand	45.9	46.5	46.5	46.5	46.5

... = data not available, – = magnitude equals zero, ADB = Asian Development Bank.

Sources: United Nations. SDG Global Database. https://unstats.un.org/sdgs/dataportal (accessed 24 July 2023).

Goal 15. Protect, restore, and promote sustainable use of terrestrial ecosystems; sustainably manage forests; combat desertification and halt and reverse land degradation; and halt biodiversity loss

Table 1.15.1: Selected Indicators for Sustainable Development Goal 15—Protection of Ecosystems and Biodiversity

ADB Regional Member	Target 15.1: By 2020, ensure the conservation, restoration, and sustainable use of terrestrial and inland freshwater ecosystems and their services, in particular forests, wetlands, mountains, and drylands, in line with obligations under international agreements					
	15.1.1: Forest Area as a Proportion of Total Land Area[a] (%)		15.1.2: Proportion of Important Sites for Terrestrial and Freshwater Biodiversity that are Covered by Protected Areas (%)			
			Terrestrial		Freshwater	
	2010	2020	2010	2022	2010	2022
Developing ADB Member Economies						
Central and West Asia	**3.9**	**4.0**	...	...	...	...
Afghanistan	1.9	1.9	5.8	46.4	-	60.9
Armenia	11.6	11.5	21.6	22.6	26.8	30.5
Azerbaijan	12.5	13.7	36.1	36.6	12.7	14.5
Georgia	40.6	40.6	34.4	42.4	22.5	38.9
Kazakhstan	1.1	1.3	26.2	28.5	19.7	20.5
Kyrgyz Republic	6.4	6.9	23.6	23.6	35.4	35.4
Pakistan	5.3	4.8	34.8	34.8	35.9	35.9
Tajikistan	2.9	3.1	15.8	16.8	27.9	30.5
Turkmenistan	8.8	8.8	14.0	14.0	12.7	12.7
Uzbekistan	7.7	8.4	15.4	17.7	13.4	13.4
East Asia	**20.1**	**21.8**	...	...	...	...
China, People's Republic of	21.3	23.3	8.6	10.1	6.9	9.6
Hong Kong, China	...	...	48.9	48.9	16.6	16.6
Korea, Republic of	65.7	64.4	33.8	37.6	36.8	36.8
Mongolia	9.1	9.1	40.7	45.2	34.9	40.5
Taipei,China	58.1 (2011)	60.8 (2021)	...	...	...	...
South Asia	**24.5**	**25.3**	...	...	...	...
Bangladesh	14.5	14.5	41.5	41.5	-	-
Bhutan	71.0	71.5	45.4	47.0	30.5	34.8
India	23.4	24.3	1.5	6.3	2.6	8.3
Maldives[c,d]	2.7	2.7	-	-	...	...
Nepal	41.6	41.6	51.7	51.7	35.1	35.1
Sri Lanka	33.6	34.2	41.4	43.7	40.2	43.9
Southeast Asia	**49.7**	**47.1**	...	...	...	...
Brunei Darussalam	72.1	72.1	41.7	41.7	50.0	50.0
Cambodia	60.0	45.7	24.7	54.5	12.9	45.0
Indonesia	53.1	49.1	19.7	25.9	36.6	39.0
Lao People's Democratic Republic	73.4	71.9	35.4	48.6	17.3	30.1
Malaysia	57.7	58.2	31.6	37.0	31.7	32.5
Myanmar	48.1	43.7	18.8	22.3	27.1	27.1
Philippines	22.9	24.1	25.4	42.8	35.4	56.1
Singapore[c,d]	25.3	21.7	21.1	21.1	...	...
Thailand	39.3	38.9	66.7	68.0	36.3	36.3
Timor-Leste[d]	62.9	61.9	40.7	45.6	...	...
Viet Nam	42.7	46.7	31.2	40.1	30.2	39.5
The Pacific	**78.3**	**77.8**	...	...	...	...
Cook Islands[d]	65.0	65.0	24.4	30.9	...	...
Fiji	58.7	62.4	11.2	11.2	0.1	0.1
Kiribati[c,d]	1.5	1.5	40.0	40.0	...	...
Marshall Islands[c,d]	52.2	52.2	8.4	10.1	...	...
Micronesia, Federated States of[d]	91.6	92.0	0.0	0.0	...	...
Nauru[c,d]	-	-	-	-	...	...
Niue[c,d]	72.2	72.6	95.3	95.3	...	...
Palau[c,d]	88.2	90.0	46.3	48.1	...	...
Papua New Guinea[d]	79.9	79.2	7.2	7.3	...	...
Samoa[d]	58.8	58.2	47.0	47.1	...	...
Solomon Islands[d]	90.4	90.1	4.5	4.8	...	...
Tonga[d]	12.4	12.4	26.1	26.1	...	...
Tuvalu	33.3	33.3	...	...	...	...
Vanuatu[d]	36.3	36.3	2.8	2.8	...	...
Developed ADB Member Economies	**19.8**	**20.3**	...	...	...	...
Australia	16.9	17.4	45.5	57.3	29.7	37.6
Japan	68.5	68.4	49.9	65.1	46.7	63.5
New Zealand	37.4	37.6	45.4	46.2	22.9	24.2
DEVELOPING ADB MEMBER ECONOMIES	**23.5**	**24.0**	...	...	...	...
ALL ADB REGIONAL MEMBERS	**22.6**	**23.0**	...	...	...	...

Goal 15. Protect, restore, and promote sustainable use of terrestrial ecosystems; sustainably manage forests; combat desertification and halt and reverse land degradation; and halt biodiversity loss

Table 1.15.1: Selected Indicators for Sustainable Development Goal 15—Protection of Ecosystems and Biodiversity *(continued)*

ADB Regional Member	Target 15.4: By 2030, ensure the conservation of mountain ecosystems, including their biodiversity, in order to enhance their capacity to provide benefits that are essential for sustainable development		Target 15.5: Take urgent and significant action to reduce the degradation of natural habitats, halt the loss of biodiversity and, by 2020, protect and prevent the extinction of threatened species	
	15.4.1: Coverage by Protected Areas of Important Sites for Mountain Biodiversity (%)		15.5.1: Red List Index[b]	
	2010	2022	2010	2022
Developing ADB Member Economies				
Central and West Asia	...	...	...	...
Afghanistan	7.6	45.8	0.84	0.84
Armenia	22.3	23.4	0.83	0.83
Azerbaijan	55.5	55.5	0.91	0.91
Georgia	34.8	43.2	0.89	0.89
Kazakhstan	38.1	45.3	0.87	0.87
Kyrgyz Republic	31.5	31.5	0.99	0.98
Pakistan	35.2	35.2	0.90	0.84
Tajikistan	15.8	16.8	0.99	0.99
Turkmenistan	15.2	15.2	0.98	0.98
Uzbekistan	30.6	35.6	0.98	0.97
East Asia	...	...	...	...
China, People's Republic of	10.2	11.8	0.77	0.73
Hong Kong, China	57.0	57.0	0.84	0.84
Korea, Republic of	20.2	20.2	0.73	0.69
Mongolia	45.0	49.3	0.96	0.96
Taipei,China	...	...	...	...
South Asia	...	...	...	...
Bangladesh	–	–	0.79	0.74
Bhutan	45.4	47.0	0.80	0.80
India	1.1	10.1	0.71	0.67
Maldives[c,d]	...	...	0.89	0.83
Nepal	62.0	62.0	0.83	0.83
Sri Lanka	29.9	30.4	0.61	0.57
Southeast Asia	...	...	...	...
Brunei Darussalam	69.5	69.5	0.86	0.85
Cambodia	60.8	93.8	0.81	0.78
Indonesia	21.8	27.5	0.80	0.75
Lao People's Democratic Republic	42.4	57.0	0.82	0.81
Malaysia	39.8	48.3	0.75	0.70
Myanmar	33.1	37.1	0.83	0.79
Philippines	22.3	43.3	0.71	0.67
Singapore[c,d]	...	...	0.89	0.84
Thailand	85.7	85.7	0.81	0.77
Timor-Leste[d]	45.4	50.8	0.88	0.84
Viet Nam	34.8	45.0	0.76	0.71
The Pacific	...	...	...	...
Cook Islands[d]	–	–	0.80	0.77
Fiji	5.5	5.5	0.72	0.69
Kiribati[c,d]	...	...	0.81	0.77
Marshall Islands[c,d]	...	...	0.87	0.83
Micronesia, Federated States of[d]	–	–	0.69	0.64
Nauru[c,d]	...	...	0.81	0.76
Niue[c,d]	...	...	0.84	0.81
Palau[c,d]	...	...	0.79	0.67
Papua New Guinea[d]	7.3	7.4	0.87	0.82
Samoa[d]	35.6	35.7	0.77	0.76
Solomon Islands[d]	0.0	0.5	0.79	0.75
Tonga[d]	–	–	0.74	0.72
Tuvalu	...	...	0.87	0.83
Vanuatu[d]	3.8	3.8	0.70	0.67
Developed ADB Member Economies	...	...	...	...
Australia	45.9	66.5	0.85	0.81
Japan	60.1	67.7	0.80	0.76
New Zealand	32.8	34.0	0.67	0.61
DEVELOPING ADB MEMBER ECONOMIES	...	...	...	...
ALL ADB REGIONAL MEMBERS	...	...	...	...

... = data not available, 0.0 = magnitude is less than half of unit employed, – = magnitude equals zero, ADB = Asian Development Bank.

a The regional aggregates are calculated by averaging the combined estimates for each economy. The aggregates for East Asia exclude Hong Kong, China.
b The Red List Index value ranges from 1, which means all species are categorized as "Least Concern" (no species expected to become extinct in the near future), to 0, meaning that all species are categorized as "Extinct". The index therefore indicates how far the set of species has moved overall towards extinction.
c Figures for SDG Indicator 15.4.1 for this economy are reported as "non-relevant" in the UN SDG database.
d Figures for SDG Indicator 15.1.2 for this economy are reported as "non-relevant" in the UN SDG database.

Sources: United Nations. SDG Global Database. https://unstats.un.org/sdgs/dataportal (accessed 15 June 2023). For Taipei,China: Government of Taipei,China, Directorate-General of Budget, Accounting and Statistics.

Goal 16. Promote peaceful and inclusive societies for sustainable development; provide access to justice for all; and build effective, accountable, and inclusive institutions at all levels

Table 1.16.1: Selected Indicators for Sustainable Development Goal 16—Peace, Justice, and Strong Institutions

	Target 16.1: Significantly reduce all forms of violence and related death rates everywhere		Target 16.3: Promote the rule of law at the national and international levels and ensure equal access to justice for all		Target 16.5: Substantially reduce corruption and bribery in all their forms	Target 16.9: By 2030, provide legal identity for all, including birth registration
ADB Regional Member	16.1.1: Number of Victims of Intentional Homicide (per 100,000 population)		16.3.2: Unsentenced Detainees as a Proportion of Overall Prison Population (%)		16.5.2: Proportion of Firms Experiencing at least One Bribe Payment Request (%)	16.9.1: Proportion of Children Under 5 Years of Age Whose Births have been Registered with a Civil Authority[a] (%)
	2010	2021	2015	2021	2021	2021
Developing ADB Member Economies						
Central and West Asia						
Afghanistan	3.5	4.0	29.5	27.7 (2018)	46.8 (2014)	42.3 (2015)
Armenia	1.9	2.2	27.9	57.2	1.5 (2020)	98.7 (2016)
Azerbaijan	2.2	1.9	16.9	19.1 (2020)	12.1 (2019)	93.6 (2006)
Georgia	4.9	2.0 (2019)	13.5	18.5 (2019)	1.3 (2019)	98.5 (2017)
Kazakhstan	8.3	3.2 (2020)	13.8	18.3 (2020)	11.6 (2019)	99.7 (2015)
Kyrgyz Republic	16.8	1.8 (2020)	18.0	18.2 (2019)	31.4 (2019)	98.9 (2018)
Pakistan	6.8	4.0	69.1	67.7	30.8 (2013)	42.2 (2018)
Tajikistan	2.4	0.9 (2020)	...	...	11.1 (2019)	95.8 (2017)
Turkmenistan	2.0	1.1 (2015)	...	...	...	99.9 (2019)
Uzbekistan	3.0 (2008)	1.4	...	...	5.9 (2019)	100.0 (2022)
East Asia						
China, People's Republic of	1.0	0.5 (2020)	...	...	11.6 (2012)	...
Hong Kong, China	0.5	0.3	18.8	32.6	...	...
Korea, Republic of	1.0	0.5	35.8	39.4	...	...
Mongolia	8.8	6.2	17.6	25.2	24.7 (2019)	99.6 (2018)
Taipei,China	0.8	0.8 (2015)	5.5	5.2 (2018)	...	...
South Asia						
Bangladesh	2.7	2.3 (2018)	73.8	81.3 (2019)	23.0 (2022)	56.0 (2019)
Bhutan	2.3	2.5 (2020)	26.9 (2017)	14.2 (2019)	0.9 (2015)	99.9 (2010)
India	3.7	2.9	67.2	77.1	27.2 (2022)	89.1
Maldives	1.7	0.6 (2019)	...	...	...	98.8 (2017)
Nepal	3.0	2.3 (2019)	...	54.4	14.5 (2013)	77.2 (2019)
Sri Lanka	3.7	3.4 (2019)	52.8	69.0 (2018)	10.0 (2011)	97.2 (2007)
Southeast Asia						
Brunei Darussalam	0.3	...	7.1	7.1 (2018)	...	...
Cambodia	2.3	...	49.3	28.7 (2018)	64.7 (2016)	73.3 (2014)
Indonesia	0.4	0.4 (2017)	33.2	16.9 (2020)	30.6 (2015)	81.3 (2022)
Lao People's Democratic Republic	...	...	...	...	40.3 (2018)	73.0 (2017)
Malaysia	1.9	0.7	25.8	40.5 (2020)	0.4 (2019)	...
Myanmar	1.6	28.4	15.1 (2016)	22.0 (2020)	29.3 (2016)	81.3 (2016)
Philippines	9.1	4.3 (2019)	69.1	64.3	17.2 (2015)	91.8 (2017)
Singapore	0.4	0.1	11.0	10.8	...	99.9 (2020)
Thailand	5.4	2.6 (2017)	18.6	14.5	9.9 (2016)	99.8 (2019)
Timor-Leste	3.6	4.1 (2015)	78.3	23.2 (2018)	9.9	60.4 (2016)
Viet Nam	1.5	...	17.6	12.8 (2019)	26.1 (2015)	98.1
The Pacific						
Cook Islands	3.5 (2012)	...	21.6	14.6 (2018)	...	100.0 (2017)
Fiji	2.2	2.2 (2020)	27.4	19.9	10.5 (2009)	86.6
Kiribati	3.7	...	9.8	5.4 (2018)	...	91.6 (2019)
Marshall Islands	...	...	...	...	...	83.8 (2017)
Micronesia, Federated States of	...	0.9 (2019)	...	...	4.6 (2009)	...
Nauru	...	...	...	...	...	95.9 (2013)
Niue	...	...	...	...	...	...
Palau	...	11.2 (2018)	...	...	...	...
Papua New Guinea	9.4	...	37.9	34.4 (2019)	26.4 (2015)	13.4 (2018)
Samoa	8.2	6.2 (2018)	5.2	23.2 (2019)	30.5 (2009)	66.9 (2020)
Solomon Islands	3.7 (2008)	...	61.3	50.4 (2018)	43.8 (2015)	88.0 (2015)
Tonga	0.9	1.0 (2019)	7.4	7.4 (2018)	24.9 (2009)	97.7 (2019)
Tuvalu	9.5	– (2019)	...	...	...	87.2 (2020)
Vanuatu	...	0.3 (2020)	12.1	32.3	11.9 (2009)	43.4 (2013)
Developed ADB Member Economies						
Australia	1.1	0.7	30.7	34.1	...	100.0 (2017)
Japan	0.4	0.2	11.0	13.3	...	100.0 (2017)
New Zealand	1.0	2.6 (2019)	25.0	48.9	...	100.0 (2017)

... = data not available, – = magnitude equals zero, ADB = Asian Development Bank.

a Changes in the definition of birth registration were made from the second and third rounds of Multiple Indicator Cluster Surveys (MICS2 and MICS3) to the fourth round (MICS4). In order to allow for comparability with the latter round, data from MICS2 and MICS3 on birth registration were recalculated according to the MICS4 indicator definition. Therefore, the recalculated data presented here may differ from estimates included in MICS2 and MICS3 national reports.

Sources: For Indicator 16.1.1: United Nations Office on Drugs and Crime. dataUNODC. https://dataunodc.un.org/ (accessed 15 July 2023). For Indicator 16.3.2: United Nations. SDG Global Database. https://unstats.un.org/sdgs/dataportal (accessed 15 July 2023). For Indicator 16.5.2: World Bank. World Development Indicators. https://data.worldbank.org/indicator (accessed 15 July 2023). For Indicator 16.9.1: United Nations Children's Fund (UNICEF). UNICEF Data Warehouse. https://data.unicef.org/dv_index/ (accessed 15 July 2023).

Goal 17. Strengthen the means of implementation and revitalize the Global Partnership for Sustainable Development

Table 1.17.1: Selected Indicators for Sustainable Development Goal 17—Financial Sustainability of Developing Economies

ADB Regional Member	Target 17.4: Assist developing countries in attaining long-term debt sustainability through coordinated policies aimed at fostering debt financing, debt relief, and debt restructuring, as appropriate, and address the external debt of highly indebted poor countries to reduce debt distress 17.4.1: Debt Service as a Proportion of Exports of Goods and Services (%)		Target 17.9: Enhance international support for implementing effective and targeted capacity-building in developing countries to support national plans to implement all the Sustainable Development Goals, including through North-South, South-South, and triangular cooperation 17.9.1: Dollar Value of Financial and Technical Assistance Committed to Developing Countries[a] (constant 2021 $ million)	
	2010	2021	Average, 2000–2010	Average, 2011–2021
Developing ADB Member Economies				
Central and West Asia	...	...	**1,721.3**	**3,875.7**
Afghanistan	0.3	2.2 (2020)	854.1	1,259.8
Armenia	2.7	8.6	72.0	107.8
Azerbaijan	1.1	6.0	38.3	129.9
Georgia	6.3	13.0	91.0	307.2
Kazakhstan	0.5	2.1	100.5	333.1
Kyrgyz Republic	3.7	5.5	56.6	102.2
Pakistan	11.5	29.5	427.6	1,216.7
Tajikistan	2.7	6.0	35.5	56.2
Turkmenistan	...	...	6.6	6.8
Uzbekistan	3.3	6.0	39.2	356.0
East Asia[b]	...	...	**441.8**	**1,096.7**
China, People's Republic of	0.8	1.3	395.4	880.3
Hong Kong, China	...	...	...	...
Korea, Republic of	...	...	...	...
Mongolia	4.3	12.4	46.3	216.4
Taipei,China	...	...	...	...
South Asia	...	...	**1,183.7**	**1,957.2**
Bangladesh	4.5	5.9	262.2	665.2
Bhutan	14.4	15.2	17.8	32.4
India	1.7	2.4	676.5	843.8
Maldives	3.0	18.6	4.8	12.0
Nepal	10.4	9.2	98.5	254.3
Sri Lanka	10.7	27.8	123.8	149.6
Southeast Asia[b]	...	...	**1,802.4**	**3,408.4**
Brunei Darussalam	...	...	...	...
Cambodia	1.0	1.9	99.5	150.7
Indonesia	6.6	14.9	916.3	1,438.4
Lao People's Democratic Republic	4.0	8.4	58.1	95.4
Malaysia	...	...	19.9	12.3
Myanmar	3.1	17.0	15.9	258.2
Philippines	16.0	7.6	167.5	630.3
Singapore	...	...	...	...
Thailand	0.4	0.5	48.3	97.2
Timor-Leste	–	2.0	59.2	47.1
Viet Nam	2.1	1.2	417.7	678.7
The Pacific	...	...	**369.4**	**450.6**
Cook Islands	...	...	2.9	4.7
Fiji	1.3	2.0	18.7	37.0
Kiribati	...	...	8.6	12.5
Marshall Islands	...	...	19.5	9.9
Micronesia, Federated States of	...	...	42.1	17.2
Nauru	...	...	11.5	6.8
Niue	...	...	2.2	7.5
Palau	...	...	1.8	4.5
Papua New Guinea	1.4	10.6 (2020)	113.3	215.6
Samoa	5.0	14.2	19.2	38.3
Solomon Islands	3.1	1.5	104.2	48.5
Tonga	9.3	3.6	12.1	19.7
Tuvalu	...	...	3.2	5.9
Vanuatu	1.4	6.6	16.1	23.4
Developed ADB Member Economies	...	...	...	...
Australia	...	...	...	...
Japan	...	...	...	...
New Zealand	...	...	...	...
DEVELOPING ADB MEMBER ECONOMIES[b]	...	...	**5,518.6**	**10,788.5**
DEVELOPING ECONOMIES WORLDWIDE[c]	...	...	**23,190.6**	**36,441.5**

... = data not available, – = magnitude equals zero, $ = United States dollars, ADB = Asian Development Bank.

a Technical assistance includes assistance through North-South, South-South, and triangular cooperation. The United Nations dataset and metadata refer to this indicator as total official development assistance (gross disbursements) for technical cooperation.

b For reporting economies only.

c The figures provided refer to aggregates for all developing economies as reported in the United Nations' SDG Global Database.

Source: United Nations. SDG Global Database. https://unstats.un.org/sdgs/dataportal (accessed 20 July 2023).

Goal 17. Strengthen the means of implementation and revitalize the Global Partnership for Sustainable Development

Table 1.17.2: Selected Indicators for Sustainable Development Goal 17—Statistical Capacity Building

ADB Regional Member	Target 17.18: By 2020, enhance capacity-building support to developing countries (or economies), including for least developed countries (or economies) and small island developing states, to increase significantly the availability of high-quality, timely, and reliable data disaggregated by income, gender, age, race, ethnicity, migratory status, disability, geographic location, and other characteristics relevant in national contexts	Target 17.19: By 2030, build on existing initiatives to develop measurements of progress on sustainable development that complement gross domestic product and support statistical capacity-building in developing countries (or economies)	
	17.18.3: Availability of National Statistical Plan[a]	19.19.1: Dollar Value of All Resources Made Available to Strengthen Statistical Capacity in Developing Countries (current $)	19.19.2: Countries (or Economies) that Have Conducted at Least One Population and Housing Census in the Past 10 Years[b]
	2022	2020	2020
Developing ADB Member Economies			
Central and West Asia			
Afghanistan	B	446,283.0	...
Armenia	A, B, C, D	153,716.0	...
Azerbaijan	A, B, C	1,029,637.0	2019
Georgia	A, B, C	1,628,371.0	2022
Kazakhstan	A, B	120,603.0	2020
Kyrgyz Republic	A, B	640,679.0	2022
Pakistan	A, B	1,179,362.0	2017
Tajikistan	C, D, E (2019)	690,718.0	2020
Turkmenistan	...	281,673.0	2022
Uzbekistan	A, B	1,347,320.0	...
East Asia			
China, People's Republic of	A, B, C	3,169,476.0	2020
Hong Kong, China	A, B	...	2016
Korea, Republic of	A, B	...	2015
Mongolia	A, B	119,617.0	2020
Taipei,China	...	...	2020
South Asia			
Bangladesh	A, B	2,261,887.0	2022
Bhutan	A, B, C, D	31,306.0	2017
India	B	4,995,897.0	...
Maldives	B	242,258.0	2022
Nepal	B, C, D	10,456,952.0	2021
Sri Lanka	B	446,189.0	...
Southeast Asia			
Brunei Darussalam	A, B, C	54,155.0	2021
Cambodia	B	833,765.0	2019
Indonesia	B	2,227,705.0	2020
Lao People's Democratic Republic	B, C, D	2,568,461.0	2015
Malaysia	A, B, C	385,125.0	2020
Myanmar	B	1,688,885.0	2014
Philippines	A, B, C, D	215,290.0	2015
Singapore	A, B, C	20,843.8 (2018)	2020
Thailand	A, B	129,553.0	...
Timor-Leste	B (2019)	470,137.0	2015
Viet Nam	B	16,403,572.0	2019
The Pacific			
Cook Islands	B, C (2019)	45,937.0	2016
Fiji	C, D	148,279.0	2017
Kiribati	...	84,450.0	2015
Marshall Islands	...	155,220.0	2021
Micronesia, Federated States of	...	13,196.0	...
Nauru	C (2019)	85,980.0	2021
Niue	...	87,817.0 (2019)	2017
Palau	C (2019)	58,270.0	2015
Papua New Guinea	B	252,373.0	...
Samoa	A, B	69,937.0	2016
Solomon Islands	B	46,507.0	2019
Tonga	A, B	316,048.0	2016
Tuvalu	B	40,329.0	2017
Vanuatu	C (2019)	14,774.0	2016
Developed ADB Member Economies			
Australia	A, B	...	2016
Japan	A, B, C	...	2015
New Zealand	B, C	47,667.4 (2018)	2018

... = data not available, $ = United States dollars, ADB = Asian Development Bank.

a A = a national statistical plan fully funded, B = a national statistical plan under implementation, C = a national statistical plan with funding from government, D = a national statistical plan with funding from donors, E = a national statistical plan with funding from others.

b Refers to the most recent year in which a population and housing census was conducted.

Sources: United Nations. SDG Global Database. https://unstats.un.org/sdgs/dataportal (accessed 20 July 2023). For 17.19.2: For Georgia: National Statistics Office of Georgia. https://www.geostat.ge/en/modules/categories/736/2002-general-population-census-results (accessed 20 July 2023); For Maldives: Maldives Bureau of Statistics. https://statisticsmaldives.gov.mv/census-in-2022 (accessed 20 July 2023); For Myanmar: Department of Population. https://dop.gov.mm/en/publication-category/2014-reports (accessed 20 July 2023); For Taipei,China: Government of Taipei,China, Directorate-General of Budget, Accounting and Statistics; and for Turkmenistan: State Statistics Committee of Turkmenistan. http://www.stat.gov.tm (accessed 20 July 2023).

Data Gaps and Other Data-Related Issues

New and huge data demands. The approved global framework for monitoring the SDGs consists of 231 unique indicators with greater disaggregation and across a wider spectrum of topics than the Millennium Development Goals. With international development support, governments are strengthening their national statistical systems to address data demands across all SDG indicators.

Limited data availability for Sustainable Development Goal indicators. While there have been many improvements to data availability and timeliness since the launch of the SDGs in 2015, there is more to be done. While only 50% of SDG indicators of internationally comparable data for monitoring are available in 2016, sufficient data availability had increased to 93% of indicators by 2022, but significant data gaps still exist in terms of geographic coverage, timeliness, and level of disaggregation.

Differing priorities among national statistics offices with regard to economic data production result in disparities in data availability. Most national statistics offices across Asia and the Pacific conduct population and housing censuses every decade. Such sources provide baseline socioeconomic data that overlap SDG indicators with economic and social dimensions. Depending on the frequency of data collection, administrative reporting systems and household surveys—such as labor force surveys, household income and expenditure surveys, demographic and health surveys, establishment surveys, and agriculture surveys—can be other good sources of data for SDG indicators.

Gaps in data granularity. Many SDG indicators require disaggregation by location, sex, gender, age, income, ethnicity, migration status, disability status, and other relevant dimensions. Granular data can illustrate disparities within and across economies.

However, the extent to which specific groups are disproportionately at risk is difficult to decipher given the lack of data disaggregation and interlinkages across indicators. Sex disaggregations, even for basic indicators such as extreme poverty rates based on the $1.90 a day (at 2011 purchasing power parity) level, are not currently available. Similarly, poverty numbers are currently unavailable for vulnerable groups, such as people with disabilities or indigenous peoples, since the sample surveys these poverty calculations are based on are designed to obtain an overview of welfare conditions. Investments are needed (e.g., in special surveys) to obtain poverty data for vulnerable groups that make up only a small proportion of the total population.

Innovative data sources, such as big data and crowdsourced data, can potentially address these data gaps and strengthen the monitoring of SDG indicators. However, some types of big data may not represent the underlying groups of interest. Therefore, it is necessary to ensure that reliable statistical inferences can be made when complementing surveys and other conventional data sources with big data (Cox, Kartsonaki, and Keogh 2018).

Lack of data comparability. Differences in definitions mean that SDG indicators, such as the proportion of the population with access to safely managed drinking water services, rely on data related to housing conditions, which may not be fully comparable across economies. Likewise, comparisons of SDG indicators across economies are difficult for urban–rural disaggregation due to various definitions of "urban" and "rural" across time and economies.

Sparse data and irregular frequency. Some indicators that provide a useful description of income inequality—such as the growth in household expenditure among those in an economy's bottom 40th percentile of income distribution in relation to national averages are only currently available for a few economies. In another example, data on progress made toward addressing climate change are sparse.

Frequency is also of concern as some indicators, such as the coverage of protected areas in relation to marine areas, are not regularly collected. Indicators on material footprint and domestic material consumption, which are widely accepted as strategic sustainability indicators of production and consumption, are not produced annually.

Further, some protected areas are not assigned management categories. While access to remote sensing data has improved in recent years, forest regrowth cannot easily be detected with remote-sensing techniques.

Data limitations. The indicators included in the framework for monitoring the SDGs, while carefully chosen, may have some limitations. For example, the labor share in GDP does not include the income of the self-employed, even though a sizeable proportion of the employed population in developing Asia comprises people who are self-employed. Current measures of poverty used by economies are largely based on income or consumption data, while the SDG indicators include a multidimensional poverty measure that has yet to be tested on a wider scale.

The many challenges facing cities—pollution, traffic congestion, and inadequate housing for the poor—can be exacerbated by migration and population growth, changes in family structures, inequality of opportunity for excluded groups, and rising insecurity. Currently available data do not allow for a simple assessment of these issues.

The Red List Index is a composite index aggregated across multiple taxonomic groups. While it can be updated annually, the index does not adequately capture the deteriorating status of common species that are abundant and widespread yet declining gradually. Data on other indicators for monitoring many targets under SDG 15 are also sparsely available. The absence of a framework for monitoring terrestrial ecosystems, low data availability, and the lack of good-quality data must be carefully addressed.

Measurement errors. The quality of data for all SDG indicators needs to be considered when identifying trends and drawing inferences. For example, self-reporting of land area and production by farmers is known to have significant biases (Dillon and Rao 2018). The calculation of under-5 mortality rates requires complete counts of live births and child deaths by a precise age, which are not always available in economies of Asia and the Pacific that lack civil registration systems. Maternal deaths are likewise not always accounted for, given incomplete or inaccurate records on causes of death. The measurement of quality education across economies is hampered by the lack of standard definitions for minimum competency. Anthropometric measures of malnutrition (including stunted heights) are subject to measurement errors and issues around reference standards (i.e., local versus international standards). Access to safely managed drinking water and sanitation services, and information on hygiene all depend on more and better data, particularly administrative data sources (WHO and UNICEF 2017).

A complete stocktaking of all statistical capacity development programs cannot be guaranteed in the data compiled by PARIS21 for measuring the dollar-value support for statistics development. Double counting of projects can occur, or the data may also be inflated by the inaccurate inclusion of multisector projects. Further, donor commitments do not always lead to actual disbursements to recipient economies.

Ultimately, the reliability of data on SDG indicators depends on the quality of the underlying data sources. Governments across Asia and the Pacific need to increase investment, look for innovative data sources, and form strategic partnerships with a range of stakeholders to enhance data quality, comparability, measurement, and timeliness. Reliable and comprehensive data supports evidence-based policymaking that leads to better development outcomes.

PART II
Regional Trends and Tables

Regional Trends and Tables

In 2022, developing Asia grew by 4.2% and is expected to grow by 4.8% by the end of 2023 (ADB 2023a; ADB 2023b). Regional inflation in 2022, meanwhile, breached 4.4%, a level unseen in nearly ten years, while in 2023, forecasts peg regional inflation at 3.6% to 4.2% (ADB 2023a; ADB 2023b). Navigating a higher-than-usual inflation environment, amidst looming economic uncertainties, is a challenging task. Use of monetary policy tools, such as raising interest rates, must strike a balance between reducing inflation, while preserving economic growth at levels that will not have a prolonged detrimental impact on the region's future economic prospects.

Part II of *Key Indicators for Asia and the Pacific 2023* examines triggers and economic consequences of price shocks. In particular, the section reviews how ongoing inflationary pressures may have been driven by policy responses designed to mitigate the impact of the pandemic. It also examines the intersectional relationships among inflation and prospects for economic growth, through multiple channels. For instance, featured data stories illuminate how the monetary stance of major economies on inflation has affected the strength of local currencies and in turn, impacted the capacity of developing economies to service their debt. The analyses presented in this section draw on the latest 2022 estimates for nominated economic, price, and other financial indicators, as compiled by national and international statistical systems.

Overall, the data presented here shows several major challenges that developing Asia confronted in 2022, including the Russian invasion of Ukraine, and a stalled global economic recovery. The impacts from some of these challenges may persist and weigh on the region's medium term growth prospects, despite inflation moderating based on more recent data for 2023 (ADB 2023b). As the region seeks to regain its economic momentum, there is a need for deeper and stronger cross-border cooperation to enhance developing Asia's ability to manage various development challenges. Insights on regional cooperation may also provide valuable guidance on how to tackle other threats that may lie ahead (ADB 2022b).

Post-pandemic recovery and economic uncertainties. In 2022, Asia and the Pacific was poised for a post-pandemic economic rebound but additional shocks emerged to unsettle the recovery, undermining development progress (photo by Al Benavente/ADB).

Navigating Inflationary Pressures and Economic Uncertainties

Inflationary pressures exacerbate lingering impacts of the COVID-19 pandemic.

For central banks and other monetary authorities, managing inflation is an important development priority as price fluctuations can have a profound impact on the economy. When prices fall, businesses may find it challenging to be profitable, which can eventually lead to higher unemployment. On the other hand, during periods with elevated levels of inflation and reduced purchasing power, people tend to reduce consumption which in turn, leads to decline in living standards. Part I also discussed how a high inflation regime can be detrimental to people with low incomes as it adds to the existing cost burden they experience from premiums paid for goods and services. High inflation also exacerbates uncertainty and unpredictability in the economy, making it challenging for businesses to plan ahead and consequently, leads to reduced investment.

The year 2022 was marked by a number of external shocks such as the Russian invasion of Ukraine which disrupted food and energy markets. It also became more apparent that the COVID-19 pandemic was having longer-term repercussions on the global (including developing Asia) socioeconomic landscape. For instance, the continued zero COVID policy in the People's Republic of China (PRC) for most of 2022 caused prolonged supply chain disruptions which disrupted the transport of raw materials, the production of finished products, and the overall distribution and consumption of certain products and services.

Box 2.1. COVID-19 Stringency and Economic Recovery: Asia and the Pacific Experience

Safeguarding human health and life was the key concern of economies during the pandemic. Within months of detecting the COVID-19 novel virus, governments moved swiftly to put in place a wide range of containment measures to curb its spread in order to protect lives. While these measures did help slow transmission of the virus, it soon became clear that they were also resulting in serious socioeconomic collateral damage. Even as social and economic life returned to normal in 2022, many economies were still experiencing the lingering impacts of the stringent lockdowns and other containment actions. In summary, while COVID-19 stringency measures were crucial in momentarily shielding populations from the disease, they inevitably brought about serious and long-lasting economic costs, including slower growth.

Are pandemic measures related to economic growth?

A study of 49 economies and their gross domestic product (GDP) growth rates found that COVID-19 stringency measures are negatively correlated with economic growth (Bajra et al. 2022). In particular, it noted that economies saw declines in growth as their governments implemented restrictive border closures and other containment measures. This shows the linkage between pandemic measures and impacts on growth in Asia and the Pacific.

Yearly COVID-19 Stringency and Declines in GDP Growth Rates During Pandemic Years by Economy

Economies that implemented more stringent COVID-19 measures experienced steeper declines in GDP growth.

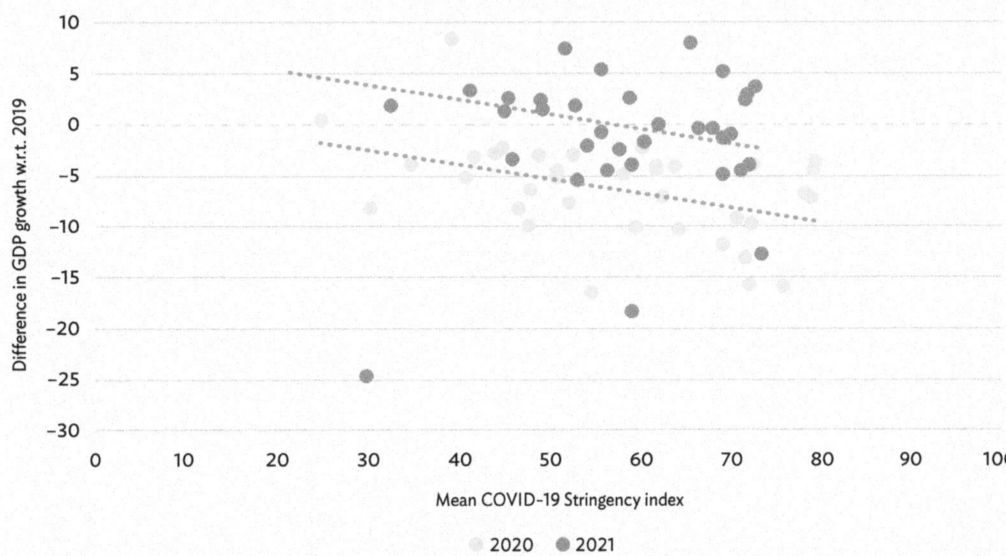

Note: The declines in GDP growth figures shown here represent the difference in GDP growth rates between a pandemic year (2020 or 2021) and pre-pandemic year (2019) per economy. Meanwhile, the mean stringency index figures represent the mean of daily stringency indices in each pandemic year per economy. The trendline for 2021 does not account for the single outlier point located in the lower left quadrant of the plot

Sources: Asian Development Bank estimates using data presented in Table 2.2.11 of *Key Indicators for Asia and the Pacific 2023*; Oxford COVID-19 Governance Response Tracker. https://www.bsg.ox.ac.uk/research/covid-19-government-response-tracker (accessed 4 September 2022).

Figure above, compiled from ADB data, shows that the real GDP growth rates of economies in the region in 2021 were generally higher than the levels seen in 2020, suggesting an overall recovery 2 years into the pandemic. It also indicates that the more restrictive the stringency measures taken, the more negative the impacts on GDP growth. This is consistent with the conclusion drawn in (Bajra et al. 2022), although it should be noted that our data shows a weaker correlation. This could be due to the annualized treatment of the data we have used, in contrast to the more granular quarterly data used in the Bajra study. At the same time, the study only captures quarterly data from the first quarter of 2020 to the first quarter of 2021, thus giving only a partial picture for the second pandemic year, 2021. Moving forward, it will be worth examining whether the same correlation can still be observed once we have data for Asia and the Pacific economies with the same temporal granularity (quarterly) and the analysis period extended to cover up to the last quarter of 2021.

(continued on next page)

Box 2.1. COVID-19 Stringency and Economic Recovery: Asia and the Pacific Experience *(continued)*

Which Asia and the Pacific economies experienced declines in growth during pandemic lockdowns?

The following line graph illustrates the fluctuations in GDP growth (top) and COVID-19 stringency (bottom) on a quarterly basis by economy.

Quarterly COVID-19 Stringency Measures and GDP Growth by Economy (Asia and the Pacific)

Most economies in Asia and the Pacific experienced at least one episode of GDP decline immediately after implementing tighter COVID-19 restrictions.

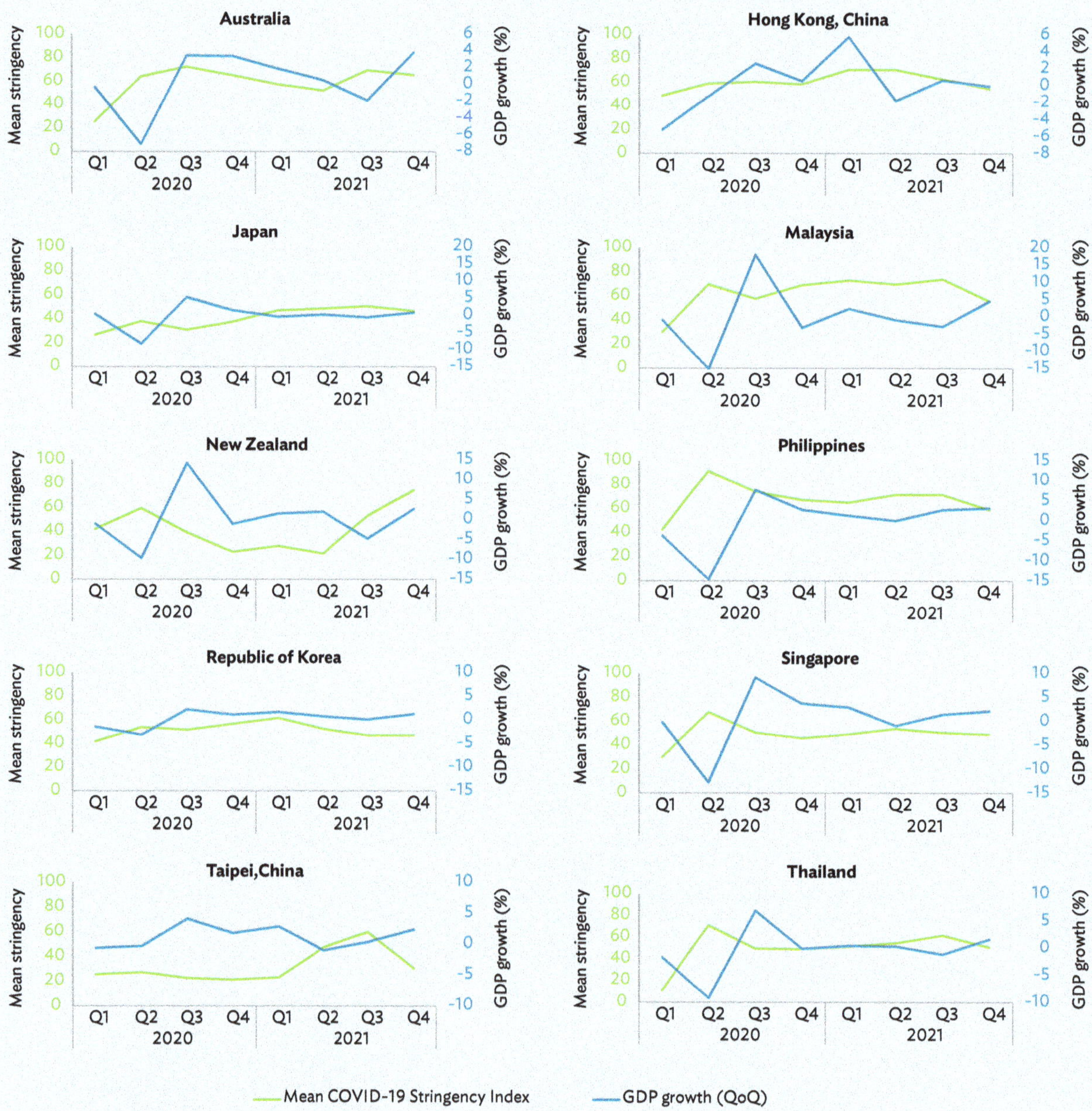

QoQ = quarter-on-quarter.

Note: The GDP growth figures shown here represent quarter-on-quarter growth rates of seasonally adjusted GDP per economy, while the stringency figures represent the mean of daily stringency indices in each quarter per economy.

Sources: CEIC Data Company database. https://www.ceicdata.com/en (accessed 11 September 2022); Oxford COVID-19 Governance Response Tracker. https://www.bsg.ox.ac.uk/research/covid-19-government-response-tracker (accessed 4 September 2022).

(continued on next page)

Box 2.1. COVID-19 Stringency and Economic Recovery: Asia and the Pacific Experience *(continued)*

Based on available quarterly data, many economies in the region saw slower economic growth during certain quarters when pandemic lockdowns were in place (either partial or total). For example, developing economies in East Asia, such as the Republic of Korea, showed sharp declines in GDP growth coinciding with tight stringency measures imposed at the onset of the pandemic.

Similarly in Southeast Asia, the Philippines and Singapore saw decreases in GDP growth during lockdowns implemented at the pandemic's onset, and in response to the Delta variant of the virus. Malaysia's economy was negatively affected by these developments and also experienced a sharp decline in GDP growth during a third wave of COVID-19 in the third quarter of 2020 (Aw et al. 2021). The same developments were largely observed in Thailand, except that it experienced a longer period of weaker growth, due to more restrictive lockdowns running from the first to the third quarters of 2021.

Developed economies were not spared either, with both Australia and Japan seeing slower growth amidst stringency measures imposed at the pandemic's onset and in response to subsequent resurgences in COVID-19 cases from 2020 to 2021.

References:

Asian Development Bank: Key Indicators Database Online. https://kidb.adb.org (accessed 11 September 2022).

S. Aw, B. Teh, G. Ling, P. Leng, W. Chan, and M. Ahmad. 2021. The Covid-19 Pandemic Situation in Malaysia: Lessons Learned from the Perspective of Population Density. *International Journal of Environmental Research and Public Health.* 18. 12. 6566.

U. Bajra, F. Aliu, B. Aver, S. Cadez. 2022. COVID-19 pandemic-related policy stringency and economic decline: was it really inevitable?. *Economic Research-Ekonomska Istraživanja*. pp. 1-17.

CEIC Database. https://www.ceicdata.com/en (accessed 30 September 2022).

Oxford COVID-19 Governance Response Tracker. Blavatnik School of Government, University of Oxford. United Kingdom. https://www.bsg.ox.ac.uk/research/covid-19-government-response-tracker. License: CC BY 4.0. (accessed 4 September 2022).

Figure 2.1: Global Energy Prices and Inflation Rates for the World and Developing Asia

As global energy prices increased, inflation rates in the world and developing Asia in 2022 both reached levels unseen in the previous 20 and almost 10 years, respectively.

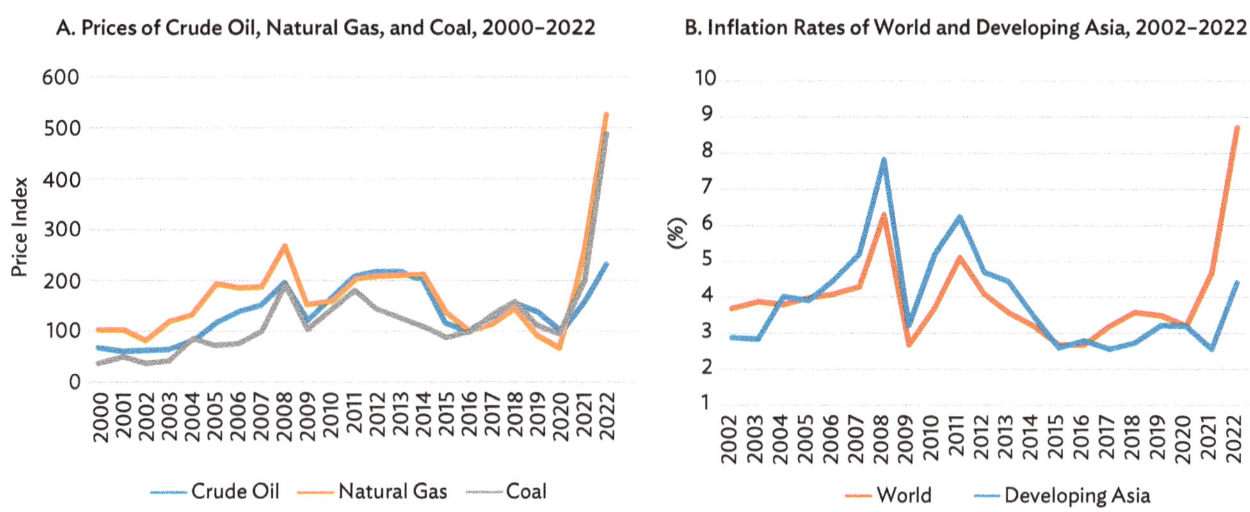

Sources: Chart A - Asian Development Bank (ADB) estimates using data from the International Monetary Fund Primary Commodity Prices website https://www.imf.org/en/Research/commodity-prices for Figure A (accessed 29 May 2023). Chart B - for Developing Asia, Asian Development Bank's Asian Development Outlook database (accessed 12 April 2023); For World: IMF website https://www.imf.org/external/datamapper/PCPIPCH@WEO/OEMDC (accessed 27 May 2023).

Along with the lingering impacts from the pandemic, inflation in 2022 also became a major global concern with prices for food, energy, and other goods increasing much more rapidly than they had in recent years. At the end of 2022, consumer price inflation reached 4.4% in developing Asia, a level unseen in almost a decade.

Figure 2.2: Food and Food-related Commodities Imports from the Russian Federation and Ukraine and Growth Rate of CPI of Food and Nonalcoholic beverages

The Asia and Pacific region has been affected by supply disruptions to select food commodities.

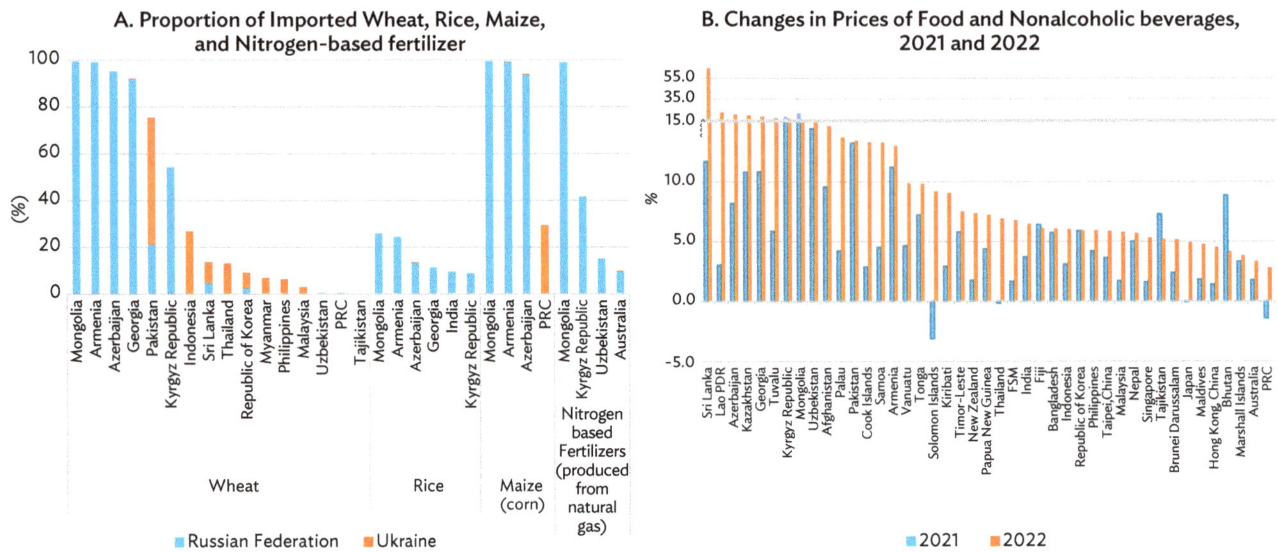

FSM = Federated States of Micronesia, Lao PDR = Lao People's Democratic Republic, PRC = People's Republic of China.

Sources: Chart A - Asian Development Bank estimates using data from UN Comtrade. https://comtrade.un.org/data (accessed 3 Nov 2022); Chart B - Asian Development Bank estimates using data presented in Table 2.3.2 of *Key Indicators of Asia and the Pacific 2023*.

Prices of fuel and agricultural products saw the steepest spikes, as a result of disruptions caused by the Russian invasion of Ukraine. Global energy prices reached their highest levels since 2000, exceeding levels seen during the last oil price bubble in 2008-2009. The impacts of these price rises on economies in Asia and the Pacific were less severe than on other regions, which are more dependent on Russian commodities. (Figure 2.2). Nonetheless, at least 15 economies in Asia and the Pacific saw retail prices of fuel increase by at least 8% from 2021 to 2022 (details provided on individual economy tables of this report).

There was also a sharp spike in fertilizer prices, which rose 80% in 2021 and almost 30% at the beginning of 2022. This was due to a broader range of factors than those driving energy prices, including increased input costs, sanctions-driven supply disruptions in Belarus and the Russian Federation, and export restrictions imposed by the People's Republic of China. Prices for urea, phosphates, and potash, which go into the production of fertilizers, either exceeded or are near their respective 2008 prices, while the Russian invasion of Ukraine resulted in both fertilizer affordability and availability concerns (WBG 2022a).

While most economies in Asia and the Pacific were less affected than those in other regions by the commodity price spikes, a number who import substantial amounts of rice, corn, wheat, and fertilizer from the Russian Federation and Ukraine, did see surges in prices in 2022 (Figure 2.2). In particular, 15 economies in Asia and the Pacific saw price indices for food (and nonalcoholic beverages) increase by at least 10% from 2021 to 2022 (Table 2.3.2).

Along with higher food and fuel costs, prices for transport, restaurants and hotels also saw a substantial increase in 2022. A surge in demand for travel and dining contributed to this, while prices for used vehicles also rose as delays and supply shortages held back sales of new vehicles (Figure 2.3).

Along with external shocks in 2022, inflationary pressures may have been driven by a number of policy responses taken to mitigate the socioeconomic impacts of the pandemic.

When the pandemic hit in 2020, many governments around the world responded by implementing programs to support health needs and provide immediate support to vulnerable households. From January 2020 to September 2021, fiscal stimulus packages announced globally reached $16.9 trillion, with $4.5 trillion in Asia and the Pacific (IMF 2021). As a result, the money supply increased in many parts of the world, including Asia and the Pacific, with year-on-year growth in the money supply in 2020 exceeding the rate of expansion seen in 2019, in 33 out of 44 economies in the region. A key effect of a sharp increase in money supply is a rise in inflationary pressures.

Figure 2.4 shows the growth in money supply from 2020 to 2022. In 2022, 11 out of 36 economies recorded money supply increases of at least 10%, compared to the year earlier.

In response to inflationary pressures, central banks hiked interest rates.

A common response to curb inflationary pressures is to raise interest rates to increase the cost of borrowing money, and as a result, push demand down. In 2022, central banks around the world announced various rate measures to control inflation and ensure price stability. In the US, the Federal Reserve increased interest rates seven times in 2022, with the policy rate rising from 0.25% in February up to 4.50% by December. In Asia and the Pacific, central banks in 18 of 22 economies hiked policy rates at least once in 2022 (Figure 2.5).

In general, an economy's rate increases can affect the trade, exchange rates, and financial market channels of other economies. In the case of trade, as aggregate demand is suppressed by higher domestic rates, an economy's demand for imports declines and it buys less from other economies. The impact of rising US interest rates on other economies financial market channels can be seen in downward pressure on local investments and consumption as economies raise rates in tandem.

Figure 2.3: Consumer Price Inflation by Group, 2022

Prices of goods and services in transport, food and nonalcoholic beverages, restaurants and hotels, and miscellaneous goods and services are among those that have shown the highest median inflation rates across Asia and the Pacific.

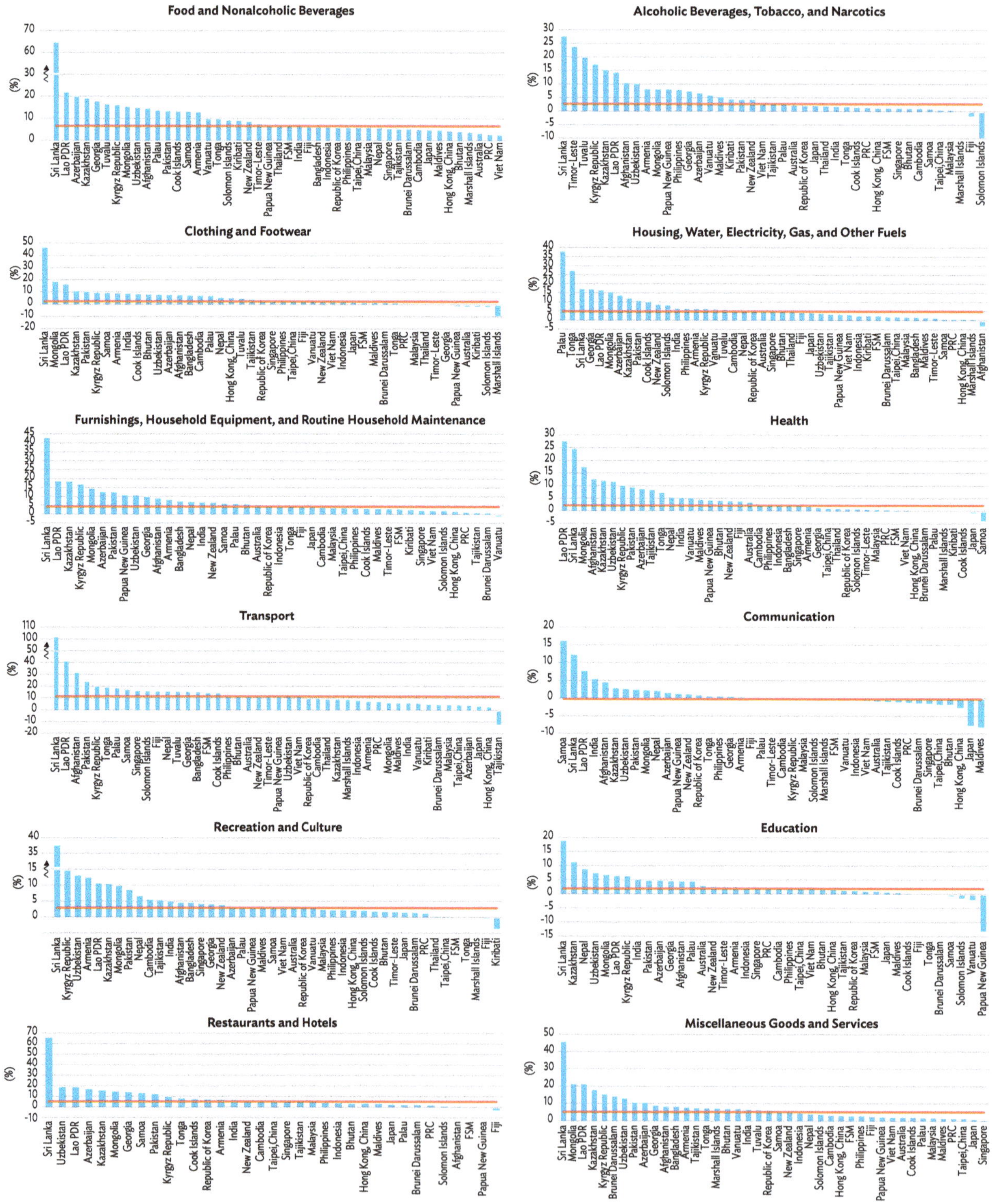

FSM = Federated States of Micronesia, Lao PDR = Lao People's Democratic Republic, PRC = People's Republic of China.

Notes: Inflation rates for Cambodia, Marshall Islands, and Sri Lanka refer to Phnom Penh, Majuro, and Colombo, respectively.
In general, the CPI data of the economies are grouped according to the Classification of individual Consumption According to Purpose (COICOP) adopted by the United Nations Statistical Commission in 1999. Other economies have switched to the most recent version, COICOP 2018.
The red horizontal line represents the median value of inflation.

Source: Asian Development Bank estimates using data presented in individual economy tables available at the Key Indicators Database https://kidb.adb.org.

Figure 2.4: Growth of Money Supply, 2020–2022

Money supply has increased since 2020, in part as a result of fiscal stimulus measures taken by governments to respond to the pandemic.

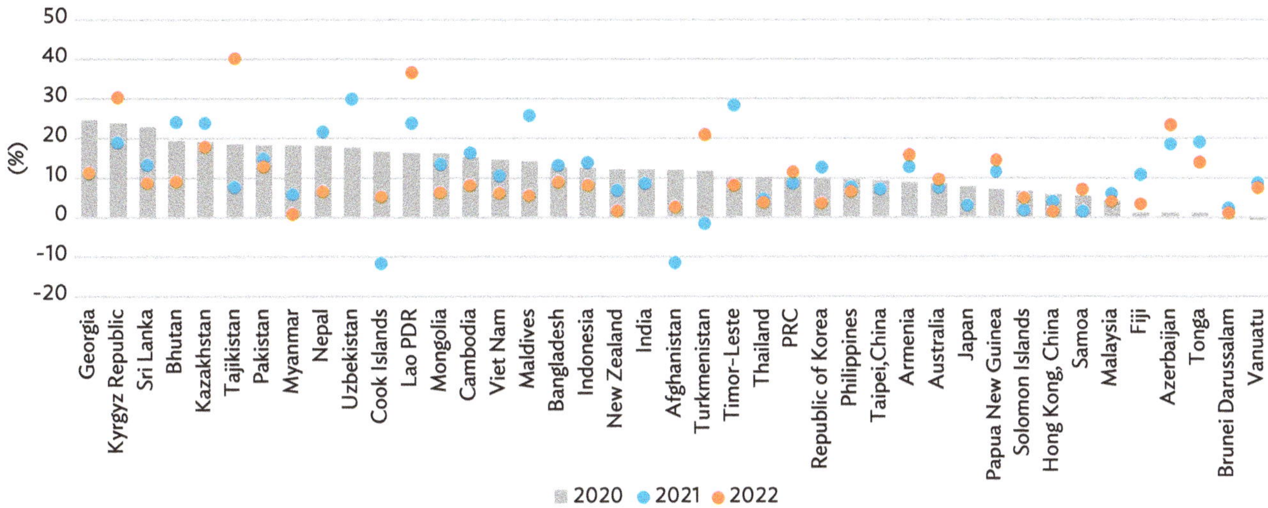

FSM = Federated States of Micronesia, Lao PDR = Lao People's Democratic Republic, PRC = People's Republic of China.
Source: Asian Development Bank estimates using data from Table 2.3.5 of *Key Indicators for Asia and the Pacific 2023.*

As inflation accelerated, economic recovery in most economies slowed.

As the two previous editions of this publication have noted, the COVID-19 pandemic caused a major setback to economic growth in developing Asia. In 2020, the region experienced its first economic contraction in the past six decades. In 2021, the region grew by 7.2%, largely as a result of a rebound in domestic economic activity and a sustained expansion in exports, but in 2022 growth slowed to 4.3%. With economies now reopened, expectations for a gradual pickup in growth have returned. At the beginning of 2022, global growth was projected at 4.4% (IMF 2022a) and 5.3% in developing Asia (ADB 2021).

As touched on in the previous section, inflation can undermine economic growth in several ways, such as reducing investments, per capita income, and efficiency in the usage of productive factors (Andres and Hernando 1997; Barro 1995; Ghazanchyan et al. 2015). Data presented in Table 2.2.11 shows that a quarter of economies registered GDP growth rates lower than 2.5% in 2022, and in 11 economies the rate of growth was at least 1 percentage point lower than the level recorded in 2021.

The aggressive monetary response of the United States to inflation may have also affected the strength of Asia and the Pacific's currencies, as Figure 2.7 suggests. In 2022, 38 out of 44 economies saw their currencies depreciate against the US dollar, 11 of which experienced depreciations of at least 10%. This relative devaluation of local currencies could further reinforce inflation pressures through increases in import prices. The latest Commodity Markets Outlook of the World Bank reports that this is propelling food and fuel prices up to the point that it could further worsen the food and energy crises, as nearly 60% of developing economies importing oil face increased local fuel prices (WBG 2022b).

Figure 2.5: Number of Central Banks That Increased or Decreased Interest Rates

The number of central banks hiking policy rates increased going in to the second half of 2022.

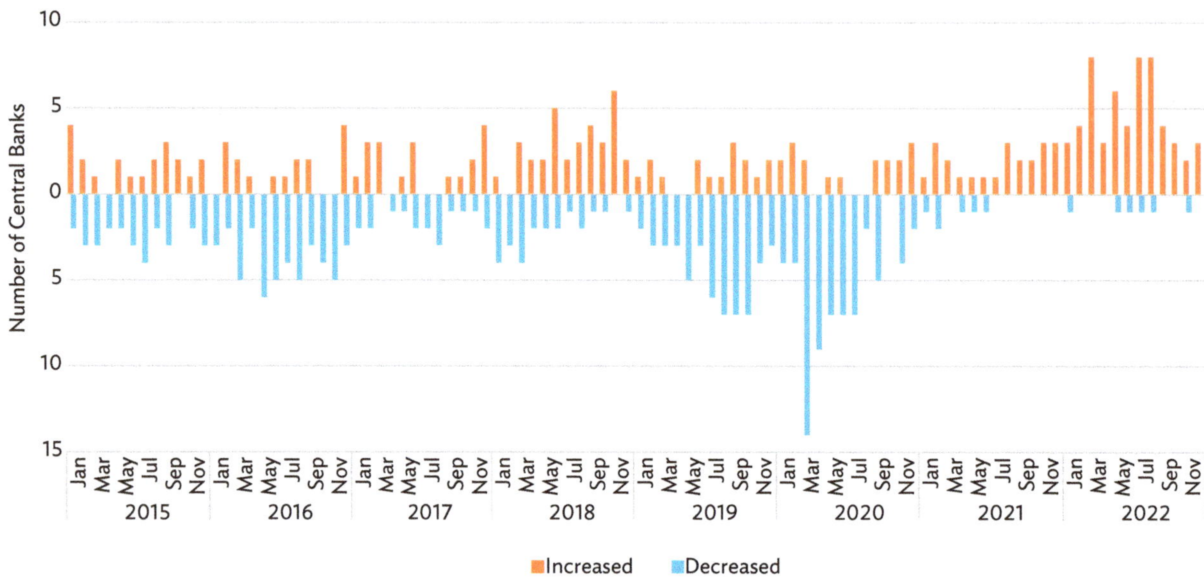

Note: Consists of ADB regional members with available data on monthly policy rates from the IMF.
Source: Asian Development Bank estimates using data from the International Monetary Fund. International Financial Statistics. http://data.imf.org/ (accessed 27 July 2023).

Figure 2.6: Developing Asia's Economic Growth

In 2022, developing Asia saw a sharp fall in growth from the year earlier, with a quarter of all economies registering growth rates below 2.5%.

A. Regional GDP Growth, 2018–2022

B. GDP Growth by Economy, 2021 and 2022

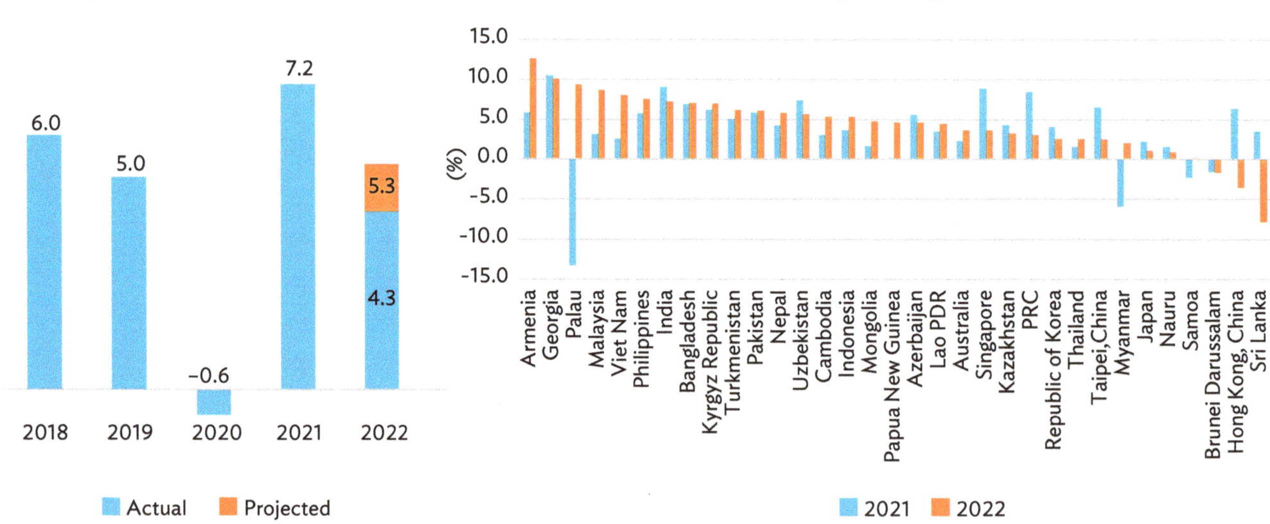

GDP = gross domestic product, Lao PDR = Lao People's Democratic Republic, PRC = People's Republic of China.

Notes: Developing Asia's actual GDP growth rates are based on the latest Asian Development Outlook 2023 figures, while the projected GDP growth rate in 2022 is an economic growth forecast based on the Asian Development Bank's *Asian Development Outlook* Supplement in 2021. Chart A - The blue bar is based on *Asian Development Outlook 2023,* and the orange bar is based on *December 2021 ADO Supplement*; Chart B - Asian Development Bank estimates using data presented in Table 2.2.11 of *Key Indicators for Asia and the Pacific 2023*.

Sources: Asian Development Bank data from the Key Indicators Database. https://kidb.adb.org/ (accessed 13 July 2023); *Asian Development Outlook 2023*; and *Asian Development Outlook Supplement 2021*.

Likewise, stock markets were also affected by higher interest rates in 2022. When interest rates are high, it becomes more expensive for businesses to borrow money which leads to decreased investment and declines in stock prices. For instance, Figure 2.7 shows that 9 out of 12 economies saw their stock price indices decrease in 2022.

Figure 2.7: Percent increase in Local Currency Units per US$ and Stock Market Price Index, 2021-2022

In 2022, nearly a quarter of economies saw their local currency depreciate by at least 10%, while stock market price indices fell in a majority of economies.

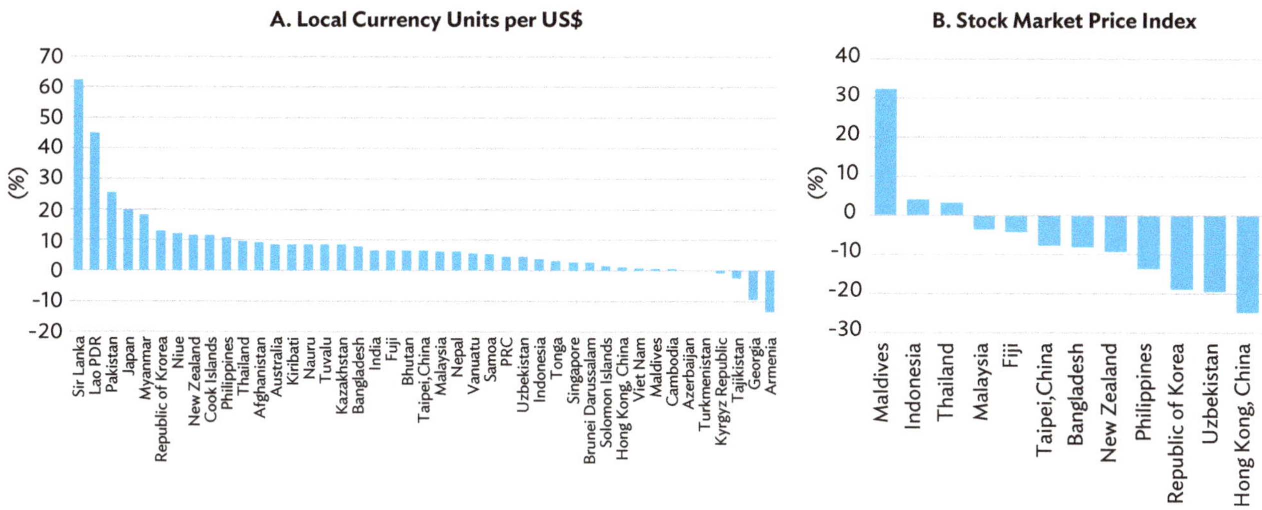

Lao PDR = Lao People's Democratic Republic, PRC = People's Republic of China.
Sources: Asian Development Bank estimates using data from Tables 2.3.10 and 2.3.12 of *Key Indicators for Asia and the Pacific 2023*.

Debt levels, meanwhile, remain above pre-pandemic levels in many parts of Asia and the Pacific.

The accumulation of more debt, especially among developing economies, was exacerbated by the COVID-19 pandemic. With a decline in economic production coinciding with an immediate need to reinforce health and social infrastructures, government debt across the globe rose to almost 100% of GDP at the onset of the pandemic in 2020. This was one of the highest levels since World War II (Ayhan Kose et al. 2021).

Figure 2.8 shows the ratio of outstanding external debt of each economy of Asia and the Pacific since the pandemic started. In 15 regional economies with available data, external debt in 2022 exceeded the levels recorded in 2019 by at least 20%.

Among economies in the region with available debt servicing data, 13 showed decreases in their debt servicing relative to their exports of goods and services from 2019 to 2020. A total of 20 experienced the same situation in 2021 (Table 2.4.23). As economic uncertainty increases, it could worsen debt distress for many economies (UNICEF 2021).

Figure 2.8: External Debt of Asia and the Pacific

External debt has increased by at least 20% from pre-pandemic levels in two out of every five economies in the region.

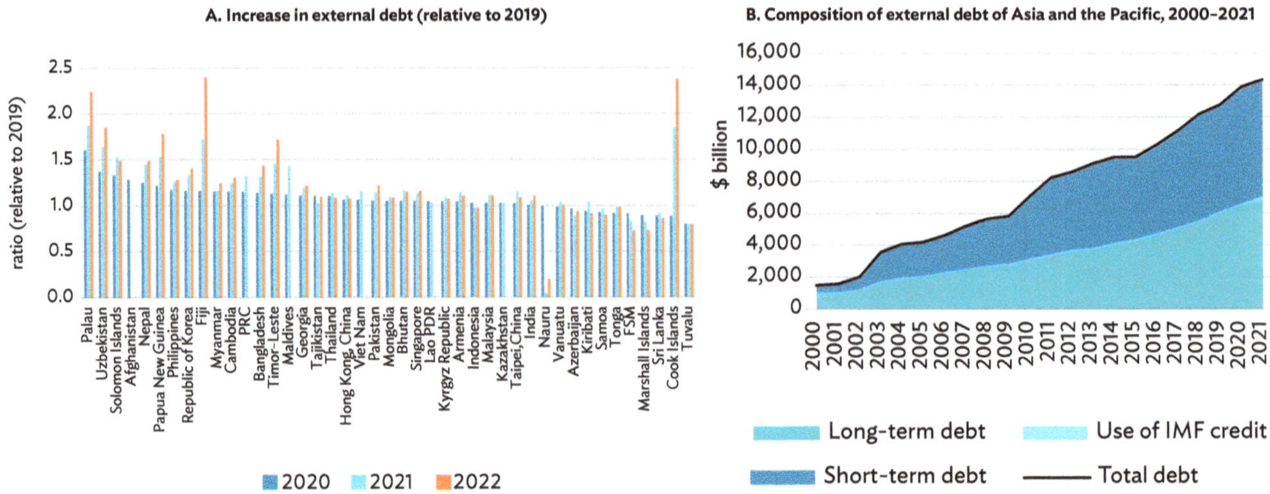

FSM = Federated States of Micronesia, Lao PDR = Lao People's Democratic Republic, PRC = People's Republic of China.

Note: Blank bars signify absence of data for the following economies and years: Afghanistan (2020, 2021); PRC (2021); Maldives (2021); Viet Nam (2021); Lao PDR (2021); and Kazakhstan (2021). For chart B, the total was calculated from ADB regional economies with available data, including developed member economies.

Sources: For chart A, Asian Development Bank estimates using data from Table A17 of *Asian Development Outlook 2023*.
For chart B, Asian Development Bank estimates using data presented in Table 2.4.20 of *Key Indicators for Asia and the Pacific 2023*, and from official sources from the individual economies.

A rise in nonperforming loans (NPL) held by banks in Asia and the Pacific is another cause for concern, with NPLs increasing in more than half of all regional member economies in 2020 (Figure 2.9). Monetary and fiscal support measures taken by governments and central banks to mitigate the impacts of the pandemic saw NPL ratios decrease in 2021 and 2022 in more than half of the economies of Asia and the Pacific (Table 2.3.9). However, high levels of NPLs remain a threat to the balance sheets of banks and undermine their ability to provide financing needed to support economic growth.

The trends in Part II highlight the need for a number of actions in response. These include reforms to support rationalization of fiscal expenditure, greater transparency of debt and its servicing, and increased mobilization of domestic resources (Ferrarini et al. 2023).

Figure 2.9: Nonperforming Loans (% of Total Gross Loans), 2019– 2022

Nonperforming loans increased in more than half of regional member economies in 2020.

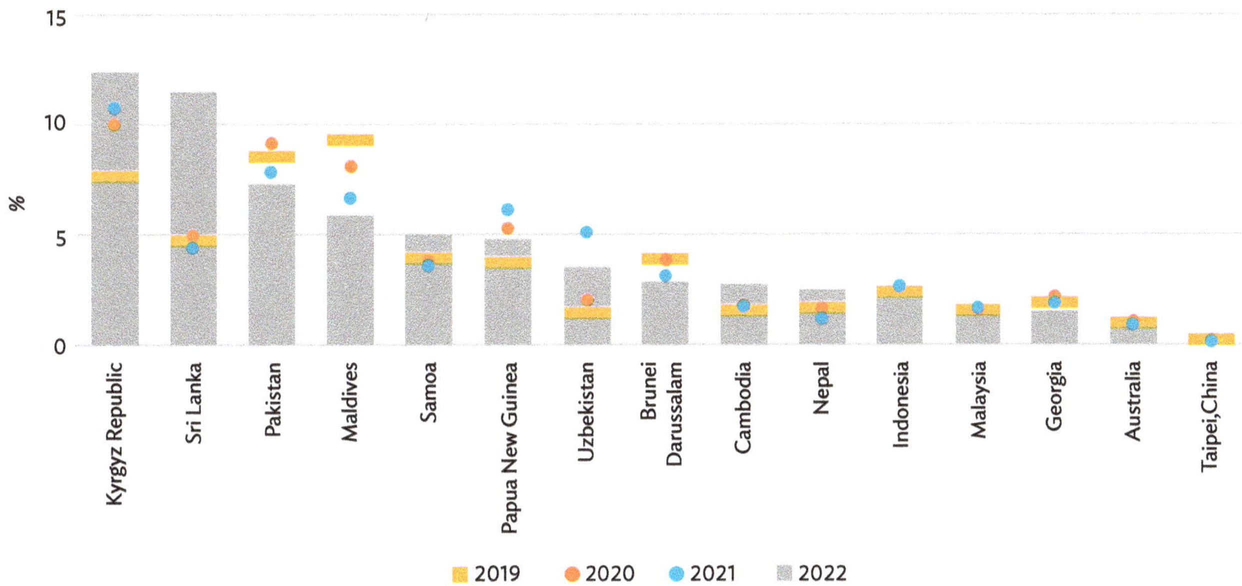

FSM = Federated States of Micronesia, PRC = People's Republic of China.

Sources: Asian Development Bank estimates using data from Table 2.3.9 of *Key Indicators for Asia and the Pacific 2023*.

References

J. Andres and I. Hernando. 1997. Does Inflation Harm Economic Growth? Evidence for the OECD. *NBER Working Paper* 6062. National Bureau of Economic Research. https://www.nber.org/papers/w6062.

Asian Development Bank (ADB). Key Indicators Database Online. https://kidb.adb.org.

ADB. 2021. *Asian Development Outlook December Supplement 2021: Recovery Continues.* Manila. https://www.adb.org/publications/ado-supplementdecember-2021.

ADB. 2022. *Asian Development Outlook Supplement 2022: Global Gloom Dims Asian Prospects.* Manila. https://www.adb.org/publications/ado-supplementdecember-2022.

ADB. 2023a. *Asian Development Outlook April 2023.* https://www.adb.org/publications/asian-development-outlook-april-2023.

ADB. 2023b. *Asian Development Outlook July 2023: Robust Growth with Moderating Inflation.* https://www.adb.org/publications/asian-development-outlookjuly-2023.

S. Aw, B. Teh, G. Ling, P. Leng, W. Chan, and M. Ahmad. 2021. The Covid-19 Pandemic Situation in Malaysia: Lessons Learned from the Perspective of Population Density. *International Journal of Environmental Research and Public Health.* 18.12. 6566.

M. Ayhan Kose, P. Nagle, F. Ohnsorge, and N. Sugawara. 2021. Debt Tsunami of the Pandemic. *Brookings Institution blogs.* 17 December. https://www.brookings.edu/blog/futuredevelopment/2021/12/17/debt-tsunami-of-the-pandemic/.

U. Bajra, F. Aliu, S. Cadez. 2022. COVID-19 pandemic-related policy stringency and economic decline: was it really inevitable? *Economic Research-Ekonomska Istraživanja.* pp. 1-17.

R. Barro. 1995. Inflation and Economic Growth. *National Bureau of Economic Research Working Paper.* No. 5326. https://www.nber.org/papers/w5326.

B. Ferrarini, S. Dagli, and P. Mariano. 2023. Sovereign Debt Vulnerabilities in Asia and the Pacific. *ADB Economics Working Paper Series.* No. 680. April. https://www.adb.org/sites/default/files/publication/879176/ewp-680-sovereign-debt-vulnerabilities-asia-pacific.pdf.

CEIC Database. https://www.ceicdata.com/en.

M. Ghazanchyan, J. G, Stotksy, and Q. Zhang. 2015. A New Look at the Determinants of Growth in Asian Countries. *IMF Working Papers.* Volume 2015. Issue 195. https://www.imf.org/en/Publications/WP/Issues/2016/12/31/A-New-Look-at-the-Determinants-of-Growth-in-Asian-Countries-43246.

International Monetary Fund (IMF). 2021. Fiscal Monitor Database of Fiscal Policy Responses to COVID-19. https://www.imf.org/en/Topics/imf-and-covid19/Fiscal-Policies-Database-in-Response-to-COVID-19.

IMF. 2022a. *World Economic Outlook Update: Rising Caseloads, A disrupted Recovery, and Higher Inflation.* https://www.imf.org/en/Publications/WEO/Issues/2022/01/25/world-economic-outlook-update-january-2022.

IMF. 2022b. Riding the Global Debt Rollercoaster. *IMF Blogs.* 12 December. https://www.imf.org/en/Blogs/Articles/2022/12/12/riding-the-global-debt-rollercoaster.

U. Kalthum and M. Masih. 2017. The Lead-Lag Relationship Between PPI, CPI and Oil Price: Malaysian Evidence. 25 November. https://mpra.ub.uni-muenchen.de/108011/1/MPRA_paper_108011.pdf.

Organisation for Economic Co-operation and Development (OECD). 2021. The COVID-19 crisis and banking system resilience: Simulation of losses on non-performing loans and policy implications. Paris. https://www.oecd.org/daf/fin/financial-markets/COVID-19-crisis-and-banking-system-resilience.pdf.

Oxford COVID-19 Governance Response Tracker. Blavatnik School of Government, University of Oxford. United Kingdom. License: CC BY 4.0. https://www.bsg.ox.ac.uk/research/covid-19-government-response-tracker.

World Bank Group (WBG). 2022a. Fertilizer Prices Expected to Remain Higher for Longer. *World Bank Blogs.* 11 May. https://blogs.worldbank.org/opendata/fertilizer-prices-expected-remain-higher-longer.

WBG. 2022b. Currency Depreciations Risk Intensifying Food, Energy Crisis in Developing Economies. 26 October. https://www.worldbank.org/en/news/pressrelease/2022/10/26/commodity-markets-outlook.

Population

Table 2.1.1: Midyear Population

ADB Regional Member	Population (million)					Population Growth Rates[a] (%)				
	2010	2015	2020	2021	2022	2010	2015	2020	2021	2022
Developing ADB Member Economies										
Central and West Asia[b]	**276.8**	**304.1**	**343.6 |**	**351.8 |**	**357.9***	**2.0**	**1.9**	**1.9 |**	**2.3 |**	**2.4***
Afghanistan[c]	24.5	27.1	31.4 |	33.6	...	2.1	2.1	2.2 |	6.9	...
Armenia[c]	3.1	3.0	3.0	3.0	3.0	-0.7	-0.2	-0.2	0.1	-0.1
Azerbaijan	9.1	9.6	10.0	10.0	10.1	1.2	1.2	0.7	0.4	0.5
Georgia	3.8	3.7	3.7	3.7	3.7	-0.7	0.2	0.1	-0.4	0.1
Kazakhstan	16.1	17.5	18.8	19.0 |	19.6	1.7	1.5	1.4	1.3 |	3.2
Kyrgyz Republic[c]	5.4	5.9	6.5	6.6	6.7	1.3	2.1	2.1	1.7	1.7
Pakistan	173.5	191.7	220.4	224.8	229.2	2.1	2.0	2.0	2.0	2.0
Tajikistan	7.5	8.5	9.4	9.8*	10.0*	2.5	2.4	2.0	1.7	1.9*
Turkmenistan	5.3	5.8	6.3	6.3	6.4	1.7	1.8	1.5	1.5	1.4
Uzbekistan	28.6	31.3	34.2	34.9	35.6	2.9	1.8	1.9	2.0	2.1
East Asia[b]	**1,423.3**	**1,468.0**	**1,498.4 |**	**1,498.6**	**1,497.4**	**0.5**	**0.5**	**0.1**	**0.0**	**-0.1**
China, People's Republic of[c]	1,340.9	1,383.3	1,412.1	1,412.6	1,411.8	0.5	0.5	0.1	0.0	-0.1
Hong Kong, China	7.0	7.3	7.5	7.4	7.3	0.7	0.9	-0.4	-0.9	-0.9
Korea, Republic of	49.6	51.0	51.8 |	51.7	51.6	0.5	0.5	0.1	-0.2	-0.2
Mongolia	2.7	3.0	3.4	3.4	3.5	1.6	2.1	1.8	1.6	1.4
Taipei,China	23.1	23.5	23.6	23.5	23.2	0.3	0.2	-0.1	-0.5	-0.5
South Asia[b]	**1,382.6**	**1,493.0***	**1,577.8***	**1,594.3***	**1,605.8***	**1.4**	**1.2***	**1.1***	**1.0***	**1.0***
Bangladesh	148.6	158.9	168.2	171.7	169.8	1.4	1.4	1.4	1.4	1.2
Bhutan	0.7	0.8	0.7	0.8	0.8	1.8	1.6	0.9	1.0	0.9
India[c]	1,186.0	1,284.0	1,357.0	1,370.0	1,383.0	1.4	1.2	1.1	1.0	1.0
Maldives	0.4	0.5*	0.6*	0.6*	0.6*	2.3	3.9*	4.4*	2.0*	1.9*
Nepal	26.3	28.0	29.4	29.2	29.4	1.4	1.4	0.9	0.9	0.9
Sri Lanka	20.7	21.0	21.9	22.2	22.2	1.0	0.9	0.5	1.1	0.1
Southeast Asia[b]	**589.2 |**	**630.7 |**	**664.6**	**670.1**	**676.6**	**1.2 |**	**1.3 |**	**1.1**	**0.9**	**1.0**
Brunei Darussalam	0.4	0.4	0.4	0.4	0.4	1.8	1.2	-2.0	-0.2	1.1
Cambodia	14.1	15.1	16.2	16.6	16.6	1.3	1.4	1.4	1.5	1.4
Indonesia	237.6	255.6	270.2	272.7	275.8	1.4	1.4	1.2	1.0	1.2
Lao People's Democratic Republic	6.0	6.5 |	7.2	7.3	7.4	1.5	1.4	1.5	1.5	1.4
Malaysia	28.6	31.2	32.5	32.6	32.7	1.8	1.6 |	...	0.4	0.2
Myanmar[c]	50.2	52.5	54.8	55.3	55.8	0.7	0.9	0.9	0.9	0.9
Philippines	93.1 |	100.8	109.0	110.2	111.6	1.0 |	1.7 (2016)	1.6	1.1	1.2
Singapore[c]	5.1	5.5	5.7	5.5	5.6	1.8	1.2	-0.3	-4.1	3.4
Thailand	65.9	68.0	69.5	69.7	69.9	0.6	0.6	0.3	0.3	0.2
Timor-Leste	1.1	1.2	1.3	1.3	1.3	1.8	1.9	2.0	1.9	-0.2
Viet Nam	87.1	92.2	97.6	98.5	99.5	1.2	1.1	1.1	1.0	1.0
The Pacific[b,d]	**9.3**	**10.6**	**12.1***	**12.4* |**	**12.8***	**2.7**	**2.7**	**2.7***	**2.7* |**	**2.7***
Cook Islands	23.7	18.4	18.5	18.3	19.2	1.1	0.9 (2016)	-2.3	0.3	0.9
Fiji	850.7	869.5	891.4	893.5	899.5	0.6	0.4	0.6	0.6	0.6
Kiribati[c]	103.1	110.1	119.4	121.4*	...	2.2	1.3	1.6	1.6*	...
Marshall Islands	52.9	54.0	55.0	55.2	55.4	1.1	0.4	0.4	0.4	0.4
Micronesia, Federated States of[c]	102.8	103.7	104.6*	104.8*	105.0*	-0.5	0.2	0.2*	0.2*	0.2*
Nauru	10.0	10.9	11.7	11.8	11.9	-0.2	1.6	1.6	1.2	0.8
Niue[c]	1.5	1.6	1.7*	1.7*	...	-4.0	3.5	–*	–*	...
Palau	18.3	17.7	17.6*	17.5* |	18.0*	-1.9	1.8	0.8	-0.6 |	0.1*
Papua New Guinea	7,055.4	8,225.6	9,589.9	9,888.8	10,197.0	3.1	3.1	3.1	3.1	3.1
Samoa	185.9	193.8	201.9	205.1	207.1	0.8	0.8	0.8	1.6	0.9
Solomon Islands	555.5	625.6	694.6	708.5	722.4	2.6 (2011)	2.3	2.0	2.0	2.0
Tonga	102.8	101.7	100.3	100.2	100.1	0.2	-0.5	-0.1	-0.1	-0.1
Tuvalu	11.1	10.7	10.6	10.5	10.0	0.5	-0.3	-1.3	-1.3	-1.3
Vanuatu	239.7	268.6	300.0	307.0	314.0	2.4	2.3	2.8	2.2	2.3
Developed ADB Member Economies[b]	**154.5**	**155.6**	**156.6**	**156.5**	**156.2**	**0.3**	**0.2**	**0.0**	**-0.1**	**-0.2**
Australia	22.0	23.8	25.7	25.7	26.0	1.5	1.4	1.2	0.1	1.2
Japan	128.1	127.1	125.8	125.7	125.1	0.0	-0.1	-0.3	-0.1	-0.4
New Zealand	4.4	4.6	5.1	5.1	5.1	1.1	2.1	2.2	0.4	0.2
DEVELOPING ADB MEMBER ECONOMIES[b]	**3,681.3 |**	**3,906.5* |**	**4,096.6* |**	**4,127.3* |**	**4,150.5**	**1.0 |**	**1.0* |**	**0.8* |**	**0.8* |**	**0.7***
ALL ADB REGIONAL MEMBERS[b]	**3,835.7 |**	**4,062.1* |**	**4,253.2* |**	**4,283.8* |**	**4,306.7**	**1.0 |**	**1.0* |**	**0.8* |**	**0.7* |**	**0.7***
WORLD	**6,985.6**	**7,426.6**	**7,841.0**	**7,909.3**	**7,975.1**	**1.3**	**1.2**	**1.0**	**0.9**	**0.8**

... = data not available; | = marks break in series; * = provisional, preliminary, estimate; – = magnitude equals zero; 0.0 = magnitude is less than half of unit employed; ADB = Asian Development Bank.

a The annual population growth rate is calculated as the percentage change in population when comparing the reference year with the year prior. For example, the population growth rates under the column heading "2020" refer to population growth from 2019 to 2020.

b Regional population totals include only reporting economies with data corresponding to the year heading, while regional population growth rates are estimated as a weighted average of the annual population growth rates of the reporting economies. Weights are based on the total population of the region for the years in which the reporting economies have published the annual growth rates.

c Estimates of population size are as of 1 January for the Kyrgyz Republic and Armenia; 10 June for Afghanistan; 30 June for Niue and Singapore; 30 September for the Federated States of Micronesia; 1 October for India and Myanmar; 7 November for Kiribati; and 31 December for the People's Republic of China.

d The total population for the Pacific subregion is expressed in millions, while estimates of population size for ADB developing member economies in the Pacific are expressed in thousands.

Sources: Economies' official sources. For Afghanistan (2021), Lao PDR (2000–2004), Pakistan (2018–2022), Palau (2022), Papua New Guinea, and Tuvalu (2018–2021): Asian Development Bank estimates using data from the economies' official sources. For Myanmar (2000–2013): World Bank. World Development Indicators. http://databank.worldbank.org/data/reports.aspx?source=world-development-indicators# (accessed 1 July 2017). For Nauru: Pacific Community. Pacific Data Hub. Stat Data Explorer. Population projections. https://stats.pacificdata.org/ (accessed 9 June 2023). For Turkmenistan and World: United Nations. World Population Prospects 2022. https://population.un.org/wpp/Download/Standard/Population/ (accessed 1 March and 30 June 2023).

Table 2.1.2: Migration and Urbanization

ADB Regional Member	Net International Migration Rate[a] (per 1,000 population)						Urban Population[b] (% of total population)					
	2010	2015	2019	2020	2021	2022	2010	2015	2019	2020	2021	2022
Developing ADB Member Economies												
Central and West Asia	...	...	...	...	...	...	39.2	40.8	39.2	39.3	39.2*	39.5
Afghanistan[c]	-5.0	-8.3	-0.2	4.3	-4.6	-1.6	23.2	24.7	25.3	25.6	24.7	...
Armenia	-10.8	-9.4	-9.0	-4.6	-4.6	-1.8	63.5	63.5	63.9	63.9	64.0	63.9
Azerbaijan	0.2	0.1	0.0	0.1	0.1	–	53.0	53.1	55.0	54.9	54.7	54.6
Georgia	-6.4	-3.5	-1.4	-0.7	-0.7	-2.7	56.5	57.5	58.9	59.2	59.5	...
Kazakhstan	1.4	-0.7	-2.0	-0.7	-1.0	–	53.8	56.8	58.3	58.8	59.2	61.6
Kyrgyz Republic	-9.5	-5.0	-5.4	-2.2	-2.5	-1.5	34.1	33.7	34.0	34.2	34.4	35.4
Pakistan	-2.2	-10.2	-5.3	-2.6	-2.0	-0.7	36.9	39.2	36.7	36.8	36.8	36.9
Tajikistan	-4.4	-2.2	-0.8	-0.4	-0.4	-2.0	26.4	26.4	26.3	26.3	26.3*	28.8
Turkmenistan[d]	-1.8	-1.7	-1.6	-0.7	-0.7	-0.6	48.5	50.3	52.0	52.5	53.0	53.5
Uzbekistan	-0.7	-0.7	-2.1	-1.2	-1.2	-0.6	51.5	50.8	50.5	50.6	50.7	50.8
East Asia	...	...	...	...	...	...	51.5	58.5	63.5	64.6	65.4	65.9
China, People's Republic of	-0.2	-0.1	-0.2	-0.0	-0.1	-0.2	50.0	57.3	62.7	63.9	64.7	65.2
Hong Kong, China	1.5	1.8	–	–	–	2.7	100.0	100.0	100.0	100.0	100.0	100.0
Korea, Republic of[d]	1.2	5.2	2.1	–	0.8	0.6	81.9	81.6	81.4	81.4	81.4	81.4
Mongolia	-3.2	1.3	3.3	–	–	-0.3	69.2	68.6	68.5	69.0	69.4	70.1
Taipei,China[e]	0.3	1.4	1.2	1.1	1.1	1.0	59.3	60.9	61.0	61.1	61.1	60.7
South Asia	...	...	...	...	...	...	29.1	32.4*	33.9*	35.0*	35.4*	35.8*
Bangladesh[d]	-3.1	-1.8	-2.1	-0.4	-1.0	-1.8	25.9	34.3	37.4	38.2	38.9	39.7
Bhutan[d]	-1.7	-1.6	0.4	0.4	0.4	0.4	34.8	38.9	40.9	42.3	43.0	40.9
India	-0.3	-0.4	-0.4	-0.0	-0.2	-0.3	29.9	32.7	34.0	34.3	34.6	34.9
Maldives	17.4	29.2	13.4	2.2	2.3	-15.2	36.4	38.5*	40.2*	40.7*	41.3*	41.7*
Nepal[f]	-10.8	-8.0	-2.4	10.5	9.9	-2.0	16.6	18.5	21.4	62.4	63.2	66.1
Sri Lanka[d]	-1.3	-4.6	-4.4	-4.2	-4.2	-3.5	18.2	18.3	18.6	18.7	18.9	19.0
Southeast Asia	-0.3	-0.1	-0.2	-0.1	-0.2	-0.3	44.2	47.3	49.5	50.2	50.7	51.2
Brunei Darussalam[d]	1.2	-1.2	-1.3	-0.9	-0.4	–	75.0	76.7	77.9	78.3	78.6	78.9
Cambodia[d]	-3.0	-3.4	-3.4	-1.4	-1.5	-1.8	20.3	22.2	23.8	24.2	24.7	25.1
Indonesia[d]	-0.3	-0.1	-0.2	-0.1	-0.1	-0.2	49.9	53.3	56.0	56.6	57.3	57.9
Lao People's Democratic Republic[d]	-4.3	-1.9	-1.4	-1.4	-1.4	-1.3	30.1	33.1	35.6	36.3	36.9	37.6
Malaysia	4.0	2.6	1.9	1.7	1.4	1.4	71.0	74.3	76.2	75.1	75.3	75.5
Myanmar[d]	-2.4	-1.8	-1.9	-1.2	-0.7	-0.6	28.9	29.9	30.9	31.1	31.4	31.8
Philippines[d]	-1.9	0.1	-0.2	-0.4	-0.7	-0.6	45.3	46.3	47.1	47.4	47.7	48.0
Singapore	21.3	7.3	7.0	3.6	3.3	4.5	100.0	100.0	100.0	100.0	100.0	100.0
Thailand[g]	0.8	0.5	0.1	0.5	0.0	0.3	42.0	48.6	53.6	54.8	56.0	57.1
Timor-Leste[d]	-1.5	-4.6	-4.1	-2.7	-1.5	-3.7	27.7	29.5	30.9	31.3	31.7	32.1
Viet Nam	-0.1	-0.1	-0.0	-0.0	-0.0	-0.8	30.4	33.5	35.0	36.8	37.1	37.3
The Pacific	...	...	...	...	...	...	18.5	18.4	18.6	18.7*	18.7	18.7
Cook Islands	21.6	-17.0	-16.1	-9.4	-9.4	-5.9	73.3	74.4	75.3	75.5	75.7	75.9
Fiji	-11.7	-12.0	-12.8	-6.5	-6.5	-3.8	52.2	54.7	56.8	57.2	57.7	58.2
Kiribati	-5.7	-7.3	-5.5	-2.3	-2.3	-3.0	47.4	51.6	54.8	55.6	56.3	...
Marshall Islands[d]	-26.1	-37.8	-41.6	-42.9	-44.2	–	73.6	75.8	77.4	77.8	78.2	78.5
Micronesia, Federated States of[d]	-16.6	-12.8	-11.5	-5.6	-5.6	-5.2	22.3	22.5	22.8	22.9	23.1	23.2
Nauru[d]	-24.3	-2.8	-8.8	-5.5	-5.3	-11.0	100.0	100.0	100.0	100.0	100.0	100.0
Niue[d]	-6.4	4.3	23.2	-2.1	-2.0	–	38.7	42.6	45.5	46.2	46.9	47.6
Palau	-19.0	0.5	0.4	0.4	0.2	-1.1	77.0	78.7	...	78.9*	...	...
Papua New Guinea[d]	6.6	3.5	2.4	1.1	1.1	-0.1	13.0	13.0	13.3	13.3	13.5	13.6
Samoa	-16.7	-15.3	-11.6	-4.9	-4.0	-6.7	19.9	19.2	18.8	18.8	17.5	17.2
Solomon Islands[d]	-4.1	-2.6	-2.4	-1.2	-1.1	-2.2	20.0	22.4	24.2	24.7	25.1	25.6
Tonga	-18.0	-23.2	-17.9	-9.0	-8.9	-7.5	23.4	23.1	21.9	21.5	21.1	20.8
Tuvalu	1.6	-14.5	-5.2	-1.4	-1.3	-5.3	54.8	59.7	63.2	64.0	64.8	65.5
Vanuatu	-3.6	-2.7	-1.3	-0.6	-0.6	–	24.4	24.6	25.1	25.2	21.7	21.2
Developed ADB Member Economies	...	...	...	...	...	...	90.0	90.5	90.7	90.8	90.9	90.9
Australia	7.6	8.8	9.3	4.6	4.6	5.4	86.2	86.8	87.3	87.3	87.2	87.3
Japan[d]	1.2	1.2	1.5	0.7	0.7	0.8	90.8	91.4	91.7	91.8	91.9	92.0
New Zealand	1.4	10.3	21.1	7.6	7.5	2.5	83.9	84.0	84.1	84.0	83.9	83.6
DEVELOPING ADB MEMBER ECONOMIES	...	...	...	...	...	...	40.9	45.2*	47.7*	48.6*	49.0*	49.4*
ALL ADB REGIONAL MEMBERS	...	...	...	...	...	...	42.9	47.0*	49.3*	50.2*	50.6*	50.9*
WORLD	–	–	–	–	–	–	51.7	53.9	55.7	56.2	56.6	57.0

... = data not available; (-/+) 0.0 = magnitude is less than half of unit employed; * = provisional, preliminary, estimate; – = magnitude equals zero; ADB = Asian Development Bank.

a Refers to annual average migration over the period shown. United Nations population estimates and projections are based on all available sources of data on population size and levels of fertility, mortality, and international migration. Statistics on international migration are sourced from population registers and other administrative sources. These estimates and projections are made for 237 distinct national economies or areas comprising the total population of the world.

b In estimating the aggregates for Asia and the Pacific, imputation was done for economies with missing data by substituting available data from the nearest years. The aggregates were derived using data on total population and percentage of urban population from economies' official sources and the United Nations' World Urbanization Prospects 2018 and World Population Prospects 2022.

c For urban population, refers to the share of urban population to total resident population, i.e., excluding the nomadic population.

d For urban population, refers to data from World Urbanization Prospects 2018 for: 2014–2022 for Bangladesh; 2016, 2018, 2020, and 2021 for Bhutan; and the whole data series for Brunei Darussalam, Cambodia, the Federated States of Micronesia, Indonesia, Japan, the Lao People's Democratic Republic, the Marshall Islands, Myanmar, Nauru, Niue, Papua New Guinea, the Philippines, the Republic of Korea, Solomon Islands, Sri Lanka, Timor-Leste, and Turkmenistan.

e For urban population, refers to localities of 100,000 or more inhabitants.

f For 2000, the figure is an estimate based on the 2001 census. For 2002–2010 and 2012 onward, the figures are estimates based on the 2011 census and refer to 58 urban municipalities. For 2020 onward, data refer to 293 urban municipalities.

g For urban population, data for 2010 onward include non-Thai citizens who are listed in the civil registration.

Sources: For net international migration rate: United Nations. World Population Prospects 2022. https://population.un.org/wpp/Download/Standard/Migration/ (accessed 1 March 2023). For urban population: economies' official sources; and United Nations. World Urbanization Prospects 2018. https://population.un.org/wup/Download/ (accessed 30 June 2023).

Table 2.1.3: Proportion of Total Population by Age Bracket, and Age Dependency Ratio

ADB Regional Member	Population Aged 0–14 Years (% of total population)				Population Aged 15–64 Years (% of total population)			
	2010	2015	2021	2022	2010	2015	2021	2022
Developing ADB Member Economies								
Central and West Asia	**37.1**	**36.5**	**35.8**	**35.6**	**58.8**	**59.3**	**59.7**	**59.8**
Afghanistan	49.0	45.8	43.4	43.1	48.7	51.8	54.2	54.5
Armenia	19.3	19.6	20.4	20.5	70.4	69.7	66.8	66.4
Azerbaijan	23.9	24.4	23.9	23.5	70.5	70.1	69.4	69.4
Georgia	18.7	19.4	21.1	21.3	67.9	66.7	64.3	64.1
Kazakhstan	24.6	27.0	29.5	29.7	68.6	66.0	62.5	62.3
Kyrgyz Republic	30.7	32.5	34.5	34.4	65.1	63.7	61.2	61.0
Pakistan	39.2	38.4	36.9	36.6	57.0	57.7	58.8	59.2
Tajikistan	36.8	36.6	36.4	36.3	60.0	60.4	60.3	60.3
Turkmenistan	30.2	30.4	31.2	31.1	65.9	65.6	63.9	63.7
Uzbekistan	29.2	28.5	30.1	30.2	66.2	67.1	64.9	64.7
East Asia	**18.3**	**18.1**	**17.4**	**17.0**	**72.9**	**71.7**	**69.3**	**69.1**
China, People's Republic of	18.5	18.4	17.7	17.2	72.9	71.6	69.2	69.0
Hong Kong, China	12.3	11.6	12.2	12.0	74.4	72.9	68.2	67.5
Korea, Republic of	16.4	13.8	11.9	11.6	72.6	73.3	71.5	70.9
Mongolia	28.1	29.3	32.4	32.5	68.1	66.9	63.2	62.9
Taipei,China	16.0	13.7	12.7	12.6	73.6	74.3	71.4	70.7
South Asia	**31.2**	**28.8**	**25.8**	**25.4**	**63.7**	**65.6**	**67.5**	**67.7**
Bangladesh	33.4	30.2	26.5	26.0	62.2	65.0	67.7	68.0
Bhutan	29.6	27.0	22.8	22.1	65.2	67.3	71.1	71.6
India	31.0	28.6	25.7	25.3	64.0	65.7	67.5	67.8
Maldives	25.7	22.9	21.7	21.7	69.8	72.9	73.7	73.5
Nepal	36.2	33.4	29.4	28.9	59.1	61.1	64.6	65.0
Sri Lanka	25.5	25.0	23.2	22.8	66.8	66.0	65.6	65.6
Southeast Asia	**27.5**	**26.2**	**24.8**	**24.5**	**66.5**	**67.3**	**67.6**	**67.6**
Brunei Darussalam	26.0	24.2	22.3	22.1	70.6	71.7	71.8	71.8
Cambodia	32.1	30.9	29.3	28.9	64.3	64.9	65.2	65.2
Indonesia	27.9	26.9	25.5	25.2	66.2	66.9	67.7	67.9
Lao People's Democratic Republic	35.9	33.1	31.0	30.6	60.2	62.7	64.6	64.9
Malaysia	27.8	25.2	23.0	22.7	67.1	68.9	69.8	69.8
Myanmar	28.3	26.6	24.9	24.6	66.5	67.8	68.5	68.5
Philippines	34.5	32.6	30.6	30.3	61.2	62.7	64.0	64.2
Singapore	14.3	12.7	12.0	11.8	78.5	78.4	73.9	73.0
Thailand	19.3	17.4	15.8	15.5	71.9	71.6	69.7	69.3
Timor-Leste	41.4	39.0	35.3	34.7	53.8	55.5	59.4	60.1
Viet Nam	24.3	23.4	22.5	22.4	69.2	69.6	68.7	68.5
The Pacific	**37.4**	**36.3**	**34.6**	**34.2**	**59.7**	**60.6**	**62.0**	**62.2**
Cook Islands	28.1	26.2	23.7	23.6	63.8	64.3	65.0	64.7
Fiji	31.1	30.2	28.9	28.6	64.7	65.0	65.4	65.5
Kiribati	36.4	35.6	36.2	36.1	60.2	61.0	60.1	60.1
Marshall Islands	39.6	37.4	33.2	32.5	58.4	60.0	62.6	63.0
Micronesia, Federated States of	35.5	33.1	30.7	30.3	61.2	62.8	63.4	63.5
Nauru	36.5	38.5	38.8	38.8	62.2	59.9	58.9	58.8
Niue	26.2	27.0	26.4	26.1	61.5	60.6	58.7	58.9
Palau	21.3	20.6	21.0	21.0	72.6	72.0	69.5	69.1
Papua New Guinea	37.9	36.5	34.6	34.2	59.5	60.7	62.3	62.6
Samoa	39.0	38.4	37.7	37.6	56.2	56.9	57.2	57.2
Solomon Islands	41.2	40.5	39.3	39.1	55.4	56.0	57.2	57.4
Tonga	37.6	36.8	34.6	34.3	56.7	57.2	59.2	59.5
Tuvalu	32.5	31.6	31.6	31.7	62.1	62.9	62.1	61.9
Vanuatu	38.9	39.6	39.6	39.4	57.3	56.6	56.7	56.9
Developed ADB Member Economies	**14.3**	**13.8**	**13.1**	**13.0**	**63.9**	**61.1**	**59.8**	**59.8**
Australia	19.1	18.9	18.4	18.2	67.4	66.2	65.1	64.9
Japan	13.2	12.7	11.8	11.6	63.2	60.0	58.4	58.5
New Zealand	20.9	20.0	18.9	18.7	66.2	65.4	65.2	65.0
DEVELOPING ADB MEMBER ECONOMIES	**26.3**	**25.1**	**23.5**	**23.2**	**67.2**	**67.6**	**67.4**	**67.5**
ALL ADB REGIONAL MEMBERS	**25.8**	**24.7**	**23.1**	**22.8**	**67.1**	**67.4**	**67.2**	**67.2**
WORLD	**27.1**	**26.4**	**25.5**	**25.3**	**65.3**	**65.2**	**64.9**	**64.9**

continued on next page

Table 2.1.3: Proportion of Total Population by Age Bracket, and Age Dependency Ratio *(continued)*

ADB Regional Member	Population Aged 65 Years and Older (% of total population)				Age Dependency Ratio for Total Population			
	2010	2015	2021	2022	2010	2015	2021	2022
Developing ADB Member Economies								
Central and West Asia	**4.1**	**4.2**	**4.5**	**4.6**	**70.0**	**68.6**	**67.6**	**67.1**
Afghanistan	2.4	2.4	2.4	2.4	105.4	93.0	84.6	83.6
Armenia	10.4	10.7	12.7	13.1	42.1	43.4	49.6	50.7
Azerbaijan	5.6	5.5	6.7	7.1	41.8	42.7	44.2	44.1
Georgia	13.4	14.0	14.6	14.6	47.3	50.0	55.4	55.9
Kazakhstan	6.8	7.0	7.9	8.0	45.8	51.5	60.0	60.5
Kyrgyz Republic	4.2	3.8	4.4	4.5	53.6	57.0	63.5	63.9
Pakistan	3.7	3.9	4.2	4.3	75.4	73.4	70.0	69.0
Tajikistan	3.2	3.0	3.3	3.5	66.6	65.6	65.9	66.0
Turkmenistan	4.0	4.0	4.9	5.1	51.9	52.5	56.6	56.9
Uzbekistan	4.6	4.3	5.0	5.1	51.1	48.9	54.0	54.7
East Asia	**8.7**	**10.2**	**13.3**	**13.9**	**37.1**	**39.4**	**44.3**	**44.7**
China, People's Republic of	8.6	10.0	13.1	13.7	37.1	39.6	44.5	44.9
Hong Kong, China	13.3	15.5	19.6	20.5	34.3	37.2	46.6	48.2
Korea, Republic of	11.0	13.0	16.7	17.5	37.8	36.5	39.9	41.0
Mongolia	3.8	3.8	4.4	4.6	46.8	49.5	58.4	58.9
Taipei,China	10.4	12.0	16.0	16.7	36.0	34.6	40.2	41.5
South Asia	**5.0**	**5.6**	**6.7**	**6.9**	**56.9**	**52.5**	**48.2**	**47.6**
Bangladesh	4.4	4.8	5.8	6.0	60.8	53.9	47.7	47.1
Bhutan	5.1	5.7	6.1	6.3	53.3	48.6	40.7	39.7
India	5.1	5.6	6.8	6.9	56.4	52.1	48.1	47.5
Maldives	4.5	4.2	4.5	4.8	43.2	37.2	35.6	36.0
Nepal	4.7	5.5	6.0	6.1	69.2	63.6	54.9	53.8
Sri Lanka	7.6	9.0	11.2	11.5	49.6	51.5	52.4	52.3
Southeast Asia	**5.9**	**6.5**	**7.7**	**7.9**	**50.3**	**48.6**	**48.0**	**47.9**
Brunei Darussalam	3.4	4.1	5.8	6.2	41.6	39.5	39.2	39.3
Cambodia	3.6	4.2	5.5	5.8	55.6	54.1	53.4	53.3
Indonesia	5.9	6.2	6.8	6.9	51.1	49.4	47.6	47.2
Lao People's Democratic Republic	3.9	4.2	4.4	4.5	66.2	59.4	54.7	54.1
Malaysia	5.1	5.9	7.3	7.5	49.1	45.0	43.3	43.2
Myanmar	5.2	5.6	6.6	6.8	50.3	47.4	46.0	45.9
Philippines	4.3	4.6	5.3	5.4	63.3	59.4	56.2	55.7
Singapore	7.2	8.9	14.1	15.1	27.3	27.6	35.4	36.9
Thailand	8.8	11.0	14.5	15.2	39.1	39.6	43.5	44.4
Timor-Leste	4.8	5.5	5.3	5.2	85.8	80.3	68.3	66.4
Viet Nam	6.5	7.0	8.8	9.1	44.5	43.8	45.6	46.0
The Pacific	**2.9**	**3.1**	**3.5**	**3.5**	**67.5**	**64.9**	**61.3**	**60.7**
Cook Islands	8.1	9.5	11.3	11.7	56.8	55.5	53.8	54.5
Fiji	4.2	4.8	5.7	5.9	54.5	53.9	53.0	52.7
Kiribati	3.4	3.4	3.7	3.8	66.1	64.0	66.4	66.4
Marshall Islands	2.0	2.7	4.3	4.5	71.3	66.7	59.9	58.7
Micronesia, Federated States of	3.2	4.1	5.9	6.2	63.3	59.2	57.7	57.4
Nauru	1.4	1.6	2.3	2.5	60.8	67.0	69.9	70.2
Niue	12.3	12.4	14.9	15.0	62.7	65.1	70.4	69.8
Palau	6.1	7.4	9.5	9.9	37.8	38.8	43.8	44.7
Papua New Guinea	2.6	2.8	3.1	3.2	68.0	64.7	60.5	59.8
Samoa	4.8	4.7	5.1	5.2	77.9	75.7	74.9	74.8
Solomon Islands	3.4	3.4	3.5	3.5	80.6	78.4	74.8	74.1
Tonga	5.7	6.0	6.2	6.2	76.4	74.7	69.0	68.0
Tuvalu	5.4	5.5	6.2	6.4	60.9	59.0	60.9	61.6
Vanuatu	3.8	3.7	3.7	3.7	74.4	76.6	76.5	75.8
Developed ADB Member Economies	**21.9**	**25.1**	**27.1**	**27.3**	**56.5**	**63.7**	**67.3**	**67.3**
Australia	13.6	14.9	16.6	16.9	48.4	51.1	53.7	54.0
Japan	23.6	27.3	29.8	29.9	58.2	66.7	71.1	71.1
New Zealand	13.0	14.5	15.9	16.3	51.1	52.8	53.4	53.9
DEVELOPING ADB MEMBER ECONOMIES	**6.5**	**7.3**	**9.1**	**9.3**	**48.7**	**47.9**	**48.3**	**48.2**
ALL ADB REGIONAL MEMBERS	**7.1**	**8.0**	**9.7**	**10.0**	**49.0**	**48.5**	**48.9**	**48.8**
WORLD	**7.7**	**8.3**	**9.6**	**9.8**	**53.2**	**53.4**	**54.1**	**54.0**

ADB = Asian Development Bank.

Notes:

1 All figures presented in this table are ADB estimates using data from the United Nations' World Population Prospects 2022.

2 United Nations population estimates are based on all available sources of data on population size and levels of fertility, mortality, and international migration for 237 distinct economies or areas comprising the total population of the world.

Source: United Nations. World Population Prospects 2022. https://population.un.org/wpp/ (accessed 01 March 2023).

Labor Force and Employment

Table 2.1.4: Labor Force Participation Rates
(%)

ADB Regional Member	2010	2015	2016	2017	2018	2019	2020	2021	2022
Developing ADB Member Economies									
Central and West Asia									
Afghanistan[a,b]	49.8 (2011)	55.4 (2013)	...	53.9	...	...	41.9	...	...
Armenia[c]	61.2	62.5	61.0	60.9	58.9	59.9	58.5	57.8	...
Azerbaijan[c]	64.8	65.4	66.0	66.2	66.3	66.5	66.8	67.1	...
Georgia[c]	51.5	55.5	55.0	54.5	52.9	51.8	50.5	50.9	51.9
Kazakhstan	71.2	69.7	70.0	69.7	70.0	70.1	69.2	69.3	68.7
Kyrgyz Republic	64.2	62.4	61.5	60.1	59.8	60.2	60.1	60.3	...
Pakistan	45.9	45.2	...	...	44.3	44.8	...	44.9	...
Tajikistan	50.3	47.7	46.7	46.2	45.7	45.5	45.5	45.8	...
Turkmenistan[d]	49.2	47.4	47.2	47.1	46.9	46.8	45.9	46.2	46.2
Uzbekistan[c]	70.7	71.9	72.5	73.5	74.3	75.0	73.8	74.1	73.9
East Asia									
China, People's Republic of[d]	71.0	69.3	68.9	68.4	67.8	67.4	65.0	67.1	66.9
Hong Kong, China	59.6	61.1	61.1	61.1	61.3	60.7	59.7	59.4	58.2
Korea, Republic of	61.1	62.8	62.9	63.2	63.1	63.3	62.5	62.8	63.9
Mongolia[c]	61.6	61.5	60.5	61.1	61.0	60.5	58.8	56.9	58.6
Taipei,China	58.1	58.7	58.8	58.8	59.0	59.2	59.1	59.0	59.2
South Asia									
Bangladesh	59.3	57.1 (2013)	58.5	58.2	...	...	...	...	61.0
Bhutan[e]	68.6	63.1	62.2	63.3	62.6	66.4	67.8	69.1	63.1
India	57.1	...	...	...	49.8*	50.2	53.5	54.9	55.2
Maldives[f]	52.1	63.8 (2014)	57.6	...	...	60.2	...	...	...
Nepal[c]	74.3 (2012)	72.2 (2014)	...	...	38.5	...	...	...	...
Sri Lanka	48.6	53.8	53.8	54.1	51.8	52.3	50.6	49.9	49.8
Southeast Asia									
Brunei Darussalam[c]	68.9 (2011)	65.6 (2014)	...	64.2	66.8	64.6	65.5	63.8	...
Cambodia	87.0	82.7	84.0	86.6	...	69.3	...	...	...
Indonesia	67.7	65.8	66.3	66.7	67.3	67.5	67.8	67.8	68.6
Lao People's Democratic Republic[c]	79.2	...	...	40.8	...	...	...	...	47.1
Malaysia[c]	63.7	67.9	67.7	68.0	68.3	68.7	68.4	68.6	...
Myanmar	67.0	64.7	...	61.2	61.5	63.2	...	...	...
Philippines	64.1	63.7	63.5	61.2	60.9	61.3	59.5	63.4	64.7
Singapore[g]	66.2	68.3	68.0	67.7	67.7	68.0	68.1	70.5	70.0
Thailand[h]	72.3	69.8	68.8	68.1	68.3	67.5	67.8	67.8	68.1
Timor-Leste[c]	24.0	30.6 (2013)	46.9	...	...	...	...	30.5	...
Viet Nam	76.7	77.4	77.3	76.9	77.0	76.8	74.4	67.7	68.0
The Pacific									
Cook Islands	71.0 (2011)	...	71.9	...	...	70.4	...	68.1	...
Fiji[i]	62.0	58.2	57.6	57.5	57.4	57.4	56.3	56.4	...
Kiribati	59.3	66.0	...	...	...	...	53.0	...	...
Marshall Islands	41.7 (2011)	...	...	...	...	...	...	...	...
Micronesia, Federated States of	57.3	56.9 (2014)	...	...	...	...	...	...	...
Nauru[b,d]	64.0 (2011)	68.7 (2013)	...	...	...	...	...	65.2	...
Niue	68.9 (2011)	...	...	68.6	...	...	...	...	...
Palau	68.1 (2012)	77.4	...	...	...	...	76.9	...	...
Papua New Guinea[d]	48.3	47.6	47.5	47.5	47.5	47.4	47.0	47.1	47.1
Samoa[b]	41.3 (2011)	...	47.4	43.3	...	...	...	43.4	...
Solomon Islands	62.9 (2009)	...	...	...	...	...	...	...	...
Tonga	94.8 (2003)	...	63.7	...	46.7	...	...	59.1	...
Tuvalu	59.4 (2012)	...	52.3	...	...	...	...	...	...
Vanuatu[d]	69.2	69.4	69.4	69.3	69.3	69.3	68.6	68.9	...
Developed ADB Member Economies									
Australia	65.4	65.0	64.9	65.2	65.6	66.0	65.0	65.9	66.6
Japan	59.6	59.6	60.0	60.5	61.5	62.1	62.0	62.1	62.5
New Zealand	67.6	68.8	70.0	70.9	70.9	70.5	70.2	70.8	71.3

... = data not available, * = provisional or preliminary, ADB = Asian Development Bank.

Note: Based on varying concepts and definitions of "labor force" across economies.

a For 2017, data cover the period from April 2016 to April 2017. For 2020, data cover the period from October 2019 to September 2020.
b Figures for different years may not be directly comparable with each other due to changes in methodology and labor concepts adopted.
c Recommendations from the 19th International Conference of Labour Statisticians were adopted by: Armenia, beginning 2018; Azerbaijan, beginning 2015; Brunei Darussalam, beginning 2017; Georgia, beginning 2010; the Lao People's Democratic Republic, for 2017; Malaysia, beginning 2019; Mongolia, beginning 2019; Nepal, for 2018; Timor-Leste, beginning 2010; and Uzbekistan, beginning 2017. Hence, data for these years may not be directly comparable with data in other years. The 19th conference provided the statistical concept of work for reference purposes; and the operational concepts, definitions, and guidelines for (i) three distinct subsets of work activities, referred to as forms of work, which include own-use production work, employment work, and volunteer work; (ii) related classifications of the population according to their labor force status and main work status; and (iii) measures of labor underutilization. The concept of employment has also been refined to refer to work for pay or profit.
d Data refer to estimates modeled by the International Labour Organization.
e For 2017, data are from the census of population. For all other years, data are from labor force surveys. Thus, data prior to and after the census year may not be directly comparable with 2017 data.
f Includes local population only.
g Refers to Singapore residents only.
h Includes the seasonally inactive labor force.
i For 2017, the reported number of employed people excludes those who are engaged in unpaid employment as of end of June. Hence, data for 2014 and 2016 are not comparable with data for 2017 because the former years include unpaid employment.

Sources: Economies' official sources. For Micronesia, Federated States of (2014), Nauru, Papua New Guinea, the People's Republic of China, Turkmenistan, and Vanuatu: International Labour Organization. ILOSTAT Database. http://www.ilo.org/ilostat/ (accessed 18 July 2023). For Tuvalu (2016): Pacific Data Hub. Explorer: National Minimum Development Indicators. https://stats.pacificdata.org/vis?lc=en&df[ds]=SPC2&df[id]=DF_NMDI&df[ag]=SPC&df[vs]=1.0&dq=A..NMDI0014%2BOTH._T._T._T..&pd=2010%2C2020&ly[rw]=GEO_PICT&ly[cl]=TIME_PERIOD&fs[0]=Development%20indicators%2C0%7CNational%20Minimum%20Development%20Indicators%23NMDI%23&pg=0&fc=Development%20indicators&lo=1 (accessed 14 July 2023).

Table 2.1.5: Employment in Agriculture, Industry, and Services
(% of total employment)

ADB Regional Member	Agriculture				
	2010	2015	2019	2020	2021
Developing ADB Member Economies					
Central and West Asia					
Afghanistan[a]	54.6	47.1	42.5	44.5	...
Armenia[b]	38.6	35.3	24.1	21.8	...
Azerbaijan[b]	38.2	36.4	36.0	36.3	36.3
Georgia[b,c]	48.1	44.1	38.2	19.8	18.9
Kazakhstan	28.3	18.0	14.9	13.5	13.4
Kyrgyz Republic	32.2	29.3	19.3	18.3	...
Pakistan	43.4	41.0	36.9	...	37.5
Tajikistan	52.6	48.6	44.7	60.9	...
Turkmenistan	29.4	24.5	20.7	...	...
Uzbekistan[b]	26.8	27.6	25.7	26.4	26.5
East Asia					
China, People's Republic of[d]	36.7	28.6	25.3	23.6	22.9
Hong Kong, China[e]	0.2	0.2	0.2	–	–
Korea, Republic of	6.6	5.2	5.1	5.4	5.3
Mongolia[b]	33.5	28.5	25.3	23.8	25.9
Taipei,China	5.4	5.1	5.0	4.8	4.7
South Asia					
Bangladesh	47.3	43.5	38.3	...	...
Bhutan	59.6	58.0	55.8	49.9	49.2
India	51.5	45.3	42.6	...	...
Maldives[f]	13.2	9.8	8.3	...	...
Nepal[b]	70.0	66.9	64.4	...	...
Sri Lanka[g]	31.8	28.7	25.0	27.1	...
Southeast Asia					
Brunei Darussalam[b]	0.7	0.7	2.0	1.3	...
Cambodia	57.3	42.5	34.5	...	...
Indonesia	39.1	33.0	28.5	29.8	28.3
Lao People's Democratic Republic[b]	71.5	65.6	61.4	...	...
Malaysia[b]	13.3	12.5	10.3	10.5	10.3
Myanmar	53.1	51.7	48.9	...	...
Philippines	32.9	29.2	22.9	24.8	24.2
Singapore[h]	0.1	0.1	0.0	0.1	0.1
Thailand	38.3	32.3	31.4	31.3	31.9
Timor-Leste[b]	50.8	42.6	39.3	...	...
Viet Nam[i]	48.7	44.0	37.2	33.0	28.9
The Pacific					
Cook Islands[j]	4.9 (2006)	...	2.5	...	...
Fiji[k]	24.4	19.9	17.6	...	...
Kiribati[l]	22.1	24.3	...	23.2	...
Marshall Islands	1.0	1.1	1.0	0.8	0.7
Micronesia, Federated States of	52.2 (2000)	1.7	2.0 (2018)	...	...
Nauru	...	...	...	...	...
Niue	15.9 (2006)	...	...	...	...
Palau[m]	7.8 (2005)	6.4	...	...	...
Papua New Guinea	65.4	59.8	56.2	...	...
Samoa	34.5	32.3	30.2	...	...
Solomon Islands[n]	45.6	40.1	37.3	...	...
Tonga	25.3	22.7	19.4	...	...
Tuvalu	...	...	...	...	...
Vanuatu	63.8	60.6	56.8	...	...
Developed ADB Member Economies					
Australia	3.2	2.6	2.6	2.8	2.4
Japan	4.1	3.6	3.4	3.2	3.1
New Zealand	6.7	6.1	5.8	6.0	6.1

continued on next page

Table 2.1.5: Employment in Agriculture, Industry, and Services *(continued)*
(% of total employment)

ADB Regional Member	Industry				
	2010	2015	2019	2020	2021
Developing ADB Member Economies					
Central and West Asia					
Afghanistan[a]	14.7	17.2	18.6	18.1	...
Armenia[b]	17.4	15.9	24.8	21.0	...
Azerbaijan[b]	13.7	14.1	14.8	14.6	14.9
Georgia[b,c]	10.6	11.0	14.3	18.2	19.0
Kazakhstan	18.7	20.6	21.0	19.7	19.7
Kyrgyz Republic	21.1	20.9	25.4	25.9	...
Pakistan	21.4	24.0	25.0	...	25.4
Tajikistan	15.6	15.5	15.8	8.6	...
Turkmenistan	35.2	37.7	39.8	...	...
Uzbekistan[b]	22.7	22.9	23.0	23.5	23.5
East Asia					
China, People's Republic of[d]	28.7	29.2	27.4	28.7	29.1
Hong Kong, China[e]	12.8	11.9	11.1	11.1	11.4
Korea, Republic of	25.0	25.4	24.6	24.7	24.6
Mongolia[b]	16.2	20.3	21.6	20.7	22.1
Taipei,China	37.3	37.3	36.8	35.4	35.5
South Asia					
Bangladesh	17.6	20.0	21.3	...	...
Bhutan	6.6	9.7	10.2	14.9	15.4
India	21.8	24.5	25.1	...	...
Maldives[f]	16.7	18.4	19.1	...	...
Nepal[b]	13.0	14.1	15.1	...	...
Sri Lanka[g]	25.6	25.8	27.9	26.9	...
Southeast Asia					
Brunei Darussalam[b]	19.5	17.9	20.8	23.7	...
Cambodia	16.0	24.9	27.9	...	...
Indonesia	18.7	22.0	22.4	21.6	22.3
Lao People's Democratic Republic[b]	8.3	11.0	12.9	...	...
Malaysia[b]	27.6	27.5	27.0	26.2	25.9
Myanmar	16.5	16.8	16.9	...	...
Philippines	15.7	16.2	19.1	18.3	18.4
Singapore[h]	21.9	17.4	15.6	14.8	14.4
Thailand	20.6	23.7	22.8	22.6	22.2
Timor-Leste[b]	9.3	13.5	16.3	...	...
Viet Nam[i]	21.7	22.7	27.4	30.8	33.2
The Pacific					
Cook Islands[j]	14.2 (2006)	...	11.3	...	...
Fiji[k]	16.7	14.6	14.1	...	...
Kiribati[l]	16.1	18.2	...	5.6	...
Marshall Islands	22.0	14.4	15.1	13.5	12.8
Micronesia, Federated States of	...	9.1	9.6 (2018)	...	...
Nauru	...	...	...	...	...
Niue	17.1 (2006)	...	...	...	...
Palau[m]	2.6 (2005)	11.7	...	...	...
Papua New Guinea	7.9	11.1	13.2	...	...
Samoa	23.4	24.6	24.9	...	...
Solomon Islands[n]	8.1	10.3	12.1	...	...
Tonga	31.5	29.7	30.9	...	...
Tuvalu	...	...	...	...	...
Vanuatu	6.9	10.9	14.1	...	...
Developed ADB Member Economies					
Australia	21.0	19.4	19.1	19.2	18.7
Japan	25.6	25.0	24.2	23.5	23.3
New Zealand	20.6	21.6	19.3	20.4	20.0

continued on next page

Table 2.1.5: Employment in Agriculture, Industry, and Services *(continued)*
(% of total employment)

ADB Regional Member	Services				
	2010	2015	2019	2020	2021
Developing ADB Member Economies					
Central and West Asia					
Afghanistan[a]	30.8	35.8	39.0	36.7	...
Armenia[b]	44.0	48.8	51.2	57.2	...
Azerbaijan[b]	48.1	49.6	49.2	49.0	48.8
Georgia[b,c]	41.3	44.9	47.6	61.9	62.1
Kazakhstan	53.0	61.4	64.2	66.8	66.9
Kyrgyz Republic	46.7	49.8	55.3	55.9	...
Pakistan	35.2	35.0	38.1	...	37.2
Tajikistan	31.8	35.9	39.5	30.5	...
Turkmenistan	35.5	37.8	39.5	...	...
Uzbekistan[b]	50.5	49.5	51.3	50.0	50.0
East Asia					
China, People's Republic of[d]	34.6	42.2	47.3	47.7	48.0
Hong Kong, China[e]	86.9	87.9	88.8	88.6	88.6
Korea, Republic of	68.4	69.4	70.3	70.0	70.1
Mongolia[b]	50.2	51.3	53.1	55.5	52.0
Taipei,China	57.3	57.6	58.2	59.8	59.8
South Asia					
Bangladesh	35.1	36.6	40.4	...	...
Bhutan	33.8	32.4	34.1	35.2	35.4
India	26.7	30.2	32.3	...	...
Maldives[f]	70.1	71.8	72.6	...	...
Nepal[b]	17.0	18.9	20.5	...	...
Sri Lanka[g]	42.6	45.6	47.2	46.0	...
Southeast Asia					
Brunei Darussalam[b]	79.8	81.3	77.3	74.9	...
Cambodia	26.7	32.6	37.6	...	...
Indonesia	42.2	44.9	49.1	48.7	49.3
Lao People's Democratic Republic[b]	20.2	23.4	25.6	...	...
Malaysia[b]	59.1	60.0	62.7	63.4	63.8
Myanmar	30.3	31.5	34.2	...	...
Philippines	51.4	54.6	58.0	56.9	57.4
Singapore[h]	78.0	82.5	84.4	85.1	85.4
Thailand	41.1	44.0	45.7	46.1	45.9
Timor-Leste[b]	39.9	44.0	44.4	...	...
Viet Nam[i]	29.6	33.2	35.3	36.2	38.0
The Pacific					
Cook Islands[j]	80.9 (2006)	...	86.3	...	...
Fiji[k]	58.8	65.6	68.3	...	...
Kiribati[l]	61.8	57.5	...	71.2	...
Marshall Islands	77.1	84.5	83.0	84.8	85.7
Micronesia, Federated States of	...	89.2	...	...	...
Nauru	...	...	...	...	...
Niue	66.9 (2006)	...	...	...	...
Palau[m]	89.6 (2005)	82.0	...	...	...
Papua New Guinea	26.7	29.1	30.6	...	...
Samoa	42.0	43.0	44.9	...	...
Solomon Islands[n]	46.4	49.7	50.6	...	...
Tonga	43.3	47.6	49.8	...	...
Tuvalu	...	...	...	...	...
Vanuatu	29.3	28.5	29.1	...	...
Developed ADB Member Economies					
Australia	75.8	78.0	78.4	78.0	78.9
Japan	70.4	71.4	72.4	73.3	73.6
New Zealand	72.6	72.3	74.9	73.6	73.9

... = data not available, (-/+) 0.0 = magnitude is less than half of unit employed, – = magnitude equals zero, ADB = Asian Development Bank.

Note: Data are based on varying labor force concepts and definitions adopted by different economies. Some values may not add up to 100% due to limitations on data availability.

a For 2017, data cover the period from April 2016 to April 2017. For 2020, data cover the period from October 2019 to September 2020. For 2011 onward, different methodologies were used in surveys for labor force estimation, therefore, data are not directly comparable overtime.
b Recommendations from the 19th International Conference of Labour Statisticians have been adopted by: Armenia, beginning 2018; Azerbaijan, beginning 2015; Brunei Darussalam, beginning 2017; Georgia, beginning 2010; the Lao People's Democratic Republic, for 2017; Malaysia, beginning 2019; Mongolia, beginning 2019; Nepal, for 2018; Timor-Leste, beginning 2010; and Uzbekistan, beginning 2017. Hence, data for these years may not be directly comparable with data for other years. The 19th conference provided the statistical concept of work for reference purposes; and the operational concepts, definitions, and guidelines for (i) three distinct subsets of work activities, referred to as forms of work, which include own-use production work, employment work, and volunteer work; (ii) related classifications of the population according to their labor force status and main work status; and (iii) measures of labor underutilization. The concept of employment has also been refined to refer to work for pay or profit.
c Prior to 2017, employment in services includes people who were engaged in construction industries.
d Refers to persons engaged in social labor and receiving remuneration or earning business income.
e Employment in services includes people who are engaged in electricity and gas supply; water supply; and sewerage, waste management, and remediation activities.
f Figures include local population only. For 2010, employment in services includes people who were engaged in industries other than agriculture, forestry, and fishing; mining and quarrying; or manufacturing.
g Some data may not add up because data for 2010 exclude the northern and eastern provinces.
h Refers to Singapore residents only.
i Refers to total number of persons engaged in any activity regardless of age.
j Covers all wage and salary earners from all islands.
k For 2010 and 2018, the reported number of employed people excludes those who are engaged in unpaid employment as of end of June. For 2016, figures are not comparable with other years because they include unpaid employment.
l Refers to cash work and unpaid village work. For 2010, employment in agriculture includes people who were engaged in mining and quarrying.
m For 2005, employment in services includes people who were engaged in electricity, gas, water, and construction industries.
n For 2009, the figure refers to paid employment.

Source: Asian Development Bank estimates using data from economies' official sources.

Table 2.1.6: Poverty and Inequality

ADB Regional Member	Proportion of Population Living on Less Than $2.15 a Day (2017 PPP)[a] (%)			Proportion of Population Living on Less Than $3.65 a Day (2017 PPP)[a] (%)			Income Ratio of Highest 20% to Lowest 20%[b]			Gini Coefficient[c]		
	2010	2015	2020	2010	2015	2020	2010	2015	2019	2010	2015	2020
Developing ADB Member Economies												
Central and West Asia												
Afghanistan	...	...	...	...	...	...	...	...	...	...	...	...
Armenia	1.0	1.1	0.5(2021)	14.0	9.4	8.7(2021)	4.3	5.0	4.0(2021)	0.300	0.324	0.279(2021)
Azerbaijan[d]	0.0(2005)	...	...	0.3(2005)	...	...	3.5(2005)	...	...	0.266(2005)	...	...
Georgia	14.4	4.9	5.5(2021)	35.7	20.0	19.1(2021)	8.0	6.5	5.9(2021)	0.395	0.365	0.342(2021)
Kazakhstan	0.2	0.0	0.0(2018)	2.9	0.7	0.5(2018)	4.0	3.7	3.9(2018)	0.280	0.268	0.278(2018)
Kyrgyz Republic	3.5	2.2	1.3	21.4	21.1	18.7	4.5	4.1	4.1(2020)	0.301	0.290	0.290
Pakistan[e]	9.4	5.1	4.9(2018)	52.4	40.0	39.8(2018)	3.9	4.4	4.1(2018)	0.288	0.313	0.296(2018)
Tajikistan	6.8(2009)	6.1	...	32.0(2009)	25.7	...	4.7(2009)	5.6	...	0.308(2009)	0.340	...
Turkmenistan	...	...	...	...	...	...	...	...	...	...	...	...
Uzbekistan[f]	81.5(2003)	...	...	94.6(2003)	...	...	5.9(2003)	...	...	0.353(2003)	...	...
East Asia												
China, People's Republic of	13.9	1.2	0.1(2019)	33.1	9.8	3.0(2019)	9.6	7.1	6.8	0.437	0.386	0.382(2019)
Hong Kong, China	...	...	...	...	...	...	...	...	...	...	...	...
Korea, Republic of	0.5	0.2(2014)	0.2(2016)	0.7	0.5(2014)	0.5(2016)	5.4	5.2(2014)	5.2(2016)	0.320	0.312(2014)	0.314(2016)
Mongolia	1.1	0.3(2014)	0.7(2018)	12.6	4.1(2014)	6.9(2018)	5.3	5.0(2014)	5.2(2018)	0.331	0.320(2014)	0.327(2018)
Taipei,China[g]	0.2	0.0(2013)	0.0(2016)	0.2	0.2(2013)	0.2(2016)	4.3	3.9	3.9(2021)	0.296	0.279	0.277(2021)
South Asia												
Bangladesh	18.2	...	13.5(2016)	59.3	...	51.6(2016)	4.7	...	4.8(2016)	0.321	...	0.324(2016)
Bhutan	5.9(2007)	1.7(2012)	0.9(2017)	26.6(2007)	11.9(2012)	9.4(2017)	6.7(2007)	6.9(2012)	6.6(2017)	0.381(2007)	0.388(2012)	0.374(2017)
India[e]	22.5(2011)	18.7	10.0(2019)	62.3(2011)	60.9	44.8(2019)	5.5(2011)	5.2	5.5	0.357(2011)	0.347	0.357(2019)
Maldives[e]	3.8(2009)	...	0.0(2019)	18.0(2009)	...	0.0(2019)	7.0(2009)	...	4.3	0.384(2009)	...	0.293(2019)
Nepal[e]	8.2	...	...	40.0	...	...	5.0	...	...	0.328	...	...
Sri Lanka	3.5(2009)	2.6(2012)	1.0(2019)	23.8(2009)	19.7(2012)	11.3(2019)	5.7(2009)	6.4(2012)	6.2	0.361(2009)	0.387(2012)	0.377(2019)
Southeast Asia												
Brunei Darussalam	...	...	...	...	...	...	...	...	...	...	...	...
Cambodia	...	...	...	...	...	...	...	...	...	...	...	...
Indonesia	18.3	8.3	2.5(2022)	50.7	35.8	20.2(2022)	6.1	6.9	6.3(2022)	0.372	0.404	0.379(2022)
Lao People's Democratic Republic[e]	19.5(2007)	10.9(2012)	7.1(2018)	58.5(2007)	40.5(2012)	32.5(2018)	5.5(2007)	5.8(2012)	6.6(2018)	0.354(2007)	0.360(2012)	0.388(2018)
Malaysia	0.1(2011)	0.0	0.0(2018)	1.8(2011)	0.4	0.2(2018)	9.5(2011)	8.2	8.3(2018)	0.439(2011)	0.411	0.412(2018)
Myanmar	...	6.2	2.0(2017)	...	30.0	19.6(2017)	...	6.3	4.5(2017)	...	0.381	0.307(2017)
Philippines[h]	11.3(2009)	6.5	3.0(2021)	35.3(2009)	27.1	17.8(2021)	9.9(2009)	9.1	7.4(2021)	0.463(2009)	0.446	0.407(2021)
Singapore	...	...	...	...	...	...	...	...	...	...	...	...
Thailand	0.3	0.0	0.0(2021)	3.9	0.8	0.6(2021)	7.0	5.8	5.6(2021)	0.394	0.360	0.351(2021)
Timor-Leste	40.9(2007)	24.4(2014)	...	80.4(2007)	69.2(2014)	...	3.9(2007)	4.1(2014)	...	0.278(2007)	0.287(2014)	...
Viet Nam	2.9	1.9(2014)	0.7	14.0	8.8(2014)	3.8	7.1	5.9(2014)	6.7(2020)	0.393	0.348(2014)	0.368
The Pacific												
Cook Islands	...	...	...	...	...	...	...	...	...	...	...	...
Fiji[e]	1.0(2008)	0.4(2013)	1.3(2019)	9.4(2008)	6.0(2013)	12.4(2019)	7.2(2008)	6.0(2013)	4.7	0.404(2008)	0.367(2013)	0.307(2019)
Kiribati	14.0(2006)	...	1.7(2019)	37.8(2006)	...	19.5(2019)	6.7(2006)	...	3.9	0.370(2006)	...	0.278(2019)
Marshall Islands	...	...	0.9(2019)	...	...	6.1(2019)	...	...	6.0	...	...	0.355(2019)
Micronesia, Federated States of	8.6(2005)	16.0(2013)	...	27.1(2005)	40.7(2013)	...	8.7(2005)	8.4(2013)	...	0.424(2005)	0.401(2013)	...
Nauru	...	1.7(2012)	...	...	20.9(2012)	...	...	5.1(2012)	...	...	0.324(2012)	...
Niue	...	...	...	...	...	...	...	...	...	...	...	...
Palau	...	...	...	...	...	...	...	...	...	...	...	...
Papua New Guinea[e]	39.7(2009)	...	...	67.7(2009)	...	...	9.3(2009)	...	...	0.419(2009)	...	...
Samoa[e]	1.1(2008)	1.2(2013)	...	10.9(2008)	10.5(2013)	...	7.7(2008)	6.8(2013)	...	0.420(2008)	0.387(2013)	...
Solomon Islands	50.6(2005)	26.6(2012)	...	74.6(2005)	61.0(2012)	...	10.4(2005)	6.4(2012)	...	0.461(2005)	0.371(2012)	...
Tonga	1.3(2009)	1.8	...	9.6(2009)	13.9	...	6.7(2009)	5.4	...	0.375(2009)	0.335	...
Tuvalu	3.6	...	...	19.6	...	...	7.0	...	...	0.391	...	...
Vanuatu	14.7	...	10.0(2019)	42.0	...	34.9(2019)	6.5	...	5.3	0.374	...	0.323(2019)
Developed ADB Member Economies												
Australia	...	...	...	...	...	...	5.8	5.7(2014)	5.7(2018)	0.347	0.344(2014)	0.343(2018)
Japan	...	...	...	...	...	...	4.9	5.3(2013)	...	0.321	0.329(2013)	...
New Zealand[i]	...	...	...	...	...	...	...	...	...	0.335	0.325	0.320

... = Data not available, (-/+) 0.0 = magnitude is less than half the unit employed, $ = United States dollars, ADB = Asian Development Bank, PPP = purchasing power parity.

a Poverty estimates are consumption-based, except for Malaysia; the Philippines; the Republic of Korea; and Taipei,China, whose estimates are income-based. The World Bank has updated the international poverty lines using 2017 purchasing power parity (PPP), however, 2011-based PPP poverty estimates are still released for SDG monitoring.
b Derived from the income or expenditure share of the highest 20% and lowest 20% groups by income.
c Inequality estimates are consumption-based, except for Malaysia; the Philippines; the Republic of Korea; and Taipei,China, whose estimates are income-based.
d The most recent year data are for 2005: 0.0% for proportion of population below $2.15 a day (2017 PPP); 0.3% for proportion of population below $3.65 a day (2017 PPP); 3.5 for income ratio of highest 20% to lowest 20%; and 0.266 for Gini coefficient.
e Household income and expenditure surveys for these economies were conducted in overlapping years. The table adopts the approach of the World Bank's World Development Indicators, i.e., using the initial year of the survey as the reference period for the poverty estimates.
f The most recent year data are for 2003: 81.5% for proportion of population below $2.15 a day (2017 PPP); 94.6% for proportion of population below $3.65 a day (2017 PPP); 5.9 for income ratio of highest 20% to lowest 20%; and 0.353 for Gini coefficient.
g The Gini coefficient reflected in the table refers to the coefficient using per capita disposable income published by the Government of Taipei,China's Directorate-General of Budget, Accounting and Statistics. The estimates using disposable income of households are 0.326 for 2000 and 0.341 for 2021. Alternative estimates for the Gini coefficient are available in the World Bank's Poverty and Inequality Platform.
h Income-based poverty estimates were used. However, consumption-based estimates are also available for $2.15 poverty line, 11.1% (2009), 8.3% (2015), and 6.8% (2021); and for $3.65 poverty line 38.3% (2009), 33.4% (2015), and 29.9% (2021).
i The Gini coefficient data are based on disposable income post taxes and transfers using the new definition.

Sources: World Bank. World Development Indicators. http://data.worldbank.org/data-catalog/world-development-indicators (accessed 31 July 2023); and World Bank. Poverty and Inequality Platform. https://pip.worldbank.org/ (accessed 17 April 2023). For New Zealand's Gini coefficient: Organisation for Economic Co-operation and Development. Income Distribution and Poverty. https://stats.oecd.org/index.aspx?queryid=66670# (accessed 31 July 2023). For Taipei,China's income ratio and Gini coefficient: Government of Taipei,China, Directorate-General of Budget, Accounting and Statistics.

Table 2.1.7: Human Development Index

ADB Regional Member	2010	2016	2017	2018	2019	2020	2021	Rank in 2021[a]
Developing ADB Member Economies								
Central and West Asia	**0.664**	**0.694**	**0.697**	**0.701**	**0.704**	**0.694**	**0.699**	...
Afghanistan	0.448	0.481	0.482	0.483	0.488	0.483	0.478	180
Armenia	0.746	0.765	0.768	0.771	0.778	0.757	0.759	85
Azerbaijan	0.727	0.750	0.753	0.757	0.761	0.730	0.745	91
Georgia	0.759	0.794	0.800	0.804	0.810	0.802	0.802	63
Kazakhstan	0.767	0.805	0.811	0.814	0.819	0.814	0.811	56
Kyrgyz Republic	0.664	0.693	0.696	0.698	0.698	0.689	0.692	118
Pakistan	0.505	0.541	0.543	0.545	0.546	0.543	0.544	161
Tajikistan	0.636	0.660	0.665	0.671	0.676	0.664	0.685	122
Turkmenistan	0.711	0.742	0.741	0.746	0.742	0.741	0.745	91
Uzbekistan	0.673	0.709	0.715	0.720	0.726	0.721	0.727	101
East Asia	**0.812**	**0.845**	**0.849**	**0.855**	**0.860**	**0.861**	**0.862**	...
China, People's Republic of	0.691	0.740	0.747	0.755	0.762	0.764	0.768	79
Hong Kong, China	0.907	0.938	0.944	0.949	0.952	0.949	0.952	4
Korea, Republic of	0.890	0.912	0.916	0.919	0.923	0.922	0.925	19
Mongolia	0.701	0.733	0.732	0.743	0.746	0.745	0.739	96
Taipei,China	0.873	0.903	0.907	0.911	0.916	0.923	0.926	...
South Asia	**0.613**	**0.664**	**0.671**	**0.678**	**0.684**	**0.681**	**0.682**	...
Bangladesh	0.553	0.612	0.622	0.635	0.644	0.655	0.661	129
Bhutan	0.581	0.638	0.647	0.658	0.671	0.668	0.666	127
India	0.575	0.639	0.644	0.645	0.645	0.642	0.633	132
Maldives	0.688	0.741	0.746	0.750	0.755	0.734	0.747	90
Nepal	0.543	0.586	0.594	0.601	0.611	0.604	0.602	143
Sri Lanka	0.737	0.767	0.771	0.776	0.778	0.780	0.782	73
Southeast Asia	**0.679**	**0.710**	**0.713**	**0.717**	**0.722**	**0.720**	**0.715**	...
Brunei Darussalam	0.828	0.835	0.834	0.830	0.830	0.830	0.829	51
Cambodia	0.540	0.581	0.586	0.591	0.598	0.596	0.593	146
Indonesia	0.664	0.699	0.704	0.710	0.716	0.709	0.705	114
Lao People's Democratic Republic	0.551	0.604	0.607	0.607	0.610	0.608	0.607	140
Malaysia	0.769	0.803	0.805	0.807	0.810	0.806	0.803	62
Myanmar	0.510	0.572	0.580	0.590	0.598	0.600	0.585	149
Philippines	0.674	0.700	0.704	0.710	0.718	0.710	0.699	116
Singapore	0.910	0.934	0.935	0.940	0.943	0.939	0.939	12
Thailand	0.737	0.785	0.790	0.795	0.804	0.802	0.800	66
Timor-Leste	0.619	0.604	0.606	0.605	0.614	0.614	0.607	140
Viet Nam	0.663	0.688	0.692	0.697	0.703	0.710	0.703	115
The Pacific	**0.638**	**0.653**	**0.656**	**0.658**	**0.660**	**0.657**	**0.655**	...
Cook Islands	...	...	...	...	...	...	...	...
Fiji	0.714	0.735	0.741	0.745	0.746	0.737	0.730	99
Kiribati	0.589	0.617	0.621	0.622	0.630	0.623	0.624	136
Marshall Islands	0.633 (2011)	0.637	0.638	0.639	0.640	0.639	0.639	131
Micronesia, Federated States of	0.625	0.629	0.632	0.633	0.633	0.629	0.628	134
Nauru	...	...	...	...	...	...	...	...
Niue	...	...	...	...	...	...	...	...
Palau	0.773	0.778	0.775	0.778	0.776	0.773	0.767	80
Papua New Guinea	0.499	0.547	0.552	0.554	0.560	0.560	0.558	156
Samoa	0.713	0.717	0.716	0.716	0.715	0.712	0.707	111
Solomon Islands	0.550	0.560	0.564	0.566	0.567	0.565	0.564	155
Tonga	0.713	0.735	0.740	0.742	0.744	0.745	0.745	91
Tuvalu	0.616	0.636	0.634	0.642	0.635	0.639	0.641	130
Vanuatu	0.591	0.596	0.599	0.603	0.611	0.608	0.607	140
Developed ADB Member Economies	**0.914**	**0.930**	**0.931**	**0.933**	**0.934**	**0.935**	**0.938**	...
Australia	0.923	0.935	0.937	0.941	0.941	0.947	0.951	5
Japan	0.898	0.921	0.922	0.923	0.924	0.923	0.925	19
New Zealand	0.922	0.934	0.935	0.936	0.937	0.936	0.937	13
DEVELOPING ADB MEMBER ECONOMIES	**0.672**	**0.701**	**0.705**	**0.709**	**0.713**	**0.709**	**0.709**	...
ALL ADB REGIONAL MEMBERS	**0.688**	**0.716**	**0.719**	**0.723**	**0.727**	**0.724**	**0.724**	...
WORLD[b]	**0.697**	**0.729**	**0.733**	**0.736**	**0.739**	**0.735**	**0.732**	...

... = data not available, ADB = Asian Development Bank.

Notes:
1 Regional indexes are calculated as an arithmetic average of the indexes of reporting economies with data corresponding to the year heading.
2 The Human Development Index (HDI) is calculated by the Human Development Report Office of the United Nations Development Programme (UNDP) using the most recently revised historical data from national and international agencies, which continually improve their data series. Hence, the HDI values and ranks presented in this table are not comparable to those published in previous editions. For this 2021-2022 edition, HDI data presented depict the state of human development during uncertain times brought about by COVID-19 pandemic, Russian Invasion of Ukraine, and climate and ecological disasters, based on available data for 2021 and previous years. More information is available at the UNDP website, https://hdr.undp.org/system/files/documents/global-report-document/hdr2021-22overviewenpdf.pdf.

a Rank in 2021 among the 191 national economies presented in the Human Development Report 2021-2022 of the UNDP.
b Calculated by the UNDP Human Development Report Office (HDRO) by applying the human development index formula to the weighted group averages of component indicators.

Sources: United Nations Development Programme. Human Development Data (1990–2021). https://hdr.undp.org/sites/default/files/2021-22_HDR/HDR21-22_Composite_indices_complete_time_series.csv (accessed 09 May 2023). For Taipei,China: Government of Taipei,China, Directorate-General of Budget, Accounting and Statistics.

Table 2.1.8: Life Expectancy at Birth
(years)

ADB Regional Member	Both Sexes		Female		Male	
	2010	2022	2010	2022	2010	2022
Developing ADB Member Economies						
Central and West Asia	...	...	...	...	...	...
Afghanistan	60.9	62.9	62.4	66.2	59.3	59.8
Armenia	73.2	73.4	77.4	78.4	68.6	67.9
Azerbaijan	69.5	73.5	72.8	76.2	66.3	70.6
Georgia	72.1	71.6	76.6	76.5	67.6	66.8
Kazakhstan	68.1	69.5	72.5	73.0	63.6	65.8
Kyrgyz Republic	68.3	70.5	72.2	74.9	64.3	66.2
Pakistan	64.4	66.4	66.9	68.9	62.3	64.1
Tajikistan	67.7	71.3	70.4	73.5	65.4	69.2
Turkmenistan	68.3	69.4	71.6	72.9	64.9	65.9
Uzbekistan	69.2	71.7	71.8	74.3	66.7	69.0
East Asia	...	...	...	...	...	...
China, People's Republic of	75.6	78.6	78.3	81.3	73.1	76.0
Hong Kong, China	83.0	84.3	85.9	86.9	80.2	81.8
Korea, Republic of	80.8	84.0	84.2	87.1	77.1	80.7
Mongolia	67.2	72.7	71.8	77.4	63.0	68.1
Taipei,China	79.2	80.9 (2021)	82.5	84.3 (2021)	76.1	77.7 (2021)
South Asia	...	...	...	...	...	...
Bangladesh	68.6	73.7	70.3	76.0	67.2	71.5
Bhutan	68.4	72.2	70.1	74.2	67.0	70.6
India	66.9	67.7	68.6	69.4	65.3	66.3
Maldives	77.7	80.8	78.8	81.8	76.8	80.1
Nepal	66.8	70.5	68.6	72.4	65.1	68.6
Sri Lanka	73.2	76.6	77.6	80.2	69.2	72.9
Southeast Asia[a]	**70.3**	**71.4**	**72.9**	**74.3**	**67.7**	**68.7**
Brunei Darussalam	74.8	74.6	77.1	76.8	72.8	72.5
Cambodia	67.7	69.9	69.8	72.6	65.4	67.1
Indonesia	68.7	68.3	70.4	70.4	66.9	66.2
Lao People's Democratic Republic	64.0	69.0	66.2	71.2	61.9	66.9
Malaysia	74.4	76.3	77.1	78.8	72.1	74.0
Myanmar	63.3	67.3	66.2	70.5	60.6	64.2
Philippines	70.8	72.2	72.4	74.2	69.1	70.2
Singapore	81.7	84.1	84.0	86.3	79.3	82.0
Thailand	76.1	79.7	80.4	83.9	72.1	75.5
Timor-Leste	65.3	69.1	67.0	70.8	63.8	67.4
Viet Nam	73.5	74.6	78.3	79.3	68.8	69.9
The Pacific	...	...	...	...	...	...
Cook Islands	73.5	75.1	77.8	79.0	69.9	71.4
Fiji	67.3	68.3	69.3	70.2	65.5	66.5
Kiribati	65.0	67.7	66.6	69.4	63.2	65.7
Marshall Islands	63.2	65.1	65.1	67.1	61.7	63.5
Micronesia, Federated States of	71.2	70.9	74.4	74.8	68.2	67.3
Nauru	59.6	64.0	63.5	67.8	56.5	60.5
Niue	68.4	71.2	70.5	72.9	66.6	69.5
Palau	65.6	65.4	68.7	69.3	63.0	62.2
Papua New Guinea	63.0	66.0	65.3	69.2	61.3	63.4
Samoa	72.2	72.6	75.0	75.3	69.7	70.1
Solomon Islands	68.7	70.7	70.6	72.4	67.1	69.3
Tonga	70.3	71.3	73.4	74.1	67.6	68.6
Tuvalu	64.0	64.9	67.7	69.4	60.6	61.1
Vanuatu	69.6	70.5	72.1	73.1	67.6	68.3
Developed ADB Member Economies	...	...	...	...	...	...
Australia	82.1	83.6	84.2	85.5	79.8	81.7
Japan	82.9	84.8	86.2	87.8	79.5	81.8
New Zealand	81.1	83.0	83.0	84.7	79.2	81.3
DEVELOPING ADB MEMBER ECONOMIES	...	...	...	...	...	...
ALL ADB REGIONAL MEMBERS	...	...	...	...	...	...
WORLD[a]	**70.1**	**71.7**	**72.7**	**74.4**	**67.6**	**69.1**

... = data not available, ADB = Asian Development Bank.

a Aggregate age-specific mortality rates by single year of age were computed by dividing aggregated deaths by age and sex by aggregated sex- and age-specific person-years of exposure. Complete life tables and related indicators were then derived from those mortality rates.

Sources: United Nations. World Population Prospects 2022. https://population.un.org/wpp/Download/Standard/Population/ (accessed 01 March 2023). For Taipei,China: Government of Taipei,China, Directorate-General of Budget, Accounting and Statistics.

Table 2.1.9: Births, Deaths, and Fertility Rates

ADB Regional Member	Crude Birth Rate (per 1,000 people)		Crude Death Rate (per 1,000 people)		Total Fertility Rate (births per woman)	
	2010	2022	2010	2022	2010	2022
Developing ADB Member Economies						
Central and West Asia	...	...	...	...	...	...
Afghanistan	40.6	35.1	8.3	6.9	6.1	4.5
Armenia	13.9	11.7	9.4	11.9	1.5	1.6
Azerbaijan	19.9	11.9	7.2	6.4	2.1	1.7
Georgia	15.1	13.1	12.3	15.2	1.9	2.1
Kazakhstan	22.2	20.8	9.3	10.2	2.6	3.0
Kyrgyz Republic	27.7	23.3	6.9	6.0	3.1	2.9
Pakistan	32.1	27.2	7.6	7.0	4.3	3.4
Tajikistan	31.0	26.0	5.9	4.7	3.5	3.1
Turkmenistan	25.3	20.8	6.4	6.6	2.8	2.6
Uzbekistan	22.6	22.4	6.4	6.0	2.4	2.8
East Asia	...	...	...	...	...	...
China, People's Republic of	13.3	7.5	6.5	7.4	1.7	1.2
Hong Kong, China	9.7	5.6	6.2	8.4	1.1	0.8
Korea, Republic of	9.3	5.5	5.2	6.6	1.2	0.9
Mongolia	23.3	20.4	6.7	5.5	2.5	2.8
Taipei,China	7.2	5.9	6.3	8.9	0.9	0.9
South Asia	...	...	...	...	...	...
Bangladesh	21.4	17.5	6.1	5.3	2.3	2.0
Bhutan	19.5	12.3	6.8	6.4	2.3	1.4
India	21.4	16.3	7.4	9.1	2.6	2.0
Maldives	21.2	13.6	3.1	2.8	2.3	1.7
Nepal	22.6	20.2	7.0	6.7	2.5	2.0
Sri Lanka	17.6	13.8	7.4	7.3	2.2	2.0
Southeast Asia[a]	**19.5**	**16.2**	**6.8**	**7.9**	**2.4**	**2.1**
Brunei Darussalam	17.1	13.5	3.8	5.4	1.9	1.8
Cambodia	23.7	19.0	6.1	6.8	2.8	2.3
Indonesia	20.2	16.2	7.4	9.6	2.5	2.2
Lao People's Democratic Republic	27.0	21.5	8.0	6.2	3.1	2.4
Malaysia	17.0	15.0	5.0	5.4	2.1	1.8
Myanmar	19.4	16.8	9.2	8.7	2.3	2.1
Philippines	25.5	21.6	5.6	5.6	3.3	2.7
Singapore	9.1	7.1	4.0	5.0	1.2	1.0
Thailand	11.9	8.8	6.3	7.5	1.6	1.3
Timor-Leste	31.4	24.6	8.0	6.5	4.8	3.0
Viet Nam	16.9	14.7	6.2	6.8	1.9	1.9
The Pacific	...	...	...	...	...	...
Cook Islands	19.2	16.1	6.8	8.4	2.6	2.2
Fiji	22.7	19.1	7.1	8.2	2.7	2.5
Kiribati	30.8	26.7	7.1	6.2	3.9	3.3
Marshall Islands	30.1	18.5	6.9	7.9	3.6	2.7
Micronesia, Federated States of	23.7	20.7	4.6	6.3	3.2	2.7
Nauru	34.4	26.8	8.2	6.6	3.9	3.5
Niue	18.0	14.0	12.6	13.8	2.9	2.4
Palau	14.0	14.9	10.6	13.4	2.0	2.4
Papua New Guinea	30.4	25.1	7.1	6.5	3.9	3.2
Samoa	30.2	27.0	5.3	5.5	4.6	3.9
Solomon Islands	33.6	29.3	5.6	4.9	4.4	3.9
Tonga	27.3	22.9	6.6	6.9	3.9	3.2
Tuvalu	22.3	23.3	10.0	10.1	3.5	3.1
Vanuatu	33.1	29.0	6.1	5.3	4.2	3.7
Developed ADB Member Economies	...	...	...	...	...	...
Australia	13.7	11.5	6.5	6.8	2.0	1.6
Japan	8.6	6.6	10.1	12.7	1.4	1.3
New Zealand	14.6	12.4	6.6	6.5	2.2	1.8
DEVELOPING ADB MEMBER ECONOMIES	...	...	...	...	...	...
ALL ADB REGIONAL MEMBERS	...	...	...	...	...	...
WORLD[a]	**20.3**	**16.8**	**7.8**	**8.4**	**2.6**	**2.3**

... = data not available, ADB = Asian Development Bank.

a Aggregate age-specific fertility rates were computed by dividing aggregated (summed) births by mothers' single-year of age by aggregated exposures of women by age. Total fertility and other fertility indicators for the economy grouping were then derived from those age-specific fertility rates. Similarly, aggregate age-specific mortality rates by single year of age were computed by dividing aggregated deaths by age and sex by aggregated sex- and age-specific person-years of exposure. Complete life tables and related indicators were then derived from those mortality rates.

Sources: United Nations. World Population Prospects 2022. https://population.un.org/wpp/Download/Standard/Population/ (accessed 01 March 2023). For Taipei,China: Government of Taipei,China, Ministry of the Interior.

Table 2.1.10: Adult (15 Years and Older) Literacy Rate
(%)

ADB Regional Member	Both Sexes				Female				Male			
	2010		2020		2010		2020		2010		2020	
Developing ADB Member Economies												
Central and West Asia												
Afghanistan	31.4	(2011)	37.3	(2021)	17.0	(2011)	22.6	(2021)	45.4	(2011)	52.1	(2021)
Armenia	99.7	(2011)	99.8		99.7	(2011)	99.7		99.8	(2011)	99.8	
Azerbaijan	99.8[a]		99.8	(2019)	99.7[a]		99.7	(2019)	99.9[a]		99.9	(2019)
Georgia	99.7	(2002)	99.6	(2019)	99.6	(2002)	99.5	(2019)	99.8	(2002)	99.7	(2019)
Kazakhstan	99.8[b]		99.8[b]	(2018)	99.7[b]		99.7[b]	(2018)	99.8[b]		99.8[b]	(2018)
Kyrgyz Republic	99.2	(2009)	99.6[b]	(2018)	99.0	(2009)	99.5[b]	(2018)	99.5	(2009)	99.7[b]	(2018)
Pakistan	55.4		58.0	(2019)	41.0		46.5	(2019)	68.9		69.3	(2019)
Tajikistan	99.5	(2000)	99.8[b]	(2014)	99.2	(2000)	99.7[b]	(2014)	99.7	(2000)	99.8[b]	(2014)
Turkmenistan	...		99.7[b]	(2014)	...		99.6[b]	(2014)	...		99.8[b]	(2014)
Uzbekistan	100.0	(2013)	100.0	(2019)	100.0	(2013)	100.0	(2019)	100.0	(2013)	100.0	(2019)
East Asia												
China, People's Republic of	95.1		96.8[b]	(2018)	92.7		95.2[b]	(2018)	97.5		98.5[b]	(2018)
Hong Kong, China	...		...		...		...		...		...	
Korea, Republic of	98.0	(2008)	...		97.6	(2008)	...		98.3	(2008)	...	
Mongolia	98.3		99.2		98.3		99.2		98.2		99.1	
Taipei,China	...		...		...		...		...		...	
South Asia												
Bangladesh	58.8	(2011)	74.9		55.1	(2011)	72.0		62.5	(2011)	77.8	
Bhutan	55.3	(2012)	66.6	(2017)	45.2	(2012)	57.1	(2017)	66.0	(2012)	75.0	(2017)
India	69.3	(2011)	74.4[b]	(2018)	59.3	(2011)	65.8[b]	(2018)	78.9	(2011)	82.4[b]	(2018)
Maldives	98.4	(2006)	97.7	(2016)	98.4	(2006)	98.1	(2016)	98.4	(2006)	97.3	(2016)
Nepal	59.6	(2011)	67.9[b]	(2018)	48.8	(2011)	59.7[b]	(2018)	71.7	(2011)	78.6[b]	(2018)
Sri Lanka	91.2		92.4		90.0		91.6		92.6		93.3	
Southeast Asia												
Brunei Darussalam	96.1	(2011)	97.2[b]	(2018)	94.7	(2011)	96.3[b]	(2018)	97.4	(2011)	98.1[b]	(2018)
Cambodia	76.1	(2009)	80.5	(2015)	69.1	(2009)	75.0	(2015)	83.9	(2009)	86.5	(2015)
Indonesia	92.8	(2011)	96.0		90.1	(2011)	94.6		95.6	(2011)	97.4	
Lao People's Democratic Republic	58.3[b]	(2011)	84.7	(2015)	49.7[b]	(2011)	79.4	(2015)	67.4[b]	(2011)	90.0	(2015)
Malaysia	93.1		95.0	(2019)	90.7		93.6	(2019)	95.4		96.2	(2019)
Myanmar	89.9	(2000)	89.1	(2019)	86.4	(2000)	86.3	(2019)	93.9	(2000)	92.4	(2019)
Philippines	95.4	(2008)	96.3	(2019)	95.8	(2008)	96.9	(2019)	95.0	(2008)	95.7	(2019)
Singapore	95.9		97.1		93.8		95.8		98.0		98.5	
Thailand	96.4		93.8	(2018)	96.4		92.4	(2018)	96.4		95.2	(2018)
Timor-Leste	58.3		68.1[b]	(2018)	53.0		64.2[b]	(2018)	63.6		71.9[b]	(2018)
Viet Nam	93.5	(2009)	95.8	(2019)	91.4	(2009)	94.6	(2019)	95.8	(2009)	97.0	(2019)
The Pacific												
Cook Islands	...		...		...		...		...		...	
Fiji	...		...		...		...		...		...	
Kiribati	...		...		...		...		...		...	
Marshall Islands	98.3	(2011)	...		98.2	(2011)	...		98.3	(2011)	...	
Micronesia, Federated States of	...		...		...		...		...		...	
Nauru	...		...		...		...		...		...	
Niue	...		...		...		...		...		...	
Palau	99.5[b]	(2013)	96.6	(2015)	99.5[b]	(2013)	96.3	(2015)	99.5[b]	(2013)	96.8	(2015)
Papua New Guinea	61.6[b]		...		57.9[b]		...		65.3[b]		...	
Samoa	99.0	(2011)	99.1[b]	(2018)	99.1	(2011)	99.2[b]	(2018)	98.9	(2011)	99.0[b]	(2018)
Solomon Islands	76.6[b]	(2009)	...		69.0[b]	(2009)	...		83.7[b]	(2009)	...	
Tonga	99.4	(2011)	99.4[b]	(2018)	99.4	(2011)	99.5[b]	(2018)	99.3	(2011)	99.4[b]	(2018)
Tuvalu	...		...		...		...		...		...	
Vanuatu	78.4[b]	(2004)	87.5[b]	(2018)	76.2[b]	(2004)	86.7[b]	(2018)	80.5[b]	(2004)	88.3[b]	(2018)
Developed ADB Member Economies												
Australia	...		...		...		...		...		...	
Japan	...		...		...		...		...		...	
New Zealand	...		...		...		...		...		...	
WORLD	**84.0**		**86.7**		**79.8**		**83.3**		**88.3**		**90.1**	

... = data not available, ADB = Asian Development Bank.

a Based on national estimation.
b Refers to UNESCO Institute for Statistics estimates.

Source: United Nations Educational, Scientific and Cultural Organization (UNESCO) Institute for Statistics. UIS.Stat Database. http://data.uis.unesco.org/ (accessed 23 May 2023).

Table 2.1.11: Years of Schooling

ADB Regional Member	Expected[a]					
	Both Sexes		Female		Male	
	2010	2021	2010	2021	2010	2021
Developing ADB Member Economies						
Central and West Asia						
Afghanistan	9.3 (2011)	10.2[c] (2018)	7.2 (2011)	7.7[c] (2018)	11.2 (2011)	12.6[c] (2018)
Armenia	13.1[c]	13.5	13.4[c]	14.1	12.8[c]	12.9
Azerbaijan	..	13.5[d]	..	13.6[d]	..	13.4[d]
Georgia	13.5[c] (2009)	15.9	13.5[c] (2008)	16.4	12.8[c] (2008)	15.5
Kazakhstan	14.6	15.8 (2020)	14.8	16.0 (2020)	14.3	15.5 (2020)
Kyrgyz Republic	12.4[d]	13.6	12.7[d]	13.8	12.2[d]	13.3
Pakistan	6.8[c] (2011)	8.7[c] (2019)	6.1[c] (2011)	8.1[c] (2019)	7.4[c] (2011)	9.2[c] (2019)
Tajikistan	11.2	11.4 (2013)	10.4	10.7 (2013)	12.0	12.1 (2013)
Turkmenistan	..	13.7	..	13.5	..	13.9
Uzbekistan	11.5	12.1	11.3	12.1	11.6	12.1
East Asia						
China, People's Republic of	12.4[c]	..	12.4[c]	..	12.4[c]	..
Hong Kong, China	15.9[c] (2012)	17.1[c]	15.7[c] (2012)	17.4[c]	15.6[c] (2012)	16.9[c]
Korea, Republic of	16.8	16.6 (2020)	16.0	16.2 (2020)	17.6	16.9 (2020)
Mongolia	14.6[c]	15.0 (2019)	15.3[c]	15.6 (2019)	13.9[c]	14.4 (2019)
Taipei,China	16.7 (2012)	16.9 (2022)	16.8 (2012)	17.1 (2022)	16.7 (2012)	16.8 (2022)
South Asia						
Bangladesh	9.2[d] (2009)	12.4[c] (2020)	9.3[d] (2009)	13.0[c] (2020)	9.1[d] (2009)	11.9[c] (2020)
Bhutan	11.7	13.1[c] (2018)	11.8	13.5[c] (2018)	11.6	12.8[c] (2018)
India	10.7[c]	12.8 (2022)	10.5[c]	12.9 (2022)	10.9[c]	12.7 (2022)
Maldives	12.2 (2003)	12.6[c] (2019)	12.3 (2003)	14.2[c] (2019)	12.0 (2003)	11.9[c] (2019)
Nepal	11.9[c]	12.9[c] (2020)	12.0[c]	12.9[c] (2020)	11.9[c]	12.8[c] (2020)
SriLanka	13.6[c]	14.1 (2018)	13.8[c]	14.5 (2018)	13.4[c]	13.8 (2018)
Southeast Asia						
Brunei Darussalam	14.1[c]	14.0 (2020)	14.3[c]	14.4 (2020)	13.8[c]	13.5 (2020)
Cambodia	10.6[c] (2008)	..	9.9[c] (2008)	..	11.2[c] (2008)	..
Indonesia	12.3	13.6 (2018)	12.4	13.7 (2018)	12.3	13.5 (2018)
Lao People's Democratic Republic	10.0	10.1 (2020)	9.2	9.9 (2020)	10.7	10.3 (2020)
Malaysia	12.9	13.3	13.2	13.8	12.5	12.9
Myanmar	8.2 (2007)	10.7 (2018)	..	10.9 (2018)	..	10.5 (2018)
Philippines	11.4 (2009)	13.1[c] (2020)	11.6 (2009)	13.5[c] (2020)	11.1 (2009)	12.8[c] (2020)
Singapore	..	16.6[d] (2020)	..	16.7[d] (2020)	..	16.5[d] (2020)
Thailand	13.3[c]	15.4[c] (2016)	13.7[c]	15.8[c] (2016)	12.8[c]	15.1[c] (2016)
Timor-Leste	12.4	..	12.0	..	12.9	..
Viet Nam	..	..	..	..	..	..
The Pacific						
Cook Islands	11.0	14.8 (2012)	11.1	14.2 (2012)	10.9	15.5 (2012)
Fiji	13.9 (2004)	..	14.1 (2004)	..	13.7 (2004)	..
Kiribati	11.8 (2008)	..	12.2 (2008)	..	11.4 (2008)	..
Marshall Islands	12.2 (2002)	10.2 (2019)	12.2 (2002)	10.4 (2019)	12.2 (2002)	10.1 (2019)
Micronesia, Federated States of	..	..	..	..	..	..
Nauru	9.6 (2008)	..	9.7 (2008)	..	9.5 (2008)	..
Niue	12.2 (2005)	..	12.4 (2005)	..	12.0 (2005)	..
Palau	14.1[c] (2000)	16.6 (2013)	14.8[c] (2000)	17.2 (2013)	13.4[c] (2000)	16.1 (2013)
Papua New Guinea	..	..	..	..	..	..
Samoa	12.0 (2000)	..	12.4[c] (2000)	..	11.7[c] (2000)	..
Solomon Islands	9.2 (2007)	..	8.8 (2007)	..	9.6 (2007)	..
Tonga	14.5[c] (2003)	16.0 (2020)	13.9[c] (2002)	17.3 (2020)	13.4[c] (2002)	14.8 (2020)
Tuvalu	10.9 (2001)	..	11.0 (2001)	..	10.8 (2001)	..
Vanuatu	10.6[c] (2004)	..	10.2[c] (2004)	..	10.9[c] (2004)	..
Developed ADB Member Economies						
Australia	..	21.1 (2020)	..	21.8 (2020)	..	20.3 (2020)
Japan	..	15.1 (2020)	..	15.1 (2020)	..	15.1 (2020)
NewZealand	..	20.3 (2020)	..	20.7 (2020)	..	19.8 (2020)
WORLD	**11.5**	**12.5**[c] (2020)	**11.3**	**12.5**[c] (2020)	**11.6**	**12.5**[c] (2020)

continued on next page

Table 2.1.11: Years of Schooling *(continued)*

ADB Regional Member	Mean[b]					
	Both Sexes		Female		Male	
	2010	2021	2010	2021	2010	2021
Developing ADB Member Economies						
Central and West Asia						
Afghanistan	...	3.0	...	2.3	...	3.4
Armenia	11.2 (2011)	11.3 (2020)	11.2 (2011)	11.3 (2020)	11.2 (2011)	11.3 (2020)
Azerbaijan	10.5	10.5 (2019)	10.2	10.2 (2019)	10.8	10.9 (2019)
Georgia	12.5 (2012)	12.8 (2019)	12.4 (2012)	12.9 (2019)	12.6 (2012)	12.8 (2019)
Kazakhstan	11.0 (2009)	12.2 (2018)	11.0 (2009)	12.2 (2018)	11.0 (2009)	12.2 (2018)
Kyrgyz Republic	10.9 (2009)	...	10.9 (2009)	...	10.8 (2009)	...
Pakistan	4.6	4.5 (2019)	2.9	3.9 (2019)	6.1	5.0 (2019)
Tajikistan	10.8 (2000)	11.4 (2017)	10.3 (2000)	10.8 (2017)	11.3 (2000)	12.0 (2017)
Turkmenistan	...	...	...	...	...	...
Uzbekistan	...	11.9	...	11.7	...	12.1
East Asia						
China, People's Republic of	6.7	...	6.2	...	7.2	...
Hong Kong, China	11.4	12.2 (2019)	11.0	11.8 (2019)	11.9	12.7 (2019)
Korea, Republic of	11.6	12.1 (2015)	10.9	11.4 (2015)	12.5	12.9 (2015)
Mongolia	10.0	9.4 (2020)	10.3	9.9 (2020)	9.7	8.8 (2020)
Taipei,China	...	...	...	...	...	...
South Asia						
Bangladesh	5.2 (2011)	7.4 (2020)	4.4 (2011)	6.8 (2020)	6.0 (2011)	8.0 (2020)
Bhutan	2.2 (2012)	4.1 (2017)	1.5 (2012)	3.2 (2017)	3.0 (2012)	4.8 (2017)
India	5.3 (2011)	6.5 (2020)	4.0 (2011)	5.4 (2020)	6.5 (2011)	7.6 (2020)
Maldives	3.8 (2006)	...	3.5 (2006)	...	4.0 (2006)	...
Nepal	3.5 (2011)	...	2.3 (2011)	...	4.9 (2011)	...
Sri Lanka	10.2 (2009)	11.2	10.1 (2009)	11.1	10.4 (2009)	11.4
Southeast Asia						
Brunei Darussalam	11.6 (2011)	...	11.3 (2011)	...	11.8 (2011)	...
Cambodia	3.9 (2009)	3.7 (2015)	3.1 (2009)	2.8 (2015)	5.0 (2009)	4.8 (2015)
Indonesia	7.5 (2011)	8.6 (2020)	7.0 (2011)	8.2 (2020)	8.0 (2011)	8.9 (2020)
Lao People's Democratic Republic	...	...	...	...	...	...
Malaysia	9.7	10.6 (2019)	9.4	10.6 (2019)	10.0	10.7 (2019)
Myanmar	...	6.4 (2019)	...	6.1 (2019)	...	6.7 (2019)
Philippines	8.9	9.0 (2019)	9.0	9.2 (2019)	8.8	8.7 (2019)
Singapore	11.2	11.9 (2020)	10.8	11.6 (2020)	11.6	12.3 (2020)
Thailand	7.6	8.7 (2019)	7.4	8.6 (2019)	7.8	8.8 (2019)
Timor-Leste	5.3	...	4.7	...	6.0	...
Viet Nam	7.5 (2009)	8.4 (2019)	7.0 (2009)	8.0 (2019)	8.1 (2009)	8.7 (2019)
The Pacific						
Cook Islands	9.9 (2006)	...	9.8 (2006)	...	10.0 (2006)	...
Fiji	9.2 (2007)	10.6 (2017)	9.2 (2007)	10.7 (2017)	9.3 (2007)	10.6 (2017)
Kiribati	...	...	...	...	...	...
Marshall Islands	10.9 (2011)	...	10.7 (2011)	...	11.1 (2011)	...
Micronesia, Federated States of	...	...	...	...	...	...
Nauru	...	...	...	...	...	...
Niue	...	...	...	...	...	...
Palau	...	12.8 (2013)	...	12.9 (2013)	...	12.8 (2013)
Papua New Guinea	...	...	...	...	...	...
Samoa	11.7 (2011)	...	11.8 (2011)	...	11.6 (2011)	...
Solomon Islands	...	...	...	...	...	...
Tonga	10.9 (2011)	...	10.9 (2011)	...	10.9 (2011)	...
Tuvalu	...	...	...	...	...	...
Vanuatu	...	...	...	...	...	...
Developed ADB Member Economies						
Australia	12.0	12.7 (2020)	12.0	12.8 (2020)	12.0	12.6 (2020)
Japan	12.5	...	12.2	...	12.9	...
New Zealand	13.4 (2011)	12.9 (2020)	13.3 (2011)	12.9 (2020)	13.5 (2011)	13.0 (2020)
WORLD	...	...	...	...	...	...

... = data not available, ADB = Asian Development Bank.

a Refers to the expected number of years of schooling from primary to tertiary level of education.
b Refers to the average number of completed years of education among the population aged 25 years and older (excluding years spent repeating individual grades), by highest level of education attained.
c UNESCO Institute of Statistics estimate.
d National estimate.

Sources: United Nations Educational, Scientific and Cultural Organization (UNESCO) Institute for Statistics. UIS.Stat Database. http://data.uis.unesco.org/ (accessed 24 May 2023). For expected years of schooling for Taipei,China: Government of Taipei,China, Ministry of Education. Gender Statistics.

Table 2.1.12: Education Resources

ADB Regional Member	Pupil/Trained Teacher Ratio[a]				Pupil/Qualified Teacher Ratio[b]			
	Primary		Secondary		Primary		Secondary	
	2010	2021	2010	2021	2010	2021	2010	2021
Developing ADB Member Economies								
Central and West Asia								
Afghanistan	...	...	...	...	...	60.4 (2019)	...	42.1 (2018)
Armenia	27.4 (2005)	26.0	...	14.9	...	19.2	...	11.1
Azerbaijan	11.0	16.1	...	8.6	...	16.0	...	8.5
Georgia	9.4 (2009)	...	8.0 (2009)	...	...	...	...	...
Kazakhstan	...	16.8 (2020)	...	8.3 (2020)	...	16.8 (2020)	...	8.3 (2020)
Kyrgyz Republic	35.5	26.1 (2017)	18.8	14.0 (2017)	48.8 (2002)	...	...	...
Pakistan	48.0	61.9 (2019)	...	...	82.2 (2011)	92.1 (2017)	...	...
Tajikistan	27.1	22.3 (2017)	17.0 (2004)	...	...	23.0 (2017)	...	...
Turkmenistan	...	26.2	...	10.1	...	26.1	...	10.1
Uzbekistan	17.8	20.4	13.0	9.8	15.4 (2012)	20.4	13.1 (2012)	9.8
East Asia								
China, People's Republic of	...	...	...	...	...	16.7	...	14.1
Hong Kong, China	15.9	13.0	17.7	11.4	...	12.5	...	10.8
Korea, Republic of	...	...	...	...	...	...	...	...
Mongolia	31.0	34.2 (2019)	14.8	15.3 (2019)	...	31.7	...	14.1 (2019)
Taipei,China	...	...	...	...	...	...	...	...
South Asia								
Bangladesh	64.1 (2011)	59.4 (2017)	57.2 (2011)	53.2	...	47.2	...	33.1
Bhutan	32.7 (2008)	28.6	28.5 (2008)	10.8 (2018)	...	28.6	...	10.8 (2018)
India	...	29.3	...	23.3	...	28.2	...	23.5
Maldives	15.2	10.9 (2019)	18.4 (2002)	5.8 (2019)	...	21.9 (2019)	...	7.2 (2019)
Nepal	43.3	17.7	49.1	35.6	...	17.8	...	33.3
Sri Lanka	29.1	26.3 (2020)	21.9	22.1 (2018)	...	26.0 (2020)	...	22.3 (2018)
Southeast Asia								
Brunei Darussalam	13.0	10.9 (2020)	10.9 (2011)	8.3 (2020)	...	9.3 (2020)	...	7.8 (2020)
Cambodia	48.9	42.1 (2020)	25.4 (2011)	21.9 (2019)	...	42.1 (2020)	...	...
Indonesia	...	...	...	...	...	17.5 (2020)	...	15.8 (2018)
Lao People's Democratic Republic	30.2	22.5	20.4	17.1 (2020)	...	24.8 (2018)	...	22.4 (2017)
Malaysia	13.2	11.9	14.6	12.2 (2020)	...	11.6	...	11.2
Myanmar	28.3	25.6 (2018)	34.5	30.6 (2018)	...	26.7 (2018)	...	28.1 (2018)
Philippines	...	25.2 (2020)	...	24.6 (2020)	...	25.3 (2020)	...	24.6 (2020)
Singapore	18.5 (2009)	14.2 (2020)	16.3 (2009)	11.6 (2019)	18.2 (2009)	13.9 (2020)	16.2 (2009)	11.5 (2020)
Thailand	...	14.4	...	23.6 (2020)	...	14.4	...	22.9
Timor-Leste	...	...	...	...	...	33.7 (2020)	...	31.0 (2020)
Viet Nam	20.2	33.2	...	...	...	33.2	...	...
The Pacific								
Cook Islands	16.5 (2011)	15.5	15.6 (2011)	15.2 (2020)	...	15.5	...	17.7
Fiji	30.8 (2011)	38.3	26.5 (2011)	19.3 (2012)	...	40.5	...	...
Kiribati	26.1	28.9 (2020)	26.0	25.8 (2013)	25.7	30.1 (2020)	...	...
Marshall Islands	...	24.9	...	11.8 (2020)	...	18.8	...	9.9 (2020)
Micronesia, Federated States of	...	52.6	...	...	...	22.1	...	...
Nauru	26.8 (2007)	40.2 (2016)	57.4 (2007)	...	...	28.1 (2019)	...	60.2 (2019)
Niue	...	17.8	...	39.8 (2019)	...	17.8	...	6.2 (2019)
Palau	...	8.0	...	...	...	8.0	...	...
Papua New Guinea	...	...	27.4 (2012)	27.4 (2012)	...	...	...	...
Samoa	21.9 (2012)	24.3 (2014)	...	...	...	30.1 (2019)	...	...
Solomon Islands	34.4	29.9 (2019)	39.6	37.1 (2012)	50.7	29.9 (2019)	...	...
Tonga	...	23.3 (2020)	...	24.8 (2015)	...	21.9 (2020)	...	18.3 (2015)
Tuvalu	...	17.1	...	25.7 (2020)	...	10.6	...	18.7
Vanuatu	46.6	27.4	36.1	23.3 (2017)	...	27.4	...	24.8
Developed ADB Member Economies								
Australia	...	...	...	...	...	...	...	...
Japan	...	...	...	...	...	...	...	...
New Zealand	...	...	...	...	...	...	...	...
WORLD	...	**26.2** (2020)	...	**19.4** (2020)	...	**24.8** (2020)	...	**18.2** (2020)

... = data not available, ADB = Asian Development Bank.

a The UNESCO Institute for Statistics (UIS) defines a trained teacher as one who has received at least the minimum organized pedagogical teacher training pre-service and in-service required for teaching at the relevant level in a given economy in a given academic year.

b The UIS defines a qualified teacher as one who has at least the minimum academic qualifications required for teaching their subjects at the relevant level in a given economy in a given academic year.

Source: United Nations Educational, Scientific and Cultural Organization (UNESCO) Institute for Statistics Database. UIS.Developer Portal. https://apiportal.uis.unesco.org/bdds (accessed 19 June 2023).

Table 2.1.13: Health Care Resources
(per 1,000 population)

ADB Regional Member	Physicians		Hospital Beds	
	2010	2020	2010	2020
Developing ADB Member Economies				
Central and West Asia				
Afghanistan	0.24	0.25	0.4	0.4 (2017)
Armenia	2.84	2.91 (2015)	3.7	4.2 (2015)
Azerbaijan	3.66	3.17 (2019)	5.1	...
Georgia	4.45	5.11	3.0	...
Kazakhstan	3.93	4.07	7.3	...
Kyrgyz Republic	2.34	...	4.8	...
Pakistan	0.81	1.12 (2019)	0.6	0.6 (2017)
Tajikistan	1.70	...	5.1	...
Turkmenistan	2.27	...	4.1	...
Uzbekistan	2.54	...	4.4	...
East Asia				
China, People's Republic of	1.43	2.23 (2019)	2.5	4.3 (2017)
Hong Kong, China	...	...	...	...
Korea, Republic of	1.98	2.48 (2019)	8.7	12.4 (2018)
Mongolia	2.76	3.85 (2018)	6.0	8.0 (2017)
Taipei,China[a]	1.96 (2011)	2.55 (2021)	6.9 (2011)	7.3 (2021)
South Asia				
Bangladesh	0.36	0.67	0.6 (2011)	0.8 (2016)
Bhutan	0.28 (2012)	0.50	1.8 (2011)	...
India	...	0.74	0.5	0.5 (2017)
Maldives	1.44	2.05 (2019)	4.3 (2009)	...
Nepal	0.52 (2012)	0.85	0.3 (2012)	...
Sri Lanka	0.72	1.23	3.5	4.2 (2017)
Southeast Asia				
Brunei Darussalam	1.45	1.61 (2017)	2.5	2.9 (2017)
Cambodia	0.23	...	0.8	0.9 (2016)
Indonesia	0.14	0.62	0.6	1.0 (2017)
Lao People's Democratic Republic	0.20 (2009)	0.35	0.7	...
Malaysia	1.17	2.29	1.8	1.9 (2017)
Myanmar	0.52	0.74 (2019)	0.9 (2012)	1.0 (2017)
Philippines	1.27	0.77	1.1	...
Singapore	1.76	2.46 (2019)	2.0 (2011)	2.5 (2017)
Thailand	0.39	0.95	2.1	...
Timor-Leste	0.08	0.76	5.9	...
Viet Nam	0.71	0.83 (2016)	2.9	...
The Pacific				
Cook Islands	1.45 (2009)	1.35 (2019)	...	...
Fiji	0.44 (2009)	0.86 (2015)	2.2 (2011)	2.0 (2016)
Kiribati	0.40	...	1.4	1.9 (2016)
Marshall Islands	0.57	...	2.7	...
Micronesia, Federated States of	0.19 (2009)	0.94	3.2 (2009)	...
Nauru	1.10	1.35 (2015)	5.0	...
Niue	1.67 (2008)	...	...	...
Palau	1.61	1.77	4.8	...
Papua New Guinea	0.05	0.07 (2019)	...	...
Samoa	0.34	0.60	1.0 (2007)	...
Solomon Islands	0.20 (2011)	0.19 (2016)	1.7 (2011)	...
Tonga	0.56	0.95	2.6	...
Tuvalu	1.15 (2009)	1.19	5.6 (2001)	...
Vanuatu	0.18 (2012)	0.17 (2016)	1.7 (2008)	...
Developed ADB Member Economies				
Australia	3.34	4.13	3.8	3.8 (2016)
Japan	2.21	2.48 (2018)	13.5	13.0 (2018)
New Zealand	2.61	3.62	2.8	2.6 (2019)
WORLD	**1.49**	**1.61 (2018)**	**2.6**	**2.9 (2017)**

... = data not available, ADB = Asian Development Bank.

a Physicians include doctors of Chinese medicine.

Sources: World Bank. World Development Indicators. https://databank.worldbank.org/source/world-development-indicators (accessed 16 May 2023); and World Health Organization. Global Health Observatory. https://www.who.int/data/gho (accessed 16 May 2023). For Taipei,China: Government of Taipei,China, Directorate-General of Budget, Accounting and Statistics.

Table 2.1.14: Adults Aged 15 Years and Older Living with HIV
('000)

ADB Regional Member	All Adults		Women	
	2010	2021	2010	2021
Developing ADB Member Economies				
Central and West Asia				
Afghanistan	4.2	10.0	1.2	3.0
Armenia	...	...	...	...
Azerbaijan	11.0	9.9	4.6	4.1
Georgia	2.9	8.0	0.9	2.4
Kazakhstan	10.0	35.0	3.7	13.0
Kyrgyz Republic	5.1	9.6	1.7	3.7
Pakistan	66.0	210.0	7.2	41.0
Tajikistan	5.0	12.0	2.3	6.0
Turkmenistan	...	...	...	...
Uzbekistan	21.0	52.0	6.4	18.0
East Asia				
China, People's Republic of	...	...	...	...
Hong Kong, China	...	...	...	...
Korea, Republic of	...	...	...	...
Mongolia	0.5	0.6	0.1	0.2
Taipei,China	...	...	...	...
South Asia				
Bangladesh	6.9	14.0	2.0	4.6
Bhutan	1.1	1.3	0.5	0.6
India	...	2,300.0	...	1,100.0
Maldives	...	...	...	...
Nepal	29.0	29.0	10.0	13.0
Sri Lanka	3.8	3.6	1.1	1.1
Southeast Asia				
Brunei Darussalam	...	...	...	...
Cambodia	78.0	72.0	41.0	38.0
Indonesia	400.0	520.0	130.0	200.0
Lao People's Democratic Republic	8.5	15.0	3.5	6.0
Malaysia	63.0	82.0	11.0	16.0
Myanmar	240.0	260.0	87.0	100.0
Philippines	17.0	140.0	1.1	9.0
Singapore	5.9	8.0	0.6	0.7
Thailand	600.0	520.0	260.0	220.0
Timor-Leste	0.5	1.4	0.2	0.5
Viet Nam	200.0	240.0	59.0	79.0
The Pacific				
Cook Islands	...	...	...	...
Fiji	0.5	1.4	0.2	0.6
Kiribati	...	...	...	...
Marshall Islands	...	...	...	...
Micronesia, Federated States of	...	...	...	...
Nauru	...	...	...	...
Niue	...	...	...	...
Palau	...	...	...	...
Papua New Guinea	30.0	56.0	17.0	33.0
Samoa	...	...	...	...
Solomon Islands	...	...	...	...
Tonga	...	...	...	...
Tuvalu	...	...	...	...
Vanuatu	...	...	...	...
Developed ADB Member Economies				
Australia	21.0	30.0	2.7	3.7
Japan	...	...	...	...
New Zealand	2.3	3.6	0.5	0.6
WORLD	**28,300.0**	**36,700.0**	**14,900.0**	**19,700.0**

... = data not available, ADB = Asian Development Bank.

Note: Figures reported in this table are based on modelled HIV estimates. According to the Joint United Nations Programme on HIV/AIDS, modelled HIV estimates provide a scientifically appropriate way of describing HIV epidemic levels and trends, and are required because it is impossible to count the exact number of people living and newly infected with HIV, or people who have died from AIDS-related causes, in any given economy. Doing so would require regularly testing every person for HIV and investigating all deaths, which is logistically impossible and ethically problematic.

Source: Joint United Nations Programme on HIV/AIDS (UNAIDS). AIDSInfo. https://aidsinfo.unaids.org/ (accessed 20 April 2023).

Data Issues and Comparability

Demographic data are based on vital registration records, censuses, and surveys. Since vital registration records in many developing ADB member economies are incomplete, they cannot be used for statistical purposes. In most economies, population censuses, which are used to provide more accurate estimates of population sizes, are conducted every 10 years. Population numbers in between census years are products of imputation methods that use various population distributional assumptions.

The United Nations (UN) Department of Economics and Social Affairs' Population Division uses future trends on fertility, mortality, and international migration to project population numbers through to 2100. The medium-fertility variant included in the UN's World Population Prospects 2022 assumes, over the remainder of the century, a decline of fertility in economies where large families are still prevalent, a slight increase of fertility in several economies where women have fewer than 2.1 live births on average over a lifetime, and special considerations for the impact on mortality of crises such as COVID-19 pandemic as well as HIV and AIDS epidemic.

Urban population statistics are compiled according to each economy's national definition, as there is no agreed international standard for defining an urban area, which poses constraints in comparability of urban and city indicators across economies. Data from World Urbanization Prospects were used when national estimates were not available.

Household surveys, which are the best source of labor force data, are not carried out in all economies on a regular basis. Some economies rely on census data supplemented by enterprise surveys and unemployment registration records, which are often incomplete and may refer only to formal employment. Furthermore, a breakdown by economic activities also may not be available. An initiative is underway to adopt new standards for work and employment statistics, following the recommendations of the 19th International Conference of Labour Statisticians in 2013. These recommendations were adopted by Armenia, beginning 2018; Azerbaijan, beginning 2015; Brunei Darussalam, beginning 2017; Georgia, beginning 2010; the Lao People's Democratic Republic, beginning 2017; Malaysia, beginning 2019; Mongolia, beginning 2019; Nepal, beginning 2018; Timor-Leste, beginning 2010; and Uzbekistan, beginning 2017. Hence, data for these years may not be directly comparable with data in other years. For all other economies, the conceptual definitions used are based on the old framework.

Table 2.2.1: Gross Domestic Product at Purchasing Power Parity
(current international dollars, million)

ADB Regional Member	2010	2015	2017	2018	2019	2020	2021	2022
Developing ADB Member Economies								
Central and West Asia	**1,563,916**	**2,003,804**	**...**	**...**	**...**	**...**	**...**	**...**
Afghanistan	51,348	74,020	74,712	77,418	81,889	81,007	67,125	...
Armenia	21,600	29,167	35,677	38,434	42,097	39,576	43,766	52,695
Azerbaijan	132,906	144,146	139,153	144,636	150,911	146,306	161,466	180,754
Georgia	28,646	45,036	50,663	54,393	58,127	54,905	63,376	74,671
Kazakhstan	313,824	407,416	448,473	478,084	508,560	502,316	547,454	612,702
Kyrgyz Republic	16,812	25,107	31,280	33,236	35,389	32,840	36,432	41,721
Pakistan	775,101	966,888	1,058,469	1,150,594	1,200,488	1,200,659	1,336,964	1,510,643
Tajikistan	17,529	26,634	28,887	31,830	34,798	36,803	42,072	48,621
Turkmenistan	49,914	76,309	...	...	...	...	...	...
Uzbekistan	156,236	209,082	221,561	240,228	259,165	267,786	300,533	339,816
East Asia	**15,208,508**	**21,275,594**	**23,611,726**	**25,668,548**	**27,464,621**	**28,405,444**	**31,950,585**	**35,081,535**
China, People's Republic of	12,380,166	17,796,747	19,887,033	21,739,729	23,446,555	24,284,245	27,518,857	30,327,320
Hong Kong, China	345,525	411,294	442,425	465,960	466,386	441,550	491,109	507,244
Korea, Republic of	1,572,680	1,933,589	2,103,651	2,220,442	2,247,127	2,316,807	2,425,556	2,585,011
Mongolia	20,623	31,928	35,392	39,050	41,978	40,587	43,105	48,360
Taipei,China	889,513	1,102,036	1,143,224	1,203,366	1,262,576	1,322,256	1,471,958	1,613,600
South Asia	**5,829,500**	**8,066,857**	**9,465,611**	**10,314,363**	**10,931,800**	**10,521,855**	**11,945,181**	**...**
Bangladesh	359,986	555,570	781,590	858,963	943,290	988,548	1,104,636	1,265,940
Bhutan	4,589	6,915	8,307	8,767	9,438	8,604	9,358	...
India	5,229,907	7,159,798	8,276,934	9,022,940	9,540,389	9,101,318	10,370,923	11,874,583
Maldives	4,650	7,628	8,964	9,925	10,820	7,290	10,798	...
Nepal	58,482	80,943	98,516	108,574	117,879	116,588	125,512	141,938
Sri Lanka	171,886	256,002	291,299	305,193	309,983	299,506	323,954	319,527
Southeast Asia	**5,157,703**	**6,752,810**	**7,538,125**	**8,128,901**	**8,664,370**	**8,490,901**	**...**	**...**
Brunei Darussalam	31,203	25,949	25,891	26,527	28,048	28,736	29,549	31,105
Cambodia	34,743	52,598	62,891	69,213	75,425	74,043	79,712	88,346
Indonesia	2,057,207	2,647,707	2,894,126	3,117,053	3,332,231	3,305,988	3,582,442	4,036,901
Lao People's Democratic Republic	22,603	41,583	50,464	54,906	58,941	60,327	65,136	69,033
Malaysia	578,575	750,777	829,297	890,363	946,334	905,625	975,574	1,134,677
Myanmar	161,769	227,959	225,517	245,730	267,024	279,093	...	...
Philippines	528,742	733,864	854,095	930,093	1,004,707	920,939	1,017,308	1,170,982
Singapore	382,734	481,405	535,039	567,492	585,363	569,868	648,363	719,084
Thailand	886,760	1,087,226	1,205,839	1,286,973	1,337,763	1,273,000	1,350,041	1,482,098
Timor-Leste[a]	2,120	3,485	3,902	3,968	4,989	6,667	7,335	...
Viet Nam	471,248	700,257	851,064	936,583	1,023,547	1,066,615	1,143,085	1,321,256
The Pacific[b]	**32,451**	**48,297**	**53,787**	**55,558**	**...**	**...**	**...**	**...**
Cook Islands	...	...	...	...	...	...	...	...
Fiji	6,805	10,782	11,784	12,527	12,678	10,660	10,569	...
Kiribati	175	231	237	255	255	253	285	...
Marshall Islands	180	201	219	233	263	262	277	281
Micronesia, Federated States of	336	365	389	399	...	...	...	...
Nauru	61	124	110	114	126	129	139	147
Niue	...	...	...	...	...	...	...	...
Palau	238	313	316	322	323	310	274	...
Papua New Guinea	21,316	32,167	36,159	36,924	39,270	38,523	40,294	45,100
Samoa	1,015	1,216	1,300	1,353	1,418	1,297	1,350	1,428
Solomon Islands	1,163	1,509	1,690	1,778	1,841	1,802	...	...
Tonga	479	582	660	677	694	707	719	...
Tuvalu	31	39	46	48	55	54	57	...
Vanuatu	651	768	880	927	974	938	...	...
Developed ADB Member Economies	**5,528,500**	**6,474,197**	**6,655,777**	**6,805,523**	**6,896,593**	**6,856,373**	**7,068,215**	**...**
Australia	867,249	1,101,523	1,190,365	1,253,150	1,315,386	1,361,436	1,437,172	1,626,940
Japan	4,525,401	5,199,915	5,262,255	5,344,061	5,352,899	5,263,053	5,383,427	5,702,287
New Zealand	135,850	172,759	203,157	208,312	228,308	231,884	247,616	...

... = data not available, ADB = Asian Development Bank.

Note: Gross domestic product figures in local currency units are obtained from the economies' official sources and converted into a common currency using the purchasing power parity (PPP) from the World Bank's World Development Indicators. For 2011 and 2017, PPP figures are based on results from the 2011 and 2017 benchmark cycles of the International Comparison Program (ICP). For 2010 (and years prior featured in the Key Indicators Database), the PPP figures are extrapolated from the revised 2011 ICP. For 2012–2016, PPP estimates are interpolated from the two ICP reference years 2011 and 2017. For 2017 onward, the PPP figures are extrapolated from the 2017 ICP PPPs or imputed based on a regression model. For Taipei,China, the PPP figures for 2010 and 2018–2022 are Asian Development Bank estimates using data from the economy's official sources and the World Bank, while the PPP conversion factor used for 2011–2017 was from the World Bank's ICP 2017 database.

a From September 2019, oil revenue from the Joint Petroleum Development Area is now included in GDP based on the new Timor-Leste Australia Maritime Boundary Treaty.
b For reporting economies only.

Source: Asian Development Bank estimates based on data from the economies' official sources.

Table 2.2.2: Gross Domestic Product
(current $ million)

ADB Regional Member	2010	2015	2017	2018	2019	2020	2021	2022
Developing ADB Member Economies								
Central and West Asia	**515,322**	**716,640**	**...**	**...**	**...**	**...**	**...**	**...**
Afghanistan	16,078	20,607	18,896	18,419	18,904	20,143	14,879	...
Armenia	9,260	10,553	11,527	12,458	13,619	12,642	13,879	19,514
Azerbaijan	52,906	53,076	40,867	47,112	48,174	42,693	54,825	78,721
Georgia	12,243	14,954	16,243	17,600	17,477	15,846	18,626	24,605
Kazakhstan	148,047	184,388	166,806	179,340	181,667	171,082	197,112	223,598
Kyrgyz Republic	4,794	6,678	7,703	8,271	8,871	7,781	8,741	10,931
Pakistan	193,759	296,060	337,137	321,692	291,919	293,752	342,751	325,204
Tajikistan	5,642	8,271	7,536	7,765	8,301	8,134	8,938	10,492
Turkmenistan	22,582	35,855	...	...	...	...	...	...
Uzbekistan	50,010	86,196	62,081	52,870	60,284	60,225	69,601	80,392
East Asia	**7,911,047**	**13,383,287**	**14,877,114**	**16,604,531**	**16,920,103**	**17,363,601**	**20,791,395**	**20,767,640**
China, People's Republic of	6,087,192	11,061,573	12,310,490	13,894,907	14,279,968	14,687,744	17,820,459	17,963,171
Hong Kong, China	228,639	309,386	341,271	361,731	363,075	344,941	368,909	359,839
Korea, Republic of	1,143,672	1,466,039	1,623,074	1,725,373	1,651,423	1,644,313	1,810,966	1,665,246
Mongolia	7,189	11,620	11,481	13,178	14,206	13,313	15,286	16,833
Taipei,China	444,354	534,670	590,798	609,342	611,431	673,290	775,773	762,552
South Asia	**1,863,181**	**2,456,146**	**3,044,311**	**3,213,709**	**3,335,701**	**3,173,052**	**3,722,884**	**...**
Bangladesh	114,508	194,466	288,958	316,206	349,474	373,562	414,907	432,906
Bhutan	1,548	2,004	2,450	2,447	2,536	2,325	2,540	...
India	1,669,620	2,146,759	2,624,329	2,763,535	2,854,799	2,676,119	3,175,276	3,460,841
Maldives	2,588	4,109	4,754	5,301	5,609	3,746	5,406	...
Nepal	16,281	23,667	29,443	31,726	34,268	32,859	36,207	38,751
Sri Lanka	58,636	85,141	94,376	94,494	89,015	84,441	88,548	74,846
Southeast Asia	**2,019,987**	**2,526,752**	**2,857,957**	**3,064,373**	**3,246,937**	**3,094,354**	**...**	**...**
Brunei Darussalam	13,707	12,930	12,128	13,567	13,469	12,006	14,006	16,682
Cambodia	11,242	18,050	22,177	24,572	27,089	25,873	26,961	29,505
Indonesia	755,094	860,854	1,015,619	1,042,272	1,119,100	1,059,055	1,186,505	1,319,100
Lao People's Democratic Republic	6,747	14,426	17,071	18,142	18,741	19,082	19,074	15,363
Malaysia	255,018	301,355	319,109	358,789	365,178	337,339	372,981	406,306
Myanmar	...	62,543	60,793	64,896	69,329	81,625	...	...
Philippines	208,369	306,446	328,481	346,842	376,823	361,751	394,087	404,284
Singapore	239,808	307,999	343,273	376,870	376,837	348,392	423,797	466,789
Thailand	341,105	401,296	456,357	506,754	543,977	500,457	505,568	495,341
Timor-Leste[a]	882	1,594	1,596	1,564	2,029	2,158	3,621	...
Viet Nam	147,201	239,258	281,354	310,106	334,365	346,616	366,138	408,802
The Pacific	**21,167**	**31,073**	**33,374**	**35,259**	**...**	**...**	**...**	**...**
Cook Islands	241	302	346	363	357	283	328	...
Fiji	3,140	4,682	5,353	5,581	5,482	4,477	4,296	...
Kiribati	155	170	189	196	175	178	228	...
Marshall Islands	160	183	213	219	232	242	260	261
Micronesia, Federated States of	297	316	367	402	...	...	...	...
Nauru	51	90	111	120	115	117	134	128
Niue	18	24	27	31	31	29	27	...
Palau	184	279	288	285	274	258	218	243
Papua New Guinea	14,251	21,723	22,743	24,110	24,751	23,848	26,312	...
Samoa	699	826	882	894	913	829	857	857
Solomon Islands	898	1,308	1,470	1,615	1,619	1,536	...	...
Tonga	371	403	461	480	508	487	472	...
Tuvalu	31	35	45	48	54	52	60	...
Vanuatu	671	731	880	915	937	909	...	...
Developed ADB Member Economies	**7,101,760**	**5,842,525**	**6,485,404**	**6,629,500**	**6,684,304**	**6,623,613**	**6,823,875**	**...**
Australia	1,196,171	1,219,530	1,348,011	1,376,732	1,353,218	1,362,254	1,562,786	1,601,656
Japan	5,759,072	4,444,931	4,930,837	5,040,881	5,117,994	5,048,790	5,005,537	4,231,141
New Zealand	146,518	178,064	206,556	211,887	213,092	212,570	255,552	...

... = data not available, $ = United States dollars, ADB = Asian Development Bank.

Note: Gross domestic product figures in local currency units are obtained from the economies' official sources and converted to United States dollars using the official exchange rates from the International Monetary Fund. The exchange rates used are expressed as the average rate for a period of time (average of period), calculated as annual averages based on the monthly averages (local currency units relative to the United States dollar). For Myanmar, the 2010 figure for gross domestic product in US dollars was converted from the domestic currency using the World Bank's alternative conversion factor to calculate the aggregate for Southeast Asia.

a From September 2019, oil revenue from the Joint Petroleum Development Area is now included in GDP based on the new Timor-Leste Australia Maritime Boundary Treaty.

Source: Asian Development Bank estimates based on data from the economies' official sources.

Table 2.2.3: Gross Domestic Product per Capita at Purchasing Power Parity
(current international dollars)

ADB Regional Member	2010	2015	2017	2018	2019	2020	2021	2022
Developing ADB Member Economies								
Central and West Asia	**5,650**	**6,588**	**...**	**...**	**...**	**...**	**...**	**...**
Afghanistan	2,097	2,731	2,647	2,574	2,665	2,581	2,000	...
Armenia	7,070	9,688	11,948	12,929	14,196	13,372	14,769	17,794
Azerbaijan	14,679	14,938	14,121	14,551	15,196	14,630	16,075	17,905
Georgia	7,565	12,089	13,590	14,596	15,625	14,749	17,089	20,113
Kazakhstan	19,433	23,226	24,868	26,164	27,478	26,776	28,799	31,225
Kyrgyz Republic	3,103	4,259	5,094	5,312	5,539	5,034	5,489	6,183
Pakistan	4,467	5,044	5,097	5,432	5,556	5,448	5,948	6,591
Tajikistan	2,331	3,151	3,269	3,531	3,777	3,912	4,293	4,871
Turkmenistan	9,475	13,233	...	...	...	...	...	...
Uzbekistan	5,470	6,680	6,841	7,289	7,718	7,823	8,608	9,533
East Asia	**10,685**	**14,493**	**15,895**	**17,213**	**18,356**	**18,957**	**21,320**	**23,428**
China, People's Republic of	9,233	12,866	14,204	15,469	16,628	17,197	19,481	21,482
Hong Kong, China	49,191	56,409	59,842	62,523	62,119	59,023	66,249	69,049
Korea, Republic of	31,737	37,902	40,957	43,044	43,410	44,695	46,875	50,070
Mongolia	7,638	10,643	11,417	12,203	12,720	11,937	12,678	13,817
Taipei,China	38,439	46,969	48,533	51,033	53,508	56,070	62,721	69,593
South Asia	**4,216**	**5,403**	**6,195**	**6,679**	**7,000**	**6,669**	**7,492**	**...**
Bangladesh	2,423	3,496	4,804	5,218	5,665	5,877	6,434	7,455
Bhutan	6,595	9,135	11,425	11,938	12,725	11,488	12,376	...
India	4,410	5,576	6,299	6,794	7,104	6,707	7,570	8,586
Maldives	11,814	16,786	18,235	19,383	20,265	13,078	18,998	...
Nepal	2,228	2,896	3,446	3,763	4,048	3,967	4,304	4,822
Sri Lanka	8,323	12,210	13,584	14,084	14,218	13,664	14,622	14,405
Southeast Asia	**8,753**	**10,736**	**11,709**	**12,492**	**13,180**	**12,779**	**...**	**...**
Brunei Darussalam	80,669	62,922	60,720	60,758	62,191	65,043	67,049	69,835
Cambodia	2,460	3,485	4,053	4,398	4,726	4,578	4,804	5,310
Indonesia	8,657	10,359	11,073	11,800	12,484	12,235	13,138	14,638
Lao People's Democratic Republic	3,741	6,405	7,313	7,829	8,275	8,343	8,877	9,275
Malaysia	20,238	24,074	25,897	27,495	29,097	27,908	29,944	34,753
Myanmar	3,225	4,346	4,224	4,562	4,914	5,091	...	...
Philippines	5,677	7,278	8,199	8,795	9,364	8,446	9,232	10,495
Singapore	75,390	86,975	95,334	100,643	102,631	100,226	118,888	127,565
Thailand	13,452	15,993	17,505	18,623	19,300	18,314	19,373	21,218
Timor-Leste[a]	1,939	2,913	3,138	3,129	3,858	5,057	5,463	...
Viet Nam	5,412	7,593	9,026	9,819	10,608	10,930	11,604	13,284
The Pacific[b]	**3,484**	**4,551**	**4,805**	**4,834**	**...**	**...**	**...**	**...**
Cook Islands	...	...	...	...	...	...	...	...
Fiji	8,000	12,401	13,317	14,136	14,255	11,958	11,829	...
Kiribati	1,701	2,099	2,081	2,205	2,167	2,122	2,351	...
Marshall Islands	3,396	3,730	4,020	4,274	4,805	4,760	5,010	5,061
Micronesia, Federated States of	3,268	3,516	3,736	3,828	...	...	...	...
Nauru	6,083	11,388	9,757	10,036	10,959	11,027	11,738	12,358
Niue	...	...	...	...	...	...	...	...
Palau	13,037	17,716	17,651	18,368	18,514	17,596	15,667	...
Papua New Guinea	3,021	3,911	4,134	4,094	4,223	4,017	4,075	4,423
Samoa	5,459	6,277	6,600	6,810	7,078	6,423	6,579	6,896
Solomon Islands	2,094	2,412	2,587	2,665	2,705	2,595	...	...
Tonga	4,665	5,725	6,559	6,740	6,916	7,047	7,174	...
Tuvalu	2,754	3,663	4,309	4,486	5,210	5,066	5,403	...
Vanuatu	2,716	2,859	3,156	3,251	3,340	3,126	...	...
Developed ADB Member Economies	**35,794**	**41,617**	**42,612**	**43,515**	**44,044**	**43,788**	**45,170**	**...**
Australia	39,364	46,251	48,400	50,193	51,909	53,066	55,947	62,584
Japan	35,335	40,899	41,505	42,236	42,394	41,825	42,834	45,573
New Zealand	31,225	37,480	42,205	42,507	45,852	45,555	48,445	...

... = data not available, ADB = Asian Development Bank.

Note: The figures in the table are calculated as gross domestic product (GDP) at purchasing power parity (PPP) divided by the midyear population. GDP figures in local currency units are obtained from the economies' official sources and converted into a common currency using the PPP from the World Bank's World Development Indicators. For 2011 and 2017, PPP figures are based on results from the 2011 and 2017 benchmark cycles of the International Comparison Program (ICP). For 2010 (and years prior featured in the Key Indicators Database), the PPP figures are extrapolated from the revised 2011 ICP. For 2012–2016, PPP estimates are interpolated from the two ICP reference years 2011 and 2017. For 2017 onward, the PPP figures are extrapolated from the 2017 ICP PPPs or imputed based on a regression model. For Taipei,China, the PPP figures for 2010 and 2018–2022 are Asian Development Bank estimates using data from the economy's official sources and the World Bank, while the PPP conversion factor used for 2011–2017 was from the World Bank's ICP 2017 database.

a From September 2019, oil revenue from the Joint Petroleum Development Area is now included in GDP based on the new Timor-Leste Australia Maritime Boundary Treaty.
b For reporting economies only.

Source: Asian Development Bank estimates based on data from the economies' official sources.

Table 2.2.4: Gross National Income per Capita, Atlas Method
(current $)

ADB Regional Member	2010	2015	2017	2018	2019	2020	2021	2022
Developing ADB Member Economies								
Central and West Asia[a]	**1,504**	**2,141**	**1,986**	**2,073**	**2,088**	**1,955**	**2,023**	**2,189**
Afghanistan	520	610	540	520	530	500	390	...
Armenia	3,390	4,080	4,070	4,410	4,880	4,470	4,850	5,960
Azerbaijan	5,410	6,610	4,110	4,080	4,510	4,480	4,910	5,630
Georgia	3,210	4,410	4,040	4,460	4,690	4,260	4,700	5,620
Kazakhstan	7,440	11,380	8,040	8,070	8,820	8,710	8,880	9,470
Kyrgyz Republic	850	1,180	1,110	1,220	1,240	1,180	1,220	1,410
Pakistan	890	1,190	1,440	1,610	1,570	1,420	1,470	1,580
Tajikistan	910	1,250	1,020	1,020	1,070	1,050	1,160	1,210
Turkmenistan	3,930	6,790	6,160	6,500	7,080	...	...	...
Uzbekistan	1,410	2,740	2,470	2,120	1,880	1,770	1,980	2,190
East Asia[b]	**5,358**	**9,017**	**9,848**	**10,801**	**11,583**	**11,761**	**13,240**	**14,181**
China, People's Republic of	4,340	7,890	8,670	9,540	10,310	10,520	11,930	12,850
Hong Kong, China	33,620	41,180	46,380	50,050	50,480	48,550	54,370	54,370
Korea, Republic of	22,290	28,720	30,300	32,750	33,830	33,040	35,110	35,990
Mongolia	2,010	3,850	3,250	3,700	3,840	3,720	3,730	4,210
Taipei,China	19,903	23,316	24,473	26,239	27,479	28,769	32,312	35,207
South Asia[a]	**1,176**	**1,568**	**1,806**	**2,005**	**2,112**	**1,961**	**2,201**	**2,425**
Bangladesh	800	1,210	1,650	2,020	2,210	2,300	2,570	2,820
Bhutan	1,980	2,470	2,760	2,940	3,130	2,840	3,040	...
India	1,210	1,590	1,800	1,980	2,080	1,900	2,150	2,380
Maldives	6,030	7,990	9,040	9,700	10,160	6,780	9,590	11,030
Nepal	540	870	970	1,110	1,220	1,180	1,230	1,340
Sri Lanka	2,380	3,860	4,210	4,360	4,220	3,880	4,000	3,610
Southeast Asia[a]	**2,982**	**4,054**	**4,159**	**4,487**	**4,763**	**4,557**	**4,804**	**5,217**
Brunei Darussalam	32,680	38,250	29,400	29,030	31,880	31,210	30,320	31,410
Cambodia	750	1,070	1,260	1,420	1,560	1,530	1,580	1,700
Indonesia	2,510	3,420	3,530	3,850	4,070	3,900	4,170	4,580
Lao People's Democratic Republic	990	1,970	2,240	2,470	2,520	2,470	2,510	2,360
Malaysia	8,110	10,400	9,680	10,360	10,960	10,320	10,710	11,780
Myanmar	630	1,200	1,210	1,250	1,300	1,370	1,170	1,210
Philippines	2,360	3,350	3,480	3,640	3,770	3,350	3,550	3,950
Singapore	44,930	53,160	54,920	56,560	58,910	55,260	63,000	67,200
Thailand	4,510	5,580	5,820	6,450	7,080	6,920	7,090	7,230
Timor-Leste	2,870	2,180	1,800	1,820	2,110	2,100	1,140	1,970
Viet Nam	1,370	2,480	2,720	3,060	3,340	3,450	3,590	4,010
The Pacific[a]	**1,980**	**2,943**	**2,743**	**2,813**	**2,920**	**2,787**	**2,747**	**3,027**
Cook Islands	9,349	17,157	17,360	19,709	18,761	15,695	...	...
Fiji	3,470	4,840	5,120	5,680	5,610	4,680	4,500	5,270
Kiribati	1,950	3,280	2,790	3,000	3,230	2,700	2,790	3,280
Marshall Islands	3,710	4,980	5,330	6,010	6,750	6,690	6,780	7,920
Micronesia, Federated States of	2,780	3,470	3,490	3,450	4,030	4,070	3,980	4,130
Nauru	9,700 (2012)	11,280	11,100	13,020	15,550	16,500	18,010	17,870
Niue	10,896 (2011)	16,820	14,016	15,990	16,247	...	...	...
Palau	11,040	15,750	16,430	17,410	17,150	14,640	12,790	...
Papua New Guinea	1,670	2,670	2,390	2,400	2,510	2,470	2,450	2,730
Samoa	3,400	3,930	4,050	4,060	4,230	4,000	3,820	3,630
Solomon Islands	1,580	2,100	2,150	2,320	2,390	2,340	2,290	2,220
Tonga	3,270	4,210	4,440	4,710	5,130	5,200	4,930	...
Tuvalu	4,510	5,690	5,350	6,160	6,650	6,470	6,830	7,210
Vanuatu	2,510	2,770	2,860	3,120	3,590	3,250	3,420	3,560
Developed ADB Member Economies[b]	**43,911**	**42,647**	**40,903**	**43,595**	**44,097**	**42,977**	**45,781**	**45,627**
Australia	46,740	60,480	51,490	53,100	54,900	53,620	57,170	60,430
Japan	43,910	39,380	38,930	41,800	41,970	40,870	43,450	42,440
New Zealand	29,670	40,660	38,860	41,680	43,110	41,590	45,770	48,460
DEVELOPING ADB MEMBER ECONOMIES[a]	**3,067**	**4,764**	**5,143**	**5,615**	**5,972**	**5,914**	**6,563**	**7,045**
ALL ADB REGIONAL MEMBERS[a]	**4,675**	**6,191**	**6,472**	**7,018**	**7,370**	**7,264**	**7,978**	**8,428**
WORLD	**9,414**	**10,587**	**10,412**	**11,100**	**11,505**	**11,052**	**12,055**	**12,804**

... = data not available, $ = United States dollars, ADB = Asian Development Bank.

Note: The Atlas method refers to a conversion factor that averages the exchange rate for a given year and the 2 preceding years, adjusted for differences in rates of inflation between the member economy and the G5 economies.

a Aggregates are weighted averages estimated using midyear population. For estimating aggregates, imputation was done for economies with missing data by substituting available data from the nearest years.

b Aggregates are weighted averages estimated using midyear population.

Sources: World Bank. World Development Indicators. https://databank.worldbank.org/source/world-development-indicators (accessed 18 July 2023). For the Cook Islands; Niue; and Taipei,China: Asian Development Bank estimates using the Atlas method based on economies' official sources.

Table 2.2.5: Gross Domestic Product per Capita
(current $)

ADB Regional Member	2010	2015	2017	2018	2019	2020	2021	2022
Developing ADB Member Economies								
Central and West Asia	**1,862**	**2,356**	**...**	**...**	**...**	**...**	**...**	**...**
Afghanistan	657	760	670	612	615	642	443	...
Armenia	3,031	3,505	3,860	4,191	4,593	4,271	4,684	6,589
Azerbaijan	5,843	5,501	4,147	4,740	4,851	4,269	5,458	7,798
Georgia	3,233	4,014	4,357	4,723	4,698	4,257	5,022	6,628
Kazakhstan	9,168	10,512	9,249	9,815	9,816	9,119	10,369	11,395
Kyrgyz Republic	885	1,133	1,255	1,322	1,388	1,193	1,317	1,620
Pakistan	1,117	1,544	1,623	1,519	1,351	1,333	1,525	1,419
Tajikistan	750	979	853	862	901	864	912	1,051
Turkmenistan	4,287	6,218	...	...	...	...	...	...
Uzbekistan	1,751	2,754	1,917	1,604	1,795	1,759	1,993	2,255
East Asia	**5,558**	**9,116**	**10,015**	**11,135**	**11,308**	**11,588**	**13,874**	**13,869**
China, People's Republic of	4,540	7,997	8,793	9,887	10,127	10,401	12,615	12,724
Hong Kong, China	32,550	42,432	46,160	48,538	48,359	46,109	49,764	48,984
Korea, Republic of	23,079	28,737	31,601	33,447	31,902	31,721	34,998	32,255
Mongolia	2,663	3,873	3,703	4,118	4,305	3,916	4,496	4,809
Taipei,China	19,202	22,788	25,081	25,841	25,912	28,551	33,056	32,888
South Asia	**1,348**	**1,645**	**1,992**	**2,081**	**2,136**	**2,011**	**2,335**	**...**
Bangladesh	771	1,224	1,776	1,921	2,099	2,221	2,417	2,549
Bhutan	2,225	2,647	3,370	3,332	3,419	3,105	3,359	...
India	1,408	1,672	1,997	2,081	2,126	1,972	2,318	2,502
Maldives	6,576	9,043	9,671	10,353	10,506	6,721	9,511	...
Nepal	620	847	1,030	1,099	1,177	1,118	1,241	1,317
Sri Lanka	2,839	4,061	4,401	4,361	4,083	3,852	3,997	3,374
Southeast Asia	**3,428**	**4,017**	**4,439**	**4,709**	**4,939**	**4,657**	**...**	**...**
Brunei Darussalam	35,437	31,354	28,443	31,074	29,865	27,175	31,781	37,453
Cambodia	796	1,196	1,429	1,561	1,698	1,600	1,625	1,773
Indonesia	3,177	3,368	3,886	3,946	4,193	3,919	4,351	4,783
Lao People's Democratic Republic	1,117	2,222	2,474	2,587	2,631	2,639	2,599	2,064
Malaysia	8,920	9,663	9,965	11,080	11,228	10,396	11,448	12,444
Myanmar	...	1,192	1,139	1,205	1,276	1,489	...	...
Philippines	2,237	3,039	3,153	3,280	3,512	3,318	3,576	3,624
Singapore	47,237	55,646	61,165	66,837	66,070	61,274	77,710	82,808
Thailand	5,174	5,903	6,625	7,333	7,848	7,200	7,255	7,091
Timor-Leste[a]	806	1,333	1,284	1,233	1,569	1,637	2,697	...
Viet Nam	1,691	2,594	2,984	3,251	3,465	3,552	3,717	4,110
The Pacific	**2,273**	**2,928**	**2,981**	**3,068**	**...**	**...**	**...**	**...**
Cook Islands	10,160	16,422	17,724	17,956	17,663	15,319	17,899	...
Fiji	3,691	5,386	6,050	6,298	6,164	5,022	4,808	...
Kiribati	1,507	1,547	1,660	1,695	1,491	1,491	1,875	...
Marshall Islands	3,031	3,389	3,910	4,017	4,235	4,395	4,700	4,711
Micronesia, Federated States of	2,887	3,051	3,522	3,854	...	...	...	...
Nauru	5,112	8,296	9,916	10,486	10,012	10,037	11,333	10,729
Niue	11,985	14,804	16,187	18,559	18,134	16,956	15,986	...
Palau	10,044	15,788	16,062	16,265	15,704	14,640	12,446	13,501
Papua New Guinea	2,020	2,641	2,600	2,673	2,661	2,487	2,661	...
Samoa	3,759	4,261	4,475	4,500	4,556	4,106	4,179	4,140
Solomon Islands	1,617	2,091	2,250	2,422	2,378	2,211	...	...
Tonga	3,612	3,966	4,588	4,773	5,063	4,857	4,711	...
Tuvalu	2,816	3,275	4,253	4,522	5,110	4,899	5,713	...
Vanuatu	2,798	2,721	3,157	3,208	3,211	3,031	...	...
Developed ADB Member Economies	**45,980**	**37,556**	**41,522**	**42,389**	**42,688**	**42,301**	**43,608**	**...**
Australia	54,293	51,206	54,810	55,143	53,402	53,098	60,837	61,611
Japan	44,968	34,961	38,891	39,840	40,534	40,122	39,827	33,815
New Zealand	33,677	38,631	42,911	43,237	42,796	41,761	49,997	...

... = data not available, $ = United States dollars, ADB = Asian Development Bank.

Note: The figures in the table are calculated as gross domestic product (GDP) in current United States (US) dollars divided by the midyear population. GDP figures in local currency units are obtained from the economies' official sources and converted to US dollars using the official exchange rates from the International Monetary Fund. The exchange rates used are expressed as the average rate for a period of time (average of period), calculated as annual averages based on the monthly averages (local currency units relative to the US dollar). For Myanmar, the 2010 figure for GDP in US dollars was converted from the domestic currency using the World Bank's alternative conversion factor to calculate the aggregate for Southeast Asia.

a From September 2019, oil revenue from the Joint Petroleum Development Area is now included in GDP based on the new Timor-Leste Australia Maritime Boundary Treaty.

Source: Asian Development Bank estimates based on data from the economies' official sources.

Table 2.2.6: Agriculture, Industry, and Services Value-Added
(% of GDP)

ADB Regional Member	Agriculture Value-Added			Industry Value-Added			Services Value-Added		
	2010	2015	2022	2010	2015	2022	2010	2015	2022
Developing ADB Member Economies									
Central and West Asia									
Afghanistan	28.8	22.7	35.0 (2021)	21.3	22.7	16.3 (2021)	49.8	54.7	48.7 (2021)
Armenia	18.8	18.9	11.4	36.3	28.2	27.7	45.0	52.9	60.9
Azerbaijan	5.9	6.8	5.1	64.1	49.3	60.4	30.0	43.9	34.4
Georgia	9.6	8.8	7.0*	19.1	21.5	24.6*	71.4	69.7	68.4*
Kazakhstan	4.7	5.0	5.1*	41.9	32.5	29.5*	53.4	62.5	52.9*
Kyrgyz Republic	18.8	15.4	13.7*	28.2	27.5	27.2*	53.1	57.1	59.0*
Pakistan	23.6	24.4	23.5	21.8	20.5	21.5	54.7	55.1	55.0
Tajikistan	21.8	23.7	27.1*	27.9	33.2	27.3*	50.3	43.1	45.6*
Turkmenistan	11.5	9.3	...	60.0	56.9	...	28.5	33.8	...
Uzbekistan	30.6	32.1	25.1*	24.1	24.8	33.4*	45.3	43.1	41.5*
East Asia									
China, People's Republic of	9.3	8.4	7.3*	46.5	40.8	39.9*	44.2	50.8	52.8*
Hong Kong, China	0.1	0.1	0.1 (2021)	7.0	7.3	6.3 (2021)	93.0	92.7	93.7 (2021)
Korea, Republic of	2.4	2.2	1.7	37.5	37.2	34.7	60.1	60.6	63.6
Mongolia	11.6	14.0	13.1*	36.1	34.1	40.2*	52.4	52.0	46.8*
Taipei,China	1.6	1.8	1.4	33.4	36.3	37.8	65.0	62.0	60.8
South Asia									
Bangladesh	17.8	15.5	11.7	26.1	28.2	35.3	56.0	56.4	53.1
Bhutan	14.8	14.4	19.2 (2021)	43.8	42.5	34.2 (2021)	41.4	43.1	46.6 (2021)
India	18.4	17.7	18.3*	33.1	30.0	28.2*	48.5	52.3	53.5*
Maldives	6.1	6.3	6.0 (2021)	10.2	12.1	10.2 (2021)	83.8	81.7	83.8 (2021)
Nepal	35.4	29.4	23.9	15.1	14.6	14.3	49.5	56.0	61.8
Sri Lanka	10.1	8.9	9.2	30.9	32.1	31.8	59.0	58.9	59.0
Southeast Asia									
Brunei Darussalam	0.7	1.1	1.1	67.4	60.2	66.9	31.9	38.7	32.0
Cambodia	36.0	28.2	23.7	23.3	29.4	40.3	40.7	42.3	36.0
Indonesia	14.3	13.9	13.0	43.9	41.4	43.3	41.8	44.7	43.7
Lao People's Democratic Republic	30.6	19.7	20.1	29.8	31.0	38.3	39.6	49.4	41.6
Malaysia	10.2	8.4	9.0	40.9	38.9	39.6	48.9	52.7	51.4
Myanmar	36.9	26.8	20.9 (2020)	26.5	34.5	38.6 (2020)	36.7	38.8	40.5 (2020)
Philippines	13.7	11.0	9.5	32.3	30.5	29.2	53.9	58.5	61.2
Singapore	0.0	0.0	0.0	28.2	25.8	25.4	71.8	74.2	74.6
Thailand[a]	10.5	8.9	8.8*	37.1	33.4	32.5*	52.4	57.7	58.7*
Timor-Leste[b]	24.7	17.8	8.5 (2021)	8.8	18.4	61.4 (2021)	66.5	63.8	30.1 (2021)
Viet Nam	15.4	14.5	11.9	33.0	34.3	38.3	40.6	42.2	41.3
The Pacific									
Cook Islands	3.4	3.2	2.8* (2021)	7.9	11.3	8.1* (2021)	88.7	85.4	79.6* (2021)
Fiji	11.0	10.0	17.0* (2021)	20.9	19.3	19.8* (2021)	68.1	70.6	63.1* (2021)
Kiribati	24.3	22.2	23.1* (2021)	12.0	15.7	11.6* (2021)	63.7	62.1	65.3* (2021)
Marshall Islands	11.0	12.6	21.5*	15.2	11.4	10.6*	73.9	76.0	67.8*
Micronesia, Federated States of	26.7	27.8	23.9 (2018)	7.8	6.5	5.2 (2018)	65.5	65.7	70.9 (2018)
Nauru	6.3	4.0	4.8*	32.7	6.1	7.4*	61.0	89.9	74.4*
Niue	23.0	21.0	19.1* (2018)	4.0	1.6	3.7* (2018)	73.0	77.5	77.2* (2018)
Palau	4.2	3.3	4.3* (2021)	11.0	8.9	13.5* (2021)	84.8	87.8	82.2* (2021)
Papua New Guinea	20.2	18.3	19.1	34.2	36.4	37.4	45.5	45.3	43.5
Samoa	9.5	9.2	11.7	16.2	16.2	11.9	74.4	74.6	76.4
Solomon Islands	34.6	33.3	34.1 (2020)	13.8	15.6	17.2 (2020)	51.6	51.2	48.6 (2020)
Tonga	18.7	19.7	19.9 (2021)	20.5	18.1	19.4 (2021)	60.9	62.3	60.6 (2021)
Tuvalu	27.3	21.4	9.1 (2021)	5.7	12.7	16.0 (2021)	67.0	65.9	74.8 (2021)
Vanuatu	20.8	24.0	24.4 (2020)	13.7	10.6	11.0 (2020)	65.6	65.4	64.6 (2020)
Developed ADB Member Economies									
Australia	2.4	2.5	3.4	27.0	25.4	29.8	70.6	72.1	66.8
Japan	1.1	1.0	1.0 (2021)	28.3	28.8	28.9 (2021)	70.6	70.2	70.1 (2021)
New Zealand	7.1	4.9	6.1 (2020)	23.0	23.1	21.4 (2020)	69.9	72.0	72.4 (2020)

... = data not available; 0.0 = magnitude is less than half of the unit employed; * = provisional, preliminary, estimate; ADB = Asian Development Bank; GDP = gross domestic product.

a Value-added for construction is included under services.
b From September 2019, oil revenue from the Joint Petroleum Development Area is now included in GDP based on the new Timor-Leste Australia Maritime Boundary Treaty.

Source: Economies' official sources.

Table 2.2.7: Household and Government Consumption Expenditure
(% of GDP)

ADB Regional Member	Household Consumption			Government Consumption		
	2010	2015	2022	2010	2015	2022
Developing ADB Member Economies						
Central and West Asia[a]	**60.7**	**65.8**	**64.2 (2021)**	**11.3**	**11.2**	**11.7 (2021)**
Afghanistan	97.4	82.9	91.8 (2020)	14.0	12.1	21.2 (2020)
Armenia[b]	82.0	77.9	68.3	13.1	13.1	12.7
Azerbaijan	38.9	56.3	52.0 (2021)	10.9	12.4	13.9 (2021)
Georgia	79.5	73.6	74.7*	15.3	14.3	12.6*
Kazakhstan[b]	45.4	53.7	49.4*	10.8	11.6	11.4*
Kyrgyz Republic[b]	84.6	90.5	78.3*	18.1	17.8	18.7*
Pakistan[b]	79.0	80.2	84.8	10.9	9.8	10.5
Tajikistan[b]	84.7	71.2	80.4 (2021)	11.3	11.6	10.8 (2021)
Turkmenistan[b]	5.0	9.3 (2013)	...	9.3	9.1 (2013)	...
Uzbekistan[b]	61.5	64.9	61.9*	12.5	13.6	16.8*
East Asia	**38.3**	**40.0**	**37.0**	**14.4**	**15.8**	**16.1**
China, People's Republic of	34.3	37.8	37.0	14.6	16.2	16.0
Hong Kong, China[b]	61.4	66.4	66.8	8.9	9.6	14.3
Korea, Republic of	49.1	46.9	46.7	14.2	15.1	18.7
Mongolia[b]	55.2	61.9	51.6*	12.7	14.9	13.7*
Taipei,China[b]	53.2	51.5	44.6 (2021)	15.1	13.9	13.7
South Asia	**56.5**	**60.5**	**62.2 (2021)**	**10.5**	**10.0**	**10.5 (2021)**
Bangladesh	74.1	72.4	69.1	5.1	5.4	5.7
Bhutan[b]	45.3	55.3	63.4 (2021)	20.5	18.3	21.7 (2021)
India[b]	54.7	59.0	60.5*	11.0	10.4	10.5*
Maldives	...	41.3	42.4 (2021)	...	18.3	19.2 (2021)
Nepal[b]	78.6	85.8	88.6	10.0	9.0	8.9
Sri Lanka	68.5	63.9	62.0	8.5	8.9	7.2
Southeast Asia	**51.9**	**53.5**	**51.7**	**10.8**	**11.4**	**11.7 (2021)**
Brunei Darussalam[b]	14.7	19.8	22.6	22.2	25.1	20.1
Cambodia[b]	81.3	76.8	64.0	6.3	5.4	10.3
Indonesia[b]	55.2	56.3	51.9	9.0	9.7	7.7
Lao People's Democratic Republic	...	...	...	...	...	...
Malaysia[b]	48.1	54.0	57.6	12.6	13.1	11.6
Myanmar[c]	67.3	74.0	73.2 (2020)	...	...	...
Philippines[b]	70.2	72.5	75.9	9.7	10.9	15.0
Singapore	36.3	37.2	29.8	9.7	10.2	10.0
Thailand	51.7	49.7	54.9*	16.0	16.9	18.1*
Timor-Leste[d]	68.7	55.2	28.8 (2021)	103.2	58.8	28.3 (2021)
Viet Nam	58.4	59.3	54.9	10.4	10.7	9.0
The Pacific	**...**	**...**	**...**	**...**	**...**	**...**
Cook Islands	...	...	...	...	...	...
Fiji[e]	72.6	60.9	82.5 (2021)	15.0	20.2	25.1 (2021)
Kiribati	87.9	84.2	83.8 (2021)	61.6	62.9	70.5 (2021)
Marshall Islands	76.7	76.1	64.5 (2021)	56.8	55.9	55.6 (2021)
Micronesia, Federated States of	...	...	...	...	...	...
Nauru	...	...	...	...	...	...
Niue	...	...	...	...	...	...
Palau	67.8	64.5	83.3 (2021)	37.4	28.7	47.6 (2021)
Papua New Guinea[b]	48.0 (2005)	...	...	16.1 (2005)	...	...
Samoa	66.9	63.2	74.1	13.9	14.4	20.9
Solomon Islands	61.6	60.5	59.6 (2020)	31.5	29.6	25.1 (2020)
Tonga	89.1	93.5	102.4 (2021)	18.7	21.3	30.7 (2021)
Tuvalu	...	...	...	...	...	...
Vanuatu	62.6	66.9	70.1 (2020)	18.3	16.5	23.4 (2020)
Developed ADB Member Economies	**55.7**	**54.9**	**50.3**	**19.1**	**19.5**	**20.9**
Australia	55.4	56.1	48.8	18.8	19.1	22.0
Japan[b]	56.9	55.8	55.5	19.2	19.6	21.8
New Zealand	56.5	56.3	56.4 (2021)	19.7	18.5	21.1 (2021)
DEVELOPING ADB MEMBER ECONOMIES[a]	**44.4**	**45.6**	**44.6 (2021)**	**13.1**	**14.4**	**14.6 (2021)**
ALL ADB REGIONAL MEMBERS[a]	**48.6**	**47.8**	**46.0 (2021)**	**15.3**	**15.6**	**15.9 (2021)**
WORLD	**57.1**	**56.8**	**54.8 (2021)**	**17.5**	**16.7**	**17.1 (2021)**

... = data not available, * = provisional or preliminary, ADB = Asian Development Bank, GDP = gross domestic product.

Note: Figures in the table are calculated as a percentage of GDP at current prices.

a For estimating aggregates, GDP figures in domestic currencies were converted to United States dollars using official exchange rates, and imputation was done for economies with missing data by substituting available data from the nearest years.
b Data for household consumption includes nonprofit institutions serving households.
c Data refer to total final consumption expenditure.
d From September 2019, oil revenue from the Joint Petroleum Development Area is now included in GDP based on the new Timor-Leste Australia Maritime Boundary Treaty.
e For years prior to 2005 (as featured in the Key Indicators Database), data for household consumption includes nonprofit institutions serving households.

Sources: Economies' official sources. For "World": World Bank. World Development Indicators. https://databank.worldbank.org/source/world-development-indicators (accessed 22 July 2023).

Table 2.2.8: Gross Capital Formation and Changes in Inventories
(% of GDP)

ADB Regional Member	Gross Capital Formation			Changes in Inventories		
	2010	2015	2022	2010	2015	2022
Developing ADB Member Economies						
Central and West Asia[a]	**22.2**	**23.9**	**22.4 (2021)**	...	...	...
Afghanistan[b,c]	17.5	19.0	11.9 (2020)	5.3	28.1	...
Armenia	32.9	20.7	21.7	-0.6	0.1	1.4
Azerbaijan	18.1	27.9	17.1 (2021)	-0.1	0.1	0.9 (2021)
Georgia	20.5	26.3	20.7*	1.6	1.9	-1.6*
Kazakhstan	25.4	27.9	24.3*	1.0	5.0	2.8*
Kyrgyz Republic[d]	28.1	33.0	23.3*	-0.7	1.7	17.8*
Pakistan	16.0	15.8	15.7	1.6	1.6	1.6
Tajikistan	23.8	44.7	34.9 (2021)	-0.6	6.0	2.9 (2021)
Turkmenistan	51.9	50.3 (2013)	...	...	...	...
Uzbekistan	27.2	26.3	38.3*	4.6	4.3	6.3*
East Asia	**42.7**	**40.4**	**41.4**	...	...	...
China, People's Republic of	46.6	43.2	43.3	2.6	1.1	1.3
Hong Kong, China	23.9	21.5	15.0	2.1	-0.9	-1.1
Korea, Republic of	32.6	29.5	33.2	2.3	0.5	1.2
Mongolia	42.1	24.5	40.2*	7.6	6.2	14.7*
Taipei,China	25.1	21.7	27.8	1.4	0.3	0.2
South Asia	**38.6**	**31.9**	**31.5 (2021)**	...	...	...
Bangladesh[b,e]	26.2	28.9	32.0	...	...	...
Bhutan	63.2	55.5	35.8 (2021)	0.5	-0.3	0.4 (2021)
India[f]	39.8	32.1	31.4* (2021)	4.4	1.9	0.7*
Maldives	...	33.7	40.6 (2021)	...	0.5	5.9 (2021)
Nepal[g]	38.3	32.1	40.0	16.1	3.8	8.5
Sri Lanka	30.4	34.3	34.4	5.9	5.6	10.6
Southeast Asia	**28.4**	**28.1**	**26.8**	...	...	...
Brunei Darussalam	23.7	35.2	25.9	0.2	0.2	0.2
Cambodia	17.4	22.5	23.4	1.2	1.0	0.8
Indonesia	32.9	34.1	29.7	1.9	1.3	0.7
Lao People's Democratic Republic	...	...	...	...	...	...
Malaysia[h]	23.4	25.4	23.9	1.0	-0.4	5.7
Myanmar	23.2	34.8	29.6 (2020)	0.3	0.2	0.1 (2020)
Philippines	20.4	21.3	24.7	0.0	-0.9	1.4
Singapore	27.7	25.4	21.9	2.1	-1.9	1.3
Thailand	25.6	22.1	28.5*	1.4	-2.1	4.6*
Timor-Leste[i]	42.7	36.8	14.4 (2021)	0.0	1.3	0.2 (2021)
Viet Nam	37.1	32.1	33.4	1.9	1.9	1.7
The Pacific	...	...	...	...	...	...
Cook Islands	...	...	...	...	...	...
Fiji	18.8	22.4	19.6 (2021)	2.9	2.6	0.7 (2021)
Kiribati	14.4	41.8	21.0* (2021)	0.3	-0.9	-0.1* (2021)
Marshall Islands	42.6	16.7	18.2 (2021)	-1.1	-0.6	-1.0 (2021)
Micronesia, Federated States of	...	...	...	...	...	...
Nauru	...	...	...	...	...	...
Niue	...	...	...	...	...	...
Palau	24.5	25.4	42.8* (2021)	0.7	-1.9	-0.6* (2021)
Papua New Guinea	17.5 (2005)	...	...	1.0 (2005)	...	...
Samoa	39.1	34.9	37.9	1.1	0.4	3.7
Solomon Islands	17.9	16.0	18.8 (2020)	-1.4 (2012)	-0.0	-2.1 (2020)
Tonga	29.6	24.6	22.0 (2021)	0.5	2.0	-1.3 (2021)
Tuvalu	...	...	...	...	...	...
Vanuatu	37.0	32.9	33.2 (2020)	1.6	0.8	0.5 (2020)
Developed ADB Member Economies	**23.2**	**25.3**	**24.9 (2021)**	...	...	...
Australia	26.8	26.3	23.2	-0.3	0.1	0.3
Japan	22.6	25.2	26.6	-0.0	0.2	0.5
New Zealand	20.2	23.1	25.4 (2021)	0.4	0.3	0.5 (2021)
DEVELOPING ADB MEMBER ECONOMIES[a]	**39.0**	**37.1**	**37.6 (2021)**	...	...	...
ALL ADB REGIONAL MEMBERS[a]	**33.2**	**34.4**	**35.2 (2021)**	...	...	...
WORLD	**24.4**	**25.8**	**27.1 (2021)**	...	...	...

... = data not available, (-/+) 0.0 = magnitude is less than half of unit employed, * = provisional or preliminary, ADB = Asian Development Bank, GDP = gross domestic product.

Note: Figures in the table are calculated as a percentage of GDP at current prices.

a For estimating aggregates, GDP figures in domestic currencies were converted to United States dollars using official exchange rates, and imputation was done for economies with missing data by substituting available data from the nearest years.
b Refers to gross fixed capital formation.
c Changes in inventories include valuables and statistical discrepancy.
d Refers to gross fixed capital formation and acquisitions less disposals of valuables.
e Includes data on changes in inventories.
f Refers to gross capital formation, which refers to the sum of gross fixed capital formation, valuables, increases in stocks, and errors and omissions.
g Changes in inventories were derived residually; hence, statistical discrepancies or errors are included in this entry.
h Changes in inventories include valuables and statistical discrepancy.
i From September 2019, oil revenue from the Joint Petroleum Development Area is now included in GDP based on the new Timor-Leste Australia Maritime Boundary Treaty.

Sources: Economies' official sources. For "World": World Bank. World Development Indicators. https://databank.worldbank.org/source/world-development-indicators (accessed 21 July 2023).

Table 2.2.9: Exports and Imports of Goods and Services
(% of GDP)

ADB Regional Member	Exports of goods and services			Imports of goods and services		
	2010	2015	2022	2010	2015	2022
Developing ADB Member Economies						
Central and West Asia[a]	**31.0**	**21.9**	**21.7 (2021)**	**27.1**	**24.7**	**25.8 (2021)**
Afghanistan	9.8	6.9	7.3 (2020)	43.9	49.0	34.7 (2020)
Armenia	20.8	29.7	48.3	45.3	42.0	51.1
Azerbaijan	54.3	37.8	46.5 (2021)	20.7	34.8	29.8 (2021)
Georgia	33.0	40.9	52.9*	49.9	57.9	63.0*
Kazakhstan	44.2	28.5	42.1*	29.9	24.5	26.6*
Kyrgyz Republic	51.6	35.2	32.4*	81.7	75.8	95.5*
Pakistan	12.6	10.0	10.5	19.4	16.7	22.5
Tajikistan	26.8	9.8	24.2 (2021)	59.0	40.1	47.6 (2021)
Turkmenistan	76.3	74.8 (2013)	...	44.5	44.1 (2013)	...
Uzbekistan	24.3	13.8	27.3*	25.0	17.0	44.3*
East Asia	**38.4**	**29.7**	**27.9**	**34.7**	**25.7**	**24.6**
China, People's Republic of	27.2	21.4	20.7	23.5	18.1	17.4
Hong Kong, China[b]	205.3	195.9	193.9	199.4	193.5	189.9
Korea, Republic of	47.1	43.0	48.3	44.3	36.1	48.5
Mongolia	46.7	44.2	68.9*	56.7	45.5	74.4*
Taipei,China	79.6	71.3	72.0	73.0	58.4	59.0
South Asia	**21.8**	**19.6**	**21.3**	**26.7**	**22.7**	**26.4**
Bangladesh	16.0	17.3	12.9	21.8	24.8	20.9
Bhutan	43.5	34.4	31.8 (2021)	72.4	63.4	52.7 (2021)
India	22.4	19.8	22.4*	26.9	22.1	26.9*
Maldives	...	78.7	77.6 (2021)	...	71.5	74.0 (2021)
Nepal	9.6	10.5	7.1	36.4	37.4	44.6
Sri Lanka	19.6	19.9	21.5	26.8	27.0	25.0
Southeast Asia	**63.6**	**59.5**	**65.7**	**56.9**	**54.2**	**60.6**
Brunei Darussalam	67.4	52.2	86.4	28.0	37.7	60.6
Cambodia	54.1	61.7	63.9	59.5	66.1	65.8
Indonesia	24.3	21.2	24.5	22.4	20.8	20.9
Lao People's Democratic Republic	...	...	...	...	...	...
Malaysia	86.9	69.4	73.8	71.0	61.9	66.9
Myanmar	19.6	17.4	27.6 (2020)	15.1	27.9	29.1 (2020)
Philippines	32.9	27.2	28.4	33.2	31.9	44.0
Singapore	198.0	178.4	186.6	171.7	151.1	150.3
Thailand	67.1	66.8	67.3*	61.3	56.5	69.7*
Timor-Leste[c]	8.6	3.0	63.9 (2021)	125.8	56.9	36.3 (2021)
Viet Nam	54.2	72.9	94.1	59.8	72.0	91.2
The Pacific	**...**	**...**	**...**	**...**	**...**	**...**
Cook Islands	...	...	...	...	...	...
Fiji	57.4	48.8	27.3 (2021)	63.8	52.4	54.6 (2021)
Kiribati	12.3	15.7	4.7 (2021)	79.0	107.9	88.7 (2021)
Marshall Islands	36.3	44.4	46.6 (2021)	109.2	94.3	69.6 (2021)
Micronesia, Federated States of	...	...	...	...	...	...
Nauru	...	...	...	...	...	...
Niue	...	...	...	...	...	...
Palau	49.7	58.6	5.0 (2021)	77.0	76.0	82.5 (2021)
Papua New Guinea	74.5 (2005)	...	...	56.1 (2005)	...	...
Samoa	28.2	28.7	19.6	53.8	46.0	58.4
Solomon Islands	35.2	40.4	27.9 (2020)	61.0	47.8	32.3 (2020)
Tonga	12.5	17.0	12.5 (2021)	58.3	64.5	60.9 (2021)
Tuvalu	...	...	...	...	...	...
Vanuatu	48.7	46.0	18.5 (2020)	55.1	67.0	51.4 (2020)
Developed ADB Member Economies	**16.1**	**18.3**	**22.7**	**15.1**	**19.0**	**23.9**
Australia	19.8	20.1	25.8	20.7	21.6	19.9
Japan	14.9	17.4	21.5	13.6	18.0	25.4
New Zealand	30.3	28.0	22.4 (2021)	28.0	27.0	26.3 (2021)
DEVELOPING ADB MEMBER ECONOMIES[a]	**39.7**	**32.0**	**30.0 (2021)**	**36.8**	**29.0**	**27.7 (2021)**
ALL ADB REGIONAL MEMBERS[a]	**31.0**	**28.8**	**28.0 (2021)**	**28.8**	**26.7**	**26.0 (2021)**
WORLD	**28.9**	**28.3**	**30.7**	**28.0**	**27.6**	**30.3**

... = data not available, * = provisional or preliminary, ADB = Asian Development Bank, GDP = gross domestic product.

Note: Figures in the table are calculated as a percentage of GDP at current prices.

a For estimating aggregates, imputation was done for economies with missing data by substituting available data from the nearest years.

b The statistics for trade in goods and services were compiled based on the change of ownership principle in recording goods sent abroad for processing and merchanting under the standards stipulated in the System of National Accounts 2008.

c From September 2019, oil revenue from the Joint Petroleum Development Area is now included in GDP based on the new Timor-Leste Australia Maritime Boundary Treaty.

Sources: Economies' official sources. For "World": World Bank. World Development Indicators. https://databank.worldbank.org/source/world-development-indicators (accessed 22 July 2022).

Table 2.2.10: Gross Domestic Saving
(% of GDP)

ADB Regional Member	2010	2015	2017	2018	2019	2020	2021	2022
Developing ADB Member Economies								
Central and West Asia[a]	**27.3**	...	...	...	...	...	...	...
Afghanistan	-11.4	5.0	5.1	-8.4	-19.9	-20.4	...	...
Armenia	4.9	9.0	7.7	8.7	4.0	9.7	15.1	19.0
Azerbaijan	49.8	30.9	31.1	35.4	31.4	22.9	33.8	...
Georgia	3.5	9.3	16.3	17.5	16.3	4.6	2.5	10.6*
Kazakhstan	43.8	34.6	36.9	39.6	38.6	34.3	37.1	...
Kyrgyz Republic	-2.7	-8.3	0.8	0.3	7.2	5.5	-2.3	2.9*
Pakistan	9.2	9.1	7.3	6.6	5.4	6.7	5.6	3.8
Tajikistan	4.0	17.2	8.2	12.4	12.6	10.8	8.7	...
Turkmenistan	85.6	81.6 (2013)	...	...	...	...	...	...
Uzbekistan	26.0	21.5	23.2	24.6	24.3	25.0	23.6	21.3*
East Asia[a]	**47.1**	**44.0**	**43.3**	**43.1**	**42.1**	**43.0**	**42.4**	...
China, People's Republic of	51.1	46.0	45.1	44.9	44.0	44.7	45.3	...
Hong Kong, China	29.8	23.9	23.1	21.8	19.7	20.9	22.3	18.9
Korea, Republic of	35.4	36.4	37.0	35.9	34.3	35.6	35.7	32.9
Mongolia	32.1	23.2	29.8	29.4	29.6	23.7	32.1	33.9*
Taipei,China	31.5	34.4	34.7	33.8	33.6	37.5	42.1	40.4
South Asia	...	...	...	...	...	...	...	...
Bangladesh	20.8	22.2	27.1	26.5	26.9	27.1	25.3	25.2
Bhutan	31.8	22.1	29.3	22.5	23.6	16.5	14.9	...
India	...	...	...	...	...	...	...	...
Maldives	...	...	...	...	...	...	...	...
Nepal	11.5	7.6	13.0	14.8	15.3	5.7	7.7	9.3
Sri Lanka	22.3	27.1	33.0	31.1	28.3	27.6	28.7	31.4
Southeast Asia	...	...	...	...	...	...	...	...
Brunei Darussalam	63.1	55.2	53.0	56.3	54.5	50.8	52.7	57.3
Cambodia	14.5	19.6	23.2	26.0	27.2	24.4	...	...
Indonesia	34.8	32.8	32.1	31.6	31.0	31.9	31.7	...
Lao People's Democratic Republic	...	...	...	...	...	...	...	...
Malaysia	39.3	33.0	32.4	30.6	28.6	26.1	29.4	30.8
Myanmar	32.7	23.4	22.3	24.2	28.3	...	...	...
Philippines	...	...	...	...	...	...	...	...
Singapore	54.0	52.7	53.9	54.3	54.1	53.8	58.3	58.2
Thailand	31.1*	32.8*	35.4*	34.1*	33.2*	29.0*	28.9*	32.3*
Timor-Leste[b]	-74.7	-17.0	-18.1	-22.9	-1.3	5.9	42.1	...
Viet Nam	31.2	30.0	31.9	33.2	33.6	34.6	35.0	36.1
The Pacific	...	...	...	...	...	...	...	...
Cook Islands	...	...	...	...	...	...	...	...
Fiji	12.4	18.9	16.4	13.3	8.9	-0.4	-7.6	...
Kiribati	-52.1	-49.2	-56.0	-50.8	-65.1	-54.7*	-56.1*	...
Marshall Islands	23.3	23.9	25.8	26.5	26.5	31.4	35.5	...
Micronesia, Federated States of	...	...	...	...	...	...	...	...
Nauru	...	...	...	...	...	...	...	...
Niue	...	...	...	...	...	...	...	...
Palau[c]	-7.5	5.0	0.9	-1.8	-0.9*	-21.6*	-35.1*	...
Papua New Guinea	35.9 (2005)	...	...	...	...	...	...	...
Samoa	10.7	19.3	18.9	19.6	17.1	5.1	-2.2	...
Solomon Islands	...	...	...	...	...	...	...	...
Tonga	-15.1	-21.5	-15.5	-16.5	-13.2	-15.4	-39.8	...
Tuvalu	...	...	...	...	...	...	...	...
Vanuatu	28.2	25.3 (2014)	...	...	...	...	...	...
Developed ADB Member Economies[a]	**25.2**	**25.6**	**26.7**	**26.4**	**26.5**	**26.3**	**26.5**	...
Australia	25.9	24.8	24.6	24.9	25.8	26.0	27.0	29.2
Japan	25.1	25.9	27.3	26.9	26.8	26.5	26.6	24.3
New Zealand	22.5	24.1	24.6	23.9	24.0	22.6	22.1	...

.... = data not available, * = provisional or preliminary, ADB = Asian Development Bank, GDP = gross domestic product.

Note: Figures in the table are calculated as a percentage of GDP at current prices.

a For estimating aggregates, GDP figures in domestic currencies were converted to United States dollars using official exchange rates.
b From September 2019, oil revenue from the Joint Petroleum Development Area is now included in GDP based on the new Timor-Leste Australia Maritime Boundary Treaty.
c Estimated as the difference between GDP by industrial origin at producer's prices and final consumption expenditure.

Source: Economies' official sources.

Table 2.2.11: Growth Rates of Real Gross Domestic Product
(%)

ADB Regional Member	2010	2015	2017	2018	2019	2020	2021	2022
Developing ADB Member Economies								
Central and West Asia								
Afghanistan	3.2	-1.8	2.6	1.2	3.9	-2.4	-20.7	...
Armenia	2.2	3.2	7.5	5.2	7.6	-7.2	5.8	12.6
Azerbaijan	5.0	1.1	0.2	1.5	2.5	-4.2	5.6	4.6
Georgia	6.2	3.0	4.8	4.8	5.0	-6.8	10.5	10.1*
Kazakhstan	7.3	1.2	6.8	4.1	4.5	-2.5	4.3	3.3*
Kyrgyz Republic	-0.5	3.9	4.7	3.8	4.6	-8.4	6.2	7.0*
Pakistan	2.3	3.8	4.6	6.1	3.1	-0.9	5.8	6.1
Tajikistan	6.5	6.0	7.1	7.6	7.4	4.4	9.4	...
Turkmenistan	16.2	10.3 (2014)	...	...	...	...	5.0	6.2
Uzbekistan	7.1	7.2	4.4	5.5	6.0	2.0	7.4	5.7*
East Asia								
China, People's Republic of	10.6	7.0	6.9	6.7	6.0	2.2	8.4	3.0*
Hong Kong, China	6.8	2.4	3.8	2.8	-1.7	-6.5	6.4	-3.5
Korea, Republic of	6.8	2.8	3.2	2.9	2.2	-0.7	4.1	2.6
Mongolia	6.4	2.4	5.6	7.7	5.6	-4.6	1.6	4.8
Taipei,China	10.3	1.5	3.3	2.8	3.1	3.4	6.5	2.5
South Asia								
Bangladesh	5.6	6.6	6.6	7.3	7.9	3.5	6.9	7.1
Bhutan	11.9	6.6	4.7	3.1	5.8	-10.0	4.1	...
India	8.5	8.0	6.8	6.5	3.9*	-5.8*	9.1*	7.0*
Maldives	7.3	2.9	7.2	8.1	7.1	-33.5	41.7	...
Nepal	4.8	4.0	9.0	7.6	6.7	-2.4	4.2	5.8
Sri Lanka	8.0	4.2	6.5	2.3	-0.2	-4.6	3.5	-7.8
Southeast Asia								
Brunei Darussalam	3.7 (2011)	-0.4	1.3	0.1	3.9	1.1	-1.6	-1.6
Cambodia	6.0	7.0	7.0	7.5	6.8	-3.1	3.0	5.3
Indonesia	6.2	4.9	5.1	5.2	5.0	-2.1	3.7	5.3
Lao People's Democratic Republic	8.1	7.3	6.9	6.2	5.5	3.3	3.5	4.4
Malaysia	7.4	5.1	5.8	4.8	4.4	-5.5	3.1	8.7
Myanmar	9.6	7.0	5.8	6.4	6.8	3.2	-5.9*	2.0*
Philippines	7.3	6.3	6.9	6.3	6.1	-9.5	5.7	7.6
Singapore	14.5	3.0	4.5	3.6	1.3	-3.9	8.9	3.6
Thailand	7.5	3.1	4.2	4.2	2.1	-6.1	1.5*	2.6*
Timor-Leste[a]	9.3	2.8	-3.1	-0.7	23.5	31.9	5.3	...
Viet Nam	6.4	7.0	6.9	7.5	7.4	2.9	2.6	8.0
The Pacific								
Cook Islands	-4.9	5.7	9.5	5.7	4.8	-25.4*	-21.3*	...
Fiji	3.0	4.5	5.4	3.8	-0.6	-17.0	-5.1	...
Kiribati	-1.1	9.9	-0.2	5.4	-2.1	-1.4*	7.9	...
Marshall Islands	5.4	2.1	3.4	4.2	10.8	-1.8	1.1	...
Micronesia, Federated States of	2.3	4.6	2.7	0.2	...	...	...	...
Nauru	13.6	2.8	-5.5	5.7	1.0	0.7*	1.5*	0.9*
Niue	0.6	4.0	3.2*	6.5*	-1.7*	-4.7*	-6.2*	...
Palau	0.1	5.0	-2.0	5.8	-1.9*	-9.7*	-13.3*	9.4*
Papua New Guinea	10.1	6.6	3.5	-0.3	4.5	-3.2	0.1	4.6
Samoa	3.1	6.1	-0.5	2.9	2.8	-10.1	-2.3	0.0
Solomon Islands	9.7	1.7	3.1	2.7	1.7	-3.4	...	...
Tonga	0.8	1.2	3.3	0.2	0.7	0.5	-2.7	...
Tuvalu	-3.3	9.2	3.3	1.4	13.8	-4.3	1.8	...
Vanuatu	1.3	0.4	6.3	2.9	3.2	-5.0	...	...
Developed ADB Member Economies								
Australia	2.2	2.2	2.3	2.9	2.2	-0.1	2.2	3.7
Japan	4.1	1.6	1.7	0.6	-0.4	-4.3	2.1	1.0
New Zealand	1.5	3.8	3.5	3.5	2.5	-0.7	5.2	...

... = data not available, 0.0 = magnitude is less than half of unit employed, * = provisional or preliminary, ADB = Asian Development Bank.

a The Timor-Leste Australia Maritime Boundary Treaty affecting mining and quarrying has caused the growth of output for the industry sector to significantly increase in 2019.

Source: Economies' official sources.

Table 2.2.12: Growth Rates of Real Gross Domestic Product per Capita
(%)

ADB Regional Member	2010	2015	2017	2018	2019	2020	2021	2022
Developing ADB Member Economies								
Central and West Asia								
Afghanistan	1.2	-3.8	0.6	-5.0	1.7	-4.5	-25.9	...
Armenia	2.9	3.5	8.0	5.7	7.9	-7.0	5.7	12.7
Azerbaijan	3.8	-0.1	-0.8	0.6	2.6	-4.9	5.2	4.1
Georgia	7.0	2.9	4.8	4.9	5.2	-6.8	10.9	10.0
Kazakhstan	5.5	-0.3	5.4	2.7	3.2	-3.8	2.9	0.1
Kyrgyz Republic	-1.8	1.8	2.7	1.8	2.4	-10.3	4.4	5.3
Pakistan	0.2	1.8	2.2	4.0	1.1	-2.9	3.7	4.0
Tajikistan	3.9	3.5	4.8	5.3	5.1	2.3	7.6	...
Turkmenistan	14.3	8.3 (2014)	...	...	...	...	3.5	4.7
Uzbekistan	4.1	5.4	2.7	3.7	4.0	0.1	5.3	3.5
East Asia								
China, People's Republic of	10.1	6.5	6.3	6.3	5.6	2.1	8.4	3.1
Hong Kong, China	6.0	1.5	3.0	2.0	-2.4	-6.1	7.4	-2.6
Korea, Republic of	6.3	2.3	2.9	2.5	1.8	-0.8	4.3	2.8
Mongolia	4.7	0.3	3.7	5.7	3.7	-6.2	0.0	3.4
Taipei,China	10.0	1.3	3.1	2.7	3.0	3.5	7.0	2.9
South Asia								
Bangladesh	4.2	5.1	5.1	5.9	6.4	2.1	5.5	5.8
Bhutan	9.9	5.0	3.3	2.0	4.7	-10.8	3.1	...
India	7.0	6.7	5.6	5.3	2.7	-6.9	8.0	6.0
Maldives	4.9	-0.9	3.0	3.8	2.7	-36.3	39.0	...
Nepal	3.4	2.6	8.0	6.6	5.7	-3.3	3.3	4.9
Sri Lanka	6.9	3.2	5.3	1.2	-0.8	-5.1	2.4	-7.9
Southeast Asia								
Brunei Darussalam	2.0 (2011)	-1.6	-0.8	-2.3	0.6	3.2	-1.3	-2.7
Cambodia	4.6	5.6	5.5	6.0	5.4	-4.4	1.5	3.9
Indonesia	4.8	3.5	3.9	4.1	3.9	-3.3	2.7	4.1
Lao People's Democratic Republic	6.6	5.7	5.4	4.7	4.0	1.8	2.0	2.9
Malaysia	5.5	3.5	4.5	3.7	4.0	...	2.7	8.5
Myanmar	8.9	6.1	4.8	5.5	5.8	2.3	-6.7	1.1
Philippines	6.3	4.6 (2014)	5.2	4.7	4.6	-10.9	4.6	6.2
Singapore	12.5	1.8	4.4	3.1	0.1	-3.6	13.5	0.2
Thailand	6.9	2.5	3.2	3.9	1.8	-6.3	1.2	2.4
Timor-Leste[a]	7.4	0.9	-4.9	-2.6	21.1	29.4	3.4	...
Viet Nam	5.1	5.8	5.8	6.2	6.1	1.7	1.6	7.0
The Pacific								
Cook Islands	-6.0	1.5 (2013)	9.3	6.6	3.1	-23.6	-21.5	...
Fiji	2.3	4.1	4.8	3.2	-1.2	-17.5	-5.7	...
Kiribati	-3.2	8.4	-1.8	3.7	-3.7	-3.0	6.2	...
Marshall Islands	4.2	1.7	3.0	3.8	10.4	-2.2	0.7	...
Micronesia, Federated States of	2.8	4.4	2.5	0.0	...	...	...	...
Nauru	13.8	1.2	-6.9	4.1	0.1	-0.9	0.3	0.1
Niue	4.7	0.5	1.6	4.9	-1.7	-4.7	-6.2	...
Palau	2.0	3.2	-2.1	8.0	-1.4	-10.5	-12.8	9.3
Papua New Guinea	6.8	3.4	0.4	-3.3	1.3	-6.1	-3.0	1.5
Samoa	2.3	5.2	-1.3	2.1	2.0	-10.8	-3.8	-0.9
Solomon Islands	4.8 (2011)	-0.6	0.9	0.6	-0.3	-5.3	...	...
Tonga	0.6	1.7	3.4	0.3	0.8	0.6	-2.6	...
Tuvalu	-3.8	9.5	3.5	2.7	15.4	-3.0	3.2	...
Vanuatu	-1.2	-1.9	3.9	0.6	0.9	-6.8	...	...
Developed ADB Member Economies								
Australia	0.7	0.7	0.6	1.4	0.7	-1.3	2.1	2.5
Japan	4.1	1.7	1.8	0.8	-0.2	-4.0	2.3	1.5
New Zealand	0.4	1.7	1.4	1.6	0.8	-2.8	4.7	...

.. = data not available, 0.0 = magnitude is less than half of unit employed, ADB = Asian Development Bank.

a The Timor-Leste Australia Maritime Boundary Treaty affecting mining and quarrying has caused the growth of output for the industry sector to significantly increase in 2019.

Source: Asian Development Bank estimates based on data from the economies' official sources.

Table 2.2.13: Growth Rates of Agriculture Real Value-Added
(%)

ADB Regional Member	2010	2015	2016	2017	2018	2019	2020	2021	2022
Developing ADB Member Economies									
Central and West Asia									
Afghanistan	-18.0	-16.9	12.4	6.4	-4.4	17.5	5.9	-2.8	...
Armenia	-16.0	13.2	-5.0	-5.1	-6.9	-5.8	-3.7	-0.8	-0.7
Azerbaijan	-4.7	6.6	2.6	4.2	4.6	7.3	1.9	3.3	3.4
Georgia	-4.2	-0.1	-2.8	-7.7	13.8	0.7	8.1	1.5	2.9*
Kazakhstan	-12.9	3.5	5.4	6.9	3.8	-0.1	5.9	-2.2	9.1*
Kyrgyz Republic	-2.6	6.2	2.9	2.2	2.6	2.5	0.9	-4.6	7.3*
Pakistan	0.3	1.8	0.4	2.2	3.9	0.9	3.9	3.5	4.3
Tajikistan	6.8	3.4	5.2	7.6	7.0	7.0	7.9	-0.3	...
Turkmenistan	25.3	1.7 (2014)	...	...	...	...	...	...	...
Uzbekistan	6.1	6.1	6.2	1.2	0.3	3.1	2.9	4.0	3.6*
East Asia									
China, People's Republic of	4.3	3.9	3.3	4.0	3.5	3.1	3.1	7.1	4.1*
Hong Kong, China[a]	3.9	-6.8	-2.0	-5.2	-1.8	-0.8	3.8	-2.5	-6.0
Korea, Republic of	-3.6	-0.2	-5.6	2.3	0.2	3.9	-5.8	3.8	-1.3
Mongolia	-16.6	10.7	5.4	-0.3	6.5	5.2	5.8	-5.5	12.0*
Taipei,China	2.1	-7.7	-9.7	8.3	4.5	-0.9	-1.5	-4.3	-1.9
South Asia									
Bangladesh	6.2	3.3	2.8	3.2	3.5	3.3	3.4	3.2	3.1
Bhutan	0.8	4.7	4.2	2.9	4.2	1.3	4.6	2.1	...
India	8.8	0.6	6.8	6.6	2.1	6.2*	4.1*	3.5*	3.3*
Maldives	-3.5	-0.4	1.5	8.3	4.8	-7.5	7.1	-0.6	...
Nepal	2.0	1.2	-0.1	5.2	2.6	5.2	2.4	2.8	2.3
Sri Lanka	7.0	5.4	-4.7	-1.8	6.3	0.5	-0.9	0.9	-4.6
Southeast Asia									
Brunei Darussalam	-2.6 (2011)	6.4	-3.6	-1.6	-1.6	-1.4	14.4	16.9	-3.3
Cambodia	4.0	0.2	1.3	1.7	1.2	-0.7	0.6	1.1	1.0
Indonesia	3.0	3.8	3.4	3.9	3.9	3.6	1.8	1.9	2.3
Lao People's Democratic Republic	3.2	3.6	2.8	2.9	1.3	1.2	1.2	2.5	3.4
Malaysia	2.4	1.4	-3.7	5.9	0.1	1.9	-2.4	-0.2	0.1
Myanmar	4.7	3.4	-0.5	-1.5	0.1	1.6	1.7	1.0*	-3.5*
Philippines	1.3	0.7	-1.0	4.2	1.1	1.2	-0.2	-0.3	0.5
Singapore[a]	2.8	-0.4	-0.4	2.9	3.3	6.7	-4.3	11.4	-7.7
Thailand	-0.5	-6.5	-1.2	4.8	6.1	-1.0	-3.3	2.3*	2.5*
Timor-Leste	4.4	-4.4	-1.3	-2.9	2.9	2.5	0.6	5.5	...
Viet Nam	3.3	2.5	1.7	3.2	4.1	2.7	3.0	3.3	3.4
The Pacific									
Cook Islands	0.4	-2.2	-3.1	3.2	-2.5	-3.0	-5.7*	-8.7*	...
Fiji	-2.6	2.9	-10.9	10.8	3.7	4.5	3.3	0.5	...
Kiribati	-3.9	-4.8	11.1	13.1	-2.6	2.5	-1.8	5.0*	...
Marshall Islands	14.1	6.3	6.4	4.0	10.0	63.0	-2.5	8.8	...
Micronesia, Federated States of	-3.1	9.5	-4.8	-0.9	0.1	...	...	...	...
Nauru	3.7	5.2	10.6	43.4	-8.7	24.9	0.7*	1.5*	3.0*
Niue	-0.4	2.0	1.2	3.5*	1.7*	1.2*	-2.4*	-0.6*	...
Palau	-5.0	-3.7	7.7	8.4	-5.2	-5.5*	-13.1*	-2.3*	...
Papua New Guinea	2.8	-2.6	2.7	2.4	4.6	2.3	1.9	1.8	2.1
Samoa	-9.0	1.9	7.2	7.1	-12.4	2.3	-5.8	-0.1	-5.6
Solomon Islands	13.0	3.2	3.4	3.6	0.4	0.1	-3.8	...	...
Tonga	4.7	-1.7	-1.3	-2.5	0.4	3.6	3.2	0.1	...
Tuvalu	12.8	-1.8	...	0.0	1.2	-5.9	-4.8	3.2	...
Vanuatu	4.6	-5.7	5.9	0.2	0.9	6.2	-2.7	...	...
Developed ADB Member Economies									
Australia	-0.7	1.5	-7.1	9.4	-2.8	-10.5	-9.6	23.0	25.1
Japan	-5.2	-4.2	-8.1	0.7	-6.7	4.4	-7.5	3.3	...
New Zealand	-7.9	2.2	0.5	-3.8	7.0	-2.1	4.8	-0.4	...

.. = data not available; 0.0 = magnitude is less than half of unit employed; * = provisional, preliminary, estimate; ADB = Asian Development Bank.

a Refers to other goods industries comprising agriculture, forestry, and fishing; and mining and quarrying.

Source: Economies' official sources.

Table 2.2.14: Growth Rates of Industry Real Value-Added
(%)

ADB Regional Member	2010	2015	2016	2017	2018	2019	2020	2021	2022
Developing ADB Member Economies									
Central and West Asia									
Afghanistan	6.3	4.5	-1.8	9.2	11.1	4.8	-4.6	-14.2	...
Armenia	5.7	2.8	-0.3	9.0	3.7	10.5	-2.5	2.6	9.2
Azerbaijan	3.7	-1.9	-5.7	-3.1	-0.7	1.0	-5.0	3.2	0.3
Georgia[a]	8.2	2.6	6.7	4.4	-0.5	2.7	-6.8	2.4	15.2*
Kazakhstan	9.5	-0.4	1.1	7.7	4.4	5.5	1.5	4.4	2.4*
Kyrgyz Republic	2.5	2.9	7.1	8.6	5.9	8.0	-9.9	2.7	10.9*
Pakistan	4.0	5.4	6.0	4.6	9.2	0.3	-5.8	8.2	6.8
Tajikistan	2.8	16.3	22.2	7.3	17.0	10.3	17.3	13.2	...
Turkmenistan	12.8	11.6 (2014)	...	...	...	...	...	...	...
Uzbekistan	5.5	8.3	5.9	5.4	11.5	8.3	2.5	8.4	5.5
East Asia									
China, People's Republic of	12.7	5.9	6.0	5.9	5.8	4.9	2.5	8.7	3.8*
Hong Kong, China[a,b]	7.7	2.4	3.0	-0.7	2.5	-6.4	-11.2	1.2	3.2
Korea, Republic of[a]	...	...	...	...	...	...	...	...	...
Mongolia	4.3	9.9	-2.4	1.4	8.5	3.1	-4.4	-2.2	-2.8*
Taipei,China[a]	21.5	0.9	3.7	4.8	2.6	1.4	7.1	13.2	2.1
South Asia									
Bangladesh	7.0	9.7	11.1	8.3	10.2	11.6	3.6	10.3	9.9
Bhutan	12.5	8.2	6.9	2.5	-5.0	2.0	-12.8	2.0	...
India	7.9	9.6	7.7	5.9	5.3	-1.4*	-0.9*	11.6*	3.6*
Maldives	7.3	18.1	8.9	13.0	15.5	2.1	-24.8	4.5	...
Nepal	4.0	2.0	-4.1	17.1	10.4	7.4	-4.0	4.5	10.2
Sri Lanka	8.4	1.1	7.4	13.0	-1.1	-4.1	-5.3	5.7	-16.0
Southeast Asia									
Brunei Darussalam	3.2 (2011)	-0.0	-2.9	1.5	-0.4	4.2	2.9	-4.2	-4.9
Cambodia	13.6	11.7	10.9	9.8	11.6	10.7	-1.4	8.6	8.8
Indonesia	4.9	3.0	3.8	4.1	4.3	3.8	-2.8	3.4	4.1
Lao People's Democratic Republic	17.5	7.0	12.0	11.6	7.8	5.6	9.2	6.1	4.4
Malaysia	8.4	5.2	4.3	4.7	3.3	2.6	-6.1	5.6	6.6
Myanmar	18.6	8.3	8.9	8.7	8.3	8.4	3.8*	-9.6*	5.0*
Philippines	9.8	6.5	8.2	7.0	7.3	5.5	-13.1	8.5	6.5
Singapore[a,b]	23.9	-2.7	2.7	6.9	5.5	-1.1	-1.1	13.5	2.9
Thailand[a,c]	10.6	1.9	2.3	2.2	3.0	-0.1	-5.7	3.7*	-0.3*
Timor-Leste	7.9	22.2	7.6	-26.5	5.3	143.5	118.2	5.7	...
Viet Nam	7.2	9.2	7.8	8.3	9.0	8.2	4.4	3.6	7.8
The Pacific									
Cook Islands	-8.9	25.4	-13.5	19.1	7.0	10.5	-33.1*	-9.5*	...
Fiji	6.5	6.9	7.2	4.2	5.5	-0.9	-10.6	-8.3	...
Kiribati	9.5	23.3	-2.3	-15.2	-13.9	-9.4	-2.8*	21.1*	...
Marshall Islands	7.8	-13.7	-3.3	0.4	8.2	14.6	-4.7	-3.7	...
Micronesia, Federated States of	18.0	-6.1	6.4	2.9	-7.3	...	...	...	...
Nauru	39.4	-17.1	77.3	-26.8	-37.9	-21.0	-4.4*	1.5*	-0.4*
Niue	14.4	0.9	2.3	-6.0	91.7*	-11.9*	-14.7*	-4.4*	...
Palau	5.2	40.2	0.2	-5.8	2.3	0.1*	0.2*	-3.5*	...
Papua New Guinea	12.0	26.4	12.0	4.7	-7.5	7.5	-7.5	-8.1	4.3
Samoa	7.2	8.6	-2.6	-8.6	-4.8	10.8	-15.3	-3.2	-2.2
Solomon Islands	13.2	-4.0	5.0	9.5	1.3	3.5	-3.8	...	...
Tonga	4.1	-0.6	12.7	9.7	-14.8	4.6	-3.1	1.2	...
Tuvalu	-41.6	36.7	...	9.5	-5.2	62.0	-26.6	2.7	...
Vanuatu	12.2	38.5	9.4	10.1	4.9	-8.3	-0.4	...	...
Developed ADB Member Economies									
Australia[a]	...	...	...	...	...	...	...	...	...
Japan[a]	...	...	...	...	...	...	...	...	...
New Zealand[a]	...	...	...	...	...	...	...	...	...

... = data not available; (-/+) 0.0 = magnitude is less than half of unit employed; * = provisional, preliminary, estimate; ADB = Asian Development Bank.

a National accounts are compiled using chain volume measures.

b Industry data refer to manufacturing, construction, and utilities comprising electricity, gas, steam, and air-conditioning supply; water supply; and sewerage, waste management, and remediation activities.

c Industry data refer to mining and quarrying; manufacturing; electricity, gas, steam, and air-conditioning supply; water supply; and sewerage, waste management, and remediation activities.

Source: Economies' official sources.

Table 2.2.15: Growth Rates of Services Real Value-Added
(%)

ADB Regional Member	2010	2015	2016	2017	2018	2019	2020	2021	2022
Developing ADB Member Economies									
Central and West Asia									
Afghanistan	18.1	1.4	2.3	-0.7	1.9	-1.4	-5.9	-32.7	...
Armenia	4.7	1.0	3.4	10.4	9.2	9.8	-8.7	7.6	17.8
Azerbaijan	8.8	4.4	-0.8	3.2	3.8	3.8	-4.4	7.8	9.7
Georgia[a]	8.2	3.8	2.8	6.4	5.8	6.1	-7.4	16.5	8.4*
Kazakhstan	6.0	3.1	0.9	6.4	3.9	4.4	-5.3	4.4	2.9*
Kyrgyz Republic	-1.3	3.5	3.2	3.3	2.9	3.3	-8.9	7.9	4.6*
Pakistan	2.6	4.2	5.0	5.6	6.0	5.0	-1.2	5.9	6.6
Tajikistan	7.3	1.9	-1.5	6.2	4.5	7.3	-1.8	14.3	...
Turkmenistan	21.1	-13.2 (2014)	...	...	...	...	...	...	...
Uzbekistan	9.6	7.6	5.9	6.0	5.7	6.7	1.1	9.5	8.5*
East Asia									
China, People's Republic of	9.7	8.8	8.1	8.3	8.0	7.2	1.9	8.5	2.3*
Hong Kong, China[a,b]	6.9	1.7	2.3	3.5	3.1	-0.6	-6.7	5.9	-3.1
Korea, Republic of[a]	5.1	3.1	2.9	2.6	3.8	3.4	-0.8	3.8	4.2
Mongolia	9.8	0.6	2.7	7.1	5.1	6.4	-6.5	3.9	5.5*
Taipei,China[a]	6.4	1.2	1.3	2.9	3.0	3.6	1.3	2.8	2.4
South Asia									
Bangladesh	5.5	5.8	6.3	6.4	6.6	6.9	3.9	5.7	6.3
Bhutan	15.2	5.6	10.3	7.1	10.3	9.8	-10.8	6.1	...
India	7.8	9.4	8.5	6.3	7.2	6.4*	-8.2*	8.8*	9.4*
Maldives	7.3	2.4	6.7	6.2	7.3	8.8	-34.3	46.8	...
Nepal	5.8	5.4	1.2	8.4	9.3	6.8	-4.5	4.2	5.9
Sri Lanka	8.0	5.3	4.7	3.6	4.3	2.9	-1.9	3.5	-2.0
Southeast Asia									
Brunei Darussalam	4.9 (2011)	-1.1	-1.7	1.1	0.8	3.4	-2.1	2.5	3.8
Cambodia	3.3	7.1	6.8	7.0	6.7	6.2	-6.3	-1.9	3.6
Indonesia	8.4	5.5	5.7	5.7	5.8	6.4	-1.5	3.5	6.5
Lao People's Democratic Republic	7.6	8.0	4.7	4.5	6.8	6.9	-1.2	1.4	5.0
Malaysia	7.4	5.3	5.7	6.5	7.0	6.2	-5.6	1.9	11.3
Myanmar	9.5	8.7	8.1	8.1	8.7	8.3	3.4	-6.3*	2.6*
Philippines	7.6	7.4	8.2	7.4	6.7	7.2	-9.1	5.4	9.2
Singapore[a,c]	10.9	4.2	3.1	3.6	3.3	2.2	-4.5	7.0	4.7
Thailand[a,d]	7.0	5.9	5.0	5.4	5.0	4.2	-6.8	0.4*	4.6*
Timor-Leste	10.2	4.6	5.7	2.7	-2.1	1.2	-7.2	6.2	...
Viet Nam	7.2	7.0	7.5	7.1	7.5	8.1	2.0	1.6	10.0
The Pacific									
Cook Islands	-5.8	2.4	12.3	6.6	5.1	6.4	-21.8*	-18.5*	...
Fiji	2.9	3.0	0.1	3.6	1.7	0.0	-16.8	-2.9	...
Kiribati	-0.4	8.3	5.7	4.8	2.2	3.1	-0.5	0.5*	...
Marshall Islands	2.5	5.3	1.5	4.9	3.1	-0.0	-0.3	-0.4	...
Micronesia, Federated States of	2.4	3.0	2.8	2.9	0.9	...	...	...	...
Nauru	4.2	11.6	-7.0	3.1	13.4	-3.3	0.2*	1.5*	2.4*
Niue	0.4	4.6	4.1	3.6	4.7*	-1.8	-4.8	-7.7	...
Palau	-0.3	8.9	-0.7	-2.8	9.3	-0.0*	-0.1*	-14.9*	...
Papua New Guinea	12.4	-2.3	2.3	1.4	5.1	2.5	-0.2	5.5	5.0
Samoa	2.9	7.3	4.7	1.4	5.4	1.4	-6.4	-4.1	-1.2
Solomon Islands	5.1	2.5	7.3	1.2	4.8	2.0	-3.0	...	...
Tonga	0.7	1.4	5.5	1.8	3.3	0.8	-0.3	-7.6	...
Tuvalu	2.3	7.1	...	2.1	3.7	5.4	1.7	1.7	...
Vanuatu	2.7	-2.5	4.5	4.6	0.8	6.1	-6.7	...	...
Developed ADB Member Economies									
Australia[a]	...	...	...	...	...	...	...	...	...
Japan[a]	...	...	...	...	...	...	...	...	...
New Zealand[a]	...	...	...	...	...	...	...	...	...

.. = data not available; (-/+) 0.0 = magnitude is less than half of unit employed; * = provisional, preliminary, estimate; ADB = Asian Development Bank.

a National accounts are compiled using chain volume measures.
b Services data refer to import, export, wholesale, and retail trades; accommodation and food services; transportation, storage, postal, and courier services; information and communications; financing and insurance; real estate, professional, and business services; public administration, social services, and personal services; and ownership of premises.
c Services data refer to services-producing industries, including ownership of dwellings.
d Services data include construction.

Source: Economies' official sources.

Table 2.2.16: Growth Rates of Real Household Final Consumption
(%)

ADB Regional Member	2010	2015	2016	2017	2018	2019	2020	2021	2022
Developing ADB Member Economies									
Central and West Asia									
Afghanistan	...	...	...	-6.2	26.2	11.3	0.0	...	...
Armenia[a]	3.9	-7.5	-2.1	14.0	4.8	11.5	-14.0	2.7	8.1
Azerbaijan[a]	10.8	10.3	1.7	0.8	4.6	5.9	-8.7	3.6	...
Georgia[a]	9.0 (2011)	3.8	-5.7	7.4	5.8	7.2	8.8	14.5	-1.8*
Kazakhstan[a]	11.5	1.8	1.2	1.5	6.1	6.1	-3.7	6.3	2.0*
Kyrgyz Republic[a]	2.7	-0.9	-0.6	6.3	5.0	0.8	-8.3	20.9	3.4*
Pakistan[a]	2.2	3.0	7.8	6.9	7.2	5.6	-2.9	9.5	6.8
Tajikistan[a]	10.5	-15.1	13.2	4.6	4.0	5.0	3.1	4.3	...
Turkmenistan[a]	-61.4	...	...	...	...	...	...	...	...
Uzbekistan[a]	10.3	11.8	8.3	4.2	6.9	5.6	0.2	11.5	11.4*
East Asia									
China, People's Republic of	...	...	...	...	...	...	...	...	...
Hong Kong, China[a]	6.1	4.8	2.0	5.5	5.3	-0.8	-10.6	5.6	-1.2
Korea, Republic of	4.6	2.2	2.3	2.8	3.1	2.1	-4.7	3.7	4.3
Mongolia[a]	15.8 (2011)	8.1	1.8	4.3	11.7	5.8	2.1	-5.9	7.4*
Taipei,China	3.7	3.1	2.7	2.7	1.7	2.5	-2.6	-0.4	...
South Asia									
Bangladesh	4.6	5.8	3.0	6.3	9.4	4.9	3.0	8.0	4.6
Bhutan[a]	5.7	10.6	-2.3	6.1	13.6	7.5	-6.8	4.9	...
India[a]	6.7	7.9	8.1	6.2	7.1	5.2*	-5.2*	11.2*	7.3*
Maldives	...	22.1	12.9	13.1	10.6	4.5	-26.8	-26.8	...
Nepal[a]	6.2	2.6	4.2	0.8	6.2	8.1	3.6	4.3	5.4
Sri Lanka	9.9 (2011)	3.7 (2014)	2.9	-0.6	4.7	3.8	-5.8	2.6	-9.0
Southeast Asia									
Brunei Darussalam[a]	5.4 (2011)	5.2	-1.3	4.7	2.2	6.1	21.5	5.6	9.9
Cambodia[a]	8.8	6.0	6.8	4.6	4.6	5.6	-1.9	-3.6	4.4
Indonesia[a]	4.7	5.0	5.0	4.9	5.1	5.0	-2.6	2.0	4.9
Lao People's Democratic Republic	...	...	...	...	...	...	...	...	...
Malaysia[a]	6.9	6.0	5.9	6.9	8.0	7.7	-4.2	1.9	11.3
Myanmar[b]	2.6	4.7	2.2	4.1	4.5	1.5	7.1	...	...
Philippines[a]	3.6	6.4	7.1	6.0	5.8	5.9	-8.0	4.2	8.3
Singapore	4.4	5.2	3.3	3.1	4.1	2.8	-13.1	6.6	9.7
Thailand[a]	5.5	2.6	2.9	3.1	4.6	4.0	-0.8	0.6*	6.3*
Timor-Leste	5.2	1.7	3.0	6.5	2.0	3.7	-3.0	-2.6	...
Viet Nam	8.2	8.8	6.4	7.2	6.9	7.0	0.4	2.0	7.8
The Pacific									
Cook Islands	...	...	...	...	...	...	...	...	...
Fiji	...	...	...	...	...	...	...	...	...
Kiribati	-2.0	11.5	5.2	4.2	-7.0	10.3	0.4	6.5*	...
Marshall Islands	0.4	-0.6	3.0	10.2	-0.9	6.7	-2.7	-3.7	...
Micronesia, Federated States of	...	...	...	...	...	...	...	...	...
Nauru	...	...	...	...	...	...	...	...	...
Niue	...	...	...	...	...	...	...	...	...
Palau	-3.1	4.2	6.0	-0.5	5.2	-2.9*	-0.7*	-4.4*	...
Papua New Guinea[a]	9.8 (2005)	...	...	...	...	...	...	...	...
Samoa	1.6	3.2	7.7	0.6	-3.7	5.6	6.9	5.3	-6.5
Solomon Islands	8.7	2.5	3.5	0.0	7.7	2.3	-14.6	...	...
Tonga	2.3	7.9	6.8	0.6	0.7	1.4	-4.1	13.5	...
Tuvalu	...	...	...	...	...	...	...	...	...
Vanuatu	2.7	1.0	8.9	-1.9	3.4	0.4	7.7	...	...
Developed ADB Member Economies									
Australia	3.5	2.6	2.5	2.4	2.7	1.6	-3.0	1.1	3.7
Japan	2.3	-0.3	-0.6	1.0	0.4	-0.7	-5.1	0.4	2.1
New Zealand	2.5	4.3	6.5	4.9	4.7	2.4	-0.3	5.9	...

... = data not available; 0.0 = magnitude is less than half of unit employed; * = provisional, preliminary, estimate; ADB = Asian Development Bank.

a Includes expenditure of nonprofit institutions serving households.
b Data refers to total final consumption expenditure.

Source: Economies' official sources.

Table 2.2.17: Growth Rates of Real Government Consumption Expenditure
(%)

ADB Regional Member	2010	2015	2016	2017	2018	2019	2020	2021	2022
Developing ADB Member Economies									
Central and West Asia									
Afghanistan	...	...	...	-6.4	-5.6	28.4	-13.0	...	...
Armenia	3.9	4.7	-2.4	-2.1	-3.0	12.9	9.2	-6.2	6.7
Azerbaijan	3.4	1.4	6.8	1.1	-3.9	2.2	3.4	4.0	...
Georgia	-3.3 (2011)	4.4	10.9	1.1	1.6	5.7	7.1	7.8	-4.6*
Kazakhstan	2.7	2.4	2.3	2.1	-14.1	15.5	12.8	-2.4	9.1*
Kyrgyz Republic	-1.1	0.9	1.5	1.3	1.3	0.5	0.9	0.4	0.3*
Pakistan	-3.1	1.9	13.9	4.5	5.5	-1.6	8.5	1.8	-1.3
Tajikistan	0.9	3.3	1.7	10.9	4.5	0.7	2.3	4.6	...
Turkmenistan	3.7	...	...	...	...	...	...	...	...
Uzbekistan	7.0	6.7	2.7	1.5	4.8	5.7	1.4	3.1	1.3*
East Asia									
China, People's Republic of	...	...	...	...	...	...	...	...	...
Hong Kong, China	3.4	3.4	3.4	2.8	4.2	5.1	7.9	5.9	8.2
Korea, Republic of	5.6	3.8	4.4	3.9	5.3	6.4	5.1	5.6	4.1
Mongolia	15.3 (2011)	-4.7	13.3	-2.4	1.1	12.3	14.6	9.2	5.4*
Taipei,China	1.2	-0.1	3.7	-0.4	4.0	0.6	2.8	3.7	3.4
South Asia									
Bangladesh	6.8	8.8	8.4	7.2	5.3	13.4	2.0	6.9	6.2
Bhutan	7.5	10.8	4.2	4.4	3.1	10.8	4.1	5.7	...
India	5.2	7.5	6.1	11.9	6.7	3.9*	-0.9*	6.6*	1.2*
Maldives	...	3.7	3.3	-10.2	8.9	-2.9	2.4	-1.0	...
Nepal	1.3	11.5	-12.0	21.4	2.1	9.8	3.8	-1.7	5.5
Sri Lanka	-2.1 (2011)	6.0 (2014)	0.1	5.5	18.7	6.6	0.0	-2.8	1.4
Southeast Asia									
Brunei Darussalam	5.3 (2011)	-3.6	-6.5	7.4	1.6	1.8	-9.6	2.6	6.9
Cambodia	12.5	4.4	5.7	6.5	6.5	5.8	15.2	78.7	43.5
Indonesia	0.3	5.3	-0.1	2.1	4.8	3.3	2.1	4.2	-4.5
Lao People's Democratic Republic	...	...	...	...	...	...	...	...	...
Malaysia	3.4	4.5	1.1	5.7	3.4	1.5	5.0	5.3	3.9
Myanmar[a]							...	...	...
Philippines	4.2	7.9	9.4	6.5	13.4	9.1	10.5	7.2	4.9
Singapore	10.2	8.9	3.7	3.4	3.0	3.2	13.0	3.7	-2.3
Thailand	8.9	2.5	2.2	0.3	2.7	1.6	1.4	3.7*	-0.0*
Timor-Leste	2.1	3.6	-1.2	-5.8	-0.3	3.2	4.9	3.5	...
Viet Nam	12.3	7.8	3.8	5.6	4.7	5.4	1.2	4.7	3.6
The Pacific									
Cook Islands	...	...	...	...	...	...	...	...	...
Fiji	...	...	...	...	...	...	...	...	...
Kiribati	-6.6	0.7	14.1	-0.2	11.5	2.7	-9.9	4.4*	...
Marshall Islands	-1.0	4.3	8.3	1.4	5.9	7.0	-3.9	1.0	...
Micronesia, Federated States of	...	...	...	...	...	...	...	...	...
Nauru	...	...	...	...	...	...	...	...	...
Niue	...	...	...	...	...	...	...	...	...
Palau	-1.5	1.3	4.1	-0.9	4.4	0.3*	23.0*	-5.9*	...
Papua New Guinea	1.1 (2005)	...	...	...	...	...	...	...	...
Samoa	17.9	-4.6	-14.6	8.3	20.9	5.5	0.5	1.8	10.5
Solomon Islands	10.0	4.9	4.2	-5.5	14.4	6.1	-13.3	...	...
Tonga	-8.3	3.1	-1.4	2.4	1.1	9.7	11.3	22.4	...
Tuvalu	...	...	...	...	...	...	...	...	...
Vanuatu	5.0	16.9	-1.4	19.5	4.5	2.6	3.7	...	...
Developed ADB Member Economies									
Australia	1.6	2.2	4.8	4.9	3.5	5.0	7.0	6.5	6.8
Japan	1.9	1.9	1.6	0.1	1.0	1.9	2.4	3.5	1.5
New Zealand	2.1	2.1	2.1	3.9	3.4	5.5	7.6	8.0	...

... = data not available; (-/+) 0.0 = magnitude is less than half of unit employed; * = provisional, preliminary, estimate; ADB = Asian Development Bank.

a For 2000–2019, real government consumption expenditure data are included in real household consumption expenditure.

Source: Economies' official sources.

Table 2.2.18: Growth Rates of Real Gross Capital Formation
(%)

ADB Regional Member	2010	2015	2016	2017	2018	2019	2020	2021	2022
Developing ADB Member Economies									
Central and West Asia									
Afghanistan[a]	...	...	...	8.2	14.7	-17.3	33.4	...	...
Armenia	0.5 |	-3.2	-8.7	10.3	34.5	-14.3	-0.5	21.5	8.0
Azerbaijan	2.0	-8.2	-19.0	1.2	-4.3	1.1	-7.3	-4.5	...
Georgia	14.3 (2011)	7.5	13.3	-2.3	6.5	-5.9	-15.2	-21.9	23.1*
Kazakhstan	2.0	5.5	2.5	3.1	2.9	12.2	-1.0	1.5	1.7*
Kyrgyz Republic	-5.2	-2.3	8.1	6.9	16.0	7.9	-29.2	21.8	73.0*
Pakistan[b]	-6.8	12.5	9.0	7.4	9.9	-9.7	-6.1	4.0	5.5
Tajikistan[c]	7.5	25.2 |	-6.6	-12.0	25.5	8.9	-4.6	12.0	...
Turkmenistan	21.5	...	...	...	...	...	...	...	...
Uzbekistan	...	...	...	...	...	...	...	...	...
East Asia									
China, People's Republic of	...	...	...	...	...	...	...	...	...
Hong Kong, China	11.3	-8.1	4.0	5.4	1.8	-16.9	-1.4	-2.3	-13.1
Korea, Republic of	17.1	6.5	6.3	10.9	-1.3	-1.9	0.9	2.3	-0.4
Mongolia	62.8 | (2011)	-26.5	-1.8	31.6	52.1	0.2	-40.7	80.7	15.5*
Taipei,China	35.6	2.6	1.7	-0.8	6.9	7.3	7.1	17.3	4.1
South Asia									
Bangladesh[d,e]	8.6	7.1	8.9 |	8.4	12.1	6.9	4.0	8.1	9.9
Bhutan	46.1	15.7	12.5	-2.4	-5.5	-16.6	-16.0	12.6	...
India[f]	20.1	7.0	9.8	14.5	6.2	-6.0*	-11.6*	22.2*	...
Maldives	...	19.7	-1.0	7.8	7.9	-9.9	-22.1	-5.1	...
Nepal	34.4 |	7.0	-7.6	55.2	12.2	11.1	-26.7	30.4	10.5
Sri Lanka	20.2 (2011)	...	12.0	18.3	-5.4	-11.9	-0.6	4.5	-24.9
Southeast Asia									
Brunei Darussalam	37.0 (2011)	6.6	-11.1	8.0	28.1	-4.4	-9.3	-13.8	-1.8
Cambodia	-7.9	9.9	10.0	6.0	6.0	6.5	12.8	6.5	-2.1
Indonesia	8.8	3.0	5.0	5.7	8.5	2.4	-6.9	4.1	4.0
Lao People's Democratic Republic	...	...	...	...	...	...	...	...	...
Malaysia	25.3	6.7	4.4	6.3	-1.6	-3.8	-12.2	7.5	7.5
Myanmar	34.6	16.1	4.3	8.1	-1.5	1.6	1.0	...	...
Philippines	30.5	13.4	20.8	10.9	11.3	3.5	-34.2	20.0	13.8
Singapore	22.5	-9.8	9.6	11.0	-3.4	0.0	-13.9	16.6	0.5
Thailand	32.0	2.1	-3.8	11.0	16.3	-3.4	-4.8	12.6*	...
Timor-Leste	2.8	-5.0	15.7	-13.6	-0.8 |	-5.4	-31.0	33.0	...
Viet Nam[g]	10.4	9.6	9.9	10.2	8.0	7.5	4.1	4.0	5.8
The Pacific									
Cook Islands	...	...	...	...	...	...	...	...	...
Fiji	...	...	...	...	...	...	...	...	...
Kiribati	-9.3	57.4	-15.6	-10.5	-17.5	-20.4	-3.7	32.6*	...
Marshall Islands	20.4	-19.0	38.2	20.4	2.0	137.8	-58.0	-2.8	...
Micronesia, Federated States of	...	...	...	...	...	...	...	...	...
Nauru	...	...	...	...	...	...	...	...	...
Niue	...	...	...	...	...	...	...	...	...
Palau	3.3	0.3	9.8	12.0	-10.0	8.5*	30.2*	-17.1*	...
Papua New Guinea	-9.8 (2005)	...	...	...	...	...	...	...	...
Samoa	54.7	3.8	10.8	-2.5	-3.1	17.4	-20.7	0.4	11.3
Solomon Islands[a]	85.2	19.9	4.9	19.3	6.5	20.0	-12.6	...	...
Tonga	4.7	9.9	10.9	17.6	-23.6	11.9	-5.8	-19.5	...
Tuvalu	...	...	...	...	...	...	...	...	...
Vanuatu	-4.7	46.5	-23.7	28.1	14.9	-3.6	30.1	...	...
Developed ADB Member Economies									
Australia	...	...	...	...	...	...	...	...	...
Japan	2.9	3.3	0.7	2.1	1.2	0.1	-5.4	0.7	0.7
New Zealand	7.4	1.8	2.9	8.0	4.3	1.7	-2.7	13.3	...

... = data not available; | = marks break in series; * = provisional, preliminary, estimate; (-/+) 0.0 = magnitude is less than half of unit employed; ADB = Asian Development Bank.

a Refers to gross fixed capital formation.
b Data are revised due to the rebasing of national accounts to the base year 2015/2016.
c Prior to 2016, figures are based on the 1993 System of National Accounts. For 2016 onward, figures are based on the 2008 System of National Accounts.
d Refers to gross fixed capital formation, which includes data on changes in inventories.
e For 2000–2006, data refer to previous growth rates calculated using the base year 1995/1996; for 2007–2016, using the base year 2005/2006; and, for 2017–2021, using the base year 2015/2016.
f Refers to gross capital formation, which refers to the sum of gross fixed capital formation, valuables, increases in stocks, and errors and omissions.
g For 2000–2004, gross domestic product data are based on unreassured/unreevaluated scale; For 2005 onward, methodology was revised and 2010 base year was used.

Source: Economies' official sources.

Table 2.2.19: Growth Rates of Real Exports of Goods and Services
(%)

ADB Regional Member	2010	2015	2016	2017	2018	2019	2020	2021	2022
Developing ADB Member Economies									
Central and West Asia									
Afghanistan	...	...	...	46.5	-24.7	-21.5	-35.6	...	...
Armenia	26.5 |	4.9	21.3	19.3	5.0	16.0	-33.5	18.6	53.8
Azerbaijan	9.1	-0.2	-2.0	-2.2	0.5	-4.3	-11.5	13.8	...
Georgia	16.6 (2011)	4.2	8.7	11.7	10.1	9.8	-37.6	24.4	38.2*
Kazakhstan	3.1	-4.1	-4.5	8.0	9.6	2.0	-11.3	2.3	10.2*
Kyrgyz Republic	-11.7	-5.6	-3.8	6.1	-2.7	16.2	-27.3	16.4	-7.3*
Pakistan[a]	7.9	-3.8	1.4	2.5	10.0	13.2	1.5	6.5	5.9
Tajikistan[b]	23.0	– |	15.1	6.8	-5.2	21.5	21.8	55.4	...
Turkmenistan	11.7	...	...	...	...	...	...	...	...
Uzbekistan	1.6	2.1	4.3	14.8 |	10.2	16.4	-20.1	13.4	24.6*
East Asia									
China, People's Republic of	...	...	...	...	...	...	...	...	...
Hong Kong, China[c]	17.6	-1.4	0.7	5.8	3.7	-6.1	-6.7	17.0	-12.6
Korea, Republic of	13.0	0.2	2.4	2.5	4.0	0.2	-1.7	10.8	3.2
Mongolia	18.2 | (2011)	0.1	15.5	3.7	6.1	12.0	-5.3	-14.6	31.3*
Taipei,China	27.6	0.4	-0.9	4.5	0.2	0.7	1.2	17.3	2.4
South Asia									
Bangladesh[d]	0.9	-2.8	2.2 |	-1.8	6.1	11.5	-17.5	9.2	29.4
Bhutan	7.5	-3.2	-5.3	6.5	4.6	14.4	-20.2	8.9	...
India	19.5	-5.6	5.0	4.6	11.9	-3.4*	-9.1*	29.3*	11.5*
Maldives	...	-11.7	9.5	8.5	10.9	6.7	-51.4	113.3	...
Nepal	-10.4 |	2.3	-17.3	8.9	7.7	5.5	-15.9	-21.1	35.0
Sri Lanka	10.2 (2011)	...	4.9	7.7	5.4	1.7	-29.6	10.1	10.2
Southeast Asia									
Brunei Darussalam	-3.0 (2011)	-9.9	-3.2	-4.1	5.7	14.9	7.5	8.8	6.9
Cambodia	20.6	7.2	8.6	5.3	5.3	7.8	1.1	13.5	4.7
Indonesia	15.3	-2.1	-1.7	8.9	6.5	-0.5	-8.4	18.0	16.3
Lao People's Democratic Republic	...	...	...	...	...	...	...	...	...
Malaysia	11.1	0.3	1.3	8.7	1.9	-1.0	-8.6	15.4	12.8
Myanmar	10.9	15.1	-0.4	13.5	12.0	11.3	1.9	...	...
Philippines	20.3	10.0	9.2	17.4	11.8	2.6	-16.1	8.0	10.9
Singapore	17.8	5.0	0.0	7.5	7.8	0.2	0.4	11.7	-1.3
Thailand	14.0	1.0	3.0	5.0	3.0	-3.0	-19.7	11.1*	6.8*
Timor-Leste[e]	28.0	-28.3	8.5	-39.1	16.6 |	...	207.5	8.2	...
Viet Nam[f]	14.6	13.9	11.0	17.3	12.3	6.2	4.1	13.9	4.7
The Pacific									
Cook Islands	...	...	...	...	...	...	...	...	...
Fiji	...	...	...	...	...	...	...	...	...
Kiribati	-20.7	34.5	21.9	-25.0	-16.8	72.0	-33.6	-62.8*	...
Marshall Islands	35.5	-0.9	-11.7	-3.0	6.0	11.9	-4.7	22.9	...
Micronesia, Federated States of	...	...	...	...	...	...	...	...	...
Nauru	...	...	...	...	...	...	...	...	...
Niue	...	...	...	...	...	...	...	...	...
Palau	5.7	12.7	-3.9	-9.3	-5.4	-13.1*	-53.3*	-78.9*	...
Papua New Guinea	6.8 (2005)	...	...	...	...	...	...	...	...
Samoa	3.1	7.2	10.3	3.9	5.6	15.4	-61.1	-15.7	77.0
Solomon Islands	32.7	-6.5	10.7	5.2	6.2	-2.8	-21.8	...	...
Tonga	-9.4	7.9	27.2	-5.8	1.3	-3.3	-5.5	-48.9	...
Tuvalu	...	...	...	...	...	...	...	...	...
Vanuatu	1.0	4.9	19.5	-1.1	3.5	-3.7	-60.1	...	...
Developed ADB Member Economies									
Australia	4.7	6.9	6.4	5.5	4.1	3.9	-1.7	-8.4	-0.3
Japan	24.9	3.2	1.6	6.6	3.8	-1.5	-11.6	11.7	4.9
New Zealand	2.8	6.7	1.9	3.9	3.4	0.1	-18.0	2.4	...

... = data not available; | = marks break in series; * = provisional, preliminary, estimate; – = magnitude equals zero; 0.0 = magnitude is less than half of unit employed; ADB = Asian Development Bank.

a For 2016 onward, data are revised due to the rebasing of national accounts to the base year 2015/2016.
b Prior to 2016, figures are based on the 1993 System of National Accounts (SNA). For 2016 onward, figures are based on the 2008 SNA.
c The statistics for trade in goods and services are compiled based on the change of ownership principle in recording goods sent abroad for processing and merchanting under the standards stipulated in the 2008 SNA.
d For 2007–2016, data refer to previous growth rates calculated using the base year 2005/2006; and, for 2017–2021, using the base year 2015/2016.
e From 2019 onward, oil revenue from the Joint Petroleum Development Area is included in gross domestic product based on the new Timor-Leste Australia Maritime Boundary Treaty.
f For 2000 and 2004, data refer to exports less imports of goods and services. For 2005 onward, methodology was revised and 2010 base year was used. Annual growth rate cannot be calculated separately for exports and imports for 2000, 2001, and 2004.

Source: Economies' official sources.

Table 2.2.20: Growth Rates of Real Imports of Goods and Services
(%)

ADB Regional Member	2010	2015	2016	2017	2018	2019	2020	2021	2022
Developing ADB Member Economies									
Central and West Asia									
Afghanistan	...	...	...	-0.5	40.3	16.5	-7.1	...	...
Armenia	12.8 |	-15.3	6.3	24.6	13.3	11.6	-31.5	12.9	34.7
Azerbaijan	12.4	8.4	-3.2	-0.8	-0.2	-3.2	-17.1	3.0	...
Georgia	15.6 (2011)	7.2	2.4	8.1	10.3	6.6	-16.6	11.0	14.4*
Kazakhstan	2.9	-0.1	-2.0	1.0	6.6	14.9	-9.0	-0.3	11.6*
Kyrgyz Republic	-6.9	-13.2	-1.1	7.4	7.4	6.1	-28.0	39.3	62.1*
Pakistan	-2.3	890.0	17.9	19.0	15.7	7.6	-5.1	14.5	11.0
Tajikistan	8.0	- |	-7.5	-6.5	9.3	6.4	-0.4	20.0	...
Turkmenistan	7.3	...	...	...	...	...	...	...	...
Uzbekistan	0.4	-10.6	-1.3	13.7 |	42.3	13.4	-14.9	23.4	13.6*
East Asia									
China, People's Republic of	...	...	...	...	...	...	...	...	...
Hong Kong, China[a]	18.2	-1.8	0.9	6.6	4.5	-7.2	-6.9	15.8	-12.2
Korea, Republic of	17.5	2.1	5.2	8.9	1.7	-1.9	-3.1	10.1	3.7
Mongolia	49.5 | (2011)	-11.4	17.5	11.5	32.7	8.6	-15.5	13.6	30.5
Taipei,China	30.1	1.3	-1.0	1.6	0.8	0.5	-3.5	18.1	4.5
South Asia									
Bangladesh[b]	0.7	3.2	-7.1 |	5.2	23.9	0.5	-11.4	15.3	31.2
Bhutan	28.7	13.5	-6.6	-0.4	6.6	-6.2	-12.4	15.7	...
India	15.8	-5.9	4.4	17.4	8.8	-0.8*	-13.7*	21.8*	18.8*
Maldives	...	1.0	9.7	8.2	12.8	-3.3	-38.7	49.7	...
Nepal	28.3 |	9.6	3.2	28.2	19.0	5.8	-20.8	16.3	15.0
Sri Lanka	23.6 (2011)	...	7.0	6.7	3.3	-3.5	-20.1	4.1	-19.9
Southeast Asia									
Brunei Darussalam	33.7 (2011)	-8.9	-10.8	1.3	28.1	13.8	-2.1	29.5	9.5
Cambodia	16.8	6.5	8.6	4.1	4.1	6.0	7.3	23.1	5.5
Indonesia	17.3	-6.2	-2.4	8.1	12.1	-7.1	-17.6	24.9	14.7
Lao People's Democratic Republic	...	...	...	...	...	...	...	...	...
Malaysia	15.6	0.8	1.4	10.2	1.5	-2.4	-7.9	17.7	14.2
Myanmar	51.9	21.6	-11.4	10.0	-2.2	-7.7	7.0	...	...
Philippines	20.7	15.0	18.8	15.1	14.6	2.3	-21.6	12.8	13.9
Singapore	16.3	3.4	0.2	8.1	7.4	-0.0	-1.1	12.0	-1.9
Thailand	23.0	0.0	-1.0	6.2	8.3	-5.2	-13.9	17.8*	4.1*
Timor-Leste[c]	-1.8	-7.4	8.1	-8.8	2.9 |	...	11.2	9.6	...
Viet Nam[d]	13.7	15.7	11.3	18.2	9.6	4.9	3.3	15.8	2.1
The Pacific									
Cook Islands	...	...	...	...	...	...	...	...	...
Fiji	...	...	...	...	...	...	...	...	...
Kiribati	-8.2	18.8	5.5	-3.8	-9.0	14.0	-18.1*	20.4*	...
Marshall Islands	10.1	-0.3	0.2	10.9	2.3	36.3	-29.3	-8.3	...
Micronesia, Federated States of	...	...	...	...	...	...	...	...	...
Nauru	...	...	...	...	...	...	...	...	...
Niue	...	...	...	...	...	...	...	...	...
Palau	0.9	2.5	8.3	-1.5	-3.6	0.6*	-0.2*	-16.0*	...
Papua New Guinea	4.7 (2005)	...	...	...	...	...	...	...	...
Samoa	27.4	-5.6	5.7	4.3	7.1	12.0	-20.1	15.1	12.4
Solomon Islands	52.2	0.8	4.1	-2.9	18.3	8.1	-37.1	...	...
Tonga	3.0	22.6	16.9	3.5	-1.4	4.8	-4.4	-13.0	...
Tuvalu	...	...	...	...	...	...	...	...	...
Vanuatu	1.2	26.2	2.3	3.3	10.4	-15.1	1.8	...	...
Developed ADB Member Economies									
Australia	6.9	1.5	-0.3	5.2	7.0	0.2	-7.0	-3.4	7.0
Japan	11.3	0.4	-1.2	3.3	3.8	1.0	-6.8	5.1	7.9
New Zealand	11.5	3.1	5.2	7.8	4.8	1.3	-16.0	17.6	...

... = data not available; | = marks break in series; * = provisional, preliminary, estimate; – = magnitude equals zero; (-/+) 0.0 = magnitude is less than half of unit employed; ADB = Asian Development Bank.

a The statistics for trade in goods and services are compiled based on the change of ownership principle in recording goods sent abroad for processing and merchanting under the standards stipulated in the System of National Accounts 2008.

b For 2007–2016, data refer to previous growth rates calculated using the base year 2005/2006; and, for 2017–2021, using the base year 2015/2016.

c From 2019 onward, oil revenue from the Joint Petroleum Development Area is included in gross domestic product based on the new Timor-Leste Australia Maritime Boundary Treaty.

d For 2000 and 2004, data refer to exports less imports of goods and services. For 2005 onward, methodology was revised and 2010 base year was used. Annual growth rate cannot be calculated separately for exports and imports for 2000, 2001, and 2004.

Source: Economies' official sources.

Table 2.2.21: Growth Rates of Agriculture Production Index
(%)

ADB Regional Member	2010	2015	2016	2017	2018	2019	2020	2021	2022
Developing ADB Member Economies									
Central and West Asia									
Afghanistan	-0.7	-5.4	6.6	-2.4	-3.5	17.2	4.6	-3.7	...
Armenia	-13.4	9.5	-10.0	-0.8	-12.4	-2.6	5.8	-1.3	...
Azerbaijan	-2.1	6.5	3.6	6.0	5.5	7.9	1.3	2.8	...
Georgia	-4.5	1.9	-4.3	-8.7	16.9	1.3	10.0	0.9	...
Kazakhstan[a]	-21.8	2.4	1.9	-2.3	0.5	-3.5	5.8	-7.5	11.6*
Kyrgyz Republic	-1.7	8.2	2.1	1.7	1.8	1.9	0.5	-4.9	...
Pakistan	-1.9	-4.8	2.6	11.5	5.8	-13.4	1.1	...	...
Tajikistan	5.0	32.1	-2.0	11.4	7.5	7.1	-0.9	-3.3	...
Turkmenistan	4.6	2.2	-3.2	-1.4	0.7	20.8	1.9	-3.8	...
Uzbekistan	...	-0.1	0.1	-5.0	-0.8	3.1	-0.6	1.2	-0.3*
East Asia									
China, People's Republic of	2.8	3.5	-0.4	1.3	1.1	0.7	0.8	3.8	...
Hong Kong, China	–	–	–	6.3	5.9	-0.6	1.7	-2.2	-0.6
Korea, Republic of	-4.5	-2.4	-1.0	-1.0	2.5	1.0	-1.7	2.9	...
Mongolia	-21.8	30.7	-4.3	1.3	17.4	3.9	27.8	-22.8	...
Taipei,China[b]	2.1	-3.4	-3.7	5.8	2.5	-3.7	0.1	-1.8	...
South Asia									
Bangladesh	5.9	1.9	0.1	7.5	-0.0	0.9	2.7	4.1	...
Bhutan	4.0	3.0	14.9	-0.7	-13.3	7.4	8.6	-10.5	...
India	8.6	-1.2	3.9	6.0	4.0	2.4	2.8	2.8	...
Maldives	-4.0	1.4	2.3	-0.5	-0.8	4.0	0.9	-11.1	...
Nepal	0.9	0.1	2.5	4.7	1.6	5.4	5.4	1.4	...
Sri Lanka	13.8	8.3	-4.9	-10.5	13.8	1.3	7.9	4.6	...
Southeast Asia									
Brunei Darussalam	4.7	-2.2	6.4	-3.3	2.2	-1.8	7.2	8.5	...
Cambodia	7.6	0.6	5.4	4.9	4.0	0.5	3.0	2.6	...
Indonesia	5.2 (2011)	2.5	2.9	-2.4	22.5	8.1	3.0	1.0	...
Lao People's Democratic Republic	9.6	15.8	1.3	-6.4	0.5	3.3	3.4	10.8	...
Malaysia	1.8	6.3	-6.0	8.4	-3.4	-0.7	-0.7	-3.9	...
Myanmar	2.9	3.0	-0.0	0.4	-20.1	-0.6	-0.3	-1.8	...
Philippines	-1.1	-0.1	-2.2	3.4	-0.3	-0.3	-0.6	-0.4	...
Singapore	3.2	4.2	6.3	26.3	-15.5	10.0	-0.1	-9.2	...
Thailand	0.9	-2.5	0.2	6.7	6.8	0.6	-3.7	0.8	0.9
Timor-Leste	-0.3	3.4	-7.8	-4.4	5.6	0.8	-3.3	-7.2	...
Viet Nam	2.7	2.2	0.0	1.8	3.3	-0.2	1.6	5.1	...
The Pacific									
Cook Islands	-2.2	-2.4	-1.6	-5.0	1.0	-4.0	-2.2	-1.4	...
Fiji	-19.6	1.7	-24.0	35.7	4.6	2.1	-4.9	0.4	...
Kiribati	0.7	0.7	30.0	0.1	-9.2	-12.7	0.2	3.1	...
Marshall Islands	-5.0	8.0	40.7	–	-36.8	12.6	–	6.0	...
Micronesia, Federated States of	-1.0	-0.6	1.1	0.5	0.1	0.2	0.2	0.4	...
Nauru	1.3	0.7	0.8	-1.3	0.6	0.5	0.5	0.7	...
Niue	-0.5	-4.5	3.2	1.0	-2.0	-0.5	-0.3	0.7	...
Palau	...	...	...	...	...	...	...	...	...
Papua New Guinea	-1.7	0.8	0.8	0.1	1.8	-0.4	0.3	1.1	...
Samoa	1.7	-26.2	-5.5	-3.9	-3.4	-7.7	8.3	5.2	...
Solomon Islands	-25.4	1.4	0.1	1.4	1.7	-0.2	0.3	1.0	...
Tonga	-0.8	11.7	-7.4	0.1	-1.7	0.1	-0.1	-2.6	...
Tuvalu	-1.4	1.4	0.8	1.0	0.1	10.3	0.4	-3.5	...
Vanuatu	28.5	-6.8	-0.2	7.6	-0.9	0.9	-1.5	1.2	...
Developed ADB Member Economies									
Australia	-0.1	-1.3	-2.6	11.3	-8.4	-8.9	-4.5	21.4	...
Japan	-2.3	-1.1	-0.3	0.4	-0.3	0.9	-0.0	0.8	...
New Zealand	–	2.1	-1.0	-1.9	3.8	-0.4	1.0	0.5	...

... = data not available; – = magnitude equals zero; * = provisional, preliminary, estimate; (-/+) 0.0 = magnitude is less than half of unit employed; ADB = Asian Development Bank.

Note: Data refer to the gross production index (2014–2016 = 100), except for Hong Kong, China; Indonesia; Kazakhstan; Pakistan; Taipei,China; Thailand; and Uzbekistan.

a Refers to the index of physical volume of the gross production (services) of agriculture.
b Refers to the index of agricultural, forestry, and fishery production.

Sources: Food and Agriculture Organization of the United Nations. FAOSTAT Database. http://www.fao.org/faostat/en/#home (accessed 22 June 2023). For Hong Kong, China; Indonesia; Kazakhstan; Pakistan; Taipei,China; Thailand; and Uzbekistan: Economies' official sources.

Table 2.2.22: Growth Rates of Manufacturing Production Index
(%)

ADB Regional Member	2010	2015	2016	2017	2018	2019	2020	2021	2022
Developing ADB Member Economies									
Central and West Asia									
Afghanistan	...	...	...	...	...	...	...	...	...
Armenia	...	...	...	...	...	...	...	...	...
Azerbaijan	18.5	4.7	-5.6	-3.0	10.2	3.2	-0.8	8.1	-12.5
Georgia	-73.8	-12.6	3.7	1.5	4.8	0.8	-6.1	5.4	8.8
Kazakhstan	17.3	-0.9	0.4	5.0	-1.0	1.2	-1.6	0.6	-1.2
Kyrgyz Republic	19.4	-4.9	14.3	2.1	-2.4	3.2	-14.3	15.3	8.8
Pakistan	0.5	3.4	3.1	...	7.0	3.4	-11.0	11.6	11.9
Tajikistan	673.7	4.8	-0.5	-1.6	-0.2	0.2	2.2	0.3	...
Turkmenistan	...	...	...	...	...	...	...	...	...
Uzbekistan	3.6	-1.9	0.8	-2.3	3.6	-1.2	1.2	0.4	-2.7
East Asia									
China, People's Republic of[a]	16.6	7.0	6.8	7.2	6.5	6.0	3.4	9.8	3.0
Hong Kong, China[b]	3.5	-1.6	-0.4	0.4	1.3	0.4	-5.8	5.4	0.2
Korea, Republic of	16.7	-0.3	2.3	2.3	1.4	0.4	-0.2	8.4	1.4
Mongolia	...	...	...	...	...	...	...	...	...
Taipei,China	29.7	-1.2	1.9	5.3	3.9	-0.4	7.6	14.3	0.9
South Asia									
Bangladesh	16.9 (2011)	10.7	13.5	11.2	15.0	14.7	1.4	12.3	-58.5
Bhutan	...	...	...	...	...	...	...	...	...
India[c]	9.0	3.0	4.1	4.6	3.9	-1.4	-9.6	11.8	4.5
Maldives	...	...	...	...	...	...	...	...	...
Nepal	4.4 (2011)	-19.4	...	17.1	10.0	7.2	-8.9	4.5	5.4
Sri Lanka	...	...	...	...	...	...	...	...	...
Southeast Asia									
Brunei Darussalam	...	...	...	...	...	...	...	...	...
Cambodia	...	...	...	...	...	...	...	...	...
Indonesia	4.1 (2011)	4.8	4.0	4.7	4.0	4.1	-10.1	7.6	2.1
Lao People's Democratic Republic	...	...	...	...	...	...	...	...	...
Malaysia	11.1	4.8	...	6.1	4.8	3.6	-2.7	9.5	8.2
Myanmar[d]	10.1 (2011)	10.2 |	9.1	...	9.7	7.3	...	...	...
Philippines	23.2	0.5	13.1	11.3	...	-8.8	-40.6	50.4	17.1
Singapore[e]	29.7	-5.1	3.7	10.4	7.0	-1.5	7.5	13.3	2.5
Thailand	14.2	0.1	...	1.7	3.8	-3.4	-9.5	5.8	0.4
Timor-Leste	...	...	...	...	...	...	...	...	...
Viet Nam	...	1.6	0.8	...	-2.0	-1.6	-5.1	1.2	1.5
The Pacific									
Cook Islands	...	...	...	...	...	...	...	...	...
Fiji	7.6	8.9	1.9	1.7	3.6	-4.5	-6.7	2.4	3.1
Kiribati	...	...	...	...	...	...	...	...	...
Marshall Islands	...	...	...	...	...	...	...	...	...
Micronesia, Federated States of	...	...	...	...	...	...	...	...	...
Nauru	...	...	...	...	...	...	...	...	...
Niue	...	...	...	...	...	...	...	...	...
Palau	...	...	...	...	...	...	...	...	...
Papua New Guinea	...	...	...	...	...	...	...	...	...
Samoa[f]	15.2	...	...	...	...	...	...	...	...
Solomon Islands	...	...	...	...	...	...	...	...	...
Tonga	...	...	...	...	...	...	...	...	...
Tuvalu	...	...	...	...	...	...	...	...	...
Vanuatu	...	...	...	...	...	...	...	...	...
Developed ADB Member Economies									
Australia	0.5	-1.6	-2.2	-0.6	2.2	-0.9	-1.8	2.2	2.7
Japan	15.6	-1.1	–	3.1	1.1	-3.0	-10.3	5.5	–
New Zealand	4.6	1.8	3.1	1.9	1.9	1.1	-4.1	3.9	-5.3

... = data not available, | = marks break in series, – = magnitude equals zero, ADB = Asian Development Bank.

a Data include only industrial enterprises above a designated size (annual revenue from principal business of over 20 million yuan).
b Starting from the reference year 2008, the index of industrial production and producer price index for manufacturing industries are compiled based on the Standard Industrial Classification Version 2.0 of Hong Kong, China, which adopts the basic framework and principles of the International Standard Industrial Classification of All Economic Activities Revision 4.
c For the fiscal year beginning 1 April.
d For 2010–2015, fiscal year is April–March. For 2016 onward, fiscal year is October–September.
e Refers to index of industrial production.
f Refers to volume indices of industrial production.

Source: Economies' official sources.

Data Issues and Comparability

Indicators in this theme were derived from national accounts statistics compiled in accordance with the UN System of National Accounts. As national statistical offices gradually adopt the latest 2008 System of National Accounts framework with regard to data compilation and methodologies, these indicators will become more consistent across economies. Currently, economies in the region have varying reference periods (e.g., calendar year versus fiscal year) and price valuation methods. Due to a lack of reliable data and limited technical and financial resources dedicated for national accounts compilation, some economies with small statistical offices are not able to provide timely estimates, while some are dependent upon the estimates of external institutions.

Table 2.3.1: Growth Rates of Consumer Price Index
(%)

ADB Regional Member	2010	2015	2016	2017	2018	2019	2020	2021	2022
Developing ADB Member Economies									
Central and West Asia									
Afghanistan	4.9	-0.7	4.4	5.0	0.6	2.3	5.6	7.8	10.9
Armenia	8.2	3.7	-1.4	1.0	2.5	1.4	1.2	7.2	8.6
Azerbaijan	5.7	4.0	12.4	12.9	2.3	2.6	2.8	6.7	13.9
Georgia	7.1	4.0	2.1	6.0	2.6	4.9	5.2	9.6	11.9
Kazakhstan	7.1	6.6	14.6	7.4	6.0	5.3	6.8	8.0	15.0
Kyrgyz Republic	8.0	6.5	0.4	3.2	1.5	1.1	6.3	11.9	13.9
Pakistan	10.1	4.5	2.9	4.8	4.7	6.8	10.7	8.9	12.2
Tajikistan	9.8	5.1	6.1	6.7	5.4	8.0	9.4	8.0	4.2
Turkmenistan	4.4	7.4	3.6	8.0	13.2	13.0	10.0	12.5	10.0
Uzbekistan[a]	7.6	5.5	5.6	9.5	17.5	14.5	12.9	10.8	11.4
East Asia									
China, People's Republic of	3.3	1.4	2.0	1.6	2.1	2.9	2.5	0.9	2.0
Hong Kong, China	2.4	3.0	2.4	1.5	2.4	2.9	0.3	1.6	1.9
Korea, Republic of	2.9	0.7	1.0	1.9	1.5	0.4	0.5	2.5	5.1
Mongolia[b]	13.0	2.0	1.3	6.4	8.1	5.2	2.6	13.9	13.2
Taipei,China	1.0	-0.3	1.4	0.6	1.4	0.6	-0.2	2.0	3.0
South Asia									
Bangladesh	6.8	6.4	5.9	5.4	5.8	5.5	5.7	5.6	6.2
Bhutan	7.0	4.5	3.2	5.0	2.7	2.7	5.6	7.3	5.6
India	10.4	4.9	4.6	3.7	3.4	4.8	6.5	5.1	6.4
Maldives	6.1	1.0	0.5	2.8	-0.1	0.2	-1.4	0.5	2.3
Nepal	9.6	7.2	9.9	4.5	4.2	4.6	6.2	3.6	6.3
Sri Lanka[c]	6.2	2.2	4.0	6.5	4.3	4.4	4.6	5.9	46.4
Southeast Asia									
Brunei Darussalam	0.4	-0.5	-0.3	-1.3	1.0	-0.4	1.9	1.7	3.7
Cambodia[c]	4.0	1.2	3.0	2.9	2.5	1.9	2.9	2.9	5.3
Indonesia[d]	5.1	6.4	3.5	3.8	3.2	2.8	2.0	1.6	4.2
Lao People's Democratic Republic	6.0	1.3	1.6	0.8	2.0	3.3	5.1	3.8	23.0
Malaysia	1.7	2.1	2.1	3.7	1.0	0.7	-1.2	2.5	3.3
Myanmar	7.7	9.5	6.9	4.6	6.8	8.9	3.8	...	...
Philippines	3.8	0.7	1.3	2.9	5.2	2.4	2.4	3.9	5.8
Singapore	2.8	-0.5	-0.5	0.6	0.4	0.6	-0.2	2.3	6.1
Thailand	3.3	-0.9	0.2	0.7	1.1	0.7	-0.9	1.2	6.1
Timor-Leste	5.2	0.6	-1.5	0.5	2.3	0.9	0.5	3.8	7.0
Viet Nam	9.2	0.6	2.7	3.5	3.5	2.8 |	3.2	1.8	3.1
The Pacific									
Cook Islands	1.5	1.1	-0.4	-0.3	0.1	0.4	1.0	2.0	8.9
Fiji	3.7	1.4	3.8	3.3	4.1	1.8	-2.6	0.2	4.3
Kiribati[c]	-3.0	0.6	1.9	0.4	0.6	-1.8	2.5	2.1	5.3
Marshall Islands[c]	1.8	-2.2	-1.5	0.1	0.8	-0.1	-0.7	2.2	3.2
Micronesia, Federated States of	3.6	0.0	-1.0 |	...	1.5	1.9	0.6	3.2	5.4
Nauru	-3.1 |	9.8	8.2	5.1	0.5	4.3	0.9*	1.2*	1.4*
Niue	5.3	1.8	1.3	5.0	9.6	2.4	2.6	...	...
Palau	1.4	0.9	-1.0	0.7	2.1	0.2	0.2	2.7	13.4*
Papua New Guinea	4.4 (2011)	6.0	6.7	5.4	4.4	3.9	4.9	4.5	5.3
Samoa	0.8	0.7	1.3	1.8	4.2	1.0	-1.5	3.2	11.6
Solomon Islands[e]	0.9	-0.6	0.5	0.5	3.5	1.6	3.0	-0.1	5.5
Tonga	3.5	-1.1	2.6	7.5	6.1	1.2	-0.3	5.6	11.0
Tuvalu	-1.9	3.1	3.5	4.1	2.2	3.5	1.6	6.7	12.6
Vanuatu	3.1	2.5	3.9	3.1	2.3	2.8	5.3	2.3	7.1
Developed ADB Member Economies									
Australia	2.3	1.7	1.4	1.7	1.9	1.6	1.3	1.6	4.4
Japan	-0.7	0.8	-0.1	0.5	1.0	0.5	-0.0	-0.2	2.5
New Zealand	2.3	0.3	0.6	1.9	1.6	1.6	1.7	3.9	7.2

... = data not available; | = marks break in series; * = provisional, preliminary, estimate; (-/+) 0.0 = magnitude is less than half of unit employed; ADB = Asian Development Bank.

Note: Data refer to the whole of each economy, unless otherwise indicated. In general, the consumer price index (CPI) data of economies are grouped according to the Classification of Individual Consumption According to Purpose (COICOP) adopted by the United Nations Statistical Commission in 1999. Other economies have switched to the most recent version, COICOP 2018. For more information on COICOP versions, please refer to United Nations' Classification of Economic Statistics available at https://unstats.un.org/unsd/classifications/econ/.

a For 2003–2015, the calculation for the consumer price index includes weights in horticulture goods. Prior to 2016, values were calculated based on the variable weights' method, while 2016 onward uses the fixed weights method. For 2021 onward, the consumer price index commodity grouping is based on the COICOP 2018.

b Data refer to end of period. For 2000–2005, figures are based on COICOP 1999. For 2006 onward, figures are based on COICOP 2018.

c Data refer to capital city.

d For 2010, data refer to the CPI for 66 cities; for 2015–2018, 82 cities; and for 2019–2022, 90 cities. For 2019–2022, the CPI commodity grouping also changed based on COICOP 2018.

e Refers to weighted average of four towns (Audi, Gizo, Honiara, and Noro).

Source: Economies' official sources.

Table 2.3.2: Growth Rates of Food and Nonalcoholic Beverages Consumer Price Index

(%)

ADB Regional Member	2010	2015	2016	2017	2018	2019	2020	2021	2022
Developing ADB Member Economies									
Central and West Asia									
Afghanistan	3.5	-0.8	5.7	6.9	-1.0	3.8	10.0	9.6	14.6
Armenia	9.4	3.1	-3.3	4.1	2.3	1.9	0.3	11.2	13.0
Azerbaijan	7.5	4.8	13.7	17.2	2.0	3.3	4.6	8.2	20.1
Georgia	11.7	4.2	1.6	6.8	2.2	8.1	10.5	10.8	17.9
Kazakhstan	5.9	5.7	12.9	8.5	4.7	8.1	10.5	10.8	19.2
Kyrgyz Republic	6.5	3.7	-6.5	2.5	-2.2	1.3	11.7	18.0	16.2
Pakistan[a]	12.6	3.5	-0.4	10.2	6.7	-4.6	15.5	13.2	13.4
Tajikistan	...	3.8	6.5	7.8	4.9	11.4	13.6	7.3	5.2
Turkmenistan	...	...	...	...	...	...	...	...	...
Uzbekistan[b]	4.9	2.7	7.9	18.1	20.1	17.0	17.5	14.4	15.0
East Asia									
China, People's Republic of[c]	7.2	2.3	4.6	-1.4	1.8	9.2	10.6	-1.4	2.8
Hong Kong, China	3.5	3.4	3.6	1.1	4.3	9.9	7.7	1.4	4.5
Korea, Republic of	6.4	1.6	2.3	3.4	2.8	0.0	4.4	5.9	5.9
Mongolia[d]	18.6	-5.9	1.7	8.7	9.1	8.3	9.0	21.0	15.4
Taipei,China	1.1	3.8	7.9	-1.8	0.6	2.2	0.4	3.6	5.8
South Asia									
Bangladesh[e]	7.7 (2012)	6.7	4.9	6.0	7.1	5.5	5.5	5.7	6.1
Bhutan	9.4	3.3	4.0	7.5	4.9	3.6	11.4	8.9	4.2
India	...	4.7	4.4	1.9	0.4	6.6	8.0	3.7	6.5
Maldives[f]	7.5	0.5	0.6	5.6	-1.1	-0.8	2.7	1.8	4.8
Nepal[g]	15.5	9.6	10.9	1.9	2.7	3.1	8.2	5.0	5.7
Sri Lanka[h]	6.9	5.5	6.1	9.3	3.4	0.8	11.4	11.7	64.8
Southeast Asia									
Brunei Darussalam	-0.0 (2011)	1.0	-0.5	0.3	1.9	-0.7	2.5	2.4	5.1
Cambodia[h]	4.3	4.0	5.6	3.4	2.5	2.1	4.6	2.7	4.9*
Indonesia[i]	9.4	7.2	7.2	2.1	4.2	3.0	3.6	3.1	6.0
Lao People's Democratic Republic	5.6 (2012)	4.5	4.3	-0.1	1.2	4.7	8.6	3.0	22.0
Malaysia	2.5	3.6	3.8	4.0	1.6	1.7	1.3	1.7	5.8
Myanmar	7.4	13.1	9.2	4.4	6.6	9.0	2.8	...	...
Philippines	4.0	1.9	1.6	3.1	6.8	1.6	2.9	4.2	5.9
Singapore	2.3	1.2	2.3	1.3	1.3	1.1	2.9	1.6	5.3
Thailand	5.4	1.1	1.6	–	0.4	2.3	1.2	-0.1	6.9
Timor-Leste	6.4	0.3	-2.1	0.9	1.7	0.9	0.9	5.8	7.5
Viet Nam	10.7	1.5	2.4	-1.1	3.2	4.1 |	10.0	0.7	2.6
The Pacific									
Cook Islands[h,j]	2.5	0.1	0.9	0.6	0.6	1.3	2.5	2.9	13.3
Fiji	4.1	4.8	5.9	-2.1	3.4	4.9	-2.4	6.4	6.1
Kiribati[k]	-4.6	-0.6	1.7	1.8	-1.1	-2.0	1.2	2.9	9.1
Marshall Islands[h,l]	-0.9	2.3	-1.4	-0.5	1.5	0.5	-0.6	3.3	3.8
Micronesia, Federated States of	2.2	0.8	-1.2 |	...	-1.0	1.3	0.7	1.7	6.8
Nauru	-0.4	0.6 (2013)	...	...	...	...	...	...	...
Niue[m]	8.2 |	2.7	-0.2	3.4	0.6	5.1	5.2	...	...
Palau	1.8	1.7	-3.0	1.6	4.0	0.6	2.2	4.2	13.7*
Papua New Guinea	-1.0 (2011)	4.9	5.1	2.8	0.8	3.0	2.2	4.4	7.2
Samoa	-6.6 |	3.3	5.9	1.4	5.6	1.0	-1.9	4.5	13.3
Solomon Islands[n]	-2.9	-3.0	0.5	-0.9	1.9	-0.4	1.3	-3.1	9.2
Tonga	3.0	1.8	1.3	8.5	6.7	1.7	1.9	7.2	9.9
Tuvalu	-5.9	4.0	3.5	4.5	3.3	3.5	0.6	5.8	16.5
Vanuatu	4.5	3.6	2.3	6.8	4.1	5.4	11.4	4.6	9.9
Developed ADB Member Economies									
Australia[o]	1.6	2.1	0.1	1.8	-0.0	2.0	3.1	1.8	3.4
Japan	-0.3	3.6	2.0	0.6	1.6	0.2	1.2	-0.0	4.9
New Zealand	1.0	-0.1	-0.6	2.2	-0.2	1.1	3.2	1.8	7.4

... = data not available; | = marks break in series; * = provisional, preliminary, estimate; – = magnitude equals zero; (-/+) 0.0 = magnitude is less than half of unit employed; ADB = Asian Development Bank.

Note: Data refer to the whole of each economy, unless otherwise indicated.

a For 2010 onward, growth rates were calculated using price indexes with base year 2007/2008 = 100 (for 2010–2019) and base year 2015/2016 = 100 (for 2020–2022) for food and nonalcoholic beverages only.
b Prior to 2016, values were calculated based on the variable weights' method, while 2016 onward uses the fixed weights method. For 2021 onward, the consumer price index commodity grouping is based on the COICOP 2018.
c For 2016 onward, excludes nonalcoholic beverages.
d Data refer to end of period. For 2000–2005, figures are based on COICOP 1999. For 2006 onward, figures are based on COICOP 2018.
e Refers to food, beverages, and tobacco.
f Refers to food (including fish) and nonalcoholic beverages. Data prior to 2004, featured in the Key Indicators Database, also include tobacco and narcotics.
g Includes alcoholic beverages, tobacco, and narcotics; and restaurants and hotels.
h Refers to capital city.
i For 2010–2018, data refer to Indonesia's consumer price index group "Foodstuff" consisting of cereals, cassava, and related products; meat and related products; fresh fish; preserved fish; eggs, milk, and related products; vegetables; beans and nuts; fruits; spices; fats and oils; and other food items. The group does not include alcoholic and nonalcoholic beverages. For 2019–2022, data refer to food, beverages, and tobacco. Both alcoholic and nonalcoholic beverages are included in this group.
j Refers to fruits and vegetables; meat, poultry, and fish; cereal products; soft drink and sweets; farm products; fats and oils; other food; and prepared food.
k Refers to the Tarawa Retail Price Index, which is based on data for South Tarawa, to represent all of Kiribati. Data refer to the weighted average of food and nonalcoholic drinks price indexes.
l Refers to food.
m For 2010, refers to food.
n Refers to weighted average of four towns (Audi, Gizo, Honiara, and Noro).
o Includes restaurants and hotels.

Source: Economies' official sources.

Table 2.3.3: Growth Rates of Wholesale and/or Producer Price Indexes
(%)

ADB Regional Member	2010	2015	2016	2017	2018	2019	2020	2021	2022
Developing ADB Member Economies									
Central and West Asia									
Afghanistan	...	...	...	...	...	...	...	...	...
Armenia	22.6	-0.8	1.5	3.9	1.6	0.5	2.4	9.9	2.6
Azerbaijan	30.5	-30.6	27.5	36.8	26.0	3.2	-24.8	69.6	84.3
Georgia	11.3	7.5	-0.1	11.0	6.1	7.2	11.8	16.7	11.4
Kazakhstan	25.2	-20.5	16.8	15.3	19.0	5.1	-8.0	32.5	27.1
Kyrgyz Republic	22.8	8.8	6.4	1.7	1.5	4.3	21.3	11.5	5.1
Pakistan	13.8	-0.3	-1.1	4.5	5.3	16.0	10.2	9.4	24.9
Tajikistan	27.2	3.0	14.7	1.6	1.8	1.1	5.4	5.9	-3.4
Turkmenistan	...	...	...	...	...	...	...	...	...
Uzbekistan	15.6	13.5	14.8	17.5	31.8	43.2	14.9	9.3	16.8
East Asia									
China, People's Republic of	5.5	-5.2	-1.4	6.3	3.5	-0.3	-1.8	8.1	4.1
Hong Kong, China	6.0	-2.7	1.3	3.8	2.0	1.0	2.3	1.2	0.8
Korea, Republic of	3.8	-4.0	-1.8	3.5	1.9	0.0	-0.5	6.4	8.4
Mongolia	...	...	11.3	17.5	-8.1	23.9	-0.4	35.2	20.3
Taipei,China	5.5	-8.9	-3.0	0.9	3.6	-2.3	-7.8	9.5	12.4
South Asia									
Bangladesh[a]	8.9 (2006)	...	...	...	...	...	...	...	...
Bhutan	5.8 (2012)	0.6	1.2	5.8	4.7	-3.7	2.3	8.9	...
India	9.6	-3.7	1.7	2.9	4.3	1.7	1.3	13.0	9.4
Maldives	3.9	-2.4	...	...	...	...	...	...	...
Nepal	12.2	6.1	6.3	2.7	1.7	6.2	6.9	7.6	9.5
Sri Lanka	2.6	1.0	4.2	7.4	3.4	3.4	5.4	...	...
Southeast Asia									
Brunei Darussalam	...	...	...	...	...	...	...	...	...
Cambodia	...	...	...	...	...	...	...	...	...
Indonesia	4.9	4.4	7.9	4.6	5.5	0.9	1.3	2.6	4.7
Lao People's Democratic Republic	...	...	...	...	...	...	...	...	...
Malaysia	12.3 (2011)	-7.4	-1.1	6.7	-1.1	-1.4	-2.7	9.5	7.8
Myanmar	...	...	...	...	...	...	...	...	...
Philippines	5.9	1.6	0.9	1.9	1.9	1.6	2.5	3.1	7.3
Singapore	4.7	-15.3	-6.9	7.0	6.4	-3.3	-8.7	15.2	18.6
Thailand	9.4	-4.1	-1.2	0.7	0.5	-0.7	-1.6	4.7	10.4
Timor-Leste	...	...	...	...	...	...	...	...	...
Viet Nam	12.6	-0.6	-0.6	2.8	3.1	1.3	-0.6	2.9	4.2
The Pacific									
Cook Islands	...	...	...	...	...	...	...	...	...
Fiji	...	...	...	...	...	...	...	...	...
Kiribati	...	...	...	...	...	...	...	...	...
Marshall Islands	...	...	...	...	...	...	...	...	...
Micronesia, Federated States of	...	...	...	...	...	...	...	...	...
Nauru	...	...	...	...	...	...	...	...	...
Niue	...	...	...	...	...	...	...	...	...
Palau	...	...	...	...	...	...	...	...	...
Papua New Guinea	...	...	...	...	...	...	...	...	...
Samoa	...	...	...	...	...	...	...	...	...
Solomon Islands	...	...	...	...	...	...	...	...	...
Tonga	...	...	...	...	...	...	...	...	...
Tuvalu	...	...	...	...	...	...	...	...	...
Vanuatu	...	...	...	...	...	...	...	...	...
Developed ADB Member Economies									
Australia	-0.1	1.0	1.5	1.0	1.6	2.0	1.0	0.5	4.3
Japan	-0.1	-2.3	-3.5	2.3	2.6	0.2	-1.2	4.6	9.7
New Zealand	2.3	-1.3	0.8	4.8	3.4	2.1	1.0	4.6	8.3

... = data not available, 0.0 = magnitude is less than half of unit employed, ADB = Asian Development Bank.

a For agricultural and industrial products only.

Source: Economies' official sources.

Table 2.3.4: Growth Rates of Gross Domestic Product Deflator
(%)

ADB Regional Member	2010	2015	2016	2017	2018	2019	2020	2021	2022
Developing ADB Member Economies									
Central and West Asia									
Afghanistan	14.3	5.1 |	...	2.4	2.1	6.5	7.8	0.5	...
Armenia[a]	7.8 |	1.2	0.3	2.1	2.8	1.0	1.8	6.9	8.0
Azerbaijan	13.6	-8.8	14.7	16.2	12.2	-0.2	-7.5	21.6	37.3
Georgia	8.5	5.8	2.6	8.5	4.4	5.2	7.3	10.3	8.6*
Kazakhstan	19.6	1.9	13.6	8.4	9.2	7.6	4.2	13.9	18.6
Kyrgyz Republic	10.0	3.4	6.1	6.3	3.4	3.9	6.1	15.8	16.1
Pakistan	10.6	4.4	0.9	4.0	3.8	9.0	9.9	10.3	14.0
Tajikistan	12.4	5.5 (2014)	...	...	2.5	3.6	1.7	10.0	...
Turkmenistan	-3.9	-4.9	...	...	...	...	...	...	...
Uzbekistan	19.9	10.5	8.9	19.1 |	26.9	17.8	11.4	13.5	13.8*
East Asia									
China, People's Republic of	6.9	0.1	1.4	4.2	3.5	1.3	0.5	4.6	2.2*
Hong Kong, China	0.3	3.6	1.6	2.9	3.7	2.0	0.6	0.7	1.8
Korea, Republic of	2.7	3.2	2.0	2.2	0.5	-0.8	1.6	2.5	1.2
Mongolia	15.1 (2011)	7.4 | (2014)	3.0	10.8	8.0	10.0	3.7	14.4	15.7*
Taipei,China	-1.3	3.4	0.8	-0.8	-0.6	-0.2	1.9	2.5	2.0
South Asia									
Bangladesh	7.1	5.9	6.7	5.0	5.8	3.7	3.8	4.1	5.0
Bhutan	6.1	3.6	4.4	5.1	1.8	0.9	7.2	4.7	...
India	10.5	2.3	3.2	4.0	3.9	2.4	4.7	8.5	8.3
Maldives[b]	2.9	7.9	0.2	1.4	3.1	-1.3	0.4	1.7	...
Nepal	14.4 |	4.5	7.1	7.0	3.1	4.3	5.1	2.9	6.3
Sri Lanka	7.3	3.0	5.4	5.5	4.3	3.9	3.3	8.5	48.8
Southeast Asia									
Brunei Darussalam	5.3	-17.6	-9.2	5.0	9.2	-3.3	-10.9	15.5	24.2
Cambodia	3.1	1.7	3.4	3.3	3.1	3.4	-0.7	1.3	4.0*
Indonesia	7.3	4.0	2.4	4.3	3.8	1.6	-0.4	6.0	9.6
Lao People's Democratic Republic	3.1	2.3	3.0	1.9	1.9	1.2	2.8	3.6	11.6
Malaysia	5.4 (2011)	-0.4	1.7	3.8	0.6	0.1	-0.8	5.7	6.5
Myanmar	7.0	4.1	...	5.4	5.4	6.3	...	...	...
Philippines	4.4	-0.7	1.3	2.3	3.7	0.7	1.7	2.3	5.4
Singapore	1.1	3.1	0.5	2.9	3.5	-0.2	-2.7	8.8	9.1
Thailand	3.9	0.2	2.4	1.8	1.3	0.6	-1.0	1.5	4.4
Timor-Leste	11.0	7.2	0.1	-0.3	-1.3	5.0	-19.3	...	...
Viet Nam	12.1	-1.7	1.8	4.4	3.6	2.4	1.5	2.8	3.9
The Pacific									
Cook Islands	1.8	6.4	-2.1	-0.2	2.0	-1.4	8.1	34.7	...
Fiji	2.5	2.5	2.6	1.7	1.4	2.2	-1.2	-3.4	...
Kiribati	0.8	4.6	6.4	2.5	1.4	-0.4	2.3	8.7*	...
Marshall Islands	-0.7	-1.6	7.2	2.0	0.3	2.8	4.3	3.1	...
Micronesia, Federated States of	3.6	-5.3	4.0	7.5	9.4	1.5	0.5	...	...
Nauru	-18.1	-8.3	10.5	11.8	4.2	2.5	2.2	3.1	2.4
Niue	7.6	-0.3	0.6	3.9*	12.2*	4.4*	-0.3*	-7.9*	...
Palau	-0.1	8.9	6.9	-1.1	-6.2	0.1	4.1	-4.8	...
Papua New Guinea[c]	10.0	-1.4	2.3	7.7	10.0	1.1	1.6	12.0*	11.6*
Samoa	4.1	4.4	1.1	1.4	-0.2	1.6	1.6	1.5	8.7
Solomon Islands	1.7	3.4	0.3	2.6	7.9	1.2	-1.3	...	...
Tonga	7.8	5.3	3.1	5.6	5.1	7.7	-4.2	-1.9	...
Tuvalu	2.5	4.6	...	3.0	7.3	6.4	0.9	4.7	...
Vanuatu	1.5	5.9	1.6	5.4	3.2	3.3	...	...	...
Developed ADB Member Economies									
Australia	1.2	-0.6	-0.6	3.7	1.8	3.4	1.7	2.8	7.0
Japan	-1.9	2.1	0.4	-0.1	-0.0	0.6	0.9	-0.2	0.2
New Zealand	3.7	0.9	2.3	2.7	1.4	3.0	1.3	4.4	...

... = data not available; | = marks break in series; * = provisional, preliminary, estimate; (-/+) 0.0 = magnitude is less than half of unit employed; ADB = Asian Development Bank.

a For 2010, estimates are based on the 1993 System of National Accounts. For 2015 onward, estimates are based on the 2008 System of National Accounts.
b For 2015 onward, the gross domestic product (GDP) at current prices includes some product taxes that were not included in the calculation of GDP at constant prices, hence, the implicit GDP deflators may be overestimated.
c Data prior to 2021 were revised using NSO data from National Accounts 2006–2020, released in November 2022. For 2021 onward, data taken from the 2023 National Budget Volume 1 of the Department of Treasury of Papua New Guinea, which provides estimates or projections based on the actual National Accounts data from the NSO.

Source: Economies' official sources.

Money and Finance

Table 2.3.5: Growth Rates of Money Supply
(%)

ADB Regional Member	2010	2015	2016	2017	2018	2019	2020	2021	2022
Developing ADB Member Economies									
Central and West Asia									
Afghanistan	39.3	3.7	9.7	4.1	2.6	5.7	12.1	-11.1	2.5
Armenia	11.8	10.8	17.5	18.5	7.4	11.2	9.0	13.1	16.1
Azerbaijan[a]	24.3	-1.3	-1.9	9.0	5.7	20.0	1.1	18.7	23.6
Georgia[a]	30.1	17.3	21.1	14.6	13.9	17.6	24.6	11.4	11.4
Kazakhstan	23.1	8.0	46.2	7.5	7.1	11.0	19.2	24.1	18.0
Kyrgyz Republic	21.1	14.9	14.6	17.9	5.5	12.8	23.9	19.1	30.6*
Pakistan	13.0	12.8	14.5	13.9	9.5	10.8	18.3	14.7	13.1
Tajikistan	18.6	18.7	37.1	21.8	5.1	17.0	18.4	8.2	40.4
Turkmenistan[a]	74.2	18.0	9.4	11.4	8.4	12.9	11.8	-1.4	21.2
Uzbekistan	52.4	24.3	23.5	40.2	14.1	13.9	17.7	29.7	30.2
East Asia									
China, People's Republic of	18.9	13.3	11.3	9.0	8.1	8.7	10.1	9.0	11.8
Hong Kong, China	8.1	5.5	7.7	10.0	4.3	2.8	5.8	4.3	1.6
Korea, Republic of	6.0	8.2	7.1	5.1	6.7	7.9	9.8	12.9	4.0
Mongolia	62.5	-5.5	21.0	30.5	22.8	8.2	16.2	13.8	6.5
Taipei,China	5.5	5.8	3.6	3.6	2.7	4.5	9.4	7.4	6.7
South Asia									
Bangladesh	22.4	12.4	16.4	10.9	9.2	9.9	12.6	13.6	9.5
Bhutan	30.1	7.8	15.8	31.5	10.4	5.6	19.3	24.4	9.4
India[a]	16.1	10.1	10.1	9.2	10.5	8.9	12.2	8.8	9.0
Maldives	14.6	12.1	-0.2	5.2	3.4	9.5	14.2	26.2	6.0
Nepal	14.1	19.9	19.5	15.5	19.4	15.8	18.1	21.8	6.8
Sri Lanka	18.0	17.2	18.9	17.5	13.5	7.6	22.9	13.5	8.9
Southeast Asia									
Brunei Darussalam	4.8	-1.8	1.5	-0.4	2.8	4.3	-0.4	2.7	1.3
Cambodia	21.3	17.0	21.0	23.1	26.6	18.2	15.3	16.4	8.2
Indonesia	15.4	9.0	10.0	8.3	6.3	6.5	12.5	14.0	8.4
Lao People's Democratic Republic	39.5	14.7	10.9	12.2	8.4	18.9	16.3	24.0	36.9
Malaysia[a]	6.8	3.0	3.2	4.9	9.1	3.5	4.0	6.4	4.3
Myanmar	42.5	30.7	17.4	20.5	14.6	15.5	18.2	6.0	1.1*
Philippines[a]	10.0	9.4	12.8	11.9	9.5	11.5	9.6	7.9	6.8*
Singapore	8.6	1.5	8.0	3.2	3.9	5.0	13.2 |	...	1.9
Thailand	10.9	4.4	4.2	5.0	4.7	3.6	10.2	4.8	3.9
Timor-Leste	18.2	7.1	14.3	12.1	3.1	-7.1	10.2	28.7	8.6
Viet Nam	33.3	16.2	18.4	15.0	12.4	14.8	14.5	10.7	6.2
The Pacific									
Cook Islands	0.1	9.5	0.1	6.4	9.9	7.9	17.1	-5.3	7.2
Fiji[a]	3.5	13.9	5.3	8.1	2.5	2.7	1.2	11.1	3.6
Kiribati	...	...	...	...	...	...	...	...	...
Marshall Islands	9.4	28.6	19.9	23.9	-3.3	-4.9	21.8	11.7	...
Micronesia, Federated States of	...	...	...	...	...	...	...	...	...
Nauru	...	...	...	...	...	...	...	...	...
Niue	...	...	...	...	...	...	...	...	...
Palau	12.0 (2011)	30.9	17.4	0.3	0.3	-3.2	10.3	-1.1*	...
Papua New Guinea[a]	11.4	8.0	10.9	-0.7	-4.0	4.4	7.0	11.7	14.8
Samoa	6.4	6.0	9.2	15.2	8.8	4.6	5.4	1.7	7.3
Solomon Islands[a]	13.3	15.5	13.4	3.5	6.8	-3.1	6.6	1.9	5.3
Tonga	5.1	9.3	-2.9	11.3	10.6	1.8	1.1	19.3	14.1
Tuvalu	...	...	...	...	...	...	...	...	...
Vanuatu	1.3	11.4	10.6	9.3	13.1	7.0	-0.7	8.9	7.3
Developed ADB Member Economies									
Australia[a]	4.5	6.7	5.8	7.8	1.9	4.0	8.5	7.7	9.9
Japan[a]	1.9	2.5	3.2	2.9	2.2	2.0	7.7	3.3	2.3
New Zealand[b]	3.2	8.1 |	-10.9	7.3	6.4	4.7	12.2	7.1	1.8

... = data not available; | = marks break in series; * = provisional, preliminary, estimate; ADB = Asian Development Bank.

Note: Data are based on money supply M2 (M2), unless otherwise stated.

a Refers to money supply M3 (M3).
b Refers to M3 prior to 2016 and M2 for 2016 onward.

Source: Economies' official sources.

Table 2.3.6: Money Supply
(% of GDP)

ADB Regional Member	2010	2015	2016	2017	2018	2019	2020	2021	2022
Developing ADB Member Economies									
Central and West Asia									
Afghanistan	30.3	29.7 |	37.2	36.9	36.6	35.0	37.2 |	41.5	...
Armenia	26.3	36.8	43.0	46.4	46.1	47.2	54.4	54.5	52.0
Azerbaijan[a]	24.8	39.1	34.6	32.4	30.0	35.2	40.2	37.2	32.0
Georgia[a]	28.4	38.7	44.3	44.7	46.5	49.5	61.7	56.4	52.6*
Kazakhstan	30.1	21.0	26.8	24.9	23.4	23.1	27.1	28.3	27.6*
Kyrgyz Republic	31.4	33.3	34.4	36.5	35.8	37.2	47.4	45.9	48.3*
Pakistan	37.7	40.2 |	38.6	40.5	40.2	39.8	43.4	42.4	40.0
Tajikistan	18.0 |	21.2	27.0	28.0	26.7	28.0	31.3	28.1	34.5*
Turkmenistan[a]	17.3	48.2	...	...	...	...	...	...	...
Uzbekistan	17.7	19.1	20.4	23.1	19.6	17.9	18.5	19.7	21.3*
East Asia									
China, People's Republic of	176.1	202.1	207.7	203.1	198.7	201.4	215.8	207.3	220.2
Hong Kong, China	401.7	484.4	502.2	517.2	506.0	518.3	583.3	567.5	586.8
Korea, Republic of	125.5	135.5	138.3	137.8	142.3	151.4	164.9	174.4	174.8
Mongolia	48.0	43.9	50.8	56.6	59.8	55.7	65.4	64.8	56.1
Taipei,China	220.2	233.9	235.3	237.8	238.9	242.7	252.0	247.8	253.3
South Asia									
Bangladesh	45.5	52.0	44.2	43.7	42.1	41.3	43.3	44.3	48.4
Bhutan	64.0	55.8	57.8	68.3	70.3	70.2	82.6	100.2	103.0
India[a]	85.2	84.4	83.1	81.7	81.7	83.6	95.0	87.3	82.0
Maldives	47.9	48.3	45.2	43.8	40.6	42.0	71.8	62.8	58.1*
Nepal	60.3	77.5	86.1	84.2	89.5	92.8	108.8	120.5	113.5
Sri Lanka	27.3	35.1	37.6	39.4	41.9	43.4	54.2	54.8	43.5
Southeast Asia									
Brunei Darussalam	67.3	80.8	92.6	86.7	81.6	84.7	93.6	84.6	70.1
Cambodia	41.6	72.4	79.2	88.2	100.7	107.7	128.9	143.8	142.1
Indonesia	36.0	39.5	40.4	39.9	38.8	38.8	44.7	46.4	43.5
Lao People's Democratic Republic	38.0	51.2	51.5	53.1	53.1	59.1	64.8	75.0	88.0
Malaysia[a]	132.2	136.3	132.5	126.5	130.9	129.7	143.9	140.5	126.7
Myanmar	23.6	46.4	53.4	57.7	58.9	60.0	66.2	...	...
Philippines[a]	47.7	60.5	62.8	64.2	63.7	66.5	79.2	79.0	74.4*
Singapore	123.3	122.9	127.5	122.4	118.6	123.0	148.9 |	128.8	116.1
Thailand	109.0	127.7	125.4	124.0	122.8	123.4	146.6	148.8	143.9
Timor-Leste[b]	33.5	40.3	44.5	51.6	54.3 |	38.9	40.3	30.9	...
Viet Nam	101.8	116.0	126.4	130.2	131.4	137.2	150.5	158.0	149.5
The Pacific									
Cook Islands	83.1	59.3	57.7	56.2	57.3	59.9	86.8	77.6	...
Fiji[a]	67.6	73.3	73.4	74.1	72.1	72.8	89.9*	108.9*	92.7*
Kiribati	...	...	...	...	...	...	...	...	...
Marshall Islands	63.0	82.9	91.4	106.7	99.3	87.2	104.1	110.6	...
Micronesia, Federated States of	...	...	...	...	...	...	...	...	...
Nauru	...	...	...	...	...	...	...	...	...
Niue	...	...	...	...	...	...	...	...	...
Palau	46.2	72.2	79.7	82.4	83.4	82.1	98.6*	115.4*	...
Papua New Guinea[a]	34.0	33.6	34.5	30.7	26.9	26.5	29.3	28.6	28.4
Samoa	43.8	41.1	42.5	48.5	51.3	51.4	59.3	60.8	64.4
Solomon Islands[a]	28.6	40.4	43.2	42.3	40.8	38.4	42.9	44.9	46.8
Tonga	41.2	47.5	42.0	42.8	45.0	42.2	44.3	55.4	...
Tuvalu	...	...	...	...	...	...	...	...	...
Vanuatu	83.3	78.6	82.5	82.9	88.3	88.8	90.1	92.0	91.8
Developed ADB Member Economies									
Australia[a]	94.2	109.5	113.5	115.3	112.1	110.3	117.8	120.7	119.5
Japan[a]	216.6	232.5	237.1	240.2	243.8	248.2	276.6	280.4	283.2
New Zealand[c]	111.6	121.6 |	102.2	102.2	102.9	102.0	113.0	115.0	107.1

... = data not available; | = marks break in series; * = provisional, preliminary, estimate; ADB = Asian Development Bank; GDP = gross domestic product.

Note: Data are based on money supply M2 (M2), unless otherwise stated.

a Refers to money supply M3 (M3).
b From September 2019, oil revenue from the Joint Petroleum Development Area is now included in GDP based on the new Timor-Leste Australia Maritime Boundary Treaty.
c Refers to M3 prior to 2016 and M2 for 2016 onward.

Source: Economies' official sources.

Table 2.3.7: Interest Rates on Savings and Time Deposits
(% per annum, period averages)

ADB Regional Member	Savings Deposits									Time Deposits[a]								
	2010	2015	2016	2017	2018	2019	2020	2021	2022	2010	2015	2016	2017	2018	2019	2020	2021	2022
Developing ADB Member Economies																		
Central and West Asia																		
Afghanistan	5.4	3.1	1.6	1.3	1.6	1.5	0.8	...	...	8.2	5.2	4.4	3.1	2.3	3.4	2.4	...	...
Armenia	...	...	...	...	...	...	...	...	...	10.7	15.4	12.5	9.6	9.4	9.3	9.2	9.2	9.2
Azerbaijan	...	...	...	...	...	...	...	...	...	11.0	8.2	5.5	12.1	9.8	9.4	8.6	8.8	...
Georgia[b]	8.7	5.3	4.5	4.0	4.3	4.7	5.2	4.9	5.5	11.6	7.0	6.7	6.1	5.8	5.7	6.6	6.6	7.5
Kazakhstan[c]	...	...	...	...	...	...	...	...	...	9.8	7.5	11.4	11.2	10.5	9.1	8.6	8.3	11.1
Kyrgyz Republic	...	...	...	...	...	...	...	...	...	11.5	14.5	13.3	10.8	10.3	9.5	9.8	11.0	12.9
Pakistan	5.0	4.7	3.7	3.5	4.1	8.6	5.9	5.0	10.7	7.2	5.9	4.7	4.3	4.6	8.0	6.2	5.2	9.1
Tajikistan	3.8	0.9	1.2	1.4	1.1	0.6	1.0	0.9	0.4	17.8	15.6	16.4	14.6	12.8	11.6	10.7	11.5	10.6
Turkmenistan	...	...	...	...	...	...	...	...	...	11.3 (2004)	...	...	...	...	...	...	...	...
Uzbekistan[d]	...	16.5	18.1	18.0	15.9	18.3	18.6	19.4	20.6	...	18.3	18.7	18.5	16.4	18.6	19.2	18.7	19.8
East Asia																		
China, People's Republic of	0.4	0.4	0.4	0.4	0.4	0.4	0.4	0.4	0.4	2.3	2.1	1.5	1.5	1.5	1.5	1.5	1.5	1.5
Hong Kong, China	–	–	–	–	0.0	0.1	0.0	0.0	0.1	0.2	0.1	0.1	0.2	0.2	0.3	0.2	0.1	0.1
Korea, Republic of[e]	3.2	1.7	1.5	1.5	1.8	1.7	1.0	1.1	2.7	3.9	1.8	1.6	1.7	2.0	1.9	1.2	1.2	3.1
Mongolia[f]	10.7	13.0	12.4	11.7	11.2	10.5	8.4	5.8	10.9	...	...	...	12.8	11.8	10.9	8.8	6.2	11.1
Taipei,China	0.2	0.3	0.3	0.2	0.2	0.2	0.1	0.1	0.4	1.0	1.3	1.1	1.1	1.1	1.1	0.8	0.8	1.2
South Asia																		
Bangladesh[g]	4.9	4.5	3.6	3.2	3.3	3.3	2.8	2.2	2.3	9.0	9.0	7.3	6.4	7.4	8.2	6.5	5.7	6.2
Bhutan[h]	4.8	5.3	5.3	5.5	5.3	5.4	5.4	5.3	...	6.8	6.8	7.0	7.0	7.8	7.8	7.6	7.8	...
India	3.5	4.0	4.0	...	...	...	...	...	...	7.5	6.2	5.5	...	...	...	...	...	...
Maldives[i]	2.3	2.2	1.7	1.5	1.5	1.5	1.5	1.5	1.5	4.3	4.0	3.4	3.5	3.7	3.3	3.8	3.6	4.0
Nepal	7.0	2.9	2.2	4.0	4.6	5.0	4.2	3.0	6.2	8.1	6.5	5.8	10.4	10.4	9.8	9.0	7.3	10.1
Sri Lanka	5.0	5.0	4.3	4.0	4.0	4.0	3.5	3.5	3.0	8.5	7.3	11.0	11.0	10.5	9.8	5.3	5.5	12.0
Southeast Asia																		
Brunei Darussalam	0.4	0.3	0.3	0.3	0.3	0.3	0.1	0.1	0.2	0.7	0.8	0.7	0.7	0.8	0.8	0.3	0.2	0.4
Cambodia	1.2	1.2	1.5	1.2	0.6	0.6	0.6	1.0	0.9	6.6	7.4	7.4	6.4	6.2	6.3	6.3	6.2	7.6
Indonesia	3.9	1.7	1.5	1.5	1.3	1.1	0.8	0.7	0.7	7.9	8.5	7.3	6.8	6.5	6.8	5.7	3.8	4.7
Lao People's Democratic Republic	3.4	2.6	1.8	1.7	1.8	1.8	1.7	1.7	1.7	9.1	7.6	5.6	5.4	5.4	5.4	5.4	5.3	5.4
Malaysia	0.9	1.1	1.0	1.0	1.0	1.0	0.6	0.5	0.7	2.8	3.3	3.2	3.1	3.3	3.2	2.1	1.7	2.1
Myanmar	...	...	...	10.0	10.0	10.0	6.2	5.0	5.0	...	...	...	8.0	8.0	8.0	5.8	5.0	5.0
Philippines[j]	1.6	0.7	0.7	0.7	0.9	1.2	0.2*	0.1*	0.2*	2.1	3.1	3.0	2.8	3.5	4.6	2.1*	1.7*	3.6*
Singapore	0.1	0.1	0.1	0.2	0.2	0.2	0.1	0.2	0.5	0.5	0.3	0.4	0.3	0.5	0.6	0.3	0.3	1.7
Thailand	0.5	0.5	0.5	0.5	0.5	0.5	0.3	0.3	0.4	1.6	1.4	1.4	1.4	1.4	1.3	0.5	0.5	1.0
Timor-Leste	0.8	0.8	0.8	0.4	0.4	0.5	0.5	0.5	0.5	1.3	1.3	1.2	0.7	0.7	0.7	0.6	0.6	0.7
Viet Nam[k]	3.0	0.7	0.6	0.6	0.5	0.5	0.2	0.1	0.4	11.5	6.3	6.8	6.9	7.1	7.3	6.8	5.5	6.6
The Pacific																		
Cook Islands	...	...	...	...	...	...	...	...	...	...	...	...	...	...	...	...	...	...
Fiji	1.0	0.9	0.9	1.3	1.3	1.2	0.9	0.5	0.4	5.6	2.6	2.9	3.2	3.4	4.6	3.3	2.3	1.3
Kiribati	...	...	...	...	...	...	...	...	...	...	...	...	...	...	...	...	...	...
Marshall Islands	0.5	0.3	0.2	0.2	0.2	0.2	0.2	0.1	...	3.5	1.5	1.5	1.3	1.1	0.9	0.8	0.7	...
Micronesia, Federated States of	...	...	...	...	...	...	...	...	...	...	...	...	...	...	...	...	...	...
Nauru	...	...	...	...	...	...	...	...	...	...	...	...	...	...	...	...	...	...
Niue	...	...	...	...	...	...	...	...	...	...	...	...	...	...	...	...	...	...
Palau	0.9	0.1	0.1	0.1	0.1	0.1	...	...	...	0.8	0.2	0.2	0.2	0.4	0.4	...	...	...
Papua New Guinea	1.0	0.4	0.6	0.5	0.7	1.0	0.9	0.3	1.5	4.8	2.1	2.0	2.0	2.0	1.3	0.1	1.5	0.3
Samoa	1.0	1.0	1.0	1.0	1.0	1.0	1.0	1.0	1.0	2.9	2.9	2.9	2.9	2.9	2.9	2.9	2.9	2.9
Solomon Islands	0.3	0.3	0.3	0.3	0.4	0.6	0.5	0.6	0.6	5.0	0.7	0.9	1.0	1.3	1.5	1.6	1.2	1.4
Tonga	1.5	2.5	2.5	2.4	2.4	2.5	2.6	2.5	...	3.0	4.9	5.3	5.4	5.2	4.8	4.8	4.0	...
Tuvalu	...	...	...	...	...	...	...	...	...	...	...	...	...	...	...	...	...	...
Vanuatu	1.8	–	–	–	–	–	–	0.1	0.5	6.0	3.4	0.5	4.4	2.3	2.0	2.0	1.9	2.0
Developed ADB Member Economies																		
Australia[l]	4.4	2.1	1.7	1.7	0.9	0.6	0.2	0.1	0.3	6.0	2.5	2.4	2.3	2.2	1.7	0.8	0.3	0.7
Japan[m]	0.0	0.0	0.0	0.0	0.0	0.0	0.0	0.0	0.0	0.1	0.1	0.0	0.0	0.0	0.0	0.0	0.0	0.0
New Zealand[n]	...	...	...	...	...	...	...	...	...	4.7	3.3	3.3	3.3	3.3	2.6	0.8	1.5	4.5

... = data not available; – = magnitude equals zero; * = provisional, preliminary, estimate; 0.0 = magnitude is less than half of unit employed; ADB = Asian Development Bank.

a Refers to interest rate on time deposits of 12 months, unless otherwise indicated.
b Refers to deposits allocated with maturity of more than 1 year.
c Refers to interest rates on deposits of more than 12 months.
d Refers to weighted average interest rate on all time household savings deposits and time deposits from 181 to 365 days.
e Refers to weighted averages of interest rates on newly extended time and savings deposits of commercial and specialized banks.
f Rates for savings deposits include both demand and time deposits. Rates for time deposits refer to the time deposit rate.
g Refers to savings bank accounts with checking facilities.
h For savings deposits, actual range of rates for 2015–2016 is 5.0%–7.0%; for 2017, 5.0%–6.0%; for 2019 and 2020, 5.0%–5.75%; and for 2021, from 5.0% to 5.6%. For time deposits, rate refers to fixed deposits of 1 year to less than 2 years for 2010 and actual range of rates is 4.5%–6.5%; for 2015–2017, 6.5%–7.5%; for 2018 and 2019, 6.0%–9.5%; for 2020, 6.0%–9.1%; and for 2021, 6.5%–9.1%.
i Refers to time deposits of 6 months to 1 year (local currency). Figures represent a weighted average.
j Rates for savings deposits refer to the annual percentage equivalent of commercial banks' actual monthly interest expenses on peso-savings deposits to the total outstanding levels of these deposits. Rates for time deposits refer to rates charged on interest-bearing deposits with maturities of over 1 year.
k For 2010, the rate for time deposit refers to maximum interest per annum for state enterprise deposits.
l Refers to interest rates of online savings deposits.
m Refers to savings deposits of at least ¥0.3 million, calculated as the arithmetic average of weekly figures. Refers to time deposits from 12 months to less than 2 years, calculated as the arithmetic average of the monthly figures.
n Refers to interest rate on time deposits of 6 months.

Sources: Economies' official sources. For the People's Republic of China: CEIC Database. https://www.ceicdata.com/en (accessed 17 July 2023).

Table 2.3.8: Yield on Short-Term Treasury Bills and Lending Interest Rates
(% per annum, period averages)

ADB Regional Member	Yield on Short-Term Treasury Bills[a]					Lending Interest Rates				
	2010	2015	2020	2021	2022	2010	2015	2020	2021	2022
Developing ADB Member Economies										
Central and West Asia										
Afghanistan	...	...	...	...	...	15.6	15.0	...	...	...
Armenia[b]	10.6	12.9	5.8	7.8	10.6	19.2	17.6	11.6	11.8	11.7
Azerbaijan	1.8	13.0 (2016)	...	...	...	20.7	17.5	17.2	16.4	14.6
Georgia	9.6	8.8	8.6	8.9	10.2	15.8	12.5	11.8	12.5	13.7
Kazakhstan[c]	3.2	4.0	10.7	86.3	12.6	...	...	...	...	...
Kyrgyz Republic	10.4	12.8	5.9	7.1	8.1	23.7	23.6	17.0	16.6	18.7
Pakistan[d]	12.5	7.1	8.6	7.6	...	14.0	10.2	10.8	8.7	...
Tajikistan[e]	6.7	0.8	...	...	...	23.4	25.8	23.5 (2019)	...	...
Turkmenistan	...	...	...	...	...	...	...	...	...	...
Uzbekistan	...	...	13.9	13.3	16.4	...	13.8	22.3	21.4	21.7
East Asia										
China, People's Republic of[f]	2.6	3.7	2.9	2.9	2.8	5.8	4.4	4.4	4.4	4.4
Hong Kong, China[g]	0.2	0.0	0.4	0.0	1.6	5.0	5.0	5.0	5.0	5.1
Korea, Republic of[h]	2.7	1.8	0.9	0.9	2.5	5.5	3.5	2.8	2.9	4.3
Mongolia[i]	13 (2012)	14.5	...	...	...	20.1	19.6	16.9	16.0	...
Taipei,China[j]	0.3	0.4	0.3	0.2	0.5	2.7	2.8	2.4	2.4	2.8
South Asia										
Bangladesh[e]	4.5	5.8	4.8	1.3	5.0	12.2	11.7	8.3	7.3	7.1
Bhutan[e]	2.0	0.1	2.8	0.4	0.3	13.9	14.9	14.0	14.0	...
India[e,k]	6.2	7.4	3.3	3.5	5.8	8.3	10.0	9.2	8.7	8.6
Maldives[l]	4.9	6.8	3.5	3.5	3.5	10.4	11.1	11.6	11.6	10.9
Nepal[e]	6.9	0.7	1.9	3.1	8.8	...	...	...	...	...
Sri Lanka[m]	8.6	6.7	9.1 (2019)	...	...	10.2	7.0	11.2 (2019)	...	...
Southeast Asia										
Brunei Darussalam	...	...	...	...	...	5.5	5.5	5.5	5.5	5.5
Cambodia	...	...	...	...	...	...	...	...	...	...
Indonesia	7.0	8.3	5.5	3.7	3.2	13.3	12.7	9.5	8.9	8.5
Lao People's Democratic Republic[n]	8.0	...	...	...	...	22.6	...	...	...	...
Malaysia	2.6	3.1	2.0	1.8	...	5.0	4.6	3.9	3.4	4.1
Myanmar	...	...	...	...	...	20.9	16.0	14.8	...	...
Philippines[e]	3.5	1.7	2.0	1.1	2.2	7.7	5.6	7.1 (2019)	...	...
Singapore	0.3	0.3 (2013)	...	...	...	5.4	5.4	5.3	5.3	...
Thailand[e]	1.4	1.6	0.6	0.4	0.7	4.3	4.7	3.3	3.1	3.1
Timor-Leste	...	...	...	...	...	11.0 (2011)	13.5	14.1	11.2	11.0
Viet Nam[o]	11.1	4.2	...	...	...	13.1	7.1	7.6	7.8	8.0
The Pacific										
Cook Islands	...	...	...	...	...	...	...	...	...	...
Fiji[e]	3.4	1.2	1.8	0.6	0.0	7.5	5.8	6.2	5.9	5.4
Kiribati	...	...	...	...	...	...	...	...	...	...
Marshall Islands	...	...	...	...	...	...	...	...	...	...
Micronesia, Federated States of	...	...	...	...	...	15.1	15.7	14.5	12.6	...
Nauru	...	...	...	...	...	...	...	...	...	...
Niue	...	...	...	...	...	...	...	...	...	...
Palau	...	...	...	...	...	...	...	...	...	...
Papua New Guinea[p]	4.6	5.3	7.2	4.3	2.8	10.4	8.7	7.8	7.7	8.0
Samoa	...	...	...	...	...	10.7	9.5	8.7	8.5	8.3
Solomon Islands[e]	3.7	0.5	0.5	0.5	0.5	14.4	10.5	10.7	5.2	...
Tonga	...	...	...	...	...	9.9 (2012)	8.2	7.8	7.8	7.9
Tuvalu	...	...	...	...	...	...	...	...	...	...
Vanuatu	...	...	...	...	...	...	10.2	9.8	9.3	8.8
Developed ADB Member Economies										
Australia[q]	4.7	2.3	0.3	0.0	1.6	7.3	5.6	5.1 (2019)	...	...
Japan	0.4	0.2	-0.0	-0.1	-0.0	1.6	1.1	...	...	...
New Zealand	2.8	3.0	0.4	0.4	2.7	6.3	5.8	- (2018)	...	...

... = data not available, - = magnitude equals zero, (-/+) 0.0 = magnitude is less than half of unit employed, ADB = Asian Development Bank.

a Refers to 3-month Treasury bills, unless otherwise indicated.
b Refers to average yield on 9-month to 12-month Treasury bills since March 2001.
c Refers to short-term Treasury bills with maturities of 3, 6, 9, and 12 months.
d Refers to weighted average yield on 6-month Treasury securities.
e Refers to 91-day Treasury bills.
f Refers to 3-month Treasury bonds trading rate.
g Refers to annualized yields on 91-day Exchange Fund bills.
h Refers to 91-day certificates of deposit.
i Refers to weighted average rate on Treasury bills of all maturities. From December 2012 onward, refers to yield on 12-week Treasury bills.
j Refers to prime lending rates.
k Figures are for fiscal year ending March.
l Refers to rate on 28-day Treasury bills.
m Refers to weighted average rate on the last monthly issuance of 364-day Treasury bills since December 2001.
n Refers to weighted average auction rate for 12-month Treasury bills.
o Refers to average monthly yield on 360-day Treasury bills sold at auction.
p Refers to rate on 182-day Treasury bills.
q Refers to estimated closing yield in the secondary market on 13-week Treasury notes.

Sources: International Monetary Fund. International Financial Statistics. http://data.imf.org/ (accessed 27 June 2023); and Organisation for Economic Co-operation and Development. Main Economic Indicators. https://stats.oecd.org/ (accessed 28 June 2023). For Bhutan; India; Kazakhstan; and Taipei,China: Economies' official sources. For Malaysia for 2017–2022: Bank Negara Malaysia. Monthly Highlights and Statistics. https://www.bnm.gov.my/-/monthly-highlights-statistics-in-april-2023 (accessed 27 June 2023).

Table 2.3.9: Domestic Credit Provided by Banking Sector, and Bank Nonperforming Loans

ADB Regional Member	Domestic Credit Provided by Banking Sector[a] (% of GDP)						Bank Nonperforming Loans[b] (% of total gross loans)						
	2010	2015	2018	2019	2020	2021	2010	2015	2018	2019	2020	2021	2022
Developing ADB Member Economies													
Central and West Asia													
Afghanistan	...	...	...	...	...	...	49.9	12.1	8.9	...	...	...	...
Armenia	27.8	48.3	62.4	65.4	83.4	74.6	3.0	7.9	4.8	5.5	6.6	...	...
Azerbaijan	...	28.1 (2016)	13.1	14.6	15.4	16.4	...	...	...	...	...	...	2.6
Georgia	33.8	52.1	64.2	69.1	83.3	77.3	5.9	2.7	2.7	1.9	2.3	1.9	1.5
Kazakhstan	...	45.7	36.3	35.0	40.2	39.0	20.9	8.0	7.4	8.1	6.9	...	...
Kyrgyz Republic	...	...	...	...	...	...	14.8	6.7	7.3	7.7	10.1	10.8	12.5
Pakistan	...	...	...	...	...	...	...	11.4	8.0	8.6	9.2	7.9	7.3
Tajikistan	7.6	19.7	15.3	15.5	13.6	10.6	6.1	26.3	31.1	27.0	23.8	13.7	...
Turkmenistan	...	...	...	...	...	...	...	...	...	...	...	...	...
Uzbekistan	...	...	...	...	...	...	1.0	1.5	1.3	1.5	2.1	5.1	3.5
East Asia													
China, People's Republic of	...	...	...	...	...	...	1.1	1.7	1.8	1.9	1.8	1.7	...
Hong Kong, China	...	...	...	...	...	...	0.8	0.7	0.5	0.6	0.9	0.9	...
Korea, Republic of	...	...	...	...	...	...	0.6	0.5	0.3	0.3	0.2	0.2	...
Mongolia	...	...	...	...	...	...	...	...	...	...	...	...	...
Taipei,China[c]	0.9	...	...	...	...	...	0.6	0.2	0.2	0.2	0.2	0.2	0.2
South Asia													
Bangladesh	...	...	...	...	...	...	1.9 (2011)	8.4	9.9	8.9	7.7	8.0	...
Bhutan	...	...	...	...	...	97.7	5.2	6.6	7.0	8.4	...	...	...
India	...	...	...	...	...	...	...	5.9	9.5	9.2	7.9	6.5	...
Maldives	76.9	61.3	64.7	64.8	124.8	95.0	...	13.6	8.9	9.4	8.2	6.7	5.9
Nepal	...	...	...	...	...	...	...	...	1.6	1.7	1.7	1.2	2.4
Sri Lanka	...	...	...	...	...	...	...	3.2	3.4	4.7	4.9	4.5	11.5
Southeast Asia													
Brunei Darussalam	22.7	40.0	27.7	29.5	66.1	54.2	6.9	4.0	3.9	3.9	3.9	3.1	2.8
Cambodia	...	...	...	...	...	...	3.1	1.6	2.0	1.6	1.8	1.7	2.7
Indonesia	34.2	46.8	47.2	46.5	53.7	54.3	2.3	2.3	2.2	2.3	2.6	2.6	2.1
Lao People's Democratic Republic	...	...	...	...	...	...	...	...	...	...	...	...	...
Malaysia	...	...	...	...	...	...	3.4	1.6	1.5	1.5	1.6	1.7	1.7
Myanmar	...	...	...	...	...	...	...	...	...	...	...	...	...
Philippines	...	82.3 (2017)	82.9	86.5	100.3	100.8	3.3	1.9	1.7	2.0	3.5	4.0	...
Singapore	...	...	...	...	...	...	1.4	0.9	1.3	1.3	...	...	...
Thailand	133.4	171.2	166.4	169.0	194.7	203.7	3.9	2.7	...	...	3.2	3.1	2.8
Timor-Leste	...	...	...	...	...	...	...	...	...	...	...	...	...
Viet Nam	...	...	...	...	...	...	2.1	2.8	2.1	1.8	1.9	1.6	...
The Pacific													
Cook Islands	...	...	...	...	...	...	...	...	...	...	...	...	...
Fiji	131.7	111.4	124.7	135.6	173.2	195.9	4.4	1.4	3.1	3.8	6.2	8.5	...
Kiribati	...	...	...	...	...	...	...	...	...	...	...	...	...
Marshall Islands	...	...	...	...	...	...	...	...	...	...	...	...	...
Micronesia, Federated States of	...	...	...	...	...	...	...	0.2	0.3	0.3	0.1	0.3	...
Nauru	...	...	...	...	...	...	...	...	...	...	...	...	...
Niue	...	...	...	...	...	...	...	...	...	...	...	...	...
Palau	...	...	...	...	...	...	...	...	...	...	...	...	...
Papua New Guinea	23.7	40.5	36.5	37.3	41.7	38.1	1.9	3.1	3.7	3.8	5.3	6.2	4.8
Samoa	60.0	72.5	75.0	77.0	76.5	86.1	...	...	3.6	4.0	3.8	3.6	5.0
Solomon Islands	20.3	21.5	24.3	25.6	27.5	28.5	9.3	4.1	7.1	10.4	10.7	10.4	...
Tonga	...	...	...	...	...	...	...	7.7	3.6	3.2	3.7	3.5	...
Tuvalu	...	...	...	...	...	...	...	...	...	...	...	...	...
Vanuatu	...	...	...	...	...	...	4.8	12.3	...	...	...	...	...
Developed ADB Member Economies													
Australia	...	...	...	...	...	...	2.1	0.9	0.9	1.0	1.1	0.9	0.7
Japan	309.7	338.7	348.2	359.9	391.5	395.0	...	...	...	...	...	...	...
New Zealand	...	160.1	163.5	167.5	185.7	...	...	...	...	...	...	...	...

... = data not available, ADB = Asian Development Bank, GDP = gross domestic product.

a Domestic credit provided by the financial sector includes all credit to various sectors on a gross basis, with the exception of credit to the central government, which is net. The financial sector includes monetary authorities and deposit money banks, as well as other financial corporations where data are available (including corporations that do not accept transferable deposits, but do incur such liabilities as time and savings deposits). Examples of other financial corporations are finance and leasing companies, money lenders, insurance corporations, pension funds, and foreign exchange companies.

b Bank nonperforming loans to total gross loans are the value of nonperforming loans divided by the total value of the loan portfolio (including nonperforming loans before the deduction of specific loan-loss provisions). The loan amount recorded as nonperforming should be the gross value of the loan as recorded on the balance sheet, not just the amount that is overdue.

c Before 1 July 2005, nonperforming loans include loans in which payment of principal is past due for three months or more, repayment of interest is past due for six months or more, and installment repayment loans for medium to long-term is past due for six months or more. Starting 1 July 2005, includes loans in which repayment of principal or interest has been overdue for more than 3 months and any loan of which the principal debtors and surety have been sued for non-payment or the underlying collateral has been disposed, although the repayment of principal or interest has not been overdue for more than 3 months.

Sources: International Monetary Fund. Financial Soundness Indicators. http://data.imf.org/ (accessed 19 June 2023); World Bank. World Development Indicators. https://databank.worldbank.org/source/world-development-indicators (accessed 19 June 2023). For Taipei,China: Central bank of Taipei,China.

Table 2.3.10: Growth Rates of Stock Market Price Index
(%)

ADB Regional Member	2010	2015	2016	2017	2018	2019	2020	2021	2022
Developing ADB Member Economies									
Central and West Asia									
Afghanistan	...	...	...	...	...	...	...	...	...
Armenia	...	...	...	...	...	...	...	...	...
Azerbaijan	...	...	...	...	...	...	...	...	...
Georgia	...	...	...	...	...	...	...	...	...
Kazakhstan	...	...	...	...	...	...	...	...	...
Kyrgyz Republic	...	...	...	...	...	...	...	...	...
Pakistan[a]	28.2	2.1	45.7	...	...	...	...	...	...
Tajikistan	...	...	...	...	...	...	...	...	...
Turkmenistan	...	...	...	...	...	...	...	...	...
Uzbekistan	...	...	...	-0.5	0.7	-42.7	8.6	40.0	-19.5
East Asia									
China, People's Republic of	3.4	66.0	-19.0	6.7	...	...	...	...	...
Hong Kong, China	19.3	4.8	-12.0	22.3	10.2	-4.3	-8.4	7.3	-24.8
Korea, Republic of	23.6	1.4	-1.2	16.5	0.5	-9.4	5.4	40.1	-18.9
Mongolia	88.7	-14.6	-14.0	33.5	30.5	-0.8	-13.0	100.2	...
Taipei,China	23.1	-0.4	-2.2	16.5	4.0	1.6	11.9	40.3	-7.8
South Asia									
Bangladesh[a]	82.8	-4.8	8.8	24.0	-13.8	-17.3	21.3	25.1	-8.1
Bhutan	...	...	...	...	...	...	...	...	...
India	29.8	10.9	-3.6	8.6	...	...	...	...	...
Maldives	-20.4	8.9	4.8	7.4	6.8	5.2	7.7	0.0	32.2
Nepal	...	...	...	...	...	...	...	...	...
Sri Lanka[a]	96.0	-5.5	-9.7	2.3	-5.0	1.3	...	...	...
Southeast Asia									
Brunei Darussalam	...	...	...	...	...	...	...	...	...
Cambodia	...	...	...	...	...	...	...	...	...
Indonesia[a]	46.1	-12.1	15.3	20.0	-2.5	1.7	-5.1	10.1	4.1
Lao People's Democratic Republic	...	...	...	...	...	...	...	...	...
Malaysia	27.1	-6.1	-3.8	5.0	2.2	-8.4	-7.3	3.3	-3.7
Myanmar	...	...	...	...	...	...	...	...	...
Philippines	43.1	5.5	0.9	8.0	0.1	2.8	-21.1	8.5	-13.7
Singapore	30.3	-2.5	-11.6	10.3	...	...	...	...	...
Thailand	45.6	0.2	-2.1	12.7	6.6	-4.7	-18.1	17.6	3.2
Timor-Leste	...	...	...	...	...	...	...	...	...
Viet Nam[a]	12.2	6.1	14.8	...	...	...	...	...	...
The Pacific									
Cook Islands	...	...	...	...	...	...	...	...	...
Fiji	-11.1	22.0	26.4	22.4	57.6	45.0	1.5	-11.2	-4.3
Kiribati	...	...	...	...	...	...	...	...	...
Marshall Islands	...	...	...	...	...	...	...	...	...
Micronesia, Federated States of	...	...	...	...	...	...	...	...	...
Nauru	...	...	...	...	...	...	...	...	...
Niue	...	...	...	...	...	...	...	...	...
Palau	...	...	...	...	...	...	...	...	...
Papua New Guinea	26.2	-6.3	...	...	7.5	-2.9	...	...	...
Samoa	...	...	...	...	...	...	...	...	...
Solomon Islands	...	...	...	...	...	...	...	...	...
Tonga	...	...	...	...	...	...	...	...	...
Tuvalu	...	...	...	...	...	...	...	...	...
Vanuatu	...	...	...	...	...	...	...	...	...
Developed ADB Member Economies									
Australia[a]	-2.6	-2.1	7.0	7.0	-6.9	...	...	...	...
Japan	2.0	22.7	-12.6	...	...	...	...	...	...
New Zealand	9.7	12.7	17.4	11.1	14.8	18.0	12.3	10.8	-9.4

... = data not available, 0.0 = magnitude is less than half of unit employed, ADB = Asian Development Bank.

Note: All data in the table refer to growth rates of stock market prices (period average), unless otherwise indicated.

a Refers to growth rates of end-of-period stock market prices.

Sources: Asian Development Bank estimates using data from the International Monetary Fund's International Financial Statistics. http://data.imf.org/IFS (accessed 16 June 2023). For Taipei,China: Annual statistics from the stock exchange corporation in Taipei,China.

Table 2.3.11: Stock Market Capitalization

ADB Regional Member	Stock Market Capitalization ($ million)					Stock Market Capitalization (% of GDP)				
	2010	2015	2020	2021	2022	2010	2015	2020	2021	2022
Developing ADB Member Economies										
Central and West Asia										
Afghanistan	...	...	...	...	...	...	...	...	...	...
Armenia	...	...	...	...	...	...	...	...	...	...
Azerbaijan	...	...	1,434.4	1,595.3	1,468.0	...	...	3.4	2.9	1.9
Georgia	...	...	...	...	...	...	...	...	...	...
Kazakhstan	26,672.7	34,891.9	38,173.2	65,696.9	45,705.6	18.0	18.9	22.3	33.3	20.7
Kyrgyz Republic	...	...	...	...	...	...	...	...	...	...
Pakistan[a]	38,007.2	...	50,278.5	43,096.6	28,713.9	21.5	...	16.7	12.4	7.6
Tajikistan	...	...	...	...	...	...	...	...	...	...
Turkmenistan	...	...	...	...	...	...	...	...	...	...
Uzbekistan	...	...	...	...	...	...	...	...	...	...
East Asia										
China, People's Republic of	4,027,840.3	8,188,019.3	12,214,465.6	14,374,520.3	11,425,343.0	66.2	74.0	83.2	80.7	63.6
Hong Kong, China	2,711,316.2	3,184,874.2	6,130,420.4	5,434,177.1	4,566,809.1	1,185.9	1,029.4	1,777.2	1,473.0	1,269.1
Korea, Republic of	1,091,911.5	1,231,199.8	2,176,189.5	2,218,658.1	1,644,507.6	95.4	84.0	132.3	122.5	98.8
Mongolia	...	...	...	...	...	...	...	...	...	...
Taipei,China	752,520.1	768,179.4	1,518,132.7	2,008,469.9	1,486,585.8	169.4	143.7	225.5	258.9	194.9
South Asia										
Bangladesh	41,616.9	65,484.9	89,773.7	108,740.8	42,894.8	36.1	33.6	24.0	26.1	9.3
Bhutan	219.0	374.0	640.4	635.9	...	14.1	18.7	27.5	25.0	...
India	1,762,461.9	1,745,169.2	2,595,465.6	...	...	105.2	83.0	97.2	...	...
Maldives	...	...	...	...	...	...	...	...	...	...
Nepal	...	...	...	...	...	...	...	...	...	...
Sri Lanka	19,923.9	20,804.1	15,981.9	27,056.9	10,598.2	34.0	24.4	18.9	30.6	14.2
Southeast Asia										
Brunei Darussalam	...	...	...	...	...	...	...	...	...	...
Cambodia	...	...	...	...	...	...	...	...	...	...
Indonesia	360,388.1	353,271.0	496,086.1	578,631.4	610,288.4	47.7	41.0	46.8	48.8	46.3
Lao People's Democratic Republic	...	...	...	...	...	...	...	...	...	...
Malaysia	408,689.1	382,976.7	436,537.9	414,285.3	381,207.2	160.3	127.1	129.4	111.1	93.8
Myanmar	...	...	...	...	...	...	...	...	...	...
Philippines	157,320.5	238,819.9	272,790.3	285,423.3	238,581.1	75.5	77.9	75.4	72.4	59.0
Singapore	647,226.4	639,955.9	652,614.7	663,388.5	619,361.7	269.9	207.8	187.3	156.5	132.7
Thailand	277,731.7	348,798.0	543,164.6	598,908.3	604,355.0	81.4	86.9	108.5	118.5	122.0
Timor-Leste	...	...	...	...	...	...	...	...	...	...
Viet Nam[b]	30,115.5	58,734.0	186,008.5	278,794.1	170,152.3	20.5	24.5	53.7	76.1	41.6
The Pacific										
Cook Islands	...	...	...	...	...	...	...	...	...	...
Fiji	...	...	...	...	...	...	...	...	...	...
Kiribati	...	...	...	...	...	...	...	...	...	...
Marshall Islands	...	...	...	...	...	...	...	...	...	...
Micronesia, Federated States of	...	...	...	...	...	...	...	...	...	...
Nauru	...	...	...	...	...	...	...	...	...	...
Niue	...	...	...	...	...	...	...	...	...	...
Palau	...	...	...	...	...	...	...	...	...	...
Papua New Guinea	11,027.3	1,718.9	...	...	...	77.4	7.9	...	...	...
Samoa	...	...	...	...	...	...	...	...	...	...
Solomon Islands	...	...	...	...	...	...	...	...	...	...
Tonga	...	...	...	...	...	...	...	...	...	...
Tuvalu	...	...	...	...	...	...	...	...	...	...
Vanuatu	...	...	...	...	...	...	...	...	...	...
Developed ADB Member Economies										
Australia[c]	1,454,490.6	1,187,083.5	1,720,556.2	1,887,400.8	1,679,171.9	126.6	87.9	129.7	121.6	100.2
Japan	3,827,774.2	4,894,919.1	6,718,219.6	6,544,303.5	5,380,475.5	66.5	110.1	133.1	130.7	127.2
New Zealand	35,506.9 (2009)	74,350.5	132,198.5	122,933.8	97,545.7	29.3 (2009)	41.8	62.2	48.1	39.5

... = data not available, $ = United States dollars, ADB = Asian Development Bank, GDP = gross domestic product.

a For 2010, data refer to Karachi Stock Exchange. For 2018 onward, data refer to Pakistan Stock Exchange.
b Data refer to the sum of Hanoi Stock Exchange and Ho Chi Minh Stock Exchange.
c Include investment funds.

Sources: For stock market capitalization ($ million): World Bank. World Development Indicators. https://databank.worldbank.org/source/world-development-indicators (accessed 20 July 2023); and World Federation of Exchanges. Statistics Portal. https://statistics.world-exchanges.org (accessed 20 July 2023). For stock market capitalization (% of GDP): Asian Development Bank (ADB) estimates using data from World Bank and World Federation of Exchanges. For Bhutan and Taipei,China: ADB estimates using data from economies' official sources. For India: World Bank. World Development Indicators. https://databank.worldbank.org/source/world-development-indicators (accessed 20 July 2023).

Table 2.3.12: Official Exchange Rates
(local currency units per $, period averages)

ADB Regional Member	2010	2015	2016	2017	2018	2019	2020	2021	2022
Developing ADB Member Economies									
Central and West Asia									
Afghanistan	46.5	61.1	67.9	68.0	72.1	77.7	76.8	82.9	90.4*
Armenia	373.7	477.9	480.5	482.7	483.0	480.4	489.0	503.8	435.7
Azerbaijan	0.8	1.0	1.6	1.7	1.7	1.7	1.7	1.7	1.7
Georgia	1.8	2.3	2.4	2.5	2.5	2.8	3.1	3.2	2.9
Kazakhstan	147.4	221.7	342.2	326.0	344.7	382.7	413.0	425.9	460.2
Kyrgyz Republic	46.0	64.5	69.9	68.9	68.8	69.8	77.3	84.6	84.1
Pakistan	85.2	102.8	104.8	105.5	121.8	150.0	161.8	162.9	204.9
Tajikistan	4.4	6.2	7.8	8.5	9.2	9.5	10.3	11.3	11.0
Turkmenistan	2.9	3.5	3.5	3.5	3.5	3.5	3.5	3.5	3.5
Uzbekistan[a]	1,578.4	2,568.0	2,965.3	5,113.9	8,069.6	8,836.8	10,054.3	10,609.5	11,050.1
East Asia									
China, People's Republic of	6.8	6.2	6.6	6.8	6.6	6.9	6.9	6.4	6.7
Hong Kong, China	7.8	7.8	7.8	7.8	7.8	7.8	7.8	7.8	7.8
Korea, Republic of	1,156.5	1,131.0	1,160.8	1,131.0	1,100.2	1,165.4	1,180.3	1,144.0	1,291.4
Mongolia	1,357.1	1,970.3	2,140.3	2,439.8	2,472.5	2,663.5	2,813.3	2,849.3	3,140.7
Taipei,China	31.6	31.9	32.3	30.4	30.2	30.9	29.6	28.0	29.8
South Asia									
Bangladesh	69.6	77.9	78.5	80.4	83.5	84.5	84.9	85.1	91.7
Bhutan	45.7	64.2	67.2	65.1	68.4	70.4	74.1	73.9	78.6
India	45.7	64.2	67.2	65.1	68.4	70.4	74.1	73.9	78.6
Maldives	12.8	15.4	15.4	15.4	15.4	15.4	15.4	15.4	15.4
Nepal	73.3	102.4	107.4	104.5	108.9	112.6	118.3	118.1	125.2
Sri Lanka	113.1	135.9	145.6	152.4	162.5	178.7	185.6	198.8	322.6
Southeast Asia									
Brunei Darussalam	1.4	1.4	1.4	1.4	1.3	1.4	1.4	1.3	1.4
Cambodia	4,184.9	4,067.8	4,058.7	4,050.6	4,051.2	4,061.1	4,092.8	4,098.7	4,102.0
Indonesia	9,090.4	13,389.4	13,308.3	13,380.8	14,236.9	14,147.7	14,582.2	14,308.1	14,849.9
Lao People's Democratic Republic	8,254.2	8,127.6	8,124.4	8,244.8	8,401.3	8,679.4	9,045.8	9,697.9	14,035.2
Malaysia	3.2	3.9	4.1	4.3	4.0	4.1	4.2	4.1	4.4
Myanmar[b]	5.6	1,162.6	1,234.9	1,360.4	1,429.8	1,518.3	1,381.6	1,615.7	1,905.8
Philippines	45.1	45.5	47.5	50.4	52.7	51.8	49.6	49.3	54.5
Singapore	1.4	1.4	1.4	1.4	1.3	1.4	1.4	1.3	1.4
Thailand	31.7	34.2	35.3	33.9	32.3	31.0	31.3	32.0	35.1
Timor-Leste[c]	1.0	1.0	1.0	1.0	1.0	1.0	1.0	1.0	1.0
Viet Nam	18,612.9	21,697.6	21,935.0	22,370.1	22,602.1	23,050.2	23,208.4	23,159.8	23,271.2
The Pacific									
Cook Islands[d]	1.4	1.4	1.4	1.4	1.4	1.5	1.5	1.4	1.6
Fiji	1.9	2.1	2.1	2.1	2.1	2.2	2.2	2.1	2.2
Kiribati	1.1	1.3	1.3	1.3	1.3	1.4	1.5	1.3	1.4
Marshall Islands[c]	1.0	1.0	1.0	1.0	1.0	1.0	1.0	1.0	1.0
Micronesia, Federated States of[c]	1.0	1.0	1.0	1.0	1.0	1.0	1.0	1.0	1.0
Nauru	1.1	1.3	1.3	1.3	1.3	1.4	1.5	1.3	1.4
Niue[d]	1.4	1.4	1.4	1.4	1.4	1.5	1.5	1.4	1.6
Palau[c]	1.0	1.0	1.0	1.0	1.0	1.0	1.0	1.0	1.0
Papua New Guinea	2.7	2.8	3.1	3.2	3.3	3.4	3.5	3.5	...
Samoa	2.5	2.6	2.6	2.6	2.6	2.6	2.7	2.6	2.7
Solomon Islands	8.1	7.9	7.9	7.9	8.0	8.2	8.2	8.0	8.2
Tonga	1.9	2.1	2.2	2.2	2.2	2.3	2.3	2.3	2.3
Tuvalu[e]	1.1	1.3	1.3	1.3	1.3	1.4	1.5	1.3	1.4
Vanuatu	96.9	109.0	108.5	107.8	110.2	114.7	115.4	109.5	115.4
Developed ADB Member Economies									
Australia	1.1	1.3	1.3	1.3	1.3	1.4	1.5	1.3	1.4
Japan	87.8	121.0	108.8	112.2	110.4	109.0	106.8	109.8	131.5
New Zealand	1.4	1.4	1.4	1.4	1.4	1.5	1.5	1.4	1.6

... = data not available; * = provisional, preliminary, estimate; $ = United States (US) dollars; ADB = Asian Development Bank.

a Data show weighted averages of the official, bank, and parallel market rates.
b Beginning 1 April 2012, the Central Bank of Myanmar adopted the managed float exchange rate regime for kyat vis-à-vis the US dollar.
c Unit of currency is the US dollar.
d Unit of currency is the New Zealand dollar.
e Unit of currency is the Australian dollar.

Sources: International Monetary Fund. International Financial Statistics. https://data.imf.org/ (accessed 14 July 2023). For Afghanistan for 2021: Official statistics from national and international sources, and for 2022: Asian Development Bank estimates based on statistics from the bank's Afghanistan Resident Mission. For the Republic of the Marshall Islands: Economic Policy, Planning and Statistics Office. Official communication, 16 May 2023. For Sri Lanka for 2022: Central Bank of Sri Lanka. https://www.cbsl.gov.lk/en/rates-and-indicators/exchange-rates (accessed 15 May 2023). For Taipei,China: Central bank of Taipei,China. Official communication, 18 April 2023. For Turkmenistan for 2000–2008: United Nations Statistics Division. UN National Accounts Main Aggregates Database. https://unstats.un.org/unsd/snaama/countryprofile (accessed 30 May 2023), and for 2009–2022: ADB estimates using data from the Central Bank of Turkmenistan. For Uzbekistan for 2000–2012: United Nations Statistics Division. UN National Accounts Main Aggregates Database. https://unstats.un.org/unsd/snaama/countryprofile (accessed 10 May 2023), and for 2013–2022: Central Bank of Uzbekistan. https://cbu.uz/en/statistics/e-gdds/data/111573/ (accessed 10 May 2023).

Exchange Rates

Table 2.3.13: Purchasing Power Parity Conversion Factor
(local currency units per $, period averages)

ADB Regional Member	2010	2011	2016	2017	2018	2019	2020	2021	2022
Developing ADB Member Economies									
Central and West Asia									
Afghanistan	14.55	16.61	17.45	17.21	17.15	17.95	19.10	18.37	...
Armenia	160.19	163.65	161.23	155.97	156.56	155.43	156.20	159.75	161.33
Azerbaijan	0.32	0.38	0.43	0.51	0.55	0.54	0.50	0.58	0.74
Georgia	0.76	0.81	0.75	0.80	0.82	0.85	0.90	0.95	0.96
Kazakhstan	69.52	82.09	110.82	121.25	129.31	136.72	140.65	153.35	167.93
Kyrgyz Republic	13.11	15.73	16.74	16.96	17.13	17.49	18.33	20.31	22.04
Pakistan	21.30	24.96	32.38	33.59	34.06	36.48	39.60	41.76	44.10
Tajikistan	1.41	1.56	2.03	2.23	2.23	2.27	2.28	2.40	2.38
Turkmenistan	1.29	1.43	1.61	1.62	1.60	1.61	1.69	...	...
Uzbekistan	505.24	602.00	1,179.96	1,432.91	1,775.98	2,055.50	2,261.19	2,457.05	2,614.18
East Asia									
China, People's Republic of	3.33	3.52	3.99	4.18	4.23	4.21	4.17	4.18	3.99
Hong Kong, China	5.14	5.23	5.93	6.01	6.09	6.10	6.06	5.84	5.56
Korea, Republic of	840.99	854.59	858.81	872.62	854.87	856.43	837.67	854.10	831.94
Mongolia	473.09	533.53	729.22	791.44	834.38	901.42	922.79	1,010.46	1,093.21
Taipei,China	15.81	15.15	15.78	15.73	15.27	14.98	15.06	14.77	14.07
South Asia									
Bangladesh	22.15	23.41	28.50	29.74	30.73	31.29	32.07	31.96	31.37
Bhutan	15.42	16.40	18.83	19.21	19.09	18.92	20.02	20.07	...
India	14.60	15.55	19.90	20.65	20.95	21.07	21.79	22.63	22.91
Maldives	7.12	7.86	8.13	8.16	8.22	7.97	7.90	7.70	7.34
Nepal	20.40	25.25	32.00	31.23	31.83	32.74	33.35	34.08	34.18
Sri Lanka	38.57	39.29	46.28	49.39	50.30	51.33	52.32	54.33	75.57
Southeast Asia									
Brunei Darussalam	0.60	0.71	0.67	0.65	0.69	0.66	0.58	0.64	0.74
Cambodia	1,354.17	1,371.24	1,402.13	1,428.35	1,438.23	1,458.59	1,430.13	1,386.32	1,369.96
Indonesia	3,336.63	3,512.75	4,518.10	4,695.66	4,760.51	4,751.37	4,671.33	4,738.86	4,852.35
Lao People's Democratic Republic	2,463.99	2,666.53	2,759.43	2,789.11	2,775.92	2,759.65	2,861.25	2,839.91	3,123.40
Malaysia	1.42	1.47	1.59	1.65	1.63	1.60	1.57	1.58	1.58
Myanmar	245.89	261.78	347.07	366.71	377.61	394.19	404.07	405.27	418.53
Philippines	17.78	18.10	18.95	19.39	19.64	19.43	19.49	19.08	18.81
Singapore	0.85	0.85	0.88	0.89	0.90	0.88	0.84	0.88	0.89
Thailand	12.19	12.39	12.73	12.84	12.72	12.62	12.30	11.97	11.72
Timor-Leste	0.42	0.45	0.43	0.41	0.39	0.41	0.32	0.49	0.49
Viet Nam	5,814.02	6,915.34	7,315.61	7,395.34	7,483.63	7,529.89	7,541.98	7,418.23	7,200.21
The Pacific									
Cook Islands	...	...	...	...	...	...	...	...	...
Fiji	0.89	0.95	0.94	0.94	0.93	0.93	0.91	0.84	0.83
Kiribati	0.97	0.96	1.03	1.04	1.03	0.99	1.02	1.06	1.04
Marshall Islands	0.89	0.94	0.97	0.97	0.94	0.88	0.92	0.94	0.93
Micronesia, Federated States of	0.88	0.88	0.89	0.94	1.01	1.00	1.00	0.98	0.97
Nauru	0.92	1.00	1.17	1.33	1.40	1.31	1.32	1.29	1.25
Niue	...	...	...	...	...	...	...	...	...
Palau	0.77	0.75	0.93	0.91	0.89	0.85	0.83	0.79	...
Papua New Guinea	1.82	1.86	1.90	2.01	2.15	2.14	2.14	2.29	2.39
Samoa	1.71	1.66	1.76	1.73	1.71	1.70	1.70	1.62	1.61
Solomon Islands	6.23	6.37	6.82	6.86	7.23	7.19	7.00	6.78	6.77
Tonga	1.48	1.45	1.49	1.54	1.58	1.68	1.59	1.49	...
Tuvalu	1.11	1.11	1.27	1.29	1.35	1.41	1.41	1.41	1.42
Vanuatu	99.82	100.51	104.31	107.85	108.70	110.29	111.90	107.84	105.74
Developed ADB Member Economies									
Australia	1.50	1.51	1.45	1.48	1.47	1.48	1.45	1.45	1.42
Japan	111.71	107.45	105.52	105.10	104.16	104.23	102.43	102.05	97.57
New Zealand	1.50	1.49	1.44	1.43	1.47	1.42	1.41	1.46	1.46

... = data not available, $ = United States dollars, ADB = Asian Development Bank.

Note: For 2011 and 2017, purchasing power parity (PPP) figures are based on results from the 2011 and 2017 benchmark cycles of the International Comparison Program (ICP). For 2010 (and years prior featured in the Key Indicators Database), PPPs are extrapolated from the revised 2011 ICP PPP estimates. For 2012–2016, figures are interpolated from the two ICP reference years 2011 and 2017. For 2018 onward, figures are extrapolated from the 2017 ICP PPPs or imputed based on a regression model.

Sources: World Bank. World Development Indicators. https://databank.worldbank.org/source/world-development-indicators (accessed 19 July 2023).
For Taipei,China: for 2010 and 2018–2022, Asian Development Bank estimates using data from the economy's official sources and World Bank data; for 2011–2017, World Bank. DataBank: ICP 2017. https://databank.worldbank.org/source/icp-2017 (accessed 19 July 2023).

Table 2.3.14: Price Level Indexes
(PPPs to official exchange rates, period averages, United States = 100)

ADB Regional Member	2010	2011	2016	2017	2018	2019	2020	2021	2022
Developing ADB Member Economies									
Central and West Asia									
Afghanistan	31.3	35.5	25.7	25.3	23.8	23.1	24.9	21.7	...
Armenia	42.9	43.9	33.6	32.3	32.4	32.4	31.9	31.7	37.0
Azerbaijan	39.8	48.6	27.0	29.4	32.6	31.9	29.2	34.0	43.6
Georgia	42.7	48.1	31.6	32.1	32.4	30.1	28.9	29.4	33.0
Kazakhstan	47.2	56.0	32.4	37.2	37.5	35.7	34.1	36.0	36.5
Kyrgyz Republic	28.5	34.1	23.9	24.6	24.9	25.1	23.7	24.0	26.2
Pakistan	25.4	29.2	31.0	32.0	31.0	26.7	25.0	26.1	24.8
Tajikistan	32.2	33.9	25.9	26.1	24.4	23.9	22.1	21.2	21.6
Turkmenistan	45.2	50.0	46.1	46.4	45.8	45.9	48.4	...	...
Uzbekistan	31.9	35.1	39.8	28.0	22.0	23.3	22.5	23.2	23.7
East Asia									
China, People's Republic of	49.2	54.5	60.0	61.9	63.9	60.9	60.5	64.8	59.2
Hong Kong, China	66.2	67.2	76.4	77.1	77.6	77.8	78.1	75.1	70.9
Korea, Republic of	72.7	77.1	74.0	77.2	77.7	73.5	71.0	74.7	64.4
Mongolia	34.9	42.2	34.1	32.4	33.7	33.8	32.8	35.5	34.8
Taipei,China	50.0	51.4	48.8	51.7	50.6	48.4	50.9	52.7	47.3
South Asia									
Bangladesh	32.0	32.9	36.4	37.6	37.4	37.2	37.8	37.7	36.4
Bhutan	33.7	35.1	28.0	29.5	27.9	26.9	27.0	27.1	...
India	32.0	32.4	29.7	32.0	30.0	29.7	29.4	30.4	28.5
Maldives	55.7	53.8	52.9	53.0	53.4	51.8	51.4	50.1	47.7
Nepal	27.4	34.9	30.1	29.4	30.5	29.0	28.7	28.9	28.3
Sri Lanka	34.1	35.5	31.8	32.4	31.0	28.7	28.2	27.3	23.3
Southeast Asia									
Brunei Darussalam	43.9	56.1	48.2	46.8	51.1	48.0	41.8	47.4	53.6
Cambodia	32.4	33.8	34.5	35.3	35.5	35.9	34.9	33.8	33.4
Indonesia	36.7	40.1	33.9	35.1	33.4	33.6	32.0	33.1	32.7
Lao People's Democratic Republic	29.9	33.2	34.0	33.8	33.0	31.8	31.6	29.3	22.3
Malaysia	44.1	47.9	38.4	38.5	40.3	38.6	37.2	38.2	35.8
Myanmar	25.2	32.9	28.2	27.2	27.3	25.7	28.3	27.2	22.5
Philippines	39.4	41.8	39.9	38.5	37.3	37.5	39.3	38.7	34.5
Singapore	62.7	67.3	63.6	64.2	66.4	64.4	61.1	65.4	64.9
Thailand	38.5	40.6	36.1	37.8	39.4	40.7	39.3	37.4	33.4
Timor-Leste	41.6	45.5	43.2	40.9	39.4	40.7	32.4	49.4	48.8
Viet Nam	31.2	33.7	33.4	33.1	33.1	32.7	32.5	32.0	30.9
The Pacific									
Cook Islands	...	...	...	...	...	...	...	...	...
Fiji	46.1	53.0	44.7	45.4	44.6	43.2	42.0	40.6	37.6
Kiribati	88.6	99.2	76.8	79.5	77.0	68.9	70.1	79.7	72.0
Marshall Islands	89.3	93.9	96.7	97.3	94.0	88.1	92.3	93.8	93.1
Micronesia, Federated States of	88.3	87.9	89.4	94.3	100.7	100.2	99.7	97.6	97.0
Nauru	80.7	98.5	85.0	100.0	108.4	94.0	88.7	95.9	90.8
Niue	...	...	...	...	...	...	...	...	...
Palau	77.0	74.9	92.9	91.0	88.6	84.8	83.2	79.4	...
Papua New Guinea	66.9	78.4	60.6	62.9	65.3	63.0	61.9	65.3	67.9
Samoa	67.4	69.6	67.3	68.3	66.6	65.1	63.1	63.2	62.0
Solomon Islands	77.2	83.4	85.8	87.0	90.9	87.9	85.2	84.4	83.0
Tonga	76.5	79.3	67.1	69.8	72.2	73.8	68.6	65.3	...
Tuvalu	102.3	114.5	94.7	98.7	100.8	98.1	96.7	105.7	98.4
Vanuatu	103.0	112.3	96.2	100.0	98.7	96.1	97.0	98.5	91.5
Developed ADB Member Economies									
Australia	132.4	149.0	105.6	111.4	114.0	105.8	97.5	108.0	103.0
Japan	127.3	134.6	97.0	93.7	94.3	95.6	95.9	93.0	74.2
New Zealand	107.9	117.4	100.3	101.7	101.7	93.3	91.7	103.2	92.8

... = data not available, ADB = Asian Development Bank, PPP = purchasing power parity.

Sources: World Bank. World Development Indicators. https://databank.worldbank.org/source/world-development-indicators (accessed 19 July 2023).
For Taipei,China: Asian Development Bank estimates using data from the economy's official sources and the World Bank's DataBank: ICP 2017. https://databank.worldbank.org/source/icp-2017 (accessed 19 July 2023).

Data Issues and Comparability

Not all reporting economies meet the standards and classifications of the International Monetary Fund (IMF) on the compilation of monetary and financial statistics available on the fund's Dissemination Standards Bulletin Board.[4]

Consumer price index coverage differs across economies. Most economies try to follow the Classification of Individual Consumption by Purpose guidelines, but the implementation varies across economies. In some instances, the basket of goods and services in the index is outdated or represents only urban areas (or the capital city). Other price measurements, such as the wholesale price index and the producer price index, are not available in Pacific economies.

Broad money supply in most economies relates to M2, which includes cash, checking deposits, savings deposits, money market securities, mutual funds, and other time deposits. However, 11 of the 44 economies with available data reported M3, thereby posing limits to comparability as M3 also includes less liquid financial assets. Not all economies publish the same types of aggregates, and even when aggregates have the same name (i.e., M1, M2, M3, etc.), their asset composition often differs significantly. For example, the definition of M2 in one economy may include time deposits with maturities of 1 year or less, whereas another economy's M2 definition may include time deposits with maturities of 2 years or less.

Finally, some economies use the central bank policy rate, while others use commercial bank rates in measuring banks' average deposit and lending rates.

4 For more information on the IMF's standards and classifications on the compilation of monetary and financial statistics, go to http:// dsbb.imf. org/Pages/SDDS/StatMethod.aspx.

Table 2.4.1: Trade in Goods Balance
(% of GDP)

ADB Regional Member	2010	2015	2018	2019	2020	2021	2022
Developing ADB Member Economies							
Central and West Asia							
Afghanistan	-27.3	-32.4	-31.2	-28.0	-25.3	-25.8	...
Armenia	-22.3	-11.2	-14.2	-12.6	-10.9	-10.9	-10.5
Azerbaijan	37.3	11.0	20.9	17.7	5.9	20.6	34.8*
Georgia	-21.5	-26.4	-23.4	-21.7	-20.0	-20.3	-20.9*
Kazakhstan	20.1	4.2	13.4	10.1	3.5	12.3	16.5*
Kyrgyz Republic	-27.8	-33.8	-36.7	-29.6	-18.5	-27.7	-62.4*
Pakistan	-6.5	-6.4	-8.7	-8.6	-7.0	-8.2	-10.6
Tajikistan	-43.9	-27.7	-24.3	-23.1	-17.8	-19.2	-28.2*
Turkmenistan	9.9	-5.3	...	...	...	...	...
Uzbekistan	1.3	-2.4	-13.0	-12.1	-10.3	-12.6	-13.9*
East Asia							
China, People's Republic of	3.9	5.2	2.7	2.8	3.5	3.2	3.7*
Hong Kong, China	1.4	-7.4	-8.9	-4.2	-1.5	0.9	-1.6
Korea, Republic of	4.2	8.2	6.4	4.8	4.9	4.2	0.9
Mongolia	-2.4	4.8	5.1	8.2	13.2	9.1	7.3*
Taipei,China	8.3	13.7	11.0	9.4	11.2	11.3	9.1
South Asia							
Bangladesh	-4.5	-3.6	-5.7	-4.5	-5.0	-5.7	-7.2*
Bhutan	-19.3	-21.8	-16.6	-16.4	-13.0	-6.9	-24.0*
India	-7.6	-6.2	-6.7	-5.6	-3.8	-6.0	-7.8*
Maldives[a]	-40.9 |	-40.4	-45.8	-42.6	-38.8	-39.0	-47.1*
Nepal[b]	-25.5	-27.4	-32.9	-33.3	-27.3	-31.7	-34.3
Sri Lanka[a]	-8.2 |	-9.9	-10.9	-9.0	-7.1	-9.2	-6.7
Southeast Asia							
Brunei Darussalam	45.3	22.4	17.4	16.4	11.5	19.1	30.9*
Cambodia	-23.9	-21.9	-23.8	-26.8	-9.8	-41.6	-29.9
Indonesia	4.1	1.6	-0.0	0.3	2.7	3.7	4.8
Lao People's Democratic Republic[a]	-4.7 |	-14.0	-5.0	-2.5	3.9	7.4	6.2
Malaysia	15.1	9.3	7.9	8.2	9.7	11.0	9.5
Myanmar[a]	0.1 |	-6.1	-6.3	...	...	...	...
Philippines	-8.1	-7.6	-14.7	-13.1	-9.3	-13.4	-17.2*
Singapore	26.4	30.1	27.7	26.0	30.5	29.7	29.2
Thailand	7.8	6.5	4.4	4.9	8.1	6.4	2.2
Timor-Leste[a,c]	-31.8 |	-39.9	-37.6 |	5.6	41.0	51.9	...
Viet Nam[a]	-3.5 |	3.1	5.2	6.3	8.9	4.3	6.3*
The Pacific							
Cook Islands	-18.2	-30.2	-30.2	-32.3	-31.0*	-30.7*	...
Fiji	-23.5	-19.5	-24.4	-25.4	-14.6	-22.0*	...
Kiribati	-41.1	-52.6	-46.8	-53.0	-54.9	-59.5*	...
Marshall Islands	-49.4	-28.6	-28.6	-54.8	-22.2	-28.6	...
Micronesia, Federated States of	-43.2	-40.4	-32.0	...	...	...	...
Nauru	33.6 (2012)	-47.9	-46.0	-45.7	-57.9*	-57.7*	-53.1*
Niue	-60.3	-40.2	-41.4*	...	...	...	...
Palau	-45.7	-49.1	-48.5	-52.1	-59.4*	-60.7*	...
Papua New Guinea[a]	15.5 |	22.1	24.9	27.2	23.0	10.3*	...
Samoa	-36.7	-32.0	-32.5	-33.6	-29.8	-36.0	-44.1
Solomon Islands	-15.2	-1.3	0.3	-2.3	-1.7	-6.3	-13.5
Tonga[d]	-53.0 |	-70.4	-80.5	-83.5	-82.0	-36.8	...
Tuvalu[d]	-54.3 |	-88.5	-32.9	-57.8	-52.2	-53.0	...
Vanuatu	-28.3	-37.0	-26.2	-29.5	-22.8	...	...
Developed ADB Member Economies							
Australia	-0.7	-0.8	0.7	2.7	3.6	3.6	6.3
Japan	1.9	-0.2	0.2	0.0	0.5	0.3	-2.8
New Zealand	1.4	-1.0	-1.5	-0.9	0.5	-2.1	...

... = data not available, | = marks break in series due to change in compilation methodology, (-/+) 0.0 = magnitude is less than half of unit employed, * = provisional or preliminary, ADB = Asian Development Bank, GDP = gross domestic product.

a Change in compilation methodology from the International Monetary Fund's Balance of Payments Manual (fifth edition) [BPM5] to the International Monetary Fund's Balance of Payments and International Investment Position Manual (sixth edition) [BPM6].

b Based on BPM5.

c From September 2019, oil revenue from the Joint Petroleum Development Area is now included in GDP based on the new Timor-Leste Australia Maritime Boundary Treaty.

d Change in compilation methodology from BPM4 to BPM6.

Source: Economies' official sources.

Table 2.4.2: Trade in Services Balance
(% of GDP)

ADB Regional Member	2010	2015	2018	2019	2020	2021	2022
Developing ADB Member Economies							
Central and West Asia							
Afghanistan	6.1	-1.4	-3.4	-2.9	-2.0	-2.7	...
Armenia	-2.8	-0.9	0.1	-0.6	0.9	2.9	8.4
Azerbaijan	-3.3	-8.0	-4.4	-5.4	-6.7	-3.9	-1.7*
Georgia	4.5	9.4	12.8	12.5	0.8	3.9	10.9*
Kazakhstan	-4.9	-2.6	-2.7	-2.1	-1.9	-1.0	-0.7*
Kyrgyz Republic	-4.2	-3.3	-1.6	0.7	-2.3	-2.5	-1.0*
Pakistan	-1.0	-1.1	-1.8	-1.5	-1.1	-0.7	-1.3
Tajikistan	-0.5	-2.5	-2.8	-3.0	-3.3	-4.3	-5.2*
Turkmenistan	...	...	...	...	...	...	...
Uzbekistan	-2.5	-0.8	-4.6	-3.8	-3.1	-3.9	-3.1*
East Asia							
China, People's Republic of	-0.2	-2.0	-2.1	-1.8	-1.0	-0.6	-0.5*
Hong Kong, China	4.4	9.8	8.7	5.8	3.5	4.7	5.5
Korea, Republic of	-1.2	-1.0	-1.7	-1.6	-0.9	-0.3	-0.3
Mongolia	-4.2	-6.2	-15.0	-14.0	-10.9	-11.1	-14.0*
Taipei,China	-2.5	-2.0	-1.1	-0.8	0.6	1.6	1.7
South Asia							
Bangladesh	-1.1	-1.6	-1.3	-0.9	-0.7	-0.7	-0.9*
Bhutan	-5.1	-3.5	-1.4	-2.1	-3.8	-4.8	-7.4*
India	2.6	3.3	3.0	3.0	3.3	3.4	4.2*
Maldives[a]	34.8 |	49.6	36.0	36.4	21.1	48.3	50.2*
Nepal[b]	-1.3	1.1	0.0	-0.4	-0.0	-1.7	-2.2
Sri Lanka[a]	1.2 |	2.7	4.0	3.2	1.0	1.8	2.7
Southeast Asia							
Brunei Darussalam	-5.9	-7.8	-7.4	-8.8	-7.1	-5.0	-5.1*
Cambodia	9.0	9.5	9.7	10.4	-1.0	-5.3	-1.5
Indonesia	-1.3	-1.0	-0.6	-0.7	-0.9	-1.2	-1.5
Lao People's Democratic Republic[a]	2.4 |	-1.6	-1.5	-0.4	-0.5	-0.7	-1.0
Malaysia	0.8	-1.8	-1.2	-0.7	-3.3	-3.9	-2.5
Myanmar[a]	-0.0 |	2.2	1.8	...	...	...	...
Philippines	2.8	1.8	3.3	3.5	3.8	3.6	3.9*
Singapore	-0.1	-2.8	1.8	3.5	0.7	5.6	7.0
Thailand	-2.1	3.9	4.4	4.5	-2.9	-6.4	-4.5
Timor-Leste[a,c]	-107.7 |	-36.5	-22.3	-21.8	-31.3	-20.8	...
Viet Nam[a]	-1.7 |	-2.0	-0.7	-0.3	-3.0	-4.2	-3.1*
The Pacific							
Cook Islands	29.8	54.2	65.3	62.7	2.5*	1.9*	...
Fiji	17.1	16.0	16.6	14.9	-1.9	-5.2*	...
Kiribati	-25.6	-39.6	-30.1	-28.4	-16.5	-24.4*	...
Marshall Islands	-19.9	-18.0	-17.2	-18.2	-12.3	-11.9	...
Micronesia, Federated States of	-15.2	-10.8	2.1	...	...	...	...
Nauru	-13.5 (2012)	-15.9	13.1	8.7	5.8*	-7.9*	-17.0*
Niue	-40.5	13.0	21.1*	...	...	...	...
Palau	19.1	32.5	15.7	9.9	-2.6*	-16.0*	...
Papua New Guinea	-17.2	-8.4	-7.8	-7.3	-6.7	-0.8*	...
Samoa	14.3	15.1	19.2	20.5	-1.5	-2.8	2.8
Solomon Islands	-10.7	-5.8	-4.6	-7.7	-6.6	-7.1	-9.7
Tonga[d]	-2.1 |	1.2	6.7	6.3	3.9	1.7	...
Tuvalu[d]	-4.1 |	-82.3	-66.5	-60.9	-51.9	-48.7	...
Vanuatu	22.3	13.5	23.1	20.8	-2.0	...	...
Developed ADB Member Economies							
Australia	-0.2	-0.7	-0.3	-0.3	0.2	0.7	-0.5
Japan	-0.5	-0.4	-0.2	-0.2	-0.7	-0.8	-1.0
New Zealand	0.9	2.0	1.4	1.2	-0.9	-1.9	...

... = data not available, | = marks break in series due to change in compilation methodology, (-/+) 0.0 = magnitude is less than half of unit employed, * = provisional or preliminary, ADB = Asian Development Bank, GDP = gross domestic product.

a Change in compilation methodology from the International Monetary Fund's Balance of Payments Manual (fifth edition) [BPM5] to the International Monetary Fund's Balance of Payments and International Investment Position Manual (sixth edition) [BPM6].

b Based on BPM5.

c From September 2019, oil revenue from the Joint Petroleum Development Area is now included in GDP based on the new Timor-Leste Australia Maritime Boundary Treaty.

d Change in compilation methodology from BPM4 to BPM6.

Source: Economies' official sources.

Table 2.4.3: Current Account Balance
(% of GDP)

ADB Regional Member	2010	2015	2018	2019	2020	2021	2022
Developing ADB Member Economies							
Central and West Asia							
Afghanistan	-4.6	-19.9	-21.1	-20.1	-15.5	-18.5	...
Armenia	-13.6	-2.7	-7.4	-7.3	-3.8	-3.7	-0.9
Azerbaijan	28.4	-0.4	12.8	9.1	-0.5	15.1	29.8*
Georgia	-9.8	-11.8	-6.8	-5.9	-12.5	-10.4	-4.1*
Kazakhstan	1.8	-5.4	-1.0	-3.9	-6.4	-1.3	3.9*
Kyrgyz Republic	-9.8	-16.2	-12.0	-12.1	4.8	-8.5	-49.6*
Pakistan	-2.2	-1.0	-5.4	-4.2	-1.7	-0.8	-4.6
Tajikistan	-10.3	-5.8	-4.9	-2.2	4.3	8.2	15.6*
Turkmenistan	-9.0	-17.3	...	...	...	0.6	6.0
Uzbekistan	4.6	1.0	-6.8	-5.6	-5.0	-7.0	-0.8*
East Asia							
China, People's Republic of	3.9	2.6	0.2	0.7	1.7	2.0	2.2*
Hong Kong, China	7.0	3.3	3.7	5.9	7.0	11.8	10.5
Korea, Republic of	2.4	7.2	4.5	3.6	4.6	4.7	1.8
Mongolia	-12.3	-8.2	-16.7	-15.2	-5.1	-14.0	-13.7*
Taipei,China	8.3	13.6	11.6	10.9	14.3	15.1	13.3
South Asia							
Bangladesh	3.2	1.8	-3.0	-1.3	-1.5	-1.1	-4.1*
Bhutan	-22.8	-29.1	-18.4	-20.5	-15.8	-11.9	-33.2*
India	-2.9	-1.1	-2.1	-0.9	0.9	-1.2	-2.0*
Maldives[a]	-13.8 |	-7.4	-28.4	-26.6	-35.5	-8.4	-16.7*
Nepal[b]	-2.3	4.5	-7.1	-6.9	-0.9	-7.8	-12.8
Sri Lanka[a]	-1.8 |	-2.2	-3.0	-2.1	-1.4	-3.7	-1.9
Southeast Asia							
Brunei Darussalam	36.5	16.6	6.9	6.6	4.5	11.2	19.6*
Cambodia	-8.7	-8.9	-11.8	-10.8	-3.4	-40.4	-25.7
Indonesia	0.7	-2.0	-2.9	-2.7	-0.4	0.3	1.0
Lao People's Democratic Republic[a]	0.4 |	-15.7	-9.1	-7.0	-1.2	2.3	1.1
Malaysia	10.1	3.0	2.2	3.5	4.2	3.8	2.6
Myanmar[a]	0.0 |	-4.9	-3.6	0.4*	-2.5*	-1.3*	-1.8*
Philippines	3.4	2.4	-2.6	-0.8	3.2	-1.5	-4.4*
Singapore	22.9	18.7	15.7	16.2	16.5	18.0	19.3
Thailand	3.4	6.9	5.6	7.0	4.2	-2.1*	-3.5*
Timor-Leste[a,c]	180.2 |	12.8	-12.2	2.2	-2.0	0.2	...
Viet Nam[a]	-2.9 |	-0.9	2.2	3.7	4.3	-2.2	-0.3*
The Pacific							
Cook Islands	11.2	31.1	38.2	35.3	-15.9*	-10.7*	...
Fiji	-7.1	-3.5	-8.5	-12.7	-13.6	-16.0*	...
Kiribati	0.1	33.0	39.3	48.7	39.9	9.1*	...
Marshall Islands	-14.8	17.2	6.5	-24.4	20.5	5.8	...
Micronesia, Federated States of	-17.5	4.5	21.0	...	...	...	...
Nauru	38.1 (2012)	-18.5	8.0	4.9	2.8*	4.1*	3.5*
Niue	-53.9	11.1	15.7*	...	...	...	...
Palau	-9.3	-8.8	-19.4	-34.6	-41.7*	-28.5*	-45.2*
Papua New Guinea	-4.4 |	7.3	13.6	14.4	14.4	11.3*	...
Samoa	-4.8	-1.5	2.7	3.8	-9.0	-13.3	-9.4
Solomon Islands	-16.0	-2.7	-3.0	-9.5	-1.6	-5.1	-14.3
Tonga[d]	-8.7 |	-9.0	4.4	-0.5	10.9	4.9	...
Tuvalu[d]	-3.8 |	-35.3	60.9	-22.2	16.3	24.1	...
Vanuatu	-5.6	0.3	12.2	13.6	2.7	...	...
Developed ADB Member Economies							
Australia	-5.0	-3.7	-2.8	-0.9	1.5	3.0	2.0
Japan	3.8	3.1	3.5	3.5	2.9	3.9	2.1
New Zealand	-2.8	-2.4	-3.9	-2.4	-2.7	-6.8	...

... = data not available, | = marks break in series due to change in compilation methodology, 0.0 = magnitude is less than half of unit employed, * = provisional or preliminary, ADB = Asian Development Bank, GDP = gross domestic product.

a Change in compilation methodology from the International Monetary Fund's Balance of Payments Manual (fifth edition) [BPM5] to the International Monetary Fund's Balance of Payments and International Investment Position Manual (sixth edition) [BPM6].

b Based on BPM5.

c From September 2019, oil revenue from the Joint Petroleum Development Area is now included in GDP based on the new Timor-Leste Australia Maritime Boundary Treaty.

d Change in compilation methodology from BPM4 to BPM6.

Source: Economies' official sources.

Table 2.4.4: Total Remittances, Inflows—Dollar Amounts
($ million)

ADB Regional Member	2010	2015	2018	2019	2020	2021	2022
Developing ADB Member Economies							
Central and West Asia	**21,282**	**32,959**	**39,844**	**41,927**	**43,785**	**52,640**	**65,673**
Afghanistan	378	349	804	829	789	300	350
Armenia	1,669	1,491	1,488	1,528	1,327	1,557	2,035
Azerbaijan	1,410	1,270	1,226	1,275	1,403	1,527	3,950
Georgia	1,184	1,459	2,034	2,258	2,110	2,644	3,854
Kazakhstan	226	294	618	506	374	310	481
Kyrgyz Republic	1,266	1,688	2,689	2,411	2,423	2,792	3,051
Pakistan	9,690	19,306	21,193	22,252	26,089	31,312	29,871
Tajikistan	2,021	2,259	2,183	2,322	2,187	2,922	5,346
Turkmenistan	–	–	–	–	–	–	–
Uzbekistan	3,438	4,843	7,610	8,546	7,084	9,277	16,736
East Asia	**59,419**	**71,964**	**76,904**	**78,423**	**69,816**	**63,627**	**61,802**
China, People's Republic of	52,460	63,938	67,414	68,398	59,507	53,000	51,000
Hong Kong, China	340	387	425	451	427	453	414
Korea, Republic of	5,854	6,464	7,125	7,166	7,435	7,742	7,825
Mongolia	266	261	441	561	549	471	399
Taipei,China	500	915	1,500	1,846	1,899	1,960	2,164
South Asia	**71,929**	**97,958**	**109,748**	**116,750**	**120,237**	**125,407**	**145,938**
Bangladesh	10,850	15,296	15,566	18,364	21,752	22,206	21,504
Bhutan	8	20	58	57	83	73	96
India	53,480	68,910	78,790	83,332	83,149	89,375	111,222
Maldives	3	4	4	4	5	5	5
Nepal	3,464	6,730	8,287	8,244	8,108	8,226	9,293
Sri Lanka	4,123	7,000	7,043	6,749	7,140	5,522	3,818
Southeast Asia	**42,429**	**58,277**	**68,630**	**72,897**	**70,392**	**74,154**	**77,035**
Brunei Darussalam	–	–	–	–	1	1	1
Cambodia	557	1,185	1,431	2,659	2,588	2,539	2,616
Indonesia	6,916	9,659	11,215	11,666	9,651	9,402	9,960
Lao People's Democratic Republic	42	189	240	297	232	221	198
Malaysia	1,103	1,644	1,686	1,597	1,427	1,565	1,640
Myanmar	115	1,934	2,673	2,553	2,671	2,000	1,900
Philippines	21,557	29,799	33,809	35,167	34,883	36,685	38,049
Singapore	–	–	–	–	–	–	–
Thailand	4,433	5,895	7,466	8,162	8,257	9,065	9,335
Timor-Leste	137	62	96	100	155	175	185
Viet Nam	7,569	7,910	10,013	10,695	10,528	12,500	13,151
The Pacific[a]	**479**	**655**	**867**	**957**	**962**	**1,206**	**1,263**
Cook Islands	...	...	...	...	...	...	...
Fiji	176	252	290	287	317	394	459
Kiribati	16	14	20	20	15	13	15
Marshall Islands	22	27	31	32	33	34	30
Micronesia, Federated States of	18	23	23	23	23	23	23
Nauru	...	...	...	...	...	...	...
Niue	...	...	...	...	...	...	...
Palau	2	2	3	3	3	3	2
Papua New Guinea	4	4	4	29	2	12	3
Samoa	139	131	148	155	204	248	280
Solomon Islands	14	19	20	25	28	51	81
Tonga	74	129	183	190	191	217	217
Tuvalu	4	3	3	2	2	3	3
Vanuatu	12	50	143	189	144	208	150
Developed ADB Member Economies	**3,919**	**6,031**	**6,746**	**6,625**	**6,513**	**6,892**	**7,359**
Australia	1,864	2,175	1,868	1,763	1,197	936	1,298
Japan	1,684	3,325	4,369	4,389	4,888	5,294	5,384
New Zealand	371	532	509	474	428	661	677
DEVELOPING ADB MEMBER ECONOMIES[a]	**195,538**	**261,813**	**295,994**	**310,954**	**305,192**	**317,034**	**351,710**
ALL ADB REGIONAL MEMBERS[a]	**199,457**	**267,845**	**302,740**	**317,579**	**311,705**	**323,926**	**359,069**
WORLD[a]	**470,037**	**596,214**	**695,443**	**726,936**	**716,885**	**791,114**	**831,103**

... = data not available, – = magnitude equals zero, $ = United States dollars, ADB = Asian Development Bank.

Note: Figures are based on the International Monetary Fund's Balance of Payments and International Investment Position Manual (sixth edition).

a Includes only reporting economies with data corresponding to the year heading.

Source: World Bank-KNOMAD. Remittances Data. https://www.knomad.org/data/remittances (accessed 3 July 2023). For Taipei,China: Ministry of Finance. Official communication, 27 June 2023.

Table 2.4.5: Total Remittances, Inflows—Proportion of Economic Activity
(% of GDP)

ADB Regional Member	2010	2015	2016	2017	2018	2019	2020	2021	2022
Developing ADB Member Economies									
Central and West Asia[a]	**4.3**	**4.8**	**5.4**	**5.6**	**6.0**	**6.5**	**6.9**	**7.2**	**8.4**
Afghanistan	2.4	1.7	3.5	4.4	4.4	4.4	3.9	2.0	...
Armenia	18.0	14.1	13.1	13.3	11.9	11.2	10.5	11.2	10.4
Azerbaijan	2.7	2.4	1.7	2.8	2.6	2.6	3.3	2.8	5.0
Georgia	9.7	9.8	10.0	11.0	11.6	12.9	13.3	14.2	15.7
Kazakhstan	0.2	0.2	0.3	0.3	0.3	0.3	0.2	0.2	0.2
Kyrgyz Republic	26.4	25.3	29.3	32.3	32.5	27.2	31.1	31.9	27.9
Pakistan	5.0	6.5	6.3	5.9	6.6	7.6	8.9	9.1	9.2
Tajikistan	35.8	27.3	26.7	29.7	28.1	28.0	26.9	32.7	50.9
Turkmenistan	–	–	...	...	...	...	...	...	...
Uzbekistan	6.9	5.6	6.7	11.5	14.4	14.2	11.8	13.3	20.8
East Asia	**0.8**	**0.5**	**0.5**	**0.5**	**0.5**	**0.5**	**0.4**	**0.3**	**0.3**
China, People's Republic of	0.9	0.6	0.5	0.5	0.5	0.5	0.4	0.3	0.3
Hong Kong, China	0.1	0.1	0.1	0.1	0.1	0.1	0.1	0.1	0.1
Korea, Republic of	0.5	0.4	0.4	0.4	0.4	0.4	0.5	0.4	0.5
Mongolia	3.7 |	2.2	2.3	2.4	3.3	3.9	4.1	3.1	2.4
Taipei,China	0.1	0.2	0.2	0.2	0.2	0.3	0.3	0.3	0.3
South Asia[a]	**3.9**	**4.0**	**3.4**	**3.2**	**3.4**	**3.5**	**3.8**	**3.4**	**3.6**
Bangladesh	9.5	7.9	5.1	4.7	4.9	5.3	5.8	5.4	5.0
Bhutan	0.5	1.0	1.6	1.8	2.4	2.2	3.6	2.9	...
India	3.2	3.2	2.7	2.6	2.9	2.9	3.1	2.8	3.2
Maldives	0.1	0.1	0.1	0.1	0.1	0.1	0.1	0.1	...
Nepal	21.3	28.4	27.2	23.5	26.1	24.1	24.7	22.7	24.0
Sri Lanka	7.0	8.2	8.3	7.6	7.5	7.6	8.5	6.2	5.1
Southeast Asia[a]	**2.5**	**2.6**	**2.6**	**2.5**	**2.6**	**2.6**	**2.6**	**2.5**	**2.4**
Brunei Darussalam	...	...	...	...	...	...	0.0	0.0	0.0
Cambodia	5.0	6.6	6.0	5.8	5.8	9.8	10.0	9.4	8.9
Indonesia	0.9	1.1	1.0	0.9	1.1	1.0	0.9	0.8	0.8
Lao People's Democratic Republic	0.6	1.3	1.2	1.4	1.3	1.6	1.2	1.2	1.3
Malaysia	0.4	0.5	0.5	0.5	0.5	0.4	0.4	0.4	0.4
Myanmar	0.0	3.1	3.8	4.0	4.1	3.7	3.3	...	...
Philippines	10.3	9.7	9.8	10.0	9.7	9.3	9.6	9.3	9.4
Singapore	–	–	–	–	–	–	–	–	–
Thailand	1.3	1.5	1.5	1.5	1.5	1.5	1.6	1.8	1.9
Timor-Leste	15.6	3.9	4.9	5.5	6.2	4.9	7.2	4.8	...
Viet Nam	5.1	3.3	3.3	3.3	3.2	3.2	3.0	3.4	3.2
The Pacific[a]	**2.3**	**2.1**	**2.3**	**2.4**	**2.5**	**2.7**	**2.9**	**2.8**	**...**
Cook Islands	...	...	...	...	...	...	...	...	...
Fiji	5.6	5.4	5.5	5.2	5.2	5.2	7.1	9.2	...
Kiribati	10.1	8.2	9.1	9.5	10.2	11.4	8.4	5.9	...
Marshall Islands	13.9	14.9	14.1	14.3	14.3	14.0	13.8	13.3	11.5
Micronesia, Federated States of	6.1	7.4	7.0	6.4	5.8	...	...	...	...
Nauru	...	...	...	...	...	...	...	...	...
Niue	...	...	...	...	...	...	...	...	...
Palau	0.9	0.8	0.9	0.9	0.9	0.9	1.0	1.2	0.8
Papua New Guinea	0.0	0.0	0.0	0.0	0.0	0.1	0.0	0.0	...
Samoa	19.8	15.9	15.0	15.4	16.5	17.0	24.6	29.0	32.7
Solomon Islands	1.6	1.4	1.5	1.1	1.2	1.6	1.8	...	...
Tonga	19.9	32.1	30.0	34.4	38.3	37.5	39.1	46.0	...
Tuvalu	12.5	7.5	6.2	6.1	5.6	4.4	4.3	4.2	...
Vanuatu	1.8	6.9	7.7	12.2	15.6	20.2	15.8	...	...
Developed ADB Member Economies[a]	**0.1**	**0.1**	**0.1**	**0.1**	**0.1**	**0.1**	**0.1**	**0.1**	0.1
Australia	0.2	0.2	0.2	0.1	0.1	0.1	0.1	0.1	0.0
Japan	0.0	0.1	0.1	0.1	0.1	0.1	0.1	0.1	0.1
New Zealand	0.3	0.3	0.3	0.3	0.2	0.2	0.1	0.0	...
DEVELOPING ADB MEMBER ECONOMIES[a]	**1.0**	**1.4**	**1.3**	**1.3**	**1.3**	**1.3**	**1.3**	**1.1**	**1.2**
ALL ADB REGIONAL MEMBERS[a]	**0.8**	**1.1**	**1.0**	**1.0**	**1.0**	**1.0**	**1.0**	**0.9**	**1.0**

... = data not available, | = marks break in series, – = magnitude equals zero, 0.0 = magnitude is less than half of unit employed, ADB = Asian Development Bank, GDP = gross domestic product.

a Aggregate percentages calculated using only reporting economies with data available for both remittances and GDP in the years specified in the column headings.

Sources: Economies' official sources; and World Bank-KNOMAD, June 2023. Remittances Data. https://www.knomad.org/data/remittances (accessed 14 July 2023). For Taipei,China: Ministry of Finance. Official communication, 27 June 2023; past communication.

Table 2.4.6: Foreign Direct Investment, Net Inflows—Dollar Amounts
($ million)

ADB Regional Member	2010	2015	2018	2019	2020	2021	2022
Developing ADB Member Economies							
Central and West Asia[a]	**20,334**	**20,069**	**8,172**	**14,038**	**12,996**	**10,681**	**...**
Afghanistan	191	169	119	23	13	21	...
Armenia	529	184	267	100	59	366	998
Azerbaijan	3,353	4,048	1,403	1,504	507	-1,708	-4,474
Georgia	921	1,735	1,305	1,382	552	1,267	...
Kazakhstan	7,456	6,578	353	3,731	7,206	4,549	4,907
Kyrgyz Republic	473	1,144	144	404	-402	226	...
Pakistan	2,022	1,673	1,737	2,234	2,057	2,147	1,339
Tajikistan	94	454	221	213	107	84	174
Turkmenistan	3,632	3,043	1,997	2,129	1,169	1,453	...
Uzbekistan	1,663	1,041	625	2,316	1,728	2,276	2,531
East Asia	**340,093**	**430,126**	**353,649**	**265,787**	**387,085**	**510,916**	**331,777**
China, People's Republic of	243,703	242,489	235,365	187,170	253,096	344,075	180,167
Hong Kong, China	82,709	181,047	97,036	58,299	117,452	137,191	120,952
Korea, Republic of	9,497	4,104	12,183	9,634	8,765	22,060	17,996
Mongolia	1,691	94	1,952	2,443	1,719	2,173	2,504
Taipei,China	2,492	2,391	7,114	8,240	6,053	5,416	10,158
South Asia[a]	**29,486**	**47,877**	**46,800**	**54,422**	**66,886**	**47,895**	**52,268**
Bangladesh	1,232	2,831	2,422	1,908	1,525	1,724	1,555
Bhutan	75	6	3	13	-3	7	10
India	27,397	44,009	42,117	50,611	64,362	44,727	49,916
Maldives	216	298	576	961	441	643	722
Nepal	88	52	68	186	127	196	65
Sri Lanka	478	680	1,614	743	434	598	...
Southeast Asia[a]	**108,413**	**132,976**	**154,474**	**176,354**	**126,494**	**227,533**	**...**
Brunei Darussalam	481	171	516	373	566	205	...
Cambodia	1,404	1,823	3,213	3,663	3,625	3,483	3,579
Indonesia	15,292	19,779	18,910	24,994	19,175	21,213	21,652
Lao People's Democratic Republic	279	1,078	1,358	756	968	1,072	...
Malaysia	10,886	9,857	8,304	9,155	4,059	18,596	15,114
Myanmar	901	4,084	1,768	1,736	1,907	2,067	...
Philippines	1,070	5,639	9,949	8,671	6,822	11,983	9,200
Singapore	55,322	69,775	81,161	105,293	78,448	138,544	140,844
Thailand	14,747	8,928	13,747	5,519	-4,947	14,641	10,046
Timor-Leste	30	43	48	75	72	69	...
Viet Nam	8,000	11,800	15,500	16,120	15,800	15,660	...
The Pacific[a]	**435**	**361**	**934**	**786**	**443**	**512**	**...**
Cook Islands	...	...	...	...	...	...	...
Fiji	178	205	469	322	239	410	104
Kiribati	-7	-1	-1	-1	3	1	...
Marshall Islands	-9	-5	10	5	3	0	...
Micronesia, Federated States of	0	20 (2014)	...	...	...	...	...
Nauru	0	0	0	...	...	...	...
Niue	...	...	...	...	...	...	...
Palau	3	35	51	54	42	33	...
Papua New Guinea	36	30	307	336	113	-11	...
Samoa	0	27	17	-2	4	9	5
Solomon Islands	166	32	25	33	9	28	41
Tonga	5	6	20	2	4	0	3
Tuvalu	0	0	0	0	0	0	...
Vanuatu	63	31	38	37	24	41	...
Developed ADB Member Economies	**42,938**	**52,072**	**88,492**	**81,836**	**82,027**	**64,044**	**122,469**
Australia	35,211	46,893	60,686	38,959	15,307	24,835	**67,119**
Japan	7,441	5,252	25,289	39,961	62,585	34,669	**47,522**
New Zealand	286	-73	2,516	2,916	4,135	4,540	**7,828**
DEVELOPING ADB MEMBER ECONOMIES[a]	**498,761**	**631,409**	**564,029**	**511,386**	**593,903**	**797,536**	**590,106**
ALL ADB REGIONAL MEMBERS[a]	**541,699**	**683,481**	**652,521**	**593,222**	**675,931**	**861,580**	**712,576**
WORLD[a]	**1,927,980**	**2,762,541**	**942,713**	**1,701,039**	**1,278,015**	**2,097,718**	**1,831,171**

... = data not available, 0 = magnitude is less than half of unit employed, $ = United States dollars, ADB = Asian Development Bank.

Note: For any given year, a negative value for net inflows of foreign direct investment shows that the value of disinvestment by foreign investors was more than the value of capital newly invested in the reporting economy.

a Includes only reporting economies with data corresponding to the year heading.

Sources: World Bank. World Development Indicators. http://data.worldbank.org/indicator/BX.KLT.DINV.CD.WD?locations=MH (accessed 17 July 2023); and International Monetary Fund. Balance of Payments Analytic Presentation. https://data.imf.org/regular.aspx?key=62805741 (accessed 17 July 2023). For Taipei,China: Central bank of Taipei,China.

Table 2.4.7: Foreign Direct Investment, Net Inflows—Proportion of Economic Activity
(% of GDP)

ADB Regional Member	2010	2015	2018	2019	2020	2021	2022
Developing ADB Member Economies							
Central and West Asia[a]	**3.9**	**2.8**	**0.9**	**1.8**	**1.9**	**1.3**	**...**
Afghanistan	1.2	0.8	0.6	0.1	0.1	0.1	...
Armenia	5.7	1.7	2.1	0.7	0.5	2.6	5.1
Azerbaijan	6.3	7.6	3.0	3.1	1.2	-3.1	-5.7
Georgia	7.5	11.6	7.4	7.9	3.5	6.8	...
Kazakhstan	5.0	3.6	0.2	2.1	4.2	2.3	2.2
Kyrgyz Republic	9.9	17.1	1.7	4.6	-5.2	2.6	...
Pakistan	1.0	0.6	0.5	0.8	0.7	0.6	0.4
Tajikistan	1.7	5.5	2.8	2.6	1.3	0.9	1.7
Turkmenistan	16.1	8.5	...	...	...	...	...
Uzbekistan	3.3	1.2	1.2	3.8	2.9	3.3	3.1
East Asia[a]	**4.3**	**3.2**	**2.1**	**1.6**	**2.2**	**2.5**	**1.6**
China, People's Republic of	4.0	2.2	1.7	1.3	1.7	1.9	1.0
Hong Kong, China	36.2	58.5	26.8	16.1	34.0	37.2	33.6
Korea, Republic of	0.8	0.3	0.7	0.6	0.5	1.2	1.1
Mongolia	23.5	0.8	14.8	17.2	12.9	14.2	14.9
Taipei,China	0.6	0.4	1.2	1.3	0.9	0.7	1.3
South Asia[a]	**1.6**	**1.9**	**1.5**	**1.6**	**2.1**	**1.3**	**1.3**
Bangladesh	1.1	1.5	0.8	0.5	0.4	0.4	0.4
Bhutan	4.9	0.3	0.1	0.5	-0.1	0.3	...
India	1.6	2.1	1.5	1.8	2.4	1.4	1.4
Maldives	8.4	7.3	10.9	17.1	11.8	11.9	...
Nepal	0.5	0.2	0.2	0.5	0.4	0.5	0.2
Sri Lanka	0.8	0.8	1.7	0.8	0.5	0.7	...
Southeast Asia[a]	**5.4**	**5.3**	**5.0**	**5.4**	**4.1**	**6.8**	**...**
Brunei Darussalam	3.5	1.3	3.8	2.8	4.7	1.5	...
Cambodia	12.5	10.1	13.1	13.5	14.0	12.9	12.1
Indonesia	2.0	2.3	1.8	2.2	1.8	1.8	1.6
Lao People's Democratic Republic	4.1	7.5	7.5	4.0	5.1	5.6	...
Malaysia	4.3	3.3	2.3	2.5	1.2	5.0	3.7
Myanmar	...	6.5	2.7	2.5	2.3	...	...
Philippines	0.5	1.8	2.9	2.3	1.9	3.0	2.3
Singapore	23.1	22.7	21.5	27.9	22.5	32.7	30.2
Thailand	4.3	2.2	2.7	1.0	-1.0	2.9	2.0
Timor-Leste[b]	3.4	2.7	3.1	3.7	3.4	1.9	...
Viet Nam	5.4	4.9	5.0	4.8	4.6	4.3	...
The Pacific[a]	**2.1**	**1.2**	**2.7**	**2.3**	**1.3**	**...**	**...**
Cook Islands	...	...	...	...	...	...	...
Fiji	5.7	4.4	8.4	5.9	5.3	9.5	...
Kiribati	-4.3	-0.5	-0.6	-0.3	1.5	0.5	...
Marshall Islands	-5.8	-2.9	4.4	2.2	1.3	0.2	...
Micronesia, Federated States of	0.0	6.3 (2014)	...	...	...	...	...
Nauru	0.0	0.0	0.0	...	...	...	...
Niue	...	...	...	...	...	...	...
Palau	1.5	12.4	17.7	19.8	16.5	14.9	...
Papua New Guinea	0.2	0.1	1.3	1.4	0.5	-0.0	...
Samoa	0.0	3.3	1.9	-0.2	0.5	1.0	0.6
Solomon Islands	18.5	2.5	1.5	2.0	0.6	...	...
Tonga	1.3	1.6	4.2	0.3	0.9	0.1	...
Tuvalu	1.4	0.9	0.6	0.6	0.2	0.3	...
Vanuatu	9.4	4.2	4.1	4.0	2.7	...	...
Developed ADB Member Economies[a]	**0.6**	**0.9**	**1.3**	**1.2**	**1.2**	**0.9**	**2.0**
Australia	2.9	3.8	4.4	2.9	1.1	1.6	4.2
Japan	0.1	0.1	0.5	0.8	1.2	0.7	1.1
New Zealand	0.2	-0.0	1.2	1.4	1.9	1.8	...
DEVELOPING ADB MEMBER ECONOMIES[a]	**4.1**	**3.3**	**2.4**	**2.1**	**2.4**	**2.8**	**2.1**
ALL ADB REGIONAL MEMBERS[a]	**2.8**	**2.7**	**2.2**	**1.9**	**2.2**	**2.4**	**2.0**

... = data not available, (-/+) 0.0 = magnitude is less than half of the unit employed, ADB = Asian Development Bank, GDP = gross domestic product.

a Aggregate percentages calculated using only reporting economies with data available for both foreign direct investment and GDP in the years specified in the column headings.
b From September 2019, oil revenue from the Joint Petroleum Development Area is now included in GDP based on the new Timor-Leste Australia Maritime Boundary Treaty.

Sources: Economies' official sources; World Bank. World Development Indicators. http://data.worldbank.org/indicator/BX.KLT.DINV.CD.WD?locations=MH (accessed 17 July 2023); and International Monetary Fund. Balance of Payments Analytic Presentation. https://data.imf.org/regular.aspx?key=62805741 (accessed 17 July 2023). For Taipei,China: Central bank of Taipei,China.

Table 2.4.8: Merchandise Exports
($ million)

ADB Regional Member	2010	2015	2018	2019	2020	2021	2022
Developing ADB Member Economies							
Central and West Asia[a]	**134,666**	**116,373**	**138,420**	**140,121**	**119,121**	**146,888**	**197,104**
Afghanistan	388	571	875	864	777	850	...
Armenia	1,041	1,485	2,412	2,649	2,537	3,016	5,360
Azerbaijan	26,374	15,586	20,794	19,868	12,588	21,692	40,869
Georgia	1,677	2,204	3,380	3,798	3,344	4,243	5,593
Kazakhstan	60,271	45,956	61,111	58,066	47,541	60,321	84,394
Kyrgyz Republic	1,756	1,483	1,837	1,986	1,973	2,752	2,187
Pakistan	19,261	23,526	21,296	21,222	21,234	25,191	27,768
Tajikistan	1,195	891	1,073	1,174	1,407	2,150	2,142
Turkmenistan	9,679	12,164	11,651	12,592*	...	...	...
Uzbekistan	13,023	12,508	13,991	17,902	15,128	14,081	15,350
East Asia	**2,713,944**	**3,552,563**	**3,962,930**	**3,887,604**	**3,961,133**	**5,095,084**	**5,345,894**
China, People's Republic of	1,577,754	2,273,468	2,486,682	2,499,482	2,589,952	3,357,143	3,593,601
Hong Kong, China	390,134	465,092	530,472	509,026	506,303	638,170	578,650
Korea, Republic of	466,384	526,757	604,860	542,233	512,498	644,400	683,585
Mongolia	2,909	4,669	7,012	7,620	7,576	9,241	12,539
Taipei,China	276,763	282,577	333,905	329,244	344,804	446,129	477,519
South Asia[a]	**274,793**	**310,212**	**386,533**	**368,206**	**335,087**	**477,101**	**522,552**
Bangladesh	16,099	30,588	35,691	39,404	32,087	36,783	46,322*
Bhutan	535	561	574	610	632	718	736
India	248,648	267,550	337,439	315,229	291,371	425,745	460,614
Maldives	62	144	181	158	156	148	156
Nepal	830	833	747	862	826	1,195	1,598
Sri Lanka	8,618	10,536	11,901	11,943	10,016	12,512	13,126
Southeast Asia[a]	**1,048,353**	**1,172,177**	**1,446,549**	**1,422,447**	**1,394,121**	**1,725,441**	**1,953,672**
Brunei Darussalam	8,887	6,338	6,577	7,247	6,611	10,517	14,232
Cambodia	3,903	9,336	12,973	14,986	18,522	19,521	23,179
Indonesia	157,779	150,366	180,013	167,683	163,192	231,609	291,979
Lao People's Democratic Republic	1,746	3,653	5,408	5,806	6,115	7,695	8,078
Malaysia	198,325	199,041	248,712	240,212	234,050	299,525	352,554
Myanmar	8,872	11,432	16,704	18,118	16,937	...	...
Philippines	51,498	58,827	69,307	70,927	65,215	74,653	74,693*
Singapore	352,553	357,730	411,957	390,361	373,725	457,081	514,966
Thailand	192,511	213,397	251,155	242,686	226,861*	270,977	285,134*
Timor-Leste	42	38	46	154	264	616	...
Viet Nam	72,237	162,017	243,697	264,267	282,629	336,311	371,304
The Pacific[a]	**7,012**	**9,287**	**11,647**	**12,724**	**10,537**	**12,126**	**...**
Cook Islands	5	14	17	18	19	15	5
Fiji	837	982	1,007	1,027	828	893*	1,055*
Kiribati	4	10	8	12	9	9*	...
Marshall Islands	44	60	64	69	72	63	...
Micronesia, Federated States of	30	40	47	...	...	...	...
Nauru	32	11	9 |	4	4	5	...
Niue	1	1	2	2	1	1	...
Palau	16	18	14	11	7	2	8*
Papua New Guinea	5,737	7,640	9,827	10,947	9,073	10,622	...
Samoa	23	34	43	51	38	29	41
Solomon Islands	227	421	536	461	379	371	341
Tonga	8	18	13	20	15	16	6
Tuvalu	1	0	0	0	0	0	0
Vanuatu	48	39	61	56	46	54	50
Developed ADB Member Economies	**1,011,217**	**846,359**	**1,034,971**	**1,016,264**	**929,221**	**1,147,279**	**1,205,047**
Australia	212,027	187,525	257,480	271,069	250,138	345,302	412,819
Japan	767,826	624,681	737,877	705,733	640,594	757,067	746,588
New Zealand	31,365	34,152	39,613	39,463	38,489	44,910	45,639
DEVELOPING ADB MEMBER ECONOMIES[a]	**4,178,767**	**5,160,613**	**5,946,080**	**5,831,102**	**5,819,999**	**7,456,639**	**8,031,473**
ALL ADB REGIONAL MEMBERS[a]	**5,189,984**	**6,006,971**	**6,981,050**	**6,847,366**	**6,749,220**	**8,603,918**	**9,236,520**
WORLD[b]	**15,224,989**	**16,418,157**	**19,312,557**	**18,743,361**	**17,370,009**	**22,048,484**	**24,581,790**

... = data not available; | = marks break in series; 0 = magnitude is less than half of unit employed; * = provisional, preliminary, estimate; $ = United States dollars, ADB = Asian Development Bank.

a For estimating aggregates, imputation was done for economies with missing data by substituting available data from the nearest years.
b The world aggregate includes estimates derived from reports of partner economies for nonreporting and slow-reporting economies.

Sources: Economies' official sources; and International Monetary Fund (IMF). International Financial Statistics. http://data.imf.org/ (accessed 30 June 2023). For Nauru: for 2002–2017: Pacific Community. Pacific Data Hub. Stat Data Explorer. Population projections. https://stats.pacificdata.org/ (accessed 9 June 2023); for 2018–2021: IMF. Staff Country Reports. Republic of Nauru: 2019 Article IV. https://www.imf.org/en/Publications/CR/Issues/2020/01/29/Republic-of-Nauru-2019-Article-IV-Consultation-Press-Release-Staff-Report-and-Statement-by-49001 (accessed 10 May 2021). For "World": IMF. Direction of Trade Statistics. http://data.imf.org/?sk=9D6028D4-F14A-464C-A2F2-59B2CD424B85 (accessed 30 June 2023).

Table 2.4.9: Growth Rates of Merchandise Exports
(%)

ADB Regional Member	2010	2015	2018	2019	2020	2021	2022
Developing ADB Member Economies							
Central and West Asia[a]	**25.3**	**-33.3**	**22.1**	**1.2**	**-15.0**	**23.3**	**34.2**
Afghanistan	-3.7	0.2	5.2	-1.3	-10.1	9.4	...
Armenia	46.6	-4.0	7.8	9.8	-4.2	18.9	77.7
Azerbaijan	25.3	-44.8	37.2	-4.5	-36.6	72.3	88.4
Georgia	48.0	-23.0	23.1	12.4	-12.0	26.9*	31.8
Kazakhstan	39.5	-42.2	26.0	-5.0	-18.1	26.9	39.9
Kyrgyz Republic	5.0	-21.3	4.1	8.1	-0.7	39.5	-20.5
Pakistan	12.0	-8.5	3.6	-0.3	0.1	18.6	10.2
Tajikistan	18.3	-8.9	-10.4	9.5	19.8	52.8	-0.4
Turkmenistan	3.8	-38.5	49.6	8.1*	...	...	...
Uzbekistan	10.6	-7.7	11.4	28.0	-15.5	-6.9	9.0
East Asia	**29.8**	**-4.3**	**8.4**	**-1.9**	**1.9**	**28.6**	**4.9**
China, People's Republic of	31.3	-2.9	9.9	0.5	3.6	29.6	7.0
Hong Kong, China	22.5	-1.8	6.7	-4.0	-0.5	26.0	-9.3
Korea, Republic of	28.3	-8.0	5.4	-10.4	-5.5	25.7	6.1
Mongolia	54.3	-19.1	13.1	8.7	-0.6	22.0	35.7
Taipei,China	35.1	-11.2	5.8	-1.4	4.7	29.4	7.0
South Asia[a]	**38.2**	**-12.2**	**11.5**	**-4.7**	**-9.0**	**42.4**	**9.5**
Bangladesh	3.7	2.6	6.7	10.4	-18.6	14.6	25.9*
Bhutan	6.5	4.1	1.3	6.3	3.7	13.6	2.5
India	42.3	-13.9	12.3	-6.6	-7.6	46.1	8.2
Maldives	-63.6	-0.6	-8.8	-13.1	-1.2	-4.7	5.1
Nepal	-4.9	-11.6	6.9	15.5	-4.3	44.7	33.7
Sri Lanka	21.7	-5.3	4.7	0.4	-16.1	24.9	4.9
Southeast Asia[a]	**29.7**	**-9.7**	**10.3**	**-1.7**	**-2.0**	**23.8**	**13.2**
Brunei Darussalam	23.9	-40.2	17.8	10.2	-8.8	59.1	35.3
Cambodia	24.4	14.3	15.5	15.5	23.6	5.4	18.7
Indonesia	35.4	-14.6	6.6	-6.8	-2.7	41.9	26.1
Lao People's Democratic Republic	65.9	11.5	11.0	7.4	5.3	25.8	5.0
Malaysia	26.5	-14.9	14.4	-3.4	-2.6	28.0	17.7
Myanmar	32.4	-0.2	20.4	8.5	-6.5	...	...
Philippines	34.0	-5.3	0.9	2.3	-8.1	14.5	0.1*
Singapore	30.5	-13.8	10.5	-5.2	-4.3	22.3	12.7
Thailand	27.2	-5.8	7.6	-3.4	-6.5*	19.4	5.2*
Timor-Leste	20.7	-1.7	91.5	232.0	71.7	133.2	...
Viet Nam	26.5	7.9	13.3	8.4	6.9	19.0	10.4
The Pacific[a]	**30.4**	**-13.5**	**3.5**	**9.2**	**-17.2**	**15.1**	**...**
Cook Islands	88.0	-20.3	-14.2	0.6	10.8	-24.4	-66.6
Fiji	25.1	-19.5	2.1	2.0	-19.4	7.9*	18.1*
Kiribati	-38.0	-1.5	-46.3	49.3	-24.2	-1.6*	...
Marshall Islands	27.4	-13.9	4.9	8.1	3.6	-12.4	...
Micronesia, Federated States of	63.5	23.0	1.7	...	...	...	...
Nauru	249.5	-50.9 |	-39.4	-52.6	-1.0	9.2	...
Niue	0.8	-19.7	17.4	-7.5	-66.4	39.4	...
Palau	15.9	-5.3	-1.9	-18.5	-40.0	-71.1	305.1*
Papua New Guinea	30.9	-13.0	3.3	11.4	-17.1	17.1	...
Samoa	114.4	23.8	14.1	18.9	-24.3	-24.3	41.3
Solomon Islands	37.4	-7.6	14.5	-14.0	-17.7	-2.0	-8.2
Tonga	7.1	-6.5	-31.2	56.1	-24.0	2.8	-65.0
Tuvalu	76.5	-12.0	-11.3	51.6	-83.0	591.2	-89.8
Vanuatu	-14.8	-33.5	4.0	-9.0	-17.6	17.3	-7.7
Developed ADB Member Economies	**33.6**	**-12.9**	**7.0**	**-1.8**	**-8.6**	**23.5**	**5.0**
Australia	38.3	-21.8	11.5	5.3	-7.7	38.0	19.6
Japan	32.6	-9.5	5.7	-4.4	-9.2	18.2	-1.4
New Zealand	26.6	-17.8	4.0	-0.4	-2.5	16.7	1.6
DEVELOPING ADB MEMBER ECONOMIES[a]	**30.2**	**-7.0**	**9.3**	**-1.9**	**-0.2**	**28.1**	**7.7**
ALL ADB REGIONAL MEMBERS[a]	**30.8**	**-7.9**	**9.0**	**-1.9**	**-1.4**	**27.5**	**7.4**
WORLD[b]	**22.7**	**-12.8**	**10.1**	**-2.9**	**-7.3**	**26.9**	**11.5**

... = data not available; | = marks break in series; * = provisional, preliminary, estimate; ADB = Asian Development Bank.

Note: Growth rates are based on the value of exports in United States dollars.

a For estimating aggregates, imputation was done for economies with missing data by substituting available data from the nearest years.
b The world aggregate includes estimates derived from reports of partner economies for nonreporting and slow-reporting economies.

Sources: Economies' official sources; and International Monetary Fund (IMF). International Financial Statistics. http://data.imf.org/ (accessed 30 June 2023). For "World": Asian Development Bank estimates using data from the IMF's Direction of Trade Statistics: http://data.imf.org/?sk=9D6028D4-F14A-464C-A2F2-59B2CD424B85 (accessed 30 June 2023).

Table 2.4.10: Merchandise Imports
($ million)

ADB Regional Member	2010	2015	2018	2019	2020	2021	2022
Developing ADB Member Economies							
Central and West Asia[a]	**109,356**	**138,059**	**154,748**	**160,768**	**145,112**	**166,721**	**209,278**
Afghanistan	5,154	7,723	7,407	6,777	6,538	5,308	...
Armenia	3,749	3,239	4,976	5,538	4,583	5,362	8,769
Azerbaijan	6,662	9,774	10,952	11,335	10,077	10,419	13,509
Georgia	5,236	7,304	9,361	9,519	8,054	10,100*	13,517
Kazakhstan	31,127	30,568	33,659	39,709	38,929	41,415	50,044
Kyrgyz Republic	3,223	4,154	5,292	4,989	3,719	5,580	9,629
Pakistan	34,169	45,394	55,189	49,869	43,466	55,181	69,756
Tajikistan	2,657	3,436	3,151	3,349	3,169	4,210	5,167
Turkmenistan	8,204	14,051	5,323	5,406*	...	...	...
Uzbekistan	9,176	12,417	19,439	24,276	21,172	23,740	28,173
East Asia	**2,512,911**	**2,876,629**	**3,563,907**	**3,437,069**	**3,375,353**	**4,373,229**	**4,511,786**
China, People's Republic of	1,396,244	1,679,565	2,135,734	2,078,409	2,065,962	2,686,731	2,715,999
Hong Kong, China	433,102	522,001	602,335	563,487	550,421	682,828	629,192
Korea, Republic of	425,212	436,499	535,202	503,343	467,633	615,093	731,370
Mongolia	3,200	3,798	5,875	6,128	5,299	6,846	8,704
Taipei,China	255,153	234,768	284,761	285,702	286,039	381,732	426,521
South Asia	**409,681**	**455,084**	**616,744**	**568,858**	**473,006**	**716,167**	**844,996**
Bangladesh	21,245	37,528	53,571	55,159	50,636	60,483	77,599*
Bhutan[b]	810	977	971	1,012	939	886	1,325
India	368,166	388,189	525,618	477,270	393,519	618,628	729,470
Maldives	909	1,890	2,953	2,875	1,770	2,486	3,480
Nepal	5,110	7,565	11,430	12,597	10,113	13,035	15,339
Sri Lanka	13,441	18,935	22,200	19,945	16,029	20,649	17,783
Southeast Asia[a]	**934,617**	**1,089,778**	**1,405,735**	**1,369,472**	**1,249,882**	**1,591,621**	**1,824,949**
Brunei Darussalam	2,536	3,235	4,168	5,100	5,319	7,234	9,185
Cambodia[b]	6,588	13,285	18,813	22,242	21,066	30,726	32,005
Indonesia	135,663	142,695	188,711	171,276	141,569	196,190	237,447
Lao People's Democratic Republic[b]	2,060	5,675	6,315	6,272	5,370	6,275	7,120
Malaysia	164,177	175,593	218,036	205,049	190,433	238,299	294,504
Myanmar	4,866	16,913	19,355	18,611	17,965	...	...
Philippines	54,933	71,067	112,841	111,593	89,812	116,883	116,885*
Singapore	312,669	307,968	370,832	358,985	328,661	406,318	475,413
Thailand	165,988	187,079	228,857	216,052	186,372	238,624	274,651*
Timor-Leste	298	491	565	597	625	873	...
Viet Nam	84,839	165,776	237,242	253,697	262,691	332,235	358,902
The Pacific[a]	**7,058**	**7,294**	**8,911**	**9,461**	**7,371**	**8,083**	**...**
Cook Islands	91	110	135	136	105	119	71
Fiji	1,806	2,268	2,729	2,781	1,731	2,166*	2,997*
Kiribati	73	103	103	112	109	146*	...
Marshall Islands	125	112	126	200	126	135	...
Micronesia, Federated States of	168	160	198	...	...	...	...
Nauru	13	93		47	58	58	64	...
Niue	9	13	18	14	12	14	...
Palau	103	156	171	171	149	156	208*
Papua New Guinea[b]	3,522	2,840	3,815	4,223	3,584	3,600	...
Samoa	280	298	333	357	285	338	405
Solomon Islands	405	485	593	553	452	526	611
Tonga	158	209	228	267	229	246	118
Tuvalu	22	37	25	33	34	34	34
Vanuatu	284	411	390	357	300	340	266
Developed ADB Member Economies	**915,836**	**885,006**	**1,020,015**	**977,235**	**875,951**	**1,071,320**	**1,242,607**
Australia	193,071	200,643	227,172	213,797	202,055	248,068	289,264
Japan	692,242	647,744	748,967	721,032	636,957	773,318	898,423
New Zealand	30,523	36,619	43,876	42,405	36,939	49,933	54,921
DEVELOPING ADB MEMBER ECONOMIES[a]	**3,973,622**	**4,566,844**	**5,750,046**	**5,545,628**	**5,250,724**	**6,855,822**	**7,399,876**
ALL ADB REGIONAL MEMBERS[a]	**4,889,458**	**5,451,850**	**6,770,060**	**6,522,863**	**6,126,675**	**7,927,141**	**8,642,483**
WORLD[c]	**15,457,040**	**16,581,654**	**19,555,418**	**19,001,606**	**17,504,363**	**22,258,863**	**25,079,198**

... = data not available; | = marks break in series; * = provisional, preliminary, estimate; $ = United States dollars; ADB = Asian Development Bank.

Note: Growth rates are based on the value of exports in United States dollars.

a For estimating aggregates, imputation was done for economies with missing data by substituting available data from the nearest years.

b The Key Indicators Database features a longer time series on trade in goods. The compilation methodology shifted from cost, insurance, and freight to free on board from 2004 onward for Bhutan; from 2005 onward for Cambodia; from 2017 onward for the Lao People's Democratic Republic; and from 2010 onward for Papua New Guinea.

c The world aggregate includes estimates derived from reports of partner economies for nonreporting and slow-reporting economies.

Sources: Economies' official sources; and International Monetary Fund (IMF). International Financial Statistics. http://data.imf.org/ (accessed 30 June 2023). For Nauru: for 2002–2017: Pacific Community. Pacific Data Hub. Stat Data Explorer. Population projections. https://stats.pacificdata.org/ (accessed 9 June 2023); for 2018–2021: IMF. Staff Country Reports. Republic of Nauru: 2019 Article IV. https://www.imf.org/en/Publications/CR/Issues/2020/01/29/Republic-of-Nauru-2019-Article-IV-Consultation-Press-Release-Staff-Report-and-Statement-by-49001 (accessed 10 May 2021). For "World": IMF. Direction of Trade Statistics. http://data.imf.org/?sk=9D6028D4-F14A-464C-A2F2-59B2CD424B85 (accessed 30 June 2023).

Table 2.4.11: Growth Rates of Merchandise Imports
(%)

ADB Regional Member	2010	2015	2018	2019	2020	2021	2022
Developing ADB Member Economies							
Central and West Asia[a]	**6.0**	**-12.5**	**8.4**	**3.9**	**-9.7**	**14.9**	**25.5**
Afghanistan	54.5	-0.1	-5.0	-8.5	-3.5	-18.8	...
Armenia	12.9	-26.8	21.4	11.3	-17.2	17.0	63.5
Azerbaijan	6.9	4.7	21.2	3.5	-11.1	3.4	29.7
Georgia	17.0	-15.1	16.2	1.7	-15.4	25.4*	33.8
Kazakhstan	9.6	-26.0	13.7	18.0	-2.0	6.4	20.8
Kyrgyz Republic	6.0	-27.6	17.7	-5.7	-25.5	50.1	72.6
Pakistan	2.5	-0.9	4.6	-9.6	-12.8	27.0	26.4
Tajikistan	3.4	-20.1	13.6	6.3	-5.4	32.9	22.8
Turkmenistan	-8.8	-15.5	-47.8	1.6	...	...	...
Uzbekistan	-2.8	-11.2	38.7	24.9	-12.8	12.1	18.7
East Asia	**35.5**	**-13.2**	**13.4**	**-3.6**	**-1.8**	**29.6**	**3.2**
China, People's Republic of	38.8	-14.3	15.8	-2.7	-0.6	30.0	1.1
Hong Kong, China	24.7	-4.1	7.7	-6.4	-2.3	24.1	-7.9
Korea, Republic of	31.6	-16.9	11.9	-6.0	-7.1	31.5	18.9
Mongolia	49.7	-27.5	35.5	4.3	-13.5	29.2	27.2
Taipei,China	44.4	-16.2	10.6	0.3	0.1	33.5	11.7
South Asia[a]	**29.1**	**-11.6**	**14.8**	**-7.8**	**-16.8**	**51.4**	**18.0**
Bangladesh	5.1	2.5	25.2	3.0	-8.2	19.4	28.3*
Bhutan	40.7	4.5	-7.0	4.2	-7.2	-5.6	49.5
India	30.7	-13.4	14.1	-9.2	-17.5	57.2	17.9
Maldives	-5.6	-4.9	25.7	-2.6	-38.4	40.5	40.0
Nepal	39.3	3.3	20.7	10.2	-19.7	28.9	17.7
Sri Lanka	31.8	-2.5	5.8	-10.2	-19.6	28.8	-13.9
Southeast Asia[a]	**31.1**	**-11.0**	**14.0**	**-2.6**	**-8.7**	**27.3**	**14.7**
Brunei Darussalam	5.6	-10.0	35.2	22.3	4.3	36.0	27.0
Cambodia	35.0	10.5	21.3	18.2	-5.3	45.9	4.2
Indonesia	40.1	-19.9	20.2	-9.2	-17.3	38.6	21.0
Lao People's Democratic Republic	41.0	14.1	11.4	-0.7	-14.4	16.8	13.5
Malaysia	33.1	-15.9	12.1	-6.0	-7.1	25.1	23.6
Myanmar	11.0	4.3	0.5	-3.8	-3.5	...	...
Philippines	27.5	8.7	17.4	-1.1	-19.5	30.1	0.0*
Singapore	26.9	-18.5	13.3	-3.2	-8.4	23.6	17.0
Thailand	38.2	-10.7	14.0	-5.6	-13.7	28.0	15.1*
Timor-Leste	1.0	-11.3	2.1	5.6	4.8	39.5	...
Viet Nam	21.3	12.1	11.3	6.9	3.5	26.5	8.0
The Pacific[a]	**18.9**	**-14.8**	**11.7**	**6.2**	**-22.1**	**9.7**	**...**
Cook Islands	11.2	-9.3	-0.1	1.1	-23.0	13.3	-40.3
Fiji	17.0	-14.6	13.4	1.9	-37.8	25.1*	38.4*
Kiribati	5.4	-3.7	-4.8	8.7	-2.4	34.4*	...
Marshall Islands	-21.2	-10.7	11.4	58.6	-37.2	7.5	...
Micronesia, Federated States of	-1.8	-0.3	7.9	...	...	...	...
Nauru	-47.3	-18.0		8.9	23.5	-0.1	9.3	...
Niue	28.2	-14.9	17.7	-23.5	-13.7	18.4	...
Palau	9.3	4.4	-1.9	0.3	-12.7	4.4	33.0*
Papua New Guinea	23.0	-22.4	15.6	10.7	-15.1	0.5	...
Samoa	36.6	-12.7	3.8	7.2	-20.1	18.4	19.9
Solomon Islands	51.2	-4.1	14.8	-6.7	-18.3	16.5	16.1
Tonga	10.3	-4.4	-4.0	17.2	-14.4	7.7	-52.0
Tuvalu	59.2	66.4	-4.3	28.1	3.9	1.0	-1.3
Vanuatu	-2.5	12.9	-1.3	-8.6	-15.9	13.3	-21.9
Developed ADB Member Economies	**25.1**	**-18.2**	**9.3**	**-4.2**	**-10.4**	**22.3**	**16.0**
Australia	23.4	-11.9	2.8	-5.9	-5.5	22.8	16.6
Japan	25.8	-20.1	11.4	-3.7	-11.7	21.4	16.2
New Zealand	21.5	-13.9	9.3	-3.4	-12.9	35.2	10.0
DEVELOPING ADB MEMBER ECONOMIES[a]	**32.7**	**-12.5**	**13.5**	**-3.6**	**-5.3**	**30.6**	**7.9**
ALL ADB REGIONAL MEMBERS[a]	**31.2**	**-13.5**	**12.9**	**-3.7**	**-6.1**	**29.4**	**9.0**
WORLD[b]	**21.5**	**-12.4**	**10.2**	**-2.8**	**-7.9**	**27.2**	**12.7**

... = data not available; | = marks break in series; 0.0 = magnitude is less than half of unit employed; * = provisional, preliminary, estimate; ADB = Asian Development Bank.

Note: Growth rates are based on the value of exports in United States dollars.

a For estimating aggregates, imputation was done for economies with missing data by substituting available data from the nearest years.
b The world aggregate includes estimates derived from reports of partner economies for nonreporting and slow-reporting economies.

Sources: Economies' official sources; and International Monetary Fund (IMF). International Financial Statistics. http://data.imf.org/ (accessed 30 June 2023).
For "World": Asian Development Bank estimates using data from the IMF's Direction of Trade Statistics: http://data.imf.org/?sk=9D6028D4-F14A-464C-A2F2-59B2CD424B85 (accessed 30 June 2023).

Table 2.4.12: Trade in Goods
(% of GDP)

ADB Regional Member	2010	2015	2018	2019	2020	2021	2022
Developing ADB Member Economies							
Central and West Asia[a]	**47.4**	**35.5**	**41.8**	**43.9**	**...**	**...**	**...**
Afghanistan	34.5	40.2	45.0	40.4	36.3	41.4	...
Armenia	51.7	44.8	59.3	60.1	56.3	60.4	72.4
Azerbaijan	62.4	47.8	67.4	64.8	53.1	58.6	69.1
Georgia	56.5	63.6	72.4	76.2	71.9	77.0	77.7
Kazakhstan	61.7	41.5	52.8	53.8	50.5	51.6	60.1
Kyrgyz Republic	103.8	84.4	86.2	78.6	73.2	95.3	108.1
Pakistan	27.6	23.3	23.8	24.4	22.0	23.4	30.0
Tajikistan	68.3	52.3	54.4	54.5	56.2	71.1	69.7
Turkmenistan	79.2	73.1	...	...	...	...	...
Uzbekistan	44.4	28.9	63.2	70.0	60.3	54.3	54.1
East Asia	**66.1**	**48.0**	**45.3**	**43.3**	**42.3**	**45.5**	**47.5**
China, People's Republic of	48.9	35.7	33.3	32.1	31.7	33.9	35.1
Hong Kong, China	360.1	319.0	313.2	295.4	306.3	358.1	335.7
Korea, Republic of	78.0	65.7	66.1	63.3	59.6	69.5	85.0
Mongolia	85.0	72.9	97.8	96.8	96.7	105.2	126.2
Taipei,China	119.7	96.8	101.5	100.6	93.7	106.7	118.6
South Asia[a]	**36.7**	**31.2**	**31.2**	**28.1**	**25.5**	**32.1**	**...**
Bangladesh	32.6	35.0	28.2	27.1	22.1	23.4	28.6
Bhutan[b]	86.9	76.7	63.1	64.0	67.6	63.2	...
India	36.9	30.5	31.2	27.8	25.6	32.9	34.4
Maldives	37.5	49.5	59.1	54.1	51.4	48.7	...
Nepal	36.5	35.5	38.4	39.3	33.3	39.3	43.7
Sri Lanka	37.6	34.6	36.1	35.8	30.8	37.4	41.3
Southeast Asia[a]	**98.2**	**89.5**	**93.1**	**86.0**	**85.4**	**...**	**...**
Brunei Darussalam	83.3	74.0	79.2	91.7	99.4	126.7	140.4
Cambodia[b]	93.3	125.3	129.4	137.4	153.0	186.4	187.0
Indonesia	38.9	34.0	35.4	30.3	28.8	36.1	40.1
Lao People's Democratic Republic[b]	56.4	64.7	64.6	64.4	60.2	73.2	98.9
Malaysia	142.1	124.3	130.1	121.9	125.8	144.2	159.3
Myanmar	...	45.3	55.6	53.0	42.8	...	...
Philippines	51.1	42.4	52.5	48.4	42.9	48.6	47.4
Singapore	277.4	216.1	207.7	198.9	201.6	203.7	212.2
Thailand	105.1	99.8	94.7	84.3	82.6	100.8	113.0
Timor-Leste[c]	38.5	33.2	39.1	37.0	41.2	41.1	...
Viet Nam	106.7	137.0	155.1	154.9	157.3	182.6	178.6
The Pacific[a]	**66.5**	**53.4**	**58.3**	**61.9**	**...**	**...**	**...**
Cook Islands	39.8	40.9	42.0	43.1	43.9	40.8	...
Fiji	84.2	69.4	66.9	69.5	57.2	71.2	...
Kiribati	49.6	66.5	56.5	70.7	66.4	68.3	...
Marshall Islands	105.0	93.8	86.8	116.1	81.6	76.3	...
Micronesia, Federated States of	66.6	63.2	60.9	...	...	...	...
Nauru	86.3	115.5	46.8	54.2	53.1	50.8	...
Niue	56.4	58.9	62.7	50.0	43.1	54.6	...
Palau	64.7	62.3	64.6	66.5	60.6	72.5	88.8
Papua New Guinea[b]	65.0	48.2	56.6	61.3	53.1	54.1	...
Samoa	43.3	40.2	42.0	44.7	39.0	42.8	52.0
Solomon Islands	70.4	69.2	69.9	62.6	54.1	...	...
Tonga	44.9	56.3	50.2	56.6	50.1	55.6	...
Tuvalu	72.7	105.7	53.3	60.7	65.5	57.3	...
Vanuatu	49.5	61.6	49.4	44.1	38.1	...	...
Developed ADB Member Economies[a]	**27.1**	**29.6**	**31.0**	**29.8**	**27.3**	**32.5**	**...**
Australia	33.9	31.8	35.2	35.8	33.2	38.0	43.8
Japan	25.4	28.6	29.5	27.9	25.3	30.6	38.9
New Zealand	42.2	39.7	39.4	38.4	35.5	37.1	...
DEVELOPING ADB MEMBER ECONOMIES[a]	**66.1**	**50.9**	**49.5**	**47.0**	**...**	**...**	**...**
ALL ADB REGIONAL MEMBERS[a]	**51.9**	**46.0**	**45.5**	**43.3**	**...**	**...**	**...**

... = data not available, ADB = Asian Development Bank, GDP = Gross Domestic Product.

Note: Trade in goods is calculated as the sum of merchandise exports and imports in United States dollars.

a For estimating aggregates, imputation was done for economies with missing data by substituting available data from the nearest years.
b The Key Indicators Database features a longer time series on trade in goods. The compilation methodology shifted from cost, insurance, and freight to free on board from 2004 onward for Bhutan; from 2005 onward for Cambodia; from 2017 onward for the Lao People's Democratic Republic; and from 2010 onward for Papua New Guinea.
c From September 2019, oil revenue from the Joint Petroleum Development Area is now included in GDP based on the new Timor-Leste Australia Maritime Boundary Treaty.

Sources: Economies' official sources; and International Monetary Fund. International Financial Statistics. http://data.imf.org/ (accessed 30 June 2023).

Table 2.4.13: Direction of Trade: Merchandise Exports
(% of total merchandise exports)

To / From / ADB Regional Member	Asia and the Pacific		Europe		North and Central America		Middle East		South America		Africa		Rest of the World	
	2010	2022	2010	2022	2010	2022	2010	2022	2010	2022	2010	2022	2010	2022
Developing ADB Member Economies														
Central and West Asia[a]	**27.6**	**31.3**	**53.4**	**55.2**	**8.8**	**4.8**	**8.3**	**4.0**	**0.4**	**0.4**	**1.2**	**1.1**	**0.4**	**3.3**
Afghanistan	63.7	75.5	21.6	11.6	1.1	1.4	13.6	11.4	0.0	0.0	0.0	0.1	0.0	0.0
Armenia	10.4	13.5	67.1	67.2	11.5	1.5	9.5	17.3	0.3	0.2	0.1	0.0	1.1	0.3
Azerbaijan	19.7	11.3	59.9	82.0	9.5	0.2	10.7	5.0	0.0	0.1	0.3	1.3	0.0	0.0
Georgia	33.8	45.9	42.0	42.3	18.6	5.1	4.6	2.8	0.4	2.8	0.6	1.0	0.0	0.0
Kazakhstan	24.2	34.1	64.5	61.6	6.0	1.7	4.5	2.1	0.1	0.1	0.1	0.3	0.7	0.0
Kyrgyz Republic	19.5	37.1	52.2	56.4	7.2	0.2	21.1	6.2	0.0	0.0	0.0	0.0	0.0	0.0
Pakistan	29.9	23.9	28.5	37.9	19.1	24.1	15.1	8.5	1.7	1.2	5.7	4.4	0.0	0.0
Tajikistan	47.4	40.6	40.8	55.6	0.0	0.8	8.1	2.9	0.0	0.1	3.6	0.1	0.0	0.0
Turkmenistan	52.0	86.2	38.4	12.0	1.9	0.5	7.1	0.2	0.0	1.1	0.7	0.1	0.0	0.0
Uzbekistan	60.2	29.7	30.6	27.0	0.0	1.0	9.0	1.2	0.1	0.0	0.0	0.1	0.0	41.0
East Asia[a]	**52.9**	**53.2**	**18.9**	**17.9**	**18.3**	**18.7**	**4.1**	**4.1**	**2.8**	**3.0**	**2.5**	**3.0**	**0.4**	**0.1**
China, People's Republic of	43.5	44.8	23.2	21.5	21.7	20.7	4.6	5.0	3.4	4.0	3.3	4.0	0.3	0.0
Hong Kong, China	72.2	79.3	12.6	9.0	12.4	7.6	1.4	2.9	0.9	0.8	0.5	0.5	0.1	0.0
Korea, Republic of	57.6	61.4	14.8	13.3	15.1	19.6	5.7	2.5	3.4	1.4	2.6	1.7	0.8	0.0
Mongolia	87.0	89.6	7.5	10.2	5.2	0.1	0.4	0.1	0.0	0.0	0.0	0.0	0.0	0.0
Taipei,China	71.1	70.8	10.6	8.6	13.0	17.6	2.3	1.4	1.3	0.6	0.8	0.6	1.0	0.5
South Asia[a]	**31.7**	**26.8**	**23.7**	**25.7**	**13.7**	**20.9**	**19.4**	**14.1**	**2.4**	**3.1**	**6.4**	**8.8**	**2.7**	**0.6**
Bangladesh	9.1	13.9	49.6	57.5	23.4	24.3	2.1	2.4	0.4	1.1	0.7	0.7	14.7	0.0
Bhutan	99.8	96.4	0.1	2.6	0.1	0.0	0.0	0.0	0.0	0.9	0.1	0.0	0.0	0.0
India	33.6	28.0	21.3	22.2	12.7	20.2	21.2	15.5	2.6	3.4	7.1	10.0	1.5	0.6
Maldives	59.2	61.3	36.4	30.5	0.7	2.2	3.2	0.4	0.0	0.0	0.6	5.7	0.0	0.0
Nepal	76.5	71.0	12.5	11.9	7.4	12.5	0.5	0.8	0.2	0.1	0.1	0.1	3.0	3.6
Sri Lanka	20.7	22.9	36.0	34.5	21.4	30.0	9.9	9.0	1.0	1.7	0.9	1.9	10.2	0.0
Southeast Asia[a]	**69.4**	**66.2**	**12.7**	**11.7**	**11.7**	**17.2**	**3.1**	**2.4**	**1.0**	**1.0**	**1.9**	**1.6**	**0.1**	**0.0**
Brunei Darussalam	99.6	99.3	0.2	0.3	0.2	0.0	0.0	0.0	0.0	0.4	0.0	0.0	0.0	0.0
Cambodia	41.6	21.7	17.6	25.4	39.7	51.1	0.3	0.5	0.4	0.6	0.1	0.5	0.2	0.3
Indonesia	70.9	71.1	12.5	10.8	10.2	12.2	3.2	2.9	1.5	1.0	1.7	2.0	0.0	0.0
Lao People's Democratic Republic	85.0	89.3	11.4	6.2	3.5	4.2	0.0	0.2	0.0	0.1	0.0	0.0	0.0	0.0
Malaysia	70.3	71.7	11.8	10.5	11.1	12.5	4.3	2.6	0.7	0.5	1.7	2.2	0.0	0.0
Myanmar	95.4	71.1	1.4	23.5	0.1	3.8	1.7	0.8	0.1	0.2	1.3	0.5	0.0	0.1
Philippines	67.3	67.7	14.8	12.9	16.0	17.8	1.1	0.8	0.5	0.5	0.4	0.2	0.0	0.0
Singapore	74.9	75.1	10.7	9.4	9.8	11.0	2.1	2.1	0.5	0.5	1.9	1.8	0.1	0.0
Thailand	62.9	62.5	14.6	11.4	12.1	18.8	5.0	3.7	2.1	1.7	3.0	1.8	0.3	0.1
Timor-Leste	57.8	92.8	23.4	1.9	0.4	5.0	6.6	0.1	0.1	0.0	11.8	0.1	0.0	0.0
Viet Nam	50.8	47.4	22.2	15.5	22.4	33.0	1.7	1.7	1.1	1.7	1.5	0.7	0.4	0.0
The Pacific[a]	**75.8**	**76.3**	**18.0**	**18.2**	**4.4**	**3.5**	**0.1**	**0.2**	**1.1**	**1.2**	**0.5**	**0.6**	**0.1**	**0.1**
Cook Islands	78.9	73.6	0.0	0.0	2.0	0.4	0.0	0.0	0.0	0.0	0.0	0.0	19.1	25.9
Fiji	71.8	66.2	7.5	6.7	18.7	26.1	0.3	0.4	0.0	0.0	0.8	0.5	0.8	0.0
Kiribati	97.8	97.8	2.2	0.2	0.0	2.1	0.0	0.0	0.0	0.0	0.0	0.0	0.0	0.0
Marshall Islands	0.3	6.3	95.5	87.8	4.2	1.4	0.0	1.1	0.0	0.0	0.0	3.5	0.0	0.0
Micronesia, Federated States of	88.2	94.9	2.6	0.7	9.2	4.4	0.0	0.0	0.0	0.0	0.1	0.0	0.0	0.0
Nauru	73.7	73.2	0.2	1.3	0.5	14.1	0.9	0.1	0.0	0.0	24.7	11.3	0.0	0.0
Niue	...	...	...	...	...	...	...	...	...	...	...	...	...	...
Palau	91.1	12.4	2.0	46.5	6.6	37.0	0.2	0.2	0.1	1.5	0.0	2.3	0.0	0.0
Papua New Guinea	80.8	86.0	17.0	11.1	2.0	1.4	0.0	0.0	0.0	1.3	0.2	0.0	0.0	0.1
Samoa	96.0	74.1	0.3	4.4	3.2	18.9	0.0	0.1	0.0	1.4	0.5	1.2	0.0	0.0
Solomon Islands	81.8	71.8	17.8	25.2	0.4	1.6	0.0	0.2	0.0	1.0	0.0	0.3	0.0	0.0
Tonga	86.5	83.8	0.0	0.0	13.5	16.1	0.0	0.0	0.0	0.0	0.0	0.0	0.0	0.0
Tuvalu	75.8	25.8	14.4	71.1	5.4	1.3	0.8	0.3	2.1	0.0	1.7	1.4	0.0	0.0
Vanuatu	31.6	58.6	1.8	3.5	20.5	9.0	0.4	0.0	45.4	27.3	0.3	1.6	0.0	0.0
Developed ADB Member Economies[a]	**63.5**	**68.3**	**12.8**	**10.2**	**16.9**	**15.5**	**3.4**	**2.8**	**1.6**	**1.2**	**1.4**	**1.1**	**0.3**	**0.9**
Australia	80.1	84.0	8.9	5.7	5.0	3.9	2.9	2.3	1.0	0.8	1.3	0.7	0.8	2.6
Japan	58.9	59.5	13.9	12.8	20.5	22.1	3.5	3.0	1.8	1.4	1.3	1.2	0.1	0.0
New Zealand	65.9	69.8	12.3	9.0	11.2	13.4	4.8	4.1	1.7	0.7	2.6	2.4	1.5	0.6
DEVELOPING ADB MEMBER ECONOMIES[a]	**55.2**	**54.2**	**18.6**	**17.8**	**16.1**	**18.1**	**4.9**	**4.3**	**2.3**	**2.4**	**2.5**	**3.0**	**0.5**	**0.2**
ALL ADB REGIONAL MEMBERS[a]	**56.8**	**56.0**	**17.5**	**16.8**	**16.2**	**17.8**	**4.6**	**4.1**	**2.1**	**2.3**	**2.3**	**2.7**	**0.5**	**0.3**
WORLD[a]	**30.9**	**33.2**	**40.1**	**37.9**	**17.2**	**18.4**	**4.6**	**4.0**	**2.9**	**2.6**	**2.7**	**2.7**	**1.6**	**1.2**

... = data not available, 0.0 = magnitude is less than half of unit employed, ADB = Asian Development Bank.

a Aggregates include estimates derived from reports of partner economies for nonreporting and slow-reporting economies.

Sources: International Monetary Fund. Direction of Trade Statistics. https://data.imf.org/?sk=9D6028D4-F14A-464C-A2F2-59B2CD424B85 (accessed 30 June 2023). For the Cook Islands and Taipei,China: Economies' official sources.

Table 2.4.14: Direction of Trade: Merchandise Imports
(% of total merchandise imports)

From / To	Asia and the Pacific		Europe		North and Central America		Middle East		South America		Africa		Rest of the World	
ADB Regional Member	**2010**	**2022**	**2010**	**2022**	**2010**	**2022**	**2010**	**2022**	**2010**	**2022**	**2010**	**2022**	**2010**	**2022**
Developing ADB Member Economies														
Central and West Asia[a]	**36.9**	**41.5**	**41.1**	**36.2**	**4.6**	**4.0**	**14.5**	**14.1**	**1.6**	**2.1**	**1.3**	**1.9**	**0.0**	**0.2**
Afghanistan	70.6	65.2	15.6	7.4	2.2	0.8	10.6	26.3	0.5	0.0	0.4	0.1	0.0	0.1
Armenia	21.9	28.7	64.4	54.1	3.8	5.7	7.4	8.1	2.0	1.4	0.4	0.5	0.1	1.5
Azerbaijan	24.1	32.6	64.8	57.1	3.8	3.9	3.7	4.1	3.2	2.2	0.3	0.2	0.0	0.0
Georgia	26.4	26.1	62.6	58.9	3.9	7.7	4.6	4.4	1.9	2.6	0.6	0.3	0.0	0.0
Kazakhstan	27.2	35.9	62.7	58.1	7.0	3.7	1.2	0.8	1.4	0.5	0.4	0.3	0.0	0.6
Kyrgyz Republic	41.9	59.6	50.3	35.8	6.6	2.8	0.9	0.7	0.3	0.7	0.1	0.4	0.0	0.0
Pakistan	40.5	42.7	13.8	8.8	5.7	4.8	35.5	34.8	1.2	3.7	3.3	5.2	0.1	0.0
Tajikistan	51.1	50.6	37.0	42.1	3.2	3.4	7.6	2.7	1.1	0.7	0.0	0.0	0.0	0.4
Turkmenistan	24.7	38.9	73.4	58.5	1.1	1.7	0.7	0.3	0.1	0.5	0.0	0.0	0.0	0.0
Uzbekistan	43.1	52.2	47.5	41.8	1.5	1.4	5.0	2.4	2.7	2.1	0.1	0.1	0.0	0.0
East Asia[a]	**57.2**	**54.8**	**13.4**	**15.3**	**9.2**	**9.5**	**8.4**	**9.3**	**3.9**	**5.3**	**2.8**	**3.0**	**5.1**	**2.9**
China, People's Republic of	50.1	46.6	15.2	18.0	9.1	9.0	6.6	9.9	5.7	7.7	4.2	4.2	9.2	4.6
Hong Kong, China	82.4	83.4	9.2	8.5	6.1	5.0	1.4	2.0	0.6	0.5	0.3	0.6	0.0	0.0
Korea, Republic of	52.8	52.8	13.1	13.2	11.2	13.8	18.9	14.4	2.7	3.0	1.2	1.8	0.0	0.9
Mongolia	48.6	53.6	44.7	42.3	5.9	3.6	0.2	0.2	0.4	0.3	0.3	0.1	0.0	0.0
Taipei,China	60.8	65.2	10.5	11.9	11.5	12.0	12.3	8.4	2.2	1.4	2.7	1.1	0.0	0.0
South Asia[a]	**37.3**	**43.5**	**19.3**	**15.8**	**6.2**	**7.7**	**25.5**	**23.5**	**3.3**	**3.1**	**7.5**	**6.3**	**1.0**	**0.0**
Bangladesh	67.6	68.6	9.8	6.7	3.8	4.9	8.4	9.7	2.5	4.6	1.0	5.2	6.9	0.3
Bhutan	93.2	97.6	5.5	1.3	0.5	0.2	0.8	0.2	0.0	0.0	0.1	0.0	0.0	0.7
India	33.1	38.6	20.4	17.3	6.5	8.3	27.6	25.9	3.4	3.1	8.4	6.8	0.6	0.0
Maldives	59.7	54.9	9.7	10.0	8.9	3.0	19.9	30.3	0.6	1.0	1.2	0.8	0.0	0.0
Nepal	86.4	86.8	4.8	3.8	1.7	3.1	5.0	4.8	1.9	1.0	0.1	0.3	0.0	0.2
Sri Lanka	64.7	73.5	16.1	11.3	4.2	2.8	13.4	10.3	0.9	0.2	0.4	1.6	0.4	0.1
Southeast Asia[a]	**67.2**	**73.0**	**12.5**	**9.4**	**9.8**	**7.6**	**7.6**	**6.3**	**1.7**	**2.0**	**0.8**	**1.4**	**0.5**	**0.2**
Brunei Darussalam	78.0	61.5	10.7	31.7	10.1	5.9	0.5	0.1	0.1	0.6	0.1	0.1	0.6	0.1
Cambodia	90.0	95.0	6.7	2.7	2.7	1.4	0.2	0.4	0.2	0.3	0.1	0.1	0.0	0.0
Indonesia	72.6	74.8	9.4	7.2	8.0	5.2	6.0	5.3	2.3	3.2	1.7	4.3	0.1	0.0
Lao People's Democratic Republic	95.0	97.5	4.5	2.0	0.5	0.5	0.0	0.0	0.0	0.0	0.0	0.0	0.0	0.0
Malaysia	68.7	72.8	11.5	9.4	12.2	8.5	3.8	5.9	1.8	1.9	1.5	1.4	0.5	0.1
Myanmar	77.7	93.0	1.7	3.5	0.6	0.8	2.1	2.0	0.2	0.7	0.1	0.1	17.6	0.0
Philippines	69.4	78.7	8.9	7.5	11.6	7.4	8.5	4.6	1.4	1.5	0.2	0.3	0.0	0.0
Singapore	60.2	64.4	15.8	13.8	12.6	11.9	9.6	7.2	1.4	1.7	0.3	0.9	0.0	0.0
Thailand	65.2	66.3	12.8	9.9	6.7	7.0	11.6	11.8	1.6	1.8	0.9	1.9	1.3	1.3
Timor-Leste	97.2	90.9	2.0	5.1	0.4	2.1	0.1	0.4	0.0	1.3	0.3	0.0	0.0	0.1
Viet Nam	80.1	83.6	10.6	5.5	5.0	4.6	1.8	3.2	2.1	2.6	0.4	0.6	0.0	0.0
The Pacific[a]	**81.6**	**87.3**	**11.4**	**7.2**	**5.6**	**2.8**	**0.1**	**0.6**	**0.1**	**1.6**	**0.6**	**0.2**	**0.5**	**0.5**
Cook Islands	91.8	84.0	0.0	0.2	2.8	4.8	0.0	0.0	0.0	0.0	0.0	0.0	5.4	11.0
Fiji	91.4	93.4	2.6	2.8	3.9	2.9	0.3	0.5	0.2	0.2	0.5	0.1	1.2	0.1
Kiribati	83.0	88.3	4.6	6.2	11.7	5.4	0.0	0.0	0.3	0.0	0.4	0.1	0.0	0.0
Marshall Islands	0.1	84.0	99.7	10.7	0.0	1.7	0.0	0.8	0.0	2.6	0.1	0.2	0.0	0.0
Micronesia, Federated States of	48.1	63.3	1.2	0.3	38.1	18.3	0.1	0.0	0.0	0.2	0.3	1.0	12.1	17.0
Nauru	80.2	97.4	3.7	0.8	16.0	1.4	0.0	0.0	0.0	0.0	0.0	0.3	0.0	0.0
Niue	...	...	...	...	...	...	...	...	...	...	...	...	...	...
Palau	63.7	68.8	0.6	6.6	34.9	24.1	0.0	0.0	0.0	0.2	0.3	0.2	0.5	0.0
Papua New Guinea	88.3	95.8	5.6	1.8	5.1	2.1	0.0	0.1	0.2	0.1	0.8	0.2	0.0	0.0
Samoa	87.0	84.0	1.3	5.6	11.4	9.5	0.0	0.0	0.0	0.4	0.0	0.0	0.2	0.4
Solomon Islands	97.1	96.0	1.1	2.0	1.7	1.8	0.0	0.0	0.0	0.0	0.1	0.1	0.0	0.0
Tonga	84.3	86.8	1.9	1.7	13.2	10.6	0.1	0.0	0.2	0.8	0.1	0.0	0.2	0.0
Tuvalu	95.0	82.5	0.1	1.5	3.6	1.8	0.4	14.0	0.0	0.1	0.9	0.2	0.0	0.0
Vanuatu	91.7	87.4	5.0	6.0	2.3	4.1	0.1	0.2	0.1	0.1	0.8	2.1	0.1	0.1
Developed ADB Member Economies[a]	**54.4**	**58.8**	**14.9**	**14.6**	**12.3**	**12.7**	**13.5**	**9.8**	**2.6**	**2.4**	**1.6**	**1.4**	**0.7**	**0.4**
Australia	59.6	65.6	20.0	17.4	12.7	12.2	2.3	1.6	1.1	0.8	1.4	1.0	3.0	1.4
Japan	52.6	55.9	13.3	13.4	12.2	12.9	17.1	13.0	3.2	3.0	1.6	1.6	0.0	0.0
New Zealand	62.9	67.2	16.7	17.7	12.3	11.0	6.2	2.2	0.7	1.3	0.8	0.6	0.2	0.0
DEVELOPING ADB MEMBER ECONOMIES[a]	**57.1**	**57.8**	**14.5**	**14.5**	**8.9**	**8.6**	**10.0**	**10.3**	**3.3**	**4.1**	**2.8**	**2.9**	**3.4**	**1.8**
ALL ADB REGIONAL MEMBERS[a]	**56.6**	**57.9**	**14.6**	**14.5**	**9.6**	**9.2**	**10.7**	**10.2**	**3.1**	**3.9**	**2.5**	**2.7**	**2.9**	**1.6**
WORLD[a]	**33.5**	**36.9**	**39.1**	**36.2**	**13.1**	**13.7**	**6.0**	**5.7**	**3.5**	**3.2**	**2.9**	**2.7**	**2.0**	**1.5**

... = data not available, 0.0 = magnitude is less than half of unit employed, ADB = Asian Development Bank.

a Aggregates include estimates derived from reports of partner economies for nonreporting and slow-reporting economies.

Sources: International Monetary Fund. Direction of Trade Statistics. https://data.imf.org/?sk=9D6028D4-F14A-464C-A2F2-59B2CD424B85 (accessed 30 June 2023). For the Cook Islands and Taipei,China: Economies' official sources.

Table 2.4.15: International Reserves and Ratio to Imports

ADB Regional Member	International Reserves[a] ($ million) 2010	2015	2021	2022	Ratio to Imports[b] (months) 2010	2015	2021	2022
Developing ADB Member Economies								
Central and West Asia[c]	**77,894**	**93,691**	**123,354**	**117,445**	**9.4**	**9.3**	**9.0**	**6.5**
Afghanistan	5,147	6,990	9,741 (2020)	...	12.9	11.6	19.9 (2020)	...
Armenia	1,866	1,775	3,230	4,112	6.9	7.6	8.1	6.5
Azerbaijan	6,409	7,910	8,307	11,290	11.5	9.7	9.6	10.0
Georgia	2,264	2,521	4,271	4,886	5.4	4.3	5.5	4.6
Kazakhstan	28,275	27,871	34,378	35,076	10.3	9.9	9.9	8.5
Kyrgyz Republic	1,720	1,778	2,978	2,799	7.0	5.6	6.9	3.7
Pakistan	17,210	20,045	22,811	9,927	6.6	5.8	5.0	1.7
Tajikistan	403	494	2,499	3,847	1.7	2.1	8.0	10.1
Turkmenistan	...	...	...	...	...	...	...	...
Uzbekistan	14,600	24,307	35,139	35,768	17.5	25.2	18.4	15.2
East Asia	**3,825,703**	**4,564,090**	**4,944,223**	**4,716,379**	**20.0**	**19.7**	**13.9**	**12.9**
China, People's Republic of	2,875,894	3,405,385	3,427,045	3,306,924	27.8	26.1	15.5	14.8
Hong Kong, China	268,743	358,727	496,856	424,025	8.4	8.2	8.9	8.2
Korea, Republic of	291,571	367,944	461,964	422,075	8.4	10.4	9.7	7.5
Mongolia	2,288	1,323	4,374	3,399	8.9	4.1	7.8	4.7
Taipei,China	387,206	430,711	553,984	559,956	18.5	19.4	18.2	16.9
South Asia[c]	**320,411**	**395,960**	**694,034**	**610,284**	**9.0**	**10.3**	**11.6**	**8.8**
Bangladesh	11,178	27,493	46,154	33,748	6.3	8.8	9.1	4.9
Bhutan	1,002	1,103	971	...	15.1	13.5	13.2	...
India	297,746	351,551	633,761	562,710	9.3	10.6	12.3	9.4
Maldives	350	564	806	832	3.3	3.6	4.0	3.0
Nepal	2,939	7,945	9,204	8,884	7.2	12.5	8.7	6.9
Sri Lanka	7,196	7,304	3,138	...	6.4	4.6	1.8	...
Southeast Asia[c]	**688,196**	**731,611**	**1,179,757**	**973,814**	**9.3**	**8.5**	**9.5**	**6.8**
Brunei Darussalam	1,563	3,367	4,980	...	7.3	12.6	7.2	...
Cambodia	3,802	7,376	20,263	17,803	6.9	6.7	7.9	6.7
Indonesia	96,211	105,929	144,905	137,233	9.7	9.4	9.2	7.2
Lao People's Democratic Republic	817	1,072	1,476	1,216	4.8	2.3	2.8	2.1
Malaysia	106,525	95,287	116,890	114,651	8.6	7.8	7.2	6.0
Myanmar	5,729	4,599	7,670 (2020)	...	16.0	4.0	...	...
Philippines	62,373	80,667	108,794	96,132	14.0	14.6	12.2	9.1
Singapore	225,715	247,746	417,896	289,465	8.7	9.8	12.9	7.8
Thailand	172,129	156,514	245,985	216,596	12.4	10.0	12.4	9.5
Timor-Leste	406	438	935	...	15.9	8.0	14.5	...
Viet Nam	12,926	28,616	109,963	87,131	2.0	2.2	4.1	3.0
The Pacific[c]	**4,582**	**3,871**	**6,362**	**...**	**8.6**	**4.1**	**13.2**	**...**
Cook Islands	...	...	...	...	...	...	...	...
Fiji	721	919	1,518	1,556	5.6	5.9	9.9	7.1
Kiribati	8	7	23	21	1.3	0.7	1.4	...
Marshall Islands	...	...	...	...	...	...	...	...
Micronesia, Federated States of	56	135	497	...	4.2	9.7	...	...
Nauru	...	...	...	...	...	...	...	...
Niue	...	...	...	...	...	...	...	...
Palau	...	...	...	...	...	...	...	...
Papua New Guinea	3,092	1,738	2,309 (2019)	...	10.5	2.7	1.9 (2019)	...
Samoa	173	112	295	321	7.4	4.5	10.5	9.5
Solomon Islands	266	534	695	662	8.9	14.6	17.8	14.5
Tonga	105	156	362	376	6.0	6.2	23.9	21.8
Tuvalu	...	...	...	...	...	...	...	...
Vanuatu	161	269	665	639	8.1	10.4	38.2	...
Developed ADB Member Economies[c]	**1,155,175**	**1,293,326**	**1,479,709**	**1,298,681**	**16.3**	**17.9**	**17.3**	**13.5**
Australia	42,268	45,412	57,846	56,705	2.6	2.7	2.9	2.5
Japan	1,096,185	1,233,214	1,405,750	1,227,576	21.0	23.5	23.0	16.9
New Zealand	16,723	14,700	16,114	14,400	6.5	5.1	3.8	...
DEVELOPING ADB MEMBER ECONOMIES[c]	**4,916,787**	**5,789,222**	**6,947,731**	**6,423,806**	**15.9**	**15.8**	**12.6**	**...**
ALL ADB REGIONAL MEMBERS[c]	**6,071,962**	**7,082,548**	**8,427,441**	**7,722,486**	**16.0**	**16.1**	**13.2**	**...**

... = data not available, $ = United States dollars, ADB = Asian Development Bank.

a Data refer to international reserves with gold at national valuation, unless otherwise specified, as of the end of the year. For Afghanistan (2000–2007 and 2021–2022), Bhutan (2000–2018 and 2022), Brunei Darussalam (2022), Kiribati, Lao People's Democratic Republic (2021–2022), Myanmar (2021–2022), Nauru, Palau, Papua New Guinea (2020–2022), Samoa, Solomon Islands (2000–2011), Sri Lanka (2022), Timor-Leste (2000–2002 and 2022), Tonga, Turkmenistan, Uzbekistan (2005–2012), and Vanuatu, data refer to international reserves without gold. For estimating regional aggregates, imputation was done for economies with missing data using available data from nearest years.

b Merchandise imports from the balance of payments were used in the calculations. The aggregate ratios were calculated using only reporting economies with data available for both reserves and imports in the years specified in the column headings.

c Aggregates include only reporting economies with data corresponding to the year heading.

Sources: For international reserves: International Monetary Fund (IMF). International Financial Statistics. http://data.imf.org/ (accessed 30 June 2023); and for Taipei,China: economy's official source. For the reserves-to-imports ratio: Asian Development Bank estimates using data from the IMF's International Financial Statistics; official communications from the IMF; and economies' official sources.

Table 2.4.16: Net Official Development Assistance from All Sources to Developing Economies
($ million)

ADB Regional Member	2010	2016	2017	2018	2019	2020	2021
Developing ADB Member Economies							
Central and West Asia[a]	**11,448**	**9,384**	**8,524**	**7,999**	**9,212**	**10,923**	**10,836**
Afghanistan	6,235	4,069	3,812	3,792	4,137	4,209	4,693
Armenia	320	326	258	142	417	135	162
Azerbaijan	156	79	124	87	119	123	10
Georgia	589	463	447	589	492	1,041	769
Kazakhstan	212	63	59	80	54	74	58
Kyrgyz Republic	372	519	465	439	443	485	479
Pakistan	2,933	2,961	2,364	1,387	2,010	2,592	2,923
Tajikistan	388	360	328	404	362	768	551
Turkmenistan	44	32	28	20	25	34	29
Uzbekistan	198	511	639	1,058	1,153	1,462	1,162
East Asia[a]	**959**	**-466**	**-224**	**-372**	**-298**	**130**	**-282**
China, People's Republic of	672	-791	-990	-705	-609	-573	-564
Hong Kong, China	...	...	...	...	...	...	...
Korea, Republic of	...	...	...	...	...	...	...
Mongolia	287	326	766	334	311	702	282
Taipei,China	...	...	...	...	...	...	...
South Asia[a]	**5,670**	**6,724**	**8,731**	**6,951**	**8,706**	**9,661**	**10,215**
Bangladesh	1,327	2,533	3,782	3,045	4,382	5,375	5,089
Bhutan	97	52	119	108	179	203	127
India	2,831	2,679	3,198	2,462	2,550	1,795	3,135
Maldives	88	23	46	131	71	311	112
Nepal	767	1,065	1,270	1,452	1,333	1,759	1,598
Sri Lanka	559	373	316	-247	192	218	154
Southeast Asia[a]	**6,365**	**6,146**	**6,180**	**5,993**	**4,788**	**9,054**	**6,637**
Brunei Darussalam	...	...	...	...	...	...	...
Cambodia	681	728	856	783	966	1,374	1,367
Indonesia	1,324	-108	280	963	-693	1,210	626
Lao People's Democratic Republic	389	399	480	589	622	529	576
Malaysia	-6	-52	-29	-34	-3	-5	14
Myanmar	355	1,537	1,542	1,712	2,044	2,870	1,507
Philippines	582	284	160	547	886	1,456	1,634
Singapore	...	...	...	...	...	...	...
Thailand	-20	228	250	-419	-352	198	132
Timor-Leste	290	224	232	208	230	250	255
Viet Nam	2,770	2,906	2,407	1,645	1,088	1,171	526
The Pacific[a]	**1,435**	**1,345**	**1,579**	**1,899**	**1,742**	**2,549**	**2,883**
Cook Islands	14	17	19	34	29	29 (2019)	...
Fiji	76	117	146	121	129	194	609
Kiribati	24	61	77	80	57	58	73
Marshall Islands	25	13	73	54	66	183	107
Micronesia, Federated States of	64	51	98	99	93	172	131
Nauru	28	23	26	38	54	28	34
Niue	15	14	15	19	19	22	28
Palau	29	18	22	85	25	66	51
Papua New Guinea	514	532	533	790	649	1,056	1,185
Samoa	124	89	136	128	124	167	84
Solomon Islands	333	176	187	196	224	214	265
Tonga	66	83	87	97	108	163	113
Tuvalu	14	24	29	27	36	43	36
Vanuatu	109	129	133	131	131	154	167
DEVELOPING ADB MEMBER ECONOMIES[a]	**25,876**	**23,134**	**24,790**	**22,470**	**24,150**	**32,316**	**30,289**
DEVELOPING ECONOMIES WORLDWIDE[b]	**129,264**	**158,811**	**165,081**	**167,562**	**163,493**	**195,210**	**203,693**

... = data not available, $ = United States dollars, ADB = Asian Development Bank.

Note: Net official development assistance refers to concessional flows to developing economies and multilateral institutions provided by official agencies, including state and local governments, or by their executing agencies, administered with the objective of promoting the economic development and welfare of developing economies, and containing a grant element of at least 25%. Net flow takes into account principal repayments for loans, offsetting entries for forgiven debt, and recoveries made on grants.

a For reporting economies only.
b Includes data for all developing economies as reported in the Organisation for Economic Co-operation and Development's OECD.Stat database.

Source: Organisation for Economic Co-operation and Development. OECD.Stat Database. http://stats.oecd.org (accessed 20 July 2023).

Table 2.4.17: Net Other Official Flows from All Sources to Developing Economies
($ million)

ADB Regional Member	2010	2016	2017	2018	2019	2020	2021
Developing ADB Member Economies							
Central and West Asia[a]	**4,070.1**	**5,540.1**	**2,663.7**	**1,869.2**	**3,028.3**	**4,634.3**	**2,301.2**
Afghanistan	71.2	97.2	56.1	0.2	14.8	–1.5	1.7
Armenia	288.3	197.2	157.6	156.7	225.3	81.8	96.8
Azerbaijan	179.9	1,114.7	1,738.5	490.7	343.6	–118.4	–559.7
Georgia	250.2	486.6	262.1	218.9	411.9	851.2	1,090.4
Kazakhstan	2,247.2	441.4	–853.7	–586.6	–53.5	568.7	401.3
Kyrgyz Republic	18.3	–43.2	–6.0	51.2	33.4	15.3	23.3
Pakistan	345.3	1,102.3	378.2	–137.1	755.9	1,536.3	864.1
Tajikistan	6.4	13.6	15.6	48.2	75.4	62.4	89.1
Turkmenistan	647.4	926.1	532.3	127.6	–811.1	171.7	–657.7
Uzbekistan	16.0	1,204.2	383.0	1,499.5	2,032.6	1,466.7	951.9
East Asia[a]	**3,355.5**	**896.3**	**1,036.2**	**818.7**	**1,086.2**	**1,287.7**	**4,487.1**
China, People's Republic of	3,196.3	139.9	1,227.3	645.4	664.0	931.2	4,004.3
Hong Kong, China	...	...	...	...	...	...	...
Korea, Republic of	...	...	...	...	...	...	...
Mongolia	159.3	756.4	–191.1	173.3	422.2	356.5	482.8
Taipei,China	...	...	...	...	...	...	...
South Asia[a]	**6,175.1**	**3,653.6**	**3,636.7**	**2,831.4**	**3,289.3**	**10,585.1**	**7,439.4**
Bangladesh	35.1	1,421.5	2,337.4	938.4	1,208.9	1,833.9	2,304.4
Bhutan	24.0	8.0	3.1	–5.2	6.4	4.2	3.9
India	5,967.5	1,935.6	1,190.1	1,650.9	1,899.4	8,224.4	4,061.4
Maldives	–33.9	–24.7	–23.8	18.0	–6.6	–16.3	51.6
Nepal	–6.9	0.7	–2.3	–0.2	51.2	–2.8	50.6
Sri Lanka	189.3	312.6	132.3	229.5	130.0	541.7	967.5
Southeast Asia[a]	**3,916.6**	**3,110.3**	**60.5**	**4,789.0**	**5,858.8**	**7,684.6**	**6,788.7**
Brunei Darussalam	...	...	...	...	...	...	...
Cambodia	–5.0	–12.3	84.1	–24.8	86.5	15.7	–7.5
Indonesia	1,783.7	3,708.7	2,963.1	3,793.7	1,804.8	2,164.1	1,710.7
Lao People's Democratic Republic	–120.5	38.6	74.7	34.1	20.6	–27.7	–223.9
Malaysia	159.2	–1,494.5	–739.8	–963.0	1,971.0	–475.3	–15.4
Myanmar	30.9	100.6	96.4	16.3	130.4	417.7	–265.2
Philippines	–680.3	203.1	–32.2	956.5	456.8	6,272.5	3,803.5
Singapore	...	...	...	...	...	...	...
Thailand	–71.5	–39.3	–1,051.6	–614.0	718.6	211.7	915.6
Timor-Leste	4.6	24.8	11.8	26.5	38.3	14.8	3.3
Viet Nam	2,815.4	580.6	–1,345.9	1,563.7	631.8	–908.9	867.6
The Pacific[a]	**4,982.0**	**–144.7**	**–164.0**	**–2.7**	**62.5**	**566.4**	**82.3**
Cook Islands	9.7	–1.2	1.8	0.6	3.4	...	...
Fiji	14.2	40.6	48.3	27.0	10.9	309.5	171.9
Kiribati	0.5	0.3	0.1	0.3	0.3	...	...
Marshall Islands	–0.6	36.7	17.1	58.7	144.5	–38.6	–21.2
Micronesia, Federated States of	0.8	2.3	1.5	0.2	0.1	–0.3	–1.0
Nauru	0.3	62.5	19.4	0.4	0.1	...	...
Niue	...	–	...	...	0.1	...	...
Palau	6.4 (2011)	6.6	9.9	8.7	4.9	17.1	9.4
Papua New Guinea	4,892.3	–320.7	–267.2	–120.7	–181.4	281.5	–74.3
Samoa	4.1	5.6	1.3	–0.2	0.7	–2.0	–0.2
Solomon Islands	59.2	19.1	0.5	10.9	73.0	0.1	0.1 (2020)
Tonga	0.3	2.5	1.2	2.3	2.0	–	– (2020)
Tuvalu	–0.1	0.2	0.1	0.2	0.2	–	– (2020)
Vanuatu	1.3	0.9	2.1	8.8	3.9	–0.9	–2.4
DEVELOPING ADB MEMBER ECONOMIES[a]	**22,499.2**	**13,055.7**	**7,233.0**	**10,305.5**	**13,325.1**	**24,758.1**	**21,098.7**
DEVELOPING ECONOMIES WORLDWIDE[b]	**70,855.8**	**29,290.3**	**30,542.3**	**38,595.9**	**28,036.8**	**56,234.7**	**65,358.5**

... = data not available, – = magnitude equals zero, $ = United States dollars, ADB = Asian Development Bank.

Note: Net other official flows refer to official sector transactions with economies on the Development Assistance Committee List of Official Development Assistance Recipients, which do not meet the conditions for eligibility as official development assistance, either because they are not primarily aimed at development or because they have a grant element of less than 25%. The Development Assistance Committee List of Official Development Assistance Recipients is available at http://www.oecd.org/dac/financing-sustainable-development/development-finance-standards/daclist.htm. Net other official flows also include net export credits. Net flow takes into account principal repayments for loans, offsetting entries for forgiven debt, and recoveries made on grants.

a For reporting economies only.
b Includes data for all developing economies as reported in the Organisation for Economic Co-operation and Development's OECD.Stat database.

Source: Organisation for Economic Co-operation and Development. OECD.Stat Database. http://stats.oecd.org (accessed 16 July 2023).

Capital Flows

Table 2.4.18: Net Private Flows from All Sources to Developing Economies
($ million)

ADB Regional Member	2010	2016	2017	2018	2019	2020	2021
Developing ADB Member Economies							
Central and West Asia[a]	**-822**	**1,243**	**-1,184**	**-6,680**	**33**	**3,921**	**4,480**
Afghanistan	-21	-5	3	1	2	–	1
Armenia	-69	179	88	88	107	4	54
Azerbaijan	798	404	146	205	483	502	392
Georgia	22	190	361	334	224	590	36
Kazakhstan	-1,511	-86	-3,000	-7,575	-1,020	2,718	3,650
Kyrgyz Republic	23	-23	15	12	-1	-12	-16
Pakistan	-75	192	703	-86	93	107	264
Tajikistan	18	-2	-42	43	-18	41	-9
Turkmenistan	-46	285	107	-26	-230	-316	-150
Uzbekistan	39	108	436	323	394	287	257
East Asia[a]	**46,322**	**42,731**	**38,835**	**31,500**	**42,949**	**20,081**	**17,244**
China, People's Republic of	46,301	42,145	38,767	31,290	42,360	21,275	18,093
Hong Kong, China	...	...	...	...	...	...	...
Korea, Republic of	...	...	...	...	...	...	...
Mongolia	22	586	68	210	589	-1,194	-849
Taipei,China	...	...	...	...	...	...	...
South Asia[a]	**20,237**	**14,937**	**19,632**	**14,914**	**20,318**	**5,987**	**12,073**
Bangladesh	-3	-380	225	30	332	359	2
Bhutan	18	-0	-1	-7	0	1	-1
India	19,976	14,812	18,961	13,980	19,550	5,961	12,267
Maldives	38	17	-1	148	148	-33	51
Nepal	-11	6	53	25	30	26	-13
Sri Lanka	218	482	394	739	259	-328	-234
Southeast Asia[a]	**21,463**	**23,520**	**25,424**	**21,095**	**69,611**	**20,638**	**15,792**
Brunei Darussalam	...	...	...	...	...	...	...
Cambodia	256	403	412	457	644	1,033	234
Indonesia	3,348	10,353	11,225	6,429	13,843	6,214	6,792
Lao People's Democratic Republic	172	44	72	27	97	9	23
Malaysia	6,573	2,133	2,961	79	9,102	2,752	2,420
Myanmar	260	356	452	415	559	395	56
Philippines	2,424	2,738	4,251	3,049	31,544	2,215	175
Singapore	...	...	...	...	...	...	...
Thailand	6,394	2,762	1,497	6,647	7,476	2,660	3,384
Timor-Leste	-3	-42	15	4	8	-0	41
Viet Nam	2,038	4,772	4,537	3,989	6,337	5,359	2,668
The Pacific[a]	**978**	**925**	**1,211**	**-2,063**	**-1,091**	**40**	**-1,160**
Cook Islands	-0	-1	0	-18	-1	...	...
Fiji	-3	-15	45	40	9	21	13
Kiribati	-0	-9	-1	9	5	...	...
Marshall Islands	974	9	572	-515	30	-178	39
Micronesia, Federated States of	3	714	453	-1,641	-1,215	55	-790
Nauru	-0 (2011)	-0	0	-0	-0	-12	...
Niue	-0 (2012)	0	0	0	0	2	9
Palau	3	9	10	9	8	8	0
Papua New Guinea	-40	211	134	8	61	153	-506
Samoa	17	8	6	54	-3	11	0
Solomon Islands	3	-1	-8	-0	3	1	1
Tonga	-10	-0	0	0	4	0	...
Tuvalu	1 (2011)	0	0	...	...	0	...
Vanuatu	31	1	-1	-10	9	-22	74
DEVELOPING ADB MEMBER ECONOMIES[a]	**88,177**	**83,357**	**83,916**	**58,766**	**131,819**	**50,666**	**48,428**
DEVELOPING ECONOMIES WORLDWIDE[b]	**324,145**	**128,540**	**235,112**	**96,429**	**216,919**	**-15,867**	**211,951**

... = data not available, – = magnitude equals zero, (-/+) 0 = magnitude is less than half of unit employed, $ = United States dollars, ADB = Asian Development Bank.

Note: Net private flows refer to the sum of direct investments and portfolio investments.

a For reporting economies only.
b Includes data for all developing economies as reported in the Organisation for Economic Co-operation and Development's OECD.Stat database.

Source: Organisation for Economic Co-operation and Development. OECD.Stat Database. http://stats.oecd.org (accessed 17 July 2023).

Table 2.4.19: Aggregate Net Resource Flows from All Sources to Developing Economies
($ million)

ADB Regional Member	2010	2016	2017	2018	2019	2020	2021
Developing ADB Member Economies							
Central and West Asia[a]	**14,696**	**16,168**	**10,004**	**3,189**	**12,273**	**20,581**	**17,617**
Afghanistan	6,285	4,162	3,871	3,794	4,154	4,207	4,696
Armenia	539	703	503	387	750	221	313
Azerbaijan	1,135	1,598	2,008	783	946	506	–158
Georgia	861	1,139	1,070	1,142	1,128	2,482	1,895
Kazakhstan	948	419	–3,794	–8,081	–1,020	3,484	4,109
Kyrgyz Republic	413	453	474	502	475	489	486
Pakistan	3,203	4,255	3,445	1,164	2,859	4,180	4,051
Tajikistan	413	371	302	495	419	872	631
Turkmenistan	645	1,244	667	122	–1,016	378	–779
Uzbekistan	253	1,823	1,458	2,880	3,579	3,761	2,371
East Asia[a]	**50,636**	**43,162**	**39,647**	**31,947**	**43,737**	**12,160**	**21,449**
China, People's Republic of	50,169	41,494	39,004	31,231	42,415	12,252	21,533
Hong Kong, China	...	...	...	...	...	...	...
Korea, Republic of	...	...	...	...	...	...	...
Mongolia	468	1,668	642	716	1,322	–92	–84
Taipei,China	...	...	...	...	...	...	...
South Asia[a]	**32,082**	**25,315**	**31,999**	**24,697**	**32,313**	**20,356**	**29,728**
Bangladesh	1,360	3,574	6,345	4,013	5,922	6,731	7,395
Bhutan	140	60	121	95	185	209	130
India	28,774	19,427	23,349	18,093	23,999	10,972	19,463
Maldives	93	15	22	297	212	255	215
Nepal	749	1,071	1,321	1,477	1,414	1,782	1,637
Sri Lanka	966	1,168	842	721	581	407	888
Southeast Asia[a]	**31,744**	**32,776**	**31,664**	**31,877**	**80,257**	**26,359**	**29,218**
Brunei Darussalam	...	...	...	...	...	...	...
Cambodia	932	1,120	1,353	1,215	1,697	2,233	1,594
Indonesia	6,456	13,953	14,468	11,186	14,954	6,435	9,129
Lao People's Democratic Republic	441	482	627	650	739	521	375
Malaysia	6,726	587	2,192	–918	11,071	332	2,419
Myanmar	646	1,993	2,090	2,143	2,733	3,893	1,297
Philippines	2,326	3,225	4,379	4,553	32,887	9,682	5,612
Singapore	...	...	...	...	...	...	...
Thailand	6,302	2,951	696	5,614	7,843	–1,031	4,432
Timor-Leste	292	207	259	238	276	258	299
Viet Nam	7,623	8,258	5,599	7,197	8,056	4,036	4,062
The Pacific[a]	**7,395**	**2,126**	**2,626**	**–167**	**714**	**3,246**	**1,805**
Cook Islands	23	15	21	17	31	31 (2019)	...
Fiji	87	143	239	188	149	525	794
Kiribati	24	52	77	90	62	58	73
Marshall Islands	998	58	661	–402	240	–102	125
Micronesia, Federated States of	68	767	552	–1,542	–1,122	165	–661
Nauru	28	85	45	38	54	17	34
Niue	15	14	15	19	19	24	37
Palau	32	33	42	102	37	85	60
Papua New Guinea	5,366	422	400	678	528	1,685	606
Samoa	145	103	143	182	121	164	84
Solomon Islands	395	194	179	206	300	215	265
Tonga	57	85	88	100	114	163	113
Tuvalu	14	25	29	28	37	43	36
Vanuatu	142	131	134	130	143	173	238
DEVELOPING ADB MEMBER ECONOMIES[a]	**136,553**	**119,547**	**115,940**	**91,542**	**169,294**	**82,703**	**99,817**
DEVELOPING ECONOMIES WORLDWIDE[b]	**524,265**	**316,641**	**430,735**	**302,587**	**408,448**	**215,275**	**481,002**

... = data not available, $ = United States dollars, ADB = Asian Development Bank.

Note: Aggregate net resource flows refer to the sum of net official development assistance, net other official flows, and net private flows.

a For reporting economies only.
b Includes data for all developing economies as reported in the Organisation for Economic Co-operation and Development's OECD.Stat database.

Source: Organisation for Economic Co-operation and Development. OECD.Stat Database. http://stats.oecd.org (accessed 17 July 2023).

External Indebtedness

Table 2.4.20: Total External Debt of Developing Economies—Dollar Amounts
($ million)

ADB Regional Member	Total External Debt			External Debt (Public and Publicly Guaranteed)		
	2010	2015	2021	2010	2015	2021
Developing ADB Member Economies						
Central and West Asia[a]	**224,402**	**294,965**	**404,192**	**68,381**	**109,812**	**183,113**
Afghanistan	2,436	2,597	3,531	1,976	1,990	1,908
Armenia	6,307	8,831	13,818	2,560	3,998	6,263
Azerbaijan	7,251	13,319	14,645	3,812	8,712	13,020
Georgia	8,790	14,875	22,053	3,274	5,721	9,081
Kazakhstan	119,151	153,470	159,755	3,845	20,404	26,490
Kyrgyz Republic	4,118	7,722	9,064	2,446	3,433	3,960
Pakistan	63,124	68,614	130,433	43,726	51,043	94,670
Tajikistan	3,561	5,144	7,046	1,806	2,093	3,186
Turkmenistan	1,682	7,004	4,851	1,513	6,869	4,386
Uzbekistan	7,981	13,390	38,995	3,423	5,550	20,148
East Asia[a]	**2,083,974**	**3,211,088**	**5,453,670**	**...**	**...**	**...**
China, People's Republic of	742,737	1,333,769	2,702,505	102,275	146,062	475,424
Hong Kong, China	879,034	1,300,348	1,818,191 (2022)	...	...	...
Korea, Republic of	354,693	396,064	664,503 (2022)	...	...	...
Mongolia	5,928	21,953	33,940	1,782	4,006	11,625
Taipei,China	101,581	158,954	202,146 (2022)	8,035	1,116	1,034 (2022)
South Asia[a]	**344,322**	**568,606**	**776,660**	**143,193**	**223,026**	**317,923**
Bangladesh	26,572	38,695	91,429	21,146	27,094	62,425
Bhutan	935	2,011	3,069	919	1,945	2,987
India	290,428	478,826	612,866	100,563	162,305	205,105
Maldives	917	1,006	3,847	628	685	3,092
Nepal	3,787	4,143	8,856	3,507	3,543	7,794
Sri Lanka	21,684	43,925	56,592	16,430	27,453	36,520
Southeast Asia[a]	**557,124 (2012)**	**625,452**	**921,508**	**255,440 (2012)**	**289,286**	**418,451**
Brunei Darussalam	...	...	...	...	...	...
Cambodia	4,010	9,436	20,020	3,060	5,638	9,452
Indonesia	198,278	307,749	416,471	102,748	159,571	242,719
Lao People's Democratic Republic	6,554	11,642	17,188	3,751	6,689	10,271
Malaysia	...	...	...	...	...	...
Myanmar	9,990	10,220	13,927	8,433	9,714	11,822
Philippines	65,350	76,270	106,428	45,086	38,864	59,284
Singapore	...	...	...	...	...	...
Thailand	106,358	132,186	210,982	15,929	22,396	36,136
Timor-Leste	...	117	279	...	46	232
Viet Nam	44,941	77,833	136,213	32,799	46,367	48,536
The Pacific[a]	**8,282**	**22,991**	**21,759 (2019)**	**...**	**...**	**...**
Cook Islands	99	75	71 (2019)	...	...	...
Fiji	1,107	1,233	2,028	426	678	1,213
Kiribati	14	33	47 (2019)	...	...	...
Marshall Islands	105	95	64 (2022)	...	...	...
Micronesia, Federated States of	...	...	...	...	...	...
Nauru	...	...	...	...	...	...
Niue	...	...	...	...	...	...
Palau	66	64	218* (2022)	...	...	...
Papua New Guinea	5,987	20,387	16,983	1,042	1,501	6,041
Samoa	325	437	443	299	408	381
Solomon Islands	231	207	483	125	81	141
Tonga	154	184	224	144	175	186
Tuvalu	15	19	3	...	...	...
Vanuatu	178	257	515	103	172	412
DEVELOPING ADB MEMBER ECONOMIES[a]	**3,096,461**	**4,723,103**	**7,576,937**	**537,610**	**776,323**	**1,416,482**
DEVELOPING ECONOMIES WORLDWIDE[a,b]	**5,627,637**	**8,245,320**	**12,013,394**	**1,573,709**	**2,306,657**	**3,487,010**

... = data not available; * = provisional, preliminary, estimate; $ = United States dollars; ADB = Asian Development Bank.

Note: Refers to the sum of public and publicly guaranteed long-term debt, private nonguaranteed long-term debt, use of International Monetary Fund credit, and estimated short-term debt.

a Regional aggregates include only reporting economies with data corresponding to the year heading.
b Refers to all low- and middle-income economies as classified by the World Bank. For developing member economies not covered by the World Bank, data are from the economies' official sources.

Sources: World Bank. International Debt Statistics. http://data.worldbank.org/data-catalog/international-debt-statistics (accessed 1 July 2023); and Asian Development Bank estimates using economies' official sources.

Table 2.4.21: Total External Debt of Developing ADB Member Economies—Proportion of Income
(% of GNI)

ADB Regional Member	Total External Debt			External Debt (Public and Publicly Guaranteed)		
	2010	2015	2021	2010	2015	2021
Developing ADB Member Economies						
Central and West Asia						
Afghanistan	15.3	13.5	15.0 (2020)	12.6	9.9	13.0
Armenia	64.9	80.4	102.6	26.3	36.4	46.5
Azerbaijan	14.6	25.9	27.5	7.7	17.0	24.3
Georgia	73.1	101.8	124.8	27.2	39.1	52.0
Kazakhstan	92.6	88.8	95.9	3.0	11.8	15.3
Kyrgyz Republic	91.7	120.3	115.8	54.5	53.5	48.8
Pakistan	36.3	25.8	38.2	25.1	19.2	27.5
Tajikistan	51.1	52.5	66.7	25.9	21.4	29.6
Turkmenistan	8.1	20.8	15.0 (2019)	7.3	20.4	11.8 (2020)
Uzbekistan	15.8	15.3	56.2	6.8	6.3	28.8
East Asia						
China, People's Republic of	12.3	12.1	15.4	1.7	1.3	2.7
Hong Kong, China[a]	384.7	420.2	503.8 (2022)	...	...	...
Korea, Republic of	31.0	26.9	39.4 (2022)	...	...	...
Mongolia	89.7	206.1	260.7	27.0	37.6	89.0
Taipei,China[a,b]	22.2	29.0	25.9 (2022)	1.8	0.2	0.1 (2022)
South Asia						
Bangladesh	21.3	18.6	20.9	17.0	13.0	14.2
Bhutan	64.0	108.1	139.8 (2020)	63.0	104.5	125.3
India	17.5	23.0	19.6	6.1	7.8	6.6
Maldives	40.3	26.6	86.8	27.6	18.1	62.9
Nepal	23.5	16.8	24.3	21.8	14.3	21.0
Sri Lanka	38.6	55.9	68.6	28.3	33.0	42.2
Southeast Asia						
Brunei Darussalam	...	...	...	...	...	...
Cambodia	37.4	55.7	78.4	28.2	33.1	37.0
Indonesia	27.0	37.0	36.1	14.0	19.2	21.0
Lao People's Democratic Republic	98.1	84.5	97.2	56.2	48.5	57.9
Malaysia	...	...	...	...	...	...
Myanmar	27.7	16.9	22.0	23.4	16.0	18.7
Philippines	28.2	22.3	26.1	19.5	11.4	14.5
Singapore	...	...	...	...	...	...
Thailand	32.5	34.7	43.2	4.9	5.9	7.4
Timor-Leste	1.8 (2012)	4.2	11.7	0.0 (2012)	1.6	12.3
Viet Nam	31.5	34.3	39.3	23.0	20.4	14.0
The Pacific						
Cook Islands[a]	41.0	25.0	12.3 (2019)	...	...	...
Fiji	36.4	28.0	46.5	14.0	15.4	30.0
Kiribati[a]	8.5	20.0	23.0* (2019)	...	...	...
Marshall Islands[a]	62.7	52.2	0.2 (2022)	...	...	...
Micronesia, Federated States of[a]	29.0	25.6	...	...	...	...
Nauru	...	...	...	...	...	...
Niue	...	...	...	...	...	...
Palau[a]	35.3	22.4	74.9	...	...	...
Papua New Guinea	45.4	95.6	65.5	7.9	7.0	24.0
Samoa	50.5	56.7	57.3	45.3	50.5	45.9
Solomon Islands	28.7	16.2	29.2	14.7	6.3	8.8
Tonga	40.6	41.8	36.7 (2020)	37.9	39.7	37.6
Tuvalu[a]	49.1	53.5	3.6 (2022)	...	...	...
Vanuatu	27.4	34.5	50.6	15.8	23.1	37.2

... = data not available; * = provisional, preliminary, estimate; 0.0 = magnitude is less than half of unit employed; ADB = Asian Development Bank; GNI = gross national income.

a For total external debt as a percentage of GNI, gross domestic product is used in lieu of GNI.
b For public and publicly guaranteed external debt as a percentage of GNI, gross domestic product is used in lieu of GNI.

Sources: For total external debt (% of GNI): World Bank. International Debt Statistics. http://data.worldbank.org/data-catalog/international-debt-statistics (accessed 1 July 2023); and economies' official sources. For public and publicly guaranteed external debt (% of GNI): Asian Development Bank estimates using the World Bank's International Debt Statistics and World Development Indicators; and economies' official sources.

External Indebtedness

Table 2.4.22: Total External Debt of Developing ADB Member Economies—Proportion of Exports
(% of exports of goods, services, and primary income)

ADB Regional Member	2010	2016	2017	2018	2019	2020	2021
Developing ADB Member Economies							
Central and West Asia							
Afghanistan	88.7	188.7	189.5	141.1	142.4	177.1	...
Armenia	193.5	223.4	188.4	183.8	176.5	294.5	255.0
Azerbaijan	25.1	78.9	72.4	59.8	62.8	92.7	53.6
Georgia	191.5	230.1	189.0	170.2	171.8	291.6	241.4
Kazakhstan	174.7	373.7	283.1	225.4	232.7	296.8	233.8
Kyrgyz Republic	181.2	327.7	312.1	294.1	268.9	353.3	269.8
Pakistan	219.7	272.4	303.5	315.3	346.2	416.6	360.0
Tajikistan	158.4	230.3	217.2	228.9	230.1	235.7	167.1
Turkmenistan	...	...	...	...	...	...	...
Uzbekistan	60.5	118.5	108.9	101.5	112.3	200.7	207.7
East Asia							
China, People's Republic of	41.3	58.3	62.7	67.2	72.8	78.0	70.6
Hong Kong, China[a]	149.2	177.6	190.5	190.6	195.1	221.6	197.2 (2022)
Korea, Republic of[a]	62.4	60.3	58.9	57.7	67.1	85.3	75.7 (2022)
Mongolia	173.2	433.8	406.6	375.2	359.2	405.2	339.0
Taipei,China[a]	30.0	45.3	43.1	44.0	43.6	44.8	35.1 (2022)
South Asia							
Bangladesh	122.1	110.1	129.9	128.2	138.3	190.0	183.5
Bhutan	154.0	343.4	349.4	310.8	331.8	372.1	401.9
India	81.1	102.1	100.7	93.3	98.5	111.4	91.9
Maldives	45.6	38.7	45.5	64.9	71.2	191.7	97.1
Nepal	212.7	166.9	165.9	163.0	190.0	347.0	297.3
Sri Lanka	189.8	265.5	263.6	258.0	285.4	423.9	375.0
Southeast Asia							
Brunei Darussalam	...	...	...	...	...	...	...
Cambodia	65.8	68.5	70.2	71.2	70.4	83.8	97.4
Indonesia	117.6	185.6	177.0	171.6	193.8	227.1	164.2
Lao People's Democratic Republic	284.0	259.8	254.3	240.3	234.1	266.4	217.1
Malaysia	...	...	...	...	...	...	...
Myanmar	127.2	72.4	72.9	63.0	59.2	86.8	106.0
Philippines	106.7	89.5	75.2	77.1	77.3	107.5	106.7
Singapore[a]	...	...	...	...	...	...	...
Thailand	45.7	49.1	51.6	51.1	53.7	73.8	68.4
Timor-Leste	1.9 (2012)	12.3	14.2	15.7	15.5	31.1	58.0
Viet Nam	56.1	45.2	45.5	41.1	41.5	42.9	39.9
The Pacific							
Cook Islands[a]	85.0	24.2	21.4	20.3	21.3	...	...
Fiji	58.7	54.6	49.8	45.6	49.8	117.5	164.5
Kiribati[a]	13.7	17.4	16.1	16.5	14.3	...	...
Marshall Islands[a]	94.1	55.5	47.7	42.7	38.1	35.5	36.7
Micronesia, Federated States of	...	...	...	...	...	...	...
Nauru	...	...	...	...	...	...	...
Niue	...	...	...	...	...	...	...
Palau[a]	62.8	43.1	51.9	59.4	66.0	161.1	190.2
Papua New Guinea	98.2	231.3	167.6	166.8	159.5	192.3	159.3
Samoa	154.0	162.7	155.8	139.4	118.9	347.0	402.9
Solomon Islands	68.9	44.2	59.3	44.7	54.7	88.4	103.2
Tonga	283.9	142.8	138.3	120.1	111.2	127.6	230.2
Tuvalu[a]	64.1	40.4	10.6	6.6	11.5	6.1	5.3
Vanuatu	48.9	69.1	91.1	79.4	82.0	174.2	197.5

... = data not available, ADB = Asian Development Bank.

a External debt as a percentage of exports of goods, services, and primary income was derived using balance-of-payments data.

Sources: World Bank. International Debt Statistics. http://data.worldbank.org/data-catalog/international-debt-statistics (accessed 1 July 2023); and Asian Development Bank estimates using economies' official sources.

Table 2.4.23: Total Debt Service Paid by Developing ADB Member Economies

ADB Regional Member	Debt Service Payment ($ million)					Debt Service Payment (% of exports of goods, services, and primary income)			
	2010	2015	2020	2021	2022	2010	2015	2020	2020
Developing ADB Member Economies									
Central and West Asia[a]	**48,060**	**48,084**	**53,787**	**57,340**	**90,287**				
Afghanistan	10	57	46	26	135	0.4	3.3	2.7	...
Armenia	969	1,546	1,966	2,051	2,045	29.7	38.4	46.0	37.8
Azerbaijan	414	1,907	1,839	1,979	1,458	1.4	9.0	10.8	7.2
Georgia	803	2,158	2,435	2,691	1,943	17.5	31.0	35.3	29.5
Kazakhstan	39,475	34,857	30,788	30,911	39,617	57.9	65.4	56.6	45.2
Kyrgyz Republic	557	413	629	570	1,429	24.5	16.8	25.6	17.0
Pakistan	4,319	4,112	9,877	12,338	35,538	15.0	14.1	35.6	34.1
Tajikistan	695	314	899	520	574	30.9	12.2	30.5	12.3
Turkmenistan	199	1,474	2,093	1,652	1,143	...	...	...	...
Uzbekistan	617	1,247	3,216	4,602	6,405	4.7	9.0	20.0	24.5
East Asia[a]	**58,803**	**134,638**	**284,935**	**350,010**	**252,754**				
China, People's Republic of	52,102	126,685	273,275	336,772	233,691	2.9	4.9	9.2	8.8
Hong Kong, China	...	...	...	...	...	...	...	...	...
Korea, Republic of[b]	2,843	...	...	...	...	...	...	...	...
Mongolia	239	1,833	2,796	2,572	8,139	7.0	35.3	35.0	25.7
Taipei,China[b]	3,620	6,119	8,864	10,667	10,924	1.1	1.6	2.3	2.1
South Asia[a]	**27,284**	**55,463**	**86,955**	**60,333**	**74,806**				
Bangladesh	1,106	1,756	4,047	5,693	5,275	5.1	5.0	10.5	11.4
Bhutan	87	129	58	118	278	14.4	17.2	7.1	15.5
India	24,413	49,662	77,064	48,749	60,009	6.8	11.2	15.2	7.3
Maldives	81	139	288	761	661	4.0	4.4	16.0	19.2
Nepal	188	226	275	280	448	10.6	8.4	12.1	9.4
Sri Lanka	1,408	3,551	5,223	4,731	8,134	12.3	20.8	39.3	31.4
Southeast Asia[a]	**56,484**	**97,704**	**116,941**	**128,496**	**177,604**				
Brunei Darussalam	...	...	...	...	...	...	...	...	...
Cambodia	65	691	1,556	2,191	2,351	1.1	5.1	7.4	10.7
Indonesia	31,569	60,273	67,398	72,999	121,128	18.7	34.6	36.7	28.8
Lao People's Democratic Republic	302	421	688	722	2,819	13.1	9.1	10.5	9.1
Malaysia	...	...	...	...	...	...	...	...	...
Myanmar	242	502	599	2,313	1,265	3.1	3.4	3.9	17.6
Philippines	11,461	10,577	9,369	12,213	8,048	18.7	12.9	10.2	12.2
Singapore	...	...	...	...	...	...	...	...	...
Thailand	10,965	18,610	20,965	18,093	21,008	4.7	6.7	7.7	5.9
Timor-Leste	0 (2012)	1	8	10	23	0.0(2012)	0.1	1.1	2.0
Viet Nam	1,880	6,631	16,358	19,955	20,963	2.3	3.8	5.6	5.9
The Pacific[a]	**931**	**1,507**	**1,645**	**4,154**	**4,834**				
Cook Islands[b,c]	3	5	4 (2019)	...	...	57.9	26.9	30.3 (2018)	...
Fiji	59	340	275	49	253	3.1	14.5	21.3	4.0
Kiribati	1	1	2 (2019)	...	...	4.4	4.0	7.0 (2019)	...
Marshall Islands	9	8	7	7	7	11.7	8.5	8.1	...
Micronesia, Federated States of	5	7	6 (2018)	...	...	13.5	7.4	3.6 (2018)	...
Nauru	...	...	...	...	...	...	...	...	...
Niue	...	...	...	...	...	...	...	...	...
Palau	...	...	...	...	...	...	...	...	...
Papua New Guinea	812	1,098	1,306	4,048	4,416	13.3	12.7	13.9	38.0
Samoa	11	21	24	16	35	5.0	8.8	18.7	14.2
Solomon Islands	21	14	9	13	76	6.2	2.4	1.9	2.8
Tonga	5	6	6	4	21	9.3	7.3	3.9	3.6
Tuvalu	...	...	...	...	...	...	...	...	...
Vanuatu	6	7	19	18	25	1.6	1.9	7.3	6.8
DEVELOPING ADB MEMBER ECONOMIES[a]	**191,562**	**337,396**	**544,264**	**600,332**	**600,284**				

... = data not available, (-/+) 0.0 = magnitude is less than half of unit employed, $ = United States dollars, ADB = Asian Development Bank.

a Aggregates include only reporting economies with data corresponding to the year heading.
b Refers to principal repayments on long-term debt plus interest on short-term and long-term debt.
c Refers to debt service as a percentage of total exports, as reflected under the "Direction of Trade" in the individual economy table available via the Key Indicators Database at https://kidb.adb.org.

Sources: World Bank. International Debt Statistics. http://data.worldbank.org/data-catalog/international-debt-statistics (accessed 1 July 2023); economies' official sources; and Asian Development Bank estimates using economies' official sources.

Table 2.4.24: International Tourist Arrivals
('000)

ADB Regional Member	2010	2016	2017	2018	2019	2020	2021	2022
Developing ADB Member Economies								
Central and West Asia[a]	**9,288**	**12,825**	**15,707**	**22,370**	**26,352**	**5,949**	**8,261***	**10,552***
Afghanistan	...	...	...	...	...	...	...	...
Armenia	684	1,260	1,495	1,652	1,894	360	876*	1,666*
Azerbaijan	1,280	2,044	2,454	2,633	2,864	519	462*	...
Georgia	1,067	3,297	4,069	4,757	5,080	1,087	1,577*	3,653*
Kazakhstan	2,991	...	...	...	...	...	...	...
Kyrgyz Republic	1,224	3,853	4,568	6,947	8,508	2,079	3,169*	...
Pakistan	907	...	...	...	...	...	...	...
Tajikistan	160	344	431	1,035	1,257	351	296*	...
Turkmenistan	...	...	...	...	...	...	...	...
Uzbekistan	975	2,027	2,690	5,346	6,749	1,553	1,881*	5,233*
East Asia[a]	**90,570**	**114,159**	**113,169**	**119,106**	**119,396**	**13,282**	**6,891***	**4,948***
China, People's Republic of	55,664	59,270	60,740	62,900	65,700	7,967	5,662*	...
Hong Kong, China	20,085	26,553	27,884	29,263	23,752	1,359	89*	568*
Korea, Republic of	8,798	17,242	13,336	15,347	17,503	2,519	967*	3,198*
Mongolia	456	404	469	529	577	59	33*	286*
Taipei,China	5,567	10,690	10,740	11,067	11,864	1,378	140*	896*
South Asia[a]	**8,005**	**19,052**	**...**	**...**	**23,367**	**7,841**	**8,811***	**...**
Bangladesh	139	182	237	267	323	182	135*	...
Bhutan	41	210	255	274	316	30	...	...
India	5,776	14,570	...	...	17,914	6,337	7,010*	...
Maldives	792	1,286	1,390	1,484	1,703	555	1,322*	1,675*
Nepal	603	753	940	1,173	1,197	230	150*	614*
Sri Lanka	654	2,051	2,116	2,334	1,914	508	194*	720*
Southeast Asia[a]	**70,471**	**110,771**	**120,569**	**128,620**	**138,592**	**25,451**	**3,092***	**...**
Brunei Darussalam	214	219	259	278	333	62	4*	...
Cambodia	2,508	5,012	5,602	6,201	6,611	1,306	196*	2,277*
Indonesia[b]	7,003 |	11,072	12,948	13,396	15,455	3,915	1,546*	...
Lao People's Democratic Republic	1,670	3,315	3,257	3,770	4,384	812	...	...
Malaysia	24,577	26,757	25,948	25,832	26,101	4,333	135*	10,071*
Myanmar	792	2,907	3,443	3,551	4,364	903	131*	...
Philippines	3,520	5,967	6,621	7,168	8,261	1,483	164*	2,650*
Singapore	9,161	12,913	13,903	14,673	15,119	2,086	325*	...
Thailand	15,936	32,530	35,592	38,178	39,874	6,696	428*	11,153*
Timor-Leste	40	66	74	75	81	18	6*	...
Viet Nam	5,050	10,013	12,922	15,498	18,009	3,837	157*	3,661*
The Pacific[a]	**1,310**	**1,619**	**1,634**	**1,693**	**1,755**	**332**	**84***	**...**
Cook Islands	104	146	161	169	172	25	26*	114*
Fiji	632	792	843	870	894	147	32*	636*
Kiribati	5	6	6	7	8	1	0*	...
Marshall Islands	5	5	6	7	6	1	0*	...
Micronesia, Federated States of	45	30	...	19	18	...	...	...
Nauru	...	...	...	...	...	...	...	...
Niue	6	9	10	11	10	1	–	...
Palau	85	138	123	106	94	18	5*	12*
Papua New Guinea	140	179	139	140	160	39	17*	...
Samoa	122	134	146	164	172	23	3*	...
Solomon Islands	21	23	26	28	29	4	1*	7*
Tonga	47	59	63	54	67	50	0*	...
Tuvalu	2	3	3	3	4	1	–	...
Vanuatu	97	95	109	116	121	22	...	...
Developed ADB Member Economies[a]	**16,836**	**35,678**	**41,061**	**44,123**	**45,050**	**6,892**	**697***	**7,526***
Australia	5,790	8,269	8,815	9,246	9,466	1,828	246*	3,694*
Japan	8,611	24,039	28,691	31,191	31,882	4,116	246*	3,832*
New Zealand	2,435	3,370	3,555	3,686	3,702	948	205*	...
DEVELOPING ADB MEMBER ECONOMIES[a]	**179,644**	**258,425**	**...**	**...**	**309,462**	**52,855**	**27,139***	**...**
ALL ADB REGIONAL MEMBERS[a]	**196,480**	**294,104**	**...**	**...**	**354,512**	**59,747**	**27,836***	**...**
WORLD	**856,653**	**1,111,617**	**1,176,959**	**1,229,353**	**1,465,000**	**407,000**	**456,000***	**963,000***

... = data not available, | = marks break in series, – = magnitude equals zero, 0 = magnitude is less than half of unit employed, * = provisional or preliminary, ADB = Asian Development Bank.

Note: For Australia; Japan; the Kyrgyz Republic; the Republic of Korea; Taipei,China; Tajikistan; Uzbekistan: and Viet Nam: Data refer to international visitor arrivals at frontiers (including tourists and same-day visitors). For the rest of the economies and the world total: Data refer to international tourist arrivals at frontiers (overnight visitors only, i.e., excluding same-day visitors).

a Includes only reporting economies with data corresponding to the year heading.

b Prior to 2015, data refer to international tourist arrivals at frontiers (overnight visitors only, i.e., excluding same-day visitors). For 2015 onward, data refer to international visitor arrivals at frontiers (including tourists and same-day visitors).

Sources: United Nations World Tourism Organization. UNWTO.eLibrary. https://www.e-unwto.org (accessed 17 May 2023) and World Tourism Barometer and Statistical Annex, May 2023. https://www.e-unwto.org/toc/wtobarometereng/21/2.

Table 2.4.25: International Tourism Receipts
($ million)

ADB Regional Member	2010	2016	2017	2018	2019	2020	2021	2022
Developing ADB Member Economies								
Central and West Asia[a]	**3,631**	**8,965**	**10,535**	**11,470**	**11,782**	**2,599**	**4,250***	**...**
Afghanistan	75	49	2	28	72	65	...	...
Armenia	646	1,017	1,204	1,329	1,528	287	784*	2,439*
Azerbaijan	657	2,714	3,012	2,634	1,792	304	313*	823*
Georgia	659	2,111	2,704	3,222	3,269	542	1,245*	3,520*
Kazakhstan	1,005	1,858	2,135	2,255	2,456	455	535*	...
Kyrgyz Republic	160	432	429	459	644	151	207*	...
Pakistan	305	322	352	390	494	439	559*	738*
Tajikistan	3	4	8	9	14	6	11*	...
Turkmenistan	...	...	...	...	...	...	...	...
Uzbekistan	121	458	689	1,144	1,513	350	596*	1,437*
East Asia	**86,731**	**103,406**	**96,347**	**108,386**	**100,536**	**24,915**	**24,749***	**24,707***
China, People's Republic of	45,814	44,432	38,559	40,386	35,832	9,951	11,330*	9,583*
Hong Kong, China	21,689	31,398	31,709	35,268	28,913	2,859	1,850*	3,147*
Korea, Republic of	10,263	16,886	13,368	18,567	20,867	10,276	10,804*	11,996*
Mongolia	244	316	396	461	513	29	21*	234*
Taipei,China	8,721	10,374	12,315	13,704	14,411	1,800	744*	2,747*
South Asia[a]	**17,244**	**29,203**	**35,119**	**37,074**	**38,697**	**15,548**	**13,027***	**...**
Bangladesh	81	214	341	353	388	217	273*	420*
Bhutan	40	92	105	103	120	21	4*	...
India	14,490	22,427	27,365	28,568	30,720	13,036	8,650*	21,360*
Maldives	1,713	2,506	2,744	3,028	3,157	1,398	3,473*	...
Nepal	344	446	639	641	705	194	120*	...
Sri Lanka	576	3,518	3,925	4,381	3,607	682	507*	1,136*
Southeast Asia[a]	**68,484**	**113,026**	**126,206**	**138,235**	**146,897**	**30,675**	**10,789***	**...**
Brunei Darussalam	...	144	177	190	217	16	2*	...
Cambodia	1,519	3,212	3,639	4,362	4,769	1,015	184*	...
Indonesia	6,958	11,206	13,139	16,426	16,911	3,382	521*	6,719*
Lao People's Democratic Republic	382	716	648	811	935	213	1*	...
Malaysia	18,152	18,085	18,385	19,608	19,829	2,974	77*	6,329*
Myanmar	72	2,197	1,969	1,652	2,483	...	...	...
Philippines	2,645	5,143	6,988	8,240	9,781	1,791	600*	4,174*
Singapore	14,178	18,979	19,922	20,422	20,300	5,355	4,109*	11,793*
Thailand	20,104	44,786	52,376	56,366	59,810	13,403	5,134*	...
Timor-Leste	24	58	73	78	70	26	12*	43*
Viet Nam	4,450	8,500	8,890	10,080	11,792	2,500	149*	3,841*
The Pacific[a]	**1,256**	**1,727**	**1,817**	**1,888**	**1,892**	**349**	**...**	**...**
Cook Islands	111	202	230	234	228	37	43*	...
Fiji	635	878	942	969	963	154	35*	693*
Kiribati	4	3	4	3	3	0	–	...
Marshall Islands	4	5	7	9	4	4	...	...
Micronesia, Federated States of	24	...	...	...	...	...	...	...
Nauru	1	3	4	2	...	...	...	...
Niue	...	7	8	...	...	...	...	...
Palau	73	121	106	98	86	47	6*	...
Papua New Guinea	2	1	2	4	2	2	1*	...
Samoa	123	148	166	192	201	24	...	58*
Solomon Islands	44	59	67	81	71	6	...	...
Tonga	16	51	48	48	57	19	9*	...
Tuvalu	2	5	6	6	8	1	–	...
Vanuatu	217	244	227	243	270	55	2*	...
Developed ADB Member Economies[a]	**48,219**	**77,544**	**86,421**	**98,152**	**102,109**	**42,271**	**24,774***	**36,875***
Australia	28,472	37,019	41,762	45,098	45,522	25,820	16,988*	23,382*
Japan	13,224	30,752	34,065	42,093	46,054	10,700	4,861*	9,328*
New Zealand	6,523	9,773	10,594	10,961	10,533	5,751	2,866*	4,165*
DEVELOPING ADB MEMBER ECONOMIES[a]	**177,345**	**256,326**	**270,023**	**297,053**	**299,804**	**74,086**	**52,911**	**...**
ALL ADB REGIONAL MEMBERS[a]	**225,564**	**333,870**	**356,444**	**395,205**	**401,913**	**116,357**	**77,685**	**...**
WORLD	**940,726**	**1,226,392**	**1,327,269**	**1,436,722**	**1,494,000**	**559,000**	**638,000**	**1,031,000***

... = data not available, – = magnitude equals zero, 0 = magnitude is less than half of unit employed, * = provisional or preliminary, $ = United States dollars, ADB = Asian Development Bank.

a Includes only reporting economies with data corresponding to the year heading.

Sources: United Nations World Tourism Organization. UNWTO.eLibrary. https://www.e-unwto.org (accessed 17 May 2023); and United Nations World Tourism Organization. 2023. World Tourism Barometer, Statistical Annex. Volume 21.

Data Issues and Comparability

Most of the data on international transactions presented in this section were taken from balance-of-payments statistics as reported by individual economies. IMF guidelines are followed by most governments in compiling these statistics. However, authorities have difficulty accurately recording nonofficial transactions such as migrant workers' remittances and private capital flows, which is one of the reasons that the IMF's Balance of Payments Manual (BPM) was updated to the sixth edition (BPM6) in 2009. All economies in the region have adopted BPM6 in recent years except two economies, which still rely on BPM5. However, there is not a single framework for an extended time series available for all economies. There are 20 economies reporting a mix of BPM5 and BPM6, and three economies reporting a mix of BPM4 and BPM6. This therefore affects the comparability of data across economies.

The World Trade Organization and other international agencies closely monitor international trade statistics. Common definitions are used by all economies, with the larger economies throughout Asia and the Pacific using standard forms and procedures for data processing.

Data on official development assistance, other official flows, and private direct investment and other private capital are compiled by the Organisation for Economic Co-operation and Development's Development Assistance Committee. These data are standardized on a calendar-year basis for all donors, but may have discrepancies for some economies owing to the fiscal-year data available in budget documents. Commitments from donors do not necessarily translate to actual disbursements to recipient economies of official development assistance.

Table 2.5.1: Road Indicators—Total Network, Passenger Kilometers Travel, Freight Kilometers Travel

ADB Regional Member	Road Indicators Network, Total (km)			Road Passenger Travel[a] (p-km million)			Road Freight Kilometers Travel[b] (t-km million)		
	2010	2015	2021	2010	2015	2021	2010	2015	2021
Developing ADB Member Economies									
Central and West Asia									
Afghanistan	19,138 (2011)	37,090	...	...	...	...	6,796.0 (2011)	4,423.0	...
Armenia	9,125	10,368	11,306	2,344.3	2,395.9	1,072.2	235.8	479.4	1,052.3
Azerbaijan[c]	18,977	19,016	78,307	16,633.0	23,825.0	16,892.0	11,728.0	16,038.0	9,425.0
Georgia	19,040	20,553	40,044	...	...	...	619.7	664.3	720.9
Kazakhstan	96,018	96,529	95,443	...	...	...	80,300.0	161,864.0	148,000.0
Kyrgyz Republic	...	...	...	7,209.5	9,005.6	8,360.6 (2022)	1,281.5	1,401.7	1,451.0 (2022)
Pakistan	260,040	265,404	270,972 (2019)	...	...	...	...	...	...
Tajikistan	...	...	...	...	510.1 (2017)	...	50,745.7	68,304.1	79,075.9 (2020)
Turkmenistan	...	...	13,773	27,657.0	...	...	11,399.0	...	...
Uzbekistan	...	...	...	78,400.0	109,100.0	124,141.2 (2019)	24,464.2	12,800.0	15,879.3 (2019)
East Asia									
China, People's Republic of	4,008,200	4,577,300	5,280,700	1,502,080.0	1,074,270.0	362,750.0	4,338,970.0	5,795,570.0	6,908,770.0
Hong Kong, China	2,076	2,101	2,223 (2022)	...	...	...	...	...	...
Korea, Republic of	...	99,024	105,083	104,671.0	385,018.1	330,991.5 (2020)	103,898.0	132,382.0	...
Mongolia	...	109,567 (2017)	111,917	1,480.2	1,940.5	1,914.9 (2022)	1,834.0	2,374.0	2,591.9 (2022)
Taipei,China	40,335	41,952	42,799	...	...	...	29,631.6	37,805.3	34,094.2
South Asia									
Bangladesh	21,269	21,365	...	...	...	...	...	...	...
Bhutan	4,661	11,177	18,270	...	...	...	...	...	...
India	4,582,439	5,472,144	6,331,757 (2019)	8,409,000.0	15,428,000.0	...	1,287,300.0	2,027,400.0	...
Maldives	...	...	...	...	...	...	...	...	...
Nepal	11,636 (2011)	12,898	11,179 (2020)	...	...	...	...	...	...
Sri Lanka	29,119	31,280	31,385	...	...	...	...	...	...
Southeast Asia									
Brunei Darussalam	3,127 (2011)	3,355	3,788	...	...	...	...	...	...
Cambodia	44,709 (2009)	...	61,534 (2019)	...	...	...	...	...	...
Indonesia	487,314	529,073	546,116	...	...	...	...	...	...
Lao People's Democratic Republic	47,491	56,332	59,101 (2020)	2,556.0	3,202.1	4,060.0 (2020)	513.0	434.7	556.7
Malaysia	144,403	214,816	267,046 (2020)	...	...	...	...	...	...
Myanmar	...	...	134,057 (2020)	...	40,840.0	28,581.8 (2019)	507.9	419.4	274.6 (2020)
Philippines	31,242	32,633	33,213	...	...	...	...	...	...
Singapore	8,895	9,246	9,608 (2022)	...	...	...	...	...	...
Thailand	...	...	702,989 (2022)	452,040.0	663,561.0	735,051.0 (2019)	185,884.0	193,911.4	187,728.0 (2020)
Timor-Leste	...	8,701	...	...	...	...	...	...	...
Viet Nam	...	309,969 (2016)	277,167 (2019)	69,197.4	105,382.2	112,740.5 (2020)	36,179.0	51,514.9	73,503.2 (2020)
The Pacific									
Cook Islands	...	...	...	...	...	...	...	...	...
Fiji	...	...	...	...	...	...	...	...	...
Kiribati	...	...	...	...	...	...	...	...	...
Marshall Islands	...	...	...	...	...	...	...	...	...
Micronesia, Federated States of	...	...	...	...	...	...	...	...	...
Nauru	...	...	...	...	...	...	...	...	...
Niue	...	...	...	...	...	...	...	...	...
Palau	...	...	...	...	...	...	...	...	...
Papua New Guinea	...	30,000 (2016)	...	...	...	...	...	...	...
Samoa	1,152 (2012)	...	...	...	...	...	...	...	...
Solomon Islands	...	...	...	...	...	...	...	...	...
Tonga	...	...	...	...	...	...	...	...	...
Tuvalu	...	120 (2017)	...	...	...	...	...	...	...
Vanuatu	1,776 (2012)	2,241 (2014)	...	...	...	...	...	...	...
Developed ADB Member Economies									
Australia	872,292	874,143	...	284,570.7	302,478.2	277,592.0* (2019)	181,480.7	202,454.0	230,114.8
Japan	1,210,000	1,221,000	1,228,100 (2020)	78,962.0	67,019.0	25,593.0 (2020)	286,538.0	240,195.0	213,419.0 (2020)
New Zealand	94,126	94,822	97,353 (2022)	...	...	...	21,268.0	23,843.0	27,502.0 (2020)

... = data not available; * = provisional/preliminary/estimate; ADB = Asian Development Bank; p-km = passenger-kilometer; t-km = ton-kilometer.

a A passenger-kilometer, abbreviated as p-km, is a unit of measurement representing the transport of 1 passenger by a defined mode of transport over 1 kilometer.

b A ton-kilometer, abbreviated as t-km, is a unit of measurement representing the transport of 1 metric ton of goods (including packaging and tare weights of intermodal transport units) by a defined mode of transport over 1 kilometer. Only the distance on the national territory of the reporting economy is taken into account for national, international and transit transport.

c For 2010 and 2015, road network only covers republican and local importance roads.

Source: Asian Development Bank. Asian Transport Outlook Database. https://data.adb.org/dataset/asian-transport-outlook-database (accessed 6 June 2023).

Table 2.5.2: Road Indicators—Registered Vehicles

ADB Regional Member	2010	2015	2016	2017	2018	2019	2020	2021
Developing ADB Member Economies								
Central and West Asia								
Afghanistan	1,197,574(2011)	1,831,900	1,849,199	1,933,931	1,927,387	1,978,846	2,009,407	2,027,598
Armenia	...	...	...	...	...	...	...	...
Azerbaijan	984,196	1,325,825	1,333,841	1,345,401	1,373,780	1,422,473	1,478,157	1,572,027
Georgia	702,700	1,081,400	1,167,200	1,228,100	1,289,000	1,339,300	1,404,400	1,490,200
Kazakhstan	3,579,200	4,397,369	4,383,139	4,382,662	4,342,159	4,325,293	4,433,522	4,386,620
Kyrgyz Republic	...	...	...	...	...	...	...	...
Pakistan	7,853,002	18,502,109	21,067,850	23,812,676	26,566,167	29,137,562	30,757,539	...
Tajikistan	...	...	...	...	...	...	...	...
Turkmenistan	...	...	...	...	...	...	...	...
Uzbekistan	...	...	...	...	...	...	...	...
East Asia								
China, People's Republic of	77,216,700	161,614,900	184,501,300	208,083,900	231,232,300	252,571,200	272,088,300	292,743,100
Hong Kong, China	664,726	798,316	818,316	840,597	865,661	879,154	913,477	...
Korea, Republic of	...	23,151,659	23,984,039	24,724,770	25,410,979	25,914,261	26,654,988	27,700,841 (2022)
Mongolia	608,274(2012)	789,720	841,552	900,145	970,880	1,043,028	1,136,734	1,234,701
Taipei,China	18,176,222	21,400,863	21,510,650	21,704,365	21,871,240	22,111,807	22,297,000	22,597,694
South Asia								
Bangladesh	1,509,028	2,441,829	2,818,752	3,238,702	3,690,000	4,075,411	4,451,671	...
Bhutan	43,581	60,651	68,149	75,490	81,160	88,264	92,167	99,194
India	129,499,241	209,284,140	229,557,955	253,310,000	272,586,500	295,771,514	326,299,000	...
Maldives	46,027	77,775	87,125	97,212	108,530	...	...	...
Nepal	1,178,911	2,339,169	2,783,428	3,221,042	3,539,519	...	...	...
Sri Lanka	3,954,311	6,302,141	6,795,469	7,247,122	7,727,921	8,095,224	8,297,852	8,331,702
Southeast Asia								
Brunei Darussalam	165,849(2009)	267,281	277,332	277,200	282,345	289,978	272,944	277,316
Cambodia	...	...	...	...	...	...	...	...
Indonesia	76,907,127	120,786,914	128,069,103	118,922,708	126,508,776	133,617,012	136,137,451	141,992,573
Lao People's Democratic Republic	1,008,788	1,717,144	1,850,020	1,979,054	2,104,655	2,233,133	2,342,844	2,997,485
Malaysia	20,188,565	26,301,952	27,613,259	26,350,246	29,277,453	30,497,054	31,642,275	...
Myanmar	2,147,404	5,077,699	5,541,361	6,337,002	6,853,995	7,420,952	7,625,110	...
Philippines	6,634,710	8,706,607	9,251,565	10,410,814	11,595,434	12,725,306	11,851,192	13,856,622 (2022)
Singapore	945,829	957,246	956,430	961,842	957,006	973,101	973,990	995,746 (2022)
Thailand	28,484,829	36,731,023	39,124,339	38,308,763	39,551,789	40,712,048	41,471,345	41,706,531
Timor-Leste	10,940	17,801	19,498	21,969	23,974	...	...	...
Viet Nam	32,362,000	46,137,400	49,646,700	56,850,000	61,317,400	65,572,500	...	...
The Pacific								
Cook Islands	...	...	...	...	...	...	...	...
Fiji	81,926	101,425	110,763	117,623	119,960	131,571	131,687	138,650
Kiribati	...	...	...	...	...	...	...	...
Marshall Islands	2,343(2008)	...	...	...	...	...	...	...
Micronesia, Federated States of	7,586	8,314	9,004	8,140	9,433	11,751	...	...
Nauru	1,737(2011)	...	...	...	...	...	...	...
Niue	846(2011)	1,392(2014)	...	...	...	...	...	...
Palau	5,643	4,120	7,413	6,656	7,592	8,140	...	...
Papua New Guinea	...	...	...	...	...	...	...	...
Samoa	16,349(2011)	17,397(2013)	...	22,045	...	...	...	...
Solomon Islands	...	...	...	...	...	...	...	...
Tonga	19,432	...	...	...	...	...	...	...
Tuvalu	...	...	...	...	...	...	...	...
Vanuatu	5,368(2009)	...	...	...	...	...	...	...
Developed ADB Member Economies								
Australia	16,061,100	18,007,767	18,387,136	18,781,204	19,173,279	19,505,241	19,805,331	20,680,152 (2022)
Japan	78,653,371	80,892,607	81,256,449	81,541,204	81,764,583	81,849,782	82,077,752	82,174,944
New Zealand	3,415,811	3,812,314	3,972,320	4,137,550	4,266,894	4,376,503	4,438,756	4,542,035

... = data not available, ADB = Asian Development Bank.

Source: Asian Development Bank. Asian Transport Outlook Database. https://data.adb.org/dataset/asian-transport-outlook-database (accessed 6 June 2023).

Table 2.5.3: Road indicators—Safety

ADB Regional Member	Estimated Road Traffic Deaths, 2016		Road User Deaths, 2016[a] (%)				
	Total	Death Rate (per 100,000 people)	Four-Wheeled Vehicles	Two- and Three-Wheeled Vehicles	Cyclists	Pedestrians	Others
Developing ADB Member Economies							
Central and West Asia	**44,846**	**14.3**					
Afghanistan	5,230	15.1	...	...	...	...	...
Armenia	499	17.1	59.6	1.5	0.4	34.8	3.7
Azerbaijan	845	8.7	51.8	0.9	0.9	42.0	4.3
Georgia	599	15.3	44.9	0.5	0.7	26.5	27.4
Kazakhstan	3,158	17.6	59.8	4.3	1.7	30.9	3.3
Kyrgyz Republic	916	15.4	27.6	2.1	0.2	40.0	30.0
Pakistan	27,582	14.3	...	...	...	...	...
Tajikistan	1,577	18.1	57.4	...	2.3	40.3	–
Turkmenistan	823	14.5	...	...	...	...	...
Uzbekistan	3,617	11.5	...	...	...	...	...
East Asia[b]	**261,669**	**17.9**					
China, People's Republic of	256,180	18.2	...	...	...	...	...
Hong Kong, China	...	...	...	...	...	...	...
Korea, Republic of	4,990	9.8	...	20.5	5.9	39.9	33.7
Mongolia	499	16.5	39.3	18.6	1.2	28.7	12.2
Taipei,China	...	...	...	...	...	...	...
South Asia	**331,906**	**21.6**					
Bangladesh	24,954	15.3	...	...	...	...	...
Bhutan	139	17.4	...	...	...	...	...
India	299,091	22.6	17.9	39.6	1.7	10.4	30.4
Maldives	4	0.9	–	75.0	–	25.0	–
Nepal	4,622	15.9	...	...	...	...	...
Sri Lanka	3,096	14.9	6.2	50.8	8.1	29.2	5.7
Southeast Asia[b]	**114,030**	**17.8**					
Brunei Darussalam	...	...	...	...	...	...	...
Cambodia	2,803	17.8	6.2	73.5	2.3	9.6	8.4
Indonesia	31,726	12.2	4.9	73.6	3.2	15.5	2.7
Lao People's Democratic Republic	1,120	16.6	...	...	...	...	...
Malaysia	7,374	23.6	...	...	...	...	...
Myanmar	10,540	19.9	10.8	64.8	3.1	14.2	7.1
Philippines	12,690	12.3	0.3	4.7	0.1	1.0	93.9
Singapore	155	2.8	7.8	44.0	14.2	33.3	0.7
Thailand	22,491	32.7	12.3	74.4	3.5	7.6	2.3
Timor-Leste	161	12.7	...	...	...	...	...
Viet Nam	24,970	26.4	...	...	...	...	...
The Pacific[b]	**1,428**	**13.7**					
Cook Islands	3	17.3	20.0	80.0	–	–	–
Fiji	86	9.6	63.3	...	...	36.7	–
Kiribati	5	4.4	40.0	20.0	–	40.0	–
Marshall Islands	...	...	...	...	...	...	...
Micronesia, Federated States of	2	1.9	50.0	–	–	50.0	–
Nauru	...	...	...	...	...	...	...
Niue	...	...	...	...	...	...	...
Palau	...	...	...	...	...	...	–
Papua New Guinea	1,145	14.2	52.5	...	...	47.5	–
Samoa	22	11.3	41.2	–	5.9	47.1	5.9
Solomon Islands	104	17.4	...	...	...	...	...
Tonga	18	16.8	66.7	–	–	27.8	5.6
Tuvalu	...	...	...	...	...	...	...
Vanuatu	43	15.9	...	...	...	...	...
Developed ADB Member Economies	**6,939**	**4.4**					
Australia	1,351	5.6	60.9	19.3	2.2	14.0	3.5
Japan	5,224	4.1	32.4	17.2	15.1	35.0	1.0
New Zealand	364	7.8	68.5	15.9	1.5	7.6	6.4
DEVELOPING ADB MEMBER ECONOMIES[b]	**753,879**	**19.0**					
ALL ADB REGIONAL MEMBERS[b]	**760,818**	**18.4**					

... = data not available, – = magnitude equals zero, ADB = Asian Development Bank.

a Nature of road user deaths might not add up to 100% due to rounding.
b Regional aggregates include reporting economies only.

Source: World Health Organization. 2018. Global Status Report on Road Safety 2018. Geneva.

Table 2.5.4: Rail Indicators—Total Route, Length per Land Area

ADB Regional Member	Rail Lines, Total Route (km)			Rail Network, Length per Land Area (km per km^2 '000)		
	2010	2015	2021	2010	2015	2021
Developing ADB Member Economies						
Central and West Asia						
Afghanistan	106.0 (2011)	106.0	...	0.2 (2011)	0.2	...
Armenia	871.1	823.6	782.1	30.6	28.9	27.5
Azerbaijan	2,792.0	2,446.0	2,499.0	33.8	29.6	30.2
Georgia	1,566.0	1,576.0	1,546.0	22.5	22.7	22.2
Kazakhstan	15,016.1	15,341.1	16,579.6	5.6	5.7	6.1
Kyrgyz Republic	...	...	...	...	...	...
Pakistan	7,791.0	7,791.0	7,791.0 (2020)	10.1	10.1	10.1 (2020)
Tajikistan	...	...	...	...	...	...
Turkmenistan	...	...	...	...	...	...
Uzbekistan	4,227.2	4,238.0	...	9.9	9.6	...
East Asia						
China, People's Republic of	91,200.0	121,000.0	150,700.0	9.7	12.8	16.0
Hong Kong, China	...	...	...	...	...	...
Korea, Republic of	3,557.3	3,873.5	...	36.6	39.8	...
Mongolia	...	1,810.0 (2016)	1,100.0 (2019)	...	1.2 (2016)	0.7 (2019)
Taipei,China	1,085.0	1,065.0	1,065.0 (2020)	30.0	29.4	29.4 (2020)
South Asia						
Bangladesh	2,460.0	2,877.0	3,094.0 (2020)	18.9	22.1	23.8 (2020)
Bhutan	...	...	...	...	...	...
India	64,460.0	66,252.0	68,103.0 (2020)	21.7	22.3	22.9 (2020)
Maldives	...	...	...	...	...	...
Nepal	...	...	...	...	...	...
Sri Lanka	1,263.0	1,568.0	1,607.0	20.1	25.3	26.0
Southeast Asia						
Brunei Darussalam	...	...	...	...	...	...
Cambodia[a]	604.0	257.0	652.0 (2019)	3.4	1.5	3.7 (2019)
Indonesia	4,816.4	5,286.0	6,466.2	2.7	2.9	3.4
Lao People's Democratic Republic	...	...	...	...	...	...
Malaysia	1,792.0	1,775.0	1,775.0 (2020)	5.5	5.4	5.4 (2020)
Myanmar	5,487.8	6,107.4	6,112.3 (2020)	8.4	9.4	9.4 (2020)
Philippines	452.0	452.0	452.0 (2020)	1.5	1.5	1.5 (2020)
Singapore	...	...	...	...	...	...
Thailand	4,507.9	4,507.9	4,801.3 (2020)	8.8	8.8	9.4 (2020)
Timor-Leste	...	...	...	...	...	...
Viet Nam	2,577.0	3,147.0	...	8.3	10.1	...
The Pacific						
Cook Islands	...	...	...	...	...	...
Fiji	...	590.0 (2014)	...	...	32.3 (2014)	...
Kiribati	...	...	...	...	...	...
Marshall Islands	...	...	...	...	...	...
Micronesia, Federated States of	...	...	...	...	...	...
Nauru	...	...	...	...	...	...
Niue	...	...	...	...	...	...
Palau	...	...	...	...	...	...
Papua New Guinea	...	...	...	...	...	...
Samoa	...	...	...	...	...	...
Solomon Islands	...	...	...	...	...	...
Tonga	...	...	...	...	...	...
Tuvalu	...	...	...	...	...	...
Vanuatu	...	...	...	...	...	...
Developed ADB Member Economies						
Australia	...	33,343.0	32,799.0	...	4.3	4.3
Japan	...	...	...	...	...	...
New Zealand	...	...	3,700.0 (2019)	...	...	14.1 (2019)

... = data not available, ADB = Asian Development Bank, km = kilometer, km^2 = square kilometer.

a Data refers to railways rehabilitated and constructed.

Sources: For rail lines, total route: Asian Development Bank. Asian Transport Outlook Database. https://data.adb.org/dataset/asian-transport-outlook-database (accessed 6 June 2023). For rail network: Asian Development Bank estimates using land area data from World Bank. World Development Indicators. https://data.worldbank.org/indicator (accessed 6 June 2023).

Table 2.5.5: Railways—Passengers Carried and Goods Transported

ADB Regional Member	Passengers Carried[a] (p-km million)			Goods Transported[b] (t-km million)		
	2010	2015	2021	2010	2015	2021
Developing ADB Member Economies						
Central and West Asia						
Afghanistan	...	...	...	...	...	...
Armenia	125.6	104.3	112.3	743.2	640.3	811.2
Azerbaijan	834.0	439.0	104.0	8,331.0	6,269.0	5,316.0
Georgia	...	544.5 (2016)	273.2	6,227.5	4,261.3	3,322.1
Kazakhstan	16,056.0	17,011.6	12,750.0	213,200.0	267,400.0	297,400.0
Kyrgyz Republic	98.7	40.8	21.6 (2022)	737.7	917.8	1,013.1 (2022)
Pakistan	20,619.0	21,201.0	20,485.0 (2020)	4,846.9	3,301.4	7,369.9 (2020)
Tajikistan	...	1.7 (2017)	...	...	...	...
Turkmenistan	1,685.0	...	...	9,715.0	...	...
Uzbekistan	3,500.0	4,180.5	4,983.3 (2019)	22,300.0	22,934.9	23,444.6 (2019)
East Asia						
China, People's Republic of	876,220.0	1,196,060.0	956,780.0	2,764,410.0	2,375,430.0	3,323,800.0
Hong Kong, China	...	...	...	...	...	...
Korea, Republic of	58,381.8	68,371.0	48,737.4 (2020)	9,452.4	9,479.3	7,357.0 (2019)
Mongolia	1,220.0	996.7	703.4 (2022)	10,286.7	11,462.6	14,948.8 (2022)
Taipei,China	20,930.8	27,110.9	19,539.9	866.3	636.2	447.1
South Asia						
Bangladesh	8,253.0 (2012)	8,711.0	...	693.0	694.0	...
Bhutan	...	...	...	...	...	...
India	978,508.0	1,149,835.0 (2016)	590,217.0	...	...	...
Maldives	...	...	...	...	...	...
Nepal	...	...	...	...	...	...
Sri Lanka	4,568.0	7,407.0	2,158.2	162.8	127.4	161.6
Southeast Asia						
Brunei Darussalam	...	...	...	...	...	...
Cambodia	...	...	...	...	...	...
Indonesia	20,340.0	22,296.0	8,699.0	6,559.0	10,057.0	15,149.0
Lao People's Democratic Republic	...	0.1	0.0	...	...	0.0 (2020)
Malaysia	1,532.2	426.1	200.9 (2019)	1,482.8	1,474.5	1,141.6 (2019)
Myanmar	5,371.4	3,416.2	1,709.5 (2020)	1,059.4	812.3	790.3 (2020)
Philippines	...	...	...	...	...	...
Singapore	7,880.0	9,391.0 (2014)	...	...	...	...
Thailand	846.0	6,133.4	...	...	2,545.3	...
Timor-Leste	...	...	...	...	...	...
Viet Nam	4,377.9	4,149.6	1,509.2 (2020)	3,960.9	4,035.5	3,819.0 (2020)
The Pacific						
Cook Islands	...	...	...	...	...	...
Fiji	...	...	...	...	...	...
Kiribati	...	...	...	...	...	...
Marshall Islands	...	...	...	...	...	...
Micronesia, Federated States of	...	...	...	...	...	...
Nauru	...	...	...	...	...	...
Niue	...	...	...	...	...	...
Palau	...	...	...	...	...	...
Papua New Guinea	...	...	...	...	...	...
Samoa	...	...	...	...	...	...
Solomon Islands	...	...	...	...	...	...
Tonga	...	...	...	...	...	...
Tuvalu	...	...	...	...	...	...
Vanuatu	...	...	...	...	...	...
Developed ADB Member Economies						
Australia	14,534.6	15,448.1	8,183.9 (2022)	258,624.0	401,597.3	460,324.4 (2022)
Japan	393,466.0	427,486.2	263,211.0 (2020)	20,398.0	21,519.0	18,340.0 (2020)
New Zealand	...	...	...	4,768.0 (2012)	4,348.0	4,443.0

... = data not available, 0.0 = magnitude is less than half of unit employed, ADB = Asian Development Bank, p-km = passenger-kilometer, t-km = ton-kilometer.

a A passenger-kilometer, abbreviated as p-km, is a unit of measurement representing the transport of 1 passenger by a defined mode of transport over 1 kilometer.
b A ton-kilometer, abbreviated as t-km, is a unit of measurement representing the transport of 1 metric ton of goods (including packaging and tare weights of intermodal transport units) by a defined mode of transport over 1 kilometer. Only the distance on the national territory of the reporting economy is taken into account for national, international and transit transport.

Source: Asian Development Bank. Asian Transport Outlook Database. https://data.adb.org/dataset/asian-transport-outlook-database (accessed 6 June 2023).

Table 2.5.6: Air Transport

ADB Regional Member	Aviation Total Passenger Kilometers[a] (p-km million)			Aviation Freight Transport[b] (t-km million)		
	2010	2015	2021	2010	2015	2021
Developing ADB Member Economies						
Central and West Asia						
Afghanistan	...	...	...	...	...	...
Armenia	1,278.6	27.4 (2016)	416.5	9.7	– (2016)	2.1
Azerbaijan	1,613.0	3,338.0	2,334.0	139.0	582.0	2,802.0
Georgia	368.9	548.9	173.0	0.9	41.3	812.8
Kazakhstan	6,469.2	11,153.3	14,849.8	90.1	42.7	76.5
Kyrgyz Republic	814.2	1,966.1	2,071.9 (2022)	64.4	57.4	20.8
Pakistan	16,209.0	13,751.0	14,938.0 (2019)	188.9	135.5	66.2 (2020)
Tajikistan	...	193.4 (2017)	...	...	...	...
Turkmenistan	2,712.0	...	...	29.0	...	...
Uzbekistan	5,800.0	6,786.0	10,998.1 (2019)	168.0	131.1	119.0 (2019)
East Asia						
China, People's Republic of	403,899.6	951,303.6 (2017)	652,970.0	17,890.0	20,807.0	27,816.0
Hong Kong, China	...	...	...	...	...	...
Korea, Republic of	135,770.8	198,443.4	62,314.4 (2020)	145.0	112.0	...
Mongolia	907.2	1,993.5	1,828.4 (2022)	...	...	...
Taipei,China	60,051.2	80,054.8	20,938.5 (2020)	11,873.3	9,079.7	10,297.6 (2020)
South Asia						
Bangladesh	5,027.0	6,645.0	...	123.0	199.0	...
Bhutan	...	...	...	...	...	...
India	103,171.0	145,787.0	81,800.0 (2022)	...	...	...
Maldives	...	...	...	...	...	...
Nepal	...	...	...	67.4	68.0	85.6
Sri Lanka	9,399.6	12,737.3	...	1,472.7	1,146.4	...
Southeast Asia						
Brunei Darussalam	...	...	...	...	...	...
Cambodia	...	...	...	–	...	...
Indonesia	75,805.2	88,464.9	41,864.4	11,591.5	5,940.6	3,326.6
Lao People's Democratic Republic	82.8	846.1	3,680.0	1.2	0.4	0.5
Malaysia	66,719.0	87,210.0	25,018.0 (2020)	...	...	...
Myanmar	566.1	1,452.2	1,639.9 (2019)	1.3	5.0	5.1 (2019)
Philippines	...	...	...	...	...	...
Singapore	...	...	...	...	...	...
Thailand	...	...	...	29,309.0	27,221.0	24,232.0 (2019)
Timor-Leste	...	...	...	...	...	...
Viet Nam	21,162.0	42,068.4	34,124.9 (2020)	426.8	599.5	922.5 (2019)
The Pacific						
Cook Islands	...	...	...	...	...	...
Fiji	...	...	...	...	...	...
Kiribati	...	...	...	...	...	...
Marshall Islands	...	...	...	...	...	...
Micronesia, Federated States of	...	...	...	...	...	...
Nauru	...	...	...	...	...	...
Niue	...	...	...	...	...	...
Palau	...	...	...	...	...	...
Papua New Guinea	...	...	...	...	...	...
Samoa	...	...	...	...	...	...
Solomon Islands	...	...	...	...	...	...
Tonga	...	...	...	...	...	...
Tuvalu	...	...	...	...	...	...
Vanuatu	...	...	...	...	...	...
Developed ADB Member Economies						
Australia	60,223.3	70,162.1	37,835.4 (2022)	321.5	281.6	266.5
Japan	133,649.0	172,984.0	...	1,032.0	1,056.0	528.0 (2020)
New Zealand	...	...	...	...	...	...

... = data not available, – = magnitude equals zero, ADB = Asian Development Bank, p-km = passenger-kilometer, t-km = ton-kilometer.

a A passenger-kilometer, abbreviated as p-km, is a unit of measurement representing the transport of 1 passenger by a defined mode of transport over 1 kilometer. For air transport, it includes both domestic and international flights.

b A ton-kilometer, abbreviated as t-km, is a unit of measurement representing the transport of 1 metric ton of goods (including packaging and tare weights of intermodal transport units) by a defined mode of transport over 1 kilometer. For air transport, it includes both domestic and international flights.

Source: Asian Development Bank. Asian Transport Outlook Database. https://data.adb.org/dataset/asian-transport-outlook-database (accessed 6 June 2023).

Table 2.5.7: Logistics

ADB Regional Member	Container Port Traffic (teu '000)			Liner Shipping Connectivity Index[a]			Logistics Performance Index[b]		
	2010	2015	2021	2010	2015	2022	2012	2018	2023
Developing ADB Member Economies									
Central and West Asia									
Afghanistan	...	...	...	...	...	...	2.3	1.9	1.9
Armenia	...	...	...	...	...	...	2.6	2.6	2.5
Azerbaijan	...	...	...	...	...	...	2.5	...	...
Georgia	242	277	553 (2020)	5.9	5.4	5.4	...	2.4	2.7
Kazakhstan	...	...	...	...	...	...	2.7	2.8	2.7
Kyrgyz Republic	...	...	...	...	...	...	2.4	2.5	2.3
Pakistan	2,224	2,706	3,548	30.9	33.7	36.6	2.8	2.4	...
Tajikistan	...	...	...	...	...	...	2.3	2.3	2.5
Turkmenistan	...	...	...	...	...	...	...	2.4	...
Uzbekistan	...	...	...	...	...	...	2.5	2.6	2.6
East Asia									
China, People's Republic of	140,552	199,840	262,606	129.6	141.3	177.6	3.5	3.6	3.7
Hong Kong, China	23,699	20,114	17,772	95.5	90.7	81.4	4.1	3.9	4.0
Korea, Republic of	19,377	25,477	29,787	85.4	95.5	112.7	3.7	3.6	3.8
Mongolia	...	...	...	...	...	...	2.3	2.4	2.5
Taipei,China	12,737	14,492	15,453	60.4	68.0	83.0	3.7	3.6	3.9
South Asia									
Bangladesh	1,364	2,066	3,272	7.7	11.7	16.1	...	2.6	2.6
Bhutan	...	...	...	...	...	...	2.5	2.2	2.5
India	9,236	12,319	19,937	43.8	50.4	64.8	3.1	3.2	3.4
Maldives	50	84	...	5.7	7.4	9.2	2.5	2.7	...
Nepal	...	...	...	...	...	...	2.0	2.5	...
Sri Lanka	4,120	5,185	7,250	38.6	52.5	71.5	2.8	2.6	2.8
Southeast Asia									
Brunei Darussalam	93	103	106 (2020)	5.4	6.0	6.5	...	2.7	...
Cambodia	224	392	600 (2020)	6.0	8.8	8.6	2.6	2.6	2.4
Indonesia	7,840	9,576	11,805	36.5	34.5	55.0	2.9	3.2	3.0
Lao People's Democratic Republic	...	...	...	...	...	...	2.5	2.7	2.4
Malaysia	18,133	24,013	28,262	79.3	92.0	100.1	3.5	3.2	3.6
Myanmar	335	827	1,090	4.9	9.5	9.2	2.4	2.3	...
Philippines	5,045	7,069	8,491	21.8	25.8	30.0	3.0	2.9	3.3
Singapore	28,431	30,922	37,470	94.0	99.9	112.4	4.1	4.0	4.3
Thailand	7,179	8,884	10,437	43.3	44.0	72.1	3.2	3.4	3.5
Timor-Leste	...	...	...	2.5	2.6	2.2	...	...	...
Viet Nam	6,431	10,615	18,360	43.3	57.5	79.2	3.0	3.3	3.3
The Pacific									
Cook Islands	...	...	...	1.5	2.6	2.5	...	...	...
Fiji	87	89	...	11.6	10.8	10.9	2.4	2.4	2.3
Kiribati	...	...	...	3.6	3.9	6.2	...	...	...
Marshall Islands	...	...	...	3.6	4.9	7.2	...	...	...
Micronesia, Federated States of	...	...	...	1.8	2.4	4.4	...	...	...
Nauru	...	...	...	1.1	2.1	...	...	...	...
Niue	...	...	...	1.1	...	2.0	...	...	...
Palau	...	...	...	3.8	3.8 (2016)	2.5	...	...	...
Papua New Guinea	142	194	205 (2020)	7.5	10.0	11.3	...	2.2	2.7
Samoa	22	28	41 (2020)	6.0	6.0	8.6	...	...	...
Solomon Islands	...	...	...	6.2	9.0	8.1	...	2.6	2.8
Tonga	...	...	...	4.9	4.9	7.8	...	...	...
Tuvalu	...	...	...	2.3	2.8	1.5	...	...	...
Vanuatu	...	...	...	4.0	7.6	7.4	...	...	...
Developed ADB Member Economies									
Australia	6,438	7,723	8,154	30.9	32.4	38.3	3.7	3.8	3.7
Japan	19,940	21,095	22,204	72.6	76.7	79.4	3.9	4.0	3.9
New Zealand	2,318	2,931	3,251	20.0	20.9	30.8	3.4	3.9	3.6

... = data not available, ADB = Asian Development Bank, teu = twenty-foot equivalent unit.

a The Liner Shipping Connectivity Index captures how well economies are connected to global shipping networks. It is based on five components of the maritime transport sector: number of ships, their container-carrying capacity, maximum vessel size, number of services, and number of companies that deploy container ships in an economy's ports. The index generates a value of 100 for the economy with the highest average index in 2004.

b The index ranges from 1 to 5, with higher scores representing better performance.

Source: Asian Development Bank. Asian Transport Outlook Database. https://data.adb.org/dataset/asian-transport-outlook-database (accessed 6 June 2023).

Communications

Table 2.5.8: Access to Fixed Telephones, Mobile Phones, and Internet—Total Subscriptions
('000)

ADB Regional Member	Fixed Telephone Subscribers		Mobile Phone Subscribers		Fixed Broadband Subscribers	
	2010	2021	2010	2021	2010	2021
Developing ADB Member Economies						
Central and West Asia	**16,633.0**	**15,892.6**	**181,113.9**	**317,248.1**	**2,558.4**	**17,063.4**
Afghanistan	16.6	145.8	10,215.8	22,678.0	1.5	26.6
Armenia	592.3	418.1	3,865.4	3,599.3	93.6	466.6
Azerbaijan	1,506.6	1,644.3	9,100.1	10,817.1	475.3	2,055.6
Georgia	1,111.9	345.3	3,978.2	5,552.6	182.4	1,009.5
Kazakhstan	4,057.6	2,980.6	19,402.6	24,471.0	869.6	2,753.6
Kyrgyz Republic	489.1	299.0	5,275.5	8,511.0	23.1	289.0
Pakistan	6,079.1	2,989.1	99,185.8	188,711.5	789.5	2,949.0
Tajikistan	367.7	502.0	5,940.8	11,584.0	4.7	6.0
Turkmenistan	520.0	801.7	3,197.6	6,254.7	0.7	10.0
Uzbekistan	1,892.2	5,766.6	20,952.0	35,069.0	118.0	7,497.5
East Asia	**343,914.6**	**220,652.8**	**953,914.0**	**1,864,162.5**	**151,087.3**	**568,389.9**
China, People's Republic of	294,383.0	180,701.0	859,003.0	1,733,006.0	126,337.0	535,786.6
Hong Kong, China	4,361.7	3,804.4	13,793.7	23,939.7	2,167.7	2,935.4
Korea, Republic of	28,543.2	23,213.2	50,767.2	72,855.5	17,194.3	22,944.3
Mongolia	193.2	399.2	2,510.5	4,687.3	76.8	380.5
Taipei,China	16,433.5	12,535.0	27,839.5	29,674.0	5,311.6	6,343.2
South Asia	**40,845.6**	**28,933.2**	**847,557.4**	**1,408,952.7**	**11,717.3**	**42,438.6**
Bangladesh	1,280.8	1,530.6	67,923.9	184,444.9	414.6	11,136.7
Bhutan	26.3	19.7	394.3	778.0	8.7	2.8
India	35,090.0	23,773.8	752,190.0	1,154,046.6	10,990.0	27,560.0
Maldives	28.4	14.0	494.4	706.0	15.6	76.5
Nepal	841.7	726.0	9,195.6	38,213.0	60.2	1,270.0
Sri Lanka	3,578.5	2,869.2	17,359.3	30,764.1	228.3	2,392.7
Southeast Asia[a]	**73,120.0**	**33,485.3**	**532,636.5**	**936,023.4**	**14,515.4**	**60,513.6**
Brunei Darussalam	79.9	112.3	435.1	603.5	21.7	79.4
Cambodia	358.9	40.3	8,150.8	19,899.8	35.7	336.2
Indonesia	40,931.1	9,019.5	211,290.2	365,872.6	2,280.3	12,419.4
Lao People's Democratic Republic	103.1	1,300.2	4,003.4	4,823.0	5.9	150.8
Malaysia	4,609.8	8,247.1	33,858.7	47,201.7	2,097.8	3,734.1
Myanmar	493.3	522.1	594.0	67,930.1	23.0	893.0
Philippines	3,335.4	4,584.4	83,150.1	163,345.2	1,791.0 (2011)	9,623.7
Singapore	1,996.1	1,901.1	7,384.6	8,761.9	1,338.4	1,526.4
Thailand	6,835.1	4,634.0	71,726.3	120,850.0	3,251.9	12,420.9
Timor-Leste	2.9	1.9	473.0	1,386.2	0.5	1.3
Viet Nam	14,374.4	3,122.5	111,570.2	135,349.5	3,669.3	19,328.2
The Pacific[a]	**338.8**	**267.0**	**3,105.0**	**6,817.3**	**38.6**	**67.5**
Cook Islands	7.2	7.0	7.8	17.0	1.7	3.0
Fiji	129.8	48.5	697.9	991.5	23.3	23.1
Kiribati	8.4	0.0	10.6	52.6	0.8	0.3
Marshall Islands	...	...	...	16.0	...	1.0 (2020)
Micronesia, Federated States of	8.5	7.0	27.5	22.0	1.0	6.0
Nauru	...	...	6.2	10.0	1.0	...
Niue	1.0	1.0	...	...	...	...
Palau	7.0	8.0	14.5	24.0	0.2	...
Papua New Guinea	121.2	166.0	1,909.1	4,818.0	6.1	21.0
Samoa	8.0	6.0	90.0	69.0	0.2	1.7
Solomon Islands	8.4	7.0	115.5	474.0	2.5	1.0
Tonga	31.0	10.8	54.3	64.3	1.1	6.8
Tuvalu	1.2	2.0	1.6	9.0	0.2	0.5
Vanuatu	7.1	3.6	169.9	249.9	0.5	3.2
Developed ADB Member Economies[a]	**78,123.7**	**65,828.6**	**150,497.1**	**236,466.0**	**40,703.8**	**56,114.6**
Australia	10,625.0	3,747.8	22,500.0	27,285.0	5,510.0	9,145.4
Japan	65,618.7	61,429.8	123,287.1	203,335.0	34,101.8	45,168.1
New Zealand	1,880.0	651.0	4,710.0	5,846.0	1,092.0	1,801.1
DEVELOPING ADB MEMBER ECONOMIES[a]	**474,856.2**	**299,235.2**	**2,518,342.9**	**4,533,204.7**	**179,918.3**	**688,475.1**
ALL ADB REGIONAL MEMBERS[a]	**552,980.0**	**365,063.7**	**2,668,840.0**	**4,769,670.6**	**220,622.1**	**744,589.8**

... = data not available, 0.0 = magnitude is less than half of unit employed, – = magnitude equals zero, ADB = Asian Development Bank.

a Regional aggregates are calculated as the sum of the reporting economies. Imputation was done for economies with missing data by substituting available data from the nearest years.

Source: International Telecommunication Union. World Telecommunication/ICT Indicators Database. http://www.itu.int/en/ITU-D/Statistics/Pages/stat/default.aspx (accessed 30 May 2023).

Table 2.5.9: Access to Fixed Telephones, Mobile Phones, and Internet—Subscriptions per 100 People

ADB Regional Member	Fixed Telephone			Mobile Cellular			Fixed Broadband			Internet Users		
	2010	2015	2021	2010	2015	2021	2010	2015	2021	2010	2015	2021
Developing ADB Member Economies												
Central and West Asia[a]	**5.5**	**4.7**	**4.4**	**59.9**	**71.9**	**87.1**	**0.8**	**2.7**	**4.7**			
Afghanistan[b]	0.1	0.3	0.4	36.2	58.4	56.6	0.0	0.0	0.1	4.0	8.3	18.4
Armenia	20.1	19.2	15.0	131.2	120.4	129.0	3.2	9.9	16.7	25.0	59.1	78.6
Azerbaijan	16.3	18.2	15.9	98.5	108.5	104.9	5.1	19.3	19.9	46.0	77.0	86.0
Georgia	29.0	25.2	9.2	103.7	147.2	147.8	4.8	16.9	26.9	26.9	47.6	76.4
Kazakhstan	24.4	23.3	15.5	116.7	147.5	127.5	5.2	12.9	14.3	31.6	70.8	90.9
Kyrgyz Republic	8.9	6.9	4.6	96.2	128.1	130.4	0.4	3.6	4.4	16.3	30.2	77.9
Pakistan	3.1	1.7	1.3	51.0	59.7	81.6	0.4	0.8	1.3	8.0	11.0	21.0
Tajikistan	4.8	5.4	5.1	77.9	99.6	118.8	0.1	0.1	0.1	11.6	19.0	...
Turkmenistan	9.9	11.2	12.6	60.7	136.0	98.6	0.0	0.1	0.2	3.0	15.0	...
Uzbekistan	6.6	9.1	16.9	73.2	70.4	102.9	0.4	5.8	22.0	15.9	42.8	76.6
East Asia[a]	**24.1**	**18.8**	**14.6**	**66.7**	**94.7**	**123.3**	**10.6**	**20.6**	**37.6**			
China, People's Republic of	21.8	16.6	12.7	63.7	92.7	121.5	9.4	19.9	37.6	34.3	50.3	73.1
Hong Kong, China	61.2	58.5	50.8	193.4	226.0	319.4	30.4	31.7	39.2	72.0	84.9	93.1
Korea, Republic of	58.5	56.6	44.8	104.0	115.6	140.6	35.2	39.3	44.3	83.7	89.9	97.6
Mongolia	7.2	8.6	11.9	92.9	103.5	140.0	2.8	7.0	11.4	10.2	22.5	84.3
Taipei,China	71.2	59.2	52.5	120.6	126.2	124.4	23.0	24.1	26.6	71.5	78.0	90.1
South Asia[a]	**2.8**	**2.0**	**1.8**	**58.9**	**77.4**	**86.4**	**0.8**	**1.5**	**2.6**			
Bangladesh	0.9	0.5	0.9	45.8	83.2	108.9	0.3	3.1	6.6	3.7	12.9	38.9
Bhutan	3.7	2.9	2.5	55.9	90.9	100.1	1.2	3.8	0.4	13.6	39.8	85.6
India	2.8	1.9	1.7	60.6	75.7	82.0	0.9	1.3	2.0	7.5	14.9	46.3
Maldives	7.8	5.0	2.7	136.7	169.8	135.4	4.3	5.3	14.7	26.5	54.5	85.8
Nepal	3.1	3.1	2.4	33.9	99.7	127.2	0.2	1.1	4.2	7.9	17.6	51.6
Sri Lanka	17.3	15.4	13.2	84.0	112.0	141.3	1.1	2.9	11.0	...	15.3	66.7
Southeast Asia[a,c]	**12.2**	**5.4**	**5.0**	**88.8**	**125.6**	**138.5**	**2.5**	**4.0**	**9.0**			
Brunei Darussalam	20.2	18.0	25.2	109.9	110.0	135.5	5.5	8.2	17.8	53.0	71.2	98.1
Cambodia	2.5	1.7	0.2	56.7	135.2	120.0	0.2	0.5	2.0	1.3	18.0	60.2
Indonesia	16.8	4.0	3.3	86.6	130.8	133.7	0.9	1.5	4.5	10.9	22.1	62.1
Lao People's Democratic Republic	1.6	14.2	17.5	63.3	54.9	65.0	0.1	0.2	2.0	7.0	18.2	62.0
Malaysia	16.1	14.5	24.6	117.9	142.0	140.6	7.3	9.9	11.1	56.3	71.1	96.8
Myanmar	1.0	1.0	1.0	1.2	79.6	126.3	0.0	0.1	1.7	0.3	10.9	44.0
Philippines[d]	3.5	3.1	4.0	87.9	114.4	143.4	1.9	2.8	8.5	25.0	36.9	52.7
Singapore	38.7	35.7	32.0	143.0	145.7	147.5	25.9	26.3	25.7	71.0	83.2	91.1
Thailand	10.0	7.6	6.5	105.1	146.4	168.8	4.8	8.9	17.3	22.4	39.3	85.3
Timor-Leste	0.3	0.2	0.1	43.5	114.2	104.9	0.0	0.1	0.1	3.0	18.6	39.5
Viet Nam	16.4	7.9	3.2	127.6	130.5	138.9	4.2	8.3	19.8	30.7	45.0	74.2
The Pacific[a,c]	**3.4**	**2.5**	**2.1**	**31.5**	**48.9**	**54.2**	**0.4**	**0.4**	**0.5**			
Cook Islands[e]	42.0	37.1	41.2	45.3	78.9	100.0	9.7	15.1	17.6	35.7	51.0	...
Fiji	14.3	7.9	5.2	77.1	105.3	107.2	2.6	1.4	2.5	20.0	42.5	87.7
Kiribati	7.8	1.3	0.0	9.8	35.1	40.8	0.8	0.1	0.2	9.1	14.9	53.6
Marshall Islands[f]	...	4.7	...	...	31.4	38.0	...	2.0	2.3	7.0	19.3	...
Micronesia, Federated States of	7.9	6.2	6.2	25.6	20.6	19.4	0.9	3.0	5.3	20.0	31.5	40.4
Nauru[g]	18.6	...	...	60.5	84.0	79.9	9.3	...	...	54.0	62.4	83.9
Niue	55.2	54.2	51.6	...	...	...	...	...	...	77.0	...	...
Palau	37.6	40.5	44.4	78.3	133.4	133.2	1.3	6.9	...	...	...	...
Papua New Guinea	1.6	1.7	1.7	25.2	41.0	48.4	0.1	0.2	0.2	1.3	7.9	32.1
Samoa	4.1	5.6	2.7	46.2	59.2	31.5	0.1	1.0	0.8	7.0	25.4	78.2
Solomon Islands	1.6	1.2	1.0	21.4	69.3	67.0	0.5	0.2	0.1	5.0	10.0	36.1
Tonga	28.9	12.5	10.2	50.6	69.3	60.7	1.0	2.3	6.4	16.0	38.7	71.6
Tuvalu	11.4	18.4	17.9	15.2	60.7	80.3	2.3	4.1	4.0	14.6	27.3	71.6
Vanuatu	2.9	1.7	1.1	69.2	63.2	78.3	0.2	1.6	1.0	8.0	22.4	66.3
Developed ADB Member Economies[a]	**50.6**	**47.6**	**42.3**	**97.4**	**123.3**	**151.9**	**26.4**	**30.3**	**36.0**			
Australia	48.3	35.7	14.5	102.2	108.2	105.3	25.0	28.7	35.3	76.0	84.6	96.2
Japan	51.2	50.1	49.3	96.2	126.2	163.2	26.6	30.5	36.2	78.2	91.1	82.9
New Zealand	43.3	40.3	12.7	108.4	122.0	114.0	25.1	31.6	35.1	80.5	85.2	95.9
DEVELOPING ADB MEMBER ECONOMIES[a,c]	**12.6**	**9.0**	**7.1**	**66.6**	**91.0**	**108.1**	**4.8**	**9.1**	**16.4**			
ALL ADB REGIONAL MEMBERS[a,c]	**14.1**	**10.5**	**8.4**	**67.8**	**92.2**	**109.6**	**5.7**	**9.9**	**17.1**			

... = data not available, 0.0 = magnitude is less than half of unit employed, ADB = Asian Development Bank.

a Regional aggregates are derived from table 2.5.8 regional aggregate levels and population data from the United Nations' World Population Prospects 2022.
b For internet users, data for 2021 refers to 2020.
c Regional aggregates are calculated as the sum of the reporting economies. Imputation was done for economies with missing data by substituting available data from the nearest years.
d For fixed broadband, data for 2010 refers to 2011.
e For fixed telephone and mobile cellular, data for 2015 refers to 2016. For fixed broadband, data for 2015 refers to 2013.
f For fixed telephone, data for 2015 refers to 2014. For fixed broadband, data for 2021 refers to 2020.
g For fixed telephone, data for 2010 refers to 2009. For internet users, data for 2010 refers to 2011 and data for 2015 refers to 2017.

Sources: International Telecommunication Union. World Telecommunication/ICT Indicators Database. http://www.itu.int/en/ITU-D/Statistics/Pages/stat/default.aspx (accessed 30 May 2023); and United Nations. World Population Prospects 2022. https://population.un.org/wpp/Download/Standard/Population/ (accessed 30 May 2023).

Data Issues and Comparability

Issues with data organization, collection, compilation, and dissemination affect the availability, quality, and timeliness of road statistics. Some regions, especially the Pacific, have incomplete or no data.

Most data on telephone and internet subscriptions came from questionnaires sent by the International Telecommunication Union to participating economies. Other information and reports were sourced from national ministries in charge of telecommunications and from staff estimates.

Table 2.6.1: Electricity Production and Sources

ADB Regional Member	Total Electricity Production (kWh billion)		Sources of Electricity (% of total): Combustible Fuels[a]		Hydropower		Solar		Others[b]	
	2010	2020	2010	2020	2010	2020	2010	2020	2010	2020
Developing ADB Member Economies										
Central and West Asia[c]	**310.1**	**412.1**	**67.7**	**72.2**	**30.4**	**22.6**	**0.0**	**0.6**	**1.9**	**4.6**
Afghanistan	0.9	1.4 (2021)	14.0	9.3 (2021)	86.0	88.4(2021)	...	2.3 (2021)	...	...
Armenia	6.5	7.8	22.2	40.4	39.4	22.7	...	1.7	38.5	35.2
Azerbaijan[d]	18.7	25.8	81.6	95.3	18.4	4.1	...	0.2	0.0 (2009)	0.4
Georgia	10.1	11.2	6.8	25.3	93.2	73.9	...	...	...	0.8
Kazakhstan	82.7	114.4 (2021)	90.3	89.0 (2021)	9.7	8.0(2021)	0.0	1.4 (2021)	0.0 (2012)	1.5 (2021)
Kyrgyz Republic[d]	12.1	15.4	8.2	9.3	91.8	90.7	...	...	...	...
Pakistan	94.4	130.5	62.7	61.9	33.7	26.1	...	0.6	3.6	11.5
Tajikistan	16.4	20.1	0.2	9.9	99.8	90.1	...	...	...	...
Turkmenistan	16.7	22.5	100.0	100.0	0.0 (2011)	0.0	...	...	...	...
Uzbekistan	51.7	66.5	79.0	92.5	21.0	7.5	...	0.0	...	0.0
East Asia[c]	**4,996.4**	**8,679.8**	**78.3**	**68.5**	**15.3**	**16.2**	**0.0**	**3.3**	**6.4**	**11.9**
China, People's Republic of	4,207.2	7,779.1	79.2	68.5	17.2	17.4	...	3.4	3.6	10.7
Hong Kong, China	38.3	37.1 (2021)	100.0	100.0 (2021)	...	...	...	...	...	...
Korea, Republic of	499.5	578.6	68.6	66.7	1.3	1.2	0.2	3.1	30.0	28.9
Mongolia	4.4	7.8 (2021)	98.9	90.2 (2021)	0.8	1.8(2021)	0.2	0.8 (2021)	0.0	7.3 (2021)
Taipei,China	247.1	288.1 (2022)	...	...	...	...	...	...	...	...
South Asia[c]	**1,017.1**	**1,652.3**	**82.6**	**78.4**	**12.9**	**11.2**	**0.0**	**3.7**	**4.4**	**6.7**
Bangladesh	40.8	84.8	98.1	98.5	1.9	1.0	...	0.5	...	0.0
Bhutan	7.3	11.1 (2021)	0.0	0.0 (2021)	100.0	100.0(2021)	0.0	0.0 (2021)	...	0.0 (2021)
India	954.5	1,533.3	83.3	78.3	12.0	10.5	...	4.0	4.7	7.2
Maldives	0.4	0.8 (2021)	99.2	97.0 (2021)	...	...	0.2	2.6 (2021)	0.6	0.4 (2021)
Nepal	3.2	6.2	0.1	0.0	99.9	99.9	...	0.0	...	0.1
Sri Lanka	10.8	15.8	47.2	64.9	52.3	31.5	0.1	1.4	0.5	2.2
Southeast Asia[c]	**676.5**	**1,122.6**	**85.3**	**80.5**	**11.8**	**15.2**	**0.0**	**1.7**	**2.9**	**2.7**
Brunei Darussalam	3.8	5.7	100.0	100.0	...	...	0.1 (2011)	0.0	...	...
Cambodia	1.0	9.3 (2021)	96.5	49.5 (2021)	3.2	44.2(2021)	0.3	6.4 (2021)	...	...
Indonesia	169.6	274.8	84.2	87.6	10.3	7.2	0.0	0.0	5.5	5.2
Lao People's Democratic Republic	8.4	40.4 (2021)	...	34.2 (2021)	100.0	65.7(2021)	0.0 (2012)	0.1 (2021)	...	...
Malaysia	116.8	182.7	94.6	84.3	5.4	14.4	0.0	1.3	...	...
Myanmar	8.6	23.6	28.2	64.3	71.8	35.4	...	0.3	...	...
Philippines	67.8	107.6 (2021)	73.7	79.0 (2021)	11.5	8.6(2021)	0.0	1.4 (2021)	14.7	11.1 (2021)
Singapore[d]	45.4	53.7	100.0	98.8	...	...	0.0	1.2	...	...
Thailand	159.5	186.9 (2021)	96.5	93.2 (2021)	3.5	2.5(2021)	0.0	2.5 (2021)	0.0	1.9 (2021)
Timor-Leste	0.1	0.5 (2021)	98.9	99.5 (2021)	1.1	0.3(2021)	...	0.2 (2021)	...	...
Viet Nam	95.4	240.5	70.5	65.1	29.4	30.5	...	3.9	0.1	0.4
The Pacific[c]	**5.1**	**6.8** (2021)	**63.9**	**66.1** (2021)	**27.6**	**26.1**(2021)	**0.0**	**1.3** (2021)	**8.4**	**6.4** (2021)
Cook Islands	0.0	0.0 (2021)	99.8	61.3 (2021)	...	...	0.2	38.7 (2021)	...	...
Fiji	0.9	1.0 (2021)	50.9	42.1 (2021)	48.4	56.5(2021)	0.1 (2012)	1.3 (2021)	0.8	0.1 (2021)
Kiribati	0.0	0.0 (2021)	97.1	84.0 (2021)	...	...	2.9	16.0 (2021)	...	...
Marshall Islands	0.1	0.1 (2021)	100.0	97.6 (2021)	...	...	0.3 (2012)	2.4 (2021)	...	...
Micronesia, Federated States of	0.1	0.1 (2021)	98.8	92.3 (2021)	...	1.8(2021)	1.2	4.3 (2021)	–	1.6 (2021)
Nauru	0.0	0.0 (2021)	99.8	91.0 (2021)	...	...	0.2	9.0 (2021)	...	...
Niue	0.0	0.0 (2021)	97.9	87.6 (2021)	...	...	2.1	12.4 (2021)	...	...
Palau	0.1	0.1 (2021)	100.0	93.9 (2021)	...	...	...	6.1 (2021)	...	...
Papua New Guinea	3.6	5.0 (2021)	62.0	68.4 (2021)	26.4	23.0(2021)	0.0	0.0 (2021)	11.6	8.5 (2021)
Samoa	0.1	0.2 (2021)	64.1	55.0 (2021)	35.9	32.4(2021)	0.0	12.5 (2021)	...	0.1 (2021)
Solomon Islands	0.1	0.1 (2021)	99.4	95.8 (2021)	0.6	0.9(2021)	1.4 (2011)	3.3 (2021)	...	...
Tonga	0.1	0.1 (2021)	100.0	86.7 (2021)	...	...	...	9.3 (2021)	...	4.0 (2021)
Tuvalu	0.0	0.0 (2021)	97.9	77.0 (2021)	...	...	2.1	23.0 (2021)	...	...
Vanuatu	0.1	0.1 (2021)	80.9	72.8 (2021)	11.6	11.0(2021)	0.1 (2011)	9.0 (2021)	7.5	7.2 (2021)
Developed ADB Member Economies	**1,468.6**	**1,327.5**	**68.6**	**75.4**	**8.8**	**9.6**	**0.3**	**7.6**	**22.4**	**7.4**
Australia	252.7	265.2	92.5	78.7	5.4	5.7	0.2	7.9	2.0	7.7
Japan	1,170.9	1,017.8	65.0	77.0	7.7	8.6	0.3	7.8	27.0	6.6
New Zealand	45.0	44.5	28.2	21.3	54.9	54.5	0.0	0.4	16.9	23.9
DEVELOPING ADB MEMBER ECONOMIES[c]	**7,005.2**	**11,873.0**	**79.1**	**71.2**	**15.3**	**15.6**	**0.0**	**3.1**	**5.5**	**10.0**
ALL ADB REGIONAL MEMBERS[c]	**8,473.7**	**13,200.5**	**77.3**	**71.7**	**14.2**	**15.0**	**0.1**	**3.6**	**8.5**	**9.7**

... = data not available, (-/+) 0.0 = magnitude is less than half of unit employed, – = magnitude equals zero, ADB = Asian Development Bank, kWh = kilowatt-hour.

a Electricity from combustible fuels refers to the production of electricity from the combustion of fuels that are capable of igniting or burning, which would include coal, natural gas, oil, and other combustible fuels.
b Includes chemical heat, geothermal, nuclear, tide, other marine electricity, wind, wave, and other sources of energy.
c Includes only reporting economies with data corresponding to the year heading.
d Partial 2021 energy data are available from the United Nations' Energy Statistics Database. However, 2020 figures were reflected in this table to ensure comparability of data.

Sources: United Nations. Energy Statistics Database. http://data.un.org/Data.aspx?d=EDATA&f=cmID%3aEL (accessed 17 June 2023). For Taipei,China: Government of Taipei,China; Directorate-General of Budget, Accounting and Statistics; Official communication, 18 April 2023.

Electricity

Table 2.6.2: Electric Power Consumption
(kWh per capita)

ADB Regional Member	2010	2015	2017	2018	2019	2020
Developing ADB Member Economies						
Central and West Asia[a]	**809.6**	**893.0**	**953.9**	**991.3**	**953.5**	**913.5**
Afghanistan	86.2	134.5	150.3	151.3	153.0	158.3 (2021)
Armenia	1,584.0	1,866.2	1,971.7	1,904.6	2,070.2	2,099.5
Azerbaijan[b]	1,452.7	2,085.8	1,984.5	2,049.2	2,115.6	2,138.8
Georgia	1,997.5	2,630.7	2,975.6	3,167.8	3,204.9	3,056.8
Kazakhstan	3,789.8	4,417.8	4,845.8	5,141.7	4,301.0	4,217.8
Kyrgyz Republic	1,298.6	1,802.7	1,828.1	1,922.6	1,967.5	1,908.5
Pakistan	396.5	428.6	477.3	498.1	508.5	474.0
Tajikistan	1,857.8	1,467.7	1,550.8	1,521.7	1,517.2	1,568.1
Turkmenistan	2,061.3	2,555.8	2,469.3	2,430.0	2,393.1	2,357.9
Uzbekistan	1,547.5	1,529.9	1,576.1	1,649.1	1,642.8	1,549.5
East Asia[a]	**3,059.9**	**3,971.7**	**4,425.5**	**4,746.1**	**4,938.1**	**5,100.6**
China, People's Republic of	2,688.6	3,629.5	4,085.9	4,419.1	4,630.0	4,807.3
Hong Kong, China	5,869.4	5,934.2	5,874.4	5,921.9	5,992.3	6,112.8 (2021)
Korea, Republic of[b]	9,392.4	9,935.3	10,451.7	10,555.7	10,390.1	10,184.2
Mongolia	1,249.1	1,782.1	1,921.4	2,038.5	2,118.1	2,316.5 (2021)
Taipei,China	10,703.0	10,979.1	11,420.1	11,613.5	11,531.5	12,059.7 (2022)
South Asia[a]	**516.8**	**721.4**	**780.7**	**794.1**	**875.2**	**799.2**
Bangladesh	232.6	327.9	407.1	430.2	478.5	477.4
Bhutan	2,735.0	2,767.7	2,890.7	2,868.1	2,970.0	2,547.0 (2021)
India	559.7	781.9	838.3	850.2	937.8	850.1
Maldives	937.6	1,336.1	1,447.8	1,490.5	1,502.5	1,455.5 (2021)
Nepal	100.9	140.1	202.6	228.0	228.2	253.3
Sri Lanka	445.5	550.3	627.2	654.2	680.8	665.4
Southeast Asia[a]	**1,008.8**	**1,264.2**	**1,398.6**	**1,451.9**	**1,500.5**	**1,502.0**
Brunei Darussalam	8,243.8	8,867.3	8,222.6	8,483.7	9,825.0	11,684.1
Cambodia	157.1	338.0	429.0	539.7	640.4	676.5
Indonesia	603.6	821.2	924.9	942.8	957.4	975.1
Lao People's Democratic Republic	386.0	624.6	709.7	762.4	914.5	951.5 (2021)
Malaysia	3,860.1	4,255.0	4,582.2	4,718.2	4,837.9	4,576.5
Myanmar	127.8	260.2	302.9	340.2	352.2	359.3
Philippines	584.0	658.1	728.8	761.0	789.3	778.2 (2021)
Singapore[b]	8,182.6	8,409.5	8,610.9	8,674.5	8,815.2	8,589.1
Thailand	2,187.2	2,476.1	2,614.6	2,643.8	2,709.0	2,782.2 (2021)
Timor-Leste	93.5	210.9	258.3	265.8	300.1	287.7 (2021)
Viet Nam	980.1	1,558.5	1,857.4	2,030.3	2,161.8	2,232.2
The Pacific[a]	**457.1**	**474.4**	**477.8**	**494.5**	**488.6**	**477.7** (2021)
Cook Islands	1,804.6	1,705.1	2,001.0	2,522.8	2,376.6	2,192.0 (2021)
Fiji	844.4	900.6	981.8	1,006.5	1,034.3	951.8 (2021)
Kiribati	177.8	188.5	199.4	207.8	206.9	186.2 (2021)
Marshall Islands	1,273.0	1,179.9	1,388.1	1,380.8	1,354.9	1,453.0 (2021)
Micronesia, Federated States of	488.7	434.6	428.5	426.8	423.2	415.9 (2021)
Nauru	1,513.5	1,732.7	2,200.8	2,356.6	2,621.3	2,745.4 (2021)
Niue	1,533.1	1,619.9	1,637.2	1,748.8	1,769.9	1,703.7 (2021)
Palau	3,894.3	4,439.7	4,714.9	4,791.8	4,967.6	4,882.4 (2021)
Papua New Guinea	425.1	447.1	438.6	458.8	448.3	446.7 (2021)
Samoa	477.7	567.1	666.6	660.0	715.9	696.6 (2021)
Solomon Islands	138.8	135.0	140.1	132.8	130.8	123.6 (2021)
Tonga	397.0	463.3	557.8	550.6	598.4	622.5 (2021)
Tuvalu	512.5	519.7	614.1	630.3	643.8	635.8 (2021)
Vanuatu	248.8	221.9	248.2	242.2	245.6	226.2 (2021)
Developed ADB Member Economies[a]	**8,490.3**	**7,895.3**	**8,019.1**	**7,916.7**	**7,817.8**	**7,693.1**
Australia	10,027.7	9,428.5	9,428.7	9,430.9	9,423.4	9,352.7
Japan	8,197.3	7,572.9	7,730.7	7,603.9	7,481.8	7,348.9
New Zealand	9,336.4	8,876.2	8,413.7	8,260.3	8,130.4	7,793.0
DEVELOPING ADB MEMBER ECONOMIES[a]	**1,580.2**	**2,026.9**	**2,234.5**	**2,363.4**	**2,462.6**	**2,480.9**
ALL ADB REGIONAL MEMBERS[a]	**1,851.5**	**2,247.3**	**2,448.3**	**2,567.0**	**2,657.4**	**2,669.0**

ADB = Asian Development Bank, kWh = kilowatt-hour.

Notes: All figures presented in this table are Asian Development Bank estimates using data from the United Nation's Energy Statistics Database, Government of Taipei,China; Directorate-General of Budget, Accounting and Statistics, and the United Nations' World Population Prospects 2022.

a Includes only reporting economies with data corresponding to the year heading.
b Partial 2021 energy data are available from the United Nations' Energy Statistics Database. However, 2020 figures were reflected in this table to ensure comparability of data.

Sources: For electric power consumption: United Nations. Energy Statistics Database. http://data.un.org/Data.aspx?d=EDATA&f=cmID%3aEL (accessed 17 June 2023). For Taipei,China: Government of Taipei,China; Directorate-General of Budget, Accounting and Statistics; Official communication, 18 April 2023. For total population: United Nations. World Population Prospects 2022. https://population.un.org/wpp/Download/Standard/Population/ (accessed 01 March 2023).

Table 2.6.3: Use of Energy

ADB Regional Member	Energy Use (PJ)			GDP per Unit Use of Energy (constant 2017 $ million PPP per PJ)		
	2010	2015	2020	2010	2015	2020
Developing ADB Member Economies						
Central and West Asia[a]	**10,359.0**	**10,658.2**	**10,857.1**	**154.6**	**188.4**	**228.2**
Afghanistan	140.6	168.9	197.4	406.2	421.3	388.5
Armenia	106.2	134.7	152.4	251.7	245.9	245.9
Azerbaijan	485.9	605.0	642.9	262.4	236.9	215.5
Georgia	139.8	197.8	208.1	263.8	237.4	249.9
Kazakhstan	3,363.4	3,180.4	2,759.2	100.7	134.0	172.4
Kyrgyz Republic	115.5	167.2	149.6	195.3	171.2	207.9
Pakistan	3,092.2	3,314.4	3,685.0	255.2	289.8	308.5
Tajikistan	143.4	166.6	204.5	125.4	151.5	170.4
Turkmenistan	951.4	988.3	1,062.4	46.1	73.2	89.8 (2019)
Uzbekistan	1,820.6	1,734.8	1,795.6	77.7	115.5	140.0
East Asia[a]	**112,823.7**	**132,599.6**	**152,704.3**	**123.8**	**149.6**	**168.0**
China, People's Republic of	101,618.2	120,324.1	140,212.6	117.0	144.6	164.0
Hong Kong, China	544.0	575.9	513.8	663.2	724.3	813.8
Korea, Republic of	10,497.6	11,426.5	11,549.4	162.4	173.4	190.3
Mongolia	164.0	273.0	428.5	123.9	120.9	89.7
Taipei,China	...	...	...	...	...	...
South Asia	**29,747.2**	**37,883.9**	**41,389.9**	**201.9**	**216.7**	**238.9**
Bangladesh	1,482.9	1,768.3	2,079.0	339.8	387.1	450.3
Bhutan	56.8	63.8	67.5	98.9	115.0	120.7
India	27,409.7	35,122.8	38,177.5	190.7	203.8	223.6
Maldives	13.4	18.4	23.6	444.9	427.5	293.0
Nepal	445.6	501.6	633.8	163.5	179.4	174.2
Sri Lanka	338.8	408.9	408.5	564.6	636.9	702.7
Southeast Asia	**21,964.5**	**25,788.5**	**29,230.0**	**241.1**	**263.6**	**274.9**
Brunei Darussalam	135.7	113.8	163.3	194.1	230.2	166.6
Cambodia	196.4	252.3	357.2	198.0	217.9	196.3
Indonesia	8,072.8	8,708.7	10,344.7	248.2	301.1	302.6
Lao People's Democratic Republic	100.3	168.8	246.0	302.2	261.4	231.0
Malaysia	2,965.0	3,424.5	3,881.5	195.4	219.1	220.9
Myanmar	659.8	847.5	957.2	211.9	227.7	276.1
Philippines	1,706.3	2,143.0	2,380.8	325.9	347.9	366.3
Singapore	883.2	1,216.8	1,135.0	449.0	405.6	473.4
Thailand	4,906.9	5,668.4	5,242.8	197.2	197.4	229.7
Timor-Leste	4.5	7.1	9.4	696.6	551.2	674.6
Viet Nam	2,333.6	3,237.7	4,512.0	236.9	230.4	223.9
The Pacific[a]	**186.9**	**233.2**	**251.1**	**209.0**	**213.3**	**210.1**
Cook Islands	1.1	1.1	1.0	...	...	...
Fiji	19.9	25.2	20.6	456.1	434.1	490.2
Kiribati	1.4	1.4	1.6	142.8	167.5	154.1
Marshall Islands	2.0	2.0	2.0	100.6	103.7	124.0
Micronesia, Federated States of	1.5	2.1	2.2	243.8	176.4	179.2
Nauru	0.6	0.8	0.7	114.7	185.7	196.5
Niue	0.1	0.1	0.1	...	...	...
Palau	2.9	2.8	2.9	94.7	115.8	97.6
Papua New Guinea	140.9	180.5	200.4	176.8	183.4	182.0
Samoa	4.2	5.0	5.3	269.9	236.9	247.8
Solomon Islands	8.0	7.6	7.6	163.5	204.7	225.7
Tonga	1.7	1.6	2.7	322.1	367.2	251.6
Tuvalu	0.1	0.1	0.1	259.2	346.4	389.9
Vanuatu	2.7	2.8	3.8	274.3	280.9	231.3
Developed ADB Member Economies	**27,248.7**	**24,437.4**	**22,594.2**	**221.3**	**264.3**	**287.9**
Australia	5,396.3	5,330.4	5,514.2	183.6	212.5	226.8
Japan	21,014.9	18,143.0	16,145.0	232.0	283.1	312.3
New Zealand	837.5	964.0	935.1	195.2	196.1	226.7
DEVELOPING ADB MEMBER ECONOMIES[a]	**175,081.4**	**207,163.4**	**234,432.3**	**153.7**	**178.1**	**196.5**
ALL ADB REGIONAL MEMBERS[a]	**202,330.1**	**231,600.8**	**257,026.4**	**162.8**	**187.2**	**204.6**
WORLD[a]	**511,022.9**	**543,579.4**	**561,518.1**	**179.6**	**200.4**	**214.8**

... = data not available, $ = United States dollars, ADB = Asian Development Bank, GDP = gross domestic product, PJ = petajoule, PPP = purchasing power parity.

a Aggregates include only reporting economies with data corresponding to the year heading.

Sources: For Energy Use: United Nations. Energy Statistics Database. https://data.un.org/SdmxBrowser/start (accessed 21 June 2023). For GDP per Unit Use of Energy: Asian Development Bank estimates using data from World Bank's World Development Indicators Database. https://databank.worldbank.org/source/world-development-indicators# (accessed 21 June 2023); and United Nation's Energy Statistics Database. https://data.un.org/SdmxBrowser/start (accessed 21 June 2023).

Table 2.6.4: Energy Production and Imports

ADB Regional Member	Energy Production (PJ)			Energy Imports, Net (% of total energy use)		
	2010	2015	2020	2010	2015	2020
Developing ADB Member Economies						
Central and West Asia	**16,391.7**	**17,420.5**	**16,680.9**	**-58.2**	**-63.4**	**-53.6**
Afghanistan	41.4	61.0	71.4	70.5	63.9	63.8
Armenia	38.9	44.5	42.0	63.4	67.0	72.5
Azerbaijan	2,758.9	2,473.7	2,411.6	-467.8	-308.8	-275.1
Georgia	57.5	55.1	43.7	58.8	72.1	79.0
Kazakhstan	6,769.9	6,812.2	6,650.5	-101.3	-114.2	-141.0
Kyrgyz Republic	53.1	75.3	102.4	54.1	55.0	31.5
Pakistan	2,251.6	2,302.5	2,219.8	27.2	30.5	39.8
Tajikistan	114.7	131.3	154.6	20.0	21.2	24.4
Turkmenistan	1,981.9	3,407.3	3,255.3	-108.3	-244.8	-206.4
Uzbekistan	2,323.7	2,057.7	1,729.7	-27.6	-18.6	3.7
East Asia[a]	**91,160.2**	**103,740.7**	**115,082.5**	**18.8**	**21.4**	**24.4**
China, People's Republic of	88,642.0	100,962.7	111,744.3	12.8	16.1	20.3
Hong Kong, China	...	...	...	...	...	...
Korea, Republic of	1,863.1	2,123.0	2,169.2	82.3	81.4	81.2
Mongolia	655.0	655.1	1,169.0	-299.5	-139.9	-172.8
Taipei,China	...	...	...	...	...	...
South Asia	**23,018.7**	**24,009.1**	**25,763.2**	**22.6**	**36.6**	**37.8**
Bangladesh	1,293.7	1,474.6	1,456.7	12.8	16.6	29.9
Bhutan	72.9	76.8	91.4	-28.4	-20.3	-35.4
India	21,104.5	21,875.0	23,599.6	23.0	37.7	38.2
Maldives	0.2	0.2	0.2	98.9	99.0	99.0
Nepal	384.4	423.6	464.5	13.7	15.5	26.7
Sri Lanka	163.0	158.8	150.8	51.9	61.2	63.1
Southeast Asia	**29,035.6**	**30,832.5**	**33,068.9**	**-32.2**	**-19.6**	**-13.1**
Brunei Darussalam	775.2	672.8	603.1	-471.3	-491.2	-269.4
Cambodia	124.4	143.0	161.3	36.6	43.3	54.8
Indonesia	16,605.0	17,364.0	20,463.6	-105.7	-99.4	-97.8
Lao People's Democratic Republic	97.7	162.1	297.2	2.6	4.0	-20.8
Malaysia	3,450.0	3,748.7	3,837.2	-16.4	-9.5	1.1
Myanmar	966.5	1,177.4	1,147.3	-46.5	-38.9	-19.9
Philippines	998.9	1,091.9	1,229.2	41.5	49.0	48.4
Singapore	24.9	26.3	25.8	97.2	97.8	97.7
Thailand	2,927.7	3,130.9	2,598.0	40.3	44.8	50.4
Timor-Leste	318.0	280.7	196.9	-6,899.1	-3,874.5	-2,003.8
Viet Nam	2,747.2	3,034.7	2,509.2	-17.7	6.3	44.4
The Pacific[a]	**106.9**	**557.1**	**608.8**	**41.3**	**-141.0**	**-144.4**
Cook Islands	0.1	0.1	0.1	94.4	93.9	89.0
Fiji	5.2	7.4	6.2	74.0	70.5	69.8
Kiribati	0.5	0.6	0.6	60.7	59.4	62.7
Marshall Islands	–	–	–	100.0	100.0	100.0
Micronesia, Federated States of	0.0	0.0	0.0	98.4	98.4	98.0
Nauru	0.0	0.0	0.0	100.0	99.9	98.9
Niue	0.0	0.0	0.0	80.3	83.7	82.9
Palau	...	0.0	0.0	...	99.7	99.3
Papua New Guinea	95.4	543.1	595.7	32.3	-200.8	-197.2
Samoa	1.5	1.6	1.7	63.3	67.6	67.6
Solomon Islands	3.2	3.3	3.4	59.6	56.4	55.7
Tonga	0.0	0.0	0.1	98.8	98.1	98.0
Tuvalu	0.0	0.0	0.0	99.6	97.7	94.8
Vanuatu	0.9	0.9	0.9	66.7	67.5	76.0
Developed ADB Member Economies	**18,624.6**	**18,144.9**	**21,489.1**	**31.6**	**25.7**	**4.9**
Australia	13,646.0	16,032.9	18,950.3	-152.9	-200.8	-243.7
Japan	4,205.4	1,321.5	1,811.4	80.0	92.7	88.8
New Zealand	773.2	790.5	727.4	7.7	18.0	22.2
DEVELOPING ADB MEMBER ECONOMIES[a]	**159,713.0**	**176,559.9**	**191,204.2**	**8.5**	**14.5**	**18.3**
ALL ADB REGIONAL MEMBERS[a]	**178,337.5**	**194,704.8**	**212,693.3**	**11.6**	**15.7**	**17.1**
WORLD[a]	**528,007.8**	**569,392.1**	**586,527.2**	**-3.4**	**-4.9**	**-4.6**

... = data not available, (-/+) 0.0 = magnitude is less than half of unit employed, – = magnitude equals zero, ADB = Asian Development Bank, PJ = petajoule.

a The aggregates for energy production include only economies with available data corresponding to the year heading. The aggregates for net energy imports include only economies with available data corresponding to the year heading for both energy use and energy production. Net energy imports are calculated as the difference between total energy use and total energy production divided by total energy use.

Sources: For Energy Production: United Nations. Energy Statistics Database. https://data.un.org/SdmxBrowser/start (accessed 21 June 2023). For Net Energy Imports: Asian Development Bank estimates using data from United Nations' Energy Statistics Database. https://data.un.org/SdmxBrowser/start (accessed 21 June 2023).

Table 2.6.5: Retail Prices of Fuel Energy
($/L)

ADB Regional Member	Gasoline (Premium)			Diesel		
	2010	2015	2022	2010	2015	2022
Developing ADB Member Economies						
Central and West Asia						
Afghanistan	...	...	...	...	...	...
Armenia	1.01	0.90	1.14	0.92	0.89	1.36
Azerbaijan	...	...	...	...	...	...
Georgia	1.03	0.82	1.17	1.00	0.82	1.37
Kazakhstan	0.58	0.56	0.39	0.53	0.44	0.62
Kyrgyz Republic	...	...	...	...	...	...
Pakistan	0.80	0.68	0.71 (2019)	0.83	0.78	0.81 (2019)
Tajikistan	...	...	...	...	...	...
Turkmenistan	...	...	...	...	...	...
Uzbekistan	...	...	...	...	...	...
East Asia						
China, People's Republic of	...	...	...	...	...	...
Hong Kong, China	1.75	1.77	2.46	1.25	1.41	2.63
Korea, Republic of	1.48	1.34	1.40	1.30	1.15	1.43
Mongolia	1.01	0.79	0.75	0.96	0.91	1.11
Taipei,China	0.94	0.75	1.00	0.82	0.68	0.92
South Asia						
Bangladesh	...	...	...	...	...	...
Bhutan	...	...	...	...	...	...
India	1.05	1.18 (2014)	...	0.83	0.91 (2014)	...
Maldives	...	...	...	...	...	...
Nepal	1.22	1.22	1.24	0.95	0.97	1.11
Sri Lanka	1.02	0.86	0.89 (2021)	0.65	0.70	0.61 (2021)
Southeast Asia						
Brunei Darussalam	...	...	...	...	...	...
Cambodia	...	...	...	...	...	...
Indonesia	0.50	0.66	0.82	0.50	0.64	1.00
Lao People's Democratic Republic	...	...	...	...	...	...
Malaysia	0.67	0.63	0.47 (2020)	0.57	0.49	0.43 (2020)
Myanmar	150.50	0.76	0.59 (2019)	1.54 (2012)	0.80	0.65 (2019)
Philippines	0.96	0.90	1.32	0.76	0.60	1.31
Singapore	1.35	1.59	2.36	0.89	0.85	1.81
Thailand	1.02	0.81	1.08	0.91	0.72	0.94
Timor-Leste	...	...	...	...	...	...
Viet Nam	1.42 (2011)	1.12	1.42 (2021)	0.93 (2011)	0.68	0.67 (2021)
The Pacific						
Cook Islands	...	...	...	...	...	...
Fiji	...	...	...	...	...	...
Kiribati	...	...	...	...	...	...
Marshall Islands	...	...	...	...	...	...
Micronesia, Federated States of	...	...	...	...	...	...
Nauru	...	...	...	...	...	...
Niue	...	...	...	...	...	...
Palau	...	...	...	...	...	...
Papua New Guinea	...	...	...	...	...	...
Samoa	...	...	...	...	...	...
Solomon Islands	1.14	1.11	1.41	1.15	1.07	1.55
Tonga	...	...	...	...	...	...
Tuvalu	...	...	...	...	...	...
Vanuatu	1.50	1.36	1.44 (2021)	...	...	...
Developed ADB Member Economies						
Australia	1.16	0.97	1.28	1.17	0.97	1.42
Japan	1.64	1.23	1.38	1.28	0.97	1.14
New Zealand	1.34	1.41	1.82	0.85	0.80	1.54

... = data not available, $ = United States dollars, ADB = Asian Development Bank, L = liter.

Source: Economies' official sources.

Data Issues and Comparability

Energy data are compiled by the United Nations Statistics Division (UNSD) using standard procedures that follow the definitions of the United Nations International Recommendations for Energy Statistics[5]. The UNSD Annual Questionnaire on Energy Statistics to the UN member economies is the primary source of information for the UNSD energy database. The UNSD sometimes prepares estimates where official data are incomplete or inconsistent. For the indicator on GDP per unit use of energy, the energy statistics adopt the territory principle, while national accounts are being compiled on the residency principle, which could be a potential source of inconsistency, although in practice differences are not huge[6].

For data on access to electricity, the Sustainable Energy for All (SE4ALL) database from the SE4ALL Global Tracking Framework—led jointly by the Energy Sector Management Assistance Program, the International Energy Agency, and the World Bank—provides data on the proportion of access for an entire economy, as well as in rural and urban areas. The data for this indicator are a combination of economy-reported data and modeled estimates by the World Bank.

5 The full definitions can be found at https://unstats.un.org/UNSD/energy/ires/.

6 More information can be found at https://unstats.un.org/unsd/energystats/methodology/documents/escm_2017850e.pdf

Table 2.7.1: Agriculture Land Use
(% of total land area)

ADB Regional Member	Agricultural Land			Arable Land			Permanent Cropland		
	2010	2015	2021	2010	2015	2021	2010	2015	2021
Developing ADB Member Economies									
Central and West Asia[a]	**67.5**	**67.5**	**67.1**	**13.8**	**14.2**	**14.2**	**0.4**	**0.4**	**0.4**
Afghanistan	58.1	58.1	58.7	11.9	11.9	12.0	0.2	0.2	0.3
Armenia	60.9	58.9	58.8	15.8	15.7	15.6	1.9	2.0	2.1
Azerbaijan	57.7	57.7	57.8	22.8	23.4	25.3	2.8	2.9	3.3
Georgia	35.4	34.8	34.2	5.7	5.3	4.5	1.8	1.6	1.8
Kazakhstan	80.4	80.1	79.2	10.6	11.0	11.0	0.0	0.0	0.0
Kyrgyz Republic	55.3	55.0	54.0	6.7	6.7	6.7	0.4	0.4	0.4
Pakistan	45.7	47.0	47.1	38.1	39.4	39.6	1.1	1.0	1.0
Tajikistan	34.0	34.9	35.4	5.3	6.0	6.0	1.0	1.0	1.5
Turkmenistan	72.4	72.0	72.0	4.1	4.1	4.1	0.1	0.1	0.1
Uzbekistan	58.7	58.0	58.3	9.6	9.2	9.1	0.8	0.9	1.0
East Asia[a]	**58.2**	**57.8**	**57.4**	**11.1**	**10.7**	**10.1**	**1.3**	**1.5**	**1.8**
China, People's Republic of	56.2	55.8	55.5	12.8	12.2	11.6	1.5	1.7	2.0
Hong Kong, China	5.2	4.9	3.8	3.3	3.0	1.9	1.0	1.0	1.0
Korea, Republic of	18.2	17.8	16.4	15.5	15.0	13.8	2.1	2.2	2.1
Mongolia	73.3	73.0	72.3	0.8	0.9	0.9	0.0	0.0	0.0
Taipei,China	23.0	22.5	22.2	16.9	16.8	16.9	6.1	5.6	5.4
South Asia[a]	**58.6**	**58.7**	**58.6**	**50.3**	**50.1**	**49.6**	**4.2**	**4.6**	**4.8**
Bangladesh	71.0	72.5	77.3	59.9	59.4	62.3	6.5	8.5	10.4
Bhutan	13.6	13.8	13.5	2.6	2.6	2.5	0.3	0.3	0.2
India	60.4	60.4	60.0	52.8	52.6	51.9	4.1	4.4	4.6
Maldives	23.0	21.3	19.7	13.0	13.0	13.0	6.7	5.0	3.3
Nepal	28.8	28.7	28.7	15.2	14.7	14.7	1.1	1.5	1.5
Sri Lanka	41.8	44.3	45.5	19.1	21.0	22.2	15.6	16.2	16.2
Southeast Asia[a]	**29.2**	**30.6**	**32.4**	**15.8**	**16.0**	**16.5**	**9.6**	**10.8**	**12.0**
Brunei Darussalam	2.5	2.5	2.5	0.8	0.8	0.8	1.1	1.1	1.1
Cambodia	30.6	32.0	34.6	21.2	22.3	23.3	0.9	1.2	2.7
Indonesia	29.5	30.8	34.1	12.5	12.7	13.9	11.2	12.3	14.4
Lao People's Democratic Republic	9.6	10.1	8.8	6.1	6.5	5.3	0.6	0.7	0.6
Malaysia	22.5	26.1	26.1	2.6	2.5	2.5	19.0	22.7	22.7
Myanmar	19.2	19.5	19.9	16.5	16.7	16.8	2.2	2.3	2.3
Philippines	40.6	42.0	42.5	17.8	18.7	18.7	17.8	18.2	18.8
Singapore	1.1	0.9	0.9	0.9	0.8	0.8	0.1	0.1	0.1
Thailand	44.7	44.7	46.0	34.3	33.1	33.6	8.8	10.1	10.9
Timor-Leste	22.7	22.9	23.0	7.8	7.7	7.5	4.8	5.2	5.4
Viet Nam	34.3	38.8	39.4	20.5	22.3	21.7	11.7	14.4	15.7
The Pacific[a]	**3.9**	**4.1**	**4.3**	**0.8**	**1.0**	**0.9**	**2.2**	**2.3**	**2.5**
Cook Islands	8.3	7.9	7.9	2.5	2.1	2.1	5.8	5.8	5.8
Fiji	17.5	17.3	17.1	3.5	3.8	4.2	4.5	4.0	3.4
Kiribati	42.0	42.0	42.0	2.5	2.5	2.5	39.5	39.5	39.5
Marshall Islands	47.2	38.9	38.9	2.8	2.8	2.8	44.4	36.1	36.1
Micronesia, Federated States of	7.1	7.1	7.1	2.9	2.9	2.9	...	...	...
Nauru	20.0	20.0	20.0	...	...	...	20.0	20.0	20.0
Niue	18.5	18.5	18.5	3.8	3.8	3.8	10.8	10.8	10.8
Palau	9.3	9.3	9.3	0.7	0.7	0.7	4.3	4.3	4.3
Papua New Guinea	2.8	2.9	3.2	0.7	0.7	0.7	1.7	1.8	2.0
Samoa	14.7	26.7	17.8	4.2	11.5	4.1	8.3	11.0	11.4
Solomon Islands	3.9	4.1	4.3	0.7	0.8	0.8	2.9	3.0	3.2
Tonga	44.4	48.6	48.6	23.6	27.8	27.8	15.3	15.3	15.3
Tuvalu	60.0	60.0	60.0	...	...	...	60.0	60.0	60.0
Vanuatu	15.3	15.3	15.3	1.6	1.6	1.6	10.3	10.3	10.3
Developed ADB Member Economies[a]	**47.3**	**43.8**	**45.5**	**3.7**	**4.3**	**4.3**	**0.1**	**0.1**	**0.1**
Australia	49.0	45.3	47.3	3.3	4.0	4.1	0.0	0.0	0.1
Japan	13.6	13.3	12.8	11.7	11.5	11.2	0.9	0.8	0.7
New Zealand	43.3	40.7	38.6	1.9	1.8	2.3	0.3	0.3	0.3
DEVELOPING ADB MEMBER ECONOMIES[a]	**54.0**	**54.1**	**54.2**	**17.6**	**17.5**	**17.3**	**3.0**	**3.3**	**3.7**
ALL ADB REGIONAL MEMBERS[a]	**52.3**	**51.5**	**52.0**	**14.1**	**14.2**	**14.0**	**2.3**	**2.5**	**2.8**
WORLD	**36.7**	**36.6**	**36.8**	**10.5**	**10.7**	**10.7**	**1.2**	**1.3**	**1.4**

... = data not available, 0.0 = magnitude is less than half of unit employed, ADB = Asian Development Bank.

a Aggregates are weighted averages estimated using total land area for the respective year headings.

Source: Food and Agriculture Organization of the United Nations. FAOSTAT Database. http://www.fao.org/faostat/en/#data/RL (accessed 23 July 2023).

Table 2.7.2: Deforestation and Pollution

ADB Regional Member	Deforestation Rate[a,b] (average % change)			Carbon Dioxide Emissions[c, d] (t '000)			Nitrous Oxide Emissions[d] (t '000 CO_2 equivalent)		
	2010	2015	2021	2010	2015	2020	2010	2015	2020
Developing ADB Member Economies									
Central and West Asia	**-0.02**	**-0.31**	**-0.20**	**606,884**	**590,093**	**653,666**	**96,891**	**106,938**	**120,322**
Afghanistan	–	–	–	8,576	10,058	8,709	4,579	5,057	4,863
Armenia	0.06	0.06	0.06	4,337	5,343	6,747	767	1,085	1,174
Azerbaijan	-0.44	-0.85	-1.02	24,312	31,773	34,305	3,360	4,098	4,794
Georgia	-0.22	–	–	5,322	9,399	10,255	1,854	2,066	2,158
Kazakhstan	0.24	-1.39	-0.85	229,702	191,060	211,897	11,050	10,887	11,597
Kyrgyz Republic	-0.40	-0.35	-1.39	6,394	10,267	9,080	1,642	1,796	2,016
Pakistan	1.01	0.81	1.11	140,379	164,152	184,111	53,511	58,250	68,972
Tajikistan	–	-0.56	-0.24	2,447	4,905	9,329	1,573	1,941	2,431
Turkmenistan	–	–	–	59,175	63,778	63,655	5,548	6,498	5,327
Uzbekistan	-1.17	-1.14	-0.70	126,241	99,358	115,578	13,008	15,260	16,989
East Asia	**-1.07**	**-0.84**	**-0.78**	**9,334,598**	**10,760,245**	**11,535,553**	**512,116**	**577,077**	**561,263**
China, People's Republic of	-1.19	-0.93	-0.85	8,474,923	9,859,281	10,944,686	488,417	549,580	536,920
Hong Kong, China	...	...	...	...	...	...	...	...	...
Korea, Republic of	0.14	0.16	0.16	575,216	607,827	569,682	9,257	9,870	10,097
Mongolia	0.06	0.01	0.01	14,311	17,301	21,185	9,416	13,034	14,246
Taipei,China	...	...	...	270,148	275,836	273,617 (2019)	5,026	4,593	4,904 (2019)
South Asia	**-0.26**	**-0.33**	**-0.31**	**1,729,639**	**2,259,989**	**2,325,614**	**271,244**	**287,476**	**317,522**
Bangladesh	0.17	0.05	–	50,488	73,157	85,493	24,449	26,675	28,077
Bhutan	-0.37	-0.07	-0.07	493	1,042	1,035	109	104	97
India	-0.27	-0.38	-0.37	1,659,983	2,158,023	2,200,836	238,635	251,795	279,004
Maldives	–	–	–	963	1,339	1,454	7	9	9
Nepal	-0.30	–	–	4,641	7,186	14,949	5,450	6,326	7,178
Sri Lanka	0.30	-0.24	0.15	13,072	19,241	21,846	2,594	2,567	3,157
Southeast Asia	**0.20**	**0.62**	**0.51**	**1,155,481**	**1,395,249**	**1,688,055**	**154,245**	**164,451**	**188,688**
Brunei Darussalam	0.45	–	–	7,171	6,398	9,588	113	121	138
Cambodia	0.18	3.79	1.93	5,141	8,433	18,653	4,322	4,584	4,785
Indonesia	0.16	0.97	0.66	415,537	489,053	563,197	57,756	63,200	75,596
Lao People's Democratic Republic	0.29	0.21	0.21	2,877	8,876	19,179	2,509	2,724	3,143
Malaysia	0.39	-0.53	0.26	199,867	236,229	245,139	9,908	9,967	9,265
Myanmar	1.08	0.96	1.01	8,131	19,034	33,875	15,867	18,653	22,957
Philippines	0.68	-0.50	-0.49	81,918	110,991	133,471	12,758	12,612	14,456
Singapore	-0.41	1.52	1.16	42,414	45,432	43,705	6,751	8,392	10,311
Thailand	-0.54	0.01	0.18	240,768	268,853	265,479	22,485	19,008	20,932
Timor-Leste	0.15	0.15	0.15	244	437	446	222	273	274
Viet Nam	-1.21	-0.97	-0.52	151,414	201,513	355,323	21,554	24,916	26,833
The Pacific	**0.01**	**0.06**	**0.07**	**7,516**	**9,029**	**7,670**	**2,229**	**2,242**	**2,143**
Cook Islands	-0.01	–	–	...	...	...	...	...	...
Fiji	-0.63	-0.61	-0.59	1,126	1,264	1,028	317	174	191
Kiribati	–	–	–	54	61	57	5	5	5
Marshall Islands	–	–	–	141	146	110	1	1	1
Micronesia, Federated States of	-0.04	-0.04	-0.05	105	145	108	24	26	28
Nauru	...	...	...	43	55	41	0	0	0
Niue	0.03	-0.05	-0.05	...	...	...	...	...	...
Palau	-0.24	-0.21	-0.19	215	201	158	–	–	–
Papua New Guinea	0.03	0.09	0.09	5,042	6,370	5,492	1,628	1,777	1,704
Samoa	0.29	0.29	0.30	192	232	207	51	61	50
Solomon Islands	0.03	0.03	0.03	343	304	223	21	22	23
Tonga	–	–	–	118	110	118	49	50	52
Tuvalu	–	–	–	10	8	7	1	1	1
Vanuatu	–	–	–	127	134	121	132	124	86
Developed ADB Member Economies	**0.13**	**-0.42**	**-0.01**	**1,584,284**	**1,596,413**	**1,424,421**	**89,167**	**105,975**	**82,740**
Australia	0.17	-0.54	–	395,993	385,782	378,997	54,166	71,867	49,332
Japan	-0.04	0.02	–	1,157,242	1,178,349	1,014,065	20,203	19,050	18,498
New Zealand	0.00	0.00	-0.16	31,049	32,281	31,360	14,797	15,057	14,910
DEVELOPING ADB MEMBER ECONOMIES	**-0.36**	**-0.15**	**-0.18**	**12,834,118**	**15,014,604**	**16,210,557**	**1,036,724**	**1,138,184**	**1,189,938**
ALL ADB REGIONAL MEMBERS	**-0.26**	**-0.21**	**-0.14**	**14,418,402**	**16,611,017**	**17,634,978**	**1,125,891**	**1,244,158**	**1,272,678**

continued on next page

Table 2.7.2: Deforestation and Pollution *(continued)*

ADB Regional Member	Methane Emissions[d] (t '000 CO_2 equivalent)			Other Greenhouse Gases[d, e] (t '000 CO_2 equivalent)		
	2010	2015	2020	2010	2015	2016
Developing ADB Member Economies						
Central and West Asia	**375,286**	**440,501**	**467,392**	**-12,708**	**-21,786**	**-2,334**
Afghanistan	15,196	15,944	16,222	2,582	-691	-1,800
Armenia	2,204	2,467	2,320	469	1,149	722
Azerbaijan	16,320	15,854	15,733	-54	-1,163	-514
Georgia	5,750	5,513	5,133	-248	1,005	1,190
Kazakhstan	65,101	63,811	69,749	-20,146	-20,260	-7,610
Kyrgyz Republic	3,887	4,375	4,865	1,569	3,669	2,918
Pakistan	126,521	147,157	169,428	-8,720	6,550	10,236
Tajikistan	4,328	5,235	5,521	-759	-753	260
Turkmenistan	86,338	132,778	124,819	-3,962	-6,292	-6,869
Uzbekistan	49,641	47,368	53,602	16,562	-4,999	-867
East Asia	**1,104,947**	**1,190,985**	**1,226,435**	**-261,624**	**-329,144**	**-304,445**
China, People's Republic of	1,065,646	1,147,404	1,186,285	-285,418	-382,872	-364,711
Hong Kong, China	...	...	...	...	...	...
Korea, Republic of	23,804	22,740	21,990	17,515	48,128	56,606
Mongolia	8,927	15,747	18,159	1,320	1,711	-224
Taipei,China	6,570	5,093	4,786 (2019)	4,959	3,890	3,382 (2019)
South Asia	**772,484**	**796,810**	**819,169**	**-176,304**	**-248,524**	**-325,548**
Bangladesh	82,725	86,145	88,904	-8,226	2,224	1,514
Bhutan	542	491	452	-676	-595	-422
India	658,933	678,829	697,655	-166,579	-254,017	-333,368
Maldives	90	114	138	213	360	737
Nepal	21,600	22,486	23,644	-124	-605	1,576
Sri Lanka	8,593	8,744	8,378	-911	4,110	4,415
Southeast Asia	**676,422**	**683,504**	**701,044**	**-1,686**	**37,794**	**15,648**
Brunei Darussalam	1,922	1,669	1,539	-301	-1,160	-902
Cambodia	18,190	17,666	17,836	963	3,006	3,983
Indonesia	312,450	319,718	333,995	-4,542	-4,638	-32,216
Lao People's Democratic Republic	6,953	7,585	8,011	88	4,531	10,919
Malaysia	33,244	37,666	37,176	-1,220	-9,767	-29,432
Myanmar	65,149	66,531	72,110	-123	3,206	5,188
Philippines	61,262	63,980	65,722	191	5,719	4,267
Singapore	3,158	3,857	4,348	411	3,025	2,728
Thailand	85,193	75,223	75,893	5,664	26,494	28,220
Timor-Leste	6,571	5,989	4,795	-28	146	204
Viet Nam	82,331	83,621	79,619	-2,789	7,232	22,688
The Pacific	**8,250**	**12,521**	**12,592**	**-752**	**-1,662**	**-715**
Cook Islands	...	...	...	...	...	...
Fiji	768	372	444	36	-18	107
Kiribati	20	22	23	25	21	17
Marshall Islands	31	32	32	...	...	...
Micronesia, Federated States of	44	49	53	...	...	...
Nauru	4	4	4	49	...	49 (2012)
Niue	...	...	...	...	...	...
Palau	18	19	20	188 (2011)	191	228
Papua New Guinea	6,200	10,795	10,855	-1,062	-1,905	-1,267
Samoa	273	300	267	75	91	130
Solomon Islands	344	381	416	143	61	108
Tonga	88	91	92	-66	-115	-91
Tuvalu	11	11	12	9	...	9 (2012)
Vanuatu	448	445	374	40	12	52
Developed ADB Member Economies	**192,728**	**212,340**	**189,510**	**-62,498**	**-59,251**	**-39,327**
Australia	129,412	151,225	131,485	-21,765	-29,898	-17,269
Japan	29,737	27,896	25,783	-39,416	-29,850	-21,412
New Zealand	33,578	33,219	32,242	-1,317	497	-646
DEVELOPING ADB MEMBER ECONOMIES	**2,937,388**	**3,124,320**	**3,226,632**	**-453,073**	**-563,321**	**-617,394**
ALL ADB REGIONAL MEMBERS	**3,130,116**	**3,336,661**	**3,416,142**	**-515,571**	**-622,571**	**-656,721**

... = data not available, - = magnitude equals zero, 0.00 = magnitude is less than half of unit employed, ADB = Asian Development Bank, CO_2 = carbon dioxide, t = metric ton.

a Rate refers to percentage change over previous year. A negative value indicates that the deforestation rate is decreasing (i.e., reforestation).
b Aggregates are calculated as the percentage change of the sum of forest land area of the reporting economies.
c Data from the World Bank are expressed in kiloton (kt), while data provided in the table are expressed in thousands of metric tons (t), using a conversion factor of 1 kt = 1,000 metric tons.
d Regional aggregates include only reporting economies with data corresponding to the year heading.
e Other greenhouse gas emissions refer to hydrofluorocarbons, perfluorocarbons, and sulphur hexafluoride.

Sources: Food and Agriculture Organization of the United Nations. FAOSTAT Database. http://www.fao.org/faostat/en/#data/RL (accessed 16 July 2023); and World Bank. World Development Indicators. https://databank.worldbank.org/source/world-development-indicators (accessed 21 July 2023). For Taipei,China: Government of Taipei,China, Directorate-General of Budget, Accounting and Statistics.

Freshwater

Table 2.7.3: Freshwater Resources

ADB Regional Member	Internal Renewable Freshwater Resources (m³ billion per year)	Internal Renewable Freshwater Resources (m³ per inhabitant per year)	Annual Freshwater Withdrawals (m³ billion)	Water Productivity[a] (constant 2015 $ per m³)
	2020[b]	2020[c]	2020[b]	2020
Developing ADB Member Economies				
Central and West Asia	**370**	**1,036**	**355**	**...**
Afghanistan	47	1,211	20	1.1
Armenia	7	2,315	3	4.2
Azerbaijan	8	800	13	4.1
Georgia	58	14,572	2	10.0
Kazakhstan	64	3,427	25	8.4
Kyrgyz Republic	49	7,500	8	0.9
Pakistan	55	249	190	1.7
Tajikistan	63	6,654	11	1.1
Turkmenistan	1	233	26	1.7
Uzbekistan	16	488	59	1.9
East Asia[d]	**2,913**	**1,870**	**598**	**...**
China, People's Republic of	2,813	1,912	568	25.7
Hong Kong, China	...	...	...	...
Korea, Republic of	65	1,265	29	55.7
Mongolia	35	10,615	0	29.3
Taipei,China	...	...	...	...
South Asia[d]	**1,880**	**1,178**	**706**	**...**
Bangladesh	105	638	36	7.4
Bhutan	78	101,088	0	6.6
India	1,446	1,048	648	3.9
Maldives	0	55	0	767.7
Nepal	198	6,802	9	3.1
Sri Lanka	53	2,466	13	7.2
Southeast Asia	**4,993**	**7,481**	**499**	**...**
Brunei Darussalam	9	19,430	0	146.0
Cambodia	121	7,213	2	10.5
Indonesia	2,019	7,380	223	4.6
Lao People's Democratic Republic	190	26,170	7	2.5
Malaysia	580	17,920	7	51.4
Myanmar	1,003	18,431	33	2.6
Philippines	479	4,371	86	4.2
Singapore	1	103	0	674.7
Thailand	225	3,216	57	7.5
Timor-Leste	8	6,231	1	2.2
Viet Nam	359	3,692	82	4.0
The Pacific[d]	**884**	**77,745**	**0**	**...**
Cook Islands	...	...	...	...
Fiji	29	31,848	0	51.0
Kiribati	...	...	...	...
Marshall Islands	...	...	...	...
Micronesia, Federated States of	...	...	...	...
Nauru	0	924	...	...
Niue	...	...	...	...
Palau	...	...	...	...
Papua New Guinea	801	89,527	0	61.0
Samoa	...	...	...	...
Solomon Islands	45	65,076	...	...
Tonga	...	...	...	...
Tuvalu	...	...	...	...
Vanuatu	10	32,558	...	...
Developed ADB Member Economies	**1,249**	**8,098**	**97**	**...**
Australia	492	19,294	9	172.6
Japan	430	3,400	78	55.7
New Zealand	327	67,811	10	20.4
DEVELOPING ADB MEMBER ECONOMIES[d]	**11,039**	**2,668**	**2,159**	**...**
ALL ADB REGIONAL MEMBERS[d]	**12,288**	**2,868**	**2,256**	**...**

... = data not available, 0 = magnitude is less than half of unit employed, $ = United States dollars, ADB = Asian Development Bank, m³ = cubic meter.

a Gross domestic product in 2015 United States dollars per cubic meter of total freshwater withdrawal.
b Regional aggregates are calculated as the sum of the economies.
c Regional aggregates are weighted averages estimated using population.
d For reporting economies only.

Sources: Food and Agriculture Organization of the United Nations. AQUASTAT Database. http://www.fao.org/nr/water/aquastat/data/query/index.html (accessed 17 July 2023); and World Bank. World Development Indicators. http://data.worldbank.org/indicator (accessed 20 July 2023).

Data Issues and Comparability

Data on greenhouse gases (GHGs) have been compiled from the Emissions Database for Global Atmospheric Research, a joint project of the European Commission Joint Research Centre and the Netherlands Environmental Assessment Agency. This database applies a technology-based emissions factor approach consistently for all economies. It utilizes a consistent set of activity data for calculating various substances, GHGs, and air pollutants; and relies on the spatial allocation of emissions on a 0.1-degree by 0.1-degree grid.

There may be substantial uncertainty in economy-level data—especially for methane, nitrous oxide, and other GHGs—due to the limited accuracy of international activity data and the emission factors selected for calculating emissions on an economy level. However, since the Intergovernmental Panel on Climate Change methodologies are consistently used, and data are based on international information sources, there is sound basis for comparability.[7]

The Food and Agriculture Organization of the United Nations monitors land use and forestry data using its own expert sources, economy reports, satellite imagery, and official data reported on through questionnaires conducted by the organization.

7 For more information on the methodologies of the Emissions Database for Global Atmospheric Research, go to https://edgar.jrc.ec.europa. eu/methodology.

Table 2.8.1: Government Net Lending/Net Borrowing
(% of GDP)

ADB Regional Member	2010	2015	2018	2019	2020	2021	2022
Developing ADB Member Economies							
Central and West Asia							
Afghanistan[a]	2.4	-1.4	0.8	-1.7	-4.4	...	...
Armenia	-5.0	-4.8	-1.6	-0.8	-5.1*	-4.6	-2.2*
Azerbaijan	15.4	-2.8	9.5	6.2	-2.8	4.8	...
Georgia	-4.3	-1.0	-0.8	-1.6	-9.0	-5.9	-2.2*
Kazakhstan	5.0	-2.2	1.4	-0.5	-6.9	-3.6	...
Kyrgyz Republic[b]	-4.9	-1.4	-1.1	-0.1	-3.3	-0.2	-1.1*
Pakistan[c]	-5.3	-4.7	-5.7	-7.8	-7.0	-6.0	-7.8
Tajikistan[d]	-9.2 |	-7.4	-10.6	-7.8	0.3	0.2	...
Turkmenistan	2.0	-0.7	...	...	...	...	...
Uzbekistan	...	3.3	3.2	0.5	-1.5	-3.7	...
East Asia							
China, People's Republic of	-1.6	-3.4	-4.1	-4.9	-6.2	-3.8	-4.7
Hong Kong, China	4.1	1.4	3.5	1.9	-8.9	...	...
Korea, Republic of	1.1 (2012)	1.2	3.1	0.8	-2.7	-0.3	...
Mongolia	-3.2	-11.1	-4.1	-8.9	-20.2	-13.9	-8.8*
Taipei,China	-2.6	0.2	0.1	0.5	-0.3	1.4	...
South Asia							
Bangladesh[c]	-1.7	-2.2	-1.9	-4.6	-4.3	-3.2	...
Bhutan[c]	1.5	1.5	-0.3	-2.3	-2.3	-6.7	-5.8
India[e]	-4.9	-3.9	-3.4	-4.7	-9.2*	-6.7*	-6.4*
Maldives[f]	-12.9	-6.5	-5.3	-6.7	-23.5	-13.8	-14.3*
Nepal[g]	-1.4	0.9	-4.8	-4.8	-4.9	-4.1	...
Sri Lanka	-6.1	-7.2	-5.0	-6.4	-12.8	-11.7	-9.2
Southeast Asia							
Brunei Darussalam[h]	15.1	-14.8	0.2	-5.6	-19.6	-5.4	...
Cambodia	-4.5	-0.9	0.4	2.2	-3.7	-7.0	1.1*
Indonesia	-0.6	-2.7	-1.7	-2.1	-6.1	-4.4	-2.5
Lao People's Democratic Republic[i]	-0.9	-3.7	-4.3	-2.9	-5.1	-0.6	...
Malaysia	-5.0	-3.1	-3.6	-3.4	-6.1	-6.4	...
Myanmar[j]	-4.4 (2012)	-4.4	-5.9 |	-4.0	...	...	...
Philippines	-3.3	-1.3	-3.1	-3.3	-7.5	-8.3	-8.6
Singapore[k]	7.5	4.2	4.8	7.4	-7.4	1.7	...
Thailand[i]	-0.7	0.2	0.2	0.4	-4.5	-6.7	-4.3*
Timor-Leste	...	7.3	5.0	-4.1	-2.9	-2.5	...
Viet Nam[l]	-2.1	-4.9	-0.9	-0.3	...	...	...
The Pacific							
Cook Islands[c]	2.9	-7.8	5.2	5.7	-6.8	-18.7*	...
Fiji[m]	-2.6	-2.2	-4.6	...	...	...	...
Kiribati	-6.9 (2011)	56.1	51.9	19.0	30.8	-3.3*	...
Marshall Islands[i]	3.5	2.8	2.6	-1.8	2.4	0.7	3.3*
Micronesia, Federated States of[i]	0.5	10.3	24.2	...	...	...	...
Nauru[c]	0.1	10.5	33.6	29.9	35.7*	43.8*	29.3*
Niue	...	...	...	...	...	...	...
Palau[i]	-1.0	5.2	6.2	0.3	-9.8*	-16.9*	-12.6*
Papua New Guinea	...	-2.4 (2017)	-2.6	-5.0*	-8.6*	-6.7	-5.6*
Samoa	-8.1 (2012)	-3.7	1.3	2.7	6.0	1.7	5.3
Solomon Islands	5.7	0.8	1.5	-1.5	-2.4	-1.2	-3.0
Tonga[c]	...	1.5 (2016)	2.9	3.1	0.9	-1.7	...
Tuvalu	11.5 (2012)	40.0	30.3	-1.1	5.0	-7.0	...
Vanuatu	-1.7 (2012)	7.2	8.4	7.0	...	...	...
Developed ADB Member Economies							
Australia[c]	-5.5	-2.9	-1.3	-1.2	-7.7	-9.3	-3.8
Japan[k]	-8.8	-3.6	-2.4	-3.1	-10.0	-5.9	...
New Zealand[c]	-3.5	0.2	1.3	1.2	-6.2	-2.5	-4.6

... = data not available; | = marks break in series; * = preliminary, provisional, estimate; ADB = Asian Development Bank; GDP = gross domestic product.

Note: In general, economies follow the guidelines of the International Monetary Fund on Government Finance Statistics (GFS). Some economies still use the 1986 version of the GFS guidelines, while others have switched to the 2001 or 2014 guidelines. The comparability of the data in this table is limited by variations in the concepts and definitions used in different versions of the GFS framework. Data refer to government net lending/net borrowing as classified in the GFS 2001 or GFS 2014 framework, except for Bhutan; Brunei Darussalam; India; the Kyrgyz Republic; Maldives; Nauru; Pakistan; the People's Republic of China; Taipei,China; Tajikistan; and Turkmenistan, where data refer to overall budgetary surplus/deficit as classified in the GFS 1986 framework. Data refer to general government, except for Bangladesh; Bhutan; Brunei Darussalam; Cambodia; the Federated States of Micronesia; Fiji; India; the Lao People's Democratic Republic; Malaysia; Maldives; the Marshall Islands; Nauru; Nepal; Palau; the Philippines; Solomon Islands; Sri Lanka; Taipei,China; Timor-Leste; Tonga; Tuvalu; Vanuatu; and Viet Nam, where data refer to central government. For Armenia: Data prior to 2010 (featured in the Key Indicators Database) refer to central government. For Azerbaijan: Data for 2000–2007 (featured in the Key Indicators Database) are based on the state budget. For Cambodia: Data refer to central government excluding extra budgetary central government. For Pakistan: Data refer to the consolidated federal and provincial governments. For the People's Republic of China: Data refer to consolidated central and local governments. For Turkmenistan: Data prior to 2011 refer to central government.

a The longer time series featured in the Key Indicators Database refers to GFS data for 2005–2011 based on fiscal year beginning 21 March. For 2012, data cover 9 months from 21 March to 20 December. For 2013 onward, GFS data are based on fiscal year ending 20 December. For 2005–2015, national accounts data are based on fiscal year beginning 21 March. For 2016 onward, national accounts data are based on fiscal year ending 20 December.
b For 2007 onward, data are calculated excluding net lending.
c Data are based on fiscal year ending 30 June.
d National accounts data prior to 2015 are based on the 1993 System of National Accounts while figures for 2015 onward are based on the 2008 System of National Accounts.
e Data are based on fiscal year beginning 1 April.
f For 2013 onward, data are calculated excluding net lending.
g Data are based on fiscal year ending 15 July.
h The longer time series featured in the Key Indicators Database refers to data for 2003 onward based on fiscal year beginning 1 April. Data are derived as excess of revenue over expenditure (ordinary plus charged) less the sum of contribution to a development fund, contribution to a government trust fund, and capital and currency adjustments.
i Data are based on fiscal year ending 30 September.
j The longer time series featured in the Key Indicators Database refers to GFS data for 2012–2018 based on fiscal year beginning 1 April. For 2019, GFS data are based on fiscal year beginning 1 October.
k Data are based on fiscal year ending 31 March.
l Until the 53rd edition of the Key Indicators of Asia and the Pacific, Viet Nam's data on government finance from the Ministry of Finance (MOF), was presented using the GFS 1986 standard. Starting in the 54th edition of the Key Indicators of Asia and the Pacific, with the support of the World Bank and International Monetary Fund (IMF), the MOF submitted its 2003–2019 government finance data following GFS 2014 standard. The MOF is currently working with IMF to convert its 2020-onward government finance data.
m The longer time series featured in the Key Indicators Database refers to GFS data for 2000–2014 based on fiscal year ending 31 December. For 2015 onward, GFS data are based on fiscal year ending 31 July.

Sources: Economies' official sources. For Hong Kong, China; Nepal; and Timor-Leste: International Monetary Fund (IMF). Government Finance Statistics. https://data.imf.org/ (accessed April–June 2023). For Nauru (2015–2016): IMF. Staff Country Reports. Republic of Nauru: 2019 Article IV. https://www.imf.org/en/Publications/CR/Issues/2020/01/29/Republic-of-Nauru-2019-Article-IV-Consultation-Press-Release-Staff-Report-and-Statement-by-49001 (accessed 9 May 2021). For Nauru (2017–2022): IMF. Staff Country Reports. Republic of Nauru: 2021 Article IV. https://www.imf.org/en/Publications/CR/Issues/2022/02/07/Republic-of-Nauru-2021-Article-IV-Consultation-Press-Release-Staff-Report-and-Statement-by-512874 (accessed 28 May 2023).

Table 2.8.2: Government Taxes
(% of GDP)

ADB Regional Member	2010	2015	2018	2019	2020	2021	2022
Developing ADB Member Economies							
Central and West Asia							
Afghanistan[a]	8.8	7.1	9.5	8.4	7.5	...	...
Armenia	17.7	21.3	21.1	22.6	22.5	22.7	22.4*
Azerbaijan	12.3	15.7	13.1	14.3	17.3	13.4	...
Georgia	22.3	23.6	23.4	24.1	22.3	22.6	24.1*
Kazakhstan	19.6	13.6	15.1	15.1	12.4	13.8	...
Kyrgyz Republic	17.9	19.7	20.5	19.6	17.8	20.4	24.9
Pakistan[b]	8.9	9.9	10.8	9.7	9.3	9.4	10.1
Tajikistan[c]	18.0	20.8	20.5	20.4	18.3	19.9	...
Turkmenistan	17.5 (2011)	15.6	...	...	...	...	...
Uzbekistan	...	20.3	19.8	19.4	19.6	18.8	...
East Asia							
China, People's Republic of	17.8	18.1	17.0	16.0	15.2	15.0	13.8
Hong Kong, China[d]	13.5	14.4	13.8	13.3	14.0	...	...
Korea, Republic of	18.0 (2012)	17.6	20.1	20.0	20.2	22.4	...
Mongolia	24.2	17.9	20.2	20.6	18.5	20.7	23.7
Taipei,China	7.7	8.6	8.9	9.0	8.1	9.2	...
South Asia							
Bangladesh[b]	10.2	8.9	7.4	8.9	7.7	8.5	...
Bhutan[b]	13.3	15.0	16.6	15.7	13.0	11.5	13.5
India[d]	7.5	6.9	7.0	6.8	7.2*	7.6*	7.6*
Maldives	8.8	19.4	19.4	19.2	19.0	17.7	19.9*
Nepal[e]	13.4	14.7	19.1	19.8	15.8	17.8	...
Sri Lanka	10.9	11.7	11.2	10.9	7.8	7.4	7.3
Southeast Asia							
Brunei Darussalam[f]	...	...	...	...	...	...	...
Cambodia	7.3	14.6	17.1	19.7	17.9	16.4	18.3*
Indonesia	12.1	12.0	11.5	11.1	9.5	10.3	11.5
Lao People's Democratic Republic[g]	13.8	13.5	11.7	11.5	9.4	10.3	...
Malaysia	13.3	14.1	12.0	11.9	10.9	11.2	...
Myanmar[h]	6.6 (2012)	7.5	7.4 |	7.0	...	...	...
Philippines	11.6	13.0	14.0	14.5	14.0	14.1	13.2
Singapore[d]	12.8	13.1	13.0	13.2	12.8	13.1	...
Thailand[g]	16.1	17.6	16.5	16.1	15.7	15.6	15.8*
Timor-Leste	...	7.8	8.5	6.3	5.5	3.5	...
Viet Nam[i]	19.3	15.8	16.3	16.1	...	...	...
The Pacific							
Cook Islands[b]	27.0	23.5	27.0	29.5	34.0	18.9*	...
Fiji	...	...	...	...	...	...	...
Kiribati[b]	18.3 (2011)	22.7	21.7	24.9	26.6	27.8	...
Marshall Islands[g]	15.9	14.1	14.7	15.0	13.9	13.8	13.9
Micronesia, Federated States of[g]	12.0	12.3	32.2	...	...	...	...
Nauru[b]	8.1 | (2012)	21.7	29.6	36.1	48.4*	48.4*	41.2*
Niue	...	...	...	...	...	...	...
Palau[g]	17.0	20.3	21.2	20.0	19.6*	18.8*	...
Papua New Guinea	...	...	13.2	13.0	11.5	11.9	12.8*
Samoa[b]	20.9 (2012)	23.6	25.5	25.6	25.9	25.0	25.2
Solomon Islands	22.0	25.7	25.5	22.2	21.1	21.5	21.2
Tonga[b]	...	...	21.9	20.9	23.0	22.9	...
Tuvalu	28.5 (2012)	33.1	26.8 (2016)	...	...	...	...
Vanuatu	17.3 (2012)	16.9	17.8	17.5	...	...	...
Developed ADB Member Economies							
Australia[b]	25.5	27.3	28.7	28.8	27.9	28.5	29.6
Japan[d]	15.6	18.6	19.1	18.9	19.9	21.2	...
New Zealand[b]	29.2	30.7	30.6	31.7	30.5	32.6	34.3

... = data not available; | = marks break in series; * = provisional, preliminary, estimate; ADB = Asian Development Bank; GDP = gross domestic product.

Note: In general, economies follow the guidelines of the International Monetary Fund on Government Finance Statistics (GFS). Some economies still use the 1986 version of the GFS guidelines, while others have switched to the 2001 or 2014 guidelines. The comparability of the data in this table is limited by variations in the concepts and definitions used in different versions of the GFS framework. Data refer to government taxes as classified in the GFS 2001 or GFS 2014 framework, except for Bhutan; Brunei Darussalam; India; the Kyrgyz Republic; Maldives; Nauru; Pakistan; the People's Republic of China; Taipei,China; Tajikistan; and Turkmenistan, where data refer to tax revenue as classified in the GFS 1986 framework. Data refer to general government, except for Bangladesh; Bhutan; Brunei Darussalam; Cambodia; the Federated States of Micronesia; Fiji; India; the Lao People's Democratic Republic; Malaysia; Maldives; the Marshall Islands; Nauru; Nepal; Palau; the Philippines; Solomon Islands; Sri Lanka; Taipei,China; Timor-Leste; Tonga; Tuvalu; Vanuatu; and Viet Nam, where data refer to central government. For Armenia: Data prior to 2010 (featured in the Key Indicators Database) refer to central government. For Azerbaijan: Data for 2000–2007 (featured in the Key Indicators Database) are based on the state budget. For Cambodia: Data refer to central government excluding extra budgetary central government. For Pakistan: Data refer to the consolidated federal and provincial governments. For the People's Republic of China: Data refer to consolidated central and local governments. For Turkmenistan: Data prior to 2011 refer to central government.

a The longer time series featured in the Key Indicators Database refers to GFS data for 2005–2011 based on fiscal year beginning 21 March. For 2012, GFS data cover 9 months from 21 March to 20 December. For 2013 onward, GFS data are based on fiscal year ending 20 December. For 2005–2015, national accounts data are based on fiscal year beginning 21 March. For 2016 onward, national accounts data are based on fiscal year ending 20 December.
b Data are based on fiscal year ending 30 June.
c National accounts data prior to 2015 are based on the 1993 System of National Accounts while figures for 2015 onward are based on the 2008 System of National Accounts.
d Data are based on fiscal year beginning 1 April.
e Data are based on fiscal year ending 15 July.
f The longer time series featured in the Key Indicators Database refers to data for 2003 onward based on fiscal year beginning 1 April.
g Data are based on fiscal year ending 30 September.
h For 2012–2018, GFS data are based on fiscal year beginning 1 April. For 2019, GFS data are based on fiscal year beginning 1 October. For 2012–2015, national accounts data are based on fiscal year beginning 1 April. For 2016 onward, national accounts data are based on fiscal year beginning 1 October.
i Until the 53rd edition of the Key Indicators of Asia and the Pacific, Viet Nam's data on government finance from the Ministry of Finance (MOF), was presented using the GFS 1986 standard. Starting in the 54th edition of the Key Indicators of Asia and the Pacific, with the support of the World Bank and International Monetary Fund (IMF), the MOF submitted its 2003-2019 government finance data following GFS 2014 standard. The MOF is currently working with IMF to convert its 2020-onward government finance data.

Sources: Economies' official sources. For Hong Kong, China; Nepal; and Timor-Leste: International Monetary Fund (IMF). Government Finance Statistics. https://data.imf.org/ (accessed April–June 2023). For Nauru (2015–2016): IMF. Staff Country Reports. Republic of Nauru: 2019 Article IV. https://www.imf.org/en/Publications/CR/Issues/2020/01/29/Republic-of-Nauru-2019-Article-IV-Consultation-Press-Release-Staff-Report-and-Statement-by-49001 (accessed 9 May 2021). For Nauru (2017–2022): IMF. Staff Country Reports. Republic of Nauru: 2021 Article IV. https://www.imf.org/en/Publications/CR/Issues/2022/02/07/Republic-of-Nauru-2021-Article-IV-Consultation-Press-Release-Staff-Report-and-Statement-by-512874 (accessed 28 May 2023).

Table 2.8.3: Government Revenue
(% of GDP)

ADB Regional Member	2010	2015	2018	2019	2020	2021	2022
Developing ADB Member Economies							
Central and West Asia							
Afghanistan[a]	23.0	23.9	29.8	26.9	24.1	...	...
Armenia	23.2	23.8	23.0	24.7	26.0	25.0	25.1*
Azerbaijan	47.0	34.4	39.7	43.0	37.9	38.1	...
Georgia	26.9	30.4	28.6	29.2	27.3	27.4	29.1*
Kazakhstan	25.5	17.6	19.6	19.1	17.4	17.9	...
Kyrgyz Republic	23.1	27.7	25.0	24.9	23.3	26.5	30.6
Pakistan[b]	12.6	12.9	13.3	11.2	13.2	12.4	12.1
Tajikistan[c]	19.3	23.7	23.3	23.0	21.9	29.8	...
Turkmenistan[d]	15.8	16.6	...	...	...	...	...
Uzbekistan	...	27.6	27.9	27.9	27.1	26.4	...
East Asia							
China, People's Republic of	20.2	22.1	19.9	19.3	18.0	17.6	16.8
Hong Kong, China[e]	22.3	21.7	23.8	23.3	23.3	...	...
Korea, Republic of	33.3 (2012)	32.2	33.4	34.1	34.3	36.9	...
Mongolia	32.0	26.1	28.3	28.8	25.2	29.2	32.5
Taipei,China	10.7	11.4	11.1	11.1	11.0	11.0	...
South Asia							
Bangladesh[b]	13.0	10.6	8.3	10.4	9.6	10.7	...
Bhutan[b]	27.4	21.4	22.8	18.2	21.8	24.9	21.3
India[e]	10.8	9.1	8.8	8.7	8.5*	9.3*	8.9*
Maldives	19.3	26.4	26.2	25.6	24.8	24.5	27.1*
Nepal[f]	18.1	18.6	23.2	23.2	20.1	21.1	...
Sri Lanka	12.6	12.6	12.6	11.9	8.8	8.3	8.3
Southeast Asia							
Brunei Darussalam[g]	49.0	20.9	32.9	26.4	12.4	25.3	...
Cambodia	13.8	18.5	22.1	24.8	21.9	19.7	20.7*
Indonesia	16.6	15.0	14.8	14.3	12.3	13.7	15.0
Lao People's Democratic Republic[h]	21.7	20.3	16.2	15.6	12.6	14.6	...
Malaysia	19.4	18.6	16.1	17.5	15.9	15.1	...
Myanmar[i]	9.8 (2012)	11.8	10.9 |	10.2	...	...	...
Philippines	12.9	14.7	15.5	16.1	15.9	15.5	14.7
Singapore[j]	16.8	18.0	18.2	20.9	18.1	17.6	...
Thailand[h]	20.6	22.2	21.2	20.9	20.7	19.8	19.8*
Timor-Leste	...	91.1	86.1	65.0	58.5	43.2	...
Viet Nam[k]	21.7	19.6	19.5	19.4	...	...	...
The Pacific							
Cook Islands[b]	38.3	39.7	42.3	43.0	51.2	44.5*	...
Fiji[l]	25.5 |	28.5	28.5	27.1	25.4	23.4	21.9
Kiribati[b]	64.4 (2011)	127.8	131.0	121.3	130.0	106.7*	...
Marshall Islands[h]	63.0	59.3	63.2	63.9	70.2	67.2	67.2*
Micronesia, Federated States of[h]	67.7	66.0	79.7	...	...	...	...
Nauru[b]	39.2 |	74.5	108.5	136.0	151.4*	137.0*	151.5*
Niue	...	...	...	...	...	...	...
Palau[h]	46.7	41.2	44.4	43.5	49.0*	51.8*	41.2*
Papua New Guinea	...	...	17.7	16.3	14.2	14.9	16.1*
Samoa[b]	30.2 (2012)	32.0	36.0	32.1	37.6	36.5	38.3
Solomon Islands	28.2	35.1	31.7	27.4	30.1	30.1	28.6
Tonga[b]	...	...	42.6	41.7	51.6	41.9	...
Tuvalu	105.3 (2012)	184.0	156.1	111.7	121.5	122.3	...
Vanuatu	22.8 (2012)	32.3	38.6	37.5	...	...	...
Developed ADB Member Economies							
Australia[b]	32.1	34.2	35.6	35.7	34.4	35.0	36.0
Japan[j]	29.9	35.0	35.5	35.4	36.7	38.1	...
New Zealand[b]	36.7	37.8	36.8	37.8	36.2	37.7	39.3

... = data not available; | = marks break in series; * = provisional, preliminary, estimate; ADB = Asian Development Bank; GDP = gross domestic product.

Note: In general, economies follow the guidelines of the International Monetary Fund on Government Finance Statistics (GFS). Some economies still use the 1986 version of the GFS guidelines, while others have switched to the 2001 or 2014 guidelines. The comparability of the data in this table is limited by variations in the concepts and definitions used in different versions of the GFS framework. Data refer to government revenue as classified in the GFS 2001 or GFS 2014 framework, except for Bhutan; Brunei Darussalam; India; the Kyrgyz Republic; Maldives; Nauru; Pakistan; the People's Republic of China; Taipei,China; Tajikistan; and Turkmenistan, where data refer to total government revenue as classified in the GFS 1986 framework. Data refer to general government, except for Bangladesh; Bhutan; Brunei Darussalam; Cambodia; the Federated States of Micronesia; Fiji; India; the Lao People's Democratic Republic; Malaysia; Maldives; the Marshall Islands; Nauru; Nepal; Palau; the Philippines; Solomon Islands; Sri Lanka; Taipei,China; Timor-Leste; Tonga; Tuvalu; Vanuatu; and Viet Nam, where data refer to central government. For Armenia: Data prior to 2010 (featured in the Key Indicators Database) refer to central government. For Azerbaijan: Data for 2000–2007 (featured in the Key Indicators Database) are based on the state budget. For Cambodia: Data refer to central government excluding extra budgetary central government. For Pakistan: Data refer to the consolidated federal and provincial governments. For the People's Republic of China: Data refer to consolidated central and local governments. For Turkmenistan: Data prior to 2011 refer to central government.

a The longer time series featured in the Key Indicators Database refers to GFS data for 2005–2011 based on fiscal year beginning 21 March. For 2012, GFS data cover 9 months from 21 March to 20 December. For 2013 onward, GFS data are based on fiscal year ending 20 December. For 2005–2015, national accounts data are based on fiscal year beginning 21 March. For 2016 onward, national accounts data are based on fiscal year ending 20 December.
b Data are based on fiscal year ending 30 June.
c National accounts data prior to 2015 are based on the 1993 System of National Accounts while figures for 2015 onward are based on the 2008 System of National Accounts.
d For 2010, data refer to central government revenue. For 2015 onward, data refer to general government revenue.
e Data are based on fiscal year beginning 1 April.
f Data are based on fiscal year ending 15 July.
g The longer time series featured in the Key Indicators Database refers to data for 2003 onward, based on fiscal year beginning 1 April.
h Data are based on fiscal year ending 30 September
i For 2012–2018, GFS data are based on fiscal year beginning 1 April. For 2019, GFS data are based on fiscal year beginning 1 October. For 2012–2015, national accounts data are based on fiscal year beginning 1 April. For 2016 onward, national accounts data are based on fiscal year beginning 1 October.
j Data are based on fiscal year ending 31 March.
k Until the 53rd edition of the Key Indicators of Asia and the Pacific, Viet Nam's data on government finance from the Ministry of Finance (MOF), was presented using the GFS 1986 standard. Starting in the 54th edition of the Key Indicators of Asia and the Pacific, with the support of the World Bank and International Monetary Fund (IMF), the MOF submitted its 2003-2019 government finance data following GFS 2014 standard. The MOF is currently working with IMF to convert its 2020-onward government finance data.
l The longer time series featured in the Key Indicators Database refers to GFS data for 2000–2014 based on fiscal year ending 31 December. For 2015 onward, GFS data are based on fiscal year ending 31 July. National accounts data are based on calendar year.

Sources: Economies' official sources. For Hong Kong, China; Nepal; and Timor-Leste: International Monetary Fund (IMF). Government Finance Statistics. https://data.imf.org/ (accessed April–June 2023). For Nauru (2015–2016): IMF. Staff Country Reports. Republic of Nauru: 2019 Article IV. https://www.imf.org/en/Publications/CR/Issues/2020/01/29/Republic-of-Nauru-2019-Article-IV-Consultation-Press-Release-Staff-Report-and-Statement-by-49001 (accessed 9 May 2021). For Nauru (2017–2022): IMF. Staff Country Reports. Republic of Nauru: 2021 Article IV. https://www.imf.org/en/Publications/CR/Issues/2022/02/07/Republic-of-Nauru-2021-Article-IV-Consultation-Press-Release-Staff-Report-and-Statement-by-512874 (accessed 28 May 2023).

Table 2.8.4: Government Expenditure
(% of GDP)

ADB Regional Member	2010	2015	2016	2017	2018	2019	2020	2021	2022
Developing ADB Member Economies									
Central and West Asia									
Afghanistan[a]	20.6	25.2	29.0	27.7	29.0	28.6	28.5	...	...
Armenia	28.2	28.6	29.3	27.7	24.6	25.5	31.1	29.5	27.3*
Azerbaijan	31.6	37.2	32.8	33.5	30.2	36.8	40.7	33.3	...
Georgia	31.2	31.4	32.3	31.2	29.4	30.9	36.3	33.3	31.3*
Kazakhstan	20.4	19.8	20.5	22.9	18.2	17.2	24.3	21.5	...
Kyrgyz Republic	31.2	31.3	31.8	31.3	27.7	27.1	28.6	28.6	33.8*
Pakistan[b]	18.2	18.2	18.3	19.4	19.0	18.9	20.4	18.5	19.7
Tajikistan[c]	27.2 |	31.9	33.4	34.6	34.0	30.8	29.6	29.6	...
Turkmenistan	13.8 |	17.3	...	...	...	...	...	...	...
Uzbekistan	...	24.3	23.6	22.8	24.7	27.4	28.5	30.1	...
East Asia									
China, People's Republic of	21.8	25.5	25.2	24.4	24.0	24.2	24.2	21.4	21.5
Hong Kong, China[d]	18.1	20.3	19.9	19.5	20.3	21.4	32.2	...	...
Korea, Republic of	32.2 (2012)	31.1	30.2	30.7	30.3	33.2	37.0	37.3	...
Mongolia	35.2	37.2	47.5	37.0	32.4	37.7	45.3	43.1	41.3*
Taipei,China	13.4	11.2	11.2	10.9	11.1	10.6	11.3	9.7	...
South Asia									
Bangladesh[b]	14.8	12.7	12.9	13.4	10.2	15.0	13.9	13.9	...
Bhutan[b]	35.6	29.8	32.6	32.8	34.5	25.5	32.8	39.5	36.1
India[d]	15.7	13.0	12.8	12.5	12.2	13.4	17.7*	16.0*	15.3*
Maldives	33.2	34.0	37.6	30.8	32.5	33.6	49.9	39.5	42.0*
Nepal[e]	19.5	17.6	18.9	23.6	28.0	28.0	25.0	25.1	...
Sri Lanka	18.7	19.8	18.2	17.8	17.6	18.4	21.6	20.0	17.5
Southeast Asia									
Brunei Darussalam[f]	34.0	35.7	39.7	36.3	32.8	32.0	31.5	30.7	...
Cambodia	18.3	19.4	20.2	21.2	21.7	22.6	25.6	26.7	19.6*
Indonesia	17.2	17.7	16.9	16.7	16.5	16.4	18.5	18.1	17.5
Lao People's Democratic Republic[g]	22.7	24.1	21.1	21.6	20.5	18.5	17.8	15.2	...
Malaysia	24.4	21.7	20.0	18.9	19.7	20.8	22.0	21.5	...
Myanmar[h]	14.2 (2012)	16.2	15.8	15.5	16.8 |	14.2	...	...	...
Philippines	16.2	16.0	16.7	17.0	18.6	19.4	23.4	23.8	23.3
Singapore[d]	9.3	13.8	13.4	12.6	13.4	13.5	25.5	15.9	...
Thailand[g]	21.3	22.0	21.0	21.2	21.0	20.5	25.2	26.5	24.1*
Timor-Leste	...	83.7	98.6	73.1	81.0	69.1	61.4	45.7	...
Viet Nam[i]	23.8	24.5	22.9	21.5	20.4	19.7	...	...	...
The Pacific									
Cook Islands[b]	35.5	47.5	37.8	30.1	37.1	37.3	58.0	63.2*	...
Fiji[j]	31.5 |	36.0	43.3	32.8	34.6	33.1	33.7	42.2	37.5
Kiribati[b]	71.3 (2011)	71.7	78.3	86.6	79.2	102.3	99.2	110.0*	...
Marshall Islands[g]	59.5	56.5	57.1	64.0	60.6	65.7	67.8	66.4	63.9*
Micronesia, Federated States of[g]	67.2	55.7	61.7	64.0	55.5	...	...	...	...
Nauru[b]	83.6 |	83.1	93.4 |	101.7	95.6	118.9	134.5*	135.5*	139.9*
Niue	...	...	...	...	...	...	...	...	...
Palau[g]	25.8	26.4	27.1	29.3	33.5	34.3	54.0*	60.2*	53.9*
Papua New Guinea	...	...	...	17.9	20.3	21.3	22.7	21.6	21.7*
Samoa[b]	38.3 (2012)	35.7	31.9	34.7	34.7	29.4	30.6	34.7	33.0
Solomon Islands	22.6	34.3	34.0	33.1	30.2	29.0	32.6	25.4	27.8
Tonga[b]	...	...	37.2	39.6	39.7	38.6	50.7	43.6	...
Tuvalu	93.8 (2012)	144.0	150.0	106.5	125.8	112.8	116.5	129.4	...
Vanuatu	24.5 (2012)	25.1	25.9	29.1	30.2	30.5	...	...	...
Developed ADB Member Economies									
Australia[b]	37.7	37.1	37.4	36.7	36.8	36.9	42.1	44.3	39.8
Japan[d]	38.7	38.6	38.2	37.9	37.8	38.5	46.7	44.0	...
New Zealand[b]	40.3	37.6	36.8	36.0	35.4	36.6	42.5	40.1	43.9

.... = data not available; | = marks break in series; * = provisional, preliminary, estimate; ADB = Asian Development Bank; GDP = gross domestic product.

Note: In general, economies follow the guidelines of the International Monetary Fund on Government Finance Statistics (GFS). Some economies still use the 1986 version of the GFS guidelines, while others have switched to the 2001 or 2014 guidelines. The comparability of the data in this table is limited by variations in the concepts and definitions used in different versions of the GFS framework. Data refer to government expenditure as classified in the GFS 2001 or GFS 2014 framework, except for Bhutan; Brunei Darussalam; India; the Kyrgyz Republic; Maldives; Nauru; Pakistan; the People's Republic of China; Taipei,China; Tajikistan; and Turkmenistan, where data refer to total government expenditure as classified in the GFS 1986 framework. Data refer to general government, except for Bangladesh; Bhutan; Brunei Darussalam; Cambodia; the Federated States of Micronesia; Fiji; India; the Lao People's Democratic Republic; Malaysia; Maldives; the Marshall Islands; Nauru; Nepal; Palau; the Philippines; Solomon Islands; Sri Lanka; Taipei,China; Timor-Leste; Tonga; Tuvalu; Vanuatu; and Viet Nam, where data refer to central government. For Cambodia: Data refer to central government excluding extra budgetary central government. For Pakistan: Data refer to the consolidated federal and provincial governments. For the People's Republic of China: Data refer to consolidated central and local governments. For Turkmenistan: Data prior to 2011 refer to central government.

a The longer time series featured in the Key Indicators Database refers to GFS data for 2005–2011 based on fiscal year beginning 21 March. For 2012, GFS data cover 9 months from 21 March to 20 December. For 2013 onward, GFS data are based on fiscal year ending 20 December. For 2005–2015, national accounts data are based on fiscal year beginning 21 March. For 2016 onward, national accounts data are based on fiscal year ending 20 December.
b Data are based on fiscal year ending 30 June.
c Prior to 2015, national accounts data are based on the 1993 System of National Accounts; and, for 2015 onward, are based on the 2008 System of National Accounts.
d Data are based on fiscal year beginning 1 April.
e Data are based on fiscal year ending 15 July.
f The longer time series featured in the Key Indicators Database showing Brunei Darussalam's government expenditure for 2003 onward are based on fiscal year beginning 1 April.
g Data are based on fiscal year ending 30 September.
h For 2012–2018, GFS data are based on fiscal year beginning 1 April. For 2019, data are based on fiscal year beginning 1 October. For 2012–2015, national accounts data are based on fiscal year beginning 1 April. For 2016 onward, national accounts data are based on fiscal year beginning 1 October.
i Until the 53rd edition of the Key Indicators of Asia and the Pacific, Viet Nam's data on government finance from the Ministry of Finance (MOF) was presented using the GFS 1986 standard. Starting in the 54th edition of the Key Indicators of Asia and the Pacific, with the support of the World Bank and International Monetary Fund (IMF), the MOF submitted its 2003–2019 government finance data following GFS 2014 standard. The MOF is currently working with IMF to convert its 2020 onward government finance data.
j The longer time series featured in the Key Indicators Database refers to GFS data for 2000–2014 based on fiscal year ending 31 December. For 2015 onward, GFS data are based on fiscal year ending 31 July. National accounts data are based on calendar year.

Sources: Economies' official sources. For Nauru (2012–2022): International Monetary Fund. Staff Country Reports. Republic of Nauru: 2021 Article IV. https://www.imf.org/en/Publications/CR/Issues/2022/02/07/Republic-of-Nauru-2021-Article-IV-Consultation-Press-Release-Staff-Report-and-Statement-by-512874 (accessed 28 May 2023). For Timor-Leste: International Monetary Fund. Government Finance Statistics. https://data.imf.org/ (accessed 28 April 2023).

Table 2.8.5: Government Expenditure by Economic Activity
(% of GDP)

ADB Regional Member	Health 2010	Health 2015	Health 2020	Health 2021	Health 2022	Education 2010	Education 2015	Education 2020	Education 2021	Education 2022	Social Protection 2010	Social Protection 2015	Social Protection 2020	Social Protection 2021	Social Protection 2022
Developing ADB Member Economies															
Central and West Asia															
Afghanistan[a]	0.9	1.2	1.8	...	...	3.6	3.6	2.1	...	...	0.5	1.4	1.1	...	...
Armenia	1.6	1.7	2.4	2.3	1.7*	3.2	2.9	2.8	2.7	2.4*	7.1	7.7	8.9	8.9	7.3*
Azerbaijan	1.0	1.3	2.3	1.5	...	2.9	3.1	4.0	3.3	...	6.8	6.8	11.4	8.6	...
Georgia	2.1	2.7	3.7	4.4	3.0*	2.8	4.4	4.4	4.2	3.8*	6.5	7.3	9.6	7.8	6.8*
Kazakhstan	2.5	2.1	2.8	2.9	...	3.5	3.3	4.8	5.2	...	4.5	4.5	6.5	5.6	...
Kyrgyz Republic	2.9	3.0	2.9	2.8	2.7*	5.4	5.9	6.6	5.9	7.0*	5.0	5.8	5.7	4.9	5.3*
Pakistan	...	...	...	...	...	...	...	...	...	...	...	...	...	...	...
Tajikistan[b]	1.4 |	2.0	3.1	2.9	...	4.0 |	5.0	5.1	5.4	...	3.5 |	5.2	4.6	4.2	...
Turkmenistan	...	...	...	...	...	...	...	...	...	...	...	...	...	...	...
Uzbekistan	...	2.5	3.3	...	...	...	6.0	6.3	...	...	...	7.4	9.3	...	...
East Asia															
China, People's Republic of	1.2	1.7	1.9	1.7	1.9	3.0	3.8	3.6	3.3	3.3	2.2	2.8	3.2	2.9	3.0
Hong Kong, China[c]	2.4	3.2	3.9	...	...	3.5	3.4	4.1	...	...	2.4	2.9	4.2	...	...
Korea, Republic of	0.2	0.3	0.4	0.8	...	2.8	3.0	3.6	3.7	...	4.3	5.3	8.1	7.8	...
Mongolia	2.5	2.5	4.5	5.7	5.8*	5.1	3.0	3.4	3.3	4.4*	11.1	7.6	10.7	12.6	11.8*
Taipei,China	0.2	0.1	0.1	0.1	...	1.7	1.4	1.5	1.3	...	3.1	3.3	3.3	3.1	...
South Asia															
Bangladesh[d]	0.8	0.7	0.6	0.7	...	2.0	2.0	2.3	2.3	...	0.9	0.7	1.2	1.2	...
Bhutan[d]	3.0	2.8	3.7	3.7	3.8	6.7	6.0	7.3	6.5	5.6	3.1	3.2	3.4	3.3	3.3
India[c,e]	1.0 (2011)	1.2	1.6	1.7	...	4.4 (2011)	4.4	4.6	4.5	...	1.4 (2011)	1.8	2.1	2.0	...
Maldives[f]	2.9	4.0	7.5	5.7	4.7*	5.3	4.6	5.7	4.5	4.6*	1.7	5.1	5.9	4.6	4.3*
Nepal[g]	1.5	1.2	1.0	1.2	...	3.9	3.3	1.0	0.9	...	0.8	0.6	1.7	1.7	...
Sri Lanka	1.1	1.5	1.5 (2019)	2.2	1.3	1.6	1.9	1.8 (2019)	1.8	1.5	1.6	4.8	...	...	...
Southeast Asia															
Brunei Darussalam[h]	1.8	2.3	2.3	2.1	...	3.6	4.1	4.2	3.7	...	0.8	0.8	0.7	0.6	...
Cambodia	1.3	1.3	1.7	2.2	0.8*	1.6	2.0	2.9	2.5	2.4*	0.5	0.8	1.2	1.1	1.2*
Indonesia	1.0	1.1	1.7	2.4	1.6	3.4	3.3	3.0	2.9	2.5	0.1	0.3	2.0	1.7	1.5
Lao People's Democratic Republic	...	...	...	...	...	...	...	...	...	...	...	...	...	...	...
Malaysia	2.0	2.0	2.2	2.3	...	6.1	4.8	4.5	4.2	...	...	...	...	...	...
Myanmar[i]	0.7 (2012)	1.0 |	0.8 (2019)	...	...	1.5 (2012)	2.1 |	2.0 (2019)	...	...	0.4 (2012)	0.8 |	0.9 (2019)	...	...
Philippines[j]	0.3	0.8	1.4	1.6	1.3	2.4	2.8	3.7	3.9	3.5	1.6	1.3	3.6	2.4	2.5
Singapore[c]	1.2	2.1	3.3	3.1	...	3.0	2.9	3.1	2.4	...	1.1	1.8	7.8	1.8	...
Thailand[k]	...	1.1	1.4	1.8	1.9*	...	3.8	3.1	3.1	2.7*	...	2.5	5.6	5.2	4.9*
Timor-Leste	4.0	3.7	3.3 (2018)	...	...	7.8	6.5	4.7 (2018)	...	...	16.3	11.7	8.5 (2018)	...	...
Viet Nam	...	...	...	...	...	...	...	...	...	...	...	...	...	...	...
The Pacific															
Cook Islands[d]	3.9	3.0	5.6	5.6	...	4.0	3.5	4.5	4.3	...	3.9	4.2	6.9	12.6	...
Fiji	...	...	...	...	...	...	...	...	...	...	...	...	...	...	...
Kiribati[d]	...	9.9	11.0	11.3*	...	...	9.9	12.2	14.2*	...	...	1.4	1.1	3.8*	...
Marshall Islands[k]	8.2	7.6	9.0	...	...	20.6	16.6	12.9	...	...	...	0.6 (2016)	2.4	...	...
Micronesia, Federated States of	...	...	...	...	...	...	...	...	...	...	...	...	...	...	...
Nauru	...	...	...	...	...	...	...	...	...	...	...	...	...	...	...
Niue	...	...	...	...	...	...	...	...	...	...	...	...	...	...	...
Palau	...	...	...	...	...	...	...	...	...	...	...	...	...	...	...
Papua New Guinea	...	...	...	...	...	...	...	...	...	...	...	...	...	...	...
Samoa[d]	3.6	5.4	5.3	5.9	5.9	5.8	4.5	4.9	6.2	6.1	1.1	2.1	1.3	2.5	2.4
Solomon Islands	...	...	...	...	...	...	...	...	...	...	...	...	...	...	...
Tonga	...	...	...	...	...	...	...	...	...	...	...	...	...	...	...
Tuvalu	8.5 (2012)	9.4	...	...	...	16.0 (2012)	23.2	...	...	...	6.1 (2012)	18.3	...	...	...
Vanuatu	3.0 (2011)	2.5	2.7 (2018)	...	...	6.4 (2011)	5.6	6.7 (2018)	...	...	0.0 (2011)	0.1	0.0 (2018)	...	...
Developed ADB Member Economies															
Australia[d]	6.6	6.8	7.5	7.8	7.9	5.9	5.5	5.8	5.6	5.4	9.8	10.4	11.0	11.7	10.7
Japan[c]	6.8	7.3	7.7	8.3	...	2.8	2.6	2.7	2.6	...	2.1	2.5	2.8	2.8	...
New Zealand[d]	7.0	6.8	7.1	7.5	8.6	6.8	6.2	6.3	5.7	5.8	12.5	11.5	11.2	11.8	12.7

... = data not available; | = marks break in series; * = provisional, preliminary, estimate; 0.0 = magnitude is less than half of unit employed; ADB = Asian Development Bank; GDP = gross domestic product.

Note: In general, economies follow the guidelines of the International Monetary Fund on Government Finance Statistics (GFS). Some economies still use the 1986 version of the GFS guidelines, while others have switched to the 2001 or 2014 guidelines. The comparability of the data in this table is limited by variations in the concepts and definitions used in different versions of the GFS framework. The table refers to government expenditure by economic activity as classified in the GFS 2001 or GFS 2014 framework, except for Bhutan; Brunei Darussalam; India; the Kyrgyz Republic; the People's Republic of China; and Taipei,China, where data refer to health, education, and social security and welfare, as classified in the GFS 1986 framework. For Maldives, data prior to 2017 are classified in the GFS 1986 framework, while data for 2017 onward follow the GFS 2014 framework. Data refer to general government, except for Bangladesh; Bhutan; Brunei Darussalam; Cambodia; India; Malaysia; Maldives; the Marshall Islands; Nepal; the Philippines; Samoa; Sri Lanka; Taipei,China; Timor-Leste; Tuvalu; and Vanuatu, where data refer to central government. For Cambodia: Data refer to central government excluding extra budgetary central government. For the People's Republic of China: Data refer to consolidated central and local governments.

a For 2010, data based on fiscal year beginning 21 March. For 2015 onward, GFS data are based on fiscal year ending 20 December. For 2010 and 2015, national accounts data are based on fiscal year beginning 21 March. For 2016 onward, national accounts data are based on fiscal year ending 20 December.
b National accounts data prior to 2015 are based on the 1993 System of National Accounts while data for 2015 onward are based on the 2008 System of National Accounts.
c Data are based on fiscal year beginning 1 April.
d Data are based on fiscal year ending 30 June.
e Data exclude local bodies.
f Prior to 2012, refers to total expenditure. For 2012 onward, refers to total budget. For 2020, GDP estimates used are projections available as of 15 March 2021, forecasted by the Government of Maldives' Ministry of Finance.
g Data are based on fiscal year ending 15 July.
h For 2003 onward, data are based on fiscal year beginning 1 April.
i For 2012-2018, GFS data are based on fiscal year beginning 1 April. For 2019, data are based on fiscal year beginning 1 October. National accounts data for 2012-2015 are based on fiscal year beginning 1 April, and for 2016 onward on fiscal year beginning 1 October.
j For 2010-2018, data refer to obligation basis. For 2019 onward, data refer to cash basis. For 2010, data on education include expenditure on recreation, culture, and religion.
k Data are based on fiscal year ending 30 September.

Sources: Economies' official sources. For Hong Kong, China and Nepal: Asian Development Bank estimates using data from the International Monetary Fund's Government Finance Statistics. https://data.imf.org/ (accessed April–June 2023).

Table 2.8.6: Corruption Perceptions Index

ADB Regional Member	2012	2015	2018	2019	2020	2021	2022	Rank in 2020[a]	Rank in 2022[a]
Developing ADB Member Economies									
Central and West Asia									
Afghanistan	8.0	11.0	16.0	16.0	19.0	16.0	24.0	174	150
Armenia	34.0	35.0	35.0	42.0	49.0	49.0	46.0	58	63
Azerbaijan	27.0	29.0	25.0	30.0	30.0	30.0	23.0	128	157
Georgia	52.0	52.0	58.0	56.0	56.0	55.0	56.0	45	41
Kazakhstan	28.0	28.0	31.0	34.0	38.0	37.0	36.0	102	101
Kyrgyz Republic	24.0	28.0	29.0	30.0	31.0	27.0	27.0	144	140
Pakistan	27.0	30.0	33.0	32.0	31.0	28.0	27.0	140	140
Tajikistan	22.0	26.0	25.0	25.0	25.0	25.0	24.0	150	150
Turkmenistan	17.0	18.0	20.0	19.0	19.0	19.0	19.0	169	167
Uzbekistan	17.0	19.0	23.0	25.0	26.0	28.0	31.0	140	126
East Asia									
China, People's Republic of	39.0	37.0	39.0	41.0	42.0	45.0	45.0	66	65
Hong Kong, China	77.0	75.0	76.0	76.0	77.0	76.0	76.0	12	12
Korea, Republic of	56.0	54.0	57.0	59.0	61.0	62.0	63.0	32	31
Mongolia	36.0	39.0	37.0	35.0	35.0	35.0	33.0	110	116
Taipei,China	61.0	62.0	63.0	65.0	65.0	68.0	68.0	25	25
South Asia									
Bangladesh	26.0	25.0	26.0	26.0	26.0	26.0	25.0	147	147
Bhutan	63.0	65.0	68.0	68.0	68.0	68.0	68.0	25	25
India	36.0	38.0	41.0	41.0	40.0	40.0	40.0	85	85
Maldives	...	...	31.0	29.0	43.0	40.0	40.0	85	85
Nepal	27.0	27.0	31.0	34.0	33.0	33.0	34.0	117	110
Sri Lanka	40.0	37.0	38.0	38.0	38.0	37.0	36.0	102	101
Southeast Asia									
Brunei Darussalam	55.0	...	63.0	60.0	60.0	...	...	...	...
Cambodia	22.0	21.0	20.0	20.0	21.0	23.0	24.0	157	150
Indonesia	32.0	36.0	38.0	40.0	37.0	38.0	34.0	96	110
Lao People's Democratic Republic	21.0	25.0	29.0	29.0	29.0	30.0	31.0	128	126
Malaysia	49.0	50.0	47.0	53.0	51.0	48.0	47.0	62	61
Myanmar	15.0	22.0	29.0	29.0	28.0	28.0	23.0	140	157
Philippines	34.0	35.0	36.0	34.0	34.0	33.0	33.0	117	116
Singapore	87.0	85.0	85.0	85.0	85.0	85.0	83.0	4	5
Thailand	37.0	38.0	36.0	36.0	36.0	35.0	36.0	110	101
Timor-Leste	33.0	28.0	35.0	38.0	40.0	41.0	42.0	82	77
Viet Nam	31.0	31.0	33.0	37.0	36.0	39.0	42.0	87	77
The Pacific									
Cook Islands	...	...	...	...	...	...	...	...	...
Fiji	...	...	...	...	...	55.0	53.0	45	49
Kiribati	...	...	...	...	...	...	...	...	...
Marshall Islands	...	...	...	...	...	...	...	...	...
Micronesia, Federated States of	...	...	...	...	...	...	...	...	...
Nauru	...	...	...	...	...	...	...	...	...
Niue	...	...	...	...	...	...	...	...	...
Palau	...	...	...	...	...	...	...	...	...
Papua New Guinea	25.0	25.0	28.0	28.0	27.0	31.0	30.0	124	130
Samoa	...	...	...	...	...	...	...	...	...
Solomon Islands	...	...	44.0	42.0	42.0	43.0	42.0	73	77
Tonga	...	...	...	...	...	...	...	...	...
Tuvalu	...	...	...	...	...	...	...	...	...
Vanuatu	...	...	46.0	46.0	43.0	45.0	48.0	66	60
Developed ADB Member Economies									
Australia	85.0	79.0	77.0	77.0	77.0	73.0	75.0	18	13
Japan	74.0	75.0	73.0	73.0	74.0	73.0	73.0	18	18
New Zealand	90.0	91.0	87.0	87.0	88.0	88.0	87.0	1	2

... = data not available, ADB = Asian Development Bank.

Note: The Key Indicators Database features a longer time series of scores on the Corruption Perceptions Index. This includes scores for 2000–2011, which refer to perceptions of the degree of corruption as seen by business people and analysts. Those scores range from 0 (highly corrupt) to 10 (very clean) and are not comparable over time. From 2012 onward, an updated methodology was used to calculate scores, and these are presented on a scale from 0 (highly corrupt) to 100 (very clean). Due to the differences in methodology, scores prior to 2012 should not be compared with scores for 2012 onward.

a Based on Transparency International's methodology, an economy's rank indicates its position relative to the Corruption Perceptions Index of other economies of the world; 2021 and 2022 rankings compare 180 economies.

Source: Transparency International. Corruption Perceptions Index. https://www.transparency.org/ (accessed 2 May 2023).

Data Issues and Comparability

Most economies generally follow the IMF's Government Finance Statistics (GFS) guidelines: some still use the 1986 version, while others have switched to the 2001 or 2014 versions. The comparability of the data is limited by variations in the concepts and definitions used in different versions of the GFS framework. Furthermore, there is no single framework for an extended time series available in most economies that are using the 2014 guidelines, with most economies recording their transactions on a cash basis (and a few on an accrual basis).

Data on government expenditures and revenue are derived from economy sources and are therefore not standard throughout Asia and the Pacific. Data refer to general government for some economies, and central government for other economies.

Statistics on perceived corruption are taken from nonofficial sources. Common procedures are used in all economies and the researchers producing these data have refined their procedures over several surveys. However, because of the subjective nature of many of the data, they can only be used to give a broad idea of trends, levels, and rankings, so small changes from one year to the next should be interpreted with caution.

PART III
Dollar Price Wedge between Nominal and Real Global Value Chain Participation

Introduction

Global value chains (GVCs) describe the flow of goods and services across economies through sequential processes of production, distribution, and value addition within supply chains, capitalizing on location-specific competitive advantages including changes in relative prices. With supply chains now highly globalized, an important question to ask is, have the significant price increases seen worldwide since mid-2021, resulted in changes in economies' participation in GVCs? Using the nominal and real multiregional input-output tables (MRIOTs) produced by the Asian Development Bank (ADB 2023) for the period 2007–2022, this chapter tracks the evolution of GVC participation indicators of certain economies, and the effects that price changes have had.

While trends in GVC participation based on nominal MRIOTs are affected by changes in economic structures, production technologies, prices, and exchange rates, those based on the real MRIOTs are affected only by the first two having been expressed in constant prices. Analyzing both the nominal and real trends provides a richer context, and this chapter reports on the effects of dollar price changes[1] on GVC participation rates, especially in the context of post-pandemic inflation.

Nominal and Real MRIOTs

ADB has been publishing nominal MRIOTs since 2015, and the real MRIOTs since 2020, with 35-industry and 5-final demand category disaggregation for 62 economies and the rest of the world. Nominal MRIOTs are compiled using the same methodology employed by the World Input-Output Database (WIOD)[2]. Real MRIOTs, expressed in 2010 prices, are compiled to remove changes in the trends driven by price fluctuations, so that these are in constant terms and relate only to other factors such as quantity, value-addition, and compositional changes[3].

Both the nominal and real MRIOTs tables are expressed in US dollars (USD). For the nominal MRIOTs, data are sourced from the official national accounts, and international trade databases such as United Nations Comtrade and Balanced Trade in Services. Data in local currency units are converted to USD using the period average exchange rates obtained from the International Monetary Fund (IMF 2022) International Financial Statistics. Real tables are calculated by deflating the nominal counterparts using implicit

1 Price changes are referred to as dollar price changes since all MRIOT are expressed in US dollars (USD).

2 World Input-Output Database is developed by the Groningen Growth and Development Centre at the University of Groningen in the Netherlands.

3 Statistical Office of the European Communities (Eurostat). 2016. Handbook on prices and volume measures in national accounts. Luxembourg: Publications Office of the European Union.

price indices (deflators)[4]. The main data source for deflators is the United Nations Statistics Division (UNSD) National Accounts Estimates of Main Aggregates database.

Table 3.1 is a simplified representation of a real MRIOT, assuming a two-economy, two-industry, and three-final use category universe. Notations with and without asterisks refer respectively to real and nominal values.

Table 3.1: Simplified Representation of a Real Multiregional Input-Output Table

		Economy A		Economy B		Economy A			Economy B			Gross Output (GO)
		Intermediate Use				Final Use						
		Industry 1	Industry 2	Industry 1	Industry 2	F1 (FCE)	F2 (GFCF)	F3 (INV)	F1 (FCE)	F2 (GFCF)	F3 (INV)	
Economy A	Industry 1	INT_{11}^{*AA}	INT_{12}^{*AA}	INT_{11}^{*AB}	INT_{12}^{*AB}	FIN_{11}^{*AA}	FIN_{12}^{*AA}	FIN_{13}^{*AA}	FIN_{11}^{*AB}	FIN_{12}^{*AB}	FIN_{13}^{*AB}	GO_1^{*A}
	Industry 2	INT_{21}^{*AA}	INT_{22}^{*AA}	INT_{21}^{*AB}	INT_{22}^{*AB}	FIN_{21}^{*AA}	FIN_{22}^{*AA}	FIN_{23}^{*AA}	FIN_{21}^{*AB}	FIN_{22}^{*AB}	FIN_{23}^{*AB}	GO_2^{*A}
Economy B	Industry 1	INT_{11}^{*BA}	INT_{12}^{*BA}	INT_{11}^{*BB}	INT_{12}^{*BB}	FIN_{11}^{*BA}	FIN_{12}^{*BA}	FIN_{13}^{*BA}	FIN_{11}^{*BB}	FIN_{12}^{*BB}	FIN_{13}^{*BB}	GO_1^{*B}
	Industry 2	INT_{21}^{*BA}	INT_{22}^{*BA}	INT_{21}^{*BB}	INT_{22}^{*BB}	FIN_{21}^{*BA}	FIN_{22}^{*BA}	FIN_{23}^{*BA}	FIN_{21}^{*BB}	FIN_{22}^{*BB}	FIN_{23}^{*BB}	GO_2^{*B}
Taxes, subsidies, international transport margins, etc. (TAX)		$TINT_1^{*A}$	$TINT_2^{*A}$	$TINT_1^{*B}$	$TINT_2^{*B}$	$TFIN_1^{*A}$	$TFIN_2^{*A}$	$TFIN_3^{*A}$	$TFIN_1^{*B}$	$TFIN_2^{*B}$	$TFIN_3^{*B}$	TAX^*
Gross value-added (GVA)		GVA_1^{*A}	GVA_2^{*A}	GVA_1^{*B}	GVA_2^{*B}							GVA^*
Gross Output (GO)		GO_1^{*A}	GO_2^{*A}	GO_1^{*B}	GO_2^{*B}	FIN_1^{*A}	FIN_2^{*A}	FIN_3^{*A}	FIN_1^{*B}	FIN_2^{*B}	FIN_3^{*B}	GO^*

Where:
- INT Intermediate Use
- FIN Final Use
- TINT Taxes, Subsidies, International transport margins, etc. on Intermediate Use
- TFIN Taxes, Subsidies, International transport margins, etc. on Final Use
- TAX Total Taxes, Subsidies, International transport margins, etc.
- GVA Gross Value-Added
- GO Gross Output
- * Value at Constant Prices

Thus:
- INT_{12}^{*BA} Intermediate Use of industry 1 of Economy B exported to industry 2 of Economy A
- INT_{21}^{*AA} Intermediate Use of industry 2 of Economy A domestically acquired by Industry 1 of Economy A
- FIN_{11}^{*BA} Final Use of Industry 1 of Economy B exported to Final Consumption Expenditure of Economy B

In general,
Let:
- M Row Economy (Exporting Economy)
- N Column Economy (Importing Economy)
- i Row Industry
- j Column Industry
- f Column Final Use
- p Implicit Price Deflator

4 The conversion to USD by the UNSD is done using appropriate annual monthly average of annual average end of month quotations of exchange rates. The market exchange rates are obtained from the International Monetary Fund (IMF 2022), International Financial Statistics, which are communicated by the Monetary Authority of each member economy or from end-of-month quotations in the market of that economy. The implicit price index is computed as the ratio of current value to constant value multiplied by 100.

Thus:

$GO_i^{*M} = \frac{GO_i^M}{p_{GOi}^M}$	to calculate the Gross Output by Economy M
$FIN_{i3}^{*MN} = \frac{FIN_{i3}^{MN}}{p_{FIN3}^N}$	to calculate the Final Use of industry i of economy M exported to inventory of economy N
$FIN_{if}^{*MN} = \frac{FIN_{if}^{MN}}{(GO_i^M - \sum_N FIN_{i3}^{MN})} \times (GO_i^{*M} - \sum_N FIN_{i3}^{*MN})$	to calculate the Final Use other than inventory of industry i of economy M exported to Final Use f of Economy N
$INT_{ij}^{*MN} = \frac{INT_{ij}^{MN}}{(GO_i^M - \sum_N FIN_{i3}^{MN})} \times (GO_i^{*M} - \sum_N FIN_{i3}^{*MN})$	to calculate the intermediate use of industry i of economy M exported to industry j
$TINT_j^{*N} = \frac{TINT_j^N}{(GO_j^N - \sum_M INT_j^{MN})} \times (GO_j^{*N} - \sum_M INT_j^{*MN})$	to calculate the Taxes, Subsidies, International transport margins, etc. on Intermediate of economy NUse by Economy N
$TFIN_f^{*N} = \frac{TFIN_f^N}{p_{TFINf}^N}$	to calculate the Taxes, Subsidies, International transport margins, etc. on Final Use by Economy N
$GVA_j^{*N} = \frac{GVA_j^N}{(GO_j^N - \sum_M INT_j^{MN})} \times (GO_j^{*N} - \sum_M INT_j^{*MN})$	to calculate the Gross Value-Added by Economy N
$TAX^* = \sum_N TINT_j^{*N} + \sum_N TFIN_j^{*N}$	to calculate the total Taxes, Subsidies, International transport margins, etc.
$GVA^* = \sum_N GVA_j^{*N}$	to calculate the total gross value added
$GO^* = \sum GO_i^{*M}$	to calculate the total gross output

Source: Asian Development Bank (ADB) framework.

Deflator indices for the gross value-added (GVA) of the industries and final use categories are critical to the construction of the real MRIOTs. GVA deflators are used to segregate the effects of price changes on outputs. Ideally, each industry has its own unique deflator. However, implicit price indices are available only at an aggregated level for some industry categories[5]. In such cases, price indices of closely related industries are used as deflators. Since changes in inventories could also be negative, using the standard inventory deflators has been shown to distort the real MRIOTs compilation process. Thus, economy-wide GDP deflators are used for inventories.

Industry-specific gross outputs are deflated using the relevant implicit price indices. The resulting gross outputs in volume or real terms serve to calibrate, from both supply (row) and use (column) perspectives, transaction values in the MRIOTs resulting from subsequent estimation processes. Gross outputs, net of inventories in real terms, are proportionally allocated row-wise based on the structure of the nominal tables (with the columns for inventories excluded). Then, the total use of intermediate inputs by economy-industry is derived by summing up the deflated values in each column. For each economy-industry, the residual derived by subtracting the deflated total intermediate inputs from the deflated gross output (column totals) is proportionally distributed to GVA, taxes, subsidies, and international transport margins based on their corresponding shares in the nominal MRIOTs. Total final use by economy-category is calculated by summing up the deflated values in each column in the final use block.

---

5 Given the limitations in the price indices adopted for the current methodology, improvements to the compilation process are underway. These include the collection of disaggregated deflators (per industry), including export and import price indices, as officially reported by National Statistics Offices. Gross value-added deflators will also be separately collected from gross output deflators, with intermediate consumption derived residually. The current methodology treats the gross value-added as a residual, while assuming that the gross output deflators are the same as the gross value-added deflators.

Prices and GVCs. Significant changes in inflation and exchange rates tend to be reflected in the statistics on global value chains (photo by Mark Floro/ADB).

To ensure that the resulting estimates in the real MRIOTs are coherent with the UN official deflators, and the nominal MRIOTs, are consistent with relevant statistical and economic concepts and identities, a series of consistency and validation checks are conducted, and adjustments are made accordingly.

Methodology

The underlying data for the statistics and analysis presented in this chapter are the nominal and real MRIOTs produced by ADB. Time series of nominal MRIOTs account for changes in production technology, economic structure, prices, and exchange rates over time. The series of real MRIOTs, on the other hand, expressed in 2010 (base year) prices, reflect only the technological and structural changes. Thus, price and exchange rate changes together account for the differences between corresponding data points in the two tables or statistics derived from them. The combined effects of such are referred to as the dollar price wedge in this chapter since all transactions in the MRIOTs are expressed in US dollars.

The objective of this chapter is to document this dollar price wedge, or the difference between nominal and real GVC participation. To this end, data on gross exports from the nominal and real MRIOTs are decomposed into value-added components following Borin and Mancini's (2019) framework.

An economy's gross exports can be decomposed as follows:

Table 3.2: Value Added Components of an Economy's Gross Exports

Component	Description
DAVAX	Traditional type of trade where value-added exports cross one international border
REX	Value-added exports that are re-exported and are ultimately absorbed abroad
REF	Value-added exports eventually absorbed back at home
FVA	Foreign value-added embedded in an economy's exports
PDC	Purely double counted trade resulting from back-and-forth trading

Economy i's GVC participation rates for any given year t are given as follows:

Let $j \in$ [constant price, current price],

$$GVC\ participation\ rate^{j}_{i,t} = \frac{REX^{j}_{i,t} + REF^{j}_{i,t} + FVA^{j}_{i,t} + PDC^{j}_{i,t}}{Gross\ exports^{j}_{i,t}} \quad (1)$$

$$Backward\ GVC\ PR^{j}_{i,t} = \frac{FVA^{j}_{i,t} + PDC^{j}_{i,t}}{Gross\ exports^{j}_{i,t}} \quad (2)$$

$$Foward\ GVC\ PR^{j}_{i,t} = \frac{REX^{j}_{i,t} + REF^{j}_{i,t}}{Gross\ exports^{j}_{i,t}} \quad (3)$$

Each of these equations provide two sets of GVC participation rates: nominal – based on nominal MRIOTs; and real – based on real MRIOTs. The two sets of GVC participation rates for selected regions and economies will be examined in the following sections.

World and Developing Asia's GVC Participation

Nominal and real GVC-related trade shares in total world exports have largely remained stable and consistent with each other since 2007, with averages of 45.2% and 45.0%, respectively, as shown in Figure 3.1. This observed stability of world GVC shares over time reflects the long-term relationships among economies, industries, and businesses involved in global production networks. Since GVCs rely on efficient coordination amongst various economic actors and integration of different stages of production across multiple jurisdictions, this consistency underlines the deep and enduring interdependencies within global supply chains.

Figure 3.1: Traditional and GVC Trade on World Exports (in Trillions USD), 2007–2022

GVC = Global Value Chains.
Note: Traditional trade refers to the value-added embedded on exports that are directly absorbed by the direct importer, while GVC trade refers to value-added embedded on exports that cross two or more borders.
Source: Asian Development Bank (ADB) calculations using the nominal and real ADB Multiregional Input-Output Tables 2007–2022.

The effect of the recent inflationary surge is apparent for 2021, when total nominal exports exceeded real estimates by nearly 8%, the largest gap in the series.
The corresponding gap in 2022 was more than 7%, the third largest gap in the series. This implies that price effects on the measurement of GVC participation have become large enough to affect our understanding of GVC levels and trends. It is therefore no longer sufficient to study GVC in nominal terms only.

The relative stability in GVC trade as a share of total exports and the consistency of the ratios in nominal and real terms seen above are also reflected in the GVC participation rates at the world level (Figure 3.2). The recent inflationary surges are reflected in 2022, which saw a 0.9 percentage point separating the nominal and real GVC participation rates that year, the highest in the series. The earlier stability could be explained by two factors. First, the combined inflation and exchange rate pass-through effects may not have caused substantial shifts in the distribution of global value chain activities at the world level. Further, long-term contracts, pricing, and hedging arrangements may have helped to stabilize prices and trade volumes within GVCs over time.

It is noteworthy, that from 2012 to 2016, globally, producer price inflation fell below consumer price inflation before increasing at a much faster rate and diverging post-pandemic. The difference between producer price inflation and consumer price inflation is a key determinant of the size of the dollar price wedge. All else being equal, given formulas (1)—(3) above, when producer price inflation is lower than consumer price inflation, real GVC participation rates tend to be higher than nominal participation rates.

Figure 3.2: World GVC Participation Rate, 2007–2022

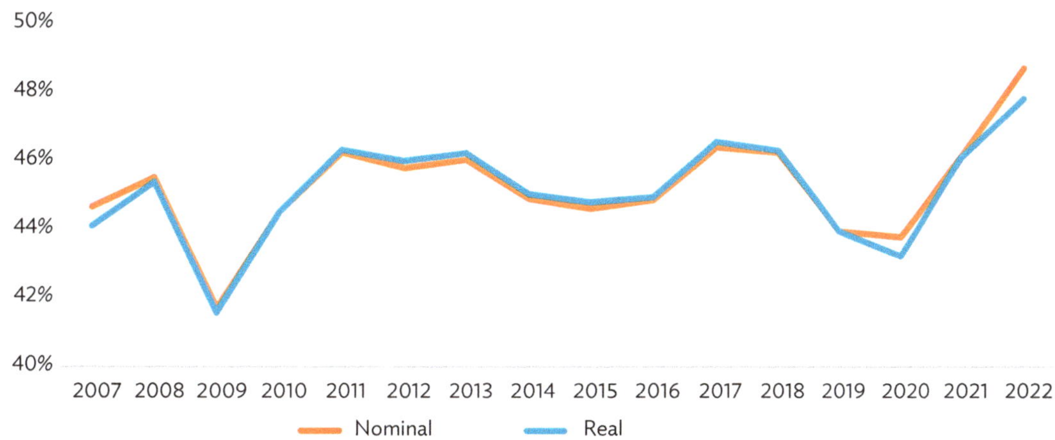

GVC = Global Value Chains.
Source: Asian Development Bank (ADB) calculations using the nominal and real ADB Multiregional Input-Output Tables 2007–2022.

While GVC trade shares to total exports have remained relatively stable since 2007, participation rates have been considerably affected by major events such as the global financial crisis (GFC) (2007–2009), the United States and People's Republic of China (US-PRC) trade conflict (2016–2019), and the COVID-19 pandemic (2020 onward). The sharpest increases in real and nominal participation rates since the GFC were seen in 2021 and 2022. However, while both series reached record-high levels by 2022, real participation fell further below nominal participation with surging producer price inflation far outpacing consumer price inflation.

Compared to the drop in GVC participation following the GFC, the decline in 2020 was significantly smaller. This could be attributed to a few key developments: (1) the normal trade cycle and the intensifying US-PRC trade conflict which had significantly dampened trade and GVC participation by 2019; (2) the unprecedented degree of fiscal and monetary measures which many governments rolled out attenuated the pandemic's impact on demand and supply; and (3) the acceleration and adoption of digital technologies which largely ensured the continuation of economic activities, created major opportunities in new and emerging areas such as e-commerce, and increased the demand for digital goods and services.

Developing Asia's nominal and real GVC participation rates have generally trodden close to global rates since 2007 (Figure 3.3). However, during the periods of major crises discussed above, the region's participation declined faster than the global average, indicating that its GVC trade was more sensitive to the impact of such events and shocks.

Moreover, the region's nominal and real participation rates were relatively less closely aligned than the global averages. The largest dollar price wedges for the region were seen between 2012 and 2016, before narrowing considerably in recent years. It should be noted that developing Asia's GVC participation is largely driven by the PRC's

Figure 3.3: Developing Asia GVC Participation Rate, 2007–2022

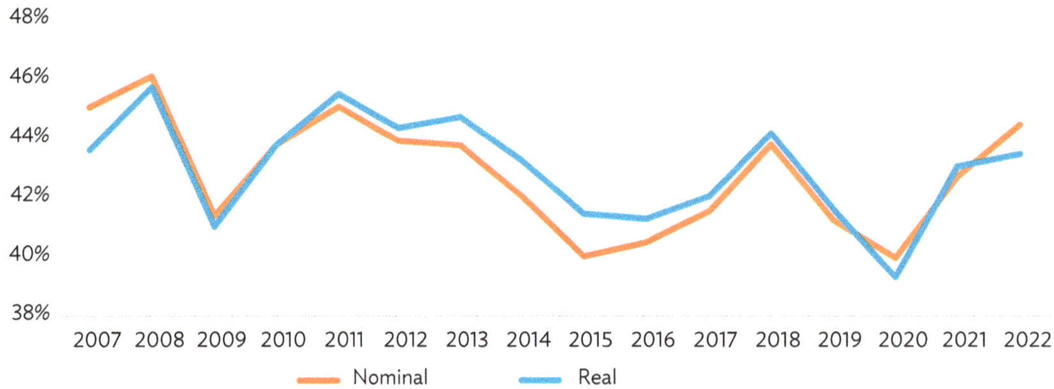

GVC = Global Value Chains.
Source: Asian Development Bank (ADB) calculations using the nominal and real ADB Multiregional Input-Output Tables 2007–2022.

GVC-related trade, which in 2022 accounted for nearly 40% of the region's total trade in intermediate products.

Between 2012 and 2016, the PRC's producer price inflation fell well below its consumer price inflation with the gap widest in 2015. The average difference between the two inflation rates narrowed quite significantly between 2017 and 2021, which seemed to be reflected in the region's dollar price wedge during the period. Producer price inflation surged between 2020 and 2022, while consumer price inflation remained relatively flat, contributing not only to the widening of the wedge but also to the surpassing of the real rate by the nominal rate for the first time in the series[6].

Economy-Specific GVC Participation

To study the effects of the dollar price changes on GVC participation statistics at a more granular level, the nominal and real participation trends of selected economies are analyzed in this subsection with statistics on backward and forward participation. The economies were chosen based on their relative importance in the global supply chains (PRC and US), and on the unique characteristics of their participation in GVCs (Türkiye, Singapore, and Kazakhstan).

Türkiye is ranked among the 20 largest economies in the world and is located at the crossroads of Asia and Europe. Between 2007 and 2022, the economy's GVC participation appeared to be rising in nominal terms (Figure 3.4.a). However, since 2008, Turkish lira has been depreciating against the US dollar, and when this is taken into consideration, Türkiye's GVC participation is shown to be flat over the course of the data series, fluctuating between 36% and 42% in real terms.

6 While the real participation rates were above nominal rates throughout 2011 to 2019, the reverse is seen in the estimates for years prior to 2010 due to the choice of that year as the base year for the MRIO deflation.

Similarly, Türkiye's backward participation rate has been rising in nominal terms (Figure 3.4.b). However, once currency depreciation and price effects have been controlled for, the trend is reversed. In real terms, Türkiye's backward participation rate has in fact been declining since 2007.

In terms of forward participation, currency depreciation has had the opposite trend effect. Türkiye's forward participation rate has been underestimated in nominal terms, as the real rates are a few percentage points higher (Figure3.4.c). The price wedge has also grown over time, with the largest gaps in 2021–2022, reflecting recent inflationary pressures.

Figure 3.4: GVC Participation Rate, Türkiye, 2007–2022

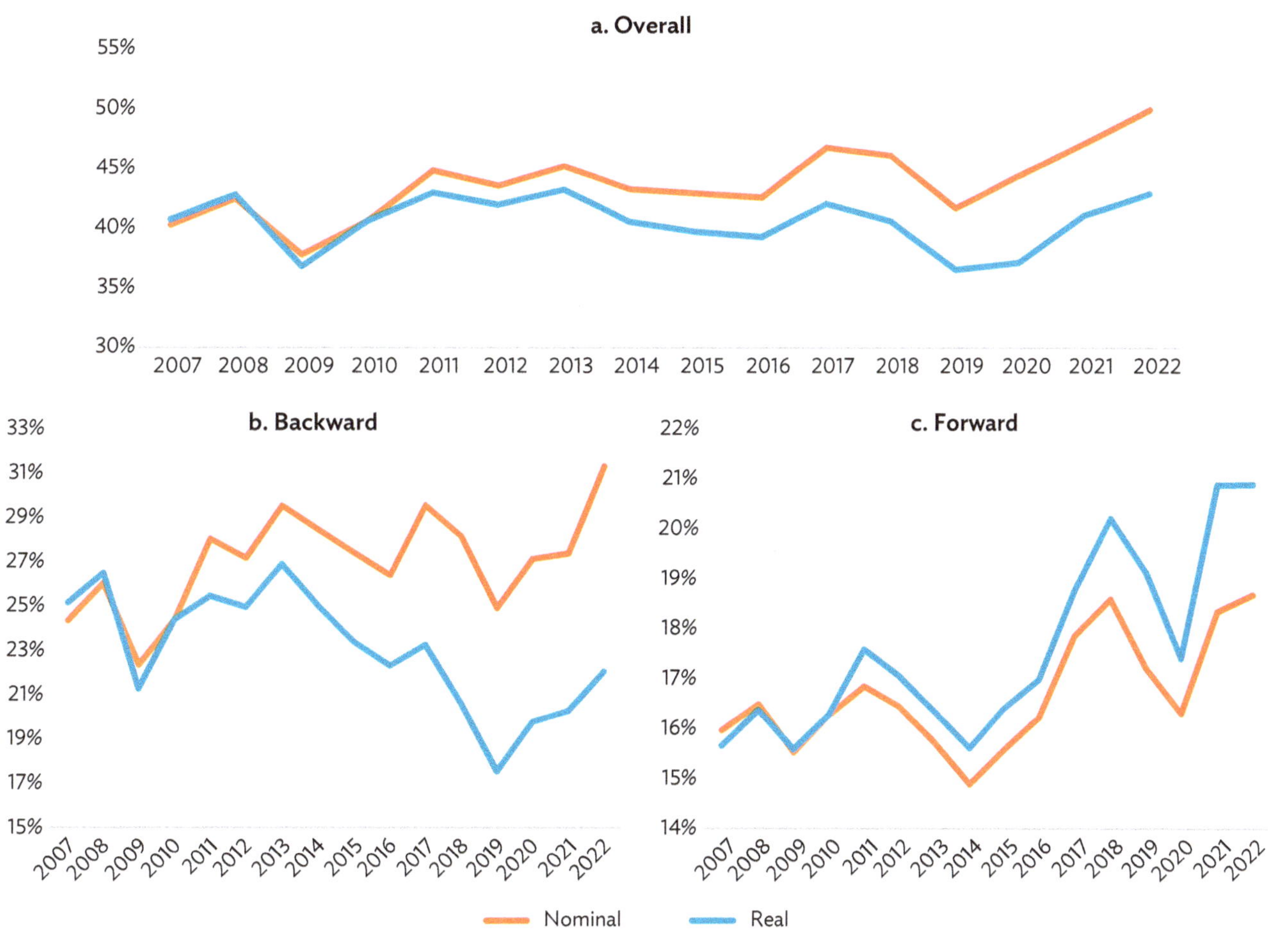

GVC = Global Value Chains.
Source: Asian Development Bank (ADB) calculations using the nominal and real ADB Multiregional Input-Output Tables 2007–2022.

High services content in trade characterizes Singapore's participation in GVCs. Although a relatively small economy, Singapore's involvement in global supply chains was quite high between 2007 and 2022, with its overall GVC participation rate averaging above 60% both in nominal and real terms (Figure 3.5.a.). Although the two series were closely aligned between 2007 and 2014, the dollar price wedge started to increase in 2015 and has sustained a relatively wide gap until 2020.

Singapore's economic slowdown in 2015–2016, which coincided with a sharp depreciation of its currency, evidently affected its GVC participation. The backward participation rates had their steepest decline during this period, subsequently creating a dollar price wedge that reached its peak in the years leading up to the US-PRC trade dispute (Figure 3.5.b). Both nominal and real forward participation rates of Singapore have been rising since 2015 before declining in 2022 (Figure 3.5.c). During this period, the combined effects of inflation and exchange rate pass-through appear to have pulled nominal rates upward relative to real rates.

Figure 3.5: GVC Participation Rate, Singapore, 2007–2022

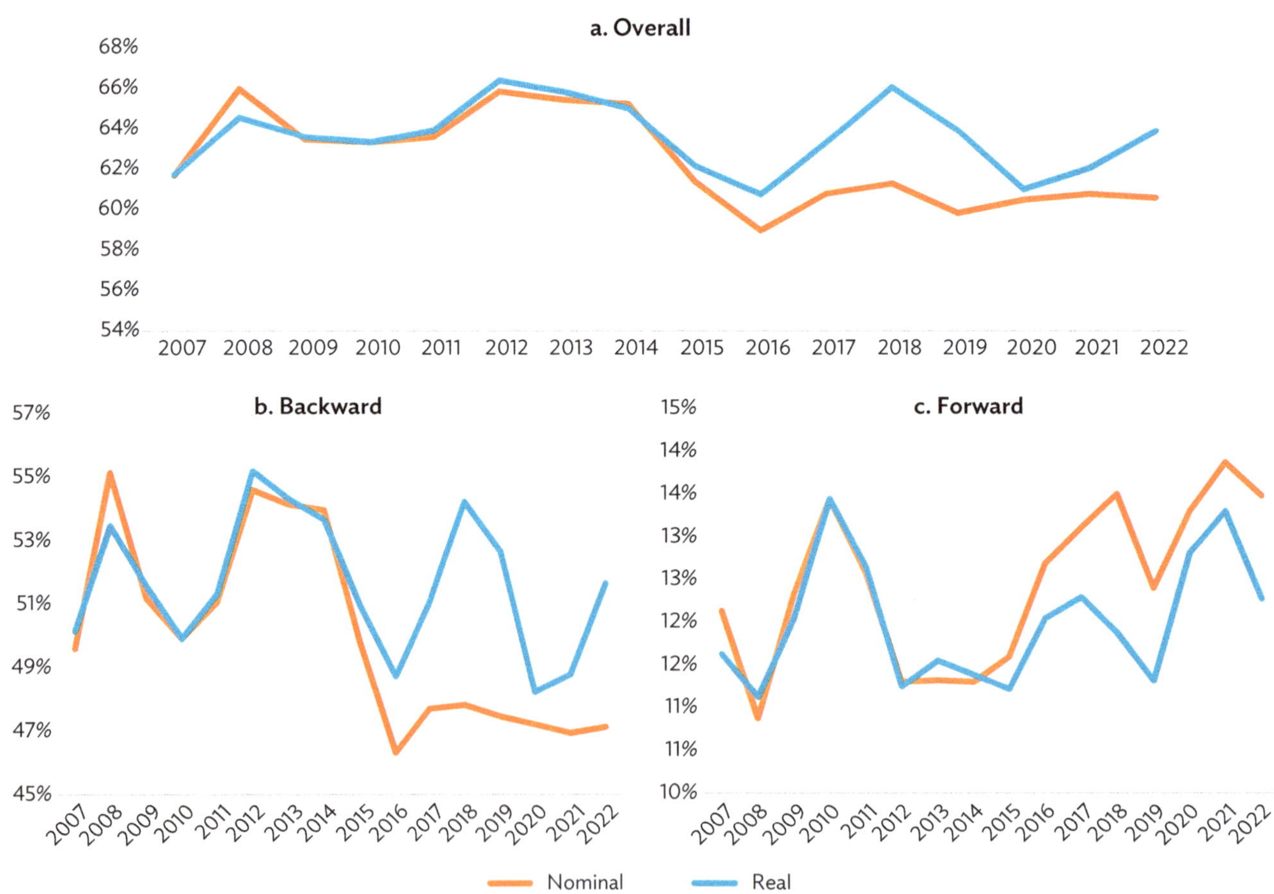

GVC = Global Value Chains.
Source: Asian Development Bank (ADB) calculations using the nominal and real ADB Multiregional Input-Output Tables 2007–2022.

Between 2007 and 2022, Kazakhstan's currency (Kazakhstani Tenge) was steadily declining. After the pandemic, the economy also experienced one of the largest surges in overall inflation in developing Asia. Yet, even with these developments, the dollar price wedge between its nominal and real GVC participation rates remained rather narrow throughout the period (Figure 3.6.a).

Kazakhstan's economy is dominated by the mining sector, with intermediate products like crude petroleum, gas and crude metals—prices of which are globally determined in US dollars—consistently constituting the bulk of its exports (averaging 70%). On the other hand, products for final use made only a small contribution to exports (10%). Imports, meanwhile, were dominated by final products (80%). Such an economic landscape may have contributed to the close alignment of nominal and real forward GVC participation rates even in times of persistent inflation and tenge depreciation (Figure 3.6.c). As for backward participation rates, although trends in nominal and real terms exhibited similarity in movement, a seemingly permanent and consistent price wedge between the two is observed from 2015 all the way to 2022.

Figure 3.6: GVC Participation Rate, Kazakhstan, 2007–2022

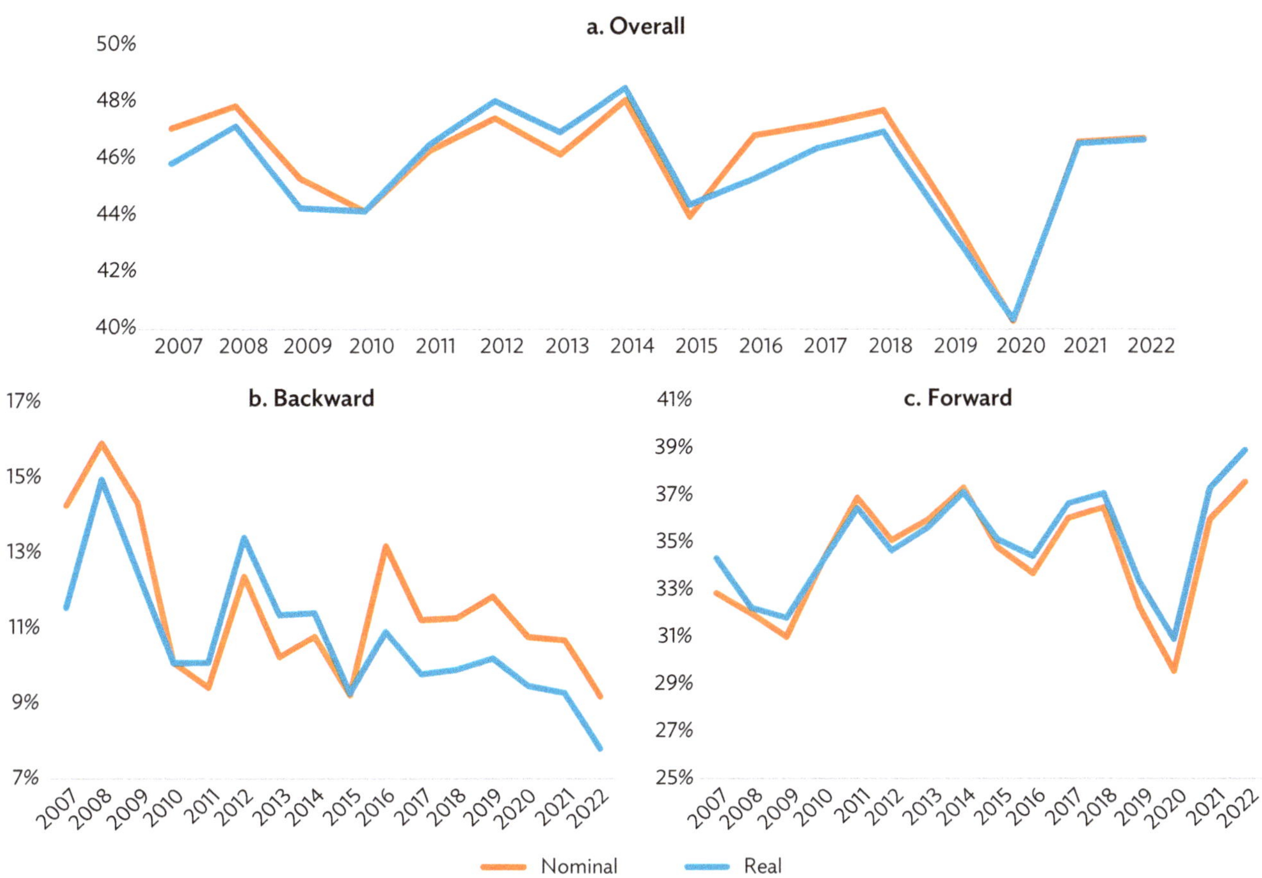

GVC = Global Value Chains.
Source: Asian Development Bank (ADB) calculations using the nominal and real ADB Multiregional Input-Output Tables 2007–2022.

Between 2007 and 2022, The PRC's nominal and real GVC participation rates were generally closely aligned with each other, although real participation had been higher since 2011, with the dollar price wedge narrowing between 2017 and 2019 before starting to widen after 2020 (Figure 3.7.a). The price wedge also changed direction in 2022, occurring alongside a producer price inflation surge and yuan depreciation.

It is striking that the PRC's GVC participation rates, in nominal and real terms, reached near peak levels in 2022 despite the US-PRC trade conflict, the pandemic and the Russian invasion of Ukraine. Interestingly, the economy's real participation trend was largely driven by its backward participation while the nominal one was driven by forward participation. Even as nominal rates showed PRC's backward participation to have stagnated since 2018, in real terms it seemed not only to have recovered from the effects of both the trade conflict and the pandemic but to have further strengthened in 2022 (Figure 3.7.b.). The converse appeared to be the case with forward participation (Figure 3.7.c.).

Figure 3.7: GVC Participation Rate, People's Republic of China, 2007–2022

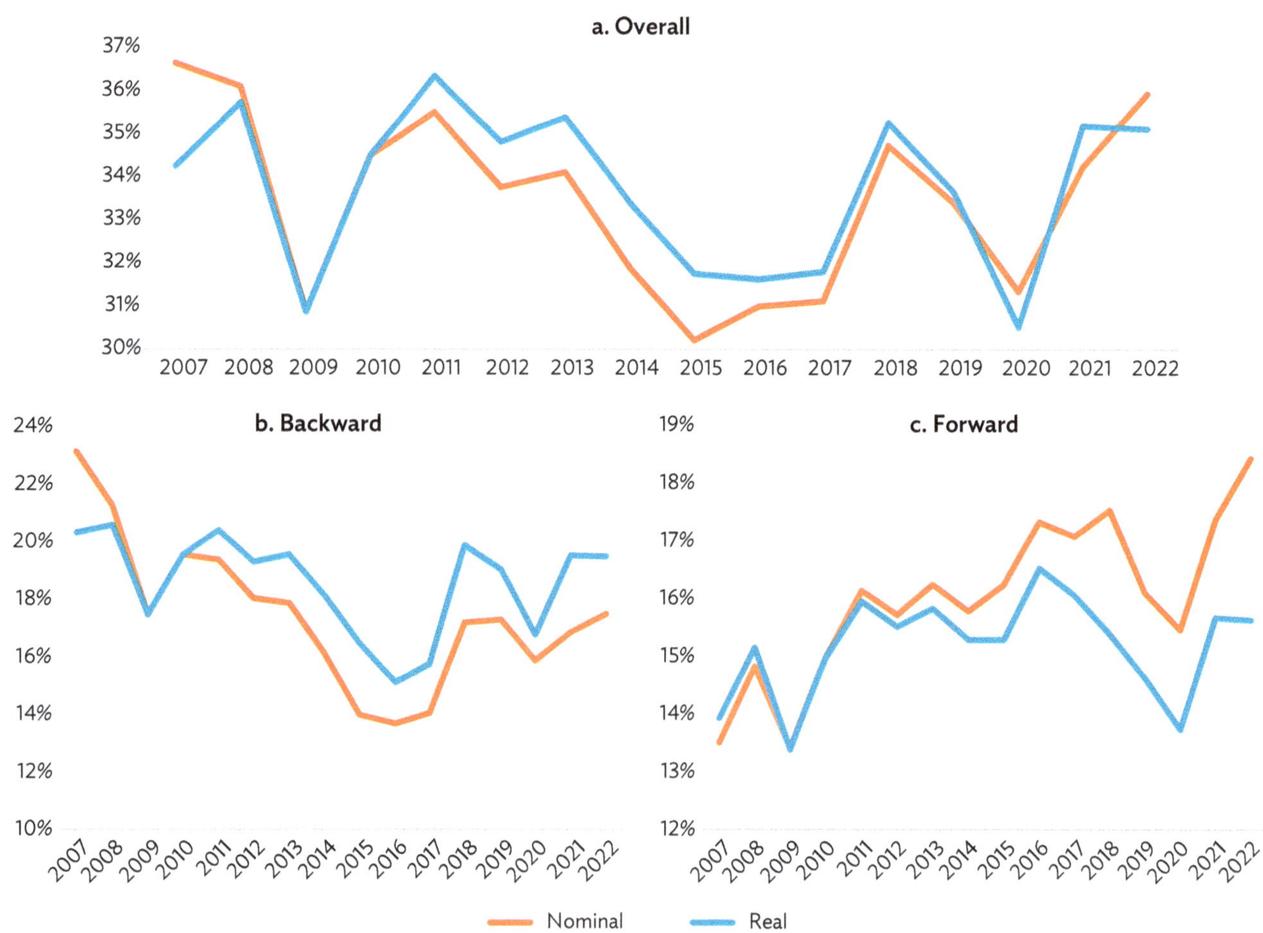

GVC = Global Value Chains.
Source: Asian Development Bank (ADB) calculations using the nominal and real ADB Multiregional Input-Output Tables 2007–2022.

Between 2007 and 2013, the nominal and real GVC participation rates of the US largely coincided with each other (Figure 3.8.a). Between 2014 and 2020, the US dollar generally appreciated against the currencies of the largest exporters to the economy, coinciding with the real series dominating, while the dollar price wedge expanded, narrowing only by 2021. Further, by 2022, the US dollar picked up strength, and the economy's participation rate reached record levels both in nominal and constant terms.

In nominal terms, the US's backward participation rates had generally been stable from 2007–2022, varying within a relatively narrow range, except in 2009, 2016, and 2020 (Figure 3.8.b.). The real participation rate, on the other hand, had been increasing overall since 2009, surging in 2018, and recovering quickly from the 2020 pandemic slump to surpass even the 2018 levels by 2022. The real trend started to diverge from the nominal trend, and dominate it from 2014. The price wedge between the nominal and real trends has been significant ever since, reaching the maximum in the series in 2022.

Figure 3.8: GVC Participation Rate, United States, 2007–2022

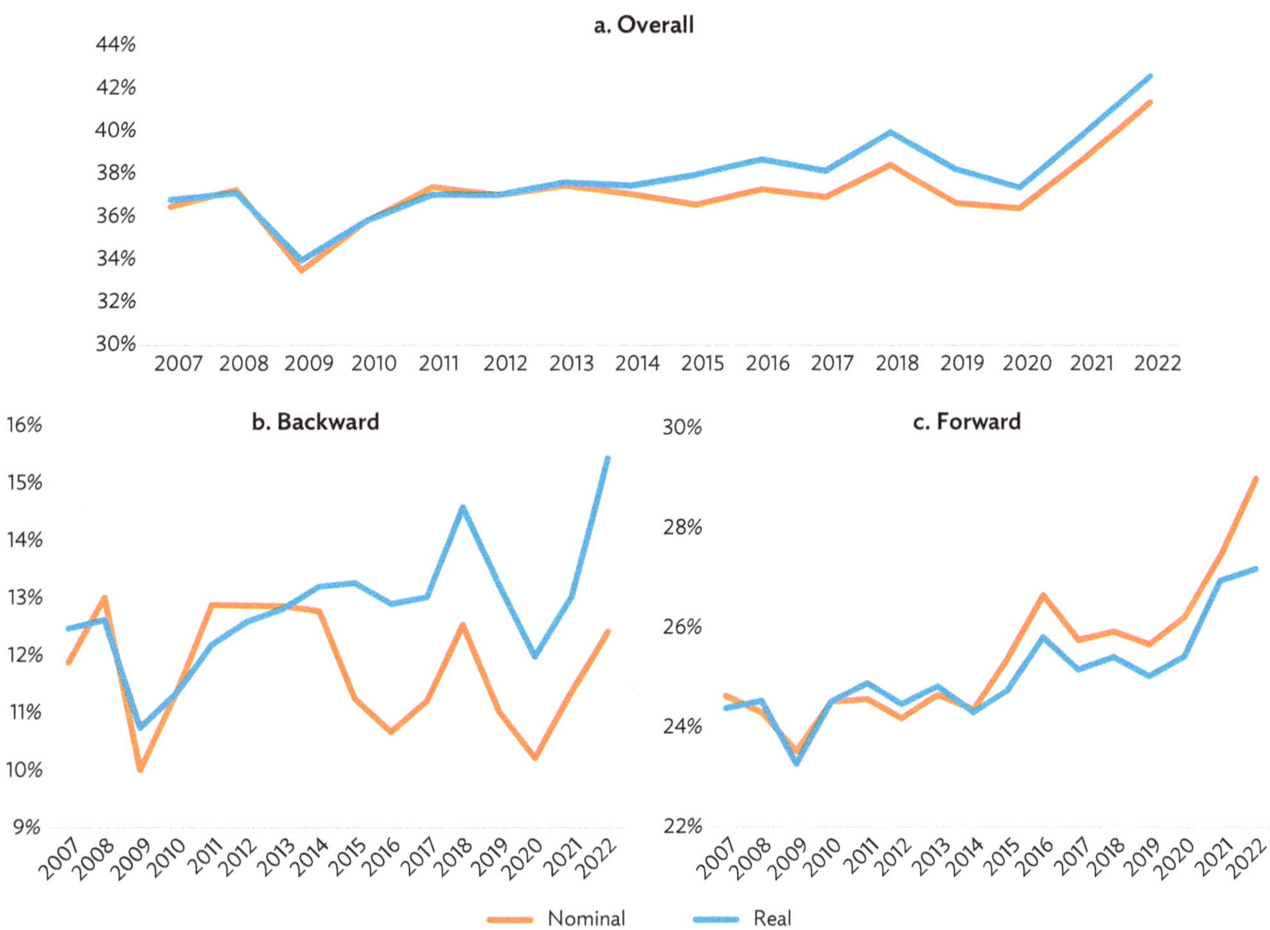

GVC = Global Value Chains.
Source: Asian Development Bank (ADB) calculations using the nominal and real ADB Multiregional Input-Output Tables 2007–2022.

Between 2007 and 2022, forward GVC participation of the US increased both in nominal and constant terms, with the nominal rates trending consistently above the real rates after 2014 (Figure 3.8.c.). Further, the corresponding wedge in the forward series was considerably smaller than the one in the backward series for any given year. While the same inflation and exchange rate factors influenced the price wedge in both series, the impact was considerably attenuated in forward participation.

Conclusion

Most of the research and analysis—whether it be for statistical, economic, or policy purposes—on GVCs are principally based on nominal value supply-use tables (SUTs), input-output tables (IOTs), and multi-regional input-output tables (MRIOTs). While these nominal statistical frameworks can be used to discern the state and evolution of GVCs and to support relevant policy formulation, their relevance and accuracy can be diminished in times of significant changes in product prices or in currency exchange rates, as seen from the analysis presented in this chapter. As is the case with gross domestic product, for instance, the relevance and accuracy issue could largely be resolved by basing the relevant estimation and analysis on real value statistical frameworks.

However, while economies with advanced statistical systems produce real value national SUTs and IOTs periodically, to date, no organization has published real value MRIOTs ever since a WIOD initiative that culminated in 2016 with the release of tables for reference years 2001–2014. With the 2023 release of the nominal and real value MRIOTs for reference years 2007–2022, ADB has served to bridge this critical data gap which has been impeding GVC-related research and analysis at a time characterized by the post-pandemic inflation surge and currency volatility.

Using nominal and real MRIOTs for 2007–2022, this chapter highlights the polarity effects that inflation and exchange rate changes have on GVC-related statistics and analysis, thereby affecting information and inferences that could illuminate policy. Further, this chapter details a method to isolate the dollar price effect on GVC statistics and discern the pure effect of technological and structural changes on the state and evolution of GVCs and of an economy's participation in them.

Revealing the presence of differences between nominal and real values at the global and select-case economy level is intended to facilitate further discourse and research on the subject matter. This would be particularly useful in cases of economies that display large, persistent, and unpredictable disparities, or even polarity. Taking further steps to capture and understand the dollar price wedge could become an important statistical and economic tool as it offers the possibility of potential interventions with more information to base decisions on.

References

Asian Development Bank (ADB). 2023. Multiregional Input-Output Database. http://kidb.adb.org (accessed 5 July 2023).

A. Borin and M. Mancini. 2019. Measuring What Matters in Global Value Chains and Value-Added Trade. *World Bank Policy Research Working Paper.* No. 8804. Washington, DC. World Bank. https://documents1.worldbank.org/curated/en/639481554384583291/pdf/Measuring-What-Matters-in-Global-Value-Chains-and-Value-Added-Trade.pdf.

Statistical Office of the European Communities (Eurostat). 2016. Handbook on prices and volume measures in national accounts. Luxembourg. Publications Office of the European Union. https://ec.europa.eu/eurostat/documents/3859598/7152852/KS-GQ-14-005-EN-N.pdf/839297d1-3456-487b-8788-24e47b7d98b2?t=1613384990563.

International Monetary Fund (IMF). 2022. Exchange Rates incl. Effective Ex. Rates. International Financial Statistics. https://data.imf.org/regular.aspx?key=61545850. (accessed 13 July 2023).

H. Jongrim, M.A. Kose, and F. Ohnsorge. 2021. One-Stop Source: A Global Database of Inflation. *Policy Research Working Paper*. No. 9737. World Bank. Washington DC. https://www.worldbank.org/en/research/brief/inflation-database. (accessed 16 May 2023).

PART IV

Stories Behind Data—Using Price Data and Statistics to Track Socioeconomic Development

Overview

Price data and statistics serve a wide range of purposes for development practitioners and policymakers. In the case of the COVID-19 pandemic, data on fluctuations in prices of consumer goods and services, in particular costs for face masks, medical equipment, and medicines, helped authorities develop pandemic-related policies to ensure these essential items were kept affordable at a time when they were needed most.

As previously mentioned in this report, the Russian invasion of Ukraine further contributed to supply chain disruptions that emerged during the pandemic, pushing prices to levels not seen for decades. These inflationary pressures have caused an increased cost of living crisis, with the impacts being felt most amongst the extreme poor. In this difficult environment, price and inflation data are critical in helping policy makers formulate actions and interventions to minimize the adverse impacts of high inflation.

Irrespective of the pandemic, price data have always been an important source of information for policymakers. In Part II of the report, we noted how central banks regularly examine inflation data to keep track of price movements over time, which in turn, become the basis for inflation targets and the setting of interest rates. Spatial variations in prices of essential goods and services also inform policies regarding cost of living, minimum wages, and determination of poverty thresholds.

National statistical systems routinely collect data on prices and among various indices, the consumer price index (CPI) is one of the most commonly compiled development indicators. The CPI is designed to measure how prices of goods and services commonly consumed by households change over time. In addition to the CPI, government statisticians also compile other price indices, such as the producer price index (PPI), export and import price index, residential property price index, and others. The CPI and other indices track price movements temporally within an economy or a geographical area.

Another key price data gathering initiative across economies of the world is the International Comparison Program (ICP), one of the largest and longest-running statistical initiatives in the world (WBG 2021a). It measures price levels across economies and produces purchasing power parities (PPPs). PPPs are the ratio of prices in the national currency of a specific basket of goods and services in an economy to the cost of purchasing the same basket in a reference economy.

While the scope of the CPI is temporal price movements over time for household consumption expenditures within a single economy, the PPPs reflect spatial price indices across economies for the same time period, with their scope covering all main categories of gross domestic product including household consumption expenditures. The PPPs allow comparisons of price levels across economies and of 'real' gross domestic product and its components across economies by expressing these metrics in a common currency.

The ICP is a global partnership implemented under the auspices of the United Nations Statistical Commission (UNSC) with the World Bank leading the implementation of the program in collaboration with regional and international development partners and national statistical agencies. Since the 2005 ICP benchmark, the Asian Development Bank has led the implementation of ICP for Asia and the Pacific (ADB 2019)[1]. The UNSC has now made the ICP a permanent part of its global statistical program, highlighting its important role for policymaking (ADB 2020; WBG n.d.).

This chapter briefly describes the importance of price statistics in policymaking and turns its focus on the ICP, highlighting the importance of ICP in providing measures of comparisons of price levels and real sizes of economies across the world through a collaborative global partnership. It discusses the critical role of statistical agencies of the participating economies of the world in its implementation, and finally presents experiences of the 22 economies that participated in the implementation of the 2017 ICP in Asia and the Pacific and their efforts to integrate ICP implementation with the regular CPI price collection.

How Are Price Data Used for Policymaking?

Data on movements in prices paid by consumers are an important resource for policy makers in formulating a wide array of programs for socioeconomic development.

Inflation has deep impacts across an economy, including on consumer spending, business investment, job creation, government programs relating to tax policies, interest rates, and other areas (Andres and Hernando 1997; Barro 1995). In general, very low inflation can signal weakness in an economy and potential risk for deflation, while very high inflation can signal an overheated economy and the threat of uncontrolled price hikes if left unchecked. National authorities typically target moderate inflation levels ranging from 2% to 4%, to ensure prices are kept relatively stable and financial stability is maintained, while governments roll out programs to promote economic growth (Ball 1992).

The term inflation is typically used in reference to the consumer price index, or CPI, one of the indicators commonly used to track changes in cost of living.[2] It includes headline CPI and core CPI, which are typically reported by government statistics offices. In general, the CPI captures temporal changes in prices paid for a market

1 Other agencies implementing the program at the regional levels are: African Development Bank (AfDB); Statistical Office of the European Communities (Eurostat); Organisation for Economic Co-operation and Development (OECD); Interstate Statistical Committee of the Commonwealth of Independent States (CIS-STAT); the United Nations Economic and Social Commission for Western Asia (UN-ESCWA); and United Nations Economic Commission for Latin America and the Caribbean (UN-ECLAC).

2 Box 4.1 presents a discussion of how cost of living is measured empirically.

basket of goods and services commonly consumed by households. The breakdown of items typically follows the categories of the Classification of Individual Consumption by Purpose (COICOP) developed by the United Nations Statistics Division (UN 2018). Core CPI excludes categories such as food and energy as these prices may be volatile or sensitive to factors outside the broader economy. Headline CPI captures all categories (IMF et al. 2020). CPI data is usually compiled monthly, highlighting the importance of it as a source of timely information on price movements for policymaking. Table 4.1, meanwhile, shows examples of specific policy uses of data derived from consumer price movements.

Table 4.1: Policy Uses of Data on Consumer Price Movements

Use	Remarks
Indexation of wage	One of the original rationales behind compilation of consumer price data was the need to link wage determination to a price index that captures cost of living.
Indexation of social security benefits	In a number of economies, it is a common practice to index the rates at which social security benefits (e.g., retirement pensions, unemployment benefits, sickness benefits, child allowances) are payable based on consumer price data.
Indexation of interest, rents, and other contractual payments	Payments for rents and interest are commonly indexed to the CPI. It is also possible for housing rent payments to be associated with the CPI or another index, like a house price index.
Taxation	Changes in CPI can impact tax payments in multiple ways. Tax laws can be modified to include some form of indexing.
Real consumption and real income	Price indices deflate expenses and income to obtain real consumption and income measures, which involve volume comparisons over time or space.

Source: Asian Development Bank summary based on IMF's Consumer Price Index Manual: Concepts and Method 2020.

Box 4.1: How is the Cost of Living Measured?

Since the cost of living has a profound effect on people's well-being it is important to collect data on it and assess the different impacts across demographic groups and how this can change over time (The Lancet Public Health 2022). National statistical systems, particularly national statistics offices, are at the forefront of collecting data on prices of goods and services used to estimate the cost of living in a specific economy.

The standard of living and cost of living are two interrelated economic concepts that are important when examining trends in quality of living. The standard of living is associated with quality of life, while cost of living represents the amount of money needed to support a specific standard of living (Latimaha, Ismail, and Bahari 2020).

At the individual level, standard of living may be quantified based on a person's income, consumption, expenditures, employment and other economic opportunities, health, and education. For economy-wide indicators, gross domestic product per capita and the Human Development Index (HDI) are among the most commonly used aggregate measures (Bérenger and Verdier-Chouchane 2007).

To compile a consumer price index, most governments gather data to monitor changes in the prices of a basket of goods and services commonly consumed by households, usually based on weights derived from the economy household consumption expenditure surveys. The price data may also help determine the living wage or the minimum amount of money a family needs to meet their basic needs (IMF et al. 2020). At the global level, the International Comparison Program (ICP) collects data on prices for the purpose of compiling purchasing power parities (PPPs), price level indexes and PPP based measures of gross domestic product (GDP) expenditures for economies of the world.

(continued on next page)

Box 4.1: How is the Cost of Living Measured? *(continued)*

As shown in the table below, data on prices are also monitored by other research agencies and private institutions, such as the Economist Intelligence Unit (EIU), Numbeo, and Mercer, that each compile their own cost-of-living index for major cities of several world economies to help companies assess the appropriate level of compensation for employees residing in different cities across world. On the other hand, price level indexes for household consumption from the ICP provide a measure of costs of living across economies.

Across the indices in the table, there are variations in the list of specific goods and services included in calculations, while data collection and index compilation methods may also differ, which must be taken into account when comparing results from these different measures.

Index	Data Collection Approach	Global Coverage	Frequency of update
Consumer Price Index	Prices collected to produce CPIs for 12 commodity groups and lower levels following COICOP classification.	National and subnational coverage	Usually, monthly
ICP's Purchasing Power Parity and Price level Index	Participating economies collect and compile data on prices of a comparable basket of household and nonhousehold items, GDP expenditures, population estimates, and market exchange rates. Follows framework of System of National Accounts and related classifications. Economy-wide collection of prices from representative sample outlets in rural and urban areas.	176 economies in the latest 2017 ICP benchmark (19 economies from East Asia and the Pacific, 6 economies from Central Asia, and 7 economies from South Asia) Non-participating economies are imputed using regression models	Usually once in six years in the past. Latest 2017 ICP benchmark available. Extrapolation for years post benchmark by - World Development Indicators (WDI) Next ICP comparison is ongoing for reference year 2021
EIU's Worldwide Cost of Living Index	Price data are collected from supermarkets, medium-priced retailers, and more expensive specialty shops. Compares more than 400 individual prices across more than 200 products and services.	172 cities (in 2022)	twice a year
Numbeo Cost of Living Index	Data collected from authoritative sources such as websites of supermarkets, taxi company websites, governmental institutions, newspaper articles, and other surveys	540 cities, 136 from Asia and the Pacific and includes indexes for cities and economy levels.	twice a year
Mercer Cost of Living Index	Evaluates more than 200 goods and services, highlights essential factors such as currency fluctuations, cost inflation, and accommodation price instability.	400 cities	twice a year

COICOP = Classification of Individual Consumption by Purpose, CPI = consumer price index, GDP = gross domestic product.

Notes: The information presented in this table corresponds to commonly used metrics for cost of living but does not constitute an exhaustive list.

Sources: Asian Development Bank summary based on information presented by International Labour Organization; International Comparison Program (ICP) – World Bank; The Economist Intelligence Unit (The EIU); Numbeo and Mercer (accessed 20 March 2023).

(continued on next page)

Box 4.1: How is the Cost of Living Measured? *(continued)*

Among different measures presented in the Table that compare cost of living across cities and/or the economies of the world, Numbeo presents such indexes for a large number of economies of the world in addition to more than 500 major cities. Despite methodological differences of Numbeo's Cost of Living Index with ICP, it presents an opportunity to compare the economy level Cost of Living Index with the Price Level Indexes (PLIs) for household consumption expenditures from ICP. The Figure below plots the rankings of 112 economies common between Numbeo and the ICP database for the year 2017 – the latest benchmark year for which ICP comparisons are available. The rankings of economies are based on the Cost of Living Index for Numbeo and PLI for household consumption expenditures from the ICP for the year 2017. The higher the Cost of Living Index or the PLI, the higher the rank for the corresponding measure. In general, the Figure shows that rankings of several economies are clustered around the diagonal of the rectangle pointing to similarities in rankings, however, for many economies the rankings are quite different from the two measures. This could be because of differences in the composition of the goods and services, methods and sources of data, and more importantly the methods and weights used in aggregating product prices to an overall measure of cost of living.

Correlation between Different Metrics of Cost of Living

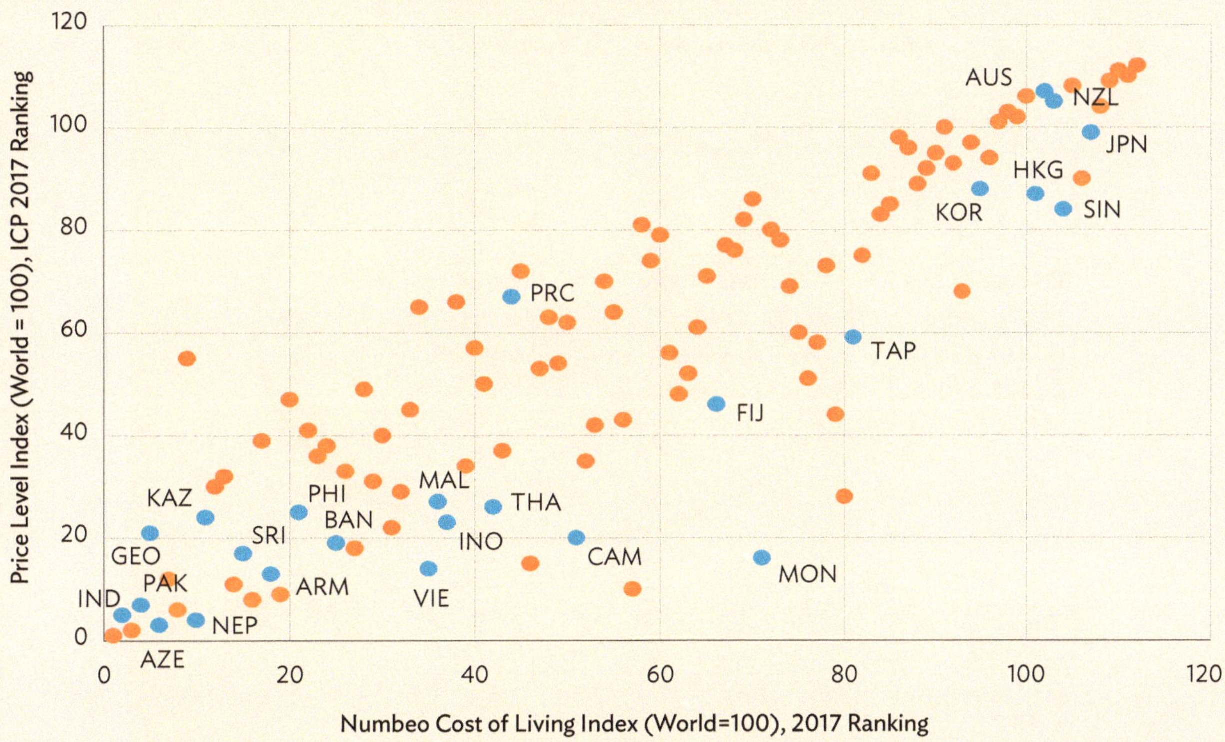

ARM = Armenia, AUS = Australia, AZE = Azerbaijan, BAN = Bangladesh, CAM = Cambodia, FIJ = Fiji, GEO = Georgia, HKG = Hong Kong, China, IND = India, INO = Indonesia, JPN = Japan, KAZ = Kazakhstan, KOR =Republic of Korea, MAL =Malaysia, MON = Mongolia, NEP = Nepal, NZL = New Zealand, PAK = Pakistan, PHI = Philippines, PRC = People's Republic of China, SIN = Singapore, SRI = Sri Lanka, TAP = Taipei,China, THA = Thailand, VIE = Viet Nam

Note: Rebased Numbeo Cost of Living Index to (World=100) from (New York=100) using average of all economies. Economies are then matched with ICP data and are ranked from the lowest (least expensive) to highest (most expensive).

Source: Asian Development Bank visualization based on Numbeo data (accessed 30 June 2023) and 2017 ICP data. https://databank.worldbank.org/source/icp-2017# (accessed 30 June 2023).

Importantly, the latest cost of living index data from the main indices available annually, all point to a significant recent spike in the cost of living. For example, the EIU's Worldwide Cost of Living Index for 2022 shows that, on average, prices in local-currency terms in the world's biggest cities increased by 8.1% compared to 2021. This is the fastest rate observed since 2000, signaling a global cost-of-living crisis triggered by the Russian invasion of Ukraine and previous COVID-19 pandemic-related restrictions.

Differences between producer and consumer prices provide insights into the evolution of global value chains over time.

While Part III of this report discussed recent trends in global value chains, differences between CPI and PPI provide additional insights into the extent to which firms continue to scale up production and allocate their resources more efficiently through the shift of production chains across borders. While the basket for CPI includes goods and services commonly consumed by the average person, including imports, the PPI is calculated based on all outputs that domestic producers sell, including intermediate goods and services, but excluding imports. This means that the PPI measures the average cost for a producer and is often used to adjust revenue streams in order to measure output growth in real terms (Figure 4.1).

Figure 4.1: Difference between CPI and PPI

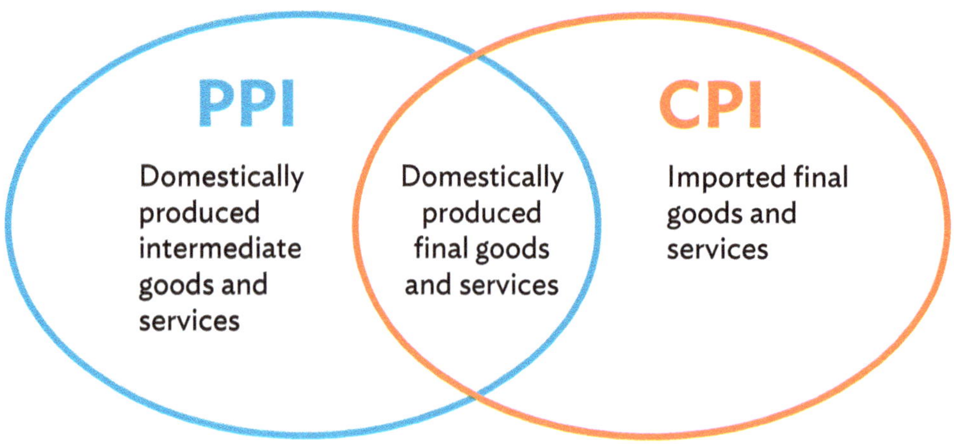

Source: Asian Development Bank visualization adopted from Box 3.1 of ADB's *Key Indicators for Asia and the Pacific 2016.*

While it is commonly expected that trends in the PPI and CPI will vary due to differences in how they are composed and weighted, there is evidence that they moved in similar patterns until the 2000s. More recent data from Asia, however, shows diverging trends. Global value chains can provide an explanation for this growing divergence as companies now conduct different stages of production in different locations, making it less likely that producer and consumer prices will move together.

This is partly due to trade liberalization and technological advancements that have made it easier for companies to find locations with lower costs and better resources. As a result, there are an increasing numbers of imported consumer goods and services not included in the basket used to calculate PPI, which explains the weaker correlation between PPI and CPI movements. Nonetheless, this issue remains an important policy concern for some economies (Wei and Xie 2019).

DB team and price experts from participating economies conducting technical
view and data validation workshops for the 2021 ICP for Asia and the Pacific.

The International Comparison Program (ICP)

The ICP is one the largest and longest running global statistical initiatives, highlighting the importance of PPPs and related indicators in policy making.

Measurements for comparisons of incomes and standards of living across economies often rely on market exchange rates. However, this method of measurement does not capture differences in price levels and real incomes. To provide reliable measures of comparable price levels across economies, the International Comparison Program (ICP) was initiated in 1968. PPPs produced from ICP are used to convert GDP expenditures recorded in currencies of individual economies to a common currency and at the same time equalize the purchasing powers of different currencies by eliminating the differences in price levels across economies, thus providing real measures to compare economic size and per capita measures. The expenditure estimates expressed in PPP terms provide real comparisons across economies as the expenditures converted using exchange rates, do not take into account, price level differences across economies, and are also affected by fluctuations in exchange rates. Evolving over time, the ICP was established as a permanent global statistical program in 2016 by the United Nations Statistical Commission (UNSC) under the overall management of the World Bank. The ICP is implemented through a unique partnership of economies, regional agencies, and multilateral agencies, with a governance structure for coordinating the program at national, regional, and global levels.

The ICP started as a small research project in 1968, in collaboration with the United Nations Statistical Office and the International Comparisons Unit of the University of Pennsylvania, funded from several sources, including the Ford Foundation and the World Bank. The goal was to set up a regular program of global PPP-based comparisons of GDP. While the first comparisons from the research project involved just 10 economies, over time it has become one of the largest global statistical programs with 176 economies participating in the most recent 2017 benchmark cycle. (Figure 4.2).

Over time ICP has continuously evolved and participation has expanded making it a truly global program.

The need for real comparisons of income and expenditure aggregates across economies in the international context, and the limitations of using market exchange rates for comparing sizes of economies, led to the establishment of the ICP. Since its creation,

Figure 4.2: Number of Participating Economies in the ICP

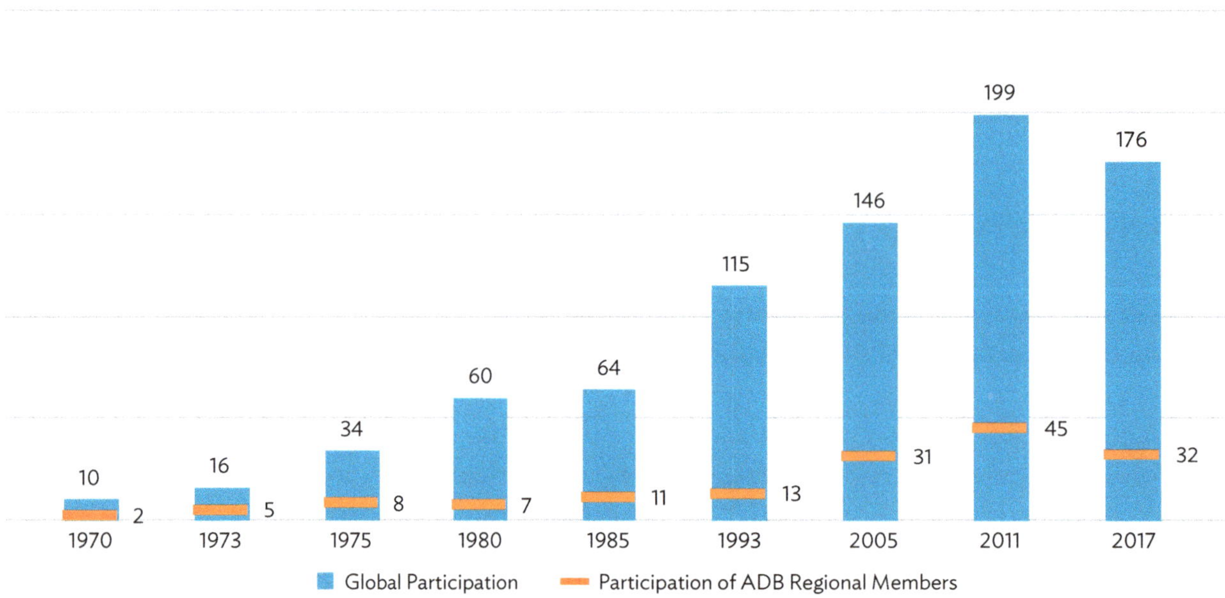

ADB = Asian Development Bank, ICP = International Comparison Program, RIA = regional implementing agency.

Notes: The number of ADB regional members is based on the current membership of ADB. ADB took the responsibility as the RIA for the ICP Asia-Pacific region from the 2005 benchmark. For the 2005 ICP, ADB as the regional implementing agency for Asia and the Pacific coordinated the participation of 21 regional members: Bangladesh; Bhutan; Brunei Darussalam; Cambodia; Fiji; Hong Kong, China; India; Indonesia; the Lao People's Democratic Republic; Malaysia; Maldives; Mongolia; Nepal; Pakistan; the People's Republic of China; the Philippines; Singapore; Sri Lanka; Taipei,China; Thailand; and Viet Nam. Some of the ADB regional members, namely, Australia, Japan, New Zealand, and the Republic of Korea are traditionally part of the comparisons undertaken by the Organisation for Economic Co-operation and Development (OECD). Additionally, ADB regional members in Central and West Asia, namely, Armenia, Azerbaijan, Georgia, Kazakhstan, the Kyrgyz Republic, and Tajikistan, are traditionally covered under the regional ICP coordinated by the Interstate Statistical Committee of the Commonwealth of Independent States (CIS-STAT). For the 2011 ICP cycle, out of 45 ADB regional members who participated, 22 regional members were coordinated by ADB; 13 Pacific Islands economies participated in Pacific Islands comparisons coordinated by the Australian Bureau of Statistics (ABS) but their participation was limited to household consumption; 4 regional members (Australia, Japan, New Zealand, and the Republic of Korea) were part of OECD comparisons and five (Armenia, Azerbaijan, Kazakhstan, the Kyrgyz Republic, and Tajikistan) were covered by CIS-STAT. Georgia participated as a singleton economy. For the 2017 ICP cycle, 32 ADB member economies participated, 22 of which were directly coordinated by ADB, while the remaining were part of OECD and CIS-STAT comparisons and Georgia as singleton participation as in 2011 ICP.

Sources: The Asian Development Bank from the *International Comparison Program for Asia and the Pacific*. https://icp.adb.org/about-icp and the World Bank from the International Comparison Program https://www.worldbank.org/en/programs/icp.

it has continuously improved by adopting new methodologies for PPP computations, strengthening its governance framework, and increasing geographic coverage to become truly global (Figure 4.3). ADB in its study (ADB 2020) provides a detailed history of the global comparisons and evolution of ICP since the early 20th century.

The earlier phases of ICP in the 1970s and 1980s saw extensive methodological developments with contributions from researchers at the University of Pennsylvania. As participation of economies increased in the 1980s, the ICP moved to the United Nations Statistical Office (now known as the United Nations Statistics Division), with ongoing technical advice from the University of Pennsylvania. Prior to 1985, the main use of PPPs from the ICP was for comparisons of real expenditures across economies. Starting with the 1985 ICP, PPPs for household consumption were used by World Bank researchers to develop an international poverty line which popularly became known as the dollar-a-day poverty line. This signaled the start of the use of PPPs from the ICP to calibrate the international poverty line to monitor absolute poverty in the world. As discussed in Part I, the extreme poverty line is currently $2.15 which is based on the PPPs for household consumption from the latest available 2017 ICP cycle.

Figure 4.3: ICP Through the Years

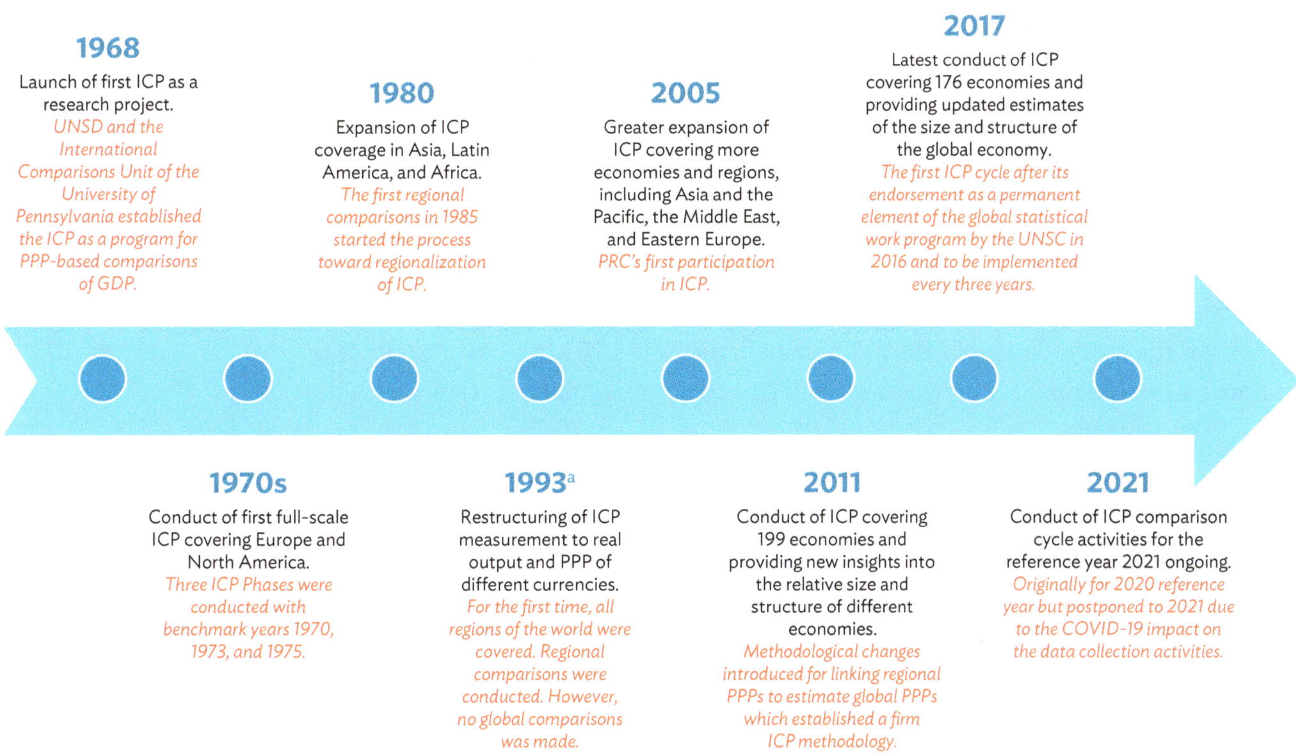

GDP = gross domestic product, ICP = International Comparison Program, PPP = purchasing power parity, UNSC = United Nations Statistical Commission, UNSD = United Nations Statistics Division.

[a] In 1990, The International Comparison Project was renamed as the International Comparison Program.

Sources: The Asian Development Bank from the *2017 International Comparison Program for Asia and the Pacific: Purchasing Power Parities and Real Expenditures* and the World Bank from the International Comparison Program https://www.worldbank.org/en/programs/icp.

The 2005 ICP began a new era as the ICP became a fully global partnership with stakeholders at the national, regional, and global levels.

The 2005 ICP was a landmark round as it ushered in a new global governance framework to address the institutional, organizational, and operational issues that emerged in the 1990s with the program increasing coverage of economies across all regions of the world. In 2005, a governance structure was established to make ICP a fully global partnership with several regional organizations invited to function as regional implementing agencies. These are the African Development Bank, ADB, Interstate Statistical Committee of the Commonwealth of Independent States (CIS-STAT), United Nations Economic Commission for Latin America and the Caribbean, United Nations Economic and Social Commission for Western Asia and the Eurostat, and OECD. Their role is to coordinate the regional comparisons and produce regional PPPs. The ICP Global Office was established at the World Bank and was given the responsibility to coordinate the program across all regions and to undertake computations of global PPPs by linking the regional PPPs.

The ICP also seeks to maximize synergies between its own operations and the statistical programs of national agencies in areas of price collection and the compilation of national accounts statistics. In the 2005 ICP benchmark, the number of participating economies grew to 146, with the People's Republic of China participating for the first time. Operational guidelines for standardized implementation and methodologies for regional and global comparisons were developed to overcome shortcomings of earlier phases. In 2011 the ICP saw some critical methodological changes, including linking regional PPPs, computed by the regional implementing agencies, to enable computation of the global PPPs by the World Bank. The number of participating economies in 2011 reached its highest level at 199, the only ICP benchmark in which 20 Pacific Island economies participated, with the Australian Bureau of Statistics taking up the coordination role[3]. With the methodologies firmly established, the 2017 ICP with 176 participating economies, saw no further changes and this allowed comparability of results with the 2011 ICP benchmark.

The International Comparison Program has become a permanent element of the global statistical program of the United Nations Statistical Commission.

Because of cost issues, ICP cycles have been implemented only for specific benchmark years. PPPs for nonbenchmark years have been conventionally estimated using extrapolation techniques. Recognizing the increasing demand from users for more frequent and reliable PPPs, the UNSC at its 47th Session in 2016 agreed to make the ICP a permanent element of the global statistical program, with benchmarks to be conducted over three-year cycles beginning with the 2017 ICP. However, due to the COVID-19

3 The participation of 20 Pacific Island economies in the 2011 ICP was limited to household consumption only. Since the 2005 ICP cycle, Fiji has been a part of the Asia Pacific region of ICP, which is coordinated by ADB.

pandemic, the 2020 cycle was postponed with 2021 becoming the new reference year instead. The 2021 ICP cycle is ongoing, with the results expected to provide insights into the impact of the pandemic on price structures and real expenditures in economies.

The governance structure of the ICP is given in Figure 4.4. It comprises the ICP Governing Board, which provides strategic leadership and sets policies and priorities for the ICP, with representatives from 11 participating economies and the regional and international agencies involved in ICP implementation. The Inter-Agency Coordination Group (IACG), which comprises the regional implementing agencies from the ICP regions responsible for steering the regional program operations and calculating regional PPPs, and the World Bank as global coordinating agency responsible for linking regional results for computation of global PPPs. The national implementing agencies, who are typically the national statistics offices of participating economies in each region, play the most important role of collecting price survey, GDP expenditure and other data, and providing it to the implementing agencies compiling the regional PPPs. And lastly, the ICP Technical Advisory Group is an independent body of experts with the responsibility of ensuring the methodological soundness and quality of ICP results.

Figure 4.4: International Comparison Program Governance Structure

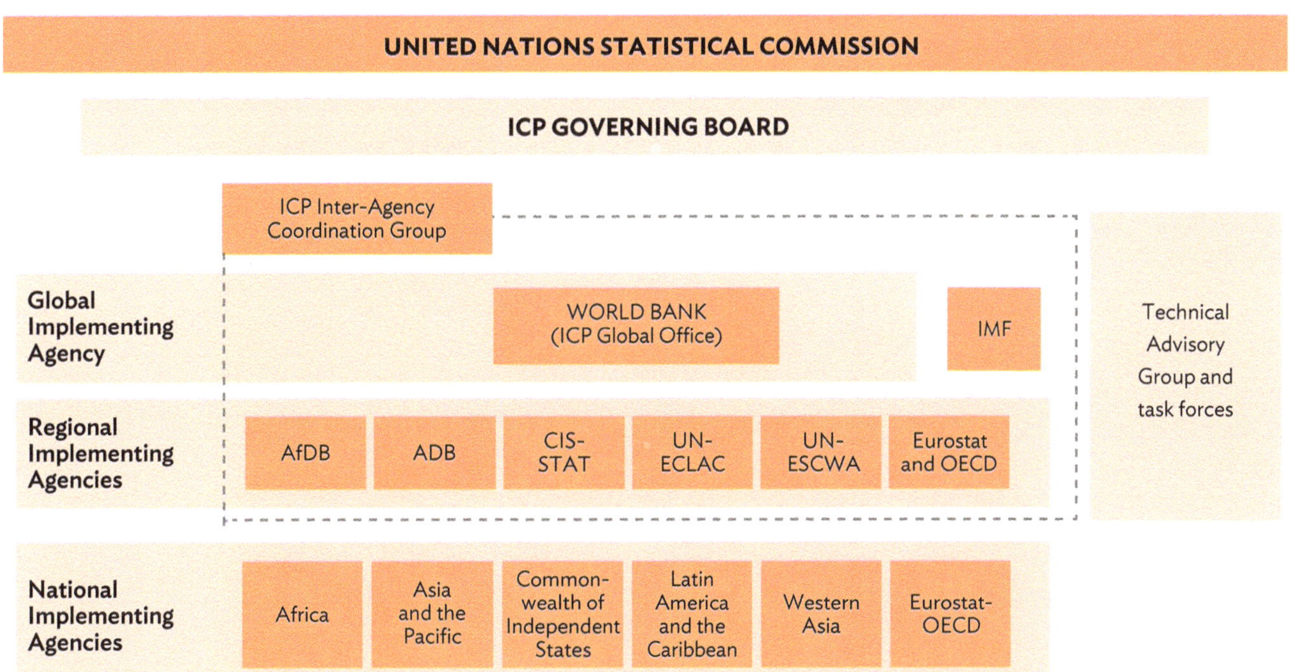

Note: AfDB = African Development Bank; ADB = Asian Development Bank; CIS-STAT = Interstate Statistical Committee of the Commonwealth of Independent States; UN-ECLAC = United Nations Economic Commission for Latin America and the Caribbean; UN-ESCWA = United Nations Economic and Social Commission for Western Asia; Eurostat = Statistical Office of the European Union; OECD = Organisation for Economic Co-operation and Development; IMF = International Monetary Fund.

Source: Adopted from p. 83 of the Asian Development Bank *2017 International Comparison Program for Asia and the Pacific: Purchasing Power Parities and Real Expenditures.*

Annual average prices for a basket of comparable and representative goods and services covering all GDP components and expenditures are used to calculate regional and global PPPs.

The computation of PPPs for GDP and its components is a data intensive exercise that is only possible as a result of the contributions of the national statistical agencies who collect the required input data. During an ICP benchmark year, participating economies in each region are required to provide specific data sets which include national annual average prices for a pre-defined basket of goods and services of household final consumption expenditures, government final consumption expenditures, gross fixed capital formation (including construction and machinery and equipment items), and gross domestic product expenditures (disaggregated into 155 subcomponents called basic headings), market exchange rates, and size of resident population (ADB 2020, WBG n.d.[4]).

The framework and scope of the ICP are defined by the *System of National Accounts*[5] and hence the price surveys are designed to be consistent with national accounts practices. This implies that the prices of products selected for price surveys from the regional item basket should be representative of the goods and services in the final consumption and investments of GDP expenditures of each economy in the region. At the same time, the representativity of the products is to be balanced with comparability of products across all economies in the region and across all regions.

To ensure comparability across all economies within a region and across all regions of the world, standard product lists of items of (i) household consumption, (ii) construction, (iii) machinery & equipment, (iv) housing rental, and (v) government compensation are used for price collection surveys. These product lists provide a 'structured product description' for each item which contains price determining characteristics to ensure that the same product specifications are priced by all economies on a 'like-with-like' basis. The balance between representativity of the products within the economy and the need for comparability across economies is achieved through consultations with participating economies and with regional and global agencies in preparing and updating the product lists for each cycle. It must also be noted that structured product descriptions are revised from one cycle to another due to changes in market conditions.

For regional comparisons, each region has its own list of items which are used for regional comparisons and estimation of regional PPPs. The region-specific items as mentioned earlier, are expected to be representative of the expenditure patterns of the economies in the region. These regional lists are supplemented with additional items selected from a global core list, which is prepared by the World Bank in consultation with regional

4 The World Bank International Comparison Program. https://www.worldbank.org/en/programs/icp/methodology.

5 The United Nations (UN), European Commission, International Monetary Fund, Organisation for Economic Co-operation and Development and World Bank. 2009. *System of National Accounts 2008*. https://unstats.un.org/unsd/nationalaccount/docs/SNA2008.pdf.

implementing agencies. The regional PPPs are estimated using the prices of items in the regional lists, while the prices of global core lists are used to derive linking factors to estimate the global PPPs from the regional PPPs. Each economy undertakes price surveys from a nationally representative sample of outlets for a subset of items that are part of the regional product lists to compile annual average prices. The items are representative of the expenditures in the economy and prices are collected on a monthly, quarterly, or six-monthly frequency, or on a once-in-a-year basis depending on the product characteristics and price variability. Table 4.2 summarizes the price surveys and number of items in the product lists used in the 2017 ICP for Asia and the Pacific, which was coordinated by ADB.

The principle of high data quality is integral to ICP implementation and sophisticated statistical tools have been developed to validate data quality and comparability across all participating economies. The price data validation process is carried out in three stages. First, is the national or intra-economy validation stage, where prices for each item compiled by a single economy are validated within the economy to correct for outlier price quotations. The prices are submitted to the regional agencies where inter-economy data validation is performed to identify outliers and inconsistent prices across economies (ADB 2020).

Table 4.2: Prices Surveys and Number of Items in Product Lists for the 2017 ICP in the Asia and Pacific Region

Survey	Survey Description	No. of Items in 2017 ICP Survey
Household consumption.	Captures the prices of goods and services typically consumed by the households in an economy. Household item prices are collected on a monthly or quarterly frequency from a representative sample of outlets to provide nationally representative prices.	1,054 items including 879 items for regional comparisons and 468 items for global linking.
Housing.	Captures annual average rents collected for a representative sample of dwellings. Additionally, indicators on number of dwellings, rooms, floor area, and facilities on access to drinking water, private toilet, and electricity are collected for housing stock in the economy.	20 dwelling types representing apartments and houses of different sizes.
Government consumption.	Captures annual average compensation paid to government employees engaged in selected occupations in production of health, education, and collective services provided by the government. The data is collected from government administrative records of payments made to the employees.	35 government occupations.
Gross fixed capital formation in construction.	Captures prices of construction items which include material inputs, rental paid for construction equipment, and labor inputs commonly used in the construction of residential buildings, nonresidential buildings, and civil engineering structures. This is a one-time survey conducted in the reference year from a representative sample of suppliers.	52 construction inputs comprising materials (34), equipment rental (10) and labor (8).
Gross fixed capital formation in machinery and equipment.	Captures prices for representative items of general and special purpose machinery, electrical and optical instruments, fabricated metal products, transport equipment, and other products that form part of the gross fixed capital formation. This is a one-time survey conducted in the reference year from a representative sample of suppliers	161 items of machinery and equipment.

ICP = International Comparison Program.
Source: Asian Development Bank.

Third, is the global or interregional validation stage, where prices are collected and compiled for all economies across all regions and are validated by the ICP global office at the World Bank. Outliers and inconsistencies identified at both regional and global levels are resolved by the participating economies cross-checking, verifying, and correcting data, if needed (ADB 2020, WBG 2020).

Results of the 2017 ICP provide data on purchasing power parities and real expenditures prior to the COVID-19 pandemic, making them especially useful to track post-pandemic economic recovery.[6]

During the 2017 ICP, 32 Asia Pacific economies participated, 22 of which were directly coordinated by ADB. These 32 regional economies account for about 56% of the global population. The results show these economies contributed 40% of the world's GDP using purchasing power parities, higher than the contribution of 34% when measured using market exchange rates.

Figure 4.5: Contribution to Global GDP, Nominal and Real

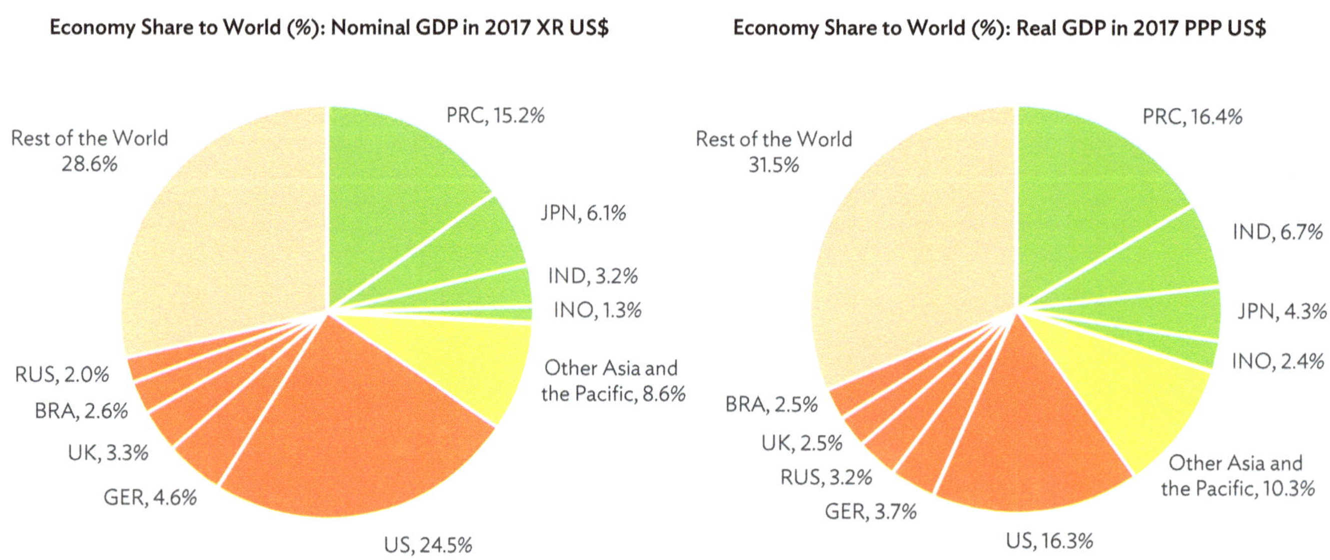

BRA = Brazil, GDP = Gross Domestic Product, GER = Germany, IND = India, INO = Indonesia, JPN = Japan, PRC = People's Republic of China, PPP = purchasing power parity, RUS = Russian Federation, UK = United Kingdom, US = United States, US$ = United States dollar, XR = Exchange Rate.

Source: The World Bank's International Comparison Program databank https://databank.worldbank.org/source/icp-2017 (accessed 7 October 2020).

[6] This section is based on the work of Joshi, Accad, and Song (2021). For additional details on the 2017 ICP Asia Pacific economies that were coordinated by the Asian Development Bank, readers may refer to the *2017 International Comparison Program for Asia and the Pacific: Purchasing Power Parities and Real Expenditures.* (ADB 2020).

Four of the regional economies are among the top 10 largest economies globally, based on purchasing power parities. The People's Republic of China ranks first with purchasing power parity-based GDP of $19.6 trillion, slightly above the United States with a GDP of $19.5 trillion. India and Japan rank third and fourth with $8.1 trillion and $5.2 trillion, respectively, while Indonesia is in 10th spot, with $2.9 trillion. The combined share of these four economies was about 30% of global GDP, and 74% of the total GDP of the 32 ADB regional members in purchasing power parity terms.

Similar to the increase in the shares of global consumption observed in the region's economies for the PPP-based GDP, eliminating differences in the prices also showed increases in the shares of household final consumptions expenditures (measured as actual consumption expenditure by households) and in shares of global investment expenditures (measured as gross fixed capital formation).

The 2017 ICP results also show that five economies—Australia, New Zealand, Japan, the Republic of Korea, and Hong Kong, China—had price levels higher than the world average (=100), while the rest had price levels below the world average of which 14 had price levels half (=50) or below half the world average.

A wide diversity is also seen in the per capita real GDP of the 32 Asia Pacific economies in comparison to the global average. The PPP-based per capita GDP for the 32 regional economies was $11,896 which is 28% lower than the world average of $16,596. Singapore was the third richest economy in the world, with per capita real GDP of $93,981—which was more than five times the global average. On the other side, Nepal had per capita income of only $2,900 which is just 17.5% of the world average. Figure 4.6 plots the Price Level Indices for 32 economies against GDP per capita in PPP terms (in log scale) with the pattern showing an expected upward sloping relationship, indicating that richer economies tend to have higher price levels as well.

At the subnational level, data on spatial variations of prices of goods and services can be used to examine a geographic area's competitive advantage and make comparisons about socioeconomic development.

From a policy perspective, it is important to collect spatially disaggregated price data to understand spatial variations in price levels and competitive advantage of locations. Significant declines or increases in prices of specific goods, commodities, or services in one geographic area relative to others may provide a basis for changes in the flow of trade or capital. At the subnational level, data on spatial price variations may help direct locale-specific policy initiatives. For example, Viet Nam publishes a Spatial Cost of Living Index (SCOLI) at subnational levels that reflects differences in the cost of living across administrative regions which provide insights on how living standards, economic performance, general productivity, and price competitiveness vary across geographic regions (Figure 4.7) (WBG 2021a).

Figure 4.6: Real Gross Domestic Product: Total, Per Capita, and Price Levels, 32 Asia Pacific Economies, 2017

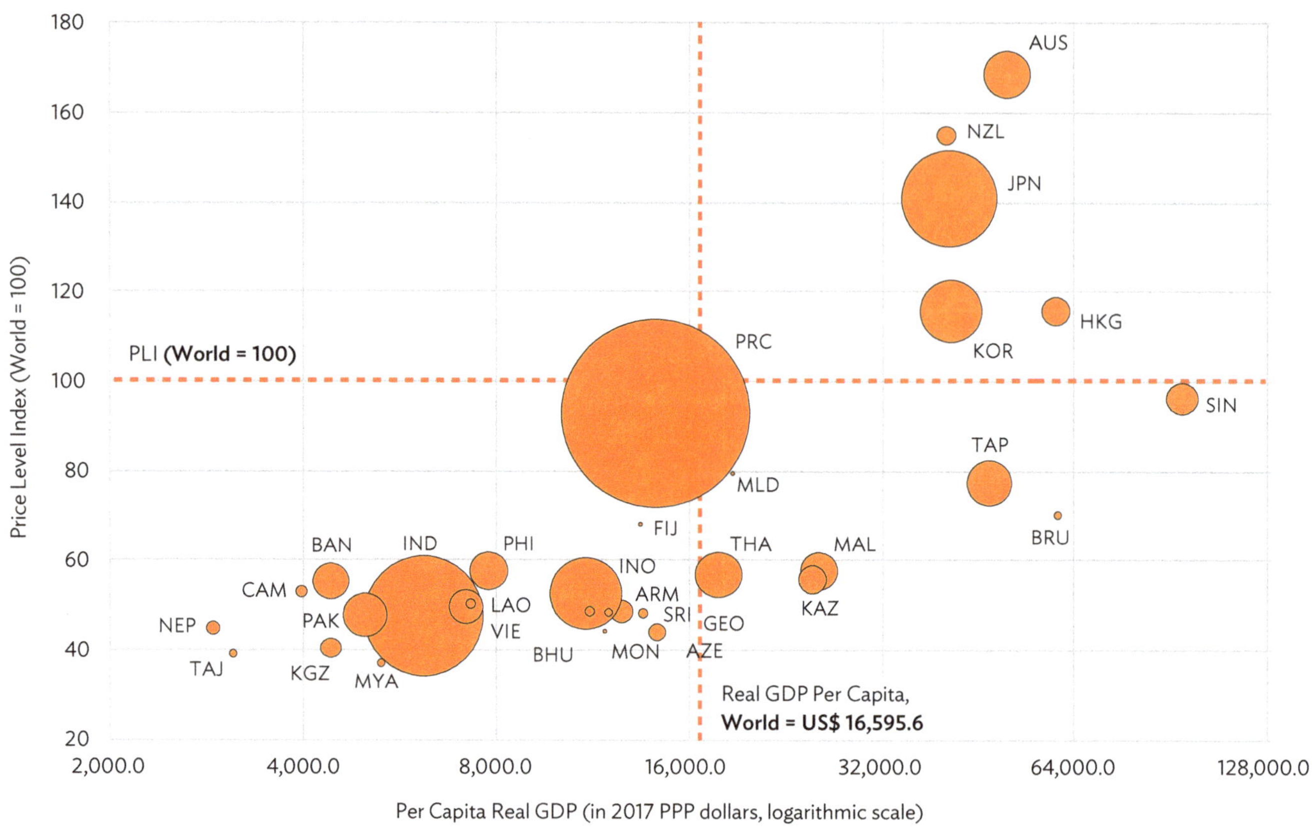

BAN = Bangladesh; BHU = Bhutan; BRU = Brunei Darussalam; CAM = Cambodia; FIJ = Fiji; GDP = gross domestic product, HKG = Hong Kong, China; IND = India; INO = Indonesia; LAO = Lao People's Democratic Republic; MAL = Malaysia; MLD = Maldives; MON = Mongolia; MYA = Myanmar; NEP = Nepal; PAK = Pakistan; PHI = Philippines; PRC = People's Republic of China; PLI = price level index, PPP = purchasing power parity, SIN = Singapore; SRI = Sri Lanka; TAP = Taipei,China; THA = Thailand; US$ = United States dollar, VIE = Viet Nam.

Notes: Bubble sizes reflect the GDP billion US$ in 2017 purchasing power parity terms. GDP is the total expenditures within the economy in the 2017 calendar year. "Real" refers to the expenditures converted using 2017 PPPs. "Asia and the Pacific" in this context consists of the 32 ADB regional members participating in the 2017 ICP.

Source: Figures are from the World Bank. 2020. *Purchasing Power Parities and the Size of the World Economies: Results from the 2017 International Comparison Program.* Washington, DC.

Figure 4.7: Spatial Cost of Living by Region in Viet Nam, 2018-2022

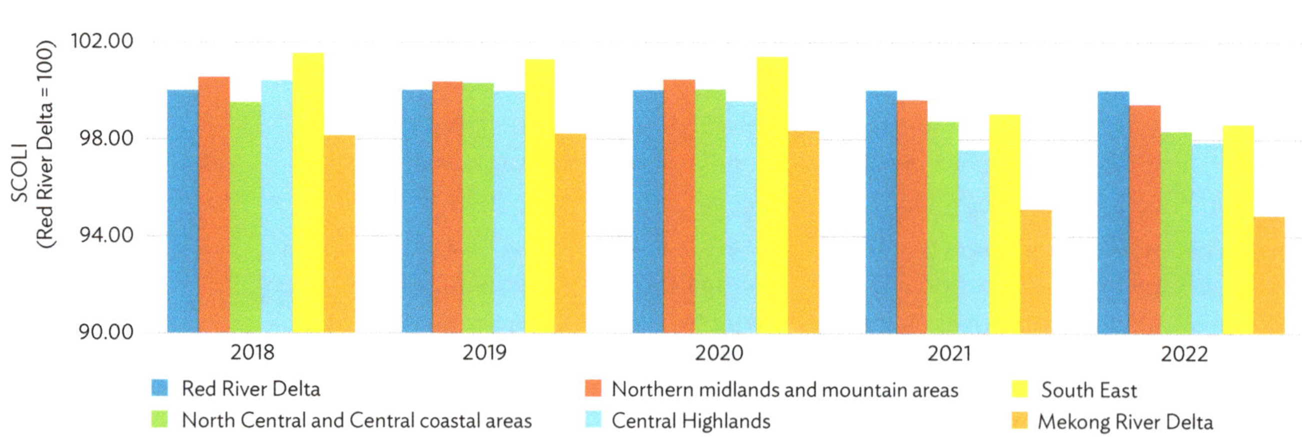

SCOLI = Spatial Cost of Living Index.

Source: General Statistics Office, Viet Nam. Statistical Yearbook 2022. https://www.gso.gov.vn/wp-content/uploads/2023/06/Sach-Nien-giam-TK-2022.pdf (accessed 11 July 2023).

Importance of PPPs

From a statistical point of view, there is a need to control the differences in price levels between economies to facilitate cross-economy comparisons that reflect only variations in the volume of economic outputs as purchasing power of different currencies are equalized. This serves as the rationale behind the ICP's compilation of purchasing power parity (PPP). The PPP measures the amount of national currency units required to purchase a basket of goods and services in an economy that can be purchased with one unit of reference currency in the reference economy (ADB 2020). By expressing this measure in a common currency, PPP-based comparisons differ from comparisons based on market exchange rates in that they distinguish between the relative price levels of different items in economies. In addition, PPP-based comparisons are also less sensitive to volatility of market exchange rates (ADB 2020; WBG n.d.). Data on PPPs can also help policymakers understand how socioeconomic development evolves over time. Along with enabling inter-economy comparisons of real GDP and its components, PPPs are used in monitoring the SDG poverty reduction target against international poverty lines expressed in PPP terms (WBG 2021a). Other PPP-based indicators in the SDG framework help monitor the human development index, income inequality, education, energy intensity, health expenditure, labor productivity, carbon dioxide emissions per unit of GDP, and they are also used in the World Economic Forum's Global Competitiveness Index (ADB 2020; WBG n.d.).

The major recommended uses of PPPs include spatial comparisons of real GDP to measure relative sizes of economies, labor productivity, income per capita, and actual individual consumption (AIC) per capita. They also enable spatial comparisons of price levels and can be used to group economies by volume index of GDP, AIC per capita, and by price levels of GDP or AIC. Other uses include analysis of temporal changes in relative GDP per capita and relative prices, to examine price convergence, and to make spatial comparison of the cost of living. (WBG 2020).

Since 1990, PPPs from the ICP have become an important tool for estimating the incidence of absolute poverty at the regional and global level, with PPP data used to establish international poverty lines and to calculate the number of people living below them in each economy. Additionally, PPPs are used by many international organizations such as the IMF, which uses PPP-converted real GDP in its current quota formula to determine subscriptions from member economies, financial assistance to members, and the share in general allocation of Special Drawing Rights. ADB's Corporate Results Framework 2019-2024, meanwhile, includes SDG indicators whose measurement depends on PPPs to track development progress in Asia and the Pacific. (ADB 2020; WBG2020).

Caveats on Use of PPPs

Amidst the diversity of potential policy uses for PPP data, there are caveats worth noting. For instance, (i) PPPs are not a precise metric to establish the strict ranking of economies; (ii) PPPs over two periods are not directly comparable and should not be used to comment on domestic inflation; (iii) PPPs are not used for temporal comparisons such as per capita real income over two benchmark years and should not be used to directly measure growth rates; (iv) PPPs are not a yardstick for comparing economic output and productivity by economic sector, and (v) PPPs should not be used as a basis for assessing whether a specific currency is undervalued or overvalued, or as equilibrium exchange rates (WBG 2021b).

Additionally, there are technical nuances worth noting. For instance, while PPPs are calculated for various expenditure components of the entire economy, the data do not necessarily correspond to expenditure patterns of a specific sociodemographic or income group. Instead, price and expenditure data used to calculate PPPs is representative of various components of an economy's GDP-related expenditure namely, final consumption expenditure by households, non-profit institutions, and government; investment expenditure in the economy, and net exports.

While using PPP data, the user must select the appropriate PPP relevant to the given problem because each PPP is representative of a specific basket of goods and services. Furthermore, while there have been attempts to compile PPPs for people living below the poverty line by collecting prices of goods and services paid by the poor in markets and outlets they frequently patronize, the results of this collection have shown that some PPPs are not significantly different from PPPs calculated for the entire population. There are also cases that show that price data collected from poverty specific surveys can affect the numerical values of the PPPs (ADB 2008).

ICP Implementation Experiences and Best Practices from the 2017 ICP in Asia and the Pacific

This section presents a summary of implementation experiences in the 2017 ICP cycle of the 22 economies participating in comparisons for Asia and the Pacific regional grouping, coordinated by ADB.[7] While ADB leads in coordinating technical operations, organizing training workshops, validating data, and computing regional PPPs, the implementing agencies of the participating economies play the most important role of conducting primary price surveys and collecting data. These survey and data collection processes follow uniform concepts and standard survey protocols. Each implementing agency conducts price surveys and provides annual average prices for a representative set of consumption and investment items from the regional product lists and detailed

7 Implementation experiences are referenced from Chapter 7 of the Asian Development Bank's *2017 International Comparison Program for Asia and the Pacific: Purchasing Power Parities and Real Expenditures.* https://www.adb.org/sites/default/files/publication/639696/icp-2017-results-methodology.pdf and information received from participating economies in ICP.

GDP expenditures which serve as basic inputs for the calculation of regional PPPs and real expenditures. ADB's partnership with regional economies is based on basic principles of transparency, cooperation, ownership, and commitment to collect high data quality that results in reliable PPPs for the region.

Successful strategies used by economies to implement program activities can serve as best practices for future ICP surveys.

The experiences of agencies implementing the ICP cover a wide range of activities involved in large-scale statistical surveys. The agencies participating in Asia and the Pacific have very diverse statistical capacities and statistical practices. An assessment of their experiences shows both commonalities, as well as diversities, along with the challenges they face in carrying out this complex process.

There are two main data requirements for the ICP. The first is GDP expenditures for 155 basic headings following a standard ICP classification, and secondly the national average prices of a basket of representative and comparable goods and services underlying different basic headings in each economy. As the price surveys cover items of household consumption, government consumption, and gross capital formation, price collection operations and validation procedures have been devised for each of these surveys.

Table 4.2 presented earlier shows the list of surveys and number of items in the product lists for the 2017 ICP cycle for Asia and the Pacific. Among them, the household price survey with a list of more than a thousand items is the biggest and most resource intensive and comprises more than 80% of the price collection work undertaken by the implementing agencies. The household price survey is to be conducted in all four quarters of the year, with prices collected monthly or quarterly for most of the products in the urban and rural markets to account for seasonal variations, giving a national annual average price for each product. The surveys of gross fixed capital formation are specialized surveys of items of construction and machinery and equipment and are conducted only once, preferably during the middle of the year to collect prices of representative products for the benchmark year.

Synergies and harmonization in the ICP price collection and regular national price surveys for consumer price index compilation is advocated as a good practice.

All ICP price surveys are equally important but with more than a thousand items in the regional household consumption basket, and with data collected nationally and throughout the year, household price surveys are the most resource intensive. The 22 participating economies collected prices for more than 4 million quotations for the household survey in 2017 ICP, reflecting the large size of survey operations. If adequate human and financial resources are not provided, the coverage and quality of price data will be consequently affected.

While recommending that the ICP benchmark cycle be implemented every three years, the UNSC also appealed to participating economies to integrate and harmonize ICP activities with their own statistical programs, especially collection of CPI data. Integrating ICP and CPI price surveys is therefore advocated as a best practice. At the same time, implementing agencies should ensure that the basic objectives of CPI as a representative and reliable indicator of tracking temporal price movements in the economy are not compromised by this harmonization process.

Integrating the ICP and CPI processes involves optimizing resources within national statistics agencies for data collection, field supervision, data entry, and data validation. This integration process can strengthen the capacity of statistical agencies to address weaknesses in CPI operations to improve the overall quality of CPI data collection. One of the biggest advantages in integrating the ICP framework at the national level is that it allows for comparisons of price levels across regions within an economy, thus facilitating subnational PPPs for which there is growing demand.

The rest of this section looks at examples of integration of the ICP and national CPI processes amongst the 22 economies coordinated by ADB in the 2017 ICP. These include practices from administrative setup, use of existing infrastructure to collect data, survey coverage and frameworks, challenges in implementation, lessons learned and future directions for use of the ICP. The same processes are being adopted in the 2021 ICP cycle.

Implementing agencies have established ICP teams comprising statistical experts with responsibilities assigned for implementation of survey activities and coordination with ADB.

One best practice that has been observed in Asia and the Pacific has been the establishment of ICP teams by implementing agencies for the express purpose of carrying out ICP surveys and data processing. These teams are led by a National Coordinator, who is a senior level statistician, along with a Deputy National Coordinator. Each team is made up of experts with clear assigned responsibilities for specific ICP survey operations, including data collection, data validation, data submission, and coordination with ADB, under the overall leadership of the National Coordinator. Participants nominated for periodic training sessions with ADB are selected from the relevant ICP team. This approach helps provide continuity to the ICP process, supports capacity building, and builds up team ownership of the program.

Conducting ICP price surveys nationally is a best practice followed by most economies in Asia and the Pacific.

Ideally, price surveys for both the CPI and ICP should be national or economy-wide (covering both rural and urban areas) for the prices to be representative of market transactions across the economy. However, in some economies, only urban locations are covered in the CPI. One reason is that urban centers reflect the bulk of household expenditures and for most nonfood items (such as clothing, footwear, electronics, durables), rural households often purchase them in urban areas.

While the CPIs are usually designed to provide reliable measures of price changes at the national and sub-national levels, the ICP is intended to capture the national average of prices, including both rural and urban locations. Typically, a subset of the entire set of CPI markets is expected to provide adequate representation for estimating national average prices.

For example, in India, while CPI coverage is from 1,181 rural markets covering almost all districts and 1,114 urban markets of 310 towns of the economy, only a subset of 320 rural and 577 urban markets representing all regions of India were selected to provide reliable estimates of national average prices for the ICP (ADB 2020). In Asia and the Pacific, all economies (except three) have economically significant rural markets and cover both rural and urban prices in their surveys, reflecting the best practice of collecting representative national annual average prices.

A number of other best practices followed in the region, which are specific to the ICP household price surveys, are summarized in Table 4.3. They aim to provide an understanding of the levels of integration of CPI and ICP activities. The summary is based on information submitted by implementing agencies in the 22 economies to ADB in response to a World Bank questionnaire on CPI-ICP integration and updated with the information submitted to ADB on the 2017 ICP household survey frameworks. It aims to provide insights into the practices followed and levels of integration of CPI and ICP activities.

CPI and ICP are implemented by the same organization.

In the 2017 ICP cycle, national statistical offices served as ICP implementing agencies in 21 of 22 participating economies. The only exception was Thailand where the ICP was the responsibility of the Trade Policy and Strategy Office in the Ministry of Commerce, which is the official agency tasked with producing the CPI in Thailand. Further, in 21 economies, price collection operations for the ICP were assigned to the units or divisions responsible for the CPI. The only exception was Nepal, where the National Statistics Office was the implementing agency for the ICP, with the Nepal Rashtra Bank responsible for CPI, highlighting slower progression in harmonization.

Nonetheless, in all 22 economies, national statistical agencies as the implementing agencies for ICP price surveys, ensured that they were managed by staff experienced in data collection, supervision, and data validation. These agencies are also best placed to identify appropriate subsets of items from the ICP regional item basket so that the items priced for ICP surveys are also representative of the household consumption expenditure of the economy.

Table 4.3: Summary of Practices that Facilitate CPI-ICP Integration

	Yes	No	Some	Overlap products	Total
1. Price Collection Infrastructure and Operations					
• CPI and ICP implementation by same organization	21	1			22
• Price collection staff for ICP make up a subset of the CPI price collection staff	11	2	9		22
• ICP survey collects prices from CPI outlets	19	3			22
• ICP price survey also incorporates price data from CPI survey	16	6			22
• Product catalogue available to assist field workers	22	0			22
• ICP and CPI price collection carried out at the same time	9	6		7	22
2. Data Processing					
• ICP data captured in the same computer system as the CPI data	8	12		2	22
• Use of the same editing/control procedures to ensure quality of CPI and ICP data	12	7		3	22
• ICP validation procedures help improve processing of CPI data.	21	1			22
3. General					
• Organizational plans to improve the integration of CPI and ICP price surveys and processes in the near future	20	2			22

CPI = Consumer Price Index, ICP = International Comparison Program.

Notes: ICP in this table only refers to the ICP household consumption price survey. The six economies which did not use CPI prices for their 2017 ICP survey, include Bangladesh, India, Myanmar, Nepal, the People's Republic of China, and the Philippines.

Source: Responses from economies participating in the World Bank's ICP-CPI Integration Questionnaire and 2017 ICP Household Survey Framework Questionnaire submitted to ADB.

Staff engaged in CPI price collection are commonly utilized for ICP in most economies.

Having skilled workers carry out data collection and data processing is an important element of the survey process. Of the 22 economies coordinated by ADB in the 2017 ICP, price collection was carried out by a subset of CPI price collectors in 11 economies and was partly undertaken by CPI staff in nine economies. The ICP uses detailed Structured Product Specifications (SPDs), while the CPI items list does not usually include such detailed product characteristics. Experienced CPI staff are familiar with the nuances of price collection and can be easily trained for ICP price surveys to ensure they can correctly identify ICP items using prescribed SPDs for 'like-with-like' comparisons.

Price outlets used in the CPI survey design are commonly used for ICP when possible.

Whenever possible, selecting CPI markets and outlets for ICP price collection helps in capturing prices for both surveys in the same visit. These selected outlets are considered representative or popular for pricing specific items. Eighteen economies reported using CPI price outlets also as the source for ICP item prices. However, it may be noted that ICP prices are also collected from non-CPI outlets, when the CPI outlet is not a representative outlet for the specific products.

Using prices of CPI items for ICP items with common characteristics is practiced in many economies.

Another key aspect of CPI-ICP integration is making use of prices of overlapping items between the CPI and ICP. As the prices for CPI items are already collected for CPI compilation, their use for ICP helps reduce the burden of data collection. However, it is essential that the CPI items meet item specifications prescribed for ICP to ensure comparability.

Reflecting the need to maintain comparability of ICP prices across economies, significant efforts have been made by implementing agencies to compare CPI specifications with the ICP SPDs.

Mapping CPI items at the national level with ICP items is challenging because often the CPI items do not have the same level of details as SPDs, such as brand type, weight/size/quantity, packaging, standard unit of measurement, and other information. In some economies with diverse CPI item baskets across several regions, identifying nationally representative CPI items with the same specifications as ICP items is not really feasible.

From the 22 economies coordinated by ADB in the 2017 ICP, (Figure 4.8) 16 made use of prices from CPI items mapped with ICP items. Of those that used CPI prices in their ICP survey, below 20% of ICP item prices were sourced from the CPI in three of the economies, around 20%-30% were sourced from five economies and between 30%–40% were sourced in four economies. Another four economies were able to make use of CPI prices for more than 40% of the ICP items priced.

Figure 4.8: Share of CPI Items in the Total ICP Items Priced: 2017 ICP Asia Pacific Participating Economies

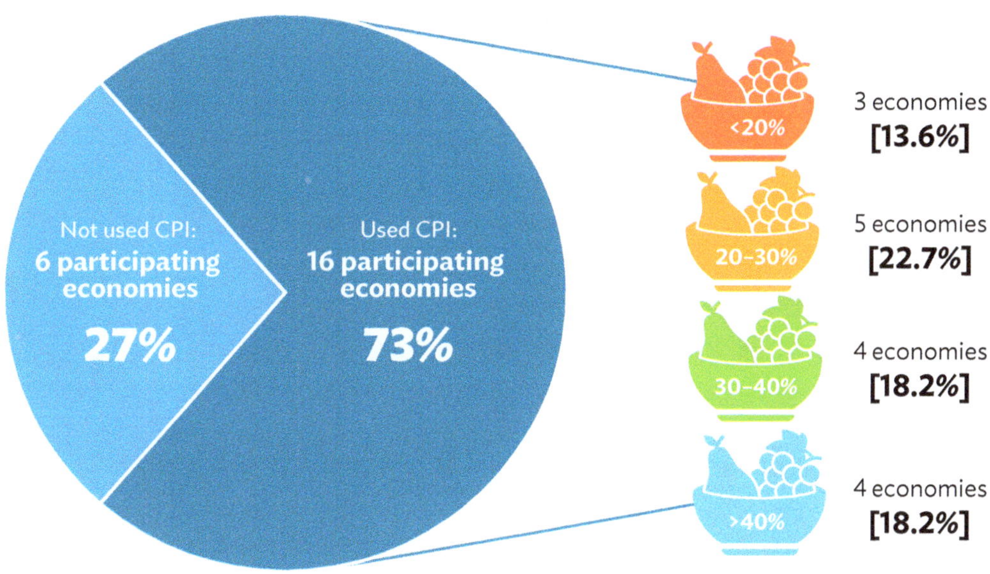

Source: Responses from economies to ADB's 2017 ICP Household Survey Framework Questionnaire.

Of the six economies that reported not having used CPI prices for their ICP survey, one did not have access to CPI prices, while the others possibly could either not gather mapping information due to the wide diversity of CPI items baskets, or because of inadequate information about product characteristics in the CPI items basket, making it difficult to map CPI items with ICP product specifications.

Food items in the CPI are more comparable with the ICP item list than other categories, although great care is needed to convert the prices to the same units of measurement as those in the ICP to ensure comparability. A large percentage of items for the ICP household survey were collected through a separate ICP survey of nonoverlapping ICP items. The larger the overlap between CPI and ICP items, the less the need for additional resources for ICP surveys.

Additionally, all 22 economies provided product catalogues prepared by ADB with item SPDs and a reference image, while some economies translated the ICP product list from English into the nationally spoken language to benefit price collectors. These practices helped underpin the quality of the surveys process, while balancing the requirements of representation and comparability.

Some economies are continuing steps to enhance product descriptions in their CPI product lists to better match them with ICP products. They are also replacing some existing CPI items with suitably representative ICP items in their CPI basket when feasible. Several economies have indicated they have future plans to enhance integration of CPI and ICP at the time of the next base-year revision.

The price collection schedule for CPI and ICP items is synchronized where feasible.

An additional feature of integrating the CPI-ICP processes is scheduling the price collection operations at the same time. In nine economies, the ICP survey was carried out at the same time as the CPI survey, while in another seven, simultaneous price collection was possible only for overlapping items. The remaining six economies chose to have largely independent price collection for ICP. The choice of timings of the two surveys depends upon available staffing, frequency of price collection for CPI items against ICP items, and internal priorities, with the timely release of monthly CPI viewed as a key macroeconomic indicator.

Use of the same data processing systems and editing protocols for CPI and ICP prices is less prevalent.

Just eight of the 22 economies coordinated by ADB in the 2017 ICP captured CPI and ICP price data using the same computer data processing system, while two reported using the same system only for overlapping products. The remaining economies have independent data processing systems for CPI and ICP. However, 12 of the 22 economies said they used the same data editing and quality control procedures for the two surveys.

In addition, all economies, except one, reported that ICP data validation procedures have helped improve their own CPI data validation processes.

The frequency of data collection is another important dimension to consider in the estimation of national annual average prices of ICP items that represent prices underpinning corresponding annual GDP expenditures. Data collection frequencies for household items can vary depending on the type of products and the specific economy. Some of the 22 economies in the 2017 ICP, collected prices of perishable food items on a weekly basis, while other food items were collected monthly. Prices for nonfood items were usually collected on a quarterly basis, and some items like durable goods, healthcare, education, package holidays, accommodation services, and others, were collected semiannually.

The experiences of the 22 economies in the 2017 ICP, show an encouraging shift to increased integration of CPI-ICP activities, as well as commitments to further synergies in future. It also reflects efforts by the participating economies to strike a balance between the need for nationally representative annual average prices for ICP, and the resources required to collect such information.

Use of Nontraditional Data in Price Collection

There are two approaches that can be taken to collect price data. The traditional approach involves choosing representative products to be surveyed, considering their specifications and data availability, selecting sampled outlets for price collection, visiting the outlets physically to collect prices on specific days of the week, month, or quarter, and using quality adjustment methods to remove the element of price change stemming from changes in quality. The nontraditional approach uses data available from big data sources, such as transaction or scanner data, or online data web scraped from the internet.

In compiling the CPI, the use of nontraditional data sources is currently being studied, and methods and challenges in their use are being tested in advanced statistical systems. These nontraditional sources and approaches are expected to improve the accuracy and frequency of index creation, while reducing the burden on price statisticians and reporting firms. However, there are several practical challenges, and their use so far has been generally limited in CPI compilation (IMF et al. 2020).

The use of nontraditional data sources for the ICP is also developing. In the current 2021 ICP cycle, pandemic constraints affected the physical collection of prices, with many economies resorting to online collection and web scraping. While the use of nontraditional methods for collecting price data for the ICP is still in its infancy, it nevertheless has the potential to improve the accuracy and frequency of the data, while reducing the burden on price statisticians and reporting outlets.

Challenges and Lessons Learned for Future ICP Implementation

The most significant challenge in the household consumption price surveys is correctly identifying products following the prescribed ICP SPDs, including the unit of measure, brands, and size measures across different regions, and within and across economies. Incorrect identification of product characteristics has contributed to high variations in national average prices and outlier prices. To resolve this concern, coordinators in national implementing agencies, along with regional coordinators, used standardized statistical tools for data validation and to identify outlier quotations and prices in the 2017 ICP. National coordinators followed up with the price collectors to clarify and correct the prices.

Similar challenges were faced in the case of items in the construction, and machinery and equipment surveys. Unlike CPI price collection, these two specialized surveys are not regularly undertaken by many national statistics agencies and are therefore only carried out for ICP purposes. The lessons from these surveys are that there is a need for more detailed product descriptions and explanatory notes along with rigorous training of price collectors ahead of the start of each survey to prevent or reduce errors at the collection stage. Taking these steps will save time at the data validation stage and improve the quality and comparability of price data.

ICP Data Governance and Privacy

Information on prices of items included in the ICP can be a valuable tool for research and under the program's data policy, researchers can access national annual average prices of ICP items. This can be done by applying for information from a regional implementing agency, and/or the World Bank. However, it should be noted that this data cannot be publicly disclosed and can only be used for the research purpose stated in the application. Confidentiality of price data is one of the principles followed by the ICP.

Additionally, requests for subnational price data for research purposes can only be made directly to a national implementing agency. It should be noted, however, that since the ICP is designed to capture 'nationally representative annual average prices' for cross-economy comparisons, it is not a suitable tool for making reliable subnational price comparisons and therefore users need to be cautious about the limitations and representativity of the data for any sub-national analysis.

References

Asian Development Bank (ADB). 2008. *Research Study on Poverty-Specific Purchasing Power Parities for Selected Countries in Asia and the Pacific*. Manila. https://www.adb.org/sites/default/files/publication/29130/poverty-specific-ppp.pdf.

ADB. 2019. *2020 International Comparison Program for Asia and the Pacific. Knowledge and Support Technical Assistance Report*. Manila. https://www.adb.org/sites/default/files/project-documents/53303/53303-001-tar-en.pdf.

ADB. 2020. *2017 International Comparison Program for Asia and the Pacific: Purchasing Power Parities and Real Expenditures*. Manila. https://www.adb.org/sites/default/files/publication/639696/icp-2017-results-methodology.pdf.

J. Andres and I. Hernando. 1997. Does Inflation Harm Economic Growth? Evidence for the OECD. *NBER Working Paper* 6062. National Bureau of Economic Research. https://www.nber.org/papers/w6062.

L. Ball. 1992. Why Does High Inflation Raise Inflation Uncertainty? *Journal of Monetary Economics*, 29. 3. pp. 371-388. https://www.sciencedirect.com/science/article/abs/pii/030439329290032W?via%3Dihub.

R. J. Barro. 1995. Inflation and Economic Growth. *NBER Working Paper* 5326. National Bureau of Economic Research. https://www.nber.org/system/files/working_papers/w5326/w5326.pdf.

V. Bérenger and A. Verdier-Chouchane. 2007. Multidimensional Measures of Well-Being: Standard of Living and Quality of Life Across Countries. *World Development*. 35. 7. pp. 1,259-1,276. https://doi.org/10.1016/j.worlddev.2006.10.011.

International Monetary Fund(IMF), International Labour Organization, Statistical Office of the European Union, United Nations Economic Commission for Europe, Organisation for Economic Co-operation and Development, and the World Bank. 2020. Consumer price index manual: concepts and methods. Washington, DC: IMF.

K. Joshi, M. Accad, and I. Song. 2021. Prices Matter When Tracking Economic Development and Recovery After the Pandemic. *Asian Development Bank Blog*. 19 April. https://blogs.adb.org/blog/prices-matter-when-tracking-economic-development-and-recovery-after-pandemic.

The Lancet Public Health. 2022. The Cost of Living: an Avoidable Public Health Crisis. *The Lancet Public Health*. 7. 6. https://www.thelancet.com/journals/lanpub/article/PIIS2468-2667(22)00120-7/fulltext.

R. Latimaha, N. Ismail, and Z. Bahari. 2020. Cost of Living and Standard of Living Nexus: The Determinants of Cost of Living. *Jurnal Ekonomi Malaysia*. 54. 3. pp. 1–14. https://www.ukm.my/jem/article/cost-of-living-and-standard-of-living-nexus-the-determinants-of-cost-of-living/.

S.J. Wei and Y. Xie. 2019. *The Wedge of the Century: Understanding a Divergence Between CPI and PPI Inflation Measures. NBER Working Paper.* No. 24319. National Bureau of Economic Research. Cambridge, MA. https://www.nber.org/system/files/working_papers/w24319/w24319.pdf.

United Nations (UN), European Commission, International Monetary Fund, Organisation for Economic Co-operation and Development and World Bank. 2009. *System of National Accounts 2008*. New York. https://unstats.un.org/unsd/nationalaccount/docs/SNA2008.pdf.

UN. 2018. Classification of Individual Consumption According to Purpose (COICOP). New York. https://unstats.un.org/unsd/classifications/unsdclassifications/COICOP_2018_-_pre-edited_white_cover_version_-_2018-12-26.pdf

World Bank (WBG). 2020. *Purchasing Power Parities and the Size of World Economies: Results from the 2017 International Comparison Program*. Washington, DC. https://openknowledge.worldbank.org/server/api/core/bitstreams/d508f4dd-1075-579f-843d-cae5631a0a61/content.

WBG. 2021a. *Purchasing Power Parities for Policy Making: A Visual Guide to Using Data from the International Comparison Program*. https://openknowledge.worldbank.org/entities/publication/dc4deba0-339b-5dca-af4c-4881445d1dce.

WBG. 2021b. *PPPs for Policy Making: A Visual Guide to Using Data from the ICP – Uses and Limitations of PPPs*. https://www.worldbank.org/en/programs/icp/brief/VC_Uses.

WBG. n.d. *International Comparison Program*. https://www.worldbank.org/en/programs/icp.

Definitions

Sustainable Development Goals

Goals and Targets	Statistical Indicators	Definition
Goal 1. End poverty in all its forms everywhere		
Target 1.1: By 2030, eradicate extreme poverty (currently measured as people living on less than $2.15 a day) for all people everywhere.	1.1.1.a: Proportion of the population living below the international poverty line, by sex, age, employment status, and geographical location (urban or rural)	Proportion of the population living on less than $2.15 a day, measured at 2017 international prices, adjusted for purchasing power parity (PPP). Note: The PPP conversion factor for private consumption is the number of units of an economy's currency required to buy the same amount of goods and/or services in the domestic market as a United States (US) dollar would buy in the US.
	1.1.1.b: Proportion of the employed population living below the international poverty line, by sex	Proportion of the employed population living in households with per capita consumption or income below the international poverty line of $1.90 a day. Note: The proportion of working poor in total employment (also known as the working poverty rate) combines data on household income or consumption with labor force framework variables measured at the individual level, and sheds light on the relationship between household poverty and employment. The numbers are International Labour Organization modeled estimates. Employed persons refer to all persons of working age who, during a short reference period such as a day or a week, performed work for others in exchange for pay or profit.
Target 1.2: By 2030, reduce at least by half the proportion of men, women, and children of all ages living in poverty in all its dimensions, according to national definitions.	1.2.1: Proportion of the population living below the national poverty line, by sex, age, and geographical location (urban or rural)	Percentage of the total population living below the national poverty line. Note: National poverty rates are defined at economy-specific poverty lines in local currencies, which are different in real terms across economies and different from the international poverty line of $2.15 a day. Thus, national poverty rates cannot be compared across economies or with the poverty rate of $2.15 a day.
Target 1.3: Implement nationally appropriate social protection systems and measures for all, including floors, and by 2030 achieve substantial coverage of the poor and the vulnerable.	1.3.1: Proportion of population covered by social protection floors/systems, by sex, distinguishing children, unemployed persons, older persons, persons with disabilities, pregnant women, newborns, work-injury victims and the poor and the vulnerable.	Percentage of the population effectively covered by a social protection system, including social protection floors, which provide old age pensions, social security, and health insurance benefits. Effective coverage of social protection is measured by the number of people who are either actively contributing to a social insurance scheme or receiving benefits (contributory or noncontributory). Coverage is expressed as a share of the respective population. (i) Population covered by at least one social protection benefit (effective coverage): proportion of the total population receiving at least one contributory or noncontributory cash benefit, or actively contributing to at least one social security scheme. (ii) Older persons: ratio of persons above statutory retirement age receiving an old-age pension to the number of persons above statutory retirement age (including contributory and noncontributory). (iii) Poor persons covered by social assistance: ratio of social assistance recipients to the population living below the national poverty line. (iv) Vulnerable persons covered by social assistance: ratio of social assistance recipients to the total number of vulnerable persons (defined as all children plus adults not covered by contributory benefits and persons above retirement age not receiving contributory benefits, i.e., pensions). (v) Children: ratio of children or households receiving child or family cash benefits to the total number of children or households with children.

(continued on next page)

Goals and Targets	Statistical Indicators	Definition
Target 1.a: Ensure significant mobilization of resources from a variety of sources, including through enhanced development cooperation, to provide adequate and predictable means for developing countries, particularly least developed economies, to implement programmes and policies to end poverty in all its dimensions.	1.a.1: Total official development assistance grants from all donors that focus on poverty reduction as a share of the recipient country's gross national income	Total official development assistance (ODA) grants from all donors that focus on poverty reduction as a share of the recipient country's gross national income. The OECD/Development Assistance Committee (DAC) defines ODA as "flows to countries and territories on the DAC List of ODA Recipients and to multilateral institutions which are i) provided by official agencies, including state and local governments, or by their executive agencies; and ii) each transaction is administered with the promotion of the economic development and welfare of developing countries as its main objective; and is concessional in character and conveys a grant element of at least 25% (calculated at a rate of discount of 10%). Poverty reduction items can be defined as ODA to basic social services (basic health, basic education, basic water and sanitation, population programmes and reproductive health) and developmental food aid.
Goal 2. End hunger, achieve food security and improved nutrition, and promote sustainable agriculture		
Target 2.1: By 2030, end hunger and ensure access by all people, in particular the poor and people in vulnerable situations, including infants, to safe, nutritious, and sufficient food all year round.	2.1.1: Prevalence of undernourishment	Proportion of the population whose habitual food consumption is insufficient to provide the dietary energy levels that are required to maintain a normal, active and healthy life. Note: Undernourishment is defined as the condition by which a person has access, on a regular basis, to an amount of food that is insufficient to provide the energy required for conducting a normal, healthy, and active life, given his or her own dietary energy requirements.
Target 2.2: By 2030, end all forms of malnutrition, including achieving, by 2025, the internationally agreed targets on stunting and wasting in children under 5 years of age, and address the nutritional needs of adolescent girls, pregnant and lactating women, and older persons.	2.2.1: Prevalence of stunting—height for age <-2 standard deviation from the median of the World Health Organization (WHO) Child Growth Standards—among children under 5 years of age	Prevalence of stunting—height-for-age <-2 standard deviation from the median of WHO Child Growth Standards—among children under 5 years of age. Note: Child stunting refers to a child who is too short for his or her age and is the result of chronic or recurrent malnutrition.
	2.2.2.a: Prevalence of wasting—weight for height >+2 standard deviation from the median of the WHO Child Growth Standards—among children under 5 years of age (overweight)	Prevalence of overweight—weight for height >+2 standard deviation from the median of WHO Child Growth Standards—among children under 5 years of age. Note: Child overweight refers to a child who is too heavy for his or her height.
	2.2.2.b: Prevalence of wasting—weight for height <-2 standard deviation from the median of the WHO Child Growth Standards—among children under 5 years of age (wasting)	Prevalence of wasting—weight for height <-2 standard deviation from the median of WHO Child Growth Standards—among children under 5 years of age. Note: Child wasting refers to a child who is too thin for his or her height as a result of recent rapid weight loss or the failure to gain weight.
Target 2.a: Increase investment, including through enhanced international cooperation, in rural infrastructure, agricultural research and extension services, technology development, and plant and livestock gene banks in order to	2.a.1: The agriculture orientation index for government expenditures	The Agriculture Orientation Index for Government Expenditures is defined as agriculture's share of government expenditure, divided by the agriculture value-added share of gross domestic product (GDP), where "agriculture" refers to the agriculture, forestry, fishing, and hunting sector. The measure is a currency-free index, calculated as the ratio of these two shares. National governments are requested to compile government expenditures according to the Government Finance Statistics system and the Classification of Functions of Government, and the agriculture value-added share of GDP, according to the System of National Accounts.

(continued on next page)

Goals and Targets	Statistical Indicators	Definition
enhance agricultural productive capacity in developing countries (or economies), particularly least developed countries (or economies).		Note: Government Expenditures are all expenses and acquisitions of nonfinancial assets associated with supporting a particular sector, as defined in the Government Finance Statistics Manual 2014 developed by the International Monetary Fund (IMF).
	2.a.2: Total official flows (official development assistance plus other official flows) to the agriculture sector	Gross disbursements of total official development assistance (ODA) and other official flows from all donors to the agriculture sector. Note: The Development Assistance Committee defines ODA as those flows to economies and territories on the committee's List of ODA Recipients and to multilateral institutions which are: (i) provided by official agencies, including state and local governments, or by their executive agencies; and (ii) each transaction is administered with the promotion of the economic development and welfare of developing economies as its main objective; and (iii) is concessional in character and conveys a grant element of at least 25% (calculated at a rate of discount of 10%). Other Official Flows are defined as transactions by the official sector which do not meet the conditions for eligibility as ODA, either because they are not primarily aimed at development, or because they are not sufficiently concessional. They also exclude officially supported export credits.
Goal 3. Ensure healthy lives and promote well-being for all at all ages		
Target 3.1: By 2030, reduce the global maternal mortality ratio to less than 70 per 100,000 live births.	3.1.1: Maternal mortality ratio	Number of maternal deaths during a given time period per 100,000 live births during the same time period. It depicts the risk of maternal death relative to the number of live births and essentially captures the risk of death in a single pregnancy (proxied by a single live birth). Note: Maternal death refers to the death of a woman while pregnant or within 42 days of termination of pregnancy, irrespective of the duration and site of the pregnancy, from any cause related to or aggravated by the pregnancy or its management (from direct or indirect obstetric death), but not from unintentional or incidental causes.
	3.1.2: Proportion of births attended by skilled health personnel	Proportion of childbirths attended by professional health personnel (generally doctors, nurses, or midwives, but can refer to other health professionals providing childbirth care). These are competent maternal and newborn health professionals educated, trained, and regulated to national and international standards. They are competent to: (i) provide and promote evidence-based, human-rights based, quality, socioculturally sensitive, and dignified care to women and newborns; (ii) facilitate physiological processes during labor and delivery to ensure a clean and positive childbirth experience; and (iii) identify and manage or refer women and/or newborns with complications. Note: Having a skilled attendant at the time of delivery is an important lifesaving intervention for both mothers and babies. Not having access to this key assistance is detrimental to the health of women and newborns because it could cause the death of the women and/or the newborn, or long-lasting morbidity. Achieving universal coverage for this indicator is therefore essential for reducing maternal and newborn mortality.

(continued on next page)

Goals and Targets	Statistical Indicators	Definition
Target 3.2: By 2030, end preventable deaths of newborns and children under 5 years of age, with all countries (or economies) aiming to reduce neonatal mortality to at least as low as 12 per 1,000 live births and under-5 mortality to at least as low as 25 per 1,000 live births.	3.2.1: Under-5 mortality rate	The probability of a child born in a specific year or period dying before reaching the age of 5 years, if subject to age specific mortality rates of that period, expressed per 1,000 live births. Note: The under-5 mortality rate as defined here is, strictly speaking, not a rate (i.e., the number of deaths divided by the number of population at risk during a certain period of time) but a probability of death derived from a life table and expressed as a rate per 1,000 live births.
	3.2.2: Neonatal mortality rate	Probability that a child born in a specific year or period will die during the first 28 completed days of life, if subject to age-specific mortality rates of that period, expressed per 1,000 live births. Note: Neonatal deaths (deaths among live births during the first 28 completed days of life) may be subdivided into early neonatal deaths, occurring during the first 7 days of life, and late neonatal deaths, occurring after the seventh day but before the 28th completed day of life.
Target 3.3: By 2030, end the epidemics of AIDS, tuberculosis, malaria, and neglected tropical diseases; and combat hepatitis, water-borne diseases, and other communicable diseases.	3.3.1: Number of new HIV infections per 1,000 uninfected population, by sex, age, and key populations	Number of new HIV infections per 1,000 persons among the uninfected population.
	3.3.2: Tuberculosis incidence per 100,000 population	Estimated number of new and relapse tuberculosis cases (all forms of tuberculosis, including cases in people living with HIV) arising in a given year, expressed as a rate per 100,000 population.
	3.3.3: Malaria incidence per 1,000 population	The number of new cases of malaria per 1,000 people at risk each year.
Target 3.4: By 2030, reduce by one third premature mortality from noncommunicable diseases through prevention and treatment, and promote mental health and well-being.	3.4.1: Mortality rate attributed to cardiovascular disease, cancer, diabetes, or chronic respiratory disease	Probability of dying between the ages of 30 and 70 years from cardiovascular diseases, cancer, diabetes, or chronic respiratory diseases, defined as the percentage of 30-year-old people who would die before their 70th birthday from cardiovascular disease, cancer, diabetes, or chronic respiratory disease, assuming that s/he would experience current mortality rates at every age and s/he would not die from any other cause of death (e.g., injuries or HIV/AIDS). Note: Probability of dying refers to the likelihood that an individual would die between two ages given current mortality rates at each age, calculated using life table methods. The probability of death between two ages may be called a mortality rate.
	3.4.2: Suicide mortality rate	The number of suicide deaths in a year, divided by the population and multiplied by 100,000.
Target 3.6: By 2020, halve the number of global deaths and injuries from road traffic accidents.	3.6.1: Death rate due to road traffic injuries	Number of road traffic fatal injury deaths per 100,000 population.
Target 3.7: By 2030, ensure universal access to sexual and reproductive health care services, including for family planning, information and education, and the integration of reproductive health into national strategies and programme.	3.7.1: Proportion of women of reproductive age (15–49 years) who have their need for family planning satisfied by modern methods	The percentage of women of reproductive age (15-49 years) currently using a modern method of contraception among those who desire either to have no (additional) children or to postpone the next pregnancy. The indicator is also referred to as the demand for family planning satisfied with modern methods.
	3.7.2: Adolescent birth rate (15–19 years) per 1,000 women in that age group	Annual number of births to females aged 15–19 years per 1,000 females in the respective age group.

(continued on next page)

Goals and Targets	Statistical Indicators	Definition
Target 3.8: Achieve universal health coverage, including financial risk protection, access to quality essential healthcare services and access to safe, effective, quality and affordable essential medicines and vaccines for all.	3.8.1 Coverage of essential health services (defined as the average coverage of essential services based on tracer interventions that include reproductive, maternal, newborn and child heath, infectious diseases, non-communicable diseases and service capacity and access, among the general and the most disadvantaged population)	Coverage of essential health services is defined as the average coverage of essential services based on tracer interventions that include reproductive, maternal, newborn and child health, infectious diseases, non-communicable diseases and service capacity and access, among the general and the most disadvantaged population. The indicator is an index reported on a unitless scale of 0 to 100, which is computed as the geometric mean of 14 tracer indicators of health service coverage. Note: The index of health service coverage is computed as the geometric means of tracer indicators. The tracer indicators are organized by four broad categories of service coverage: (i) reproductive, maternal, newborn, and child health; (ii) infectious diseases; (iii) noncommunicable diseases; and (iv) service capacity and access.
Target 3.9: By 2030, substantially reduce the number of deaths and illnesses from hazardous chemicals and air, water, and soil pollution and contamination.	3.9.1: Mortality rate attributed to household and ambient air pollution	The mortality rate attributable to the joint effects of household and ambient air pollution can be expressed as: crude death rate or age-standardized death rate. Crude rates are calculated by dividing the number of deaths by the total population (or indicated if a different population group is used, e.g. children under 5 years), while the age-standardized rates adjust for differences in the age distribution of the population by applying the observed age-specific mortality rates for each population to a standard population. Note: Evidence from epidemiological studies has shown that exposure to air pollution is linked to, among others, the important diseases taken into account in this estimate: - acute respiratory infections (estimated in all age groups); - cerebrovascular diseases (stroke) in adults (estimated above 25 years); - ischemic heart diseases (IHD) in adults (estimated above 25 years); - chronic obstructive pulmonary disease (COPD) in adults (estimated above 25 years); and - lung cancer in adults (estimated above 25 years).
	3.9.2: Mortality rate attributed to unsafe water, unsafe sanitation, and lack of hygiene—exposure to unsafe water, sanitation, and hygiene for all (WASH) services	Number of deaths from unsafe water, unsafe sanitation, and lack of hygiene through exposure to unsafe water, sanitation and hygiene for all (WASH) services in a year, divided by the population, and multiplied by 100,000.
Target 3.c: Substantially increase health financing and the recruitment, development, training, and retention of the health workforce in developing economies, especially in least developed economies and small island developing states.	3.c.1: Health worker density and distribution	Density of medical doctors: The density of medical doctors is defined as the number of medical doctors, including generalists and specialist medical practitioners, per 10,000 population in a given national and/or subnational area. The International Standard Classification of Occupations (ISCO) unit group codes included in this category are 221, 2211, and 2212 of ISCO-08. Density of nursing and midwifery personnel: The density of nursing and midwifery personnel is defined as the number of nursing and midwifery personnel per 10,000 population in a given national and/or subnational area. The ISCO-08 codes included in this category are 2221, 2222, 3221, and 3222.

(continued on next page)

Goals and Targets	Statistical Indicators	Definition
Target 3.d: Strengthen the capacity of all economies, in particular developing economies, for early warning, risk reduction, and management of national and global health risks.	3.d.1: International Health Regulations (IHR) capacity and health emergency preparedness	The revised International Health Regulations (IHR) were adopted in 2005 and entered into force in 2007. Under the IHR, States Parties are obliged to develop and maintain minimum core capacities for surveillance and response, including at points of entry, in order to detect early, assess, notify, and respond to any potential public health events of international concern. Article 54 of the IHR states that: States Parties and the Director-General shall report to the Health Assembly on the implementation of these Regulations as decided by the Health Assembly. The State Party Self-Assessment and Reporting (SPAR) tool captures the level of self-assessed national capacities. They are essential public health capacities that States Parties are required to have in place throughout their territories pursuant to Articles 5 and 12, and Annex 1A of the IHR (2005) requirements. Based on the lessons learned from the COVID-19 pandemic, the World Health Organization published the revised second edition of the IHR State Parties Self-Assessment Tool in 2021, with new indicators related to gender equality in health emergencies, advocacy for IHR implementation, and community engagement, to name a few. The revisions are intended to improve the assessment of the IHR core capacities and the preparedness of States Parties for health emergencies. The indicator SDG 3.d.1 reflects the capacities State Parties of the International Health Regulations (2005) had agreed and committed to developing. Note: The second edition SPAR tool has been expanded from 13 to 15 capacities. The 15 core capacities are (1) Policy, legal and normative instruments to implement IHR; (2) IHR Coordination and National Focal Point Functions; (3) Financing; (4) Laboratory; (5) Surveillance; (6) Human resources; (7) Health emergency management (8) Health Service Provision; (9) Infection Prevention and Control; (10) Risk communication and community engagement; (11) Points of entry and border health; (12) Zoonotic diseases; (13) Food safety; (14) Chemical events; (15) Radiation emergencies.
Goal 4. Ensure inclusive and equitable quality education and promote lifelong learning opportunities for all		
Target 4.1: By 2030, ensure that all girls and boys complete free, equitable, and quality primary and secondary education leading to relevant and effective learning outcomes.	4.1.1.a: Proportion of children and young people in grades 2/3 achieving at least a minimum proficiency level 4.1.1.b: Proportion of children and young people at the end of primary achieving at least a minimum proficiency level 4.1.1.c: Proportion of children and young people at the end of lower secondary achieving at least a minimum proficiency level	Percentage of children and young people achieving at least a minimum proficiency level in (i) reading and (ii) mathematics during primary education (Grade 2 or 3), at the end of primary education, and at the end of lower secondary education. The minimum proficiency level will be measured relative to new common reading and mathematics scales currently in development. Note: This indicator is expressed as the proportion of children and/or young people at the relevant stage of education in a given year, achieving or exceeding the pre-defined proficiency level in a given subject.

(continued on next page)

Goals and Targets	Statistical Indicators	Definition
	4.1.2: Completion rate (primary education, lower secondary education, upper secondary education)	Percentage of a cohort of children or young people aged 3–5 years above the intended age for the last grade of each level of education who have completed that grade. Note: A completion rate at or near 100% indicates that all or most children and adolescents have completed a level of education by the time they are 3 to 5 years older than the official age of entry into the last grade of that level of education. A low completion rate indicates low or delayed entry into a given level of education, high drop-out, high repetition, late completion, or a combination of these factors.
Target 4.2: By 2030, ensure that all girls and boys have access to quality early childhood development, care, and preprimary education, so that they are ready for primary education.	4.2.2: Participation rate in organized learning (1 year before the official primary entry age), by sex	Percentage of children in the given age range who participate in one or more organized learning programs, including programs which offer a combination of education and care. Participation in early childhood and in primary education are both included. The age range will vary by economy depending on the official age for entry to primary education. Note: An organized learning program is one that consists of a coherent set or sequence of educational activities designed with the intention of achieving predetermined learning outcomes or the accomplishment of a specific set of educational tasks. Early childhood and primary education programs are examples of organized learning programs. The official primary entry age is the age at which children are obliged to start primary education, according to national legislation or policies.
Target 4.c: By 2030, substantially increase the supply of qualified teachers, including through international cooperation for teacher training in developing countries (or economies), especially least developed countries (or economies) and small island developing states.	4.c.1.a: Proportion of teachers in preprimary education who have received at least the minimum organized teacher training 4.c.1.b: Proportion of teachers in primary education who have received at least the minimum organized teacher training 4.c.1.c: Proportion of teachers in lower secondary education who have received at least the minimum organized teacher training 4.c.1.d: Proportion of teachers in upper secondary education who have received at least the minimum organized teacher training	Percentage of teachers by level of education taught (pre-primary, primary, lower secondary, and upper secondary education) who have received at least the minimum organized pedagogical teacher training pre-service and in-service required for teaching at the relevant level in a given economy. Note: Number of teachers in a given level of education who are trained is expressed as a percentage of all teachers in that level of education. A teacher is trained if they have received at least the minimum organized pedagogical teacher training pre-service and in-service required for teaching at the relevant level in each economy.
Goal 5. Achieve gender equality and empower all women and girls		
Target 5.3: Eliminate all harmful practices, such as child, early, and forced marriage, and female genital mutilation.	5.3.1: Proportion of women aged 20–24 years who were married or in a union before age 15 and before age 18	Proportion of women aged 20–24 years who were married or in a union before age 15 years and before age 18 years. Note: Both formal (i.e., marriages) and informal unions are covered under this indicator. Informal unions are generally defined as those in which a couple lives together (i.e., cohabits) for some time, intends to have a lasting relationship, but for which there has been no formal civil or religious ceremony.

(continued on next page)

Goals and Targets	Statistical Indicators	Definition
Target 5.5: Ensure women's full and effective participation in, and equal opportunities for leadership at, all levels of decision-making in political, economic, and public life.	5.5.1: Proportion of seats held by women in national parliaments	The proportion of seats held by women in national parliaments, as of 1 January of the reporting year, is currently measured as the number of seats held by women members in single or lower chamber of national parliaments, expressed as a percentage of all occupied seats. Note: National parliaments can be bicameral or unicameral. This indicator covers the single chamber in unicameral parliaments and the lower chamber in bicameral parliaments. It does not cover the upper chamber of bicameral parliaments. Seats are usually won by members in general parliamentary elections. Seats may also be filled by nomination, appointment, indirect election, rotation of members, and by-election. Seats refer to the number of parliamentary mandates, or the number of members of parliament.
	5.5.2: Proportion of women in managerial positions	Proportion of females in the total number of persons employed in senior and middle management. Senior and middle management correspond to major group 1 in International Standard Classification of Occupations (ISCO)-08 and ISCO-88, minus category 14 in ISCO-08 (hospitality, retail, and other services managers) and minus category 13 in ISCO-88 (general managers), since these comprise mainly managers of small enterprises. Note: The indicator provides information on the proportion of women who are employed in decision-making and managerial roles in government, large enterprises, and institutions, thus providing some insight into women's power in decision-making and in the economy (especially compared to men's power in those areas).
Goal 6. Ensure availability and sustainable management of water and sanitation for all		
Target 6.1: By 2030, achieve universal and equitable access to safe and affordable drinking water for all.	6.1.1: Proportion of population using safely managed drinking water services	Proportion of the population using safely managed drinking water services is currently being measured by the proportion of the population using an improved basic drinking water source that is located on premises, available when needed, and free of fecal (and priority chemical) contamination. Note: Improved drinking water sources include the following: piped water into a dwelling, yard, or plot; public taps or standpipes; boreholes or tubewells; protected dug wells; protected springs; packaged water; delivered water and rainwater. "Located on premises": a water source at the point of collection is within the dwelling, yard, or plot. "Available when needed": households are able to access sufficient quantities of water when needed. "Free from fecal (and priority chemical) contamination": water complies with relevant national or local standards. In the absence of such standards, reference is made to the WHO Guidelines for Drinking Water Quality https://www.who.int/teams/environment-climate-change-and-health/water-sanitation-and-health/water-safety-and-quality/drinking-water-quality-guidelines. E. coli or thermotolerant coliforms are the preferred indicator for microbiological quality, and arsenic and fluoride are the priority chemicals for global reporting.

(continued on next page)

Goals and Targets	Statistical Indicators	Definition
		The WHO/UNICEF Joint Monitoring Programme (JMP) for Water Supply, Sanitation, and Hygiene estimates access to basic services for each economy, separately in urban and rural areas, by fitting a regression line to a series of data points from household surveys and censuses. This approach was used to report on use of 'improved water' sources for Millennium Development Goal monitoring. The JMP is evaluating the use of alternative statistical estimation methods as more data become available. The JMP 2017 update and SDG baselines report describes in more detail how data on availability and quality from different sources, can be combined with data on use of different types of supplies, as recorded in the current JMP database to compute the safely managed drinking water services indicator. https://washdata.org/report/jmp-methodology-2017-update https://washdata.org/report/jmp-2017-report-final
Target 6.2: By 2030, achieve access to adequate and equitable sanitation and hygiene for all, and end open defecation, paying special attention to the needs of women and girls and those in vulnerable situations.	6.2.1.a: Proportion of population using safely managed sanitation services	The proportion of the population using a basic sanitation facility, including handwashing facility with soap and water, that is not shared with other households and where excreta is safely disposed in situ or treated off-site. Note: Improved sanitation facilities include flush or pour-flush toilets to sewer systems, septic tanks or pit latrines, ventilated improved pit latrines, pit latrines with a slab, and composting toilets. "Safely disposed in situ": when pit latrines and septic tanks are not emptied, the excreta may still remain isolated from human contact and can be considered safely managed. For example, with the new SDG indicator, households that use twin pit latrines or safely abandon full pit latrines and dig new facilities, a common practice in rural areas, would be counted as using safely managed sanitation services. "Treated offsite": not all excreta from toilet facilities conveyed in sewers (as wastewater) or emptied from pit latrines and septic tanks (as faecal sludge) reaches a treatment site. For instance, a portion may leak from the sewer itself or, due to broken pumping installations, be discharged directly to the environment. Similarly, a portion of the faecal sludge emptied from containers may be discharged into open drains, to open ground or water bodies, rather than being transported to a treatment plant. And finally, even once the excreta reach a treatment plant a portion may remain untreated, due to dysfunctional treatment equipment or inadequate treatment capacity, and be discharged to the environment. For the purposes of SDG monitoring, adequacy of treatment will initially be assessed based on the reported level of treatment. "A handwashing facility with soap and water": a handwashing facility is a device to contain, transport or regulate the flow of water to facilitate handwashing.

(continued on next page)

Goals and Targets	Statistical Indicators	Definition
Target 6.4: By 2030, substantially increase water-use efficiency across all sectors and ensure sustainable withdrawals and supply of freshwater to address water scarcity and substantially reduce the number of people suffering from water scarcity.	6.4.2: Level of water stress: freshwater withdrawal as a proportion of available freshwater resources	The level of water stress: freshwater withdrawal as a proportion of available freshwater resources is the ratio between total freshwater withdrawn by all major sectors and total renewable freshwater resources, after taking into account environmental water requirements. Note: Total freshwater withdrawal is the volume of freshwater extracted from its source (rivers, lakes, aquifers) for agriculture, industries, and municipalities. Freshwater withdrawal includes primary freshwater (not withdrawn before), secondary freshwater (previously withdrawn and returned to rivers and groundwater, such as discharged wastewater and agricultural drainage water), and fossil groundwater. Main sectors, as defined by International Standard Industrial Classification standards, include agriculture, forestry and fishing, manufacturing, electricity industry, and services. Environmental water requirements are the quantities of water required to sustain freshwater and estuarine ecosystems. This indicator is also known as water withdrawal intensity. Total renewable freshwater resources are expressed as the sum of internal and external renewable water resources. Internal renewable water resources are defined as the long-term average annual flow of rivers and recharge of groundwater, generated from endogenous precipitation, for a given economy. External renewable water resources refer to the flows of water entering the economy, taking into consideration the quantity of flows reserved to upstream and downstream economies through agreements or treaties.
Target 6.a: By 2030, expand international cooperation and capacity-building support to developing economies in water- and sanitation-related activities and programmes, including water harvesting, desalination, water efficiency, wastewater treatment, recycling, and reuse technologies.	6.a.1: Amount of water- and sanitation-related ODA that is part of a government-coordinated spending plan	Amount of water- and sanitation-related ODA that is part of a government-coordinated spending plan is defined as the proportion of total water- and sanitation-related ODA disbursements that are included in the government budget. Note: The amount of water- and sanitation-related ODA is a quantifiable measurement as a proxy for "international cooperation and capacity development support" in financial terms. A low value of this indicator (near 0%) would suggest that international donors are investing in water- and sanitation-related activities and programs in the economy, outside the purview of the national government. A high value (near 100%) would indicate that donors are aligned with the national government and national policies and plans for water and sanitation.
Goal 7. Ensure access to affordable, reliable, sustainable, and modern energy for all		
Target 7.1: By 2030, ensure universal access to affordable, reliable, and modern energy services.	7.1.1: Proportion of population with access to electricity	Percentage of the population with access to electricity. Note: Access to electricity addresses major critical issues in all the dimensions of sustainable development. The target has a wide range of social and economic impacts, including facilitating development of household-based income-generating activities and lightening the burden of household tasks.
	7.1.2: Proportion of population with primary reliance on clean fuels and technology	Number of people using clean fuels and technologies for cooking, heating and lighting divided by total population, and expressed as a percentage. "Clean" is defined by the emission rate targets and specific fuel recommendations (i.e., against unprocessed coal and kerosene) included in the normative guidance WHO guidelines for indoor air quality: household fuel combustion.

(continued on next page)

Goals and Targets	Statistical Indicators	Definition
Target 7.2: By 2030, increase substantially the share of renewable energy in the global energy mix.	7.2.1: Renewable energy share in total final energy consumption	Percentage of final consumption of energy that is derived from renewable resources. Note: Renewable energy consumption includes consumption of energy derived from hydro, solid biofuels, wind, solar, liquid biofuels, biogas, geothermal, marine sources, and waste. Total final energy consumption is calculated from national balances and statistics as total final consumption minus nonenergy use.
Target 7.3: By 2030, double the global rate of improvement in energy efficiency.	7.3.1: Energy intensity measured in terms of primary energy and GDP	Energy supplied to the economy per unit value of economic output. Note: Total energy supply, as defined by the International Recommendations for Energy Statistics, is made up of production, plus net imports, minus international marine and aviation bunkers, plus-stock changes. GDP is the measure of economic output. For international comparison purposes, GDP is measured in constant terms at PPP.
Goal 8. Promote sustained, inclusive, and sustainable economic growth, full and productive employment, and decent work for all		
Target 8.1: Sustain per-capita economic growth in accordance with national circumstances and, in particular, at least 7% GDP growth per annum in the least developed countries (or economies).	8.1.1: Annual growth rate of real GDP per capita	Percentage change in the real GDP per capita between 2 consecutive years. Note: Real GDP per capita is calculated by dividing GDP at constant prices by the population of an economy or area. The data for real GDP is measured in constant US dollars to facilitate the calculation of economy growth rates and aggregation of the economy data.
Target 8.2: Achieve higher levels of economic productivity through diversification, technological upgrading, and innovation, including through a focus on high-value-added and labor-intensive sectors.	8.2.1: Annual growth rate of real GDP per employed person	Annual percentage change in real GDP per employed person. Note: The real GDP per employed person is a measure of labor productivity, and this indicator represents a measure of labor productivity growth, thus providing information on the evolution, efficiency, and quality of human capital in the production process.
Target 8.5: By 2030, achieve full and productive employment and decent work for all women and men, including for young people and persons with disabilities, and equal pay for work of equal value.	8.5.2: Unemployment rate, by sex, age, and persons with disabilities	Percentage of persons in the labor force who are unemployed. Note: Unemployed persons are defined as all those of working age (usually persons aged 15 and above) who were not in employment, carried out activities to seek employment during a specified recent period, and were currently available to take up employment given a job opportunity, where: (i) "not in employment" is assessed with respect to the short reference period for the measurement of employment; (ii) to "seek employment" refers to any activity when carried out, during a specified recent period comprising the past 4 weeks or 1 month, for the purpose of finding a job or setting up a business or agricultural undertaking; (iii) the point when the enterprise starts to exist should be used to distinguish between search activities aimed at setting up a business and the work activity itself. This is evidenced by the enterprise's registration to operate, or when financial resources become available, or when necessary infrastructure or materials are in place, or the first client or order is received, depending on the context; and

(continued on next page)

Goals and Targets	Statistical Indicators	Definition
		(iv) "currently available" serves as a test of readiness to start a job in the present, assessed with respect to a short reference period that is used to measure employment (depending on national circumstances, the reference period may be extended to include a short subsequent period not exceeding 2 weeks in total, so as to ensure adequate coverage of unemployment situations among different population groups).
Target 8.6: By 2020, substantially reduce the proportion of youth not in employment, education, or training.	8.6.1: Proportion of youth (aged 15–24 years) not in education, employment, or training	Proportion of youth (aged 15–24 years) who are not in education, employment, or training, also known as "the youth NEET rate". It conveys the number of young persons not in education, employment, or training, as a percentage of the total youth population.
Target 8.7: Take immediate and effective measures to eradicate forced labor, end modern slavery and human trafficking, and secure the prohibition and elimination of the worst forms of child labor, including recruitment and use of child soldiers, and, by 2025, end child labor in all its forms.	8.7.1: Proportion of children aged 5–17 years engaged in child labor	The number of children aged 5–17 years reported to be in child labor during the reference period (usually the week prior to the survey). The proportion of children in child labor is calculated as the number of children in child labor, divided by the total number of children in the population.
Target 8.10: Strengthen the capacity of domestic financial institutions to encourage and expand access to banking, insurance, and financial services for all.	8.10.1: Number of commercial bank branches and ATMs per 100,000 adults	The number of commercial bank branches per 100,000 adults refers to the number of commercial banks branches reported by the central bank or the main financial regulator of the economy every year. To make it comparable, this number is presented as a reference per 100,000 adults in the respective economy. The number of ATMs per 100,000 adults, refers to the number of ATMs in the economy for all types of institutions, such as commercial banks, non-deposit-taking microfinance institutions, deposit-taking microfinance institutions, credit unions, financial cooperatives, and others. This information is reported every year by the central bank or the main financial regulator of the economy. To make it comparable, this number is presented as a reference per 100,000 adults in the respective economy.
	8.10.2: Proportion of adults (aged 15 years and older) with an account at a bank or other financial institution or with a mobile-money service provider	Percentage of adults (aged 15+) who report having an account (of their own or held with someone else) at a bank or another type of financial institution, or have personally used a mobile-money service in the past 12 months.
Target 8.a: Increase Aid for Trade support for developing economies, in particular least developed economies, including through the Enhanced Integrated Framework for Trade-related Technical Assistance to Least Developed Economies	8.a.1 Aid for Trade commitments and disbursements	Aid for Trade commitments and disbursements is the gross disbursements and commitments of total Official Development Assistance (ODA) from all donors for aid for trade.

(continued on next page)

Goals and Targets	Statistical Indicators	Definition
Goal 9. Build resilient infrastructure, promote inclusive and sustainable industrialization, and foster innovation		
Target 9.1: Develop quality, reliable, sustainable, and resilient infrastructure, including regional and transborder infrastructure, to support economic development and human well-being, with a focus on affordable and equitable access for all.	9.1.a: Passenger volume by road transport, measured in millions of passenger-kilometers	Passenger and freight volumes are the sums of the passenger and freight volumes reported for the road and rail carriers in terms of number of people and metric tons of cargo, respectively. Note: The International Transport Forum collects data on transport (rail and road) statistics on an annual basis from all its member economies. Data are collected from transport ministries, statistical offices, and other institutions designated as official data sources. Although there are clear definitions for all the terms used in this survey, economies might have different methodologies to calculate passenger-kilometers and ton-kilometers. Methods could be based on traffic or mobility surveys, using very different sampling methods and estimating techniques, which could affect the comparability of the statistics.
	9.1.b: Freight volume by road transport, measured in millions of ton-kilometers	
	9.1.c: Passenger volume by rail transport, measured in millions of passenger-kilometers	
	9.1.d: Freight volume by rail transport, measured in millions of ton-kilometers	
Target 9.2: Promote inclusive and sustainable industrialization and, by 2030, significantly raise industry's share of employment and GDP, in line with national circumstances, and double its share in least developed countries (or economies).	9.2.1: Manufacturing value added as a proportion of GDP and per capita	Manufacturing value added (MVA) as a proportion of GDP is a ratio between MVA and GDP, both reported in constant 2015 US dollars. MVA per capita is calculated by dividing MVA in constant 2015 US dollars by the population of an economy or area.
	9.2.2: Manufacturing employment as a proportion of total employment	Share of manufacturing employment in total employment.
Target 9.4: By 2030, upgrade infrastructure and retrofit industries to make them sustainable, with increased resource-use efficiency and greater adoption of clean and environmentally sound technologies and industrial processes, with all countries (or economies) taking action in accordance with their respective capabilities.	9.4.1: Carbon dioxide (CO_2) emissions per unit of value-added	CO_2 emissions per unit of value-added is an indicator calculated as the ratio between CO_2 emissions from fuel combustion and the value added of associated economic activities. The indicator can be calculated for the whole economy (total CO_2 emissions to GDP) or for specific sectors, notably the manufacturing sector (CO_2 emissions from manufacturing industries per MVA). CO_2 emissions per unit of GDP are expressed in kilograms of CO_2 per constant 2010 US dollar PPP of GDP. CO_2 emissions from manufacturing industries per unit of MVA are measured in kilograms of CO_2equivalent per unit of MVA in constant 2015 US dollars.

(continued on next page)

Goals and Targets	Statistical Indicators	Definition
Target 9.5: Enhance scientific research and upgrade the technological capabilities of industrial sectors in all countries (or economies), in particular developing countries (or economies), including, by 2030, encouraging innovation and substantially increasing the number of research and development workers per 1 million people and public and private research and development spending.	9.5.1: Research and development expenditure as a proportion of GDP	Amount of research and experimental development expenditure divided by the total output of the economy.
	9.5.2: Researchers (full-time equivalent) per million inhabitants	Number of research and experimental development workers per 1 million people.
Target 9.a: Facilitate sustainable and resilient infrastructure development in developing economies through enhanced financial, technological, and technical support to African economies, least developed economies, landlocked developing economies, and small island developing states.	9.a.1: Total official international support (ODA plus other official flows) to infrastructure	Gross disbursements of total ODA and other official flows from all donors in support of infrastructure.
Target 9.b: Support domestic technology development, research, and innovation in developing countries (or economies), including by ensuring a conducive policy environment for, among other things, industrial diversification and value addition to commodities.	9.b.1: Proportion of medium- and high-tech industry value-added in total value-added	Ratio of the value added by medium- and high-tech (MHT) industry to total MVA. Note: Industrial development generally entails a structural transition from resource-based and low-tech activities to MHT activities. A modern, highly complex production structure offers better opportunities for skills development and technological innovation. MHT activities are also the high-value addition industries of manufacturing with higher technological intensity and labor productivity. Increasing the share of MHT sectors also reflects the impact of innovation.
Target 9.c: Significantly increase access to information and communications technology and strive to provide universal and affordable access to the Internet in least developed economies by 2020.	9.c.1.a: Proportion of population covered by narrowband (2G) mobile networks	Proportion of the population covered by a mobile network, broken down by technology, refers to the percentage of inhabitants living within range of a mobile-cellular signal, irrespective of whether or not they are mobile-phone subscribers or users. This is calculated by dividing the number of inhabitants within range of a mobile-cellular signal by the total population and multiplying by 100. Note: Coverage refers to Long-Term Evolution (LTE), broadband (3G), and narrowband (2G) mobile-cellular technologies: 2G mobile population coverage refers to the percentage of inhabitants within range of a mobile networks with access to data communications (e.g. Internet) at downstream speeds below 256 Kbit/s. This includes mobile-cellular technologies such as general packet radio service (GPRS), code division multiple access (CDMA) 2000 1x and most enhanced data for GSM (global system for mobile communications) evolution (EDGE) implementations. 3G population coverage refers to the percentage of inhabitants that are within range of at least a 3G mobile-cellular signal, irrespective of whether or not they are subscribers.
	9.c.1.b: Proportion of population covered by 3G mobile networks	
	9.c.1.c: Proportion of population covered by LTE mobile networks	

(continued on next page)

Goals and Targets	Statistical Indicators	Definition
		Long-term evolution (LTE) population coverage refers to the percentage of inhabitants that live within range of LTE/LTE-Advanced, mobile WiMAX/WirelessMAN or other more advanced mobile-cellular networks, irrespective of whether or not they are subscribers.
Goal 10. Reduce inequality within and among economies		
Target 10.1: By 2030, progressively achieve and sustain income growth of the bottom 40% of the population at a rate higher than the national average.	10.1.1.a: Growth rates of household expenditure or income per capita among the bottom 40% of the population	The growth rate in the welfare aggregate of the bottom 40% of the population is calculated as the annualized average growth rate in per capita real consumption or income of the bottom 40% of the income distribution in an economy from household surveys over a period of approximately 5 years.
	10.1.1.b: Growth rates of household expenditure or income per capita	The national average growth rate in the welfare aggregate is calculated as the annualized average growth rate in per capita real consumption or income of the total population in an economy from household surveys over a period of approximately 5years.
Goal 11. Make cities and human settlements inclusive, safe, resilient, and sustainable		
Target 11.1: By 2030, ensure access for all to adequate, safe, and affordable housing and basic services, and upgrade slums.	11.1.1: Proportion of the urban population living in slums, informal settlements, or inadequate housing	The proportion of the urban population that lives in slums or informal settlements as well as those living in inadequate housing. Note: Most of the criteria for defining slums, informal settlements, and inadequate housing overlap. The criteria for informal settlements are essentially captured in the definition of slums, which combines both slums and informal settlements as one entity. Slums and informal settlements are therefore combined into one component of the indicator, providing some continuity with what was captured under Millennium Development Goal 7. At a later stage, a composite index will be developed that will incorporate all measures (combining slums, informal settlements, and inadequate housing) to provide one estimate.
Target 11.5: By 2030, significantly reduce the number of deaths and the number of people affected, and substantially decrease the direct economic losses relative to global GDP caused by disasters, including water-related disasters, with a focus on protecting the poor and people in vulnerable situations	11.5.2: Direct economic loss in relation to global GDP, damage to critical infrastructure, and number of disruptions to basic services, attributed to disasters	Direct economic loss is the monetary value of total or partial destruction of physical assets existing in the affected area. Direct economic loss is nearly equivalent to physical damage. Note: The original national disaster loss databases usually register physical damage value (housing unit loss, infrastructure loss, etc.), which needs conversion to a monetary value according to the United Nations International Strategy for Disaster Reduction methodology. The converted global value is divided by global GDP (inflation adjusted, constant US dollars) calculated from the World Bank Development Indicators.
Target 11.6: By 2030, reduce the adverse per capita environmental impact of cities, including by paying special attention to air quality and municipal and other waste management.	11.6.2: Annual mean levels of fine particulate matter (PM), e.g., PM2.5 and PM10, in cities, measured in total (population weighted) micrograms per cubic meter	The mean annual concentration of fine suspended particles of less than 2.5 microns in diameters (PM2.5) is a common measure of air pollution. Note: The mean is a population-weighted average for the urban population in a economy and is expressed in micrograms per cubic meter
Goal 12. Ensure sustainable consumption and production patterns		
Target 12.2: By 2030, achieve the sustainable management and efficient use of natural resources	12.2.1: Material footprint, material footprint per capita, and material footprint per GDP	Material footprint is the attribution of global material extraction to domestic final demand of a economy. The total material footprint is the sum of the material footprint for biomass, fossil fuels, metal ores, and nonmetal ores. This indicator is calculated as raw material equivalent of imports, plus domestic extraction, minus raw material equivalents of exports. For the attribution of the primary material needs of final demand, a global, multiregional input-output framework is employed.

(continued on next page)

Goals and Targets	Statistical Indicators	Definition
	12.2.2: Domestic material consumption, domestic material consumption per capita, and domestic material consumption per GDP	Domestic material consumption (DMC) is a standard material flow accounting indicator and reports the apparent consumption of materials in a national economy. Note: DMC reports the amount of materials that are used in a national economy. DMC is a territorial (production side) indicator. DMC also presents the amount of material that needs to be handled within an economy, which is either added to material stocks of buildings and transport infrastructure or used to fuel the economy as material throughput. DMC describes the physical dimension of economic processes and interactions. It can also be interpreted as long-term waste equivalent. Per capita DMC describes the average level of material use in an economy – an environmental pressure indicator – and is also referred to as metabolic profile.
Goal 13. Take urgent action to combat climate change and its impacts		
Target 13.1: Strengthen resilience and adaptive capacity to climate-related hazards and natural disasters in all economies.	13.1.1.a: Number of persons affected by disasters	Number of people who were directly affected by disasters per 100,000 population. Note: Directly affected means people who have suffered injury, illness, or other health effects; who were evacuated, displaced, or relocated; or have suffered direct damage to their livelihoods, economic, physical, social, cultural, and/or environmental assets.
	13.1.1.b: Number of deaths due to disasters	The number of people who died during a disaster, or directly after, as a direct result of the hazardous event.
	13.1.2: Number of economies that adopt and implement national disaster risk reduction strategies in line with the Sendai Framework for Disaster Risk Reduction 2015–2030	Number of economies that adopt and implement local disaster risk reduction strategies in line with national disaster risk reduction strategies. Note: The score of adoption and implementation of national disaster risk reduction strategies in line with the Sendai Framework (Index) was developed to monitor progress and achievement against Indicator 13.1.2. The score of an economy indicates its compliance to alignment of national strategies with the Sendai Framework based on self-assessments of the economy using 10 criteria for monitoring the progress of national disaster risk reduction strategies.
Goal 14. Conserve and sustainably use the oceans, seas, and marine resources for sustainable development		
Target 14.5: By 2020, conserve at least 10% of coastal and marine areas, consistent with national and international law and based on the best available scientific information.	14.5.1: Coverage of protected areas in relation to marine areas	The indicator shows trends over time in the mean percentage of each important site for marine biodiversity (i.e., those that contribute significantly to the global persistence of biodiversity) that is covered by designated protected areas and other effective area-based conservation measures. Note: The International Union for Conservation of Nature (IUCN) defines protected areas as clearly defined geographical spaces, recognized, dedicated, and managed through legal or other effective means, to achieve the long-term conservation of nature with associated ecosystem services and cultural values. Importantly, a variety of specific management objectives are recognized within this definition, spanning conservation, restoration, and sustainable use. The status “designated” is attributed to a protected area when the corresponding authority, according to national legislation or common practice (e.g., by means of an executive decree or the like), officially endorses a document of designation. The designation must be made for the purpose of biodiversity conservation, not de facto protection arising because of some other activity (e.g., military).

(continued on next page)

Goals and Targets	Statistical Indicators	Definition
Goal 15. Protect, restore, and promote sustainable use of terrestrial ecosystems, sustainably manage forests, combat desertification, halt and reverse land degradation, and halt biodiversity loss		
Target 15.1: By 2020, ensure the conservation, restoration, and sustainable use of terrestrial and inland freshwater ecosystems and their services, in particular forests, wetlands, mountains, and drylands, in line with obligations under international agreements.	15.1.1: Forest area as a proportion of total land area	Size of forest cover in relation to land area. Note: Forest is defined as "land spanning more than 0.5 hectares with trees higher than 5 meters and a canopy cover of more than 10%, or trees able to reach these thresholds in situ. It does not include land that is predominantly under agricultural or urban land use". Land area is the area of an economy excluding area under inland waters and coastal waters.
	15.1.2: Proportion of important sites for terrestrial and freshwater biodiversity that are covered by protected areas, by ecosystem type	Proportion of important sites for terrestrial and freshwater biodiversity that are covered by protected areas and contribute significantly to the global persistence of biodiversity. They are covered by designated protected areas and Other Effective Area-based Conservation Measures (OECMs). The status "designated" is attributed to a protected area when the corresponding authority, according to national legislation or common practice (e.g., by means of an executive decree or the like), officially endorses a document of designation. The designation must be made for the purpose of biodiversity conservation, not de facto protection arising because of some other activity (e.g., military). OECMs are defined by the Convention on Biological Diversity (CBD) as "A geographically defined area other than a Protected Area, which is governed and managed in ways that achieve positive and sustained long-term outcomes for the in-situ conservation of biodiversity, with associated ecosystem functions and services, and where applicable, cultural, spiritual, socioeconomic, and other locally relevant values."
Target 15.4: By 2030, ensure the conservation of mountain ecosystems, including their biodiversity, in order to enhance their capacity to provide benefits that are essential for sustainable development	15.4.1: Coverage by protected areas of important sites for mountain biodiversity	Coverage by protected areas of important sites for mountain biodiversity shows temporal trends in the mean percentage of each important site for mountain biodiversity (i.e., those that contribute significantly to the global persistence of biodiversity) that is covered by designated protected areas and Other Effective Area-based Conservation Measures (OECMs). The status "designated" is attributed to a protected area when the corresponding authority, according to national legislation or common practice (e.g., by means of an executive decree or the like), officially endorses a document of designation. The designation must be made for the purpose of biodiversity conservation, not de facto protection arising because of some other activity (e.g., military). OECMs are defined by the Convention on Biological Diversity (CBD) as "A geographically defined area other than a Protected Area, which is governed and managed in ways that achieve positive and sustained long-term outcomes for the in-situ conservation of biodiversity, with associated ecosystem functions and services, and where applicable, cultural, spiritual, socio-economic, and other locally relevant values."

(continued on next page)

Goals and Targets	Statistical Indicators	Definition
Target 15.5: Take urgent and significant action to reduce the degradation of natural habitats, halt the loss of biodiversity and, by 2020, protect and prevent the extinction of threatened species.	15.5.1: Red List Index	The Red List Index measures changes in aggregate extinction risk across groups of species. It is based on genuine changes in the number of species in each category of extinction risk on the IUCN Red List of Threatened Species (www.iucnredlist.org), which is expressed as changes in an index ranging from 0 to 1. Note: The Red List Index value ranges from 1 (all species are categorized as "Least Concern") to 0 (all species are categorized as "Extinct"), indicating how far the set of species has moved overall toward extinction. Threatened species are those listed on The IUCN Red List of Threatened Species in the categories Vulnerable, Endangered, or Critically Endangered (i.e., species that are facing a high, very high, or extremely high risk of extinction in the wild in the medium-term future).
Goal 16. Promote peaceful and inclusive societies for sustainable development; provide access to justice for all; and build effective, accountable, and inclusive institutions at all levels		
Target 16.1: Significantly reduce all forms of violence and related death rates everywhere.	16.1.1: Number of victims of intentional homicide per 100,000 population	Total count of victims of intentional homicide divided by the total population, expressed per 100,000 population. Intentional homicide is defined as the unlawful death inflicted upon a person with the intent to cause death or serious injury (International Classification of Crime for Statistical Purposes, ICCS 2015). Population refers to total resident population in a given economy in a given year. Note: This indicator is widely used at national and international levels to measure the most extreme form of violent crime, providing a direct indication of lack of security.
Target 16.3: Promote the rule of law at national and international levels and ensure equal access to justice for all.	16.3.2: Unsentenced detainees as a proportion of the overall prison population	Total number of persons held in detention who have not yet been sentenced, as a percentage of the total number of persons held in detention, on a specified date.
Target 16.5: Substantially reduce corruption and bribery in all their forms.	16.5.2: Proportion of businesses that had at least one contact with a public official and that paid a bribe to a public official, or were asked for a bribe by those public officials during the previous 12 months	Proportion of firms that were asked for a gift or informal payment when meeting with tax officials. Note: This indicator aims to ascertain whether or not firms have been solicited for gifts or informal payments (i.e., bribes) when meeting with tax officials. Paying taxes are required of formal forms in most economies, and the rationale for this indicator is to measure the incidence of corruption during this routine interaction.
Target 16.9: By 2030, provide legal identity for all, including birth registration.	16.9.1: Proportion of children under 5 years of age whose births have been registered with a civil authority, by age	Proportion of children under 5 years of age whose births have been registered with a civil authority.

(continued on next page)

Goals and Targets	Statistical Indicators	Definition
Goal 17. Strengthen the means of implementation and revitalize the Global Partnership for Sustainable Development		
Target 17.4: Assist developing economies in attaining long-term debt sustainability through coordinated policies aimed at fostering debt financing, debt relief, and debt restructuring, as appropriate, and address the external debt of highly indebted poor economies to reduce debt distress	17.4.1: Debt service as a proportion of exports of goods and services	Percentage of debt services (principle and interest payments) to the exports of goods and services. Debt services covered in this indicator refer only to public and publicly guaranteed debt. Note: Concepts of public and publicly guaranteed external debt and exports of goods and services data are in accordance with the sixth edition of the Balance of Payments and International Investment Position Manual (BPM6) methodology
Target 17.9: Enhance international support for implementing effective and targeted capacity-building in developing economies to support national plans to implement all the Sustainable Development Goals, including through North-South, South-South, and triangular cooperation.	17.9.1: Dollar value of financial and technical assistance (including through North-South, South-South, and triangular cooperation) committed to developing economies	Gross disbursements of total ODA and other official flows from all donors for capacity-building and national planning. Note: ODA refers to "those flows to economies and territories on the Development Assistance Committee List of ODA Recipients and to multilateral institutions which are (i) provided by official agencies, including state and local governments, or by their executive agencies; and (ii) each transaction is administered with the promotion of the economic development and welfare of developing economies as its main objective; and is concessional in character and conveys a grant element of at least 25% (calculated at a rate of discount of 10%). Other official flows (excluding officially supported export credits) are defined as transactions by the official sector that do not meet the conditions for eligibility as ODA, either because they are not primarily aimed at development or because they are not sufficiently concessional.
Target 17.18: By 2020, enhance capacity-building support to developing economies, including for least developed economies and small island developing states, to increase significantly the availability of high-quality, timely, and reliable data disaggregated by income, gender, age, race, ethnicity, migratory status, disability, geographic location, and other characteristics relevant in national contexts.	17.18.3: Number of economies with a national statistical plan that is fully funded and under implementation, by source of funding	Count of economies that are either (i) implementing a strategy, (ii) designing a strategy, or (iii) awaiting adoption of a strategy in the current year. Note: The indicator is based on the annual Status Report on National Strategies for the Development of Statistics. In collaboration with its partners, PARIS21 reports on the progress of an economy in designing and implementing national statistical plans. This indicator can be disaggregated by geographical area. Regional-level aggregates are based on the total count of national strategies.
Target 17.19: By 2030, build on existing initiatives to develop measurements of progress on sustainable development that complement GDP, and support statistical capacity-building in developing economies.	17.19.1: Dollar value of all resources made available to strengthen statistical capacity in developing economies	US dollar value of ongoing statistical support in developing economies. Note: The indictor is based on the Partner Report on Support to Statistics, which is designed and administered by PARIS21 to provide a snapshot of the US dollar value of ongoing statistical support in developing economies.
	17.19.2: Number of economies that have conducted at least one population and housing census in the past 10 years	Economies that have conducted at least one population and housing census in the past 10 years. This includes economies that compile their detailed population and housing statistics from population registers, administrative records, sample surveys, other sources, or a combination of those sources.

Regional Trends and Tables

Indicator	Definition
PEOPLE	
Population	
Midyear Population	Estimates of the midyear de facto population. De facto population includes all persons physically present in the economy during the census day, including foreign, military, and diplomatic personnel and their accompanying household members; and transient foreign visitors in the economy or in harbors. Note: Some economies have population data referenced to different period end points (e.g., 1 January for the Kyrgyz Republic, 31 December for the People's Republic of China, and 1 October for India).
Growth Rates in Population	Number of people added to (or subtracted from) a population over a given period of time because of natural increase and net migration, expressed as a percentage of the population at the given period of time.
Net International Migration Rate	Number of immigrants minus the number of emigrants over a period, divided by the person-years lived by the population of the receiving economy over that period. It is expressed as net number of migrants per 1,000 population.
Urban Population (as % of total population)	Population living in urban areas, defined in accordance with the national definition or as used in the most recent population census. Because of national differences in the characteristics that distinguish urban from rural areas, the distinction between urban and rural populations is not amenable to a single definition that would be applicable to all economies. National definitions are most commonly based on size of locality. Population that is not urban is considered rural. The estimated population living in urban areas at midyear as a percentage of the total midyear population in an economy.
Age Dependency Ratio	Ratio of the nonworking-age population to the working-age population. Since economies define working age differently, a straightforward application of the definition will lead to noncomparable data. The Asian Development Bank therefore uses the following United Nations definition that can be calculated directly from an age distribution: $\frac{\text{Population aged (0–14) + (65 and over) years}}{\text{Population aged (15–64) years}} \times 100$
Labor Force and Employment	
Labor Force Participation Rate	Percentage of the labor force to the working-age population. The labor force is the sum of those employed and unemployed but seeking work. The labor force participation rate measures the extent of the economically active working-age population in an economy. It provides an indication of the relative size of the supply of labor available for the production of goods and services in the economy. It must be noted that the definition of working-age population varies across economies. Note: Recommendations from the 19th International Conference of Labour Statisticians have been adopted by some economies, and hence these economies may not have comparable data across years. The conference provides the statistical concept of work for reference purposes; and the operational concepts, definitions, and guidelines for (i) three distinct subsets of work activities, referred to as forms of work, which include own-use production work, employment work, and volunteer work; (ii) related classifications of the population according to their labor force status and main work status; and (iii) measures of labor underutilization. The concept of employment has also been refined to refer to work for pay or profit.
Employment in Agriculture	Employment in agriculture, including forestry and fishing, that corresponds to division 1 (International Standard of Industrial Classification [ISIC] revision 2), tabulation categories A and B (ISIC revision 3), and category A of ISIC revision 4.

(continued on next page)

Indicator	Definition
Employment in Industry	Employment in industry includes mining and quarrying; manufacturing; electricity, gas, steam, and air-conditioning supply; water supply; sewage, waste management, and remediation activities; and construction.
Employment in Mining and Quarrying	Employment in mining and quarrying that corresponds to division 2 (ISIC revision 2), tabulation category C (ISIC revision 3), and category B of ISIC revision 4.
Employment in Manufacturing	Employment in manufacturing that corresponds to division 3 (ISIC revision 2), tabulation category D (ISIC revision 3), and category C of ISIC revision 4.
Employment in Electricity, Gas, Steam, and Air-Conditioning Supply; Water Supply; Sewerage, Waste Management and Remediation Activities	Employment in electricity, gas, steam, and air-conditioning supply; water supply; sewerage, waste management, and remediation activities that corresponds to division 4 (ISIC revision 2), tabulation category E (ISIC revision 3), and categories D and E of ISIC revision 4.
Employment in Construction	Employment in construction that corresponds to division 5 (ISIC revision 2), tabulation category F (ISIC revisions 3), and category F of ISIC revision 4.
Employment in Service	Employment in service includes wholesale and retail trade; repair of motor vehicles and motorcycles; accommodation and food service activities; transportation and storage; information and communication; financial and insurance activities; real estate activities; and other services.
Employment in Wholesale and Retail Trade; Repair of Motor Vehicles and Motorcycles	Employment in wholesale and retail trade; repair of motor vehicles and motorcycles that corresponds to division 6 (subdivisions 61 and 62, ISIC revision 2); tabulation category G (ISIC revision 3); and category G of ISIC revision 4.
Employment in Transportation and Storage	Employment in transport and storage that corresponds to division 7 (subdivision 71, ISIC revision 2); tabulation category I (subcategories 60–63, ISIC revision 3); and category H of ISIC revision 4.
Employment in Accommodation and Food Service Activities	Employment in accommodation and food service activities that corresponds to division 6 (subdivision 63, ISIC revision 2); tabulation category H (ISIC revision 3); and category I of ISIC revision 4.
Employment in Information and Communication	Employment in information and communication that corresponds to division 7 (subdivision 72, ISIC revision 2); tabulation category I (subcategory 64, ISIC revision 3); and category J of ISIC revision 4.
Employment in Financial and Insurance Activities	Employment in financial and insurance activities that corresponds to division 8 (subdivisions 81–82, ISIC revision 2), tabulation category J (ISIC revision 3), and category K of ISIC revision 4.
Employment in Real Estate Activities	Employment in real estate activities that corresponds to division 8 (subdivision 83, ISIC revision 2); tabulation category K (subcategory 70, ISIC revision 3); and category L of ISIC revision 4.
Employment in Other Services	Employment in other services that corresponds to divisions 9 and 0 (ISIC revision 2), tabulation categories L to Q (ISIC revision 3), and categories M to U of ISIC revision 4.
Underemployment	Persons in time-related underemployment comprise all persons in employment who satisfy the following three criteria during the reference period: a) are willing to work additional hours; b) are available to work additional hours i.e., are ready, within a specified subsequent period, to work additional hours given opportunities for additional work; and c) worked less than a threshold relating to working time (i.e., persons whose hours actually worked in all jobs during the reference period were below a threshold, to be chosen according to national circumstances). The time-related underemployment rate is calculated as follows: $\text{TRU (\%)} = \frac{\text{Persons in time-related underemployment}}{\text{Persons employed}} \times 100$
Poverty Indicators	
Proportion of Population below \$2.15 a Day (2017 PPP)	Percentage of the population living on less than \$2.15 a day at 2017 purchasing power parity (PPP).

(continued on next page)

Indicator	Definition
Proportion of Population below $3.65 a Day (2017 PPP)	Percentage of the population living on less than $3.65 a day at 2017 PPP.
Income Ratio of Highest 20% to Lowest 20%	Income or consumption share that accrues to the richest 20% of the population, divided by the income or consumption share of the lowest 20% of the population.
Gini Coefficient or Index	Measure of the degree to which an economy's income distribution diverges from perfect equal distribution. A value of zero (0) implies perfect equality while a value of one (1) implies perfect inequality.
Human Development Index	Composite index of long and healthy life (measured by life expectancy at birth), knowledge (measured by expected years of schooling and mean years of schooling), and decent standard of living (measured by gross national income per capita in United States [US] PPP dollars).
Social Indicators	
Life Expectancy at Birth	Number of years that a newborn is expected to live if prevailing patterns of mortality at the time of his or her birth are to stay the same throughout his or her life.
Crude Birth Rate	Ratio of the total number of live births in a given period to the midyear total population of the same period, expressed per 1,000 people.
Crude Death Rate	Ratio of the number of deaths occurring within a given period to the midyear total population of the same period, expressed per 1,000 people.
Total Fertility Rate	Number of children that would be born to a woman if she were to live to the end of her childbearing years and bear children in accordance with current age-specific fertility rates.
Adult Literacy Rate	The percentage of the population aged 15 years and older who can both read and write (with understanding) a short simple statement on his or her everyday life. Generally, literacy also encompasses numeracy, i.e., the ability to make simple arithmetic calculations.
Expected years of schooling, primary to tertiary	Number of years a person of school entrance age can expect to spend within the specified level of education (from primary to tertiary level).
Mean years of schooling	Average number of completed years of education of an economy's population aged 25 years and older, excluding years spent repeating individual grades.
Pupil to qualified teacher ratio	The total number of pupils and students in the relevant level in a given academic year expressed as a percentage of the number of qualified teachers in the same level in that academic year. A qualified teacher has the minimum academic qualifications necessary to teach at a specific level of education in a given economy. This is usually related to the subject(s) they teach. The higher the pupil to qualified teacher ratio, the lower the relative access of pupils to qualified teachers.
Pupil to trained teacher ratio	The total number of pupils and students at a given level in a given academic year expressed as a percentage of the number of trained teachers at the same level in that academic year. A trained teacher has fulfilled at least the minimum organized pedagogical teacher-training requirements (pre-service or in-service) to teach a specific level of education, according to the relevant national policy or law. The higher the pupil to trained teacher ratio, the lower the relative access of pupils to trained teachers. Results can be compared with established national norms on the number of pupils per trained teacher for each level of education.
Physicians	Physicians, including general and specialist medical practitioners, expressed in terms of the number per 1,000 people.
Hospital Beds	In-patient beds for both acute and chronic care available in public, private, general, and specialized hospitals and rehabilitation centers expressed in terms of the number per 1,000 people.
Number of Adults Living with HIV	All adults, defined as men and women aged 15 years and older, with HIV infection, whether or not they have developed symptoms of AIDS, estimated to be alive at the end of a specific year.

(continued on next page)

Indicator	Definition
ECONOMY AND OUTPUT	
National Accounts	
Gross Domestic Product	Unduplicated market value of the total production activity of all resident producer units within the economic territory of an economy during a given period. It is calculated without making deductions for depreciation of fabricated assets or for depletion and degradation of natural resources. Transfer payments are excluded from the calculation of gross domestic product (GDP). GDP can be calculated using the production, expenditure, and income approaches. Production-based GDP is the sum of the gross value added by all resident producers in the economy, plus any taxes and minus any subsidies not included in the value of the products. Gross value-added is the net output of an industry after adding up all outputs and subtracting intermediate inputs. Income-based GDP is the sum of the compensation of employees, mixed income, operating surplus, consumption of fixed capital, and taxes, less subsidies on production and imports. Expenditure-based GDP is the sum of final consumption expenditure of households, nonprofit institutions serving households, and the government; gross capital formation; and exports minus imports of goods and services. GDP can be measured at current prices (the prices of the current reporting period), and constant prices (obtained by expressing values in terms of a base period and chain volume measure).
GDP at PPP	Measures obtained by using PPP to convert the GDP into a common currency, and by valuing them at a uniform price level. They are the spatial equivalent of a time series of GDP for a single economy expressed at constant prices. At the level of GDP, they are used to compare the economic size of economies.
GDP at Current US Dollar	GDP at local currency units are obtained from the economy sources and are converted to US dollars using the official exchange rates from the International Monetary Fund (IMF). The exchange rates used are expressed as the average rate for a period of time (average of period), calculated as annual averages based on the monthly averages (local currency units relative to the US dollar).
GDP per Capita at PPP	GDP at PPP, divided by the midyear population.
GNI per Capita, Atlas Method	The gross national income (GNI) converted to US dollars using the World Bank Atlas method, divided by the midyear population. GNI is the sum of value added by all resident producers, plus any product taxes (less subsidies) not included in the valuation of output, plus net receipts of primary income (compensation of employees and property income) from abroad. GNI, calculated in national currency, is usually converted to US dollars at official exchange rates for comparisons across economies, although an alternative rate is used when the official exchange rate is judged to diverge by an exceptionally large margin from the rate actually applied in international transactions. To smooth fluctuations in prices and exchange rates, a special Atlas method of conversion is used by the World Bank. This applies a conversion factor that averages the exchange rate for a given year and the 2 preceding years, adjusted for differences in rates of inflation between the economy, and through 2000, the G-5 economies (France, Germany, Japan, the United Kingdom, and the US). From 2001, these economies include the Euro area, Japan, the United Kingdom, and the US.
GDP per Capita at Current US Dollar	GDP at current US dollar value, divided by the midyear population.
Agriculture Value Added	The gross output of the agriculture sector, less the corresponding value of intermediate consumption. The industrial origin of value-added is determined by ISIC revision 4, where agriculture corresponds to ISIC Section A and includes agriculture, forestry, and fishing.

(continued on next page)

Indicator	Definition
Industry Value Added	The gross output of industry sectors, less the corresponding value of intermediate consumption. The industrial origin of value-added is determined by ISIC revision 4, where industry corresponds to ISIC Sections B-F and includes mining and quarrying (B); manufacturing (C); electricity, gas, steam, and air-conditioning supply (D); water supply; sewerage, waste management, and remediation activities (E); and construction (F).
Services Value Added	The gross output of services sectors, less the corresponding value of intermediate consumption. The industrial origin of value-added is determined by ISIC revision 4, where services corresponds to ISIC Sections G-U and includes wholesale and retail trade; repair of motor vehicles and motorcycles (G); transport and storage (H); accommodation and food service activities (I); information and communication (J); financial and insurance activities (K); real estate activities (L); professional, scientific, and technical activities (M); administrative and support service activities (N); public administration and defense; compulsory social security (O); education (P); human health and social work activities (Q); arts, entertainment, and recreation (R); other service activities (S); activities of households as employers; undifferentiated goods- and services-producing activities of households for own use (T); and activities of extraterritorial organizations and bodies (U).
Household Consumption Expenditure	Market value of all goods and services, including durable products (such as cars, washing machines, and home computers), purchased or received as income in kind by households. It excludes purchases of dwellings but includes imputed rent for owner-occupied dwellings. It also includes payments and fees to governments to obtain permits and licenses. The expenditure of nonprofit institutions serving households is generally included for most economies.
Government Consumption Expenditure	Includes all current outlays on purchases of goods and services (including wages and salaries of government employees). It also includes most expenditure on national defense and security but excludes government military expenditures that are part of public investment.
Gross Capital Formation	Total value of gross fixed capital formation, changes in inventories, and acquisitions less disposals of valuables. Gross fixed capital formation is the total value of a producer's acquisitions, less disposals, of tangible goods (such as buildings) and intangible goods (such as computer software) that are intended for use in production during several accounting periods, plus certain specified expenditure on services that adds to the value of non-produced assets. Changes in inventories are changes in stocks of produced goods and goods for intermediate consumption, and the net increase in the value of work in progress. Valuables are goods (such as precious metals and works of art) that are not used up in production but are acquired as stores of value in the expectation that they will retain or increase their value over time.
Exports of Goods and Services	Consist of sales, bartering, or gifts or grants of goods and services from residents to nonresidents. The treatment of exports in the System of National Accounts is generally identical with that in the balance of payments accounts as described in the IMF's Balance of Payments Manual.
Imports of Goods and Services	Consist of purchases, bartering, or receipts of gifts or grants of goods and services by residents from nonresidents. The treatment of imports in the System of National Accounts is generally identical to that in the balance of payments accounts as described in the IMF's Balance of Payments Manual.
Gross Domestic Saving	Difference between GDP and final consumption expenditure, where final consumption expenditure is the sum of the final consumption of household, nonprofit institutions serving households, and the government.
Production	
Agriculture Production Index	Relative level of the aggregate volume of agricultural production for each year in comparison with the base period. It is based on the sum of price-weighted quantities of different agricultural commodities produced.
Manufacturing Production Index	An index covering production in manufacturing. The exact coverage, the weighting system, and the methods of calculation vary from economy to economy, but the divergences are less important than, for example, in the case of price and wage indexes.

(continued on next page)

Indicator	Definition
MONEY, FINANCE, AND PRICES	
Prices	
Consumer Price Index	An index that measures changes in prices against a reference period of a basket of goods and services purchased by households. Based on the purpose of the consumer price index, different baskets of goods and services can be selected. For macroeconomic purposes, a broad-based basket is used to represent the relative price movement of household final consumption expenditure.
Food and Nonalcoholic Beverages Price Index	An index that covers food and nonalcoholic beverages purchased by the household mainly for consumption or preparation at home including services for food processing for own consumption. The index corresponds to Classification of Individual Consumption by Purpose (COICOP) Version 1999 and 2018 division 01. Excluded are food and nonalcoholic beverages that are provided as part of a food-serving service under COICOP division 11: restaurants and hotels (COICOP Version 1999) or restaurants and accommodation services (COICOP Version 2018).
Alcoholic Beverages, Tobacco, and Narcotics Price Index	An index that covers the purchase of alcoholic beverages, tobacco, and narcotics, regardless of where these are consumed, but not provided as part of a food-and-beverage-serving service under hotels and restaurants. Services for the production of alcohol for own consumption are also included. The index corresponds to COICOP division 02. Excluded are alcoholic beverages purchased for immediate consumption in hotels, restaurants, cafes, bars, kiosks, street vendors, automatic vending machines, etc. classified under restaurants, cafes, and the like (COICOP Group 11.1.1).
Clothing and Footwear Price Index	An index that covers all clothing materials, garments, articles and accessories, footwear and related services, including cleaning, repair, and hire of clothing and footwear, and the purchase of secondhand clothing and footwear. The index corresponds to COICOP division 03.
Housing, Water, Electricity, Gas, and Other Fuels Price Index	An index that covers goods and services for the use of the house or dwelling and its maintenance and repair; the supply of water and miscellaneous services related to the dwelling; and energy used for heating or cooling. The index corresponds to COICOP division 04.
Furnishings, Household Equipment, and Routine Household Maintenance Price Index	An index that covers a wide range of products to equip the house or dwelling and the household durables, semidurables, and nondurables as well as some household services. Includes all kinds of furniture (including lighting equipment, household textiles, glassware, tableware and household utensils), major and smaller electric household appliances, tools and equipment for house and garden, and goods for routine household maintenance. The index also includes the repair, installation, and rental services of the goods. Domestic services by paid staff in private service, supplied by enterprises or self-employed persons, window-cleaning and disinfecting services, as well as dry-cleaning and laundering of household textiles and carpets, are also included. The index corresponds to COICOP division 05.
Health Price Index	An index that covers health services provided during an overnight stay, services that do not require an overnight stay, diagnostic imaging services, medical laboratory services, patient emergency transportation, and emergency rescue services. The index also includes medicines and health products, covering all products that are separately invoiced from health services, except when administered under the direct supervision of a health care professional during an overnight stay. The index corresponds to COICOP division 06.
Transport Price Index	An index that covers four main categories of goods and services for transportation: (i) purchase of vehicles covers motor cars, motor cycles, bicycles, and animal-drawn vehicles; (ii) goods and services for the operation of the personal transport equipment cover parts and accessories for personal transport equipment, fuels and lubricants, and the repair and maintenance of personal transport equipment including expenditures for parking spaces in garages or in public places, expenditures for tolls, and expenditures to acquire a driving certificate; (iii) transport services provided by the market, structured by the mode of transport; and (iv) transport services of goods covers postal and courier services, removal and storage services, and the delivery of any kinds of goods when charged separately. The index corresponds to COICOP division 07. It excludes purchases of recreational vehicles such as camper vans, caravans, trailers, aeroplanes, and boats that are classified under the Recreation and Culture Price Index (COICOP Version 1999) or Recreation, Sport, and Culture (COICOP Version 2018).

(continued on next page)

Indicator	Definition
Communication Price Index/Information and Communication Price Index	The index corresponds to division 08 in COICOP versions 1999 and 2018. In COICOP Version 1999, this index covers three main groups of goods and services: (i) information and communication equipment, including equipment for the capture, recording, and reproduction of sound and vision; software; and information and communication services; (ii) information and communication services, including telephones and other communication services; internet access services; television and radio licenses; fee and subscription services, including streaming services of films and music; and (iii) repair, maintenance, and rental of information and communication equipment. In COICOP Version 2018, this index covers three main groups and services: (i) information and communication equipment, including equipment for the reception, recording, and reproduction of sound and vision; (ii) software; and (iii) information and communication services, which include telephone and other communication services, internet access services, television and radio licences, fee and subscription services (including streaming services of films and music); and repair, maintenance, and hire of information and communication equipment.
Recreation and Culture Price Index/Recreation, Sport, and Culture Price Index	An index that covers a wide range of goods and services for recreation, sport, and culture and is structured into eight groups: (i) recreation durables such as photographic equipment, other major durables for recreation, such as camper vans, boats, yachts, aeroplanes, and the like; (ii) nonmajor durable recreational goods such as games and toys, including video game computers, celebration articles, equipment for sport, camping, and open-air recreation; (iii) garden products and plants and flowers and purchases of pets and expenditures for pets, excluding veterinary services; (iv) recreational services cover rental, maintenance, and repair of goods, veterinary and other services for pets, recreational and leisure services, such as amusement parks, games of chance and expenditures for sporting services, both expenditures for practicing sports as well as expenditures for attendance of sport events; (v) cultural goods such as musical instruments and audio-visual media; (vi) cultural services such as cinemas, theatres, concerts, museums, and other cultural sites, and photographic services; (vii) newspapers, all kinds of books, stationery and drawing materials; and (viii) package holidays that include transportation, accommodation, food provision, or tour guide. The index corresponds to COICOP division 09.
Education Price Index/Education Services Price Index	An index that covers educational services only. It includes: (i) education by radio or television broadcasting as well as e-learning and correspondence courses; (ii) admission and registration fees as well as tuition fees; and (iii) other education-related fees such as camps and/or field trips, course fees, diploma fees, examination fees, graduation fees, laboratory fees, physical education fees, etc. The index corresponds to COICOP division 10. It excludes expenditures on other education-related goods and services such as school uniforms, education support services, such as health-care services, transport services (except in the case of excursions that are part of the normal school program), text books and academic journals, stationery, catering services, and accommodation services.
Restaurants and Hotels Price Index/Restaurants and Accommodation Service Price Index	An index that covers food and beverage services provided by restaurants, cafes, and similar facilities, either with full or limited- or self-service, or by canteens, cafeterias, or refectories at work or at school and other educational establishment's premises. It also includes catering services and accommodation services. Services for visitors and other travellers away from their principal or secondary residence are included. If not separately invoiced, it also includes food and beverage services and other serving services, such as housekeeping, parking, laundry, swimming pools and exercise rooms, recreational facilities, and conference and convention facilities.The index corresponds to COICOP division 11.
Insurance and Financial Services Price Index	An index that covers insurance and financial services. Insurance and financial services are provided by financial corporations. Insurance services are subdivided by type of insurance. Financial services are subdivided by financial intermediation services indirectly measured and by other forms of actual and indirect charges and remittance fees for financial services. For the definition and measurement of insurance and financial services, specific national accounts concepts (under the 2008 System of National Accounts) do apply. The index corresponds to COICOP Version 2018 division 12.

(continued on next page)

Indicator	Definition
Miscellaneous Goods and Services Price Index	An index that covers insurance and financial services. It also includes personal care, prostitution, personal effects not elsewhere classified, social protection, financial services not elsewhere classified, and other services not elsewhere classified. The index corresponds to COICOP Version 1999 division 12.
Personal Care, Social Protection, and Miscellaneous Goods and Services Price Index	An index that covers goods and services for personal care, jewelry and watches, services of social protection, and all other services for households, which are not elsewhere classified. Goods and services for personal care cover electric and nonelectric appliances for personal care as well as hairdressing services. Goods of personal effects cover jewelry and watches, celebratorial and devotional items, and travel goods and items. Social protection services cover childcare, nonmedical retirement homes for elderly persons and disabled persons, and services to maintain persons in their private homes and related services. This index also covers all the other services for households, which are not elsewhere classified, such as fees for legal and administrative services, fees for real estate agencies, charges for undertaking, and payments for various personal services. This index also includes religious services. The index corresponds to COICOP Version 2018 division 13.
Wholesale Price Index	A measure that reflects changes in the prices paid for goods at various stages of distribution up to the point of retail. It can include prices of raw materials for intermediate and final consumption, prices of intermediate or unfinished goods, and prices of finished goods. The goods are usually valued at purchasers' prices.
Producer Price Index	A measure of the change in the prices of goods and services, either as they leave their place of production or as they enter the production process. A measure of the change in the prices received by domestic producers for their outputs or of the change in the prices paid by domestic producers for their intermediate inputs.
GDP Deflator	A measure of the annual rate of price change in the economy as a whole for the period shown, obtained by dividing GDP at current prices by GDP at constant prices.
Money and Finance	
Money Supply	Refers to the total amount of money in circulation in a specific economy. Money supply can be measured in different ways: M1 (Narrow Money) is a measure of money supply that includes all coins and notes (M0) as well as personal money in current accounts. M2 (Intermediate Money) is the sum of M1 and personal money in deposit accounts. M3 (Broad Money) is the sum of M2 and government and other deposits. According to the Organisation for Economic Co-operation and Development, M3 includes currency, deposits with an agreed maturity of up to 2 years, deposits redeemable at notice of up to 3 months and repurchase agreements, money market fund shares or units, and debt securities up to 2 years. Not all economies publish the same types of aggregates, and even when aggregates are the same name (e.g., M1, M2, M3, etc.), their asset composition often differs significantly. Cross-economy differences in national definitions of lowered-ordered aggregates also arise from differences in the maturity categories of nontransferable deposits included in a particular money aggregate. For example, the definition of M2 in one economy may include time deposits with maturities of 1 year or less, whereas another economy's M2 definition may include time deposits with maturities of 2 years or less. When the monetary policy strategy consists of monetary aggregate targeting, the choice of the definition of the targeted aggregate is guided mainly by two considerations. The aggregate should be sufficiently sensitive to interest rate changes for the central bank to be able to control it and display a stable relationship over time to the movement of the overall price level. Liabilities excluded from broad money are the sum of all exclusions from broad money. They may include deposits; debt securities; loans; insurance, pension, and standardized guarantee schemes; financial derivatives and employee stock options; trade credit and advances; equity; or other items.

(continued on next page)

Indicator	Definition
Interest Rate on Savings Deposits	Rate paid by commercial and similar banks for savings deposits.
Interest Rate on Time Deposits	Rate paid by commercial and similar banks for time deposits.
Lending Interest Rate	Bank rate that usually meets the short- and medium-term financing needs of the private sector. This rate is normally differentiated according to creditworthiness of borrowers and objectives of financing.
Yield on Short-Term Treasury Bills	Rate at which short-term securities are issued or traded in the market.
Domestic Credit Provided by Banking Sector	Includes all credits to various sectors on a gross basis, except credit to the central government, which is net. The banking sector includes monetary authorities, deposit money banks, and other banking institutions for which data are available (including institutions that do not accept transferable deposits but do incur such liabilities as time and savings deposits). Examples of other banking institutions are savings and mortgage loan institutions and building and loan associations.
Ratio of Bank Nonperforming Loans to Total Gross Loans	Value of nonperforming loans divided by the total value of the loan portfolio (including nonperforming loans before the deduction of loan loss provisions). The amount recorded as nonperforming should be the gross value of the loan as recorded in the balance sheet, not just the amount that is overdue.
Stock Market Price Index	Index that measures changes in the prices of stocks traded in the stock exchange. The price changes of the stocks are usually weighted by their market capitalization.
Stock Market Capitalization	The share price times the number of shares outstanding (including their several classes) for listed domestic companies. Investment funds, unit trusts, and companies whose only business goal is to hold shares of other listed companies are excluded. Data are end of year values converted to US dollars using corresponding year-end foreign exchange rates. Also known as market value.
Exchange Rates	
Official Exchange Rate	The exchange rate determined by national authorities or the rate determined in the legally sanctioned exchange market. It is calculated as an annual average based on the monthly averages (local currency units relative to the US dollar).
Purchasing Power Parity Conversion Factor	Number of units of economy B's currency that are needed in economy B to purchase the same quantity of an individual good or service, which one unit of economy A's currency can purchase in economy A.
Price Level Index	Ratio of the relevant PPP to the exchange rate. It is expressed as an index on a base of 100. A price level index (PLI) greater than 100 means that, when the national average prices are converted at exchange rates, the resulting prices tend to be higher on average than prices in the base economy (or economies) of the region (and vice versa). At the level of GDP, PLIs provide a measure of the differences in the general price levels of economies. PLIs are also referred to as comparative price levels.
GLOBALIZATION	
Balance of Payments	
Trade in Goods Balance	Difference between exports and imports of goods.
Trade in Services Balance	Difference between exports and imports of services.
Current Account Balance	Sum of net exports of goods, services, net income, and net current transfers.
Total Remittances	Sum of personal remittances and social benefits. Personal remittances include personal transfers (part of current transfers); compensation of employees less taxes, social contributions, transport, and travel; and capital transfers between households. Social benefits include benefits payable under social security funds and pension funds: they may be in cash or in kind. Includes income from individuals working abroad for short periods, income from individuals residing abroad, and social benefits from abroad.
Foreign Direct Investment	Refers to net inflows of investment to acquire a lasting management interest (10% or more of voting stock) in an enterprise operating in an economy other than that of the investor. It is the sum of equity capital, reinvestment of earnings, other long-term capital, and short-term capital as shown in the balance of payments.

(continued on next page)

Indicator	Definition
External Trade	
Merchandise Exports and Imports	Covering all movable goods, with a few specified exceptions, the ownership of which changes between a resident and a foreigner. For merchandise exports, it represents the value of the goods and related distributive services at the customs frontier of the exporting economy, i.e., the free on board (FOB) value. Merchandise imports, on the other hand, are reported in cost, insurance, and freight (CIF) values.
Trade in Goods	Sum of merchandise exports and merchandise imports.
Direction of Trade	
Direction of Trade: Merchandise Exports and Imports	The direction of trade represents the value of merchandise exports and imports disaggregated according to an economy's primary trading partners. Imports are reported on a CIF basis and exports are reported on a FOB basis, with the exception of a few economies for which imports are also available in FOB. Time series data includes estimates derived from reports of partner economies for nonreporting and slow-reporting economies.
International Reserves	
International Reserves	External assets that are readily available to, and controlled by, monetary authorities for meeting balance-of-payments financing needs, for intervention in exchange markets to affect the currency exchange rate, and for other related purposes (such as maintaining confidence in the currency and the economy and serving as a basis for foreign borrowing). Consist of monetary gold, special drawing rights holdings, reserve position in the IMF, currency and deposits, securities (including debt and equity securities), financial derivatives, and other claims (loans and other financial instruments).
Ratio of International Reserves to Imports	International reserves outstanding at the end of the year as a proportion of imports of goods from the balance of payments during the year, where imports of goods are expressed in terms of a monthly average. It is a useful measure for reserve needs of economies with limited access to capital markets.
Capital Flows	
Net Official Development Assistance	Concessional flows to developing economies and multilateral institutions provided by official agencies, including state and local governments, or by their executing agencies, administered with the objective of promoting the economic development and welfare of developing economies, and containing a grant element of at least 25%. Net flow takes into account principal repayments for loans, offsetting entries for forgiven debt, and recoveries made on grants.
Net Other Official Flows	Official sector transactions with economies on the Development Assistance Committee List of Official Development Assistance Recipients, which do not meet the conditions for eligibility as official development assistance, either because they are not primarily aimed at development, or because they have a grant element of less than 25%. The Development Assistance Committee list of recipients of official development assistance is available at http://www.oecd.org/dac/financing-sustainable-development/development-finance-standards/daclist.htm. Net flow takes into account principal repayments for loans, offsetting entries for forgiven debt, and recoveries made on grants.
Net Private Flows	Sum of direct investment and portfolio investment. Direct investment is a category of international investment made by a resident entity in one economy (direct investor) with the objective of establishing a lasting interest in an enterprise that is resident in an economy other than that of the investor (direct investment enterprise). "Lasting interest" implies the existence of a long-term relationship between the direct investor and the enterprise and a significant degree of influence by the direct investor on the management of the direct investment enterprise. Direct investment involves both the initial transaction between the two entities and all subsequent capital transactions between them and among affiliated enterprises, both incorporated and unincorporated.

(continued on next page)

Indicator	Definition
	Portfolio investment is the category of international investment that covers investment in equity and debt securities, excluding any such instruments that are classified as direct investment or reserve assets.
Aggregate Net Resource Flows	Sum of net official development assistance, net other official flows, and net private flows.
External Indebtedness	
Total External Debt	Debt owed to nonresidents repayable in currency, goods, or services. It is the sum of public, publicly guaranteed, and private nonguaranteed long-term debt, use of IMF credit, and short-term debt. Short-term debt includes all debt having an original maturity of 1 year or less and interest in arrears on long-term debt.
Public and Publicly Guaranteed Debt	Comprises long-term external obligations of public debtors, including the national government, political subdivisions (or an agency of either), and autonomous public bodies, and external obligations of private debtors that are guaranteed for repayment by a public entity.
External Debt as a Percentage of GNI	Total external debt as a percentage of GNI. GNI is the sum of value added by all resident producers plus any product taxes (less subsidies) not included in the valuation of output, plus net receipts of primary income (compensation of employees and property income) from abroad.
External Debt as a Percentage of Exports of Goods and Services and Primary Income	Total external debt as a percentage of exports of goods, services, and primary income. Exports of goods, services, and primary income constitute the total value of exports of goods and services, receipts of compensation of nonresident workers, and investment income from abroad.
Total Debt Service Paid	The sum of principal repayments and interest actually paid in currency, goods, or services on long-term debt, interest paid on short-term debt, and repayments (repurchases and charges) to the IMF.
Total Debt Service Paid as a Percentage of Exports of Goods and Services and Primary Income	Total debt service paid as a percentage of exports of goods, services, and primary income.
Tourism	
International Tourist Arrivals	The number of tourists (overnight visitors) who travel to an economy other than that in which they usually reside, and outside their usual environment, for a period not exceeding 12 months, and whose main purpose of visit is other than the activity remunerated from within the economy visited. In some cases, data may also include same-day visitors when data on overnight visitors are not available separately. Data refer to the number of arrivals and not to the number of people.
International Tourism, Receipts	The receipts earned by a destination economy from inbound tourism and covering all tourism receipts resulting from expenditures made by visitors from abroad. These include lodging, food and drinks, fuel, transport in the economy, entertainment, shopping, etc. This concept includes receipts generated by overnight visits as well as by same-day trips. It does, however, exclude the receipts related to international transport by contracted residents of the other economies (for instance ticket receipts from foreigners travelling with a national company).
TRANSPORT AND COMMUNICATIONS	
Transport	
Road Network	This includes both paved and unpaved roads. Paved roads are roads surfaced with crushed stone (macadam) with hydrocarbon binder or bituminized agents, with concrete, or with cobblestones. Unpaved roads are roads surfaced with a stabilized base, but not surfaced with crushed stone, hydrocarbon binder or bituminized agents, concrete, or cobblestones.

(continued on next page)

Indicator	Definition
Passenger Kilometers Traveled	A passenger-kilometer is a unit of measurement representing the transport of 1 passenger by a defined mode of transport, e.g., road, over 1 kilometer.
Freight Kilometers Traveled	A ton-kilometer is a unit of measurement representing the transport of 1 metric ton of goods (including packaging and tare weights of intermodal transport units) by a defined mode of transport, e.g., road, over a distance of 1 kilometer. Only the distance on the national territory of the reporting economy is taken into account for national, international, and transit transport.
Registered Vehicles	Mode-specific vehicle registrations refer to the number of newly (first-time) registered vehicles recorded by the authorities. This publication reports cumulative number of vehicle registrations.
Road Traffic Deaths	Death caused by a road traffic crash and occurring within 24 hours (Kiribati, the Federated States of Micronesia, Solomon Islands, Timor-Leste, Tonga); 7 days (Azerbaijan, Bhutan, the People's Republic of China, Tajikistan, Turkmenistan, Viet Nam); 30 days (Armenia, Australia, Cambodia, Fiji, India, Indonesia, Japan, Kazakhstan, the Republic of Korea, Lao PDR , Malaysia, Mongolia, Myanmar[1], Nepal, New Zealand, Papua New Guinea, Singapore, Sri Lanka, Uzbekistan); unlimited time period (Afghanistan[2], the Cook Islands, Georgia, Maldives, the Philippines, Samoa, Thailand); within a year (the Kyrgyz Republic); no definition for other economies.
Rail Lines	Rail lines are the length of railway route available for train service, irrespective of the number of parallel tracks.
Rail Network	Length of rail lines divided by the land area.
Railways, Passengers Carried	Passengers carried by railway are the number of passengers transported by rail multiplied by kilometers traveled.
Railways, Goods Transported	Goods transported by railway are the volume of goods transported by railway, measured in metric tons multiplied by kilometers traveled.
Aviation Total Passenger Kilometers	The number of aviation passengers carried, including both domestic and international aircraft passengers of air carriers registered in a given economy, multiplied by kilometers traveled.
Aviation Freight Transport	The volume of aviation freight, express, and diplomatic bags carried on each flight stage (operation of an aircraft from takeoff to its next landing), measured in metric tons, multiplied by kilometers traveled.
Container Port Traffic	Measures the flow of containers from land to sea transport modes, and vice versa, in twenty-foot equivalent units (TEU), a standard-size container. Data refer to coastal shipping as well as international journeys. Transshipment traffic is counted as two lifts at the intermediate port (once to offload and again as an outbound lift) and includes empty units.
Liner Shipping Connectivity Index (LSCI)	The current version of the LSCI is generated from the following six components: (i) the number of scheduled ship calls per week in the economy; (ii) deployed annual capacity in TEU: total deployed capacity offered at the economy; (iii) the number of regular liner shipping services from and to the economy; (iv) the number of liner shipping companies that provide services from and to the economy; (v) the average size in TEU of the ships deployed by the scheduled service with the largest average vessel size; and (vi) the number of other economies that are connected to the economy through direct liner shipping services.
Logistics Performance Index	An interactive benchmarking tool created by the World Bank to help economies identify the challenges and opportunities they face in their performance on trade logistics and what they can do to improve their performance.

1 ADB has temporarily put on hold its assistance in Myanmar effective 1 February 2021 (https://www.adb.org/publications/myanmar-fact-sheet).

2 ADB placed on hold its assistance in Afghanistan effective 15 August 2021 (https://www.adb.org/news/adb-statement-afghanistan)

(continued on next page)

Indicator	Definition
Communications	
Telephone Subscribers	Fixed-telephone subscriptions refer to the sum of active number of analogue fixed telephone lines, voice-over-IP subscriptions, fixed wireless local loop subscriptions, ISDN voice-channel equivalents, and fixed public payphones.
Mobile Phone Subscribers	The proportion of individuals who used a mobile telephone in the 3 months prior to data collection. A mobile (cellular) telephone refers to a portable telephone subscribing to a public mobile telephone service using cellular technology, which provides access to the PSTN. This includes analogue and digital cellular systems and technologies such as IMT-2000 (3G) and IMT- Advanced. Users of both postpaid subscriptions and prepaid accounts are included.
Fixed-Broadband Subscribers	Fixed-broadband subscriptions refer to fixed subscriptions to high-speed access to the public internet (a TCP/IP connection), at downstream speeds equal to, or greater than, 256 kilobits per second. This includes cable modem, DSL, fiber-to-the-home/building, other fixed (wired)- broadband subscriptions, satellite broadband and terrestrial fixed wireless broadband. This total is measured irrespective of the method of payment. It excludes subscriptions that have access to data communications (including the Internet) via mobile-cellular networks. It should include fixed WiMAX and any other fixed wireless technologies. It includes both residential subscriptions and subscriptions for organizations.
Internet Users	The frequency of internet use by individuals who used the internet from any location in the 3 months prior to data collection. Internet can be used via a computer, mobile, phone, personal digital assistant, games machine, digital TV etc.
ENERGY AND ELECTRICITY	
Energy	
GDP per Unit of Energy Use	The ratio of GDP to total energy use (measured per petajoule) with GDP converted to 2017 constant international dollars using PPP rates. An international dollar has the same purchasing power over GDP as a US dollar has in the US.
Energy Production	Primary energy production that is the capture or extraction of fuels or energy from natural energy flows, the biosphere, and natural reserves of fossil fuels within the national territory in a form suitable for use. Inert matter removed from the extracted fuels and quantities reinjected, flared, or vented are not included. The resulting products are referred to as primary products.
Energy Use	Energy production plus imports minus exports, minus international marine bunkers, minus international aviation bunkers, minus stock changes. Also referred to as energy supply.
Energy Imports, Net	Energy imports, net estimated as energy use less production, both measured in petajoules.
Electricity	
Electricity Production	Gross production, which is the sum of the electrical energy production by all the generating units and/or installations concerned (including pumped storage), measured at the output terminals of the main generators. Also referred to as electricity generation.
Sources of Electricity	Refers to the different types of technology and/or processes for the generation or production of electricity, including: (i) electricity from combustible fuels, which refers to the production of electricity from the combustion of fuels that are capable of igniting or burning, i.e., reacting with oxygen to produce a significant rise in temperature; (ii) hydroelectricity, which refers to electricity produced from devices driven by flowing, or falling fresh water; (iii) nuclear electricity, which refers to electricity generated by nuclear plants; and (iv) other electricity, which includes solar, wind, wave, tidal, other marine electricity, geothermal, electricity generated from chemical heat, and electricity from other sources not elsewhere specified.

(continued on next page)

Indicator	Definition
Electric Power Consumption Per Capita	Total electricity consumption divided by midyear population, where consumption refers to energy-industries-own-use and final consumption. Energy-industries-own-use refers to the consumption of electricity for the direct support of the production and preparation for use of fuels and energy. Final consumption refers to the consumption of electricity by manufacturing, construction and nonfuel mining, transport, and households and other consumers (nonenergy use being irrelevant for electricity).
ENVIRONMENT	
Land	
Agricultural Land or Area	Land area that is arable, under permanent crops, and/or under permanent meadows and pastures.
Arable Land	Land under temporary agricultural crops (double-cropped areas are counted only once), temporary meadows for mowing or pasture, land under market, and kitchen gardens and land temporarily fallow (less than 5 years). The abandoned land resulting from shifting cultivation is not included. Data for arable land are not meant to indicate the amount of land that are potentially cultivable.
Permanent Cropland	Land cultivated with long-term crops that do not have to be replanted for several years (such as cocoa and coffee); land under trees and shrubs producing flowers, such as roses and jasmine; and nurseries (except those for forest trees, which should be classified under "forestry"). Permanent meadows and pastures are excluded from land under permanent crops.
Deforestation Rate	Rate of permanent conversion of natural forest area into other uses, including shifting cultivation, permanent agriculture, ranching, settlements, and infrastructure development. Deforested areas do not include areas logged but intended for regeneration or areas degraded by fuelwood gathering, acid precipitation, or forest fires. A negative rate indicates reforestation or increase in forest area.
Pollution	
Carbon Dioxide Emissions	Carbon dioxide emissions, largely by-products of energy production and use, account for the largest share of greenhouse gases, which are associated with global warming. Anthropogenic carbon dioxide emissions result primarily from fossil fuel combustion and cement manufacturing. In combustion, different fossil fuels release different amounts of carbon dioxide for the same level of energy used: oil releases about 50% more carbon dioxide than natural gas, while coal releases about twice as much. Cement manufacturing releases about half a metric ton of carbon dioxide for each metric ton of cement produced. Data for carbon dioxide emissions include gases from the burning of fossil fuels and cement manufacture but excludes emissions from land use such as deforestation.
Nitrous Oxide Emissions	Nitrous oxide emissions are mainly from fossil fuel combustion, fertilizers, rainforest fires, and animal waste. Nitrous oxide is a powerful greenhouse gas, with an estimated atmospheric lifetime of 114 years, compared with 12 years for methane. The per-kilogram global warming potential of nitrous oxide is nearly 310 times that of carbon dioxide within 100 years.
Methane Emissions	Methane emissions are those stemming from human activities including but not limited to agriculture and from industrial methane production. A kilogram of methane is 21 times as effective at trapping heat in the earth's atmosphere as a kilogram of carbon dioxide within 100 years.
Other Greenhouse Gases	By-product emissions of hydrofluorocarbons, perfluorocarbons, and sulfur hexafluoride. Although emissions of these artificial gases are small, they are more powerful greenhouse gases than carbon dioxide, with much higher atmospheric lifetimes and high global warming potential.

(continued on next page)

Indicator	Definition
Freshwater	
Internal Renewable Water Resources	Internal renewable water resources (IRWR) refer to the long-term average annual flow of rivers and recharge of aquifers generated from endogenous precipitation. Double-counting of surface water and groundwater resources is avoided by deducting the overlap from the sum of the surface water and groundwater resources.
	IRWR in billion cubic meters per year refers to surface water produced internally, plus groundwater produced internally deducted by the overlap between surface water and groundwater. IRWR in cubic meters per inhabitant per year is calculated as total annual IRWR divided by total population.
Annual Freshwater Withdrawals	Sum of surface water withdrawal and groundwater withdrawal. Total water withdrawal summed by sector deducted by desalinated water produced, direct use of treated wastewater, and direct use of agricultural drainage water.
Water Productivity	Water productivity is the ratio of the net benefits from crop, forestry, fishery, livestock, and mixed agricultural systems to the amount of water used to produce those benefits. It is calculated as GDP in constant US dollar prices, divided by annual total water withdrawal.
GOVERNMENT AND GOVERNANCE	
Government Finance	
Government Net lending/Net borrowing	Net lending (+) / net borrowing (−) is a summary measure indicating the extent to which government is either putting financial resources at the disposal of other sectors in the economy or abroad, or utilizing the financial resources generated by other sectors in the economy or from abroad. It may be viewed as an indicator of the financial impact of government activity on the rest of the economy and the rest of the world. Net lending (+) / net borrowing (−) is a balancing item calculated as the net operating balance (revenue minus expense) minus the net investment in nonfinancial assets. Net lending/net borrowing is also equal to the net acquisition of all financial assets minus the net incurrence of all liabilities from transactions. For economies following the IMF's Government Finance Statistics 1986 framework, the indicator refers to the overall budgetary surplus/deficit measured as the difference between total revenue (including grants) and total expenditure (including net lending).
Government Taxes	Taxes are compulsory, unrequited amounts receivable by government units from institutional units. Certain compulsory receivables, such as fines, penalties, and most social security contributions are not considered taxes. For economies following the IMF's Government Finance Statistics 1986 framework, tax revenue are compulsory transfers to the central government for public purposes, which includes social security contributions.
Government Revenue	Government revenue is an increase in net worth resulting from a transaction. Revenue transactions have counterpart entries either in an increase in assets or in a decrease in liabilities - thereby increasing net worth. General government units have four types of revenue: (i) compulsory levies in the form of taxes and certain types of social contributions; (ii) property income derived from the ownership of assets; (iii) sales of goods and services; and (iv) other transfers receivable from other units. For economies following the IMF's Government Finance Statistics 1986 framework, the total revenue (including grants) consists of current and capital revenues. Current revenue is the revenue accruing from taxes as well as all current nontax revenues, except transfers received from foreign governments and international institutions. Capital revenue constitutes the proceeds from the sale of nonfinancial capital assets.

(continued on next page)

Indicator	Definition
Government Expenditure	Government expenditure is the sum of expense and the net investment in nonfinancial assets. Expense is a decrease in net worth resulting from a transaction. The major types of expense are compensation of employees, use of goods and services subsidies, grants, social benefits, and other expense. The acquisition of a nonfinancial asset by purchase or barter is not an expense because it has no effect on net worth. Similarly, amounts payable on loans extended and repayments on loans incurred are not classified as expense. Nonfinancial assets are economic assets other than financial assets. Nonfinancial assets are stores of value and provide benefits either through their use in the production of goods and services or in the form of property income and holding gains. These assets are classified as fixed assets, inventories, valuables, and nonproduced assets. For economies following the IMF's Government Finance Statistics 1986 framework, total expenditure (including net lending) consists of current and capital expenditures. Current expenditure comprises purchases of goods and services by the central government, transfers to noncentral government units and to households, subsidies to producers, and interest on public debt. Capital expenditure covers outlays for the acquisition or construction of capital assets and for the purchase of intangible assets, as well as capital transfers to domestic and foreign recipients. Loans and advances for capital purposes are also included.
Government Expenditure on Education	Government expenditure on education includes expenditure on services provided to individual pupils and students and expenditure on services provided on a collective basis. Expenditure on education is allocated to pre-primary and primary education, secondary education, post-secondary nontertiary education, tertiary education, subsidiary services to education, education not definable by level, and research and development (R&D) education. For economies following the IMF's Government Finance Statistics 1986 framework, the indicator refers to government expenditure on education affairs and services.
Government Expenditure on Health	Government expenditure on health includes expenditure on services provided to individual persons and services provided on a collective basis. Expenditure on health is allocated to medical products, appliances, and equipment; outpatient services; hospital services; public health services; R&D health; and health not elsewhere classified. For economies following the IMF's Government Finance Statistics 1986 framework, the indicator refers to government expenditure on health affairs and services.
Government Expenditure on Social Protection	Government expenditure on social protection includes expenditure on services and transfers provided to individual persons and households and expenditure on services provided on a collective basis. Expenditure on social protection is allocated to sickness and disability, old age, survivors, family and children, unemployment, housing, social exclusion not elsewhere classified, and R&D social protection. For economies following the IMF's Government Finance Statistics 1986 framework, the indicator refers to government expenditure on social security and welfare affairs and services.
Governance	
Time Required to Start Up a Business	Number of calendar days needed to complete the procedures to legally operate a business. If a procedure can be accelerated at additional cost, the fastest procedure, independent of cost, is chosen.
Score (Starting a Business)	The score for starting a business is the simple average of the scores for each of the component indicators: the procedures, time and cost for an entrepreneur to start and formally operate a business, and the paid-in minimum capital requirement.

(continued on next page)

Indicator	Definition
Rank (Starting a Business)	The ranking of economies on the ease of starting a business is determined by sorting their scores for starting a business.
Corruption Perceptions Index	Ranks economies and territories based on how corrupt or otherwise their public sector is perceived to be. It is a composite index—a combination of polls—drawing on corruption-related data collected by a variety of reputable institutions. The index reflects the views of observers from around the world, including experts living and working in the economies and territories evaluated. From 2000 to 2011, scores ranged from 10 (highly clean) to 0 (highly corrupt). From 2012 onward, calculation of the score has used an updated methodology and is now presented on a 100 (very clean) to 0 (highly corrupt) scale. Due to this difference in methodology, scores from years prior to and including 2011 should not be compared with scores from 2012 onward. A economy's rank indicates its position relative to the other economies or territories included in the index. It is important to keep in mind that a economy's rank can change simply because new economies enter the index or others drop out.

www.ingramcontent.com/pod-product-compliance
Lightning Source LLC
Chambersburg PA
CBHW041751220926
51847CB00014B/171
* 9 7 8 9 2 9 2 7 0 2 8 3 0 *